# Accounting
## A Foundation

# ROBERT HODGE

# Accounting
## A Foundation

SOUTH-WESTERN
CENGAGE Learning™

Australia • Brazil • Japan • Korea • Mexico • Singapore • Spain • United Kingdom • United States

**Accounting: A foundation**
**Robert Hodge**

Publishing Director: John Yates

Publisher: Patrick Bond

Development Editor: James Clark

Content Project Editor: Jamina Ward

Manufacturing Manager: Helen Mason

Senior Production Controller: Maeve Healy

Marketing Manager: Anne-Marie Scoones

Typesetter: Newgen, India

Cover design: Adam Renvoize

Text design: Design Deluxe, Bath, UK

For product information and technology assistance, contact
**emea.info@cengage.com**

For permission to use material from this text or product, and for permission queries, email
**clsuk.permissions@cengage.com**

Products and services that are referred to in this book may be either trademarks and/or registered trademarks of their respective owners. The publishers and author/s make no claim to these trademarks.

*British Library Cataloguing-in-Publication Data*
A catalogue record for this book is available from the British Library.

ISBN: 978-1-84480-805-2

Cengage Learning EMEA
High Holborn House, 50-51 Bedford Row
London WC1R 4LR

Cengage Learning products are represented in Canada by Nelson Education Ltd.

For your lifelong learning solutions, visit
**www.cengage.co.uk**
Purchase e-books or e-chapters at:
**http://estore.bized.co.uk**

Printed by G Canale&C, Italy
1 2 3 4 5 6 7 8 9 10 – 10 09 08

# BRIEF CONTENTS

# CONTENTS

## 16 Final accounts: a simple Profit & Loss Account 113

## 17 Profit and the accounting equation 125

## 18 A simple balance sheet 131

## 19 Opening stock and cost of sales 139

## 20 The Stock Account and profit 147

## 21 Elements of the full length Profit & Loss Account 155

## 22 The Income Statement and the P&L Account 167

## PART FIVE Understanding company financial statements 511

### 68 Profitability 513

### 69 Borrowing and the effects of gearing 521

### 70 The gearing ratio 527

### 71 Working capital and liquidity 533

### 72 The working capital cycle 539

### 73 Profit and sales ratios 549

### 74 Investment ratios 557

# PREFACE

## AIMS

This book is an attempt to demystify accounting. It assumes no previous knowledge of accounting or of business, and I have tried to make it useful and accessible to all of those who may be interested.

In particular it offers a practical text for students taking many of the specialist courses and qualifications now available in accounting, and its new approach will directly benefit those who are taking the AAT certificates at Foundation (NVQ/SVQ level 2) and Intermediate level (NVQ/SVQ level 3), the ACCA Certified Accounting Technician Qualification (CAT) at Introductory level, and Module 3 of the Intermediate level.

With an emphasis throughout on understanding, and a clear new model of the business, it will also be suitable for the Financial Accounting component of the CIMA Certificate in Business Accounting, and the book-keeping elements of the Open University Certificate in Accounting.

Finally, the book is also written with sufficient rigour and breadth of scope to serve as a text for undergraduates on courses which demand a real understanding of accounting practice as a foundation for further study in management, finance, and accounting itself. I hope it may also appeal to thinking members of the general public who simply wish to understand the nature of modern business and accounting information.

## INNOVATION

A strong foundation in accounting must address at least three questions:

- What is accounting for?
- How does it work?
- What does it tell us?

These in turn revolve around the nature of a business, for accounting is the way in which we represent the sprawling mass of modern enterprise, to make it comprehensible and put it under our control. The book therefore begins with its most basic innovation – a simple drawing of the accounting model of a business.

This picture makes it possible at last to use the double entry as a powerful aid to understanding. We can, for example, say for the first time what a debit or a credit *is*, instead of merely listing arbitrary rules for how to use them. We can address the issues of accountability and fraud, and show exactly how accountants have the power to make a firm's reported profit what it ought to be, or turn it into something else that really it ought not to be. And because the picture tells a story, with a time-line and a motive, it can help us use financial statements to advantage, reading them more easily and understanding them more clearly.

## STRUCTURE

The structure of the book reflects the scope and ambition outlined above. Part 1 describes the new accounting model. Part 2 shows how to use the model to record and summarize events. Part 3 uses the model to show how and why accountants have to intervene in the reporting process. Part 4 describes the structure of the limited company, and how its peculiarities impinge upon accounting. Part 5 develops the new model to deal with ratio analysis, using small and striking real world examples to show how much a proper reading of financial statements can reveal about the underlying business.

Throughout the text, the basic accounting standards and principles are introduced in general terms as moral or professional constraints on the use of accounting judgement. Part 6 lays a foundation for further study of the standards with a brief description of the standard-setting bodies, and their purpose.

While using the model to show the inherent logic of accounting methods, at appropriate points in the text I have departed from the usual pattern and tried to show how the aims of accounting have evolved in response to changes in the economic, social, and business environment. Part 6 therefore concludes with a short list of further reading, designed to show the place of accounting in a broader social context.

## APPROACH

After the introduction, each major point of method in the text is supported with a separate worked example. Examples are tightly focused on the point at issue, and illustrated in successive steps, with simple numbers to avoid distractions in arithmetic. As far as possible, numbers are avoided in the text. In the worked examples, a major innovation is the use of colour and simple graphic devices to draw attention to the numbers that matter, and the relations between them.

Chapters are deliberately short. Each chapter deals with a small coherent unit of knowledge, and is followed in most cases with drills to practise relevant techniques, and exercises to provoke more thoughtful comprehension. Many more practice questions and answers are available on the book's website at www.cengage.co.uk/hodge.

The drills and exercises have been especially written for their place and purpose in the book. Mindful of the division between teaching and testing, I have avoided the recycling of past examination questions. Once they have grasped the subject, candidates for examinations should download and practise on the latest questions relevant to their specific examination.

## IFRS LANGUAGE

The published accounts of major companies are governed by International Financial Reporting Standards (IFRSs). The standards are written in English, but one of their proper purposes is the creation of an international language of accounting, with terms contrived to cover the general case, such as may arise in any jurisdiction or commercial culture. In a text for beginners, so as not to cloud the issue with abstractions, I have judged it better in most cases to use the more natural language associated with particular examples in a home environment.

However, those who wish to read the accounts of major companies will need to know the language of the international standards. Below is a list of the more important international terms, where they differ from the names I have normally used in the text. For the moment, the differences are few in number, and the correspondences are fairly easily understood.

| IFRS | NAME USED IN THE TEXT |
| --- | --- |
| (*worldwide general term*) | (*particular local example*) |
| Income statement | Profit & loss account |
| Retained earnings | Retained profit |
| Receivables | Debtors, or promises from debtors |
| Payables | Creditors, or promises to creditors |
| Inventory | Stock |
| Non-current asset | Fixed asset |

# WALK THROUGH TOUR

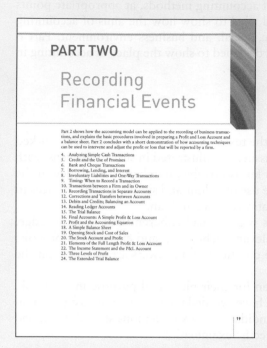

**Part openers** divide the chapters into clearly defined groups arranged to help your understanding of the subject.

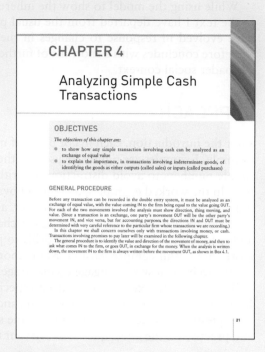

## CHAPTER 4

## Analyzing Simple Cash Transactions

### OBJECTIVES

*The objectives of this chapter are:*

- to show how any simple transaction involving cash can be analyzed as an exchange of equal value
- to explain the importance, in transactions involving indeterminate goods, of identifying the goods as either outputs (called sales) or inputs (called purchases)

### GENERAL PROCEDURE

Before any transaction can be recorded in the double entry system, it must be analyzed as an exchange of equal value, with the value coming IN to the firm being equal to the value going OUT. For each of the two movements involved the analysis must show direction, thing moving, and value. (Since a transaction is an exchange, one party's movement OUT will be the other party's movement IN, and vice versa, but for accounting purposes the directions IN and OUT must be determined with very careful reference to the particular firm whose transactions we are recording.)

In this chapter we shall concern ourselves only with transactions involving money, or cash. Transactions involving promises to pay later will be examined in the following chapter.

The general procedure is to identify the value and direction of the movement of money, and then to ask what comes IN to the firm, or goes OUT, in exchange for the money. When the analysis is written down, the movement IN to the firm is always written before the movement OUT, as shown in Box 4.1.

21

**Objectives** summarize the core content of each chapter in a list of key points.

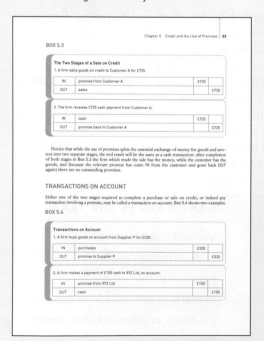

Chapter 5  Credit and the Use of Promises  33

BOX 5.3

**The Two Stages of a Sale on Credit**

1. A firm sells goods on credit to Customer A for £725.

| IN | promise from Customer A | £725 | |
| OUT | sales | | £725 |

2. The firm receives £725 cash payment from Customer A.

| IN | cash | £725 | |
| OUT | promise back to Customer A | | £725 |

Notice that while the use of promises splits the essential exchange of money for goods and services into two separate stages, the end result will be the same as a cash transaction: after completion of both stages in Box 5.3 the firm which made the sale has the money, while the customer has the goods, and (because the relevant promises have come IN from the customer and gone back OUT again) there are no outstanding promises.

### TRANSACTIONS ON ACCOUNT

Either one of the two stages required to complete a purchase or sale on credit, or indeed any transaction involving a promise, may be called a transaction on account. Box 5.4 shows two examples.

BOX 5.4

**Transactions on Account**

1. A firm buys goods on account from Supplier P for £320.

| IN | purchases | £320 | |
| OUT | promise to Supplier P | | £320 |

2. A firm makes a payment of £150 cash to XYZ Ltd, on account.

| IN | promise from XYZ Ltd | £150 | |
| OUT | cash | | £150 |

**Boxes** throughout every chapter clearly explain each example discussed in the text, in a step-by-step manner.

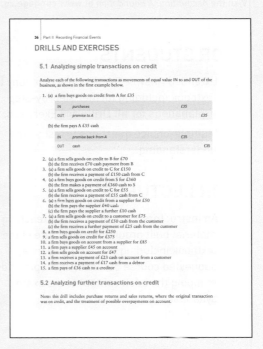

**Review** sections recap each chapter in helpful bitesize form.

**Drills and exercises** at the end of each chapter provide activities designed to enhance your understanding of each chapter and instil a working knowledge of each concept discussed.

**Answer section** at the back of the book provides solutions for key drills and exercises.

# ACCOMPANYING WEBSITE

Visit the *Accounting: A Foundation* at **www.cengage.co.uk/hodge** to find valuable teaching and learning material including:

## FOR STUDENTS

- Extended Answer Section to accompany the textbook including further step-by-step explanations for all Drills and Exercises.
- Multiple-choice questions to test your understanding.

## FOR LECTURERS

- An Instructors Manual including teaching material built around the structure of the textbook including teaching guidance, suggested course outlines, and topic grids mapping the book content to the exam syllabuses of various accounting organisations.

## FURTHER RESOURCES

- ExamView® – This testbank and test generator provides a huge amount of different types of questions, allowing lecturers to create on-line, paper and local area network (LAN) tests. This CD-based product is only available from your Cengage Learning sales representative.
- This textbook is also available in ebook format, please visit the companion website for further details.

# ACKNOWLEDGEMENTS

First, I thank many former students for their curiosity and interest. Their questions provoked, challenged and changed many of the following ideas, and tested many others to destruction.

Among former colleagues, I must thank especially Chrissie Williams, for creating an environment which made it possible to teach and learn with freedom and enjoyment, and Wayne Marshall for the generous loan of equipment at a vital stage.

Malcolm Rice had the courage and tenacity to read and comment on the whole of an early draft. I thank him for his friendship, and for the sharing of his wisdom, which contributed much and saved me from many embarrassing lapses.

I would also like to thank my editors, Pat Bond and James Clark, for their enthusiasm, effort and advice.

Without the loving moral and material support of my wife Filly, and her patience, encouragement and gentle criticism over many years, this book would not have seen the light of day. The book is hers as much as mine. Now it is complete, I offer deepest heartfelt thanks.

Robert Hodge
roberthodge@hotmail.co.uk

## REVIEWERS ACKNOWLEDGMENTS

The publishers and the author would like to thank the following academics who kindly gave their time to review the textbook proposal and draft chapters of the manuscript.

| | |
|---|---|
| Gail Farnworth | Blackpool and The Fylde College |
| Kevin Hogarth | Newbury College |
| Namasiku Liandu | University of Abertay |
| Tracey Meechan | Newbury College |
| Ruth O'Leary | National College of Ireland |
| Jayne Smith | Staffordshire University |

## ABOUT THE AUTHOR

Robert Hodge has lived and worked in various parts of the world, including ten years with the London office of one of the Big Four accounting firms. Since then he has been an independent teacher and lecturer on accounting.

# PART ONE

# Introduction

Part 1 contains a short description of the scope and purpose of financial accounting, with an overview of its distinctive method. The method is based on *the accounting model of a business*, which is drawn for the first time in Chapter 2.

1. Accounting: Subject, Method, and Purpose
2. The Accounting Model of a Business
3. Money and Value

# CHAPTER 1

# Accounting: Subject, Method, and Purpose

## OBJECTIVE

*The objective of this chapter is:*

- to outline the nature and scope of accounting, as it will be treated in the chapters that follow

## WHAT IS FINANCIAL ACCOUNTING?

Financial accounting, often called simply *accounting*, is a practical activity, which can be described, if not fully defined, in terms of its subject, its method, and its purpose.

## SUBJECT

To account for something means, in general, to give a reasoned explanation of why it is so. In terms of its subject matter, therefore, it is fair to say that financial accounting means giving a reasoned explanation of financial events, which are called *transactions* – stating *what* happened, *why* it happened, and what in the end were the *consequences*.

## METHOD

Modern financial accounting is also fairly defined by its method, which is called the double entry. The particular feature of double entry accounting, from which its name derives, is the requirement to enter (i.e. to record) the value involved in any transaction not just once but twice in the accounts – once under a heading for *what* happened, and once again under a heading to explain *why* it happened.

Given that writing itself may have been developed for accounting purposes (some 5 000 years ago), the development of double entry accounting for transactions is remarkably recent, although it was clearly well established in practice by the time it was first described in print by Luca Pacioli, a Franciscan friar, in 1494. Other methods have been used, and no doubt some still are, but the double entry method is now dominant worldwide, to the extent that the idea of financial accounting and the practice of double entry have become inseparable in the popular imagination. Reasons for the success of double entry may become clear as we study the method in detail, but in addition to its built-in requirement to explain (not just to record) what happens, the advantages of the method include the ease with which eventual consequences can be summarized, and the way in which it incorporates controls against the loss or corruption of data, with checks to prevent or detect arithmetical errors and safeguards against the duplication or neglect of information held within the system.

## PURPOSE

Financial accounting is finally distinguished by its purpose, which is, broadly speaking, to help those who own the wealth of society, to impose some degree of control over those who manage that wealth on their behalf. (The related field of management accounting is concerned with helping those who manage economic resources, to manage them efficiently.)

Historically, a division of some sort between the owners of wealth and their agents or managers is not unusual, but the sophistication of modern accounting is largely occasioned by the depth and extent of that division in the modern economy. To capture the benefits of technology and economies of scale, modern industry and commerce require the investment of very large amounts of capital. Typically, such large amounts are gathered by combining the relatively small separate investments of many hundreds and even thousands of individual owner/investors. Those individuals are so numerous that they cannot personally manage the firms in which they invest, and so they appoint managers or directors to manage each firm on their behalf.

These arrangements clearly place investors in a weak and anxious position. Unable to see for themselves what happens inside the firms in which they have invested, they may well fear that the managers they have appointed will waste or misappropriate the capital they have invested. They invest their capital in the hope of receiving an income in the form of payments or dividends out of profits. Yet when they do receive their dividends, investors also need some reassurance that what they receive as income or profit from a firm, is *truly* income or profit, which can safely be withdrawn from the firm and spent without reduction of the firm's capacity to generate further income into the future.

One way in which investors have been able to strengthen their position, reduce their anxieties, and impose some degree of control over the directors or managers they appoint, is by making them accountable – requiring them in fact to present regular financial accounts (explaining *what* they have done, *why* they did it, and what the *consequences* have been).

## ACCOUNTABILITY

Accountability works in three ways. First, it establishes a formal hierarchy. Managers may control a firm, but in accounting for their actions they formally acknowledge the duty they owe to their masters – the investors who employ them. Secondly, awareness of the requirement to give an account is in itself a pre-emptive control over undesirable behaviour. Under the requirement to account for their actions, any potentially deviant managers or directors know that they must desist or be prepared to lie and render false accounts. Crucially however, and unfortunately for them, false accounting is often easier to prove and punish than the wrongdoing it may have attempted to conceal.

Thirdly, accountability works as a general requirement to render information, the scope of which can be modified or extended as and when required. This is important, insofar as those who have wealth or capital need information as well as reassurance. It means that the financial accounts that directors or managers must prepare in order to acknowledge their responsibilities and explain their actions, can also be made to include much of the additional information needed by the firm's owners or investors, for the proper exercise of their rights of ownership and as a basis for their investment decisions.

It is these last two aspects of accountability which continue to drive the development of modern accounting. New financial abuses are checked, at least in part, by new and more detailed accounting disclosure requirements. Meanwhile legal and economic changes in society at large – changes in the rights and responsibilities of ownership – are also reflected by changes in the scope and nature of the accounting information that must be disclosed, and indeed by changes in the very concept of accounting.

## ACCOUNTING AND ACCOUNTANTS

We could also say that accounting is what accountants do. Individually, accountants may do many things, but collectively they have assumed the role of experts in financial information and control. Over the past 150 years, accountants have evolved out of the more general class of managers and business agents, emerging as members of a separate profession in response to the increasing complexity of modern business. The modern firm is like a living organism, in which mechanisms for the collection, processing and distribution of financial information have come together to resemble the nervous system. The vast majority of accountants now work inside the firm as part of that system, but there are also those who work outside the firm as independent experts. These independent accountants are employed largely but not exclusively as auditors, for the reassurance of investors. Auditors are an essential part of the apparatus of accountability, by which a firm's directors are required to give an account of their actions and achievements to the firm's investors. Independent auditors are qualified accountants who are paid to test those accounts, to form an opinion of their truth and fairness, and to make a public declaration of the opinion they have formed. Within the modern structure of industry and finance, the auditor therefore occupies a central position, and one that carries high risk as well as high responsibility.

## ACCOUNTING AND SOCIETY

It is clear from the discussion of its purpose above, that financial accounting is a matter of public interest as well as a source of private profit for those with accounting expertise. *Who* should account *to whom* reflects the distribution of wealth and power within society. What those accounts should contain, and how they should be presented, are questions which soon become matters of law and even politics. The study of accounting therefore moves rapidly from a description of accounting techniques, to a discussion of how those techniques should and should not be used, if we are to give a true and fair view of all the different actions and events that may need to be accounted for. Because of its specialized nature, this debate, and with it the power to impose their own conclusions, has to a large extent been left to the accountants. As a result accountants have become, effectively, not just experts but also unelected makers of the law within their field of expertise.

## FINANCIAL ACCOUNTING AND FINANCIAL REPORTING

Accountants have lately begun to discuss their professional role in terms of financial *reporting*, rather than financial *accounting*, with financial reporting itself described along the lines of 'providing information that is useful to economic decision-makers'. It is not yet clear whether this change in language reflects any real change in what accountants actually do, but it would be careless to assume that 'reporting' and 'accounting' mean much the same sort of thing in any case. They differ in at least two important respects. First, accounting means explaining, while reporting needs no more than a statement of the facts. (Accounting for the motion of the planets means more than just reporting changes in their position.) Secondly, reporting, as no more than a recital of the facts, is morally neutral (except of course for the moral obligation to report the truth). Accounting, by contrast, carries with it all the moral concepts involved in accountability, including the acknowledgement of higher authority, and the acceptance of responsibility for one's actions and their consequences. A real shift from accounting into reporting would be a very significant social change, and perhaps not one that would be welcomed universally.

# REVIEW

This introductory chapter has described accounting in terms of its subject matter, its method, and its purpose. The subject matter of financial accounting is the reasoned explanation of financial events or transactions. Its distinctive method is the double entry. Its primary purpose is to control the behaviour of those who manage economic resources, insofar as that is possible, by making them accountable to the owners and investors who provided those resources. Its secondary purpose is to provide owners and investors with the information they need to make investment decisions. The chapter also noted how, in view of its purpose, accounting has increasingly become a matter of public interest and a source of law, as well as a source of private profit. Finally, the chapter remarked on the recent trend within the profession to discuss the accountant's work in terms of financial reporting (providing information), as opposed to financial accounting (providing control and reassurance).

# DRILLS AND EXERCISES

At the end of each following chapter there will be a selection of drills and exercises to reinforce the main points in the text. Learning to do financial accounting is in some respects like learning to speak a foreign language or learning to drive a car – certain responses or patterns of thought require practice and must become almost automatic. Appropriate drills, therefore, are often simple and repetitive. The exercises, on the other hand, will consist of more open-ended questions, demanding a more thoughtful response

# CHAPTER 2

# The Accounting Model of a Business

## OBJECTIVES

*The objectives of this chapter are:*

- to describe the accounting model of a business
- to explain how the model works to generate profit or loss, and define the substance of profit
- to outline some of the model's limitations

## DOUBLE ENTRY AND THE ACCOUNTING MODEL

Modern financial accounting is distinguished by its use of the double entry method of accounting for transactions. It also employs a distinctive accounting model or view of what a business is and how it operates. The double entry method applies to transactions in general, and can be used by accounting entities (individuals and organizations) of any kind. The accounting model is more recent and more complex. It applies in full and properly to one kind only of accounting entity – the profit-seeking enterprise, normally called a business or a firm. It is in effect a picture of the business as a whole, built around a double entry view of its transactions. In this model:

- the firm or business itself is represented as a box or corridor;
- a transaction is a movement of money or promises IN to or OUT of the business; and
- every transaction (every movement of money or promises) must be recorded as part of an exchange of equal value.

'The double entry view of a transaction' is expressed in the last of the points above. It is the idea that every movement of money or promises IN to or OUT of a firm should be recorded as part of an exchange, which in fact involves two movements, one coming IN to the firm, and another going OUT, with the value coming IN being equal to the value going OUT. In short, the double entry method of accounting requires us to record not only the movement of money (or promise) in which we are interested, but also a movement in the opposite direction of something else of equal value, which the business gives or receives in exchange for the money or promise. The recording of this opposite movement is essentially intended to explain *why* the transaction has occurred.

## HOW THE MODEL WORKS

Box 2.1 presents a simple drawing of the accounting model (where money and/or promises to pay money are shown as M&P).

## BOX 2.1

**The Accounting Model of a Business and its Transactions**

- a transaction is a movement of money or promises (M&P) across the boundary IN to or OUT of a business

- every transaction is recorded as an exchange of equal value

- inside the business, inputs are consumed while outputs are created

This model is dynamic, with things moving and happening for a purpose. It represents not only financial events (transactions between the business and the outside world), but also the essential process that takes place inside the firm. Its motive force is the desire to generate a profit, and it works like this:

- on the left the firm buys things – it gives out money or promises to pay later, receiving *inputs* of equal value in exchange;
- inside the business, there is some *process* by which inputs are consumed, while different things called outputs are created with a different value;
- on the right the firm sells things – it takes in money or promises, while *outputs* of equal value are given out of the firm in exchange.

## THE PROFIT-MAKING PROCESS

The object of the action in the model is to generate a profit, which is done by arranging the process inside the business in such a way that the value of outputs created will be greater than the value of inputs consumed. Profit then will be the difference between the value of outputs created and the value of inputs consumed, as shown by the formula in Box 2.2, which reveals not only the value of profit, but also the process by which profit is made.

BOX 2.2

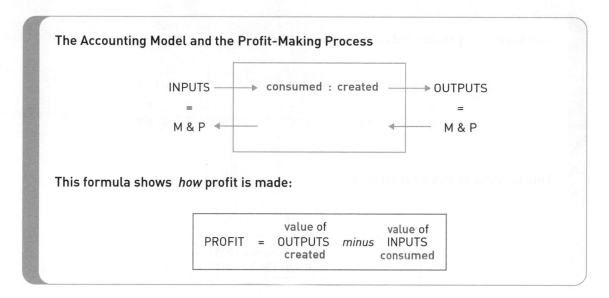

**The Accounting Model and the Profit-Making Process**

INPUTS ⟶ consumed : created ⟶ OUTPUTS

= =

M & P ⟵ ⟵ M & P

This formula shows *how* profit is made:

$$
\text{PROFIT} = \begin{array}{c} \text{value of} \\ \text{OUTPUTS} \\ \text{created} \end{array} \ minus \ \begin{array}{c} \text{value of} \\ \text{INPUTS} \\ \text{consumed} \end{array}
$$

## CONSUMPTION AND CREATION

Notice the assumption embedded in the profit formula, that inputs do not simply pass through the business and emerge unchanged as outputs. Inputs and outputs must be different things with different values. Otherwise the model cannot work to generate a profit or a loss. We may think sometimes of inputs being converted into outputs as they pass on their way through the firm, but a better view, at least to begin with, is the model as we have drawn it, with the idea that inputs really are consumed inside the business, while quite different things called outputs are actually created, as from nothing.

Also notice that consumption and creation are parts of a non-financial process which takes place wholly inside the business. This process is not a transaction – a transaction is a movement of money or promises across the boundary between the business and the outside world. This is significant. It means that accountants can never directly observe the profit-making process. Why? Because accountants observe only the transactions that occur between the business and the outside world. For accountants, whatever happens to the value of something inside the business must remain a matter of inference and conjecture, until its value is realized in the course of a transaction. (We say that the value of something is *realized*, or made real, when it is exchanged for money or the promise of money.)

## THE SUBSTANCE OF PROFIT

Looking again at our drawing of the model, and keeping in mind our description of the profit-making process, we can also identify the actual substance of profit. If a business is successful, and the value of outputs created is in fact greater than the value of inputs consumed, then of course the business will report a profit. More to the point, however, if the business is profitable, the value of money and promises coming IN to the business will be greater than the value of money and promises going OUT. Thus money and promises will accumulate inside the business. And that is not all. If the process of consumption and creation takes some time, there may also be a build-up of inputs awaiting consumption inside the firm. It is this accumulation of money, promises, and unconsumed inputs inside a business which makes up the substance of profit.

We therefore need the formula in Box 2.3 to describe the substance of profit, and although it stands in need of some refinement, it will serve for the moment to tell us what profit *is*, as opposed to how it is made.

BOX 2.3

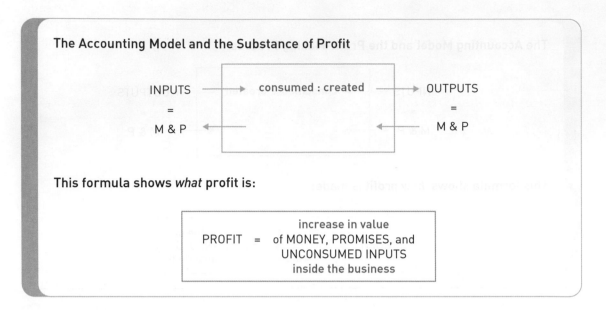

**The Accounting Model and the Substance of Profit**

This formula shows *what* profit is:

## THE MODEL AT WORK

For an example of how the model might work in practice, consider a firm which operates a fuel-burning power station, generating electricity for sale on the open market. First, the firm buys fuel. This is a transaction: money or promises are given out in exchange for fuel of equal value. The fuel, as an input, is then consumed inside the firm – in this case, the input is literally consumed by burning – and an output, electricity, is created, almost as from nothing. The firm then sells the electricity. This is a further transaction: money or promises are received in exchange for electricity of equal value. As a result, if the value of electricity sold is greater than the value of the fuel consumed to make it, the firm will make a profit. Money, promises, and perhaps a stock of fuel waiting for consumption, will accumulate inside the firm.

## GENERAL APPLICATION OF THE MODEL

The example of the power station is of course much simplified, and was carefully chosen to emphasize the process of consumption and creation that occurs within the firm. In real life there are few cases like the power station, in which the principal input is so literally consumed, with an utterly different output almost literally created out of nothing. In real life we would also have to account for many more inputs, including some, like the machinery (also an input) used in the process, whose value may be consumed or used up only very slowly, over a long period. However, with a little imagination, a similar process of consumption and creation can be seen at work in any business. Manufacturing is probably the simplest case. For example in a firm making motor vehicles, various inputs like metal, plastic, paint, labour and machinery are all consumed, while visibly different outputs are created, which are cars or trucks. Or in a tailoring firm, the major inputs, which are cloth, buttons, thread and labour, are all consumed to make quite different outputs which are clothes; and so on.

For firms in a service industry like law or education, inputs and outputs are both less tangible. The principal input consumed is human time or labour. The output is whatever service may be sold by the firm in question – for example legal advice or educational courses.

It requires a little more imagination to apply the same idea to a purely trading business – that is, a business which seems to do nothing but buy and then sell the very same goods, with apparently no intervening process of consumption and creation. To apply the model here, since no physical difference appears to exist, we must first identify some other significant difference between inputs and outputs (any difference at all will serve as evidence of an intervening process). The difference might be one of place, or time, or simply packaging. So, for example, we might say that the inputs of a fashion shop are 'clothes from the factory', while the outputs are 'clothes on the High Street', with some unspecified intervening process by which one is converted into the other. Likewise we might say that a market trader buys 'fruit at night' or 'fruit in boxes', and then after some process of conversion, sells 'fruit in the day' or 'fruit in bags'; and so on.

## LIMITATIONS

Finally, observe three limitations of the model. The first is that it concerns itself only with *transactions* – movements of money or promises across the boundary between the business and the outside world. (It is true as we have seen that the model must also assume some internal process by which inputs are consumed and outputs are created, but that process is only assumed. It is not directly observed or recorded by the accountant.) Thus it is not quite true to say that accounting reduces all things to the common denominator of money (the so-called 'money measurement' concept). The truth is, that accounting is just not interested in anything that is not, was not, or cannot be represented as, a movement of money or promises IN to or OUT of the business.

A second and unexpectedly serious limitation concerns the measurement of profit or loss. We have already observed that profit arises from a non-financial process of consumption and creation which is not directly seen by the accountant. This fact need not bother us, as long as the business consists of a series of separate ventures, with each lot of inputs fully converted into outputs and sold before the next lot of inputs is acquired. Profit in that case is easily determined by counting the money in the business when each venture ends. But modern business does not work like that. There is more often a continuous flow of inputs into the process, with some inputs consumed immediately and others sometimes taking years before their value is consumed. In that case, it becomes almost impossible to measure profit or loss with any degree of certainty, because we cannot clearly see which inputs were consumed in order to create the outputs that were sold in any period. This is a difficult problem to which we shall return.

A third limitation is the more general point made earlier, that the accounting model, as we have drawn it, represents only a profit-seeking enterprise. It cannot pretend to represent a body with any other object than the preservation of its capital and the making of a profit from the sale of goods or services. Organizations with other objects may quite properly use the double entry method of accounting for transactions, but the accounting model of a business does not truly fit. Many organizations, up to and including the state itself, cannot properly be forced into that mould.

## REVIEW

This chapter has introduced the accounting model of a business, with the associated definition of a transaction and the rule for recording every transaction as part of an exchange of equal value. It described the profit-making process of consumption and creation that occurs within the firm, and it identified the substance of profit as an accumulation of money, promises and unconsumed inputs inside the business. Finally, the chapter briefly mentioned three of the model's major limitations. Future chapters will show in detail how the logic of the model is applied to specific transactions and events.

# DRILLS AND EXERCISES

## 2.1 Transactions

State whether or not each of the following events fits the double entry definition of a transaction, giving reasons. (Observe that not every interesting event is a transaction.)

1. a firm pays wages of £50 cash
2. a farmer buys a cow for £1 000
3. a farmer's cow gives birth to a calf worth £300
4. a firm buys a machine for £10 000
5. goods worth £5 000 are destroyed in a fire
6. a person finds a £10 note in the street
7. a person inherits gold and jewellery worth £25 000
8. an uncle promises to give his nephew £20 000 in three years' time
9. a mother promises to pay the bank if her son fails to repay his overdraft
10. an oil company discovers oil reserves worth £10 billion

## 2.2 Consumption and creation (simple cases)

For each of the following firms or industries, identify the major inputs and outputs, and outline the process that takes place inside the firm.

1. an oil refinery
2. a chocolate factory
3. a flourmill
4. a bakery
5. a restaurant
6. a ship-builder
7. a tailor
8. a shoe manufacturer
9. a shoe shop
10. a firm of lawyers or accountants
11. an orchestra
12. a hospital
13. a private school
14. a newspaper
15. an hotel
16. an airline
17. a car hire company
18. a market research company
19. a software house
20. a second-hand furniture shop

## 2.3 Consumption and creation (some less obvious cases)

For each of the following firms or industries, identify the major inputs and outputs, and outline the process involved.

1. a water company
2. a timber-logging company
3. a fishing company
4. a scientific research company
5. a coal mining company
6. an arable farmer
7. a cattle farmer
8. a television station
9. an insurance company
10. a bank
11. an estate agency
12. a betting shop

## 2.4 Profit

Define profit in terms of the double entry model of a business, and explain why the calculation of profit should be such a difficult problem for accountants.

## 2.5 The double entry model and non-commercial organizations

For each of the organizations below, identify the major inputs and outputs if possible, and consider whether the double entry model of a business is fully applicable. If the model is not applicable, at what point does it fail? What legal or administrative changes would make the organization more conformable to the double entry model of a business? Would such changes be desirable?

1. the Roman Catholic Church
2. an amateur football club
3. the International Olympic Committee
4. Oxfam
5. Oxford University
6. the United Nations
7. the House of Commons
8. the police force
9. a national government
10. a regiment in the army
11. the stock exchange
12. the Conservative Party
13. the Institute of Chartered Accountants
14. the accounting department of a large firm
15. a trade union

# CHAPTER 3

# Money and Value

## OBJECTIVES

*The objectives of this chapter are:*

- to explain what is meant by money and what is meant by value in accounting, and why the distinction is important
- to explain how most statements in accounting that may appear to be about money, are in fact about value in some other form

## MONEY AND VALUE

In the accounting model of a business, a transaction is a movement of money or promises in to or out of a business, and every transaction must be recorded as an exchange of equal value. The crucial elements are money, value and exchange.

In accounting, *money* means whatever is immediately acceptable in exchange for other things. Historically money has taken many forms (leaves, stones, shells, pieces of precious metal, and so on), but in a modern economy money most obviously takes the form of local currency notes and coins. These are things which can be counted.

Meanwhile *value*, in accounting, means only exchange value, or the value at which a thing could be bought or sold. Value in this sense may take many forms and is present in anything that can be exchanged by way of trade – a house, a car, a pencil, a right of access or whatever. However, there can be no exchange value in anything that cannot be bought or sold. Thus it is important to note from this definition that many things normally considered very precious – fresh air or personal freedom, for example – can have no record in accounting. They cannot be bought and sold and therefore have no value in exchange.

Value (from now on we shall drop the explicit reference to *exchange* value) has two characteristics that are especially troublesome for accountants, as we shall see in later chapters. First, value is not an unchanging attribute. Things may gain or lose value, sometimes very rapidly, as circumstances change. Secondly, value can never be known with certainty, except at the very moment when it is realized or turned into money in the course of a transaction. At any other time, the value of an object or a service can only be estimated, with varying degrees of probability.

## MEASURING VALUE

Unlike money, value cannot be counted. It can however be quantified, and therefore needs some unit of measurement. The chosen unit may vary from place to place, but in the UK value is generally measured in pounds, while in most of western Europe it is measured in euros, and so on.

Here is considerable scope for error and confusion. On the one hand considering value we have pounds or euros as units of measurement, which are always purely abstract. On the other hand considering money we have pounds or euros as notes and coins, which are familiar physical objects. The problem is that the authorities who make the things we use for money – notes and coins – have a tendency to name their notes and coins after the value they are made to represent (the value for which they are supposed to be accepted in exchange). Thus in the UK the coin that is made to carry the value of £1, is also called 'one pound', and this gives rise to ambiguity. A simple statement such as 'this is £3' could refer to £3 *of money* – objects called pounds – or it could refer to £3 *of value*, in the form of (say) a book or a pen.

In accounting and financial affairs, and in the thinking of accountants, this ambiguity must be avoided, for the difference between money and value in some other form may be of critical significance. At the level of the individual, for example, someone owning millions of pounds' worth of value in the form of houses, cars, shares in companies, and works of art might also starve to death in a great city if they have no access to a few pence worth of value in the form of money to buy food. Likewise in business, a firm which has millions of pounds of value invested in buildings or machinery might be forced to close if it has no immediate access to value in the form of money, and cannot pay its creditors when payment falls due.

## MONEY AND VALUE IN ACCOUNTING

Statements in accounting are in general references to value, not to money. Or rather, to be quite precise: in accounting any reference to £x or $y is *always* a reference to value, but the value referred to may exist in any form, and is *not* usually in the form of money. If a statement refers in fact to value in the form of money, the reference to money must be made explicit. Thus, it may be true to say that some very rich person has billions of pounds or dollars (of value in many different forms), but if you wish to imply that their house and pockets are stuffed with bank-notes, then you must say that they have billions of pounds or dollars *in cash* (which will very seldom be the case).

## THINGS AND VALUES OF THINGS

Financial accounting is especially concerned with relations between values: every transaction is recorded as an exchange of *equal* value; profit is a *difference* between values; and so on. As it happens though, accountants often drop the explicit reference to value. Instead of saying for example:

$$value \text{ of } x = value \text{ of } y$$

as they should, accountants tend to say just '$x = y$'. This too is a likely source of confusion. Statements about things are not the same as statements about their values, and relations between things are not the same as relations between their values. If for example I have a shiny, fast, and expensive car, worth £100 000, and a less extravagant house, also worth £100 000, I can write without ambiguity that for me:

$$\begin{matrix} value \text{ of} & & value \text{ of} \\ \text{CAR} & = & \text{HOUSE} \end{matrix}$$

But it would be seriously misleading to omit the reference to value and write that for me:

$$\text{CAR} = \text{HOUSE}$$

because I do not live in my car, and the equality between my car and my house is only in the dimension of value.

## REVIEW

Financial accounting is essentially descriptive. It proceeds from observation, and not by deduction from a set of definitions. However, description depends on words, and while we may properly prefer description over definition in respect of things, it remains important to define the words we use, or at least to point very clearly to whatever it is we mean when certain words are used.

This short chapter is designed to remove two potential sources of confusion. It tries to make clear the distinction between money and value (or, to be exact, the distinction between value in the form of money, and value in the abstract, which is measured in pounds, but which may exist in any form). It also draws attention to the way in which many statements in accounting, which appear to be about things, are in fact about the value of things.

# DRILLS AND EXERCISES

## 3.1 Money or value?

Comment on each of the statements or expressions below in the light of the distinction between money and value.

1. In the year 2000, Britain's Gross Domestic Product was €950 billion.
2. US foreign aid amounts to $28 billion per year.
3. 'Celebrity wins million pound divorce settlement.'
4. 'Win a £10 000 holiday.'
5. '£10 million bank robbery.'
6. '£4 million art theft.'
7. 'Russian tycoon R.A. is today £7 billion richer after the sale of his shares in a major oil company.'
8. 'ABC plc announces £9 million profit.'

## 3.2 Value and exchange value

1. Identify at least three valuable resources whose existence cannot be recognized in the context of financial accounting, and explain why.
2. Explain how carbon trading brings environmental effects within the ambit of financial accounting.

# PART TWO

# Recording Financial Events

Part 2 shows how the accounting model can be applied to the recording of business transactions, and explains the basic procedures involved in preparing a Profit and Loss Account and a balance sheet. Part 2 concludes with a short demonstration of how accounting techniques can be used to intervene and adjust the profit or loss that will be reported by a firm.

# CHAPTER 4

# Analyzing Simple Cash Transactions

## OBJECTIVES

*The objectives of this chapter are:*

- to show how any simple transaction involving cash can be analyzed as an exchange of equal value
- to explain the importance, in transactions involving indeterminate goods, of identifying the goods as either outputs (called sales) or inputs (called purchases)

## GENERAL PROCEDURE

Before any transaction can be recorded in the double entry system, it must be analyzed as an exchange of equal value, with the value coming IN to the firm being equal to the value going OUT. For each of the two movements involved the analysis must show direction, thing moving, and value. (Since a transaction is an exchange, one party's movement OUT will be the other party's movement IN, and vice versa, but for accounting purposes the directions IN and OUT must be determined with very careful reference to the particular firm whose transactions we are recording.)

In this chapter we shall concern ourselves only with transactions involving money, or cash. Transactions involving promises to pay later will be examined in the following chapter.

The general procedure is to identify the value and direction of the movement of money, and then to ask what comes IN to the firm, or goes OUT, in exchange for the money. When the analysis is written down, the movement IN to the firm is always written before the movement OUT, as shown in Box 4.1.

## BOX 4.1

**The Double Entry Analysis of a Transaction**

A firm buys some raw material for £800 cash.

Cash or money with a value of £800 is going OUT of the firm. What comes IN to the firm is raw material, which we must assume to be of equal value. The analysis will be written as:

| direction | thing moving | value IN | value OUT |
|---|---|---|---|
| IN | raw material | £800 | |
| OUT | cash | | £800 |

The column headings shown for convenience in Box 4.1 are usually omitted. Notice, however, the important convention already stated, that the movement IN is *always* written before the movement OUT, and also that relevant values are written away off to the right, with separate columns for the value moving IN and the value moving OUT. Also notice that the thing moving (not just its value) must always be specified. This is especially important when the thing that moves is money. Readers should avoid the temptation to assume that 'OUT £5' is enough to indicate that the movement is one of cash or money. Value can exist in many forms. If a movement concerns cash, then we must say so – '*OUT cash £5*'.

## PURCHASES AND SALES

In everyday language it is quite acceptable to talk about the purchase or the sale of indeterminate 'goods'. In accounting, however, it is vitally important to specify whether the goods in question are inputs or outputs. When the goods are *inputs* we must call them *purchases*, as shown in Box 4.2.

## BOX 4.2

**Purchases**

A firm buys goods for £100 cash.

We must identify these goods as inputs by calling them purchases. The analysis will be

| IN | purchases | £100 | |
|---|---|---|---|
| OUT | cash | | £100 |

When the goods are *outputs*, we must call them *sales*, as shown in Box 4.3.

## BOX 4.3

### Sales

A firm sells goods for £150 cash.

In this case the goods going OUT have been sold. They are outputs, and we must call them sales. The analysis will be

| IN | cash | £150 | |
|---|---|---|---|
| OUT | sales | | £150 |

The same use of the words 'sales' and 'purchases' may also be necessary, when the nature of the goods is specified (for example as apples or oranges) but the firm merely buys and sells the goods, and there is no physical change or change in name to accompany the change in value that occurs as the goods pass through the firm. So for example if a firm simply buys and sells 'cars' or 'fruit', then the cars or fruit will be called *purchases* when they are inputs, and *sales* when they are outputs.

Notice however that 'purchases' is not properly applied to everything a firm may buy. It is used here in a restricted, quasi-technical sense. If a firm buys, say, equipment in order to use it, what comes IN to the firm is equipment, not purchases. Purchases means only those goods that are bought by the firm with the intention of converting them into sales. Likewise, not everything sold by a firm is rightly called sales. Sales means only those things that are normally sold in the usual course of business.

## RETURNS

It is not the case that all things going OUT of a firm must be outputs or sales just because of their direction going out, nor that all things coming IN must be inputs or purchases just because of their direction coming in. On the contrary, some of the things coming IN to a firm may in fact be sales coming back in to the firm from dissatisfied customers. Likewise some of the things going OUT of a firm may in fact be unsatisfactory or unwanted inputs going back out to the supplier.

The rule is that inputs and outputs, or purchases and sales, are distinguished not by their direction, but by their position relative to the value-changing process that takes place inside the firm. Goods remain classified as purchases or inputs until they have passed through the value-changing process and been sold. Goods that have passed through the process and been sold are classified as sales, even when they come back in again. This general rule is especially important when dealing with returns.

Sales returns are goods that have previously gone out as sales, but are now returned to the firm by customers. When they come back in, these goods still count as sales despite their inward - direction. Box 4.4 shows an example.

## BOX 4.4

### Sales Returns

A firm takes back some goods from a dissatisfied customer, and gives the customer a full refund of £500 cash.

Money is going OUT of the firm, but the goods coming IN are not purchases. They are simply sales coming back again, so the analysis will be

| IN | sales (or 'sales returns') | £500 | |
|----|----------------------------|------|------|
| OUT | cash | | £500 |

Purchase returns are purchases that go back out of the firm, being returned by the firm to its suppliers, as shown in Box 4.5.

## BOX 4.5

### Purchase Returns

A firm returns some goods to the supplier, receiving a full refund of £250 in cash.

Coming IN to the firm is the cash receivedas a refund. The goods going OUT have not yet passed through the value-changing process. They are simply purchases which have been turned around and sent back out.

| IN | cash | £250 | |
|----|------|------|------|
| OUT | purchases (or 'purchase returns') | | £250 |

# IDEAS OF PERMISSION AND SERVICE

Inputs and outputs need not be tangible objects. They can include such abstract things as permission to do something, or the performance of a service. Box 4.6 shows an example involving the sale of a permission.

## BOX 4.6

### Ideas of Permission and Service

A farmer charges someone £50 in cash to park a caravan in his field.
From the farmer's point of view, the analysis will be:

| IN | cash | £50 | |
|----|------|------|------|
| OUT | permission to park in field | | £50 |

## WAGES AND SALARIES

Wages and salaries are payments for work done by employees. Money goes OUT of the business. What comes IN is work or labour, as shown in Box 4.7.

### BOX 4.7

**Payment of Wages**

A firm pays wages of £150 in cash. The analysis will be:

| IN | labour | £150 | |
|-----|--------|------|------|
| OUT | cash | | £150 |

## HIRE OF GOODS OR EQUIPMENT

Hiring goods or equipment means making payments in exchange for permission to use the goods or equipment, as shown in Box 4.8.

### BOX 4.8

**Hire of Equipment**

A firm pays £450 cash to hire a crane. The analysis will be:

| IN | permission to use crane | £450 | |
|-----|-------------------------|------|------|
| OUT | cash | | £450 |

## RENT

Rent is a payment, usually of money, in exchange for permission to use property (land or buildings). A firm may pay rent or receive it. Box 4.9 shows the analysis of a rental payment received.

### BOX 4.9

**Rent**

A firm receives rent of £360 in cash from a tenant. The analysis will be:

| IN | cash | £360 | |
|-----|------------------------------|------|------|
| OUT | permission to use building | | £360 |

# INTEREST PAYMENTS

Interest is like rent on money – it is a payment for permission to use money. (If I give you my money, expecting you to keep it safe, then I should pay you for guarding it. If on the other hand I allow you to use my money and risk losing it, then you should pay me for giving you that permission, and the payment – or reason for the payment – will be called interest.) Most firms borrow money, and therefore pay interest for permission to use it. Box 4.10 shows how the payment of interest should be analyzed.

## BOX 4.10

### Payment of Interest

A firm pays £60 interest to a lender, in cash.

What goes OUT of the firm is cash. The payment is called interest because it is given in exchange for permission to use money. The analysis will be:

| IN | permission to use money | £60 | |
|-----|-------------------------|-----|-----|
| OUT | cash | | £60 |

# PRICE, QUANTITY, AND TRADE DISCOUNTS

While a business may publish a list of prices for the goods it sells, it may also negotiate special prices for individual customers, or offer price discounts to special groups such as students, or persons above or below a certain age. Alternatively a firm may offer quantity discounts for large orders, or special discounts to business customers (trade discounts). Where such discounts are involved, the final selling price could then be analyzed into two elements (as list price, minus discount). By convention however, the list price and the discount are *not* separately recorded in the accounts. The only value to be used in accounting for a transaction at a discounted price is the value after discount. Box 4.11 shows an example.

## BOX 4.11

### Transactions at Discounted Prices

A firm sells goods at a list price of £1 each, with a discount of 10% for orders of 100 units or more.

The firm makes a cash sale of 100 units, allowing the usual discount for quantity.

The agreed price of the goods, and the transaction value to be accounted for, is £90. The transaction will be recorded as:

| IN | cash | £90 | |
|-----|-------|-----|-----|
| OUT | sales | | £90 |

## EVERYDAY LANGUAGE AND DOUBLE ENTRY ANALYSIS

In everyday language, some single words – like 'refund', 'wages', 'rent', or 'interest' – are used to combine two separate ideas. Their meaning covers not only the money used to make a payment, but also the purpose of the payment. Thus a refund means 'money given back', for whatever reason, while wages means 'money paid in exchange for labour', rent means 'money paid in exchange for permission to use land or buildings', and so on, as we have seen above. These words, and others like them, are dangerous in double entry, because the double entry analysis depends precisely upon the separation of the two ideas which they so neatly bundle up together. To use the double entry we must first unpick the combination, so that each separate element of meaning can be separately recorded. In the double entry, a movement of money is recorded as a movement of money. That is *what* happened. The reason for the movement (what was got or given in exchange) is separately recorded as an input or an output. That is *why* it happened.

## REVIEW

This chapter has shown how a variety of ordinary commercial transactions can be analyzed as an exchange of equal value. Examples included the sale and purchase of goods, the treatment of returns, and extensive use of the idea that payments may be made or received in exchange for a service, or for permission to use something or do something. In the context of payments for a service or permission, the chapter dealt with wages and salaries, payments for the hire of equipment, rents, and interest.

# DRILLS AND EXERCISES

## 4.1 Analyzing simple cash transactions

Analyze each of the following transactions as movements of equal value IN to and OUT of the business, as shown in the first example below.

1. a firm buys goods for £600 cash

| IN | *purchases* | £600 | |
|----|-------------|------|------|
| OUT | *cash* | | £600 |

2. a firm sells goods for £700 cash
3. a building firm buys a cement-mixer for £5 000 cash
4. a firm pays wages £150 cash
5. a firm pays £15 cash for window cleaning
6. a firm receives £250 rent, in cash
7. a clothes shop sells clothes for £70 cash
8. a firm pays a manager's monthly salary £1 500 in cash
9. a business pays £500 cash for advertising
10. a professional business collects £450 cash from a client for advice

11. a hotel business charges a customer £100 cash for a room for the night
12. a business which runs buses collects 50p cash from a passenger for a ticket
13. a business pays an insurance premium of £800 for the year, in cash
14. the business above (in Q13) cancels its insurance half-way through the year, and receives a refund of £400 in cash
15. a business pays £125 cash for a licence to trade in the market
16. a business pays £300 cash to hire a machine for a week
17. a business pays £25 cash as interest to a lender
18. a business pays £85 in cash for electricity
19. a business pays £350 in cash for use of the telephone
20. the business above (in Q19) was overcharged, and receives a cash refund of £50 from the telephone company
21. a business pays £1 500 cash for one of its employees to attend a management training course
22. a money-lending business receives £15 cash, interest from a borrower
23. a business buys goods for £500 cash on Monday, and sells the same goods for £750 cash on Tuesday
24. a firm of inventors receives royalties of £1 000 in cash, from a firm which uses one of their patented inventions
25. a firm allows a 10% discount to regular customers. The firm sells goods with a list price of £200 to a regular customer, therefore receiving £180 in cash
26. a firm pays a refund of £20 cash to a customer who has returned some unwanted goods previously bought from the firm
27. a firm returns some goods to the supplier, and receives a refund of £25 cash
28. a restaurant firm receives payment of £45 cash from a customer
29. a firm pays £36 cash for one year's membership of a trade association
30. a firm pays £20 cash to a student for handing out advertising material

## 4.2 Understanding analyzed transactions

Describe in words each of the transactions below, which have already been analyzed in terms of the double entry system as an exchange of equal value.

1.

| IN | cash | £80 |
|-----|-------|------|
| OUT | sales | £80 |

2.

| IN | purchases | £100 |
|-----|-----------|------|
| OUT | cash | £100 |

3.

| IN | labour | £60 |
|-----|-------|------|
| OUT | cash | £60 |

4.

| | | | |
|---|---|---|---|
| IN | permission to use property | £450 | |
| OUT | cash | | £450 |

5.

| | | | |
|---|---|---|---|
| IN | sales | £95 | |
| OUT | cash | | £95 |

6.

| | | | |
|---|---|---|---|
| IN | cash | £18 | |
| OUT | purchases | | £18 |

7.

| | | | |
|---|---|---|---|
| IN | permission to use money | £55 | |
| OUT | cash | | £55 |

8.

| | | | |
|---|---|---|---|
| IN | use of telephone | £105 | |
| OUT | cash | | £105 |

9.

| | | | |
|---|---|---|---|
| IN | cash | £150 | |
| OUT | legal advice | | £150 |

10.

| | | | |
|---|---|---|---|
| IN | taxi ride | £12 | |
| OUT | cash | | £12 |

11.

| | | | |
|---|---|---|---|
| IN | insurance | £180 | |
| OUT | cash | | £180 |

12.

| | | | |
|---|---|---|---|
| IN | cash | £290 | |
| OUT | lessons | | £290 |

13.

| | | | |
|---|---|---|---|
| IN | machinery | £150 | |
| OUT | cash | | £150 |

14.

| IN | trade association membership | £48 | |
|----|------------------------------|-----|-----|
| OUT | cash | | £48 |

15.

| IN | vehicle licence | £55 | |
|----|-----------------|-----|-----|
| OUT | cash | | £55 |

# CHAPTER 5

# Credit and the Use of Promises

## OBJECTIVES

*The objectives of this chapter are:*

- to explain the practice of trading on credit and the use of promises
- to show how any transaction involving a promise can be analyzed as an exchange of equal value
- to explain some of the related terminology including: *debtor, creditor, receivables,* and *payables*

## TRANSACTIONS ON CREDIT

Each party to a commercial exchange must attend to the completion of two quite separate tasks: transfer of goods or services, and transfer of money to pay for them. In a cash transaction, these two tasks must be completed simultaneously – so money, goods or services, and people to receive and deliver them must be brought together in the same place at the same time.

Where there is trading on credit, however, these different tasks may be separated from each other in terms of time, place, or personnel responsible. This separation is effected by the use of promises as a form of interim payment – a transaction on credit being one in which goods or services are exchanged for a promise to pay later. Thus with trading on credit, goods may be delivered today in location *X*, by person *A* to person *B*, in exchange for a promise of payment tomorrow in location *Y*, by person *C* to person *D*, and so on. The ease and flexibility of trading on credit are such that nowadays almost all business-to-business transactions are conducted on credit, as well as an increasing proportion of transactions involving the consumer.

## ORIGINAL PROMISES

A firm may buy on credit or sell on credit. In the case of buying on credit, goods or services come IN to the firm, and a promise to pay goes OUT to the supplier, as shown in Box 5.1.

## BOX 5.1

### Analyzing a Purchase on Credit

A firm buys goods on credit for £300 from Supplier S.

| IN | purchases | £300 | |
|------|----------------------|------|------|
| OUT | promise to Supplier S | | £300 |

In the case of selling on credit, goods or services go OUT of the firm, and a promise to pay comes IN from the customer, as shown in Box 5.2.

## BOX 5.2

### Analyzing a Sale on Credit

A firm sells goods on credit to Customer C for £450.

| IN | promise from Customer C | £450 | |
|------|-------------------------|------|------|
| OUT | sales | | £450 |

## THE NATURE OF PROMISES TO PAY

It may be worth remarking that the promises involved in a transaction on credit need not be written down and handed from one party to the other. They are understood to exist in law, even if they have no physical form.

## MONEY PAYMENT

When payment is finally made in money, the original promise will be returned to the party who first gave it. Thus a transaction on credit is part of a process which is completed in two stages:

1. exchange of goods or service for promise; and
2. exchange of promise for money.

The two stages in respect of a sale on credit are shown in Box 5.3.

## BOX 5.3

### The Two Stages of a Sale on Credit

1. A firm sells goods on credit to Customer A for £725.

| IN | promise from Customer A | £725 | |
|---|---|---|---|
| OUT | sales | | £725 |

2. The firm receives £725 cash payment from Customer A.

| IN | cash | £725 | |
|---|---|---|---|
| OUT | promise back to Customer A | | £725 |

Notice that while the use of promises splits the essential exchange of money for goods and services into two separate stages, the end result will be the same as a cash transaction: after completion of both stages in Box 5.3 the firm which made the sale has the money, while the customer has the goods, and (because the relevant promise has come IN from the customer and gone back OUT again) there are no outstanding promises.

## TRANSACTIONS ON ACCOUNT

Either one of the two stages required to complete a purchase or sale on credit, or indeed any transaction involving a promise, may be called a transaction on account. Box 5.4 shows two examples.

## BOX 5.4

### Transactions on Account

1. A firm buys goods on account from Supplier P for £320.

| IN | purchases | £320 | |
|---|---|---|---|
| OUT | promise to Supplier P | | £320 |

2. A firm makes a payment of £150 cash to XYZ Ltd, on account.

| IN | promise from XYZ Ltd | £150 | |
|---|---|---|---|
| OUT | cash | | £150 |

## DEBTORS AND CREDITORS, RECEIVABLES AND PAYABLES

*Debtor* and *creditor* are terms which describe the different parties to the transfer of a promise. Specifically:

- a debtor is a firm or a person who has given a promise; and
- a creditor is a firm or person who has received a promise.

The word debtor is related to the word duty – debtors have a duty to make the payments they have promised. The word creditor, along with others like credible and credulous, is related to the idea of belief – creditors are believers in the promises they receive. Giving credit means giving belief, by accepting promises. Taking credit means taking advantage of belief, by giving promises.

Promises that have come in from debtors are also called *receivables*, with reference to the value of money ultimately receivable when the debt is paid. Similarly promises that have gone out to creditors are also called payables, this time with reference to the value of money ultimately payable by the firm to the creditor.

## TRADE DEBTORS AND TRADE CREDITORS, RECEIVABLES AND PAYABLES

Debtors and creditors who have given or received promises in the course of trade (buying or selling), are usually identified as trade debtors or trade creditors. It is fair to say therefore that:

- trade debtors are *customers* who have not yet made payment in money, and trade receivables are the promises they have given; while
- trade creditors are *suppliers* who are waiting for payment, and trade payables are the promises they have accepted in the interim.

## PROMISES FROM, AND PROMISES TO

A promise IN from a firm or person may cancel all *or part* of a promise OUT to the same firm or person, and vice versa. This means that the full amount of any original promise need not be paid all at once. Any payment of a smaller amount will serve to reduce the value of the promise that remains to be paid. Box 5.5 shows an example.

## BOX 5.5

**Promises From and Promises To**

1. A firm buys goods on credit from Supplier S for £600.

| IN | purchases | £600 | |
|---|---|---|---|
| OUT | promise to Supplier S | | £600 |

2. The firm pays £200 cash to Supplier S.

| IN | promise back from Supplier S | £200 | |
|---|---|---|---|
| OUT | cash | | £200 |

This £200 promise coming IN from Supplier S will be set off against the original promise to pay £600 that went OUT to Supplier S in transaction 1.

It leaves a net promise of £400 which the firm must still pay to Supplier S.

Since promises IN from and OUT to the same person will cancel each other, it is important in - practice to record *to whom* the business gives each promise, and *from whom* it receives each promise. As far as possible our analysis should reflect this – not just 'IN promise' or 'OUT promise', but 'IN promise *from X*' and 'OUT promise *to Y*'. In textbook examples, if no name is given, the other party to the transaction can be identified as 'customer' or 'supplier' (or 'debtor' or 'creditor') as appropriate.

# REVIEW

This chapter has introduced the idea of credit and the use of promises in business, describing transactions on credit and showing how the two stages of a transaction on credit are analyzed and recorded in the double entry system. The chapter also defined some relevant terms, including debtor and creditor, payable and receivable.

# DRILLS AND EXERCISES

## 5.1 Analyzing simple transactions on credit

Analyze each of the following transactions as movements of equal value IN to and OUT of the business, as shown in the first example below.

1. (a) a firm buys goods on credit from A for £35

| IN | purchases | £35 | |
|---|---|---|---|
| OUT | promise to A | | £35 |

(b) the firm pays A £35 cash

| IN | promise back from A | £35 | |
|---|---|---|---|
| OUT | cash | | £35 |

2. (a) a firm sells goods on credit to B for £70
   (b) the firm receives £70 cash payment from B
3. (a) a firm sells goods on credit to C for £150
   (b) the firm receives a payment of £150 cash from C
4. (a) a firm buys goods on credit from S for £360
   (b) the firm makes a payment of £360 cash to S
5. (a) a firm sells goods on credit to C for £55
   (b) the firm receives a payment of £55 cash from C
6. (a) a firm buys goods on credit from a supplier for £50
   (b) the firm pays the supplier £40 cash
   (c) the firm pays the supplier a further £10 cash
7. (a) a firm sells goods on credit to a customer for £75
   (b) the firm receives a payment of £50 cash from the customer
   (c) the firm receives a further payment of £25 cash from the customer
8. a firm buys goods on credit for £250
9. a firm sells goods on credit for £375
10. a firm buys goods on account from a supplier for £85
11. a firm pays a supplier £45 on account
12. a firm sells goods on account for £47
13. a firm receives a payment of £23 cash on account from a customer
14. a firm receives a payment of £17 cash from a debtor
15. a firm pays of £36 cash to a creditor

## 5.2 Analyzing further transactions on credit

Note: this drill includes purchase returns and sales returns, where the original transaction was on credit, and the treatment of possible overpayments on account.

Analyze each of the following transactions as movements of equal value IN to and OUT of the business.

1. (a) a firm buys goods on credit from a supplier for £15
   (b) the firm sends the entire consignment of goods back to the supplier
2. (a) a firm sells goods on credit for £10
   (b) all of the goods involved in the sale above are sent back by the customer
3. (a) a firm buys goods on credit for £65
   (b) the firm sends goods, which originally cost £45, back to the supplier
4. (a) a firm sells goods on credit for £80
   (b) half of the goods involved in the sale above are sent back by the customer
5. (a) a firm buys goods on credit from a supplier for £95
   (b) the firm pays the supplier £100 cash
   (c) the supplier repays £5 cash to the firm
6. (a) a firm sells goods on credit to a customer for £40
   (b) the firm receives a payment of £50 cash from the customer
   (c) the firm repays £10 cash to the customer
7. (a) a firm buys goods on credit for £100
   (b) the firm returns goods value £40 to the supplier
   (c) the firm pays the supplier £50 cash
8. (a) a firm sells goods on credit for £160
   (b) £60 of the goods above are returned by the customer
   (c) the firm receives payment of £100 cash from the customer
9. (a) a firm buys goods on credit for £56
   (b) the firm returns goods value £16 to the supplier
   (c) the firm pays the supplier £56 cash
   (d) the firm receives £16 cash repayment from the supplier
10. (a) a firm sells goods on credit for £227
    (b) £27 of the goods above are returned by the customer
    (c) the firm receives payment of £100 cash from the customer

## 5.3 Understanding analyzed transactions

Describe in words each of the transactions below, which have already been analyzed in terms of the double entry system as an exchange of equal value.

1.

| IN  | promise from A | £80 |     |
| --- | -------------- | --- | --- |
| OUT | sales          |     | £80 |

| IN  | cash         | £80 |     |
| --- | ------------ | --- | --- |
| OUT | promise to A |     | £80 |

2.

| IN | purchases | £60 | |
|---|---|---|---|
| OUT | promise to S | | £60 |

| IN | promise from S | £60 | |
|---|---|---|---|
| OUT | cash | | £60 |

3.

| IN | purchases | £145 | |
|---|---|---|---|
| OUT | promise to X | | £145 |

| IN | promise from X | £45 | |
|---|---|---|---|
| OUT | purchases | | £45 |

| IN | promise from X | £100 | |
|---|---|---|---|
| OUT | cash | | £100 |

4.

| IN | promise from customer | £105 | |
|---|---|---|---|
| OUT | sales | | £105 |

| IN | sales | £65 | |
|---|---|---|---|
| OUT | promise to customer | | £65 |

| IN | cash | £40 | |
|---|---|---|---|
| OUT | promise to customer | | £40 |

5.

| IN | purchases | £115 | |
|---|---|---|---|
| OUT | promise to supplier | | £115 |

| IN | promise from supplier | £125 | |
|---|---|---|---|
| OUT | cash | | £125 |

| IN | cash | £10 | |
|---|---|---|---|
| OUT | promise to supplier | | £10 |

6.

| IN | promise from customer | £57 | |
|----|----|----|----|
| OUT | sales | | £57 |

| IN | cash | £77 | |
|----|----|----|----|
| OUT | promise to customer | | £77 |

| IN | promise from customer | £20 | |
|----|----|----|----|
| OUT | cash | | £20 |

## 5.4 Exercises

1. If you were determined to sabotage a firm, would you cause more damage by destroying the record of the firm's debtors, or the record of its creditors?
2. As an industrial spy, what useful information would you hope to gain from
   (a) copying a firm's records of its debtors?
   (b) copying a firm's records of its creditors?
3. A firm has bought goods on credit from A for £100, and sold goods on credit to B for £100.
   Is it fair to say that the firm's £100 payable to A is fully covered (i.e. equalled in value) by its £100 receivable from B?
4. 'Neither a debtor nor a creditor be.'
   Is this good advice? ('good' for the individual, or 'good' for society at large?)
5. (a) If you had to choose, would you rather be a debtor or a creditor?
   (b) What difference would it make to your choice if you lived in a time of rising prices (or of falling prices)?
6. 'In revolutionary politics, the class of debtors will aspire to dismantle the state, while the class of creditors will try to take it over.'
   Is this theory plausible?

# CHAPTER 6

# Bank and Cheque Transactions

## OBJECTIVES

*The objectives of this chapter are:*

- to show how any transaction between a firm and its bank can be analyzed as an exchange of equal value
- to explain the use of bank promises as an alternative form of money
- to explain how cheques are used to make payments by instructing a bank to transfer its promises to another person

## BANK DEPOSITS AND WITHDRAWALS

When a firm takes cash to the bank and makes a deposit, it gives money to the bank and receives in exchange the bank's promise that when asked, it will return money of equal value. This is a transaction, involving the exchange of money for a promise. Box 6.1 shows the analysis.

### BOX 6.1

---

**Depositing Cash at the Bank**

A firm puts £500 cash into the bank.

Going OUT of the firm is cash; coming IN is a promise from the bank.

| IN | promise from bank | £500 | |
|-----|-------------------|------|------|
| OUT | cash | | £500 |

---

When a firm withdraws cash from the bank, it must give a promise back to the bank in exchange for the money it is taking. Again this is a transaction, as shown in Box 6.2.

BOX 6.2

### A Withdrawal from the Bank

The firm above takes £400 cash out of the bank.

What comes IN to the firm is cash; what goes OUT is a promise returned to the bank.

| | | | |
|---|---|---|---|
| IN | cash | £400 | |
| OUT | promise given back to bank | | £400 |

## BANK PROMISES AND MONEY

When banks are well regulated and responsibly managed, as nowadays they usually are, bank promises become an alternative form of money. Firms and individuals will generally hold bank promises in preference to holding money in the form of notes and coins, especially where large sums are concerned. More importantly, the transfer of bank promises becomes accepted as a means of payment that is more secure and convenient than the transfer of cash itself. To make payment using this new form of money requires only a means of transferring bank promises, which is most commonly done by cheque.

## PAYMENT BY CHEQUE

A cheque is an instruction to a bank, from the person writing (or 'drawing') the cheque, instructing the bank to take a promise away from the writer of the cheque, and give money or a promise of equal value to some other named person, who is called the payee. (If the payee uses a different bank, then the bank receiving the instruction may give its promise to the payee's bank, with further instructions for that bank to give money or a promise of equal value to the payee.)

Writing a cheque is therefore a way of giving a promise OUT to one's own bank, on the understanding that the payee will in the end get money or a promise from their own bank, which will be accepted as equivalent to money. In the double entry analysis, what matters when a firm makes a payment by cheque, is that the movement of 'money' must be recorded as a promise going OUT to the bank, in exchange for whatever comes IN, as shown in Box 6.3.

BOX 6.3

### Recording a Payment by Cheque

A firm buys goods for £45, paying by cheque.

| | | | |
|---|---|---|---|
| IN | purchases | £45 | |
| OUT | promise to bank | | £45 |

Conversely, when a firm receives a payment by cheque, it must record a promise coming IN from the bank, as shown in Box 6.4.

## BOX 6.4

**Recording the Receipt of a Cheque**

A firm sells goods for £90, receiving payment by cheque.

| IN | promise from bank | £90 | |
|---|---|---|---|
| OUT | sales | | £90 |

## 'BANK' AND 'CASH'

In summary, a cheque is a way of transferring bank promises, which are a form of money often preferable to notes and coins. There is therefore much accounting to be done for the movement of bank promises, and in practice it is usual to drop the reference to promises, calling this form of money simply 'bank', as opposed to the other form of money – notes and coins – which we call cash or petty cash. Box 6.5 shows an example.

## BOX 6.5

**'Bank'**

A firm pays a window cleaner £15 by cheque.

| IN | window cleaning | £15 | |
|---|---|---|---|
| OUT | bank | | £15 |

Although 'bank' means only promises from the bank, and 'petty cash' means only notes and coins, there is unfortunately some ambiguity about the word 'cash' on its own. Depending on the context, 'cash' may mean *all* forms of money (including notes, coins, *and* promises from the bank), or it may mean only notes and coins. There is also the expression 'cash at bank' which must be interpreted to mean the cash that the bank would have to give you, if you went along and asked for it. 'Cash at bank' is frequently opposed to 'cash in hand', which of course means notes and coins.

## CHEQUES AND THE BANKING SYSTEM

Although it is quite simple to record the issue or receipt of a cheque, writing a cheque will actually set in motion a complex sequence of events and transactions, all of which must be completed before the relevant payment is definitively made.

Imagine that X buys goods from Y, paying immediately by cheque.

1. When Y receives the cheque, she will record a promise coming IN from her bank, and sales going OUT.

2. Y will then take the cheque to her bank, which will record a promise going OUT to Y, and a promise coming IN from X's bank.
3. Y's bank will then send the cheque to X's bank, which (finally in accordance with X's instructions) will record a promise going OUT to Y's bank, and a promise coming IN from X.
4. Meanwhile X has already recorded the promise going OUT to his bank, and purchases coming IN.

It is only at stage 3, when X's bank receives the cheque and agrees to give a promise OUT to Y's bank, that the payment is definitively made. The process is illustrated in Box 6.6.

## BOX 6.6

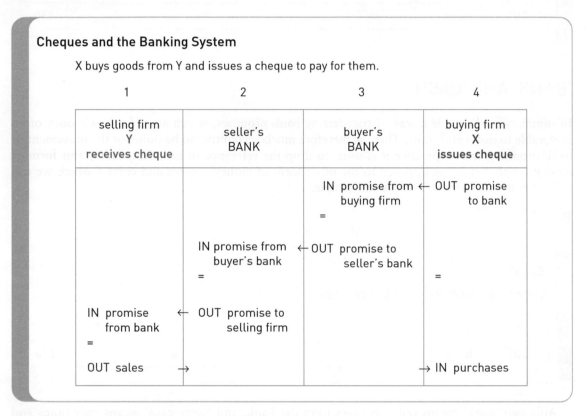

### Cheques and the Banking System

X buys goods from Y and issues a cheque to pay for them.

| 1 | 2 | 3 | 4 |
|---|---|---|---|
| selling firm Y receives cheque | seller's BANK | buyer's BANK | buying firm X issues cheque |
| | | IN promise from buying firm = | OUT promise to bank |
| | IN promise from buyer's bank = | ← OUT promise to seller's bank | = |
| IN promise from bank = OUT sales → | ← OUT promise to selling firm | | → IN purchases |

Notice in Box 6.6 how the series of promises is not *pushed* through the system by X who issues the cheque, as one might expect, but rather *pulled* through the system by Y, the payee, who sets the machinery in motion when she presents the cheque to her own bank.

## DISHONOURED CHEQUES AND OVERDRAFTS

A person who holding promises from a bank is perfectly entitled to instruct the bank to take its promises away from him or her, and give them to some other person, and the bank is obliged to obey the instruction. However it may be that a person writes a cheque when he or she holds no promises from the bank, or when the promises he or she does hold are not enough to cover the value of the cheque.

In this case when the cheque has been passed through the system and finally arrives at the issuer's bank, the bank has a choice. It may simply dishonour the cheque, refusing to honour or obey the instructions it contains. If this happens, the whole sequence of events and transactions will have to be reversed through the banking system, until the cheque itself is returned to the payee. In everyday language, we say that the cheque has bounced. More properly and politely though, it has been dishonoured.

Alternatively, the bank may allow the issuer of the cheque to overdraw, or have an overdraft. This means that the issuer's bank, having no promises of its own to take back, will instead take in a new promise from the issuer of the cheque, who will then owe money to the bank. However, unless previously agreed the bank has no obligation to allow the issuer to overdraw, and any overdraft that may be allowed is repayable on demand.

## DRAWING A CHEQUE AND CROSSING A CHEQUE

In the language of banking, cheques are not written or issued, they are drawn. The person or firm who writes a cheque is called the drawer of the cheque, and if the cheque is drawn on, say, the Royal Bank of Scotland, it means that the instructions it carries are addressed to the Royal Bank of Scotland.

A crossed cheque is one with two parallel lines drawn across it, often with 'account payee only' written between the lines. If a cheque is crossed, it means that the relevant bank is instructed not to give cash but, in the first instance, to give only a promise to the payee. This in turn means that the payee (or any other person claiming to be the payee) must have a bank account to receive the promise, and therefore should be identifiable and easily traced, in the event of any future query or suspicion. Thus it is difficult to benefit from stealing a crossed cheque, and as a security measure most banks now issue pre-printed cheque books with cheques already crossed.

## REVIEW

This chapter has described the analysis of transactions between a firm and its bank, and in particular the recording of cheque transactions, and the idea of bank promises as an alternative form of money, often called simply 'bank' or 'cash at bank'.

# DRILLS AND EXERCISES

## 6.1 Bank and cheque transactions

Analyze each of the following transactions as movements of equal value IN to and OUT of the business.

1. a firm pays wages of £50 by cheque
2. a firm sells goods for £300, receiving payment by cheque
3. a firm buys goods for £450, paying by cheque
4. a firm pays £75 cash into the bank
5. a firm takes £100 cash out of the bank
6. (a) a firm sells goods on credit to a customer for £35
   (b) the firm receives a payment of £20 by cheque from the customer
   (c) the firm receives a further payment of £15 in cash from the customer
7. (a) a firm buys goods on credit for £650
   (b) the firm pays the supplier £650 by cheque

8. a firm pays a supplier £90 on account, paying by cheque
9. a firm receives payment of £24 by cheque from a debtor
10. a firm receives and immediately pays an electricity bill of £260 by cheque
11. a firm takes £30 cash out of the bank
12. a market trader delivers the day's takings, £500 cash, to the bank
13. a customer returns some goods, and the firm gives a refund of £150 by cheque
14. a firm pays £240 by cheque for a year's subscription to a trade journal
15. a firm pays £600 by cheque to a newspaper, for placing an advertisement in the paper

## 6.2 Understanding analyzed bank transactions

Describe in words each of the transactions below, which have already been analysed in terms of the double entry system as an exchange of equal value.

1.

| IN | bank | £30 | |
| OUT | sales | | £30 |

2.

| IN | purchases | £40 | |
| OUT | bank | | £40 |

3.

| IN | labour | £50 | |
| OUT | bank | | £50 |

4.

| IN | bank | £56 | |
| OUT | cash | | £56 |

5.

| IN | promise from A | £37 | |
| OUT | bank | | £37 |

6.

| IN | cash | £100 | |
| OUT | bank | | £100 |

7.

| IN | sales | £45 | |
| OUT | bank | | £45 |

8.

| IN | bank | £95 | |
|---|---|---|---|
| OUT | promise to B | | £95 |

9.

| IN | rent (permission to use building) | £250 | |
|---|---|---|---|
| OUT | bank | | £250 |

10.

| IN | bank | £78 | |
|---|---|---|---|
| OUT | purchases | | £78 |

11.

| IN | club membership | £110 | |
|---|---|---|---|
| OUT | bank | | £110 |

12.

| IN | machinery | £500 | |
|---|---|---|---|
| OUT | bank | | £500 |

13.

| IN | insurance | £64 | |
|---|---|---|---|
| OUT | bank | | £64 |

14.

| IN | bank | £14 | |
|---|---|---|---|
| OUT | insurance | | £14 |

15.

| IN | bank X | £400 | |
|---|---|---|---|
| OUT | bank Y | | £400 |

## 6.3 Some exercises on banking arrangements

1. Why are bank promises considered to be almost as good as money, when your promises, or mine, are not?
2. Most of the large modern banks were founded in the 19th century and established themselves in grand, impressive local buildings. Some recent banks have been established with only an internet presence. Comment on the change in customer mentality that has allowed this development.
3. Explain the importance of reliable banking arrangements for the efficient conduct of business.

# CHAPTER 7

# Borrowing, Lending, and Interest

## OBJECTIVES

*The objectives of this chapter are:*

- to explain the difference between borrowing things and borrowing money
- to show how borrowing, lending and the repayment of loans can be analyzed as exchanges of equal value
- to emphasize the distinction between payment of interest and repayment of principal

## BORROWING THINGS AND BORROWING MONEY

There is a difference between borrowing or lending an object like a bicycle, and borrowing or lending money. When you borrow a bicycle, you receive possession but not ownership. The bicycle does not belong to you, and ultimately you must return it (the very same machine) to its owner. By convention borrowing or lending of this kind would not be regarded as a transaction. Money is not involved, and if there is a promise (to return the object), it relates to the thing itself, not to its value.

Borrowing money is different because when you borrow money you receive full ownership. You are not expected to return the very same notes and coins to the lender, and you may dispose of the money as you wish. Indeed the whole purpose of borrowing money is to spend it. However, while you may do as you like with the actual money that you borrow, you must promise the lender that ultimately you will repay money of equal value. Thus borrowing or lending money will qualify as a transaction, in which money is exchanged for a promise, as shown in Box 7.1.

## BOX 7.1

**Borrowing**

A firm borrows £750 cash from a lender.

From the firm's point of view, the transaction is:

| IN | cash | £750 | |
|------|-------------------|------|------|
| OUT | promise to lender | | £750 |

When a borrower makes any repayment, the lender must of course return all or part of the borrower's original promise, depending on how much is repaid. This transaction is shown in Box 7.2.

## BOX 7.2

**Repayment**

The firm above repays £500 to the lender by cheque. The analysis will be:

| IN | promise back from lender | £500 | |
|------|--------------------------|------|------|
| OUT | bank | | £500 |

## LENDING

Lending is the mirror image of borrowing. While the borrowing firm takes money IN and gives a promise OUT, the lending firm gives money OUT and takes a promise IN. Examples are given in the drills at the end of the chapter.

## PAYMENT OF INTEREST AND REPAYMENT OF PRINCIPAL

Transactions between borrowers and lenders may involve either payment of interest or repayment of principal, and sometimes the same transaction may contain elements of both. It is important to distinguish between the two.

In connection with a loan, 'principal' means the value borrowed and still to be repaid. 'Interest' means payment for permission to keep and use the money borrowed, just as rent means payment for permission to use property. The distinction between principal and interest is important because, just as one can pay rent on a house forever without ever gaining ownership, so one can pay interest on a loan forever without ever reducing the liability to repay the whole of the value originally borrowed. A repayment of principal however, does reduce the borrower's liability, and this must recognized by a return of all or part of the borrower's initial promise to repay.

Confusion between the two is perhaps only likely where one payment includes elements of both, as in the example shown in Box 7.3.

## BOX 7.3

### Payment of Interest and Repayment of Principal

A firm has previously borrowed £1 000 from XYZ, agreeing to pay interest at 10% per year on the value of the loan outstanding during the year, and to repay the principal by five equal instalments of £200.

Now, at the end of YEAR 1, the firm makes a single payment of £300 to XYZ by cheque.

Of the total £300 payment:
- £100 is interest, paid in exchange for permission to keep and use the money borrowed, and
- £200 is repayment of principal, paid in exchange for a partial return of the firm's original promise to repay.

The analysis will be:

| IN | interest (or permission to use money) | £100 | |
|----|----------------------------------------|------|------|
| IN | promise back from XYZ | £200 | |
| OUT | bank | | £300 |

## COMPOUND TRANSACTIONS

A simple transaction is one in which a single movement IN to the firm is matched against a single movement OUT. In Box 7.3, however, we saw an example of a compound transaction. A compound transaction is one in which the total value IN or OUT is composed of more than one element. Compound transactions are perfectly permissible as long as for every transaction the analysis shows *total* value IN equal to *total* value OUT. A further example is given in Box 7.4.

## BOX 7.4

### A Compound Transaction

A restaurant firm buys meat value £500 and vegetables value £400, paying the supplier £900 by cheque.

The analysis will be:

| IN | meat | £500 | |
|----|------|------|------|
| IN | vegetables | £400 | |
| OUT | bank | | £900 |

## 'TRADE' AND 'FINANCE'

The general class of debtors will now include borrowers who have given promises to repay the values lent to them, as well as customers who have given promises to pay for goods or services sold to them on credit. Likewise the general class of creditors will include lenders who have taken promises of repayment, as well as suppliers who have taken promises of payment, for goods or services supplied by them on credit). To distinguish between all of these:

- trade debtors are customers, and trade receivables are the promises they have given;
- finance debtors are borrowers, and finance receivables are the promises they have given;
- trade creditors are suppliers, and trade payables are the promises they have given;
- finance creditors are lenders, and finance payables are the promises they have given.

## REVIEW

This chapter has distinguished between borrowing and lending money, and borrowing and lending things. It described the double entry analysis of borrowing and lending money as an exchange of money for a promise to repay money of equal value at some later date. In connection with borrowing and lending the chapter also drew attention to the importance of the distinction between payment of interest and repayment of principal; and to the existence of compound transactions where total values IN or OUT may be composed of more than one element. Finally the chapter outlined the use of the terms 'trade' and 'finance' to distinguish between the different kinds of debtors and creditors, receivables and payables.

## DRILLS AND EXERCISES

### 7.1 Borrowing, lending and interest

Analyze each of the following transactions as movements of equal value IN to and OUT of the business.

1. (a) a business borrows £1 000 from XYZ, receiving the money by cheque
   (b) the business pays £40 interest by cheque to XYZ
   (c) the business repays £600 by cheque to XYZ
2. (a) a business lends £800 to ABC, paying the money by cheque
   (b) the business receives a cheque from ABC for £20 interest
   (c) the business receives repayment of £500 by cheque from ABC
3. a business pays £450 by cheque to a lender, being £250 interest, and £200 repayment of principal
4. a business receives a cheque for £275 from a borrower, being £25 interest and £250 repayment of principal
5. a business borrows £1 200, receiving £1 000 by cheque, and £200 in cash
6. a business pays a lender £350 by cheque and £50 cash, being a repayment of £300, and a payment of £100 interest

## 7.2 Other compound transactions

Analyze each of the following transactions as movements of equal value IN to and OUT of the business.

1. a firm buys computer equipment for £500, and software for £200, paying £300 immediately by cheque, with the rest on credit
2. a firm buys a truck (value £20 000), a trailer (value £5 000), a refrigerator unit (value £7 000) and fuel (value £200), paying the total immediately by cheque

## 7.3 Understanding analyzed transactions

Describe in words each of the transactions below, which have already been analyzed in terms of the double entry system as an exchange of equal value.

**1.**

| | | | |
|---|---|---|---|
| IN | bank | £3 000 | |
| OUT | promise to XYZ | | £3 000 |

**2.**

| | | | |
|---|---|---|---|
| IN | promise back from XYZ | £1 000 | |
| OUT | bank | | £1 000 |

**3.**

| | | | |
|---|---|---|---|
| IN | permission to use money (interest) | £200 | |
| IN | promise from lender | £800 | |
| OUT | bank | | £1 000 |

**4.**

| | | | |
|---|---|---|---|
| IN | equipment | £900 | |
| OUT | cash | | £100 |
| OUT | bank | | £300 |
| OUT | promise to supplier | | £500 |

**5.**

| | | | |
|---|---|---|---|
| IN | sales | £100 | |
| OUT | cash | | £30 |
| OUT | promise to customer | | £70 |

6.

| IN | bank | £50 | |
|---|---|---|---|
| IN | promise from supplier | £400 | |
| OUT | purchases | | £450 |

# CHAPTER 8

# Involuntary Liabilities and One-way Transactions

## OBJECTIVES

*The objectives of this chapter are:*

- to explain the relation between promises, claims and liabilities
- to show how the emergence of an involuntary liability or a one-way transaction can be analyzed within the accounting model as an exchange of equal value
- to discuss the true nature and purpose of an input or an output in the accounting model

## PROMISES, CLAIMS, AND LIABILITIES

Promises, claims, and liabilities are terms describing different aspects of the same reality. Whoever agrees to accept a promise, will thereby have a claim on the giver of the promise. And whoever gives a promise will also have a liability or obligation to fulfil the promise. Thus if I give you a promise, you will have a claim on me, and I will have a liability to you.

When we analyze transactions, we focus on the movement of promises, and so it may seem to be the issue of a promise that causes the existence of a claim or liability. However, it is possible for a claim or liability to exist, which is not the result of a transaction. For example, a firm may face a legal claim for damages, or it may have a liability to pay tax. In such cases, if the firm wishes to record the existence of the claim or liability in its accounts, it can do so by the device of recording a promise going OUT to pay the claim or liability. In this case, it will be the existence of the claim or liability that will cause the issue of the promise. The relation between promises, claims and liabilities is shown in Box 8.1 on the following page.

## INVOLUNTARY LIABILITIES

The power to recognize a liability in the accounts of a business by recording the issue of a promise is most useful in the case of involuntary liabilities. An involuntary liability is a liability imposed on the firm against its will, in exchange for no identifiable benefit. Such perhaps is the liability to pay a tax, or the liability to pay a fine or damages for committing a wrong. Thus if a firm has a liability to pay a tax or a fine or damages, and wishes to record that liability in its accounts, it may do so by recording the issue of a promise to pay the liability.

## BOX 8.1

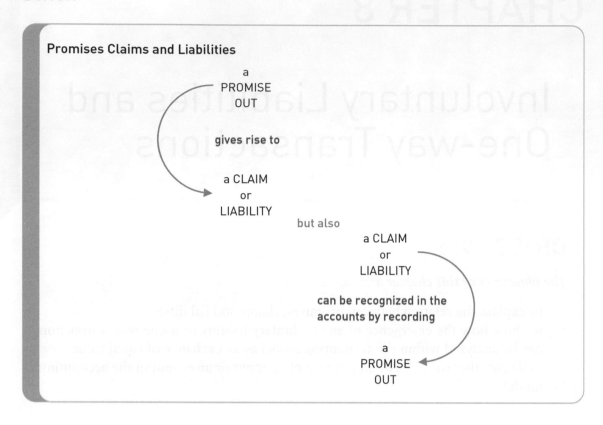

**Promises Claims and Liabilities**

a
PROMISE
OUT

**gives rise to**

a CLAIM
or
LIABILITY

but also

a CLAIM
or
LIABILITY

**can be recognized in the
accounts by recording**

a
PROMISE
OUT

The issue of a promise (for whatever reason) is of course a transaction, which in this case, as in any other, must be analyzed as an exchange of equal value, with an input coming IN to explain why the promise has been given OUT. Naming the relevant input may demand some ingenuity, but not much. Box 8.2 presents an example.

## BOX 8.2

**Recognising an Involuntary Liability**

A firm has a liability to pay tax of £750. In order to show the liability in its accounts, the firm may record the issue of a promise to pay the relevant amount.

The firm will explain the issue of the promise by recording 'tax' as the *input* or *reason why* it has been issued.

| IN | tax (= reason why promise is given) | £750 | |
|----|--------------------------------------|------|------|
| OUT | promise to tax authority (= recognition of liability) | | £750 |

When payment is eventually made, the promise initially shown as going OUT to record the existence of the liability will now be shown as coming back IN (therefore cancelling the record of the liability) as shown in Box 8.3.

## BOX 8.3

### Recording the Payment of an Involuntary Liability

A firm has previously recorded a liability to pay tax of £750. The firm now pays the tax by cheque.

The payment cancels the liability, so in exchange for the money that goes OUT, the firm will show the original promise to pay coming back IN.

| | | | |
|---|---|---|---|
| IN | promise back from tax authority | £750 | |
| OUT | bank | | £750 |

## ONE-WAY TRANSACTIONS

Involuntary liabilities are just part of a larger group of what might be called 'one-way transactions' – that is, transactions where in fact nothing is given or received in exchange for the movement of money or promise. Examples would include fraud, free gifts, theft, discoveries, accidental loss, and so on. One-way transactions undoubtedly occur in the real world, but they are not exempt from the rule in double entry that every transaction must be recorded as an exchange of equal value.

In such cases, where it is necessary to record a one-way transaction as an exchange of equal value, we are free to invent an input or an output with the relevant value, giving it whatever name may be necessary to explain the movement of money or promise. Box 8.4 shows two examples of the procedure.

## BOX 8.4

### Recording One-way Transactions

1. A firm receives a cheque for £500, being a grant in recognition of its contribution to economic development in the region. To record the transaction as an equal exchange, and explain the money coming IN, the firm must record an output of equal value, which it might call 'grant'.

| | | | |
|---|---|---|---|
| IN | bank | £500 | |
| OUT | grant (= reason for inward movement of money) | | £500 |

2. A firm is the victim of a theft, in which £80 cash is stolen. To record this transaction in terms of the double entry model, and explain the money going OUT, the firm must record an input of equal value, which it might call 'theft'.

| | | | |
|---|---|---|---|
| IN | theft (= reason for outward movement of money) | £80 | |
| OUT | cash | | £80 |

# THE TRUE NATURE OF INPUTS AND OUTPUTS

The existence of one-way transactions, and the requirement to invent an input or an output, if necessary, so that every transaction can be recorded as an exchange of equal value, must be deeply disturbing to the credibility of the double entry model. How can the model claim to represent reality, when it seems to be based on such an arbitrary fiction? The answer lies in a more subtle understanding of the true nature of inputs and outputs.

In our drawing of the accounting model of a business, shown again in Box 8.5, inputs and outputs are shown as *things* taken in or given out in exchange for money and promises. These inputs and outputs serve to explain movements of money or promises by answering the question *what for*? While they need not be physical objects, they are at least substantial enough to have movement and direction. This simple understanding of the model is not wholly true.

## BOX 8.5

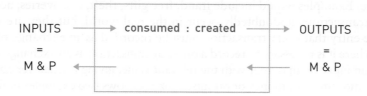

**The Accounting Model of a Business and its Transactions**

INPUTS → consumed : created → OUTPUTS
=                                    =
M & P ←                         ← M & P

- a transaction is a movement of money or promises (M&P) across the boundary IN to or OUT of a business;

- every transaction is recorded as an exchange of equal value;

- inside the business, inputs are consumed while outputs are created.

With respect to inputs, the point is that in order to generate a profit or a loss, all inputs are ultimately consumed inside the business. That is to say, unlike real things, inputs in the accounting model must have the capacity to vanish. Now, given that sooner or later all inputs are consumed and vanish in any case, the question of their 'real' existence, or not, at any point in time, is of little consequence. The function of an input in the model is only to explain an outward movement of money or a promise, and then to disappear.

Outputs are equally unreal. Always regarded as different from inputs, and created from nothing inside the business as inputs are consumed, outputs vanish immediately as they pass OUT of the business in exchange for money and promises coming IN. Once again, the question of their 'real' existence, or not, at any time, need cause us no concern. The true function of an output in the model is only to explain an inward movement of money or a promise.

Inputs and outputs in the accounting sense, therefore, are very different from inputs and outputs in the physical or engineering sense. In the physical sense an input would be anything that comes in to the business. In accounting however, an input means only any *reason why* money or promises move OUT of the business. Likewise with outputs. In the physical sense, an output would be anything that goes out of the business. But in accounting, an output means only any *reason why* money or promises move IN to the business.

In relation to the movement of money or promises, therefore, inputs and outputs do not really seek to answer the question *what for*? (which seems to imply an exchange). In truth they answer the question *why?* (which implies nothing more than a reason). Notice here that money and promises are now the only solid stuff remaining in the universe of double entry. Inputs and outputs are a kind of antimatter – products of the imagination with a transient existence, being no more than reasons given for the movements of the real things, and, crucially, always moving in a direction opposed to the movement of money or promises which it is their function to explain.

## REAL VALUE

In order to fulfil its purpose, an input or output must be given the same value as the movement of money or promise whose movement it serves to explain. We need not concern ourselves with any 'real' value that an input or an output may or may not have. In the analysis of transactions, our purpose is to account for the movement of money or promises. It is not, in the first instance, to account for the movement of goods or services. An example is shown in Box 8.6.

### BOX 8.6

#### The Real Value of an Output (or an Input)

A firm sells a barrel of rotten and worthless apples for £75 cash.

The event to be accounted for here is the movement of money, not the movement of apples. An output is needed to explain the movement of money, and the output must be assigned a value of £75, because that is the value of the movement of money it serves to explain.

The analysis therefore will be

| IN | cash | £75 | |
|----|------|-----|-----|
| OUT | bad apples | | £75 |

## REVIEW

This chapter has shown the relation between promises and liabilities, and has shown how that relation can be used to record the existence of an involuntary liability by the issue of a promise to pay the liability. The chapter also dealt with the problem of recording one-way transactions. It described the nature of inputs and outputs in the accounting model, pointing out that the real value, even the real existence, of an input and or an output is irrelevant as long as it serves its purpose, which is to explain a movement of money or promises in an opposite direction.

# DRILLS AND EXERCISES

## 8.1 Recording involuntary liabilities and one-way transactions

Show how each of the following situations could be recorded in the form of a transaction within the double entry system.

1. a restaurant business pays £1 400 cash to a gangster for 'protection'
2. a firm wins a prize of £500 for ethical advertising
3. a firm gives £1 000 cash as a gift to a political party
4. a lottery company pays a prize of £20 million in cash
5. a firm pays a parking fine of £60 in cash
6. a firm receives a prize of £5 000 for environmental awareness
7. a parcel delivery business pays £50 cash as compensation to a customer for damaging a parcel
8. a business receives a cheque for £1 000 in settlement of an insurance claim
9. a firm is tricked into buying worthless goods for £1 000 cash
10. a firm sells a worthless second-hand car for £2 000 cash
11. (a) a firm is found guilty of infringing health and safety regulations, and ordered to pay a penalty of £2 000
    (b) the firm pays the penalty by cheque
12. (a) a firm receives a tax assessment showing a liability to pay tax of £700
    (b) the firm pays the tax by cheque
13. a business is broken into and £1 800 cash is stolen from the safe
14. a charity receives a donation of £250 in cash
15. a business is found to have been negligent and ordered to pay damages of £750 to the victim

## 8.2 Understanding analyzed transactions

Describe in words the events or situations that could be analyzed and recorded in the double entry system as below:

1.

| IN | theft | £100 |
|----|-------|------|
| OUT | cash | £100 |

2.

| IN | tax charge | £450 |
|----|------------|------|
| OUT | promise (liability) to pay tax | £450 |

3.

| IN | promise (liability) to pay tax | £120 |
|----|--------------------------------|------|
| OUT | bank | £120 |

**4.**

| IN | blackmail | £60 | |
|----|-----------|-----|-----|
| OUT | cash | | £60 |

**5.**

| IN | parking fine | £16 | |
|----|--------------|-----|-----|
| OUT | cash | | £16 |

**6.**

| IN | bank | £300 | |
|----|------|------|------|
| OUT | government grant | | £300 |

**7.**

| IN | charitable donation | £250 | |
|----|---------------------|------|------|
| OUT | bank | | £250 |

**8.**

| IN | bank | £600 | |
|----|------|------|------|
| OUT | prize | | £600 |

## 8.3 Inputs and outputs

1. A firm operates a factory which creates smoke, noise and pollution.
   (a) Are these inputs or outputs, or neither?
   (b) Under what circumstances might the pollution generated by a firm become one of the firm's inputs?
2. 'Water is not an input to the water industry, and fish are not an input to the fishing industry.' Comment.

| | | |
|---|---|---|
| IN | blackmail | £40 |
| OUT | cash | £40 |
| | | |
| IN | parking fine | £10 |
| OUT | cash | £10 |
| | | |
| IN | bank | £300 |
| OUT | government grant | £300 |
| | | |
| IN | charitable donation | £250 |
| OUT | bank | £250 |
| | | |
| IN | bank | £800 |
| OUT | prize | £800 |

## 8.3 Inputs and outputs

1. A firm operates a factory which creates smoke, noise and pollution.
   (a) Are these inputs or outputs, or neither?
   (b) Under what circumstances might the pollution generated by a firm become one of the firm's inputs?

2. Water is not an input in the water industry, and fish are not an input to the fishing industry. Comment.

# CHAPTER 9

# Timing: When to Record a Transaction

## OBJECTIVES

*The objectives of this chapter are:*

- to explain the need for an operational rule to determine when a transaction should be recorded
- to describe and justify the basic operational rule that is usually adopted
- to show how using the movement of money or an invoice as the trigger for recording a transaction, rather than the movement of goods or services, may distort a firm's accounts and require correction at a later stage

## THE BASIC OPERATIONAL RULE

Every accounting system must seek to ensure as far as possible that every transaction is recorded, and that no transaction is recorded more than once. This overall objective can only be achieved only through a set of clear operational rules. Details of such rules will vary from one firm to another, but for most firms, the basic operational rule is this: a transaction must be recorded:

1. when there is a movement of money (bank or cash) IN to or OUT of the firm, or
2. when the firm issues or receives an invoice.

This rule is purely operational. It may be overridden by higher authority, for example as we have seen in the case of involuntary liabilities, but its object is to put policy into practice at the basic level, by the removal of doubt as to what should be done and when. The idea is to select *unmistakable* events as *exclusive* triggers for *automatic* response. If there is a movement of money, or if an invoice is issued or received, then a transaction must be recorded. If there is no movement of money, and no invoice is issued or received, then no transaction must be recorded.

## MOVEMENTS OF MONEY

A movement of money means a payment or receipt of cash, or the issue or receipt of a cheque. Each of these events is of course a transaction in itself, but, more importantly for present purposes, in respect of its suitability as a trigger for action, it is also an easily observed and unmistakable physical event. With a movement of money, therefore, the occurrence of the transaction and the trigger for recording the transaction are one and the same. This is the ideal situation. With promises, however, things are not so simple.

## PROMISES AND THE ROLE OF THE INVOICE

The promises involved in transactions on credit are not usually written down and handed from one party to the other. Usually, therefore, with a transaction on credit, there is no physical event, and nothing in the movement of the promise itself, that can be observed and taken as the trigger for recording the transaction. The next best alternative trigger for action is usually taken to be the issue or receipt of an invoice.

An invoice is a written request for payment. An invoice may or may not be issued in connection with a cash sale, but as a matter of business practice, every sale on credit is marked by the issue of an invoice, and for each sale on credit only one authentic invoice can be issued (it may of course be followed by copies and reminders). There is therefore a 1:1 match between authentic invoice and actual transaction, such that the *issue* of an invoice (as an unmistakable physical event) is ideally suited to be the trigger for action to record a sale on credit, while the *receipt* of an invoice is equally suited to be the trigger for action to record a purchase on credit.

## SALES INVOICE AND PURCHASE INVOICE

Because an invoice may be issued or received, for the avoidance of doubt in any given firm a *sales invoice* means an invoice issued by the firm to a customer, requesting the customer to pay for goods or services which the firm has sold. A *purchase invoice* means an invoice received by the firm from a supplier, requesting the firm to make payment for goods or services which the firm has purchased.

## CHOOSING THE INVOICE AS A TRIGGER FOR ACTION

When a firm makes a sale, there is a movement of goods or services out of the firm, *and* the firm issues an invoice requesting payment. But within the accounting office, the trigger for recording the transaction is the movement of the document, not the movement of the goods or services. Likewise, when the firm makes a purchase, goods or services come into the firm, but the transaction is recorded when the firm receives the relevant invoice, not when the firm receives the goods or services. Why do accountants choose to take the movement of a document (the invoice) as a trigger for action, rather than the movement of goods or services? At least three reasons may be offered.

First, many goods and services – like water, electricity, or labour – are not supplied in lumps that can easily be identified. They enter the firm in a continuous flow. It would not be practical, however, to update the accounting record continuously, minute by minute as these inputs flow into the firm. The accountant cannot stand by the electricity meter and record a transaction every time it ticks over to show more electricity coming in to the firm. Better to wait and do nothing until the bill arrives. (Note, though, that future developments in information technology will almost certainly weaken the power of this argument.)

A second argument against using the movement of goods or services as a trigger for recording a transaction, is the fact that goods and services come in to the firm at the various different points at which they are needed, and they leave at many different points of delivery to customers. It is impossible for the accountant or accounting staff to be present and observe these events in so many different places. By contrast, the issue or receipt of an invoice – the movement of paperwork and documentation – is easily centralized in or near the accounting office, where it can be observed by the accounting staff and taken as the trigger for further action.

A third argument in favour of using the movement of the invoice as a trigger for recording a transaction, rather than the movement of goods or promises, is the answer it offers to the problem of avoiding duplicate records of the same transaction. An invoice which has been used as a trigger to record a transaction can be marked to show that the transaction has been recorded, thus ensuring that the same transaction will not be recorded a second time. Goods and services cannot easily be marked in such a way. Using the movement of goods or services instead of the invoice as the trigger for recording a transaction would therefore mean reducing the firm's defences against the duplicate recording of transactions.

## TIMING

The rule that a transaction should be recorded when an invoice is issued or received, is designed to ensure the completeness of the record (so that every transaction gets to be recorded), and the avoidance of duplication (so that no transaction gets to be recorded more than once). Except in the case of movements of money, the rule is *not* designed to ensure that a transaction is recorded at, or near to, the time at which it actually occurs. Indeed the rule fails even to come close to meeting that desirable objective. For various reasons, an invoice may be issued well before, or long after the relevant transaction. As a result, at any particular moment, some transactions which have already taken place will be excluded from the accounting records of a firm, while other transactions may well be included, which have not yet occurred. Two examples are shown in Box 9.1.

## BOX 9.1

### The Timing of the Record

1. A firm orders an emergency supply of goods from a regular supplier. The goods are delivered immediately.

   At this point, the transaction has already occurred: the goods have arrived, and by accepting them the firm has in effect promised to pay for them. However, no transaction will be recorded until the supplier's invoice is received.

2. A firm receives an order from a customer for the construction of a specialized piece of machinery. The firm requires payment in advance before work can commence, and issues an invoice to the customer.

   The sale will be recorded at this point, with the issue of the invoice, even though the real life transaction has not yet occurred.

Although it may be unavoidable, this result is clearly undesirable. As we shall see, it means that the accounting system must be equipped with further rules and techniques, sometimes to override the basic rule, and sometimes to work around it, and adjust for the distortion it would otherwise bring into a firm's accounts.

# REVIEW

This chapter introduced the basic operational rule for determining when a transaction should be recorded in a firm's accounts: a transaction should be recorded when there is a payment or receipt of money, or when an invoice is issued or received. The chapter offered three arguments to justify the basic rule, but concluded with a warning that the accounting system must also incorporate devices to overcome the distortion that the basic rule will tend to introduce into a firm's accounting records.

# DRILLS AND EXERCISES

## 9.1 When to record a transaction – drill

State *whether*, *when*, and *how* each of the events below would normally be recorded as a transaction.

1. (a) Monday: a firm orders goods value £500 from a supplier
   (b) Tuesday: the firm receives the goods
   (c) Wednesday: the firm sells the goods for £700 cash
   (d) Thursday: the firm receives an invoice for £500 from the supplier
   (e) Friday: the firm pays the supplier £500 by cheque
2. (a) Monday: a firm orders goods value £250 from a supplier, sending a cheque with the order
   (b) Tuesday: the firm receives the goods
3. (a) Monday: a firm receives an order from a customer for goods value £325
   (b) Tuesday: the firm sends a sales invoice to the customer
   (c) Wednesday: the firm dispatches the goods to the customer
   (d) Thursday: the firm receives a cheque for £325 from the customer
4. (a) Monday: a firm receives an order from a customer for goods value £850, with cheque payment enclosed
   (b) Tuesday: the firm delivers the goods
5. (a) Monday: firm receives order for goods value £50
   (b) Tuesday: firm delivers goods value £50
   (c) Friday: the firm sends a sales invoice to the customer
6. (a) Monday: a firm uses electricity value £25
   (b) Tuesday: the firm uses electricity value £25
   (c) Wednesday: the firm uses electricity value £25
   (d) Thursday: the firm uses electricity value £25
   (e) Friday: the firm receives an electricity bill for £75

## 9.2 When to record a transaction – exercise

1. A firm signs an agreement with a customer to deliver £100 of goods per month for a year. Identify at least three ways in which this contract could be accounted for, and for each way identified, state the practical steps necessary to ensure that the contract would be accounted for in the way identified.
2. A firm signs an agreement with a customer to provide maintenance and support for the customer's computer facilities over the next two years for a fee of £2 000. Identify at least three ways in which this contract could be accounted for. State which way you think the firm would prefer, and which way you would recommend. Give reasons for your answers.

## 5.2 When to record a transaction – exercise

1. A firm signs an agreement with a customer to deliver £100 of goods per month for a year. Identify at least three ways in which this contract could be accounted for, and for each way identified, state the practical steps necessary to ensure that the contract would be accounted for in the way identified.

2. A firm signs an agreement with a customer to provide maintenance and support for the customer's computer facilities over the next two years for a fee of £2,000. Identify at least three ways in which this contract could be accounted for. State which way you think the firm would prefer and which way you would recommend. Give reasons for your answers.

# CHAPTER 10

# Transactions Between a Firm and its Owner

## OBJECTIVES

*The objectives of this chapter are:*

- to describe the separate entity concept and show how transactions between a firm and its owner can be analyzed as exchanges of equal value
- to explain the use of the word capital in double entry analysis
- to comment on the nature of capital in general

## THE SEPARATE ENTITY CONCEPT

In the accounting model of a business, the owner stands outside the firm and engages in transactions with the firm on (almost) the same basis as any other person. This view of the relation between owner and business is called the separate entity concept, which is the idea that the firm should be regarded as an entity, or being complete in itself and separate from its owner. Whether or not a business is *in fact* separate from its owner(s) is of course a matter of law. (In fact, various options are available, and the law provides for owners to choose the relationship they prefer.) But the separate entity concept is an accounting doctrine, not a legal fact. It is *always* applied in accounting, regardless of its truth or otherwise in law.

## THE SOLE TRADER

A sole trader is a single person who has complete, direct, and undivided ownership and control over a business. This represents the most basic legal structure for a firm. Other forms of business organization exist and are widely used (notably partnerships and limited companies), but these alternative structures are probably best understood by comparison with the sole trader as the norm. In the examples that follow in this and the next part of the book, we shall assume for simplicity that the owner of the business is in fact a sole trader. This will be enough to illustrate the relevant general principles, although readers should be aware that the full rights and responsibilities of ownership, as found in the sole trader, may be variously abridged in other forms of business organization, such as the limited company. The structure of the limited company, and related accounting problems, will be examined in Part 4.

# TRANSACTIONS WITH THE OWNER

When an owner makes an investment by putting resources into a firm, the event is recorded as a transaction: in exchange for the resources coming IN to the firm, a promise of equal value is given OUT to the owner. This promise serves to acknowledge the owner's claim on the business, in respect of the value he has invested. Box 10.1 shows an example.

## BOX 10.1

### Money Received from the Owner

An owner puts £600 of his own money into the bank account of his firm.

Coming IN to the firm is 'bank' (or more strictly, a promise from the bank). In exchange, a promise goes OUT to the owner. The firm's analysis therefore will be:

| IN | bank | £600 | |
|----|------|------|------|
| OUT | promise to owner | | £600 |

Value put into the firm by the owner need not be in the form of money. It may be in the form of land, buildings, machinery, stock of goods, etc, as shown in Box 10.2.

## BOX 10.2

### Equipment Received from the Owner

An owner declares that from now on his personal computer, value £750, should be regarded as the property of his firm.

The firm must issue a promise to the owner in exchange for the value it receives. The firm's analysis of the transaction therefore will be:

| IN | computer | £750 | |
|----|----------|------|------|
| OUT | promise to owner | | £750 |

The owner is also at liberty to take things OUT of a firm, but in such a case the firm will take a promise back IN from the owner, because his or her claim on the firm must be reduced. Box 10.3 shows an example.

## BOX 10.3

### Value Withdrawn by the Owner

The owner takes £100 out of a firm's bank account, for his own personal use.

Money in the form of bank promises goes OUT of the firm. But firm will take a promise back IN from the owner, to reduce his claim in consequence of the value he has taken out. The firm's analysis will be:

| IN | promise from owner | £100 | |
|-----|--------------------|------|------|
| OUT | bank | | £100 |

## POINT OF VIEW

In everyday language, transactions between a firm and its owner are usually described from the owner's point of view (as actions performed by the owner) because the owner is the active party. For accounting purposes, however, note that

- all transactions – including transactions with the owner – must be analyzed from the firm's point of view.

## GOODS TAKEN BY THE OWNER

If the owner takes indeterminate 'goods' out of a business, the goods must be analyzed as purchases. The idea is that the goods in question cannot be sales, because they are not *sold* to the owner but *taken* by him or her before they have had the chance to be consumed and turned into sales. Box 10.4 shows an example.

## BOX 10.4

### Goods Taken by the Owner

The owner takes goods value £65 out of a firm, for his or her own personal use.

These goods are not sales being sold, but purchases being taken. The firm's analysis will be:

| IN | promise from owner | £65 | |
|-----|--------------------|------|------|
| OUT | purchases | | £65 |

## CAPITAL, EQUITY, AND OWNERSHIP INTEREST

In a general context, capital means value invested or available for investment, no matter by whom. That is its central meaning. In the present context of double entry accounting, however, the word is used in a narrower sense, and refers only to the value invested in a business *by the owner*. Moreover, in double entry, capital is seen from a particular point of view.

We have seen above that the owner has a claim on the firm in respect of the value he or she has invested. In view of the equality between value invested and claim to value invested, in double entry accounting 'capital' is taken to mean not the value of the things the owner has put in, but the promises he or she has got out – that is, capital means primarily *the owner's claim on a business*, represented by promises going OUT of the business to the owner. Other expressions for this same concept are 'equity' and 'ownership interest'.

## CAPITAL IN THE ANALYSIS OF TRANSACTIONS

Since it is promises going OUT of the firm to the owner that constitute the owner's claim on the business, and since the owner's claim is called capital, accountants have formed the habit of using the word capital to apply to the promises that move OUT to the owner when he or she puts resources into a firm.

Thus in the analysis of transactions when resources come in to the firm from the owner, and the firm issues a promise to acknowledge the owner's claim to their value, we usually write 'OUT capital' instead of the more precise 'OUT promise to owner'. Or when the owner takes resources out of a firm, and the firm takes a promise back in from the owner to reduce his or her claim, we may write 'IN capital', instead of 'IN promise from owner'. Box 10.5 shows two examples.

### BOX 10.5

**Capital and the Analysis of Transactions**

1. An owner puts £900 of his own personal cash into a business. The firm's analysis will be:

| IN | cash | £900 | |
|----|------|------|---|
| OUT | capital (*meaning* promise to owner) | | £900 |

2. The owner takes goods value £350 out of a business for his own personal use. The firm's analysis will be:

| IN | capital (*meaning* promise back from owner) | £350 | |
|----|---------------------------------------------|------|---|
| OUT | purchases | | £350 |

Notice that because of the separate entity concept, with the owner standing outside the business and the owner's claim represented by promises going OUT of the business, the analysis of transactions involving the owner may at first be somewhat counter-intuitive. Thus any increase in capital, the owner's claim, is recorded by 'capital' (promises to the owner) going OUT of the firm, in exchange for whatever it is that the owner has put IN to the firm. Conversely any decrease in capital is recorded by 'capital' (promises from the owner) coming IN to the firm, in exchange for whatever it is the owner has taken OUT of the firm. The matter is possibly clearer if we constantly recall that

- *capital is the owner's claim on a firm* (it is not money or anything else of substance); and
- *capital must be seen from the firm's point of view* as a promise or promises going OUT of the firm to the owner.

## CAPITAL AS CLAIM AND VALUE OF CLAIM

In accounting, most references to capital are statements about its value. Thus while we have defined capital in this context as the owner's claim on a business, we might say at greater length that capital means *the value of* the owner's claim on a business, being equal to the value he or she has invested in the business. This would explain such statements as 'the firm's capital is £*x*', or 'capital in the business is $*y*' and so on. Such statements are a powerful source of confusion between the idea of capital and money. Once more for the avoidance of doubt: in accounting, *capital is not money* – it is a claim, or the value of a claim.

## OBJECTS AND CLAIMS

The fact that capital is a claim and not an object (or set of objects) is a matter of great significance. Objects exist in the physical world. They are lumpy, immobile, often indivisible, and generally inconvenient because they are made out of stuff. By contrast claims exist in the world of law and ideas. They can be shaped and divided at will, they are present wherever the law exists to recognize them, and they can be transferred at the stroke of a pen (nowadays at electronic speed). Consider the difference between a business and the owner's claim to a business. A business is stuck in one place (it can move, but at a very lumbering pace). It is an assemblage of things, people and knowledge that cannot be cut into separate pieces without the risk of destruction. But the owner's claim to a business can be moved around at no cost. It can be divided into an infinite number of parts. If written down on paper it can be locked in a drawer or pledged to a bank. Recognition of this difference between things and claims to things, and the power to exploit it, is one of great founding principles of capitalism – a system in which claims to things are traded with vastly more intensity than things themselves are traded.

## CAPITAL AND LIABILITIES

As a claim on the business, capital is very like a liability. In the double entry system it is recognized in the same way as liabilities, by the issue of promises going OUT of the firm. However, as we shall see in later chapters, there is a profound difference between the owner's claim on a business, and the claims of other people. For this reason it is useful to point the contrast: capital is the owner's claim on a business, and liabilities are the claims of other people.

## REVIEW

This chapter has introduced the separate entity concept, and has described how it is applied to the analysis of transactions between a business and its owner. It has also introduced the word capital in its narrower meaning of 'owner's claim on a business', and has shown how that claim is recognized by promises going OUT from the firm to the owner.

# DRILLS AND EXERCISES

## 10.1  Analyzing transactions with the owner

Analyze each of the following transactions as movements of equal value IN to and OUT of the business.

1. an owner puts £300 cash into her business
2. an owner puts a machine, value £450, into his business
3. an owner puts £500 of her own money into the business bank account
4. an owner takes £50 cash out of his own business
5. an owner takes £40 of goods out of the stock of her own business

## 10.2  Understanding analyzed transactions

Describe in words the events or situations that could be analyzed and recorded in the double entry system as below:

1.

| | | |
|---|---|---|
| IN | cash | £100 |
| OUT | capital | £100 |

2.

| | | |
|---|---|---|
| IN | capital | £20 |
| OUT | cash | £20 |

3.

| | | |
|---|---|---|
| IN | machinery | £500 |
| OUT | capital | £500 |

4.

| | | |
|---|---|---|
| IN | capital | £40 |
| OUT | purchases | £40 |

For revision find more questions and answers at our website www.cengage.co.uk/hodge

# CHAPTER 11

# Recording Transactions in Separate Accounts

## OBJECTIVES

*The objectives of this chapter are:*

- to describe what is meant by an account in the double entry system
- to show how a sequence of transactions can be recorded on a set of accounts
- to explain the significance of the net movement recorded on each individual account

## SEPARATE ACCOUNTS AND THE LEDGER

We have now seen how to analyze any transaction as part of an exchange, with movements of equal value crossing IN to and OUT of the business. The benefit of this analysis will become clear when we learn how to record all movements of the same thing in the same place, which will be called an account.

Before we begin however, it is worth remarking that double entry was developed in the age of paper, ink and mental arithmetic, which means it is most easily described in terms appropriate to those technologies. Faster and more reliable forms of information technology became very cheaply available only towards the end of the last century. No doubt those relatively recent advances in hardware will in the end occasion some progress in the essential software of accounting (the double entry system itself), but it has not happened yet. In accounting, modern technology is still used largely to mimic (albeit with greater speed and accuracy) all of the previously necessary paper-based human activities, many of which were necessary only because the system was in fact paper-based and subject to human error. For the moment, therefore, nothing is lost if the system is described in traditional terms, which readers can translate for themselves into more modern form.

So, in this context, 'an account' means a place, by tradition a page in a book, reserved to record all movements of the same thing, in the same place. Meanwhile, a ledger is a set of accounts – traditionally a book containing accounts.

## CREATING AN ACCOUNT

To record all movements of, say, cash, in one place, we need an account for cash. To create an account for cash, we simply write the title *Cash* at the top of a page, draw a horizontal line beneath it, and from that line, draw a vertical line down the middle of the page. The page is now an account. All movements of cash coming IN to the firm will be recorded on one side of the account, and all movements of cash going OUT of the firm will be recorded on the other side. By arbitrary but universal convention, movements IN are recorded on the left of an account, and movements OUT are recorded on the right. And regardless of its direction, each movement recorded in or on an account is called an *entry* in or on the account.

In the real world, every entry on an account (each movement recorded) should conform with three strict rules of practice. First, the date of each entry must be given. In the explanation of an event, *when* it occurred or when it was recorded is always of prime importance. Secondly, each entry should be given an explanation, or a reference number pointing the way back to some documentary evidence of the original transaction. (In computerized systems a simple reference number is given, although in some traditional systems it is customary in respect of every movement IN to state where the movement OUT has been recorded, and vice versa.) Thirdly, on each side of the account, the values recorded should be entered in a neat column to the right of the reference, so that the total value of movements IN and the total value of movements OUT can be found easily, and then compared to find the value of the net movement in any period.

As far as concerns this introductory text, the first two of these rules will be quite frequently ignored. Dates and references will mostly be omitted, not because they are unimportant in practice, but because their inclusion is not needed to present the theory, and would tend to obscure the working of the system beneath a weight of detail.

## T ACCOUNTS

Students of accounting obviously cannot waste a whole page for each account that they prepare, so instead they use small 'T accounts', created by stripping away all unnecessary headings and framework, and leaving a bare T to represent the account, as will be shown in future examples.

## RECORDING TRANSACTIONS ON ACCOUNTS

The procedure for recording transactions on accounts is more easily shown than described. Box 11.1 presents an example of the analysis and recording of a firm's first transaction, where blobs of colour have been added to clarify the presentation.

## BOX 11.1

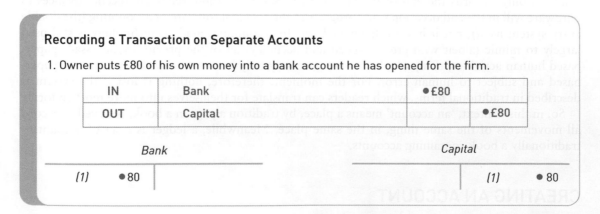

**Recording a Transaction on Separate Accounts**

1. Owner puts £80 of his own money into a bank account he has opened for the firm.

| IN | Bank | ●£80 | |
|----|------|------|------|
| OUT | Capital | | ●£80 |

| *Bank* | | *Capital* | |
|--------|--|-----------|--|
| (1)  ● 80 | | (1)  ● 80 | |

Promises IN from and OUT to the same person should be recorded in the same account, as shown in the further transactions recorded in Box 11.2.

## BOX 11.2

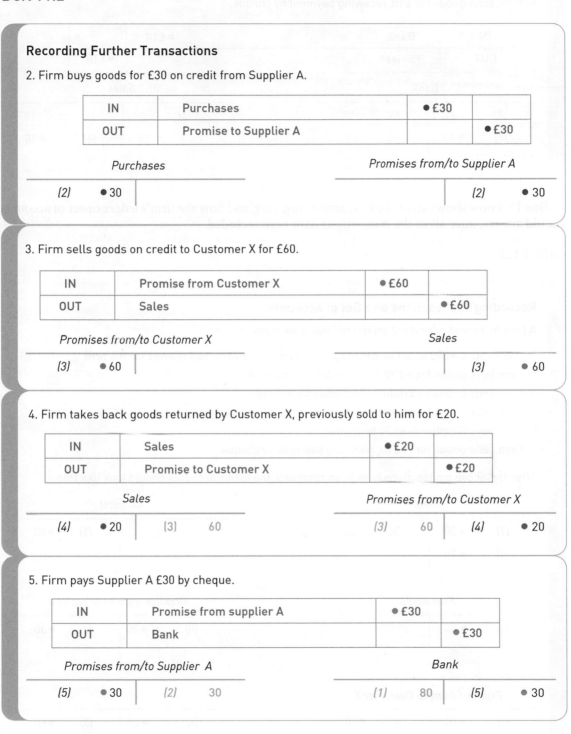

**Recording Further Transactions**

2. Firm buys goods for £30 on credit from Supplier A.

| IN | Purchases | ● £30 | |
|----|-----------|-------|-------|
| OUT | Promise to Supplier A | | ● £30 |

| Purchases | | | Promises from/to Supplier A | | |
|-----------|---|---|------------------------------|---|---|
| (2) | ● 30 | | | (2) | ● 30 |

3. Firm sells goods on credit to Customer X for £60.

| IN | Promise from Customer X | ● £60 | |
|----|-------------------------|-------|-------|
| OUT | Sales | | ● £60 |

| Promises from/to Customer X | | | Sales | | |
|-----------------------------|---|---|-------|---|---|
| (3) | ● 60 | | | (3) | ● 60 |

4. Firm takes back goods returned by Customer X, previously sold to him for £20.

| IN | Sales | ● £20 | |
|----|-------|-------|-------|
| OUT | Promise to Customer X | | ● £20 |

| Sales | | | Promises from/to Customer X | | |
|-------|---|---|------------------------------|---|---|
| (4) | ● 20 | (3) | 60 | (3) | 60 | (4) | ● 20 |

5. Firm pays Supplier A £30 by cheque.

| IN | Promise from supplier A | ● £30 | |
|----|-------------------------|-------|-------|
| OUT | Bank | | ● £30 |

| Promises from/to Supplier A | | | Bank | | |
|-----------------------------|---|---|------|---|---|
| (5) | ● 30 | (2) | 30 | (1) | 80 | (5) | ● 30 |

**BOX 11.2** Continued

6. Firm sells goods for £10, receiving payment by cheque.

| IN | Bank | ● £10 | |
|----|------|-------|---|
| OUT | Sales | | ● £10 |

| | Bank | | | | Sales | | |
|---|---|---|---|---|---|---|---|
| (1) | 80 | (5) | 30 | (4) | 20 | (3) | 60 |
| (6) | ● 10 | | | | | (6) | ● 10 |

Box 11.3 now shows all of the transactions together, and how the firm's ledger or set of accounts should appear, after all of the transactions have been recorded.

**BOX 11.3**

### Recording Transactions on a Set of Accounts

A firm in its first period enters the following six transactions:

1. Owner puts ● £80 of his own money into a bank account he has opened for the firm.
2. Firm buys goods for ● £30 on credit from Supplier A.
3. Firm sells goods on credit to Customer X for ● £60.
4. Firm takes back goods returned by Customer X, previously sold to him for ● £20.
5. Firm pays Supplier A ● £30 by cheque.
6. Firm sells goods for ● £10, receiving payment by cheque.

After the above transactions have been recorded, the firm's accounts should look like this:

| | Bank | | | | Capital | | |
|---|---|---|---|---|---|---|---|
| (1) | ● 80 | (5) | ● 30 | | | (1) | ● 80 |
| (6) | ● 10 | | | | | | |

| | Purchases | | | | Promise from/to Supplier A | | |
|---|---|---|---|---|---|---|---|
| (2) | ● 30 | | | (5) | ● 30 | (2) | ● 30 |

| | Promise from/to Customer X | | | | Sales | | |
|---|---|---|---|---|---|---|---|
| (3) | ● 60 | (4) | ● 20 | (4) | ● 20 | (3) | ● 60 |
| | | | | | | (6) | ● 10 |

# THE NET MOVEMENT ON AN ACCOUNT

A glance at Box 11.3 shows the great advantage of recording all movements of the same thing in the same place: we can see at once the overall effect of the individual movements of each thing, by considering the *net* movement on each account (the net movement being the difference between the total value of the movements IN to the account, and the total value of the movements OUT).

Thus, as shown below in Box 11.4, after all of the transactions have been recorded we can tell immediately that the firm holds £60 of promises from the bank, that the firm owes nothing to Supplier A, that Customer X owes the firm £40, and so on.

## BOX 11.4

### The Net Movement on an Account

With total movements of value £90 IN, and a movement of value £30 OUT, this account shows that the firm holds **net promises value £60 IN** from the bank.

| Bank | | | |
|---|---|---|---|
| (1) | 80 | (5) | 30 |
| (6) | 10 | | |

| Promises from/to Supplier A | | | |
|---|---|---|---|
| (5) | 30 | (2) | 30 |

With movements of equal value IN and OUT, this account shows that the firm owes **nothing** to Supplier A.

This account shows a promise value £60 coming IN from Customer X, and a promise value £20 being given back OUT. We see at once that the firm now holds **net promises  value £40 IN** from Customer X.

| Promises from/to Customer X | | | |
|---|---|---|---|
| (3) | 60 | (4) | 20 |

| Sales | | | |
|---|---|---|---|
| (4) | 20 | (3) | 60 |
| | | (6) | 10 |

With total sales value £70 going OUT and sales value £20 coming back IN, we see from this account that the firm has made **net sales value £50 OUT**.

# REVIEW

This chapter has introduced the idea of an account as a place reserved to record all movements of the same thing, in the same place. It has shown how to create an account, and how to use T accounts to simulate the real accounts of a business. Finally, it has shown the great advantage of using accounts to record transactions. When the relevant transactions have been recorded, each account readily reveals a net movement IN or OUT, which indicates the overall effect of all transactions involving the particular thing which is the subject of the account

# DRILLS AND EXERCISES

## 11.1 Recording transactions on accounts

For each separate business below, analyze the given transactions as movements IN to and OUT of the business, and record the transactions on a separate account for each item that moves.

Practical advice: unless your handwriting is very small, you should not attempt to draw more than two T accounts across a sheet of A4 paper, and no more than three down the sheet.

### BUSINESS A

1. owner puts £1 000 cash into the business
2. business buys goods value £800 on credit from X
3. business sells goods on credit to Y for £900
4. business pays £750 cash to X
5. business receives £900 cash from Y
6. business sells goods for £100 cash
7. business buys goods value £200 from X on credit
8. business pays £220 cash to X
9. business puts £500 cash into the bank
10. owner takes £30 out of the bank for his own use

### BUSINESS B

1. owner puts £750 of her own money into bank for her business
2. business borrows £250 from XYZ, receiving a cheque for this amount
3. business buys goods on credit from S for £500
4. business sells goods on credit to C for £400
5. C returns goods previously sold to him for £100
6. business returns goods to S, previously bought for £80
7. business pays wages of £80 by cheque
8. business receives cheque for £250 from C
9. business pays £110 by cheque to XYZ, being £10 interest and £100 repayment of principal
10. business pays wages £20 by cheque

### BUSINESS C

1. owner puts £2 000 of her own money into bank for the business
2. business buys goods for £1 500 on credit from P
3. business sells goods on credit for £1 300 to Q
4. business pays rent £200 by cheque
5. business receives cheque for £1 200 from Q
6. Q returns goods previously sold to him for £100
7. business pays insurance £250 by cheque
8. business pays parking fine £50 by cheque
9. business pays £1 000 by cheque to P
10. owner takes goods value £50 out of business for her own use

# CHAPTER 12

# Corrections and Transfers Between Accounts

## OBJECTIVES

*The objectives of this chapter are:*

- to explain how the double entry can be used to correct errors in accounts, without destroying the original record
- to show how the double entry method of 'cancel and replace' can also be used to move, separate and combine different values recorded in the accounts

## THE SIGNIFICANCE OF THE NET MOVEMENT ON AN ACCOUNT

Once we have recorded a number of transactions on an account, we may switch our attention away from the individual movements, towards the net movement on the account – the difference in value between the total movements IN and the total movements OUT. This does not mean that the individual movements recorded on an account somehow cease to be important. They show in detail what was done and when, and this historical evidence is a major part of the apparatus of accountability. However, it is the net movement on an account that shows the overall effect of the various individual movements.

This understanding of the net movement on an account has interesting and useful technical consequences within the double entry system. It means above all that within the same account, we can use a movement IN to cancel the effect of a movement OUT, and vice versa. The power to do this can be useful in several ways, not only to correct errors, but also to combine, separate, and move information around in the accounts.

## CORRECTING ERRORS

In accounting systems, it is clearly desirable to reduce the need and the opportunity to eliminate any part of the record, even if mistakes are made. Licence to obliterate an error is too easily misused, possibly to destroy incriminating evidence of the truth. Double entry scores the highest marks with respect to this requirement. Once an entry has been made in an account, however wrong it may be, there is no need ever to simply blot or scratch it out, nor should it ever be allowed. The correct procedure is to let the error stand, but to neutralize or cancel its effect by recording a further movement or movements in the opposite direction. As shown in Box 12.1, if a whole transaction has been recorded by mistake, opposite movements can be recorded in the accounts to cancel the effect of the mistake, while leaving the original record still intact.

## BOX 12.1

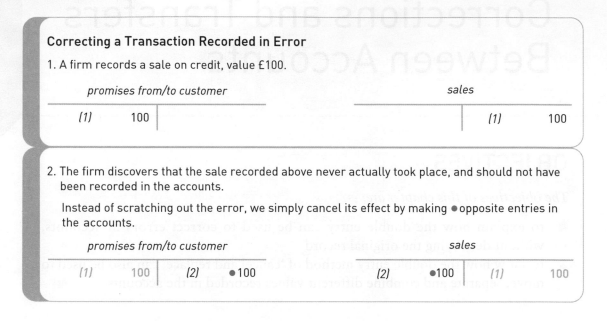

**Correcting a Transaction Recorded in Error**

1. A firm records a sale on credit, value £100.

| *promises from/to customer* | | | *sales* | | |
| --- | --- | --- | --- | --- | --- |
| (1) | 100 | | | (1) | 100 |

2. The firm discovers that the sale recorded above never actually took place, and should not have been recorded in the accounts.

   Instead of scratching out the error, we simply cancel its effect by making ●opposite entries in the accounts.

| *promises from/to customer* | | | *sales* | | |
| --- | --- | --- | --- | --- | --- |
| (1) | 100 | (2) | ●100 | (2) | ●100 | (1) | 100 |

Correcting an error need not involve cancelling the whole transaction. Sometimes it is only the value recorded that requires adjustment, as shown in Box 12.2.

## BOX 12.2

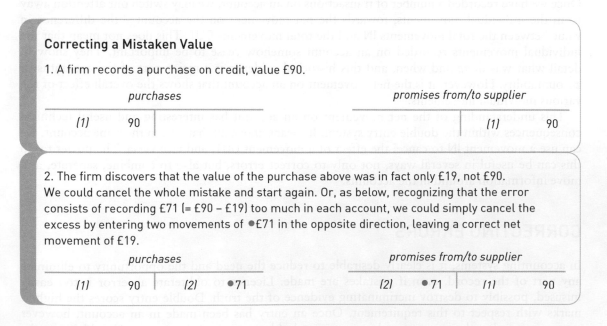

**Correcting a Mistaken Value**

1. A firm records a purchase on credit, value £90.

| *purchases* | | | *promises from/to supplier* | | |
| --- | --- | --- | --- | --- | --- |
| (1) | 90 | | | (1) | 90 |

2. The firm discovers that the value of the purchase above was in fact only £19, not £90. We could cancel the whole mistake and start again. Or, as below, recognizing that the error consists of recording £71 (= £90 – £19) too much in each account, we could simply cancel the excess by entering two movements of ●£71 in the opposite direction, leaving a correct net movement of £19.

| *purchases* | | | *promises from/to supplier* | | |
| --- | --- | --- | --- | --- | --- |
| (1) | 90 | (2) | ●71 | (2) | ●71 | (1) | 90 |

Sometimes only one side of the transaction requires correction, as when it is mistakenly entered in the wrong account, and must be corrected as shown in Box 12.3.

## BOX 12.3

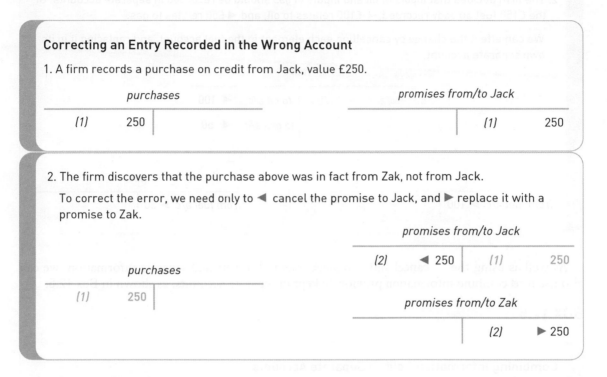

**Correcting an Entry Recorded in the Wrong Account**

1. A firm records a purchase on credit from Jack, value £250.

| purchases | | promises from/to Jack | |
|---|---|---|---|
| *(1)* 250 | | | *(1)* 250 |

2. The firm discovers that the purchase above was in fact from Zak, not from Jack.

To correct the error, we need only to ◄ cancel the promise to Jack, and ► replace it with a promise to Zak.

| | promises from/to Jack | |
|---|---|---|
| *(2)* ◄ 250 | *(1)* | 250 |

| purchases | | promises from/to Zak | |
|---|---|---|---|
| *(1)* 250 | | | *(2)* ► 250 |

# CANCEL AND REPLACE – MOVING BETWEEN ACCOUNTS

The '◄ cancel and ► replace' technique that we used to correct a mistake in Box 12.3, can also be used simply to move information from one account to another. This power to move information around within the system can be used in various ways. For example, elements of information currently lumped together in a single account, can be sorted and shown in two or more separate accounts, as shown in Box 12.4.

## BOX 12.4

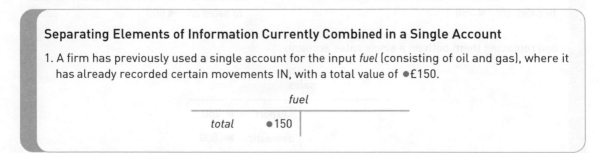

**Separating Elements of Information Currently Combined in a Single Account**

1. A firm has previously used a single account for the input *fuel* (consisting of oil and gas), where it has already recorded certain movements IN, with a total value of ●£150.

| fuel | |
|---|---|
| *total* ●150 | |

**BOX 12.4** Continued

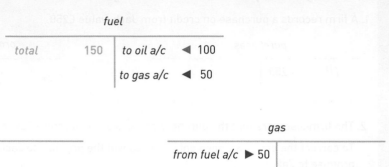

2. The firm decides that inputs of *oil* and inputs of *gas* should be recorded in separate accounts. Of the £150 fuel already recorded,◀ £100 relates to oil, and ◀ £50 relates to gas.

We can effect the change by cancelling each element in the fuel account, and replacing it in its own separate account.

|  | *fuel* |  |  |
|---|---|---|---|
| *total* | 150 | *to oil a/c* ◀ 100 |  |
|  |  | *to gas a/c* ◀ 50 |  |

| *oil* |  | *gas* |  |
|---|---|---|---|
| *from fuel a/c* ▶ 100 |  | *from fuel a/c* ▶ 50 |  |

As well as using the ' cancel and replace' method to sort and separate information, we can also use it to combine information previously kept in separate accounts, as shown in Box 12.5.

**BOX 12.5**

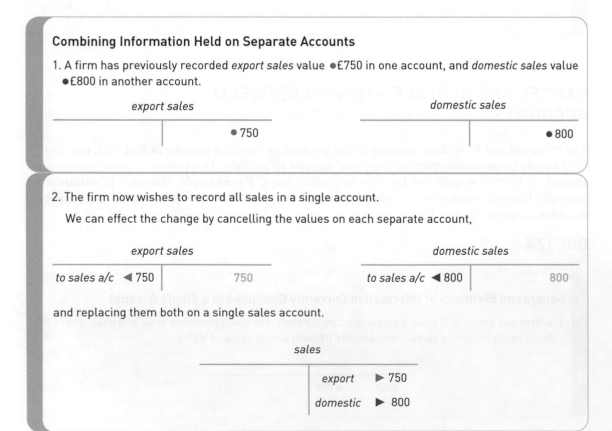

### Combining Information Held on Separate Accounts

1. A firm has previously recorded *export sales* value ●£750 in one account, and *domestic sales* value ●£800 in another account.

| *export sales* |  | *domestic sales* |  |
|---|---|---|---|
|  | ● 750 |  | ● 800 |

2. The firm now wishes to record all sales in a single account.

We can effect the change by cancelling the values on each separate account,

| *export sales* |  | *domestic sales* |  |
|---|---|---|---|
| *to sales a/c* ◀ 750 | 750 | *to sales a/c* ◀ 800 | 800 |

and replacing them both on a single sales account.

| *sales* |  |
|---|---|
| *export* ▶ 750 |  |
| *domestic* ▶ 800 |  |

# DRAWINGS

The ability to record information on one account at first, and then transfer it to another account, is especially useful in the case of drawings.

'Drawings' relates to values drawn or taken out of the business by its owner. The difficulty of accounting for drawings is that the owner may take all manner of different things out of a business (money, goods, equipment, etc.). Later if we need to know the total value of all things taken out by the owner, it is useless to look directly at all the accounts recording the relevant movements OUT, first because there may be very many of them, and secondly because in those separate accounts the values going OUT to the owner will be mixed up with all the other values going OUT to different people and for different reasons.

On the other hand, whenever the owner takes anything OUT of the business, double entry requires the business to record a promise coming back IN from the owner. So to find the total value of things taken OUT by the owner, we need only look at the Capital Account to find the total value of promises taken back IN. Except that there may be promises coming IN from the owner for other reasons. The solution is to have a separate account, called the *Drawings Account*.

The Drawings Account is a place reserved to record only those promises which come IN from the owner in exchange for the values that he or she has taken OUT. The total value of *promises* coming in to the Drawings Account in any period will therefore be equal to the total value of *things* taken out by the owner in that period. Box 12.6 shows an example.

## BOX 12.6

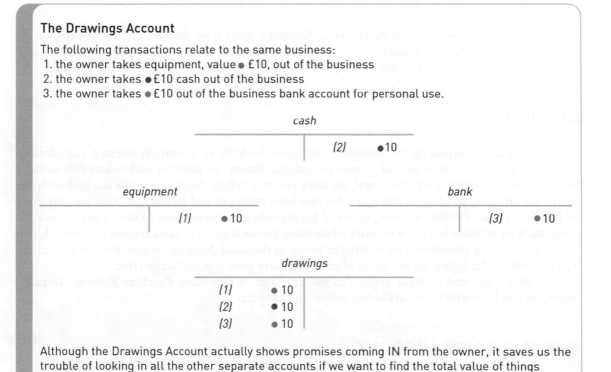

### The Drawings Account

The following transactions relate to the same business:
1. the owner takes equipment, value ●£10, out of the business
2. the owner takes ●£10 cash out of the business
3. the owner takes ●£10 out of the business bank account for personal use.

cash

|  | (2) ●10 |
|---|---|

equipment

| (1) ●10 |  |
|---|---|

bank

|  | (3) ●10 |
|---|---|

drawings

| (1) ●10 |  |
|---|---|
| (2) ●10 |  |
| (3) ●10 |  |

Although the Drawings Account actually shows promises coming IN from the owner, it saves us the trouble of looking in all the other separate accounts if we want to find the total value of things taken OUT by the owner.

In this case, it is clear from the Drawings Account that the total value of things taken out by the owner must have been £10 + £10 + £10 = £30.

At the end of a period when the Drawings Account has done its work, the total value of promises coming IN to the business from the owner can be transferred from the Drawings Account to its proper home in the Capital Account, as shown in Box 12.7.

## BOX 12.7

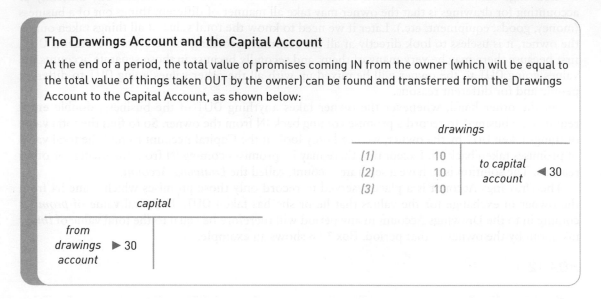

**The Drawings Account and the Capital Account**

At the end of a period, the total value of promises coming IN from the owner (which will be equal to the total value of things taken OUT by the owner) can be found and transferred from the Drawings Account to the Capital Account, as shown below:

*drawings*

| | | | | |
|---|---|---|---|---|
| (1) | 10 | to capital account | ◄ 30 |
| (2) | 10 | | |
| (3) | 10 | | |

*capital*

| | |
|---|---|
| *from drawings account* ► 30 | |

Notice, through all of this, that the Drawings Account is never more than an intermediate step on the way to the Capital Account. It may be useful, but it is not strictly necessary. The Capital Account remains the primary account (and in fact still the only *essential* account) for promises to or from the owner.

# RETURNS

Sales which are returned by the customer and come back IN to a firm represent a considerable waste of time and effort as well as a cause of disappointment. To monitor and reduce this waste, a firm may well require a separate total for sales returns, before combining it in the end with the figure for all sales, to find the value of sales that have gone out and stayed out. This is easily done by keeping a *Sales Returns* account, reserved for recording the movement of sales coming back IN. Once such an account has done its work of showing the total value of sales returns in a period, that total value can be transferred to its proper home in the Sales Account, where the net movement will then show the figure for the value of sales that have gone out and stayed out.

A similar logic and method applies to the problem of recording *Purchase Returns*. Detailed examples can be found in the drills that follow this chapter.

# THE SUSPENSE ACCOUNT

A Suspense Account is an account in which we can make a temporary record of one of the movements involved in a transaction, when we do not know the account in which it ought to be recorded. Later, when we discover where the movement ought to be recorded, we can transfer the relevant value from the Suspense Account to its proper place in another account. This procedure allows us to follow the rules of the double entry, even when we are not quite sure of exactly how we should deal with any particular transaction. BOX 12.8 presents an example.

BOX 12.8

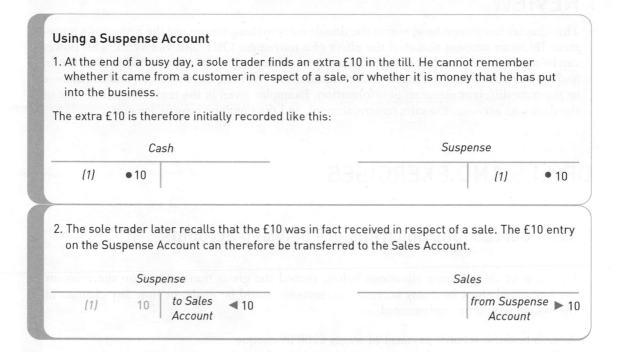

**Using a Suspense Account**

1. At the end of a busy day, a sole trader finds an extra £10 in the till. He cannot remember whether it came from a customer in respect of a sale, or whether it is money that he has put into the business.

The extra £10 is therefore initially recorded like this:

| Cash | | Suspense | |
|---|---|---|---|
| (1) ●10 | | | (1) ●10 |

2. The sole trader later recalls that the £10 was in fact received in respect of a sale. The £10 entry on the Suspense Account can therefore be transferred to the Sales Account.

| Suspense | | Sales | |
|---|---|---|---|
| (1) 10 | to Sales ◀10 Account | | from Suspense ▶10 Account |

# CANCEL AND REPLACE – A NOTE ON METHOD

An event can never be undone and can never be repeated. The record of an event, however, is easily lost and almost as easily multiplied, with adverse effects on our knowledge and understanding. With no record of an event, we will have no knowledge of its occurrence. With many records of a single event, we may falsely believe in the occurrence of many events.

Against this background, notice that the 'cancel and replace' method of moving information from one account to another, actually gives to financial records some of the solid qualities of real stuff, and so makes them harder to lose, and harder to multiply. Once it is recorded in the system, financial information cannot be lost – the rule of cancel and replace means that a record cannot be taken from one place, without being put in another place. Neither can reports of the same event be multiplied within the system – the rule of cancel and replace means that information cannot be moved or included in a new place, unless it is first removed from its old place.

This feature of the double entry system is a particular source of strength and stability. It is certainly one of the reasons for the worldwide dominance of double entry over other methods of accounting for transactions.

Finally, notice also that we have now begun to deal with movements IN to and OUT of separate accounts, rather than movements IN to and OUT of the business. Nevertheless, we have preserved the fundamental rule of double entry, that any value coming IN (to one account), must be equalled by the value going OUT (of another account), and vice versa.

# REVIEW

This chapter has shown how, within the double entry system, we can use the power of a movement IN to an account to cancel the effect of a movement OUT, and vice versa. This power can be used to correct errors without destroying evidence. Also, through the method of 'cancel and replace', it can be used to move information from one account to another, and to combine or separate different elements of information. Examples given in the text included the use of the drawings account, the sales returns account, and the purchase returns account.

# DRILLS AND EXERCISES

## 12.1 Corrections and transfers between accounts

For each of the separate situations below, record the given transactions on the relevant accounts, and show how any necessary corrections would be made, or how any changes in the system would be implemented.

A 1. a business records payment of wages £100 by cheque
   2. in fact the wages above were paid in cash, not by cheque

B 1. a business records a sale on credit to P, value £300
   2. the sale above was actually made to Q, not to P

C 1. a business records the purchase of goods for £250, with payment by cheque
   2. the business discovers that the transaction above was recorded in error, and never in fact took place

D 1. a business receives an invoice for goods purchased from X, value £1 000
   2. the invoice above contained an error. The actual value of the goods purchased was only £900

E 1. a business sends an invoice to Y, for goods sold to him, value £1 500
   2. the invoice above was sent by mistake. The customer was actually Z, and not Y

F 1. a business buys goods on credit for £3 000
   2. the goods above were apples and oranges, and the business decides that it would like to record the purchase of apples and the purchase of oranges on separate accounts. The purchase consisted of apples £1 000, and oranges £2 000

G 1. a business buys pencils for use in the office, cost £10, paid by cheque
   2. the business buys paper for the office, value £40, paid by cheque
   3. the business decides that it would prefer to have one single account for 'Stationery', instead of separate accounts for pencils and for paper

H 1.  a business sells goods for £100 cash
   2.  the business sells goods on credit to Z for £400
   3.  the business decides it would prefer to keep separate records of its cash sales and its credit sales

I 1.  a business buys goods on credit from S, value £1 200
   2.  some of the goods above, value £200, are unsatisfactory, and are returned to the supplier
   3.  since the process of buying and returning unsatisfactory goods is a waste of time, the business decides to monitor the value of goods it has to return, by keeping a separate account for 'Purchase Returns'

J 1.  a business pays wages of £10 000 cash
   2.  the business then decides to keep separate records for the cost of factory labour and shop labour
     The original payment of £10 000 consisted of £7 000 factory wages and £3 000 office wages

K 1.  a business makes sales on credit by mail order, value £2 000
   2.  goods value £500 are returned to the business by customers
   3.  in order to monitor levels of customer satisfaction, the business decides to record the value of goods returned by customers in a separate account for 'Sales Returns'

L 1.  a business receives a cheque for £50 from X, a customer who has previously bought goods on credit
   2.  X's cheque is dishonoured

M 1.  a business pays factory wages of £4 000 and factory rent of £1 000, each by cheque
   2.  the business then decides it would like to have a single account to record all factory costs

N A business maintains separate accounts for 'Sales' and for 'Sales Returns'
   1.  during a year the business sells goods on credit for £10 000
   2.  during the year, customers return goods value £2 000
   3.  at the end of the year, the business needs to know the value of its final sales for the year (i.e. the value of goods that were sold and kept by customers)

O 1.  a business pays wages £95 cash to a part-time employee
   2.  the wages above were overpaid. £5 cash is recovered from the employee

# CHAPTER 13

# Debits and Credits; Balancing an Account

## OBJECTIVES

*The objectives of this chapter are:*

- to explain what is meant by the words debit and credit in double entry accounting
- to show the procedures involved in balancing an account
- to explain the difference between an entry on an account and the balance on an account
- to describe what is meant by a journal entry
- to explain the use of the words debit and credit in certain other contexts, including bank statements, credit cards and debit cards, credit notes and debit notes

## DEBITS AND CREDITS

We began with the very solid notion of movements IN to and OUT of *the business*. In recent chapters we have subtly progressed to the more abstract idea of movements IN to and OUT of *an account*. These more abstract movements demand more abstract names. We call them debits and credits. A debit is a movement IN to an account, and a credit is a movement OUT of an account. By extension, the left side of an account, where we record movements IN, is called the debit side, and the right side of an account, where we record movements OUT, is called the credit side.

Although always pronounced in full, the words debit and credit are usually written in abbreviated form, as DR and CR. (The anomalous presence of the R in DR shows that DR and CR were formed in the beginning from the first and last letters of 'debtor' and 'creditor', but that was a long time ago, and now no longer strictly relevant.)

Observe that DR and CR are subject to the same rules that govern the use of IN and OUT. Just as we cannot record a movement IN to the business without also recording a movement of equal value going OUT of the business, so we cannot record a DR in any account without a corresponding CR in some other account, and we cannot record a DR in any account without a corresponding CR in some other account. Thus in terms of value, it is true to say that 'for every DR there must be a CR, and for every CR there must be a DR'.

Since DR and CR are so entirely abstract, we shall continue to use IN and OUT from time to time as practical substitutes, wherever it may help to present a more concrete mental picture of what is happening, or what we are trying to do. Readers should be aware however that DR and CR are the terms in general use.

## THE BALANCE ON AN ACCOUNT

The balance on an account is the net movement recorded on the account – that is, the difference between the total value of DRs or movements IN recorded on the account, and the total value of CRs or movements OUT. A net movement IN is called a DR balance, and a net movement OUT is called a CR balance. Thus an account with total movements IN value £700, and total movements OUT value £600, would be said to have a DR balance (a net movement IN) of £100. As we know, it is this net movement or balance on an account which shows the overall effect of the various individual movements recorded on the account.

For simplicity in our examples up to now (and in most of our examples still to come), we have seen at most three or four DRs or CRs on an account, matched against only one or two movements in the opposite direction. In such cases the balance on the account is easily determined by inspection. In real life however, there may be very many DRs and CRs on any single account, and the balance on the account may be quite difficult to determine without some serious arithmetic. We therefore need some formal procedure not just to find the balance, but also to show the balance on an account once we have found it. This procedure is called balancing the account.

## BALANCING AN ACCOUNT

Balancing an account means using one entry to *cancel* all the individual movements previously recorded on the account, and another entry to *replace* them with a single net movement showing their overall effect. The procedure involves five steps:

1. *Make space* to show the final total on each side of the account.
2. *Calculate the net movement* on the account, which is the difference between the total individual movements already recorded on each side.
3. *Cancel the individual movements* by inserting the difference, above the space for totals, on the side that was underweight. (Inserting the difference on the side that was underweight will make both sides equal, with no net movement down to that point. With no net movement, any individual movements recorded on the account will be of no effect – that is, they will be cancelled.)
4. Now *replace all of the individual movements* with a single net movement, by inserting the difference below the space for totals, on the side that was overweight. (This will show the overall effect of the individual movements that were cancelled in step 3 above.)
5. *Tidy up* by labelling the balancing entries that have just been made, and by writing the total on each side in the space provided, to prove that both sides are now equal down to that point. (It is important to show these equal totals next to each other, as a sign that any individual movements above that point are now of no effect because they have been summarized below.)

The value inserted above the totals in step 3, which serves to cancel all previous individual movements, is called the balance *carried forward* (bal c/f). Meanwhile, the same value, inserted below the totals in step 4, which serves to replace the individual movements with a single net movement, is called the balance *brought forward* (bal b/f).

Box 13.1 shows how the balancing procedure works in practice.

BOX 13.1

**Balancing an Account**

(We assume various individual entries have been previously made on the account.)

*Any account*

|  |  |  |  |  |
|---|---|---|---|---|
| (1) | 200 | (2) | | 700 |
| (3) | 400 | | | |

1. Draw lines to make space for final totals, level with each other on each side of the account.

*Any account*

|  |  |  |  |  |
|---|---|---|---|---|
| (1) | 200 | (2) | | 700 |
| (3) | 400 | | | |
| | 600 | | | 700 |

2. Calculate the net movement, or difference between the two sides.

Here the total coming IN on the DR side is £600, and the total going OUT on the CR side is £700, so the difference is £100 and the excess is on the CR side.

*Any account*

|  |  |  |  |  |
|---|---|---|---|---|
| (1) | 200 | (2) | | 700 |
| (3) | 400 | | | |
| ◄ | 100 | | | |

3. ◄ *Cancel* all previous individual movements by inserting the difference *above* the space for totals, on the side that was underweight.

   This will make both sides equal, with zero net movement down to the totals.

*Any account*

|  |  |  |  |  |
|---|---|---|---|---|
| (1) | 200 | (2) | | 700 |
| (3) | 400 | | | |
| | 100 | | | |
| | | | ► | 100 |

4. ► *Replace* the individual movements by inserting the difference *below* the space for totals, on the side that was overweight.

   This is the balance on the account, which replaces all the individual movements with a single net movement to summarize their effect.

## BOX 13.1    Continued

4. Finally tidy up:
   write equal *totals* in the space provided on each side
   ◀ above the totals, label the *balance carried forward*
      (*bal c/f*)
   ▶ below the totals, label the *balance brought forward*
      (*bal b/f*).

|  | *Any account* |  |  |
|---|---|---|---|
| *(1)* | 200 | *(2)* | 700 |
| *(3)* | 400 |  |  |
| *bal c/f* ◀ | 100 |  |  |
|  | 700 |  | 700 |
|  |  | *bal b/f* ▶ | 100 |

Notice that the final totals on each side of the account convey no useful information in themselves, except to mark the point down to which both sides are now equal, and thus to show that individual movements above that point can be ignored in future calculations. Likewise the balance *carried* forward: while it has a definite function in the system (it serves to cancel the individual movements already recorded), it carries no useful information. It is the balance *brought* forward on an account which carries all the useful information, representing the net movement on the account. Thus any reference to '*the balance*' on an account is always a reference to the balance *brought forward*.

Notice also that to describe the balance on an account we must always state direction (DR or CR) as well as value, as shown in Box 13.2.

## BOX 13.2

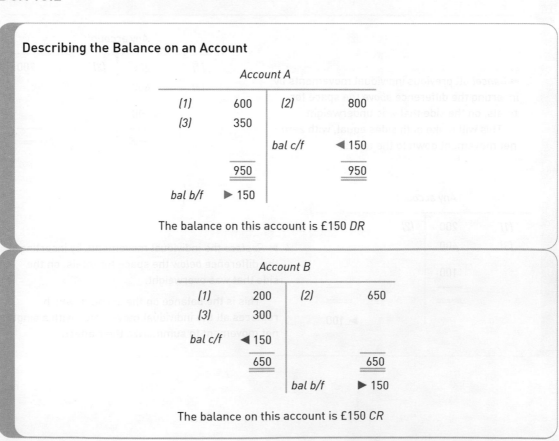

**Describing the Balance on an Account**

|  | *Account A* |  |  |
|---|---|---|---|
| *(1)* | 600 | *(2)* | 800 |
| *(3)* | 350 |  |  |
|  |  | *bal c/f* ◀ | 150 |
|  | 950 |  | 950 |
| *bal b/f* ▶ | 150 |  |  |

The balance on this account is £150 *DR*

|  | *Account B* |  |  |
|---|---|---|---|
| *(1)* | 200 | *(2)* | 650 |
| *(3)* | 300 |  |  |
| *bal c/f* ◀ | 150 |  |  |
|  | 650 |  | 650 |
|  |  | *bal b/f* ▶ | 150 |

The balance on this account is £150 *CR*

If the movements recorded on each side of an account are already equal when we come to balance it, the account is said to carry a nil balance. In such a case, we need only insert totals level with each other on each side of the account, with nothing beneath them. The totals will demonstrate the equality and prove no net movement down to that point.

## MOVEMENTS, ENTRIES, AND BALANCES

Since the object of balancing an account is to replace many individual movements with a single net movement, there is no need to balance an account which has only one entry to begin with. In such a case, the balance on the account will be the same as the single existing entry. In general however, it is worth making a strong mental distinction between what is meant by an *entry* on an account, and what is meant by the *balance* on an account.

An entry in an account means any single movement recorded on the account, regardless of its direction. Thus a DR entry is the record of a movement IN, and a CR entry is the record of a movement OUT. An entry in an account, therefore, may record one side of an equal exchange, or it may record one side of a transfer between accounts.

By contrast, the balance on an account shows the overall effect of a number of entries. In other words, an entry is part of the record of an *event*, while a balance shows a *state of affairs*. The difference is significant. If you want to know what happened, you look at the entries on a firm's accounts. If you want to know the effect of what happened, you look at the balances on the firm's accounts.

## THE JOURNAL AND JOURNAL ENTRIES

In traditional accounting, 'the Journal' is a notebook, used to make a preliminary note of any entries that we are about to make in the accounts. Thus, a journal entry would consist of a set of balancing DRs and CRs, with a short narrative or explanation of why the entries are to be made. Box 13.3 presents an example.

### BOX 13.3

**A Journal Entry**

| | | | |
|----|---------|------|------|
| DR | bank | £600 | |
| CR | capital | | £600 |

to record £600 paid into business bank account by owner.

## SOME ALTERNATIVE NOTATION

Readers should be aware that debit and credit may also be abbreviated as dr and cr, or as Dr and Cr. Also, some accountants prefer to write 'carried down' (c/d) and 'brought down' (b/d) instead of 'carried forward' and 'brought forward'. These are matters of purely personal preference.

## DRS AND CRS IN A BANK STATEMENT

Previous acquaintance with debits and credits as they appear on a bank statement may generate some confusion with respect to the description given above. The difficulty is not with any ambiguity in debits and credits as such, but with the relevant point of view.

A bank statement is a copy of the bank's account for promises IN from, and OUT to its customer. When you pay money into the bank, the bank will give a promise OUT to you. That promise will be recorded by the bank as a CR on its account for promises to you, and will therefore appear on your bank statement as a CR. When you write a cheque instructing the bank to pay someone, the bank will take a promise IN from you, in order to give it OUT to the other person, and the promise coming IN from you will appear in your bank statement as a DR.

In effect, from your point of view, the bank statement is the wrong way round. When you look at your bank statement (the bank's account for promises to you), what you would like to see is a lot of CR entries and a CR balance, showing promises from the bank being given OUT to you. On the other hand, when you look at your own account for promises from the bank, what you would like to see is lots of DR entries and a DR balance, showing promises coming IN from the bank to you.

## CREDIT CARDS AND DEBIT CARDS

A credit card gets its name because it provides a means of purchasing goods or services on credit. Use of a credit card involves two transactions which are in practice simultaneous, but which in logic must take place in sequence. First, the relevant goods are sold by the retailer to the credit card company, in exchange for the company's promise of prompt payment (within days). At the same time, the credit card company sells the goods to the cardholder, in exchange for the cardholder's promise to pay at leisure (in accordance with the terms and conditions of the card). Thus, the retailer enjoys almost immediate payment, while the cardholder, the ultimate purchaser, may enjoy a period of extended credit. Meanwhile, the credit card company benefits in two ways: it collects a commission from the supplier, and it may charge interest to any cardholder who chooses not to pay the full amount owing at the end of each accounting period.

The debit card is a later invention, and was named in deliberate contrast to its older brother, the credit card, because it does *not* allow the cardholder to make purchases on credit. Payment by debit card is effectively equivalent to immediate payment by cheque, except that the process is automated and does not involve the expense and delay entailed in the physical transfer of cheques. With a debit card, the retailer is in direct communication with the bank at the time of the transaction, and the bank immediately takes a promise IN from the cardholder (the bank 'debits the cardholder's account') and gives a promise OUT to the retailer. The cardholder benefits from not having to carry cash or write a cheque, the retailer benefits from not having to handle cash or take the risk of a bouncing cheque, and the card company benefits from a commission collected from the retailer.

## CREDIT NOTES AND DEBIT NOTES

A credit note is a document issued to cancel all or part of a previous sales invoice. When a firm issues a sales invoice, requesting payment for a sale, it records money or a promise coming IN from the customer, and sales going OUT. If the customer returns the goods or objects to the invoice, the firm may issue a credit note, giving a promise back OUT to the customer (and at the same time, recording all or some of the sale value coming back IN).

A debit note is a document issued to inform another business or individual that you have made a DR entry in their account – that is to say that you have recorded a promise coming IN from them for some reason. A debit note may therefore be used to add further charges to an invoice that has already been issued, or it may be used as a substitute for a sales invoice, especially when a firm is requesting payment for services rather than goods. A debit note may also be issued to inform a supplier that you are taking back IN a promise that you have previously given out to them – perhaps, for example, because you have been overcharged or you have discovered an error in their invoice.

## REVIEW

This chapter has introduced and defined the terms debit and credit. It has also shown how to balance an account, and explained the important difference between an entry on an account, which records an event, and the balance on an account, which shows a state of affairs.

Finally, as a matter of general interest and to clarify possible confusion, the chapter made some remarks on the meaning of debit and credit as they may appear on a bank statement, and as they are used in connection with credit cards and debit cards, and credit notes and debit notes.

# DRILLS AND EXERCISES

## 13.1  Balancing accounts

Balance each of the following separate accounts. (Guidelines for positioning of the totals have been inserted in the first two.)

| A | | B | |
|---:|---:|---:|---:|
| 200 | 100 | 200 | 700 |
| 300 | | 400 | |

| C | | D | |
|---:|---:|---:|---:|
| 750 | 50 | 30 | 25 |
| 250 | 150 | 10 | 80 |
| | 300 | 60 | |
| | 100 | | |

| E | | F | |
|---:|---:|---:|---:|
| | 1 000 | | 600 |
| | 4 500 | | 400 |
| | 1 500 | | 250 |
| | | | 750 |
| | | | 500 |

| G | | H | |
|---:|---:|---:|---:|
| 10 | 460 | 350 | 625 |
| 40 | 15 | 450 | 325 |
| 70 | 25 | 200 | |
| 30 | | 300 | |
| 50 | | 175 | |
| | | 225 | |

| I | | J | |
|---:|---:|---:|---:|
| 113 | 789 | 555 | 2 361 |
| 378 | 436 | 476 | 1 567 |
| 16 | 154 | 450 | 552 |
| 205 | | 3 287 | 4 513 |
| 1 330 | | 881 | |
| | | 1 858 | |
| | | 97 | |

| K | | L | |
|---:|---:|---:|---:|
| 113 | 4 361 | 5 234 | 1 442 |
| 378 | 4 570 | 2 839 | 926 |
| 330 | | 542 | 2 654 |
| 2 699 | | | 65 |
| 3 713 | | | 1 457 |
| | | | 146 |

## 13.2 Accounts and balances

1. show an example of an account with at least three entries, carrying a DR balance
2. show an example of an account with at least three entries, carrying a CR balance
3. show an example of an account with two DR entries and a CR entry, carrying a CR balance
4. show an example of an account with three CR entries and a DR entry, carrying a CR balance
5. show an example of an account with five entries, carrying a nil balance

# CHAPTER 14

# Reading Ledger Accounts

## OBJECTIVES

*The objectives of this chapter are:*

- to explain how and why certain accounts may have names which are initially slightly confusing
- to offer some practice in reading and understanding the content of ledger accounts

## ACCOUNT NAMES

In principle an account is given the name of the thing whose movements are recorded there – the account for recording movements of cash is called the Cash Account; the account for recording sales is called the Sales Account, and so on. However, there are departures from this general rule, some of which are very trying for beginners. These occur in connection with 'personal accounts', and in connection with the naming of certain accounts for inputs and outputs, where the explanation or *'reason why'* concept of an input or output predominates over the equal exchange or *'what for'* concept.

## PERSONAL ACCOUNTS

A *personal account* is an account for promises IN from and OUT to any particular person or firm. (Any other account is called an *impersonal account*.) The title of a personal account should properly be 'Promises from/to *Name*', but accountants usually drop the reference to promises, leaving only the name of the person or firm as the name of the account. So an account under the heading *Smith* or *Jones* would in fact record the movement of *promises* from or to Smith or Jones. The DR and CR analysis of relevant transactions would be abbreviated accordingly, as shown in Box 14.1 on the following page.

There is little harm in shortening the name of an account. But once an account has been given the name of a person, it seems only natural to refer to it as that person's account. So for example, the account in Box 14.1 for promises from or to Smith is first labelled simply 'Smith', and then referred to as 'Smith's Account'. Here is scope for confusion, because 'Smith's Account' (in the singular) must be very carefully distinguished from 'Smith's accounts' (in the plural).

'Smith's Account' in the singular, means the place where a firm records the movement of promises IN from or OUT to Smith, who evidently will be a debtor or creditor of the firm in

## BOX 14.1

**Personal Accounts and Promises**

1. A firm sells goods on credit to Smith for ● £80

| DR | Smith | £80 | |
|----|-------|------|------|
| CR | Sales | | £80 |

2. The firm receives payment of ● £60 by cheque from Smith

| DR | Bank | £60 | |
|----|------|------|------|
| CR | Smith | | £60 |

The relevant accounts will look like this:

| | | *bank* | | | | *sales* | |
|------|------|------|------|------|------|------|------|
| *(2)* | ● 60 | | | | | *(1)* | ● 80 |

| | | *Smith* | | |
|------|------|------|------|------|
| *(1)* | ● 80 | *(2)* | ● 60 | |

question. By contrast, 'Smith's accounts' in the plural, means the set of accounts maintained by Smith for recording his transactions. If we are preparing the accounts of our firm, we may make an entry in 'Smith's Account' (our account for promises from or to Smith, recorded from our point of view), but we have no business meddling in Smith's accounts, which are entirely his responsibility.

## NOMINAL ACCOUNTS AND REAL ACCOUNTS

The division between personal accounts (for promises to and from other firms or persons) and impersonal accounts (for every other thing) derives from a scheme of analysis produced in the nineteenth century, in which impersonal accounts were further divided into real accounts and nominal accounts.

Nominal accounts (not to be confused with personal accounts) were for things thought to exist in name only. These consisted in fact of outputs, and of the inputs consumed or likely to be consumed within a single period (both being thought to exist in name only because at the end of a period, there would be no trace of them inside the firm). Real accounts were for things that would really exist inside the firm at the end of a period – such things as money, stocks of goods, machinery, and so on.

Though the underlying scheme of analysis is no longer made much use of, this system still survives and merits our attention as the basis of an ad hoc division of the firm's accounts. Thus in practice, when the number of accounts becomes too many to be included in a single book or ledger, personal accounts are separated off into a Debtors' Ledger and a Creditors' Ledger, while a 'Nominal Ledger' is used to group together all the 'nominal' accounts.

## INPUTS, OUTPUTS, AND REASONS WHY

The fundamental rule of double entry accounting is that the value involved in each transaction must be recorded once under a heading to show *what* happened (the movement of money or promise), and once again under a heading to show *why* it happened, or *what for* (the movement of an input or an output). For accountants, the *fact* of a payment and the *reason* for the payment are separate things, to be recorded separately. This distinction is the essence of the double entry.

However, in everyday language, as we have previously remarked, the distinction is often lost, with both aspects of a transaction neatly wrapped up in a single word like *wages*, *rent*, or *interest* which answers both our questions: *what* happened (a payment of money or promises) and *why* did it happen (in exchange for labour, use of space, or use of money)?

Despite their potential for confusion, these words and others like them are often used as names or titles of accounts. Thus, many firms will have a Wages Account, a Rent Account, or an Interest Payable Account, and so on. In this context, such words must be stripped of their association with the *fact* of payment (any actual movements of money can only be recorded on the Cash Account or the Bank Account). Their role is reduced to indicating only the *reason* for a payment. This leads to some rather strange-looking double entry, as may be seen in the examples in Box 14.2.

### BOX 14.2

**The Double Entry Analysis of a Transaction**

1. A firm pays wages of £150 by cheque.

The *fact* of the payment – that is, the movement of money OUT of the business – is recorded with a CR in the account for Bank. The *reason* for the payment is recorded with a DR in the Wages Account.

The analysis therefore will be

| DR | Wages | £150 | |
|----|-------|------|------|
| CR | Bank | | £150 |

Here it is strange to see a DR coming IN to the Wages Account, when we think in everyday terms of wages being paid out. However, it is money that is paid out, while 'Wages' represents the reason why.

2. A firm lets out part of its premises, and receives a payment of £200 rent, by cheque.

Here, the *fact* that money comes IN to the firm is recorded with a DR in the account for Bank. The *reason* for the receipt of money is recorded with a CR in the Rent Receivable Account.

The analysis therefore will be

| DR | Bank | £200 | |
|----|------|------|------|
| CR | Rent Receivable | | £200 |

Here it is strange to see a CR going OUT of the Rent Receivable Account, when we think in everyday terms of the rent coming in to the firm. However, it is money that is received by the firm, while 'Rent Receivable' represents the reason why.

The table of account names and their content or interpretation in Box 14.3 is probably more useful than further explanation in the abstract. The table contains only a sample from the range of tricky possibilities, but many of them are initially counter-intuitive, and the table will repay study.

## BOX 14.3

### Account Names: Meaning and Content

| ACCOUNT NAME | MEANING and CONTENT |
|---|---|
| Wages | name explains an outward movement of money: account records the INPUT 'labour' |
| Fee Income | name explains an inward movement of money: account records the OUTPUT 'professional work' |
| Rent Payable | name explains an outward movement of money: account records the INPUT 'permission to use property' |
| Rent Receivable | name explains an inward movement of money: account records the OUTPUT 'permission to use property' |
| Interest Payable | name explains an outward movement of money: account records the INPUT 'permission to use money' |
| Interest Receivable | name explains an inward movement of money: account records the OUTPUT 'permission to use money' |
| Tax Charge | name explains an outward movement of money: account records an INPUT |
| Fine (for criminal offence) | name explains an outward movement of money: account records an INPUT |
| Sundry Expenses | name explains an outward movement of money: account records small unspecified INPUTs |
| Loan | name explains inward movement of money: account records a liability or promise OUT to repay the money. |

# REVIEW

This chapter has outlined some problems in the use of language and the meaning of account names. These problems are not in themselves central to the practice of double entry, but they can cause interference and make obstacles to proper understanding.

In connection with personal accounts, the chapter showed how a firm's account for promises from or to a person can be referred to as that person's account, with potentially misleading consequences.

In connection with accounts for inputs and outputs, the chapter showed how certain words like 'rent' or 'wages' have a double meaning in everyday language, and how they must be restricted to a single explanatory meaning in the context of the double entry, when they are used as account names or titles.

# DRILLS AND EXERCISES

## 14.1 Account names and balances

State the balance you would reasonably expect to find (DR balance, CR balance, nil balance, or could be either) on each of the following accounts.

1. a sales account
2. a purchases account
3. a debtor's account
4. a creditor's account
5. an account for bank
6. a cash account
7. a capital account (for promises to or from the owner)
8. an electricity account
9. an account for rent (permission to use a building)
10. a customer's account
11. a lender's account
12. an account for wages or labour
13. a supplier's account
14. an account for purchase returns
15. a borrower's account
16. an account for a customer who has overpaid the business by mistake
17. an account for interest (permission to use money)
18. an account for sales returns
19. an account for a supplier who has been overpaid by mistake
20. an account for advertising
21. the account for a lender who has been completely repaid
22. the account for a borrower who has repaid the whole amount originally borrowed
23. the account for bank, if the business has an overdraft
24. an account (in a retail shop) for refunds
25. an account for machinery and equipment

## 14.2 Accounting entries

State where you would reasonably expect to find the DR or the CR corresponding to each of the accounting entries listed below, and describe the likely events or circumstances that the entries are intended to record.

1. a CR in a sales account
2. a DR in a sales account
3. a DR in a purchases account
4. a CR in a purchases account
5. a DR in a debtor's account
6. a CR in a debtor's account
7. a CR in the account for bank
8. a DR in the account for bank
9. a DR in a creditor's account
10. a CR in a creditor's account
11. a DR in the cash account
12. a CR in the cash account
13. a CR in the capital account
14. a DR in the capital account
15. a DR in the account for electricity
16. a CR in the account for electricity
17. a DR in the account for rent payable
18. a CR in the account for rent payable
19. a DR in a customer's account
20. a CR in a customer's account
21. a DR in a supplier's account
22. a CR in a supplier's account
23. a CR in a lender's account
24. a DR in a lender's account
25. a DR in a wages account
26. a CR in a wages account
27. a CR in the account for purchase returns
28. a DR in the account for purchase returns
29. a CR in the account for sales returns
30. a DR in the account for sales returns
31. a DR in the account for advertising
32. a CR in the account for advertising

## 14.3 Understanding balances

State the significance of the following (possibly unusual) situations.

1. a CR balance on a customer's account
2. a DR balance on a supplier's account
3. a CR balance on the account for bank
4. a CR balance on the cash account
5. a DR balance on the capital account

# CHAPTER 15

# The Trial Balance

## OBJECTIVES

*The objectives of this chapter are:*

- to describe the form and content of the trial balance
- to outline the traditional use of the trial balance as a partial check on the accuracy and completeness of the accounting records
- to explain how the modern trial balance still marks a point in the division of labour between book-keeping and accounting

## THE TRIAL BALANCE

In previous chapters we have seen how to record transactions in a set of accounts, and how to balance those accounts. It would be possible to repeat such procedures indefinitely, merely recording transactions as they happen and balancing accounts from time to time, to summarize the net movement on each account. However, the usual practice is in fact to *stop* from time to time, to determine the consequences of a firm's transactions up until the stopping point. Such consequences are shown in two ways:

- in terms of the profit or loss made by the firm; and
- in terms of the state of affairs at which the firm has arrived.

This working out of consequences requires the transfer of certain balances to a *Profit & Loss Account*, and the listing of the remaining balances in a *balance sheet*. But before that, it is good practice to prepare a trial balance (TB).

A trial balance is:

- a list of all balances on all accounts;
- before transfers to or from the Profit & Loss Account.

Box 15.1 on the following page shows a series of transactions, with a balanced set of accounts on which the transactions have been recorded, and a trial balance which lists the balances on those accounts. Notice the standard format of the TB. Every trial balance should be given a title and a date – the title indicating the name of the relevant business, as well as stating the fact that the list is in fact a trial balance and not some other list of numbers. In the trial balance itself, accounts may be listed in any order, but notice how DR balances and CR balances are listed in separate columns, so that totals can be found easily and compared against each other.

## BOX 15.1

### Transactions, Balances, and the Trial Balance

FIRM A has recorded the following transactions in the course of YEAR1, and balanced its accounts at the end of the period.

1. owner puts £80 into a bank account for the firm
2. firm buys goods for £60 on credit
3. firm sells goods for £90 on credit
4. firm pays wages £50 by cheque
5. owner takes goods value £10 out of the business for his own personal use
6. firm receives cheque for £90 from customer
7. firm sells goods for £5, receiving payment by cheque
8. firm pays £45 by cheque to supplier

The firm's accounts will look like this

| | bank | | | | capital | | | | purchases | |
|---|---|---|---|---|---|---|---|---|---|---|
| (1) | 80 | (4) | 50 | | | (1) | ● 80 | (2) | 60 | (5) | 10 |
| (6) | 90 | (8) | 45 | | | | | | | c/f | 50 |
| (7) | 5 | c/f | 80 | | | | | | | 60 | 60 |
| | 175 | | 175 | | | | | b/f | ● 50 | | |
| b/f | ● 80 | | | | | | | | | |

| | supplier | | | | customer | | | | sales | |
|---|---|---|---|---|---|---|---|---|---|---|
| (8) | 45 | (2) | 60 | | (3) | 90 | (6) | 90 | | | (3) | 90 |
| c/f | 15 | | | | | | c/f | 95 | (7) | 5 |
| | 60 | | 60 | | | | | 95 | | 95 | 95 |
| | | b/f | ● 15 | | | | | | b/f | ● 95 |

| | wages (labour) | | | drawings | |
|---|---|---|---|---|---|
| (4) | ● 50 | | (5) | ● 10 | |

The trial balance based on these accounts will look like this

FIRM A Trial Balance at end of YEAR 1

| | DR | CR |
|---|---|---|
| | £ | £ |
| bank | ● 80 | |
| capital | | ● 80 |
| purchases | ● 50 | |
| supplier | | ● 15 |
| sales | | ● 95 |
| wages (labour) | ● 50 | |
| drawings | ● 10 | |
| total | £190 | £190 |

# PRACTICAL USES OF THE TRIAL BALANCE

The trial balance in Box 15.1 is said to balance because the total of the DR balances is equal to the total of the CR balances. This should always be the case, as long as:

- every original entry in the accounts has been made as part of a set of equal, balancing, DRs and CRs;
- all of the accounts have been correctly balanced; and
- the list itself is accurate and complete.

A trial balance that fails to balance is evidence that one or more of the three conditions above has not been met. Conversely a trial balance that *does* balance is reassuring evidence that those conditions have been met. However, a balancing TB is by no means any guarantee of complete reliability. Many accounting errors may occur without causing the TB to fall out of balance. For example:

- transactions may be recorded with equal DR and CR entries, but with one or both entered in the wrong account;
- both sides of a transaction (DR and CR) may be recorded in the right accounts, but at the wrong value;
- DRs and CRs may be reversed, through ignorance or by accident;
- some transactions may have been omitted altogether from the accounts;
- other transactions may have been recorded more than once in the accounts.

For all its limitations, the trial balance remained an important, if partial, test of accuracy in accounting records, until the introduction and widespread use of electronic data processing towards the end of the last century. Arguably, it is no longer so important as a test of accuracy. Recall the errors that reveal themselves by causing a trial balance not to balance: unequal DRs and CRs to record a transaction; arithmetical errors in balancing the accounts; and error, omission, or duplication in the list of balances. These are all errors in processing, and they are errors of a kind unlikely to occur when the human element is replaced by electronic processing. Meanwhile, the errors that will *not* reveal themselves by throwing the trial balance out of balance, are precisely those human operating errors (notably errors of input) that electronic processing cannot prevent or detect.

Technology therefore has made the trial balance almost obsolete as a test of accuracy, except for that dwindling number of firms where accounts are still prepared by hand. Which is not to say that the trial balance is a waste of time. As a matter of convenience, it remains extremely useful. If balances are all you want or need, a list of balances in the form of a TB is vastly more convenient than a whole set of accounts, showing every individual entry.

# SOCIAL AND PROFESSIONAL SIGNIFICANCE OF THE TRIAL BALANCE

Beyond whatever practical uses it still has, the trial balance also marks an interesting sociological divide. The work involved in recording transactions, balancing accounts, and producing a trial balance, is called book-keeping. What follows the production of the trial balance is the work of preparing a Profit & Loss Account and balance sheet. This work is held to require more thorough knowledge of theory and practice than the largely clerical work of book-keeping, and, significantly, it is believed to require the exercise of officially qualified skill and judgement, which merits more generous remuneration.

The trial balance therefore marks the stage in the division of labour at which the qualified accountant takes over from the book-keeper. It is for this reason perhaps that the accounting texts, written for aspiring professionals, may tend to overstate the continuing importance of the trial balance as a test of accuracy, even in the face of the last century's advances in technology.

## WHAT DO WE DO IF THE TRIAL BALANCE DOESN'T BALANCE?

If a trial balance fails to balance, we first of all force it to balance, by creating a Suspense Account with the necessary balance. Box 15.2 presents a simple example.

**BOX 15.2**

### Correcting Errors

1. A firm has only two accounts in its ledger, but with the balances shown below, its trial balance does not balance.

| Account A | | Account B | |
|---|---|---|---|
| balance | 750 | balance | 800 |

2. We must first force the trial balance into balance by opening a Suspense Account and giving it the necessary balance, as shown below.

| Account A | | Account B | |
|---|---|---|---|
| balance | 750 | balance | 800 |

| Supense Account | |
|---|---|
| 50 | |

Once we have a balancing trial balance, we begin to look for the error(s) that caused it to fall out of balance. In our example, it is clear that:

- *either* there are not enough DRs in Account A;
- *or* there are too many CRs in Account B.

If we now discover that the cause of the trouble is a missing DR in Account A, we can replace it on Account A by transferring the spare DR we have on the Suspense Account. If on the other hand we discover that the cause of the trouble is an excess CR in Account B, then we can cancel it by transferring the spare DR we have on the Suspense Account.

In either event, by using a Suspense Account when the trial balance fails to balance:

- we can use proper balancing double entry to correct the errors when we find them; and
- when we have found and corrected all errors, the Suspense Account will carry a nil balance.

Box 15.3 demonstrates and concludes our simple example.

## BOX 15.3

### Correcting Errors

1. A firm has forced its trial balance to balance with the use of a Suspense Account, as shown below.

| | Account A | | | | Account B | |
|---|---|---|---|---|---|---|
| balance | 750 | | | | balance | 800 |

| | Supense Account | |
|---|---|---|
| | 50 | |

2. The firm discovers that the original failure to balance was caused by an excess CR in Account B.

The excess CR in Account B is therefore cancelled by transferring the spare DR that is in the Suspense Account.

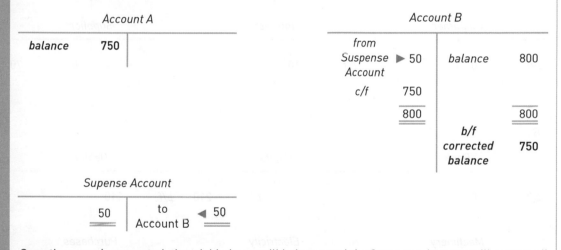

Once the error is corrected, the trial balance will balance and the Suspense Account will carry a nil balance.

# REVIEW

This chapter has defined the trial balance as a list of all balances on all accounts before transfers to or from the Profit & Loss Account, and has described the standard format of the trial balance. It also described the historic function of the TB as a partial check on the accuracy and completeness of the accounting records. In addition, it briefly discussed the continuing role of the TB as a marker of the predominantly social distinction between the work of the book-keeper, and the work of the accountant. Finally, the chapter outlined the logic of the procedures involved in making corrections when a trial balance has failed to balance (nowadays a most unlikely event, since accounting software will not allow original non-balancing entries to be made).

# DRILLS AND EXERCISES

## 15.1 Producing a trial balance

Prepare a trial balance for each of the separate sets of accounts below, which have already been balanced.

In each case (depending on whether the TB actually balances) state which errors may, or may not, have occurred in the work already done to record transactions and balance the accounts.

A

| Sales | | Purchases | | Capital | |
|---|---|---|---|---|---|
| | b/f 350 | b/f 260 | | | b/f 400 |

| Wages | | Furniture | | Bank | |
|---|---|---|---|---|---|
| b/f 150 | | b/f 380 | | | b/f 80 |

| Customer | | Interest | | Supplier | |
|---|---|---|---|---|---|
| b/f 100 | | b/f 10 | | | b/f 70 |

B

| Bank | | Capital | | Debtor | |
|---|---|---|---|---|---|
| b/f 40 | | | b/f 210 | b/f 110 | |

| Machinery | | Electricity | | Purchases | |
|---|---|---|---|---|---|
| b/f 200 | | b/f 25 | | b/f 130 | |

| Sales | | Creditor | | Wages | |
|---|---|---|---|---|---|
| | b/f 250 | | b/f 75 | b/f 50 | |

## 15.2  Recording, balancing, and producing a trial balance

For each of the separate situations below, record the given transactions on the relevant accounts, balance the accounts, and prepare a trial balance at the end of the period.

A    1. an owner puts £500 into a bank account for his business
     2. business buys goods for £400 on credit from X
     3. business sells goods for £700 on credit to Y
     4. business pays £400 by cheque to X
     5. business receives payment of £500 by cheque from Y
     6. business takes back goods from Y, previously sold to him for £200
     7. business pays wages of £100 by cheque
     8. business buys goods for £300 on credit from X
     9. business sells goods for £350, receiving payment by cheque
   10. business pays £40 for electricity

B    1. an owner puts £750 into a bank account for his business
     2. business borrows £500 from ABC finance
     3. business buys production machinery for £600, paying by cheque
     4. business buys raw materials for £300 on credit from S
     5. business sells goods for £850 on credit to C
     6. business pays wages of £150 by cheque
     7. owner takes £50 cash out of business bank account
     8. business pays £300 by cheque to S
     9. business sells goods on credit to C for £150
   10. business receives cheque for £900 from C

## 15.3  Recording, balancing, and producing a trial balance

Return to the drills at the end of Chapter 11, and, for each separate business, record the given transactions on the relevant accounts, balance the accounts, and prepare a trial balance at the end of the period.

Find more questions and answers at www.cengage.co.uk/hodge.

# CHAPTER 16

# Final Accounts: A Simple Profit & Loss Account

## OBJECTIVES

*The objectives of this chapter are:*

- to explain the basic idea of the Profit & Loss Account
- to show the steps involved in preparing a very simple Profit & Loss Account, with only sales, purchases, and closing stock

## FINAL ACCOUNTS

'Final accounts' refers to a set of two financial statements, drawn up at the end of any period, to summarize the consequences of a firm's activities. The first of these statements is the Income Statement, or Profit & Loss (P&L) Account, which reports the profit or loss made by the firm in the period, and shows how that profit or loss was made. The second is the balance sheet, which reports the state of affairs arrived at by the firm at the end of the period.

In this chapter and the next we shall present the basic idea of the P&L Account, and outline the procedures involved in its preparation. The balance sheet will be described in Chapter 18.

## THE IDEA OF THE PROFIT & LOSS ACCOUNT

In our model of a business, profit is the difference between the value of outputs created in a period, and the value of inputs consumed. The idea of the P&L Account therefore is to bring these two elements together on one account so that the difference between them – the balance on the P&L Account – will represent profit or loss for the period. The basic form of the P&L Account, in abstract, is shown in Box 16.1.

BOX 16.1

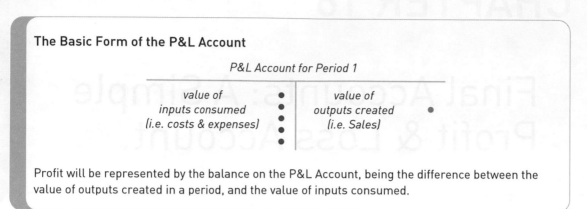

**The Basic Form of the P&L Account**

*P&L Account for Period 1*

| value of<br>inputs consumed<br>*(i.e. costs & expenses)* | value of<br>outputs created<br>*(i.e. Sales)* |
|---|---|

Profit will be represented by the balance on the P&L Account, being the difference between the value of outputs created in a period, and the value of inputs consumed.

## THE PERIOD COVERED BY A P&L ACCOUNT

Because the P&L Account is intended to summarize the consequences of a firm's activities over a particular period or length of time, the relevant period must be stated in the title of the account. The length of time may be as short as a week or a month, but the usual assumption in textbooks is that the P&L Account will cover a period of one year.

Whatever may be the length of the period (a week, a month, a year, etc.), the particular period covered by each P&L Account is in practice identified by its closing date – as for example in 'Profit & Loss Account for the year ended 30 June 2050'. However, to reduce the level of noise and detail in most of our examples, including Box 16.1, particular stretches of time will be identified only as 'Period 1' or 'Period 2', etc.

## PREPARATION OF THE P&L ACCOUNT: FIRST STEPS

Box 16.1 presents no more than a sketch of the basic form of a P&L Account. In practice there are complications. For example, the many different inputs consumed by a typical firm are usually divided into 'cost of sales', 'operating expenses', and 'financial costs'.

Avoiding such details for the moment, we shall start with the very simplest case – a trading firm (not a manufacturer) which *only* buys and sells indeterminate goods. In this and the next four chapters then, our examples will assume a firm in which sales are the only outputs, and purchases the only inputs. As a result the P&L Accounts that we prepare will contain only sales and cost of sales. (Such a truncated form of P&L Account is often called a Trading Account.) These simplifying assumptions are of course unrealistic, but they will serve to illustrate the basic principles.

In this chapter we shall also assume a brand new firm, at the end of its very first period of trading. Once the firm's transactions for the period have been recorded, and the accounts have been balanced, preparation of the P&L Account for Period 1 involves only four steps.

First, we transfer the value of sales from the Sales Account to a newly opened P&L Account for the period, using the standard ◄ cancel and ► replace technique that was shown in Chapter 12. The balance on the Sales Account (a movement OUT) is cancelled with a movement IN, and replaced with a movement OUT on the P&L Account. Box 16.2 shows an example.

Next we transfer the value of purchases to the P&L Account. Here the original movement IN to the Purchases Account is cancelled with a movement OUT, and replaced with a movement IN to the P&L Account. Box 16.3 continues the example.

## BOX 16.2

### Transferring the Value of Sales to the P&L Account

At the end of Period 1, after a firm has recorded all of its transactions for the period and balanced its accounts, the balance on the Sales Account is as shown below.

*Sales*

| | |
|---|---|
| | balance at end of period  300 |

To transfer the value of Sales to the P&L Account,

first we ◄ cancel the value
shown on the Sales Account ...

*Sales*

| | | | |
|---|---|---|---|
| to P&L A/c  ◄ 300 | | balance at end of period | 300 |

*P&L Account for Period 1*

| | |
|---|---|
| from Sales A/c  ► 300 | then we ► replace it on the P&L Account. |

## BOX 16.3

### Transferring the Value of Purchases to the P&L Account

At the end of Period 1, the balance on a firm's Purchases Account is as shown below:

*Purchases*

| | |
|---|---|
| balance at end of period   250 | |

To transfer the value of purchase to the P&L Account:

*Purchases*

| | | | |
|---|---|---|---|
| balance at end of period   250 | to P&L A/c   ◄ 250 | | |

first we ◄ cancel the value
shown on the Purchases Account ...

*P & L Account for Period 1*

| | | | |
|---|---|---|---|
| from Purchases A/c  ► 250 | from Sales A/c | 300 |

then we ► replace it
on the P&L Account.

# CLOSING STOCK

The P&L Account in Box 16.3 is not yet ready to balance. As it stands, it allows us to compare the value of sales and purchases. But profit is not the difference between sales and purchases. It is the difference between the value of outputs created in a period and the value of inputs consumed. While it may be fair to say that 'outputs created' means sales, it is not so easy to imagine that 'inputs consumed' is quite the same as purchases. In most firms, trading is continuous. It does not consist of a series of separate ventures, each one complete before the next one is undertaken. It follows that a firm will not wait until it has sold all its stocks before it makes more purchases, and that some of the goods purchased in a period may well be left in the business at the end of the period, waiting to be sold. Indeed this is very likely.

A stock of unconsumed purchases remaining in a business at the end of a period is called closing stock. The accounting records do not tell us the value of closing stock, and in practice the only way to discover how much closing stock remains on hand at the end of a period, is to go and look at the physical evidence in the warehouse, or the factory, or the shop. Most firms that deal in goods do actually conduct an annual stock-take precisely for this purpose. Stocktaking procedures are not central to the theory of accounting, but the principles of stock valuation are surprisingly complex and must be dealt with later. For the moment we shall assume that we are simply given a figure for the value of any firm's closing stock. It is important to recognize however, that *this figure cannot be found within the accounting system.* The value of closing stock must always be found and brought in to the accounts from some external source.

# THE TREATMENT OF CLOSING STOCK

Closing stock, representing purchases that have not yet been transformed into sales, should not be included in the P&L Account. However, in our example we have already transferred the value of *all* purchases into the P&L Account. The solution is simple: having identified the value of unsold purchases (closing stock), we must now take that value out of the P&L Account, so as to leave the P&L with only the value of purchases that have been sold. Closing stock taken OUT of the P&L Account could be replaced back IN the Purchases Account, but in fact it is placed in a Stock Account created for the purpose. The procedure is shown in Box 16.4.

## BOX 16.4

### The Treatment of Closing Stock

Sales and purchases have already been transferred to the P&L Account for Period 1 as shown below:

| P&L Account for Period 1 | | | |
|---|---|---|---|
| *purchases* | 250 | *sales* | 300 |

BOX 16.4   Continued

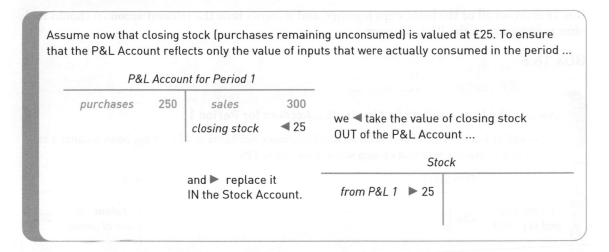

Assume now that closing stock (purchases remaining unconsumed) is valued at £25. To ensure that the P&L Account reflects only the value of inputs that were actually consumed in the period …

In summary: first we put the value of *all* purchases IN to the P&L Account, then we take the value of any unsold purchases OUT again as closing stock. After which it follows that the net value of purchases remaining IN the P&L must be the value consumed or turned into sales in the period.

## BALANCING THE P&L ACCOUNT

Our P&L Account now contains the value of sales, and the value of all the purchases that were consumed or turned into sales in Period 1. On the initial simplifying assumption that there are no other inputs except purchases, the P&L Account can now be balanced to determine the profit or loss that the firm will report for the period.

Notice that if outputs are greater than inputs consumed (i.e. if, as in our example, the firm has made a profit), then the P&L Account will carry a CR balance. Conversely if the firm has made a loss, then the P&L Account will carry a DR balance. Box 16.5 continues our example and shows the balancing of the P&L Account.

## BOX 16.5

### Balancing the P&L Account

The balance on the P&L Account represents the profit or loss for the period.

*P&L Account for Period 1*

| | | | | |
|---|---|---|---|---|
| purchases | 250 | sales | | 300 |
| bal c/f | ◄ 75 | closing stock | | 25 |
| | 325 | | | 325 |
| | | bal b/f<br>= profit | ►75 | |

A CR balance on the P&L Account will represent a profit.
A DR balance on the P&L Account will represent a loss.

## AN OVERVIEW OF THE PROCESS

Box 16.6 shows all of the basic steps together, and it shows how the relevant accounts should look after preparation of the P&L Account.

### BOX 16.6

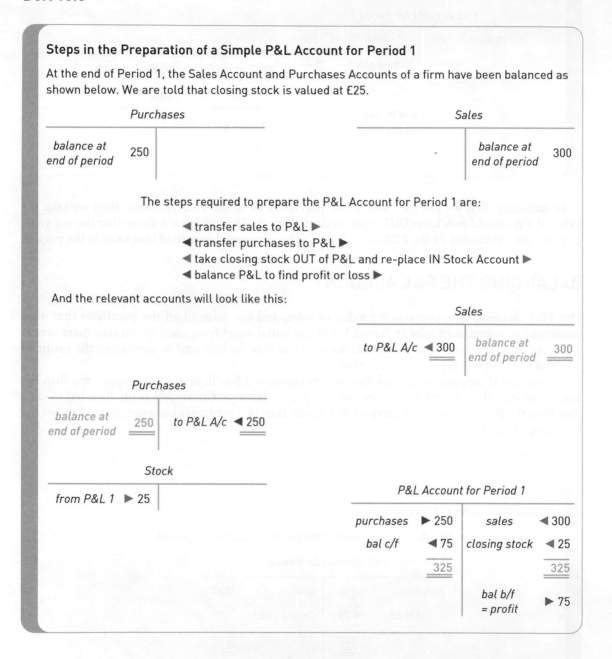

**Steps in the Preparation of a Simple P&L Account for Period 1**

At the end of Period 1, the Sales Account and Purchases Accounts of a firm have been balanced as shown below. We are told that closing stock is valued at £25.

| Purchases | | Sales | |
|---|---|---|---|
| balance at end of period | 250 | | balance at end of period 300 |

The steps required to prepare the P&L Account for Period 1 are:

◄ transfer sales to P&L ►
◄ transfer purchases to P&L ►
◄ take closing stock OUT of P&L and re-place IN Stock Account ►
◄ balance P&L to find profit or loss ►

And the relevant accounts will look like this:

**Sales**

| | | |
|---|---|---|
| to P&L A/c ◄ 300 | balance at end of period | 300 |

**Purchases**

| balance at end of period | 250 | to P&L A/c ◄ 250 |
|---|---|---|

**Stock**

| from P&L 1 ► 25 | |
|---|---|

**P&L Account for Period 1**

| purchases ► 250 | sales ◄ 300 |
|---|---|
| bal c/f ◄ 75 | closing stock ◄ 25 |
| 325 | 325 |
| | bal b/f = profit ► 75 |

Notice that the firm's accounts for money and promises do not appear at all in Box 16.6. Accounts for money and promises can be left out of the picture because we are dealing with the preparation of the P&L Account, which contains only outputs created and inputs consumed. Money and promises are not involved. Also observe that the *process* of preparing the P&L Account is just as important as the *product*. It is actually necessary to go through each of the steps as described, so that:

- the discipline and benefits of the double entry method are preserved;
- the Sales Account and the Purchases Account are left with nil balances, ready to start afresh recording the transactions of the following period; and
- the Stock Account properly shows the value of unconsumed inputs held in the firm at the end of the period.

## A SUMMARY OF THE BASIC STEPS

The four steps involved in the preparation of a very simple P&L Account for Period 1 can now be summarized with the relevant double entry in terms of DRs and CRs, as shown in Box 16.7.

### BOX 16.7

#### Steps in the Preparation of a Simple P&L Account for Period 1

1. ◀ Cancel the value on the Sales Account and ▶ replace it on the P&L Account

| DR | Sales Account | ◀ | |
|----|---------------|----|----|
| CR | P&L Account | | ▶ |

2. ◀ Cancel the value on the Purchases Account and ▶replace it on the P&L Account

| DR | P&L Account | ▶ | |
|----|-------------|----|----|
| CR | Purchases | | ◀ |

3. Take the value of closing stock OUT of the P&L Account and put it IN to the Stock Account

| DR | Stock Account | ▶ | |
|----|---------------|----|----|
| CR | P&L Account | | ◀ |

4. Balance the P&L Account to find profit (indicated by a CR balance) or loss (indicated by a DR balance).

## OPENING STOCK

Notice that closing stock at the end of one period will stay on the Stock Account and reappear as opening stock at the beginning of the next period. In due course we shall consider how to account for opening stock, but for the moment we shall avoid the problem by restricting our examples to the case of a firm at the end of its first trading period, when opening stock cannot exist.

# REVIEW

This chapter has described the idea of the P&L Account and outlined the procedures involved in preparing a very simple Profit & Loss Account for the first period of a firm's existence, showing the treatment of sales, purchases, and closing stock.

# DRILLS AND EXERCISES

## 16.1 A drill to practise making transfers to and from the P&L Account

### BUSINESS 1

Business 1 has balanced its accounts as shown below at the end of Period 1 (its first period of trading). Make the relevant transfers to and from the firm's P&L Account for Period 1, and determine the profit or loss for the period.

At the end of Period 1, Business 1's closing stock is valued at £100.

| Bank | | | | Capital | |
|---|---|---|---|---|---|
| balance at end of period | 250 | | | balance at end of period | 50 |

| Purchases | | | | Sales | |
|---|---|---|---|---|---|
| balance at end of period | 600 | | | balance at end of period | 800 |

| P&L Account for Period 1 | | | | Stock | |
|---|---|---|---|---|---|
| | | | | | |

## BUSINESS 2

Business 2 has balanced its accounts as shown below at the end of Period 1 (its first period of trading). Make the relevant transfers to and from the firm's P&L Account for Period 1, and determine the profit or loss for the period.

At the end of Period 1, Business 2's closing stock is valued at £50.

| Bank | |
|---|---|
| balance at end of period   100 | |

| Capital | |
|---|---|
| | balance at end of period   140 |

| Purchases | |
|---|---|
| balance at end of period   450 | |

| Sales | |
|---|---|
| | balance at end of period   430 |

| Promises from/to Customer A | |
|---|---|
| balance at end of period   120 | |

| Promises from/to Supplier X | |
|---|---|
| | balance at end of period   100 |

| P&L Account for Period 1 | |
|---|---|
| | |

| Stock | |
|---|---|
| | |

## BUSINESS 3

Business 3 has balanced its accounts as shown at the end of Period 1 (its first period of trading). Make the relevant transfers to and from the firm's P&L Account for Period 1, and determine the profit or loss for the period.

At the end of Period 1, Business 3's closing stock is valued at £20.

|  | Purchases |  | Bank |  |
|---|---|---|---|---|
| balance at end of period | 900 |  | balance at end of period | 50 |

|  | Promises from/to Customer B |  | Promises from/to Supplier Y |  |
|---|---|---|---|---|
| balance at end of period | 250 |  | balance at end of period | 150 |

|  | Sales |  | Capital |  |
|---|---|---|---|---|
|  | balance at end of period | 750 | balance at end of period | 200 |

| P&L Account for Period 1 |  | Stock |  |
|---|---|---|---|
|  |  |  |  |

## BUSINESS 4

Business 4 has balanced its accounts as shown below at the end of Period 1 (its first period of trading). Make the relevant transfers to and from the firm's P&L Account for Period 1, and determine the profit or loss for the period.

At the end of Period 1, Business 4's closing stock is valued at £80.

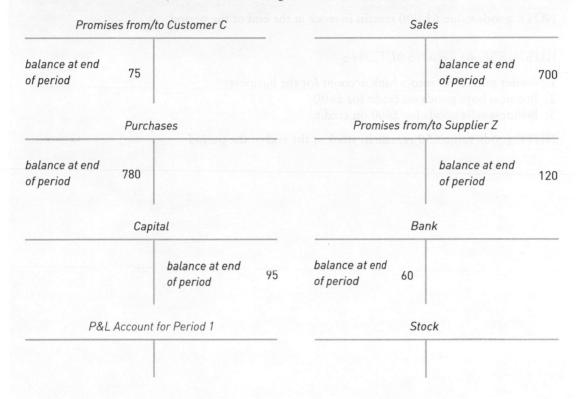

## 16.2

For each separate business below, record the given transactions on the relevant accounts, balance the accounts if necessary, and prepare a P&L Account at the end of the period

### BUSINESS 1: TRANSACTIONS

1. owner puts £1 500 into a bank account for the business
2. business buys goods on credit for £1 800
3. business sells goods on credit for £2 100

NOTE goods value £800 remain in stock at the end of the period

### BUSINESS 2: TRANSACTIONS

1. owner puts £5 000 into a bank account for the business
2. business buys goods on credit for £4 700
3. business sells goods on credit for £3 000

NOTE goods value £700 remain in stock at the end of the period

## BUSINESS 3: TRANSACTIONS

1. owner puts £3 000 into a bank account for the business
2. business buys goods on credit for £1 900
3. business returns goods value £400 to supplier
4. business sells goods on credit for £500

NOTE goods value £1 000 remain in stock at the end of the period

## BUSINESS 4: TRANSACTIONS

1. owner puts £750 into a bank account for the business
2. business buys goods on credit for £600
3. business sells goods for £600 on credit

NOTE goods value £50 remain in stock at the end of the period

# CHAPTER 17

# Profit and the Accounting Equation

## OBJECTIVES

*The objectives of this chapter are:*

- to explain how we account for the owner's claim to the extra value in a business as a result of its operations
- to introduce the accounting equation as a definition of ownership and show how the owner's claim to profit is derived from this definition
- to make clear the distinction between capital and liabilities

## ACCOUNTING FOR THE CLAIM TO PROFIT

Our presentation of the accounting model of a business is shown again in Box 17.1.

## BOX 17.1

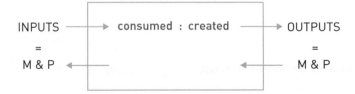

**The Accounting Model of a Business**

INPUTS ────→ consumed : created ────→ OUTPUTS

= M & P ←──────────────────←── = M & P

- a transaction is a movement of money or promises (M&P) across the boundary IN to or OUT of a business

- every transaction is recorded as an exchange of equal value

- inside the business, inputs are consumed while outputs are created

Recall from our discussion of the model in Chapter 2 that a firm which makes a profit (creating outputs with a higher value than the inputs it consumes) will accumulate value inside itself in the form of money, net promises, and inputs waiting to be consumed. This accumulation of value is the substance of profit, as opposed to the abstract measure of profit represented in the P&L Account.

The question now is: who claims that extra value? Or, in the case of loss: who suffers from the decrease in value? These are matters of law, but in accounting the assumption is that profits are claimed by the owner of a business, who also suffers any loss that may arise. (For simplicity we continue to assume a business with a single owner, but the same general principles will apply in the case of multiple ownership.)

We account for the owner's claim to profit or loss by transferring the eventual balance on the P&L Account to the Capital Account (the account which shows the details of the owner's claim).

Profit is represented by a CR balance on the P&L Account. When that CR balance is transferred to the Capital Account, it will appear as an extra promise going OUT to the owner, causing the Capital Account to show an increase in the owner's claim. An example is shown in Box 17.2.

## BOX 17.2

### Accounting for the Claim to Profit

A firm has prepared its first P&L Account, reporting a profit of £75 as shown below:

*Profit & Loss Account for Period 1*

| purchases | 250 | sales | 300 |
|---|---|---|---|
| bal c/f | 75 | closing stock | 25 |
| | 325 | | 325 |
| | | bal b/f = profit | 75 |

Now to account for the owner's claim to profit, we must

*Profit & Loss Account for Period 1*

| purchases | 250 | sales | 300 |
|---|---|---|---|
| bal c/f | 75 | closing stock | 25 |
| | 325 | | 325 |
| to Capital A/c | ◄ 75 | bal b/f = profit | 75 |

◄ cancel the balance on the P&L Account

Capital

| b/f | ● |
|---|---|
| profit from P&L 1 | ► 75 |

and ► replace it on the Capital Account,

where it will add to the owner's existing claim in respect of the value he or she has put into the business.

Notice that claiming the extra value in a business does not involve taking it away. To claim something is merely to say 'that is mine'.

## ACCOUNTING FOR A LOSS

Our example in Box 17.2 takes the case of a P&L Account with a CR balance, representing a profit. A loss would be represented by a DR balance on the P&L Account. When such a DR is transferred to the Capital Account, it will appear there as a promise coming IN from the owner, thereby causing the Capital Account to show a decrease in the owner's claim on the business.

## CAPITAL AND LIABILITIES

Accounting for the claim to profit or loss presents us with the essential difference between capital and liabilities, to which we referred in Chapter 10. We see now that capital, the owner's claim, is *adjustable*. Owners begin with a claim to the value they put into a firm, but if the firm makes a profit (that is, if the value inside the firm increases), the owner will claim the extra value, and the owner's claim will increase. If the firm makes a loss (if the value inside the firm decreases) then the owner's claim will also decrease. But liabilities, by contrast, can never be adjusted (except in extreme cases, following negotiation, by legal agreement with the creditor). Liabilities are claims whose value is fixed in law until they are paid, regardless of whatever profit or loss the firm may make.

## THE ACCOUNTING EQUATION

The adjustable nature of capital is summarized in *the accounting equation*, which is written as:

CAPITAL = ASSETS *minus* LIABILITIES

where *capital* is the owner's claim on the business, *assets* are things of value in, or owned by, the business, and *liabilities* are the claims of other people. 'Assets minus liabilities' is also called *net assets*, so the equation can be written more briefly as:

CAPITAL = NET ASSETS

Though we have written it here without explicit reference to value, it is important to recognize that the accounting equation is in fact about an equality of values. It is not about the equality or identity of things. Specifically, the accounting equation is about the value of capital, and in telling us what the value of capital is equal to, it tells us *the only way to determine the value of the owner's claim* on a business, which is:

1. find the value of assets (unconsumed inputs, money, and promises held in the business);
2. find the value of liabilities (promises given out to other people); and then
3. the value of capital will be equal to the difference between them.

Notice how this method works: the value of assets can be determined independently. So can the value of liabilities. But there is no other independent way to determine the value of capital, except by reference to the value of assets and liabilities. The accounting equation is therefore always true because there is no way in which it can be contradicted.

Box 17.3 shows the accounting equation, and defines its various elements.

BOX 17.3

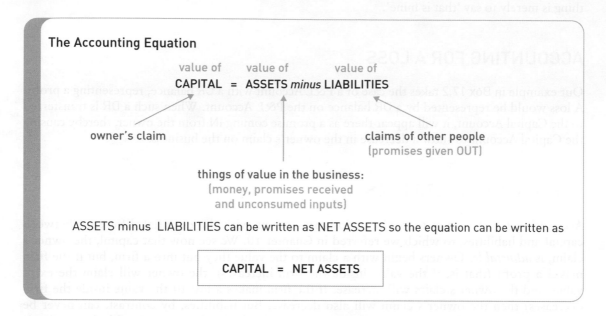

**The Accounting Equation**

value of      value of      value of
**CAPITAL   =   ASSETS** *minus* **LIABILITIES**

owner's claim                       claims of other people
(promises given OUT)

things of value in the business:
(money, promises received
and unconsumed inputs)

ASSETS minus LIABILITIES can be written as NET ASSETS so the equation can be written as

**CAPITAL = NET ASSETS**

## THE ACCOUNTING EQUATION AND THE NATURE OF OWNERSHIP

Aside from its function in determining the value of the owner's claim on a business, the accounting equation also defines the nature of the owner's claim. In our society, ownership (of a business) is a residual claim – which is to say that, looking at the assets of a business, the owner gets to claim whatever value may be left, after the claims of other people. Or, to put it another way, whoever gets to claim the value left in a business after all other legal claims are met, that person is the owner. This idea of the owner as the last person in the queue, who takes whatever is left, contrasts very strongly with the ancient, non-commercial idea of property, defined as recently as the 18th century, in Blackstone's Commentaries, as 'that sole and despotic dominion which one man claims and exercises over the external things of the world, in total exclusion of the right of any other individual in the universe'.

## PROFIT, NET ASSETS, AND THE ACCOUNTING EQUATION

At the start of this chapter and in Chapter 2, we described the substance of profit as an accumulation of money, net promises, and unconsumed inputs inside the firm. Now, using the terms of the accounting equation, we can describe that accumulation of things much more simply as *an increase in the value of net assets*, and we can write, with reference to the substance of profit, that:

**PROFIT = INCREASE in NET ASSETS**

Since extra net assets in a business are claimed by the owner, we can also write, with reference to the claim to profit, that:

**PROFIT = INCREASE in CAPITAL**

Notice however, that these equations are not reversible. An increase in net assets and capital does not necessarily indicate a profit: it may arise because the owner has put more assets into the business. Likewise, a decrease in net assets and capital may arise because the owner has taken assets out of the business, and not because the business has made a loss.

# REVIEW

The measure of profit or loss in the abstract, as reported in a P&L Account, is embodied in an increase or a decrease in the value of a firm's net assets. This chapter has shown how the owner's claim to that extra value is accounted for, by transfer of the balance on the P&L Account to the Capital Account. The chapter showed how this reflected the notion of ownership that is summarized in the accounting equation, by which capital is a residual claim. The owner of a business is the person who claims whatever is left in the business, after the claims of other people. It follows, then, that the owner of a business is the person who claims its profits or suffers its losses.

# DRILLS AND EXERCISES

## 17.1  A drill to practise preparing a simple P&L Account and transferring profit or loss to the Capital Account

For each separate business below, record the given transactions on the relevant accounts, balance the accounts if necessary, prepare a P&L Account at the end of the period, and transfer the eventual profit or loss from the P&L Account to the Capital Account.

### BUSINESS 1: TRANSACTIONS

1. owner puts £750 into a bank account for the business
2. business buys goods on credit for £900
3. business sells goods on credit for £1 000

NOTE goods value £400 remain in stock at the end of the period

### BUSINESS 2: TRANSACTIONS

1. owner puts £2 500 into a bank account for the business
2. business buys goods on credit for £2 350
3. business sells goods on credit for £1 500

NOTE goods value £350 remain in stock at the end of the period

### BUSINESS 3: TRANSACTIONS

1. owner puts £1 500 into a bank account for the business
2. business buys goods on credit for £950
3. business returns goods value £200 to supplier
4. business sells goods on credit for £250

NOTE goods value £500 remain in stock at the end of the period

## BUSINESS 4: TRANSACTIONS

1. owner puts £375 into a bank account for the business
2. business buys goods on credit for £300
3. business sells goods for £300 on credit

NOTE goods value £25 remain in stock at the end of the period

## 17.2  An exercise on the nature of the accounting equation

An inexperienced examiner has prepared a test for students who are learning the accounting equation, as shown below:

*Accounting Equation: fill in the gaps in this table*

| BUSINESS | ASSETS £ | LIABILITIES £ | CAPITAL £ |
|----------|----------|---------------|-----------|
| A | 800 | 200 | ? |
| B | 450 | ? | 300 |
| C | ? | 100 | 400 |

Carefully explain why rows B and C may give a misleading impression of the accounting equation and the nature of capital.

## 17.3  An exercise on profit and changes in net assets

Determine the profit or loss made in the period by each separate business whose assets and liabilities are given below.

1. Business begins with assets £400 and liabilities £300, and ends with assets £500, liabilities £350. There were no transactions with the owner during the period.
2. Business begins with assets £950 and liabilities £600, and ends with assets £900, liabilities £500. There were no transactions with the owner during the period.
3. Business begins with assets £750 and liabilities £700, and ends with assets £600 liabilities £200. There were no transactions with the owner during the period.
4. Opening assets £250, closing assets £500. Opening liabilities £200, closing liabilities £600.

Now answer these questions:

5. What difference would it make to your answer in (1) above if during the period the owner had taken assets value £30 out of the business?
6. What difference would it make to your answer in (2) above if during the period the owner had put assets value £200 into the business?
7. What difference would it make to your answer in (3) above if during the period the owner had put assets value £400 into the business, and taken assets value £900 out of the business?

# CHAPTER 18

# A Simple Balance Sheet

## OBJECTIVES

*The objectives of this chapter are:*

- to describe the form and content of a simple balance sheet
- to discuss the purpose of the balance sheet
- to describe the use and importance of an opening balance sheet

## THE CONTENT OF THE BALANCE SHEET

A balance sheet is:

- a list of all balances remaining on the accounts of a business;
- done after transfers to and from the P&L Account;
- arranged to represent the accounting equation.

It is intended to show the consequences of a firm's activities up to the balance sheet date, in terms of the state of affairs at which the firm has arrived.

Notice first, that when the balance sheet is prepared, the only accounts with balances remaining on them will be accounts for money, promises, or unconsumed inputs. (Any accounts for outputs created or inputs consumed will carry nil balances at this time, because the balance sheet is prepared after all such balances have been transferred to the P&L Account.)

Also notice that as shown in Box 18.1 on the following page, any DR balances remaining on the accounts at this stage must represent assets or things IN the business – that is, money, promises IN from debtors, or unconsumed inputs. Meanwhile any CR balances remaining at this stage can only represent claims on the business – that is, promises going OUT, either to the owner in respect of capital or to other people in respect of liabilities.

## BOX 18.1

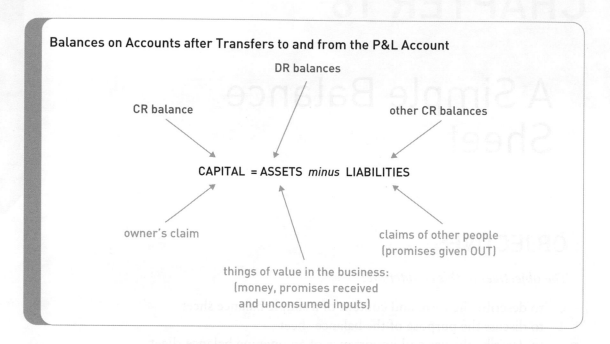

**Balances on Accounts after Transfers to and from the P&L Account**

DR balances

CR balance                                                        other CR balances

**CAPITAL = ASSETS** *minus* **LIABILITIES**

owner's claim                                            claims of other people
                                                                   (promises given OUT)

things of value in the business:
(money, promises received
and unconsumed inputs)

## FORM OF THE BALANCE SHEET

Every balance sheet should be clearly labelled as a balance sheet, to distinguish it from any other list of numbers or values. The name of the relevant firm should also be given, and the date at which the accounts were balanced. In a set of final accounts:

- the balance sheet will be dated *at* or *as at* a given date; while
- the P&L Account will be labelled *for the (period) ended on* the given date.

(Thus if a P&L Account is drawn up *for the year ended 30 June 2050*, the balance sheet will be dated *as at 30 June 2050*, and so on.) However, in most of the examples that follow, to avoid distractions of detail the balance sheet will be dated simply 'at the end of Period 1' or 'at the end of Period 2', etc. The basic form of a simple balance sheet is shown below in Box 18.2, with a note of some of the standard typographical conventions usually followed in the presentation of financial statements of this kind.

## BALANCE SHEET HEADINGS

A large firm in the real world may have hundreds or even thousands of accounts with balances for inclusion in the balance sheet. For this reason, to make the balance sheet comprehensible, many balances representing similar items may be included in the balance sheet under a single generic heading, which itself does not correspond to the name of any individual account. Thus, for example, a business of any reasonable size would have a variety of unconsumed inputs, like stock, waiting for consumption at the end of any period, and the balances representing these would be added together and included in the balance sheet as a single figure under the heading *inventory*. Similarly the general heading *receivables* may be used to cover the value of promises from debtors as well as the value of any other benefits that the firm may be expecting to receive from others (such as goods or services that have been paid for in advance). Likewise, the general heading

## BOX 18.2

**The Form of a Simple Balance Sheet**

XYZ – BALANCE SHEET at end of Period 1

|  | £ | £ |
|---|---|---|
| **ASSETS** | | |
| Stock | | 100 |
| Trade Debtors | | 150 |
| Bank | | 50 |
| Cash | | 25 |
| | | 325 |
| **LIABILITIES** | | |
| Trade Creditors | 20 | |
| Loan | 80 | |
| | | (100) |
| NET ASSETS | | £225 |
| CAPITAL | | £225 |

Typographical conventions

- in a column of numbers, brackets are used to indicate number that should be subtracted from the numbers above them

- in financial statements of this kind, columns are *not* used to separate DRs and CRs. Inner columns are used if necessary *for workings*, generating sub-totals which can be carried into outer columns

- underlining is used to indicate the arrival or presence of totals and sub-totals

- a single line beneath a figure, indicates that what follows will be a total or a sub-total of the figures above

- a double line beneath a figure indicates that the figure is a final total and a stopping point

*payables* may be used to cover not only the value of promises given out to creditors but also any other values that the firm is expecting to pay out. We shall draw attention to such headings and use them as the need arises, but with simple examples with only a few separate accounts, we shall not attempt to use them consistently throughout the text.

## HISTORICAL COST AND THE PURPOSE OF THE BALANCE SHEET

The purpose of the balance sheet is to show the *state of affairs* at which the firm has arrived, at the balance sheet date. But the balance sheet is not wholly successful in meeting this objective. While it purports to show assets and liabilities – what the firm has got, and what it owes to other people – in actual fact, it shows a list of balances, and by the time the balance sheet is prepared, the balance on an account may not correspond with the real value of any actual asset or liability.

The problem is most evident with unconsumed inputs and promises from debtors. These are recorded in the accounts at the value they had in the transaction that brought them into the business. This is called their *historical cost*. But once inside the business, their value may change, and the change in value cannot be known with certainty until they leave the business once again in the course of a transaction. Thus an input recorded in the accounts at its historical cost – the value it had when it was acquired – may well be worth considerably more, or even less, by the time the balance sheet is prepared. Similarly a promise accepted yesterday for £100, may be worth considerably less today, if the debtor who gave the promise has gone out of business or left the country.

As we shall see in later chapters, it is possible to make adjustments so that the balance sheet reflects more accurately the real value of a firm's assets and liabilities, and this would seem to be desirable, but the extent to which it can and should be done remains a matter of debate.

## THE P&L ACCOUNT AND THE CAPITAL ACCOUNT

In the previous chapter we saw how the balance on the P&L Account is transferred to the Capital Account. Notice now what this means: in effect, the P&L Account is just a stage on the way to the Capital Account. Thus, if all or some of the values transferred to the P&L Account were transferred instead directly to the Capital Account, the final balance sheet would remain in balance and would be exactly the same, even though the P&L Account and the firm's reported profit would of course be different.

## THE BALANCE SHEET AND THE ACCOUNTING EQUATION

Although the balance sheet is arranged to reflect the accounting equation, the fact that (in the absence of errors) the balance sheet does always balance, with capital equal to net assets, is only a simple consequence of the double entry system. It proves nothing about the nature of capital. The balance sheet will always balance because it is essentially no more than a peculiar form of trial balance, prepared at a particular time. Recall that a trial balance is a list of balances arranged in such a way as to show that the total of DR balances is equal to the total of CR balances. The balance sheet simply varies the arrangement by isolating one CR balance, representing capital, and showing it to be equal to the total of DR balances (representing assets) minus all the other CR balances (representing liabilities).

The fact that the balance sheet always balances, therefore, cannot be taken in any way to confirm the abstract truth of the accounting equation. (Neither does it support the widespread belief that the double entry system is somehow derived from the accounting equation. Double entry is about transactions. The accounting equation is about the nature of commercial ownership. Conceptually, the two are not related.)

## THE OPENING BALANCE SHEET

Any balances left on a firm's accounts at the end of one period will still be there at the start of the next period and transactions will continue to be recorded in the same accounts. Thus, one period's closing balance sheet, will become the next period's opening balance sheet (a list of all balances already on the accounts at the start of the next period).

With this idea of an opening balance sheet, we need no longer start our examples with a firm's very first transaction. We can now begin at any time, as long as we have an opening balance sheet to show what balances are already recorded on the firm's accounts, as shown in Box 18.3.

BOX 18.3

**Opening Balances**

Given this balance sheet at 30 June 2050

XYZ – BALANCE SHEET at end of Period 1

|  | £ | £ |
|---|---|---|
| ASSETS |  |  |
| Stock |  | ● 100 |
| Trade Debtors |  | ● 150 |
| Bank |  | ● 50 |
| Cash |  | ● 25 |
|  |  | 325 |
| LIABILITIES |  |  |
| Trade Creditors | ● 20 |  |
| Loan | ● 80 |  |
|  |  | (100) |
| NET ASSETS |  | £225 |
| CAPITAL |  | ● £225 |

we can begin recording transactions at 1 July 2050 with these balances already on the accounts

| Stock | | Trade Debtors | | Bank | |
|---|---|---|---|---|---|
| b/f ● 100 | | b/f ● 150 | | b/f ● 50 | |

| Cash | | Trade Creditors | | Loan | |
|---|---|---|---|---|---|
| b/f ● 25 | | | b/f ● 20 | | b/f ● 80 |

| Capital | |
|---|---|
| | b/f ● 225 |

# REVIEW

This chapter has shown the basic form and content of the closing balance sheet, and the use of the opening balance sheet. The chapter also explained the meaning of historical cost in accounting, and acknowledged the problems that may arise when there are changes in the value of assets or liabilities that are not realized or recorded in the form of a transaction.

# DRILLS AND EXERCISES

## 18.1 A drill to practise transfers to and from the P&L Account, and the listing of remaining balances in a balance sheet

### BUSINESS 1

Business 1 has balanced its accounts as shown below at the end of Period 1 (its first period of trading). Transfer the relevant balances to and from a P&L Account for the period, and present the firm's balance sheet at the end of the period.

NOTE: at the end of Period 1, Business 1's closing stock is valued at £80.

| Sales | | Purchases | |
|---|---|---|---|
| | balance at end of period 700 | | balance at end of period 500 |

| Bank | | Debtors | |
|---|---|---|---|
| balance at end of period 250 | | balance at end of period 100 | |

| Creditors | | Capital | |
|---|---|---|---|
| | balance at end of period 50 | | balance at end of period 100 |

| P&L Account for Period 1 | | Stock | |
|---|---|---|---|

## BUSINESS 2

Business 2 has balanced its accounts as shown below at the end of Period 1 (its first period of trading). Transfer the relevant balances to and from a P&L Account for the period, and present the firm's balance sheet at the end of the period.

NOTE: at the end of Period 1, Business 2's closing stock is valued at £50.

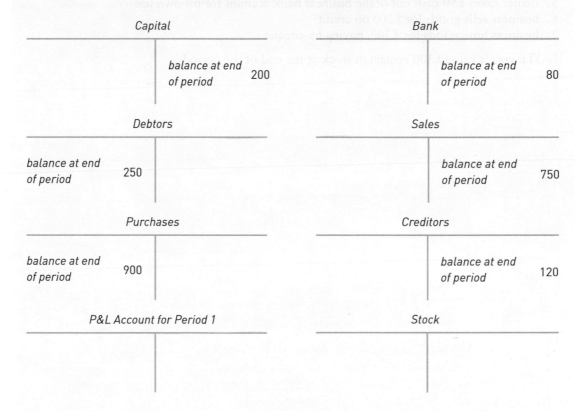

## 18.2  A drill to practise recording transactions and producing a simple P&L Account and a balance sheet

For each separate business below, record the transactions on the relevant accounts, balance the accounts if necessary, and prepare a P&L Account for the period and a balance sheet as at the end of the period.

### BUSINESS 1: TRANSACTIONS

1. owner puts £900 into a bank account for the business
2. business buys goods on credit for £850
3. business sells goods on credit for £950

NOTE goods value £350 remain in stock at the end of the period

## BUSINESS 2: TRANSACTIONS

1. owner puts £800 cash into a business
2. business buys goods on credit for £600
3. business sells goods for £850 cash
4. business deposits £1 500 at the bank
5. owner takes £50 cash out of the business bank account for his own use
6. business sells goods for £200 on credit
7. business buys goods for £300, paying by cheque

NOTE goods value £300 remain in stock at the end of the period

# CHAPTER 19

# Opening Stock and Cost of Sales

## OBJECTIVES

*The objectives of this chapter are:*

- to show the treatment of opening stock in the P&L Account
- to show and explain the roundabout way in which we must determine the cost of sales in a period

## OPENING STOCK

Any goods that are unconsumed at the end of one period, will be available for consumption during the next period. In accounting terms, one period's closing stock will become the next period's opening stock, and, like the purchases made in the next period, opening stock will be available for consumption or conversion into sales.

At the end of the next period, therefore, any existing balance on the Stock Account (representing opening stock) must be transferred in to the P&L Account along with purchases. Box 19.1 shows an example.

## CLOSING STOCK

With the value of purchases made in the period, plus opening stock, the DR side of the P&L Account in Box 19.1 now shows the total value of the goods that could have been sold in Period 2. Next we must conduct a stock-take to find how much of that value was *not* consumed or turned into sales, and therefore remains in stock at the end of Period 2. Having found that value, which is closing stock for the period, we take it OUT of the P&L Account and re-place it IN the Stock Account, where it will wait until the end of the following period. Box 19.2 on the following page shows the procedure.

## BOX 19.1

### The Treatment of Opening Stock

Inputs available for consumption in Period 2 will include closing stock from Period 1.

Assume closing stock at the end of Period 1 was valued at £100.

This will become the *opening stock* of Period 2.

|  | Stock |  |
|---|---|---|
| from | | |
| P&L (1) | 100 | |

Because Period 1's closing stock is available for consumption in Period 2,

|  | Stock |  |
|---|---|---|
| from | | to |
| P&L (1) | 100 | P&L (2) ◄ 100 |

at the end of Period 2, it must be taken OUT of the Stock Account...

**Profit & Loss Account for Period 2**

| Purchases | • | Sales | • |
|---|---|---|---|
| opening stock | | | |
| (from Stock A/c) ► 100 | | | |

... and replaced IN the P&L Account as opening stock for Period 2

## BOX 19.2

### The Treatment of Closing Stock

Assume that closing stock for Period 2 is valued at £150.

**Profit & Loss Account for Period 2**

| Purchases | • | Sales | • |
|---|---|---|---|
| opening stock | | closing stock | |
| (from Stock A/c) 100 | | (to Stock A/c) ◄ 150 | |

As usual, the value of closing stock is taken OUT of the P&L Account ...

|  | Stock |  |
|---|---|---|
| from | | to |
| P&L (1) 100 | | P&L (2) 100 |
| from | | |
| P&L (2) ►150 | | |

...and replaced IN the Stock Account.

## DETERMINING THE COST OF SALES

Cost of sales means the cost of getting or making the goods that are sold in a period. In our case, with a purely trading firm (not a manufacturer), cost of sales will mean what it cost to buy the goods that were sold in a period.

The P&L Account in our example now contains all the elements involved in the calculation of cost of sales, but notice how clumsy the procedure has to be, with three separate elements involved (purchases, opening stock, and closing stock), and consider the reason for this roundabout approach. The problem is, that in the accounts of a business we record transactions (that is, movements of money or promises). The accounts can therefore tell us the value of inputs paid for (in money or promises) during a period, but we do not record or even directly observe the movement or consumption of goods. This means that we cannot tell directly which goods have been sold, and we must pursue a very roundabout approach to determining their cost. First we find the total value that *may* have been consumed (by adding together the value of purchases and the value of any goods held in the firm as opening stock at the start of the period). Then we find and deduct (as closing stock) any value that was *not* consumed in the period. In the end, by calculation, we arrive at the value that *was* consumed in the period. A very clumsy method, but the only one we have.

## A SUMMARY OF THE PROCEDURE

Assuming for simplicity that no other inputs have been consumed in the period, all that remains to complete the procedure in our example is to balance the P&L Account, and so determine the profit or loss that the firm will report for the period.

All of the steps (transfer of sales and purchases, plus treatment of opening and closing stock) are shown together in Box 19.3, which also shows how the relevant accounts should look, on completion of the procedure.

BOX 19.3

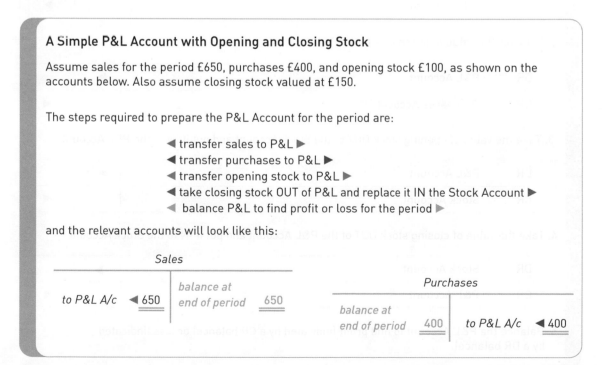

**A Simple P&L Account with Opening and Closing Stock**

Assume sales for the period £650, purchases £400, and opening stock £100, as shown on the accounts below. Also assume closing stock valued at £150.

The steps required to prepare the P&L Account for the period are:

◀ transfer sales to P&L ▶
◀ transfer purchases to P&L ▶
◀ transfer opening stock to P&L ▶
◀ take closing stock OUT of P&L and replace it IN the Stock Account ▶
◀ balance P&L to find profit or loss for the period ▶

and the relevant accounts will look like this:

*Sales*

|  |  | balance at |  |
|---|---|---|---|
| to P&L A/c  ◀ 650 | | end of period  650 | |

*Purchases*

|  |  |  |  |
|---|---|---|---|
| balance at |  |  |  |
| end of period  400 | | to P&L A/c  ◀ 400 | |

**BOX 19.3** Continued

| | Stock | | |
|---|---|---|---|
| from P&L (1) | 100 | to P&L (2) ◄ 100 | |
| from P&L (2) ► 150 | | | |

| Profit & Loss Account for Period 2 | | | |
|---|---|---|---|
| Purchases | ► 400 | Sales | ► 650 |
| opening stock (from Stock A/c) | ► 100 | closing stock (to Stock A/c) | ◄ 150 |
| bal c/f | ◄ 300 | | |
| | 800 | | 800 |
| | | bal b/f = profit | ► 300 |

The double entry for each of the five steps is also shown in Box 19.4.

**BOX 19.4**

### Preparation of a Simple P&L Account with Opening and Closing Stock

1. Transfer the value of sales to the P&L Account

| DR | Sales Account | ◄ | |
|---|---|---|---|
| CR | P&L Account | | ► |

2. Transfer the value of purchases to the P&L Account

| DR | P&L Account | ► | |
|---|---|---|---|
| CR | Purchases Account | | ◄ |

3. Take the value of opening stock OUT of the Stock Account and put it IN to the P&L Account

| DR | P&L Account | ► | |
|---|---|---|---|
| CR | Stock Account | | ◄ |

4. Take the value of closing stock OUT of the P&L Account and put it IN to the Stock Account

| DR | Stock Account | ► | |
|---|---|---|---|
| CR | P&L Account | | ◄ |

5. Balance the P&L Account to find profit (indicated by a CR balance) or loss (indicated by a DR balance).

## REVIEW

This chapter has shown how opening stock and closing stock are treated in the P&L Account of any period, as elements (along with purchases) in the calculation of cost of sales. The chapter also briefly explained why we must adopt such a clumsy approach to determining the cost of sales.

# DRILLS AND EXERCISES

## 19.1  A drill mainly to practise the transfer of opening stock IN to and closing stock OUT of the P&L Account

### BUSINESS 1

At the start of a period, the opening balance sheet of Business 1 is as shown below:

| BUSINESS 1 OPENING BALANCE SHEET | | |
|---|---|---|
| | **£** | **£** |
| ASSETS | | |
| Stock | | 120 |
| Trade debtors | | 100 |
| Bank | | 150 |
| | | 370 |
| LIABILITIES | | |
| Trade Creditors | 60 | |
| Loan | 130 | |
| | | (190) |
| NET ASSETS | | £180 |
| CAPITAL | | £180 |

Put the opening balances onto the relevant accounts and record the following transactions:

1. business buys goods for £700 on credit
2. business sells goods on credit for £900
3. business receives cheque value £750 from trade debtor

Balance the accounts at the end of the period and produce a P&L Account for the period and a balance sheet as at the end of the period.

NOTE: at the end of the period, Business 1's closing stock is valued at £160.

## BUSINESS 2

At the start of a period, the opening balance sheet of Business 2 is as shown below:

|  | £ | £ |
|---|---|---|
| **BUSINESS 2** | | |
| **OPENING BALANCE SHEET** | | |
| ASSETS | | |
| Stock | | 250 |
| Trade debtors | | 420 |
| Bank | | 130 |
| | | 800 |
| LIABILITIES | | |
| Trade Creditors | 200 | |
| Loan | 500 | |
| | | (700) |
| NET ASSETS | | £100 |
| CAPITAL | | £100 |

Put the opening balances on to the relevant accounts and record the following transactions:

1. business sells goods for £200 on credit
2. business buys goods on credit for £600
3. business pays supplier £700 by cheque
4. business receives cheque for £620 from customer

Balance the accounts at the end of the period and produce a P&L Account for the period and a balance sheet as at the end of the period.

NOTE: at the end of the period, Business 2's closing stock is valued at £200.

## 19.2 A drill to practise recording transactions in successive periods

For each separate business below, record the transactions of Period 1 on the relevant accounts, and produce a P&L Account for Period 1 and a balance sheet at the end of Period 1.

Then record the transactions of Period 2, and produce a P&L Account for Period 2 and a balance sheet at the end of Period 2.

## BUSINESS 1

Period 1

1. owner puts £1 000 into a bank account for the business
2. business buys goods on credit for £900
3. business sells goods on credit for £1 100

NOTE: goods value £300 remain in stock at the end of the period.

Period 2

4. business pays supplier £850 by cheque
5. business receives cheque for £1 000 from customer
6. business buys goods on credit for £1 200
7. business sells goods on credit for £2 500

NOTE: goods value £800 remain in stock at the end of the period.

## BUSINESS 2

Period 1

1. owner puts £7 000 into a bank account for the business
2. business buys goods on credit for £8 000
3. business sells goods for £7 000, receiving payment by cheque

NOTE: goods value £90 remain in stock at the end of the period.

Period 2

4. business pays supplier £8 000 by cheque
5. business buys goods for £6 000 on credit
6. business sells goods for £10 000 on credit

NOTE: goods value £1 500 remain in stock at the end of the period.

## BUSINESS 3

Period 1

1. owner puts £2 500 into a bank account for the business
2. business buys goods on credit from S for £2 000
3. business sells goods on credit to C for £1 500

NOTE: goods value £400 remain in stock at the end of the period.

Period 2

4. business sells goods on credit for £700
5. business receives cheque for £2 100 from customer
6. business buys goods on credit for £1 100
7. business sells goods on credit for £1 300

NOTE: goods value £150 remain in stock at the end of the period.

# CHAPTER 20

# The Stock Account and Profit

## OBJECTIVES

*The objectives of this chapter are:*

● to describe the use of the Stock Account as a parking place between one P&L Account and the next, and its limited information content
● to show how the value put on closing stock will directly affect a firm's reported profit
● to explain how easily reported profit may be overstated by the fraudulent overvaluation of closing stock

## THE STOCK ACCOUNT

The Stock Account is essentially a parking place on the journey between one P&L Account and the next. At the end of each period, the value of closing stock is taken OUT of the P&L Account and parked IN the Stock Account, where it remains for the duration of the following period. In due course it is taken OUT of the Stock Account and put IN to the P&L Account of the next period, this time as opening stock. Box 20.1 shows an example.

Notice that the only way IN to the Stock Account is OUT of one P&L Account, and the only way OUT of the Stock Account is IN to the next P&L Account. This means that the *only* time at which entries are made in the Stock Account is when the P&L Account is being prepared at the end of a period. For the rest of the time, nothing happens on the Stock Account. This in turn has interesting consequences.

**BOX 20.1**

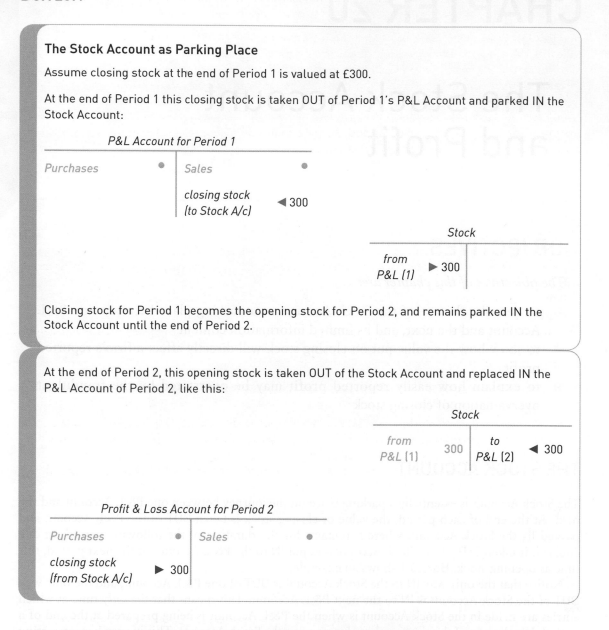

### The Stock Account as Parking Place

Assume closing stock at the end of Period 1 is valued at £300.

At the end of Period 1 this closing stock is taken OUT of Period 1's P&L Account and parked IN the Stock Account:

*P&L Account for Period 1*

| *Purchases* ● | *Sales* ● |
| --- | --- |
| *closing stock (to Stock A/c)* ◄ 300 | |

*Stock*

| *from P&L (1)* ► 300 | |
| --- | --- |

Closing stock for Period 1 becomes the opening stock for Period 2, and remains parked IN the Stock Account until the end of Period 2.

At the end of Period 2, this opening stock is taken OUT of the Stock Account and replaced IN the P&L Account of Period 2, like this:

*Stock*

| *from P&L (1)* 300 | *to P&L (2)* ◄ 300 |
| --- | --- |

*Profit & Loss Account for Period 2*

| *Purchases* ● | *Sales* ● |
| --- | --- |
| *closing stock (from Stock A/c)* ► 300 | |

## INFORMATION CONTENT OF THE STOCK ACCOUNT

Most of the separate accounts in the double entry system have a dual purpose. The individual entries on the account will provide a record of individual transactions, while at any time the balance on the account will show the up-to-date effect of those transactions. For example, the entries on the Cash Account will show each separate movement of cash, while the balance on the account will show how much cash remains in the business as a result of those transactions. The Stock Account is different in two ways:

- the Stock Account is not used to record transactions between the business and the outside world. It records only transfers IN from one P&L Account, and OUT to the next P&L Account; and

● the balance on the Stock Account will almost never tell us anything about the value of stock currently held in the business at any particular time.

It is this last point which severely limits the information content of the Stock Account. If we need to know the value of stock in the business at any time, it is useless to look at the Stock Account. Why? Because the only time at which the Stock Account will give the value of stock currently held in the business, is when that value has just been put there, transferred IN to the Stock Account from the P&L Account, following a stock-take at the end of a period. Thereafter goods will come and go, and physical stock levels will change, but the balance on the Stock Account will stay the same until the end of the next period. As we remarked in Chapter 16, the *only* way to find the value of stock at any time is to go and conduct a stock-take – the Stock Account will not provide the answer.

## STOCK AND PROFIT

All other things being equal, *more closing stock means more profit*. If two firms have the same value of opening stock, and the same value of sales and purchases, then the firm with more closing stock will have made a bigger profit.

This is so because if a firm's level of sales is given, its profit will depend on the value of inputs consumed to make those sales. Recall that closing stock is unconsumed inputs. If a firm has made the same value of sales and *has more goods left over* to sell in the next period, then *it must have used less* to make its current sales, and therefore it will have made a bigger profit. The same can be explained at least three different ways in terms of pure accounting:

● The more inputs that are taken OUT of the P&L Account as closing stock, the fewer will be left IN the P&L Account to be deducted from outputs, so the firm will report a greater profit.

● Closing stock is a CR in the P&L Account – the same side of the P&L Account as sales. Increasing the figure for closing stock in the P&L Account will therefore have the same effect as increasing the figure for sales – it will increase reported profit.

● Closing stock is an asset in the balance sheet, and the substance of profit is an increase in net assets. More stock means more net assets, and therefore greater profit.

An example of the effect of stock valuation on profit is shown in Box 20.2.

## BOX 20.2

### The Effect of Stock Valuation on Reported Profit

Assume a P&L Account with sales £700, purchases £600, and, for simplicity, no *opening* stock.

| Profit & Loss Account | | | |
|---|---|---|---|
| Purchases | 600 | Sales | 700 |

Now consider two different possible values of closing stock.

**BOX 20.2**   Continued

| Profit & Loss Account A | | | | |
|---|---|---|---|---|
| Purchases | 600 | Sales | 700 | |
| c/f | 120 | closing stock (to Stock A/c) | • 20 | IF closing stock is valued at • £20 |
| | 720 | | 720 | |
| | | b/f = profit | ▶ 120 | reported profit will be ▶ £120. |

| | | | | BUT |
|---|---|---|---|---|
| Profit & Loss Account B | | | | |
| Purchases | 600 | Sales | 700 | |
| c/f | 190 | closing stock (to Stock A/c) | • 90 | IF closing stock is valued at • £90 |
| | 790 | | 790 | |
| | | b/f = profit | ▶ 190 | reported profit will be ▶ £190. ... and so on. |

## CLOSING STOCK: BALANCE SHEET EFFECTS

In the balance sheet, a higher value for closing stock will have two effects: it will increase the value of net assets, and also increase the reported value of capital. The effect on net assets is direct and obvious: closing stock is an asset in the balance sheet; more stock means more net assets.

The effect on capital is indirect and to some extent less obvious. Recall that a higher value of closing stock means a higher profit in the P&L Account. But profit is claimed by the owner, and the balance on the P&L Account is transferred to the Capital Account. So a higher value for closing stock in the P&L Account, through its effect on profit, will result in a higher value for capital in the balance sheet – which, fortunately, will balance the higher value for net assets.

Notice the unintended consequence. Whatever arbitrary and possibly *mistaken or untrue* value may be assigned to closing stock, the balance sheet will nevertheless remain in balance, as long as the value put IN to the Stock Account is the same as the value taken OUT of the P&L Account.

## STOCK VALUATION AND FRAUD

We have seen that the value of closing stock is not a figure taken from within the accounting system. It must be brought in from elsewhere. We have also seen that a firm's reported profit is directly affected by the value of closing stock, and that the balance sheet will automatically remain in balance, whatever figure for closing stock is brought in to the accounts.

It follows that the deliberate overstatement of closing stock, in order to inflate reported profit, is one of the simplest frauds in financial accounting. It is easy to commit, and hard to detect (because at any time after the balance sheet date, the balance on the Stock Account is not even supposed to represent the value of stock that is currently in the firm).

Notice, however, that while changes in the valuation of closing stock can make a difference to the reported profit of any one period, they can make no difference to the aggregate reported profits of a firm over a number of periods. Recall that the Stock Account is only a parking place between one P&L Account and the next. Whatever is taken OUT of one P&L Account as closing stock will only be put IN to the next P&L Account as opening stock. Thus, while the overstatement of closing stock may boost the reported profit of one period, it will also serve to depress the reported profit of the next period. This reversal effect can only be avoided if closing stock in successive years is consistently overstated forever afterwards.

Also observe the difference, quite crucial now, between actual profit and reported profit. *Reported* profits may be open to manipulation, but the *actual* profit of a firm remains the same, no matter what accounting entries may be made. (Accountants are human, and are not the most careful users of language here: putting a higher value on closing stock, for example, will not actually increase *profit*, as we are tempted to say – it will increase *reported profit*, which is something rather different.)

## STOCK IN THE TRIAL BALANCE AND IN THE BALANCE SHEET

The trial balance is a list of all balances on the accounts *before* transfers to and from the P&L Account, while the balance sheet is a list of all balances on the accounts *after* transfers to and from the P&L Account.

It follows that stock in the trial balance (before transfers) must be the current period's *opening* stock (i.e. last period's closing stock, which has been sitting in the Stock Account for the whole of the current period, waiting to be transferred to the current P&L Account). And stock in the balance sheet (after transfers) will be the current period's *closing* stock, which has just been transferred out of the current period's P&L Account. In accounting drills and exercises, the value of opening stock is given in the trial balance, while the value of closing stock must be given in a note.

## REVIEW

This chapter has described some of the peculiarities of the Stock Account, especially concerning the only time at which entries are made in the account, and its limited information content. The chapter also explained how profit is affected by the value of closing stock, how this is reflected in the P&L Account and the balance sheet, and how easily reported profits can be manipulated by simply adjusting the figure used for the value of closing stock.

# DRILLS AND EXERCISES

## 20.1 A drill to practise the effect of stock valuation on reported profit

### CASE 1

In Period 1 a firm records purchases £800 and sales £900.

State what would be the firm's profit or loss for Period 1 in each of the following circumstances:

1. closing stock is valued at £75
2. closing stock is valued at £50
3. closing stock is valued at £25

### CASE 2

A firm begins a period with opening stock valued at £100. During the period, the firm records purchases £450, and sales £600.

State what would be the firm's profit or loss for the period in each of the following circumstances:

1. closing stock is valued at £100
2. closing stock is valued at £80
3. closing stock is valued at £130

### CASE 3

During a period, a firm records purchases £500, and sales £700.

State what would be the firm's profit or loss for the period in each of the following circumstances:

1. if stock levels increase by £50 during the period (i.e. if the value of closing stock is £50 greater than the value of opening stock
2. if stock levels decrease by £30 during the period
3. if there is no increase or decrease in stocks over the course of the period

### CASE 4

In Period 1 a firm records purchases £400, and sales £400.
In Period 2, the firm also records purchases £400 and sales £400.
There is no closing stock at the end of Period 2.

State what would be the firm's profit or loss for Period 1 and for Period 2, in each of the following circumstances:

1. if there is no closing stock at the end of Period 1
2. if closing stock at the end of Period 1 is valued at £50
3. if closing stock at the end of Period 1 is valued at £100

## 20.2 Exercises to consider some problems in accounting for stock

1. Explain why it is easier to mis-state the value of closing stock in a set of accounts, than it is to mis-state the value of sales or purchases.
2. A firm sells a single line of stock, which it buys at constant prices. Purchases are recorded immediately in a Stock Account, and when goods are sold, their cost is transferred out of the Stock Account and in to a Cost of Sales Account. In this way, the firm's Stock Account will always show an up-to-date cost of stock currently in the business.

   (a) Explain how this system would work, using entries on a set of T accounts.
   (b) This system involves no account for purchases. How would you be able to use information from the accounts to determine the value of purchases in a period?
   (c) Why do you think that this, or a similar system of accounting for stock, is not more widely used?

# CHAPTER 21

# Elements of the Full Length Profit & Loss Account

## OBJECTIVES

*The objectives of this chapter are:*

- to show the procedures involved in preparing a full length P&L Account
- to describe the different categories of costs and expenses in the P&L Account, the different levels of profit, and the different parts into which the P&L Account can be divided
- to show how all the balances remaining on accounts after transfers to and from the P&L Account are included in the balance sheet

## COST OF SALES

In general, *cost of sales* means the cost of getting or making the goods that were sold in a period. In a trading business, cost of sales means what it cost to buy the goods that were sold in the period – that is, cost of sales consists of:

- purchases in the period;
- plus opening stock;
- minus closing stock.

Cost of sales (sometimes shortened to COS) may also be called *cost of goods sold* (COGS).

## GROSS PROFIT

Gross profit is the difference between sales and cost of sales. In our previous examples, purchases have been the only inputs, so gross profit has been final profit, and the end-point of the P&L Account. But normally a firm will also consume many other and different inputs.

# EXPENSES

After cost of sales, the value of any other input consumed in a period is called an expense. Expenses are divided into operating expenses and financial expenses. Operating expenses means the value of all non-financial inputs consumed in a period – for example, including labour, rent, power, light and heat, insurance and so on. Financial expenses are essentially interest charges, and the various other costs of borrowing.

# OPERATING PROFIT AND NET PROFIT

Operating profit is what remains of gross profit after deduction of operating expenses. Alternatively, operating profit is profit before financial expenses.

Net profit is profit after *all* costs and expenses. (In a company which is subject to tax, net profit is called profit before tax. After the government's share of profit has been deducted, the remainder is called profit after tax.)

# THE PREPARATION OF A PROFIT & LOSS ACCOUNT WITH EXPENSES

When a firm has incurred expenses during a period (i.e. when the firm has consumed a variety of different inputs), the P&L Account must be extended to include them. This is done in stages, with the account being balanced after the transfer of each different class of input consumed. Standard procedure for the preparation of a full P&L Account is therefore:

1. make relevant transfers to and from the P&L Account concerning sales and cost of sales (purchases, opening stock, and closing stock);
2. *balance* the P&L Account to find *Gross Profit*;
3. transfer operating expenses to the P&L Account;
4. *balance* the P&L Account again to find *Operating Profit*;
5. transfer financial expenses (interest) to the P&L Account;
6. *balance* the P&L Account again to find *Net Profit*;
7. finally transfer Net Profit from the P&L Account to the Capital Account.

(We assume above and throughout this chapter that we shall be dealing with a net *profit* in the P&L Account. The assumption simplifies the presentation, although of course a loss could arise at any level.)

An example of the overall appearance of a full length P&L Account, with sample numbers, is shown in Box 21.1 on the following page.

## BOX 21.1

### A Full Length Profit & Loss Account

*Profit & Loss Account for Period...*

| | | | | |
|---|---:|---|---:|
| Purchases | 500 | Sales | 700 |
| opening stock | 100 | closing stock | 200 |
| *(from Stock A/c)* | | *(to Stock A/c)* | |
| *bal c/f* | 300 | | |
| | 900 | | 900 |
| | | *bal b/f* | |
| | | *= Gross Profit* | 300 |
| electricity | 40 | | |
| rent | 60 | | |
| advertising | 70 | | |
| wages | 20 | | |
| etc | 10 | | |
| *bal c/f* | 100 | | |
| | 300 | | 300 |
| | | *bal b/f* | |
| | | *= Operating Profit* | 100 |
| interest | 25 | | |
| *bal c/f* | 75 | | |
| | 100 | | 100 |
| | | *bal b/f* | |
| | | *= Net Profit* | 75 |
| to Capital | 75 | | |
| | 75 | | 75 |

## NAMING SEPARATE PARTS OF THE P&L ACCOUNT

Certain parts or sections of the P&L Account have their own names. The first part, containing sales and cost of sales, down to gross profit, is called the Trading Account. The final part, showing the transfer of profit or loss to the Capital Account, is called the Appropriation Account. The parts containing operating expenses and financial expenses however, have no name of their own. Box 21.2 on the following page shows an example.

**BOX 21.2**

### A Full Length Profit & Loss Account

*Profit & Loss Account for Period...*

| | | | | | |
|---|---|---|---|---|---|
| Purchases | 500 | Sales | 700 | This part of the P&L is called the Trading Account. | |
| opening stock (from Stock A/c) | 100 | closing stock (to Stock A/c) | 200 | | |
| *bal c/f* | *300* | | | It shows sales and cost of sales, going down to Gross Profit. | |
| | *900* | | *900* | | |
| | | bal b/f = Gross Profit | 300 | | |
| electricity | 40 | | | | |
| rent | 60 | | | | |
| advertising | 70 | | | This part shows operating expenses, going down to Operating Profit | |
| wages | 20 | | | | |
| etc | 10 | | | | |
| *bal c/f* | *100* | | | | |
| | *300* | | *300* | | |
| | | bal b/f = Operating Profit | 100 | | |
| interest | 25 | | | This part shows financial expenses, going down to Net Profit | |
| *bal c/f* | *75* | | | | |
| | *100* | | *100* | | |
| | | bal b/f = Net Profit | 75 | | |
| to Capital | 75 | | | This part is called the Appropriation Account | |
| | *75* | | *75* | | |

## THE TRADING AND PROFIT & LOSS ACCOUNT

A full length P&L Account may also be called a 'Trading and Profit & Loss Account'. This seems to imply that the Trading Account and the P&L Account are separate, with the P&L Account being a bit tacked on to the end of the Trading Account. Such an implication would be false: the P&L Account covers everything from sales down to net profit, and the Trading Account is only a part of the P&L Account.

Notice however, that a firm which provides services and does not trade in goods, will probably not have a separately identifiable 'Trading Account' section in its P&L Account. With a firm of accountants, lawyers, or window cleaners, for example, it may be difficult or pointless to distinguish 'cost of sales' from any other inputs consumed in a period, and so for them a P&L Account would proceed straight from sales to expenses and operating profit, without the intervening calculation of gross profit.

# TRANSFERS TO AND FROM THE P&L ACCOUNT

Box 21.3 starts a new example with a set of accounts which have already been balanced as at the end of a period. All of the subsequent transfers to and from the P&L Account are shown, with particular emphasis on the transfer of expenses.

## BOX 21.3

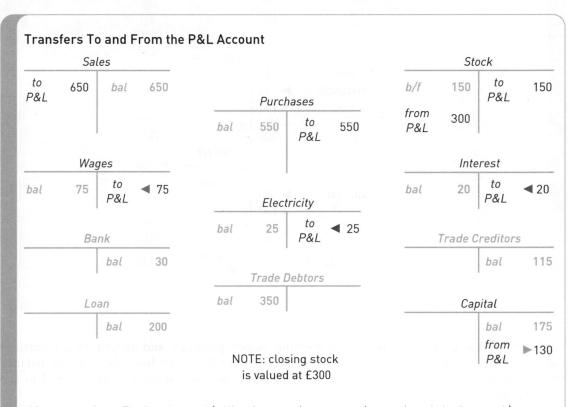

**Transfers To and From the P&L Account**

After preparing a Trading Account (with sales, purchases, opening stock and closing stock) to find **Gross Profit**, we extend the Trading Account to form a full length P&L Account as follows:

- transfer operating expenses to the P&L:
    - ◀ wages ▶
    - ◀ electricity ▶
    - ◀ balance the P&L to find **Operating Profit** ▶
- transfer financial expenses to P&L:
    - ◀ interest ▶
    - ◀ balance the P&L to find **Net Profit** ▶
- finally ◀ transfer Net Profit from the P&L to the Capital Account ▶

**BOX 21.3**   Continued

*Profit & Loss Account for Period...*

| | | | |
|---|---|---|---|
| purchases | 550 | sales | 650 |
| opening stock | 150 | closing stock | 300 |
| bal c/f | 250 | | |
| | 950 | | 950 |
| | | bal b/f<br>= Gross Profit | 250 |
| wages | ▶ 75 | | |
| electricity | ▶ 25 | | |
| bal c/f | ◀ 150 | | |
| | 250 | | 250 |
| | | bal b/f<br>= Operating<br>Profit | ▶ 150 |
| interest | ▶ 20 | | |
| bal c/f | ◀ 130 | | |
| | 150 | | 150 |
| to Capital | ◀ 130 | bal b/f<br>= Net Profit | ▶ 130 |

Notice in Box 21.3 that balances representing money, promises, and unconsumed inputs are *not* transferred to the P&L Account. These balances are left to be listed later in the balance sheet. It is only the values created and consumed in a period that must be transferred to the P&L Account.

## PREPARATION OF THE BALANCE SHEET

Box 21.4 continues the same example to show how the balance sheet is drawn up after transfers to and from the P&L Account. It also demonstrates how the steps involved in the preparation of the P&L Account are an essential element in the working of the double entry model. There can be no question of preparing a P&L Account by leaving the accounts untouched and merely copying the relevant figures into a P&L Account format. All of the relevant transfers must be properly made and recorded in the accounts, or else the balance sheet ('a list of all balances remaining on the accounts after transfers to and from the P&L Account . . .') will lose its meaning and purpose.

## BOX 21.4

### Preparation of the Balance Sheet

After transfers to and from the P&L Account, the firm's accounts will look like this:

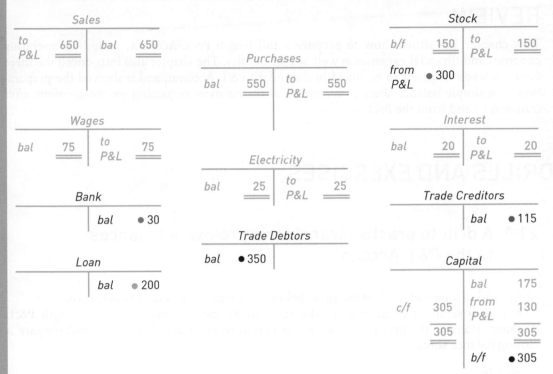

NOTE: after net profit has been transferred to the Capital Account, the P&L Account will carry a nil balance. The P&L Account itself therefore need not be shown above.

Notice that balances on the accounts are *copied* and listed in the balance sheet. They are not transferred to the balance sheet.

*ABC Balance Sheet*
*as at End of Period ...*

|  | £ | £ |
|---|---|---|
| Assets |  |  |
| Stock | ● 300 |  |
| Trade Debtors | ● 350 |  |
|  | 650 |  |
| Liabilities |  |  |
| Bank | ● 30 |  |
| Trade Creditors | ● 115 |  |
| Loan | ● 200 |  |
|  |  | (345) |
| Net Assets |  | £305 |
|  |  |  |
| Capital |  | ● £305 |

Notice, however, that the balance sheet is merely a list of values *copied* from the relevant accounts. There is no question of transferring values from the accounts to the balance sheet. Relevant values are left where they are in the accounts, and just copied in the balance sheet. Preparation of the balance sheet is not in itself an integral part of the double entry system.

## REVIEW

This chapter has shown how to prepare a full length P&L Account, including operating expenses and financial expenses as well as cost of sales. The chapter also introduced the three separate levels of profit to be found in a standard P&L Account, and it showed the preparation of a simple balance sheet by listing all of the balances remaining on the accounts after transfers to and from the P&L Account.

# DRILLS AND EXERCISES

## 21.1 A drill to practise transferring relevant balances to the P&L Account

At the end of a period, each of the firms below has balanced its accounts as shown.

For each separate firm, transfer the relevant balances to prepare a full-length P&L Account, transfer the profit or loss for the period to the Capital Account, and prepare a closing balance sheet.

*Firm A*

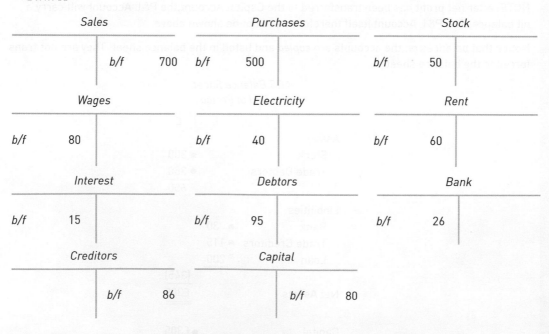

| Sales | | | Purchases | | | Stock | | |
|---|---|---|---|---|---|---|---|---|
| | b/f | 700 | b/f | 500 | | b/f | 50 | |

| Wages | | | Electricity | | | Rent | | |
|---|---|---|---|---|---|---|---|---|
| b/f | 80 | | b/f | 40 | | b/f | 60 | |

| Interest | | | Debtors | | | Bank | | |
|---|---|---|---|---|---|---|---|---|
| b/f | 15 | | b/f | 95 | | b/f | 26 | |

| Creditors | | | Capital | | |
|---|---|---|---|---|---|
| | b/f | 86 | | b/f | 80 |

NOTE: closing stock is valued at £75

*Firm B*

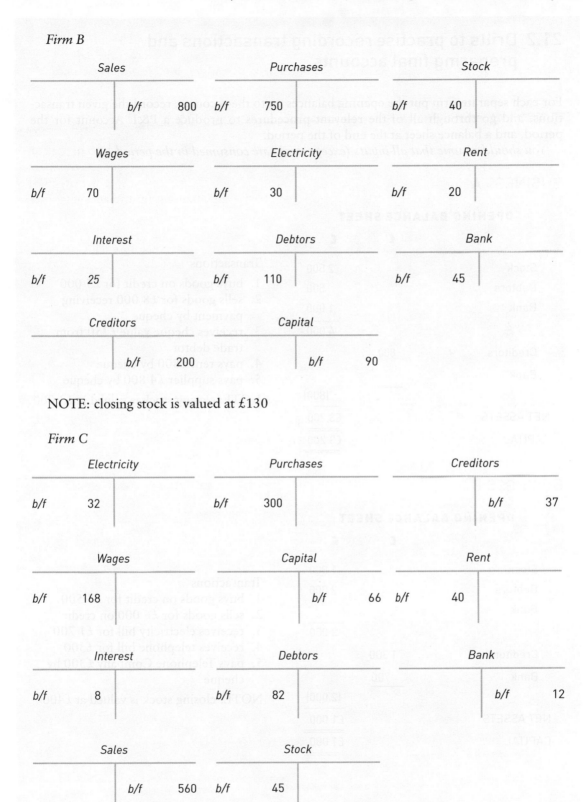

| Sales | | | Purchases | | | Stock | | |
|---|---|---|---|---|---|---|---|---|
| | b/f | 800 | b/f | 750 | | b/f | 40 | |

| Wages | | | Electricity | | | Rent | | |
|---|---|---|---|---|---|---|---|---|
| b/f | 70 | | b/f | 30 | | b/f | 20 | |

| Interest | | | Debtors | | | Bank | | |
|---|---|---|---|---|---|---|---|---|
| b/f | 25 | | b/f | 110 | | b/f | 45 | |

| Creditors | | | Capital | | |
|---|---|---|---|---|---|
| | b/f | 200 | | b/f | 90 |

NOTE: closing stock is valued at £130

*Firm C*

| Electricity | | | Purchases | | | Creditors | | |
|---|---|---|---|---|---|---|---|---|
| b/f | 32 | | b/f | 300 | | | b/f | 37 |

| Wages | | | Capital | | | Rent | | |
|---|---|---|---|---|---|---|---|---|
| b/f | 168 | | | b/f | 66 | b/f | 40 | |

| Interest | | | Debtors | | | Bank | | |
|---|---|---|---|---|---|---|---|---|
| b/f | 8 | | b/f | 82 | | | b/f | 12 |

| Sales | | | Stock | | |
|---|---|---|---|---|---|
| | b/f | 560 | b/f | 45 | |

NOTE: closing stock is valued at £53

## 21.2 Drills to practise recording transactions and preparing final accounts

For each separate firm put the opening balances on to the accounts, record the given transactions, and go through all of the relevant procedures to produce a P&L Account for the period, and a balance sheet at the end of the period.

*You should assume that all inputs (except stock) are consumed in the period.*

### BUSINESS A

| OPENING BALANCE SHEET | | |
|---|---|---|
| | £ | £ |
| Stock | | 2 500 |
| Debtors | | 500 |
| Bank | | 1 000 |
| | | 4 000 |
| Creditors | 800 | |
| Bank | | |
| | | (800) |
| NET ASSETS | | £3 200 |
| CAPITAL | | £3 200 |

Transactions
1. buys goods on credit for £5 000
2. sells goods for £8 000 receiving payment by cheque
3. receives cheque value £250 from trade debtor
4. pays rent £800 by cheque
5. pays supplier £4 800 by cheque

NOTE: closing stock is valued at £3 000

### BUSINESS B

| OPENING BALANCE SHEET | | |
|---|---|---|
| | £ | £ |
| Stock | | 1 000 |
| Debtors | | 2 000 |
| Bank | | |
| | | 3 000 |
| Creditors | 1 300 | |
| Bank | 700 | |
| | | (2 000) |
| NET ASSETS | | £1 000 |
| CAPITAL | | £1 000 |

Transactions
1. buys goods on credit for £3 500
2. sells goods for £6 000 on credit
3. receives electricity bill for £1 700
4. receives telephone bill for £300
5. pays Telephone Company £300 by cheque

NOTE: closing stock is valued at £400

## BUSINESS C

| OPENING BALANCE SHEET | | |
|---|---|---|
| | **£** | **£** |
| Stock | | 1 700 |
| Debtors | | 3 000 |
| Bank | | |
| | | 4 700 |
| Creditors | 2 400 | |
| Bank | 600 | |
| | | (3 000) |
| NET ASSETS | | £1 700 |
| CAPITAL | | £1 700 |

Transactions

1. buys goods on credit for £16 500
2. sells goods on credit for £27 000
3. receives rent demand for £1 300
4. borrows £5 000 from ABC finance, receiving the money by cheque
5. pays landlord £1 200 by cheque
6. pays interest £250 by cheque
7. pays salaries £1 800 by cheque
8. receives electricity bill for £700
9. pays interest £100 by cheque
10. repays £3 000 by cheque to ABC finance

NOTE: closing stock is valued at £1 500

## BUSINESS D

| OPENING BALANCE SHEET | | |
|---|---|---|
| | **£** | **£** |
| Stock | | 1 500 |
| Debtors | | 30 000 |
| Bank | | |
| | | 31 500 |
| Suppliers | 18 900 | |
| Bank | 1 950 | |
| Landlord | 100 | |
| Electricity Co | 700 | |
| ABC Finance | 2 000 | |
| | | (23 650) |
| NET ASSETS | | £7 850 |
| CAPITAL | | £7 850 |

Transactions

1. receives cheque for £24 000 from customer
2. pays supplier £18 000 by cheque
3. pays £100 interest to ABC Finance
4. repays ABC Finance £2 000 by cheque
5. pays £300 interest on bank overdraft
6. buys goods on credit for £27 000
7. sells goods on credit for £29 300
8. receives rent demand for £1 300
9. pays landlord £1 400 by cheque
10. receives electricity bill for £1 000
11. pays Electricity Co £1 700 by cheque
12. pays wages £3 200 by cheque
13. receives cheque for £30 000 from customer
14. pays supplier £20 000 by cheque
15. owner takes £1 500 out of business bank for his own use

NOTE: closing stock is valued at £5 000

# CHAPTER 22

## The Income Statement and the P&L Account

### OBJECTIVES

*The objectives of this chapter are:*

- to introduce the Income Statement as an alternative way of presenting the information in the standard P&L Account
- to emphasize that the presentation of an Income Statement is not a substitute for the preparation of a P&L Account, which is an essential part of the double entry system

The chapter also covers some minor points of terminology in connection with items in the P&L Account or Income Statement.

### THE INCOME STATEMENT

A major purpose of the P&L Account is to reveal information about the business to various interested parties, many of whom may know little about debits and credits, and care even less.

Measured against this objective, the standard DR and CR format of the P&L Account is evidently defective. We cannot imagine that its meaning would be at all clear to non-accountants on first or even second inspection. For this reason it is customary to copy the information from the regular P&L Account into a more user-friendly format called an *Income Statement*. Box 22.1 on the following page shows an example.

Notice in the income statement that the columns are used, as in the balance sheet, only to distinguish workings from totals and main figures. Columns to the left are used for workings, while totals and main figures are shown in columns to the right. In this format the columns are nothing to do with DRs and CRs.

### COMPARING THE FORMATS

Each format has its advantages. The income statement is undeniably simpler, and it shows a useful total for cost of sales, which is missing from the P&L Account (DR and CR format). On the other hand, the significance of stock valuation is somewhat obscured in the income statement. In the DR

## BOX 22.1

### P&L Account and Income Statement

*Profit & Loss Account for Period ...*

| | | | |
|---|---|---|---|
| purchases | 550 | sales | 650 |
| opening stock | 150 | closing stock | 300 |
| bal c/f | 250 | | |
| | 950 | | 950 |
| wages | 75 | bal b/f | 250 |
| electricity | 25 | = Gross Profit | |
| bal c/f | 150 | | |
| | 250 | | 250 |
| | | bal b/f | 150 |
| interest | 20 | = Operating Profit | |
| bal c/f | 130 | | |
| | 150 | | 150 |
| to Capital | 130 | bal b/f = Net Profit | 130 |

Here is *the same information* in the form of an Income Statement:

*Income Statement for Period ...*

| | £ | £ |
|---|---|---|
| Sales | | 650 |
| Purchases | 550 | |
| opening stock | 150 | |
| closing stock | (300) | |
| Cost of Sales | | (400) |
| Gross Profit | | 250 |
| wages | 75 | |
| electricity | 25 | |
| | | (100) |
| Operating Profit | | 150 |
| interest | | (20) |
| Net Profit | | £130 |

and CR format it is strikingly obvious that assigning a higher value to closing stock (a CR in the P&L Account) will automatically result in a higher reported profit.

Whatever one's preference, however, it is essential to realize that the income statement is not a substitute for the production of a P&L Account in proper DR and CR format. It is only an alternative way of presenting the same information – the point being, however, that the P&L Account is *more* than just a statement of information. The steps involved in the preparation of the P&L Account in DR and CR format have a vital function within the double entry system. It is always necessary to go through those steps, making transfers to and from the P&L Account, so that the accounts for sales and inputs consumed are cleared, ready to start afresh recording the next period's transactions; and so that the remaining balances can be identified for listing in the balance sheet.

Readers who are preparing for examinations will find it quicker and easier to answer questions with an Income Statement (often called a P&L Account in vertical format). Those who want to read and understand the published accounts of limited companies will almost certainly find that they are presented with information in the format of an Income Statement. However, both sets of readers will find it enormously helpful if they are able to switch mentally at will between the two formats.

The rest of this chapter deals with some points of terminology and the position or classification of certain items in the P&L Account or Income Statement. These are of no great theoretical interest, although they have some capacity to cause confusion.

# TURNOVER AND REVENUE

The words 'turnover', 'revenue' and even 'income' are frequently used instead of 'sales'. Indeed they are generally preferred, because their meaning is slightly wider than sales. Sales seems to imply the delivery of physical goods, while turnover or revenue will comfortably explain the receipt of money or promises for many other reasons as well, including, for example, the supply of services. A hotel business, for example, does not actually sell things, but it does have turnover, generate revenue, or gain income, as does a firm of lawyers or estate agents.

# CARRIAGE IN AND CARRIAGE OUT

'Carriage in' is an input. It is the work or service of carrying goods in to the firm. Sometimes the cost of carriage in is included in the purchase price of goods (suppliers call this 'free delivery'). Where carriage in is paid for separately, it is usually added to the figure for purchases, or written immediately below it, in the Trading Account. Carriage in is therefore treated as part of the cost of sales, and not as an expense.

'Carriage out' is the firm's cost of delivering goods to customers. This is an expense, and is included in the P&L Account as an operating expense, after Gross Profit.

# CUSTOMS DUTIES

Any customs duties or import taxes paid on purchases or raw materials should also be included in the Trading Account as part of cost of sales.

# OTHER INCOME

When a firm generates revenue somehow outside its normal run of activities, the additional profit is included in the P&L Account as 'Other Income', which is inserted in the P&L Account or Income Statement after Gross Profit, and before operating expenses.

# INTEREST PAYABLE AND INTEREST RECEIVABLE

For most commercial firms, 'interest' will be an expense – a payment made in exchange for permission to use money. Some firms may also receive interest. In such cases for the avoidance of doubt, 'interest payable' means the expense or DR in the P&L Account, while 'interest receivable' means the income or CR in the P&L Account.

All interest is shown in the third part of the P&L Account, after Operating Profit. Interest payable is often included under the more general heading 'finance cost', while interest receivable is included under the heading 'finance income'. Finance income or interest receivable is indicated by a CR in the P&L Account (as an output to explain the money coming in), while in the Income Statement, finance income is shown below finance cost as a negative expense.

# REVIEW

This chapter has introduced the Income Statement as an alternative presentation of the information shown in the standard DR and CR format of the P&L Account. It has also dealt briefly with some minor points of meaning and presentation, including the use and meaning of the terms turnover, revenue, carriage in, carriage out, finance cost and finance income.

# DRILLS AND EXERCISES

The Income Statement is undoubtedly a more efficient means of conveying information than the P&L Account, and this section offers a number of drills for students to develop confidence with both formats, and the ability to switch from one to another.

## 22.1  A drill to present the information in each P&L Account or Income Statement below in its alternative format

### A: PROFIT & LOSS ACCOUNT

| | | | |
|---|---|---|---|
| purchases | 20 900 | sales | 30 000 |
| opening stock | 2 250 | closing stock | 2 150 |
| c/f | 9 000 | | |
| | 32 150 | | 32 150 |
| wages | 1 400 | b/f gross profit | 9 000 |
| electricity | 600 | | |
| insurance | 300 | | |
| advertising | 200 | | |
| c/f | 6 500 | | |
| | 9 000 | | 9 000 |
| interest payable | 150 | b/f operating profit | 6 500 |
| c/f | 6 350 | | |
| | 6 500 | | 6 500 |
| to capital | 6 350 | b/f net profit | 6 350 |

## B: PROFIT & LOSS ACCOUNT

| | | | |
|---|---:|---|---:|
| purchases | 11 000 | sales | 14 800 |
| opening stock | 1 200 | closing stock | 1 700 |
| c/f | 4 300 | | |
| | 16 500 | | 16 500 |
| wages | 2 400 | b/f gross profit | 4 300 |
| rent | 1 000 | | |
| transport | 800 | | |
| c/f | 100 | | |
| | 4 300 | | 4 300 |
| interest payable | 125 | b/f operating profit | 100 |
| | | c/f | 25 |
| | 125 | | 125 |
| b/f net loss | 25 | to capital | 25 |

## C: INCOME STATEMEMT

| | £ | £ |
|---|---:|---:|
| Sales | | 50 000 |
| purchases | 36 000 | |
| opening stock | 4 000 | |
| closing stock | (5 000) | |
| Cost of Sales | | (35 000) |
| Gross Profit | | 15 000 |
| wages | 10 000 | |
| rent | 2 000 | |
| insurance | 1 000 | |
| advertising | 500 | |
| | | (13 500) |
| Operating Profit | | 1 500 |
| interest payable | | (2 000) |
| Net Loss | | £(500) |

## D: PROFIT & LOSS ACCOUNT

| | | | |
|---|---|---|---|
| purchases | 32 000 | sales | 46 600 |
| opening stock | 3 600 | closing stock | 4 000 |
| c/f | 15 000 | | |
| | 50 600 | | 50 600 |
| wages | 11 350 | b/f gross profit | 15 000 |
| rent | 2 650 | | |
| insurance | 1 900 | | |
| | | c/f | 900 |
| | 15 900 | | 15 900 |
| b/f operating loss | 900 | | |
| interest payable | 100 | interest receivable | 1 200 |
| c/f | 200 | | |
| | 1 200 | | 1 200 |
| to capital | 200 | b/f net profit | 200 |

## E: INCOME STATEMEMT

| | £ | £ |
|---|---|---|
| Sales | | 87 400 |
| purchases | 65 500 | |
| opening stock | 5 700 | |
| closing stock | (4 200) | |
| Cost of Sales | | (67 000) |
| Gross Profit | | 20 400 |
| wages | 12 150 | |
| electricity | 1 850 | |
| transport | 4 400 | |
| | | (18 400) |
| Operating Profit | | 2 000 |
| interest payable | | (3 000) |
| interest receivable | | 700 |
| Net Loss | | £(300) |

# CHAPTER 23

# Three Levels of Profit

## OBJECTIVES

*The objectives of this chapter are:*

- to explain the significance of the three levels of profit shown in the standard P&L Account
- to explain the grouping of different inputs in the P&L Account into cost of sales, operating expenses, and financial expenses, on the basis of their different behaviour and how they are controlled

## LEVELS OF PROFIT AND THE DIFFERENT INPUTS CONSUMED

This chapter attempts to justify the convention under which the P&L Account or Income Statement is divided into three sections by the insertion of three successive levels of profit (gross profit, operating profit, and net profit). Box 23.1 begins the argument by showing how the three levels of profit also serve to separate three different kinds of inputs consumed (cost of sales, operating expenses, and interest).

## BOX 23.1

| Levels of Profit and Inputs Consumed | |
|---|---|
| XYZ Summary P&L Account | |
| | £ |
| Sales | 1 000 |
| – cost of sales | (600) |
| **Gross Profit** | 400 |
| – operating expenses | (300) |
| **Operating Profit** | 100 |
| – interest | (25) |
| **Net Profit** | 75 |

The three levels of profit shown here in red ...

**BOX 23.1**   Continued

---

### XYZ Summary P&L Account

| | £ |
|---|---:|
| Sales | 1 000 |
| – cost of sales | (600) |
| Gross Profit | 400 |
| – operating expenses | (300) |
| Operating Profit | 100 |
| – interest | (25) |
| Net Profit | 75 |

also serve to separate the three different kinds of input consumed that are shown here in red

---

## COST OF SALES AND EXPENSES

Gross profit acts as a dividing line between cost of sales and expenses. This separation is useful because cost of sales and expenses behave in different ways. In general, cost of sales will vary with quantity sold – a trader who wants to sell twice as many units, must spend about twice as much to buy them, and so on. Meanwhile, expenses tend not to vary with the quantity sold, or not to vary very much. A trader who wants to sell twice as many units will probably not need to pay for twice as much labour, rent, or light and heat, and so on. Indeed if the trader is lucky, these expenses may not increase at all.

In summary, though the rule is hardly true in every case, cost of sales is very much like a *variable cost* (it varies with output), while expenses are more like *fixed costs* (which do not vary with output). In practice, in the absence of finer analysis, cost of sales and expenses are often used as surrogates for variable and fixed costs, but the likeness is by no means exact, and may well be misleading. However that may be, the difference between cost of sales and expenses, in terms of their behaviour, is enough to justify their separation in the P&L Account or Income Statement.

## OPERATING EXPENSES AND INTEREST

Operating profit divides operating expenses from financial expenses or interest. Both of these tend to behave like fixed costs, but their separation is useful because they arise for different reasons, and are subject to different levels of decision-making and control.

In terms of how they arise, the difference is that operating expenses arise from operations – what the firm actually makes or does; while interest charges depend on how the firm is financed. The point here is that every firm will incur operating expenses, because it must consume goods and services in order to function at all. But payment of interest depends upon the firm's financial structure – how much or how little it has borrowed – and borrowing is a matter of choice.

The difference in terms of decision-making and control is that control of operating expenses depends upon ensuring the efficient use of inputs, which is a constant duty, or a task at every level of the firm. By contrast, the question of whether or not to borrow, how much, for how long, and at what rates, is a strategic decision made at the highest levels in the firm. Once that decision has been made, interest payments are not an expense over which lower level managers can exercise any degree of day to day control.

## OPERATING PROFIT AND NET PROFIT

The need to consider operating profit separately from net profit follows from the discussion of financial structure above. Two firms may be identical in their assets and operations, and differ only in that one of them is financed entirely by the owner's investment, while the other is financed partly by borrowing. Despite being identical in its operations, the second firm will report a lower net profit because it must pay interest. The operating profit of the two firms, however, will be the same. The presentation of a figure for operating profit, before interest, therefore allows us to see the results of a firm's operations, without the distorting effects of interest payments, which are attributable only to the firm's financial structure. Box 23.2 gives an example.

### BOX 23.2

**Operating Profit, Interest and Net Profit**

These two firms have the same assets, and their operations are identical, but their financial structure is different.

| FIRM A Balance Sheet | | FIRM B Balance Sheet | |
|---|---|---|---|
| | £ | | £ |
| Assets | 2 000 | Assets | 2 000 |
| Liabilities | – | Liabilities | (1 000) |
| Net Assets | £2 000 | Net Assets | £1 000 |
| | | | |
| Capital | £2 000 | Capital | £2 000 |

Firm A is wholly financed by the investment of its owner, while Firm B is financed partly by borrowing £1 000 at 10 per cent per year.

With identical operations, as shown with sample figures below, the two firms will generate the same operating profit.

BUT Firm B's net profit will be lower, because it must pay interest of £100 per year.

| FIRM A P&L Account | | FIRM B P&L Account | |
|---|---|---|---|
| | £ | | £ |
| Sales | 900 | Sales | 900 |
| cost of sales | (400) | cost of sales | (400) |
| Gross Profit | 500 | Gross Profit | 500 |
| operating expenses | (200) | operating expenses | (200) |
| Operating Profit | 300 | Operating Profit | 300 |
| | – | interest | (100) |
| Net Profit | £300 | Net Profit | £200 |

# GROSS PROFIT AND THE GROSS PROFIT RATIO

The absolute value of a firm's gross profit is probably of less interest than its gross profit ratio. The *gross profit ratio* is gross profit as a percentage of sales. This ratio, sometimes called the gross profit *margin*, shows how much gross profit is generated by each £1 of sales. Box 23.3 shows examples of the relevant calculation.

## BOX 23.3

**Gross Profit Margin**

| P&L Account X | | P&L Account Y | |
|---|---|---|---|
| | £ | | £ |
| Sales | 800 | Sales | 450 |
| cost of sales | (600) | cost of sales | (90) |
| Gross Profit | 200 | Gross Profit | 360 |

GrossProfit Margin X

(200/800) × 100%

=

25%

Gross Profit Margin Y

(360/450) × 100%

=

80%

Ratios and the interpretation of financial statements are discussed more fully in Part 5. Here it is enough to say that the gross profit ratio or margin can reveal much about a firm's competitive strength. High margins may indicate that a firm can force up the price of its sales, because it faces little competition and can dominate its customers. Or it may indicate that the firm can drive down the cost of its purchases, because it dominates its suppliers, or because its suppliers operate in a very competitive industry. In either case, market power reveals itself in a high gross profit ratio, and loss of market power will usually reveal itself in falling gross profit ratios.

# OPERATING PROFIT

Operating profit is profit before the deduction of interest charges. Recall that part of the total value invested in a firm may be provided by lenders as well as owners. It is therefore possible to see operating profit as the reward available for *all* investors in the firm – lenders as well as owners. Operating profit is then shared between lenders, whose reward is a fixed amount of interest, and owners, who claim whatever extra value may be left.

Notice though, that unlike profit, interest is not a reward for success. Interest is an inducement to take the risk of loss. Lenders have a claim to the payment of interest in full, regardless of the operating profit (or even loss) made by the firm. If a firm's operating profit is not big enough to cover the interest due to its lenders, then the owners of the firm will suffer a loss in order for the interest to be paid. Interest therefore can turn a firm's operating profit into a net loss for its owners, or it can make a firm's operating loss into an even bigger net loss for its owners.

## NET PROFIT

Finally, net profit is the increase in value as a result of operations that can be claimed by the owners of a firm. Recall however that the owner's claim is always a residual. Owners have no *right* to claim anything from a firm unless there is some value left for them to claim, after meeting all the claims of other people; and they have no right to claim any profit unless there has in fact been an increase in net assets over the period. Also observe that claiming profit is not the same as taking it away. Owners always claim the net profit of a business, but they do not always take it out of the business. They may choose to leave some or all of the extra net assets in the business, to generate higher profits in the future. (This contrasts with the behaviour of lenders, who require actual payment of their interest, and are not content with a mere claim to extra value.)

## REVIEW

This chapter has attempted to justify the main divisions of the Income Statement or P&L Account. It briefly outlined the differences between the three main categories of input consumed by a business, and the significance of the three levels of profit shown in the standard P&L Account. The chapter also introduced the calculation and possible interpretation of the gross profit ratio.

## DRILLS AND EXERCISES

There are no drills or exercises on this chapter.

# CHAPTER 24

# The Extended Trial Balance

## OBJECTIVES

*The objectives of this chapter are:*

- to show how an extended trial balance can be used to divide ledger account balances between the P&L Account and the balance sheet
- to explain how the profit or loss reported by a firm depends essentially on which balances are assigned by the accountant to the P&L Account, and which are assigned to the balance sheet

## THE EXTENDED TRIAL BALANCE

The extended trial balance offers a quick way of preparing an Income Statement and balance sheet, assuming that we are given a trial balance at the end of a period, and all other necessary information, such as the value of closing stock. Although this approach avoids the full double entry procedures that are a necessary part of the accounting system, it also offers some insight into how the full procedures actually work, because it allows us to see the treatment of all the relevant values at a glance.

The first step is to *extend* the trial balance by adding a pair of columns (DR and CR) for values that should be included in the P&L Account, and a similar pair of columns for values that should be included in the balance sheet. Box 24.1 on the following page offers an illustration.

## COPYING VALUES INTO THE EXTENSION COLUMNS

The next step is to identify all values in the trial balance that would normally be transferred to the P&L Account (that is, all values representing *outputs created* or *inputs consumed*). These should be copied into the appropriate column for P&L Account values. Thus the figure for sales, which is a CR in the trial balance, will be copied into the CR column for the P&L Account, while figures for purchases, opening stock, wages, and similar DRs in the trial balance will be copied into the DR column for the P&L Account. (Recall that stock in the trial balance is *opening* stock.)

BOX 24.1

**Extending the Trial Balance – First Step**

|  | Trial Balance | | P&L Account | | Balance Sheet | |
| --- | --- | --- | --- | --- | --- | --- |
|  | DR | CR | DR | CR | DR | CR |
| sales |  | 5 000 |  |  |  |  |
| purchases | 4 000 |  |  |  |  |  |
| stock | 1 600 |  |  |  |  |  |
| wages | 200 |  |  |  |  |  |
| rent | 100 |  |  |  |  |  |
| insurance | 50 |  |  |  |  |  |
| electricity | 30 |  |  |  |  |  |
| interest | 20 |  |  |  |  |  |
| bank | 800 |  |  |  |  |  |
| trade debtors | 700 |  |  |  |  |  |
| trade creditors |  | 300 |  |  |  |  |
| loan |  | 1 000 |  |  |  |  |
| capital |  | 1 200 |  |  |  |  |
|  |  |  |  |  |  |  |
| total | 7 500 | 7 500 |  |  |  |  |

At the same time, all values in the trial balance that would normally be listed in the balance sheet (that is, all values for *money, promises,* and *unconsumed inputs*) will be copied into the appropriate DR or CR column for the balance sheet. Box 24.2 on the following page continues the example.

## CLOSING STOCK

The next step is to deal with closing stock. Remember that the value of closing stock can only be obtained from direct observation in a stock-take. It cannot be found in the trial balance. Once the value of closing stock is known, the normal accounting procedure is to take it OUT of the P&L Account and put it IN to the Stock Account, where it will remain as a balance to be listed in the balance sheet. In the extended trial balance therefore, the value of closing stock should be entered in the CR column of the P&L Account, and the DR column of the balance sheet. Box 24.3 on page 182 continues the example to show how this is done.

## BOX 24.2

### Copying Values into the Extension Columns

| | Trial Balance | | P&L Account | | Balance Sheet | |
|---|---|---|---|---|---|---|
| | DR | CR | DR | CR | DR | CR |
| sales | | 5 000 | | 5 000 | | |
| purchases | 4 000 | | 4 000 | | | |
| stock | 1 600 | | 1 600 | | | |
| wages | 200 | | 200 | | | |
| rent | 100 | | 100 | | | |
| insurance | 50 | | 50 | | | |
| electricity | 30 | | 30 | | | |
| interest | 20 | | 20 | | | |
| bank | 800 | | | | 800 | |
| trade debtors | 700 | | | | 700 | |
| trade creditors | | 300 | | | | 300 |
| loan | | 1 000 | | | | 1 000 |
| capital | | 1 200 | | | | 1 200 |
| | | | | | | |
| total | 7 500 | 7 500 | | | | |

Notice incidentally that all values maintain their original polarity. What starts as a DR in the trial balance, will end as a DR in the P&L Account or the balance sheet; and what starts as a CR in the trial balance will end as a CR in the P&L Account or the balance sheet.

## PROFIT IN THE EXTENDED TRIAL BALANCE

Finally we deal with profit (it could of course be a loss, but with the figures in our example the firm will report a profit).

Consider first what we have done. We have simply divided the balances in the TB into *P&L Account* DRs and CRs, and *balance sheet* DRs and CRs. However, we have not divided them equally: in terms of value, there are more CRs than DRs in the P&L Account, and more DRs than CRs in the balance sheet.

Now, since we started with a trial balance in which DRs and CRs were equal, any difference in total value between CRs and DRs copied into the P&L Account, must be equal and opposite to the difference between DRs and CRs copied into the balance sheet. Box 24.4 on page 183 continues the example and shows this equality of differences.

## BOX 24.3

### Closing Stock in the Extended Trial Balance

Assume that closing stock is valued at £1 500 (this value must be imported from outside the accounting system)

Closing Stock is entered as a CR in the P&L Account, and a DR in the balance sheet.

|  | Trial Balance | | P&L Account | | Balance Sheet | |
|---|---|---|---|---|---|---|
|  | DR | CR | DR | CR | DR | CR |
| sales |  | 5 000 |  | 5 000 |  |  |
| purchases | 4 000 |  | 4 000 |  |  |  |
| **stock** | 1 600 |  | 1 600 | 1 500 | 1 500 |  |
| wages | 200 |  | 200 |  |  |  |
| etc |  |  |  |  |  |  |

(Note that opening stock, as listed in the trial balance, has already been dealt with.)

What does all this mean? In the P&L Account, more CRs than DRs (by value) will indicate a profit – the value of outputs created being greater than the value of inputs consumed. Meanwhile, in the balance sheet, more DRs than CRs will indicate some extra value IN the business that is so far unclaimed – being unmatched by promises going OUT. This unclaimed value represents the substance of profit, which is now claimed by the owner. Thus, our final step is to insert a line for profit.

To show an increase in capital, the owner's claim, and to make the balance sheet balance, the value of profit must be included in the balance sheet as a CR. To close the P&L Account and make both sides equal, the value of profit must be included in the P&L Account as a DR. This last step is slightly troubling. Should not profit always be a CR? Yes, it should. But recall that profit is not an *entry* on the P&L Account, it is the *balance* on the P&L Account. What we are doing here with the DR is *cancelling* the CR balance in the P&L Account, so that we can show it as a CR in the balance sheet, which will ultimately be added to capital. The procedure is shown in Box 24.5 on page 184.

## DEBITS AND CREDITS

The extended trial balance offers a clue to the two questions that beginners in accounting often find most vexing. Why is it that a DR can represent either an expense (surely a bad thing), or an asset (which has got to be a good thing)? And, why is it that a CR can represent either a sale (which is good), or a liability (which is bad)? It is easy to dismiss these questions as childish and misconceived, with the insistence that DR and CR mean no more than left and right.

A better answer is to recognize that a DR is the record of something moving IN to the business. If that something has been used up or consumed, it must be recognized as an expense. If it remains in the business, and is still available for use or exchange, then it must be recognized as an asset. Conversely a CR is the record of something moving OUT of the business. If that something

BOX 24.4

**The Extended P&L Account, before Making Entries for Profit**

|  | Trial Balance | | P&L Account | | Balance Sheet | |
|---|---|---|---|---|---|---|
|  | DR | CR | DR | CR | DR | CR |
| sales |  | 5 000 |  | 5 000 |  |  |
| purchases | 4 000 |  | 4 000 |  |  |  |
| stock | 1 600 |  | 1 600 | 1 500 | 1 500 |  |
| wages | 200 |  | 200 |  |  |  |
| rent | 100 |  | 100 |  |  |  |
| insurance | 50 |  | 50 |  |  |  |
| electricity | 30 |  | 30 |  |  |  |
| interest | 20 |  | 20 |  |  |  |
| bank | 800 |  |  |  | 800 |  |
| trade debtors | 700 |  |  |  | 700 |  |
| trade creditors |  | 300 |  |  |  | 300 |
| loan |  | 1 000 |  |  |  | 1 000 |
| capital |  | 1 200 |  |  |  | 1 200 |
|  |  |  |  |  |  |  |
| total | 7 500 | 7 500 | 6 000 | 6 500 | 3 000 | 2 500 |

At this stage in our example:

in the **P&L Account** – total CRs exceed total DRs by £500.
in the **balance sheet** – total DRs exceed total CRs by £500.

represents goods or services which have moved out of the business in exchange for payment, then the CR must be recognized as a sale. If that something moving out of the business is a merely a *promise* to deliver some value at a later stage, then it must be recognized as a liability. If it is a promise going out to the owner, then it is part of capital, the owner's claim.

## A LESSON FROM THE EXTENDED TRIAL BALANCE

The extended trial balance also shows very clearly how, in a formal sense, the final accounts presented by a firm (its P&L Account and balance sheet) will depend entirely on where we decide to show the balances recorded in the trial balance. Technically (and without regard to

## BOX 24.5

### The Extended Trial Balance, showing Profit

| | Trial Balance | | P&L Account | | Balance Sheet | |
|---|---|---|---|---|---|---|
| | DR | CR | DR | CR | DR | CR |
| sales | | 5 000 | | 5 000 | | |
| purchases | 4 000 | | 4 000 | | | |
| stock | 1 600 | | 1 600 | 1 500 | 1 500 | |
| wages | 200 | | 200 | | | |
| rent | 100 | | 100 | | | |
| insurance | 50 | | 50 | | | |
| electricity | 30 | | 30 | | | |
| interest | 20 | | 20 | | | |
| bank | 800 | | | | 800 | |
| trade debtors | 700 | | | | 700 | |
| trade creditors | | 300 | | | | 300 |
| loan | | 1 000 | | | | 1 000 |
| capital | | 1 200 | | | | 1 200 |
| profit | | | 500 | | | 500 |
| total | 7 500 | 7 500 | 6 500 | 6 500 | 3 000 | 3 000 |

The entry for profit in the P&L Account actually serves to cancel the balance on the account, so that it can be shown in the balance sheet as a CR (which will be added to capital).

Notice how, on completion of the extended trial balance, there are equal DRs and CRs in the P&L columns (the account is closed), and there are equal DRs and CRs in the balance sheet columns (the balance sheet will balance).

where it *should* be shown), it is true that any DR in the trial balance *could* be shown either in the P&L Account as an expense, or in the balance sheet as an asset. Likewise any CR in the trial balance *could* be shown either in the P&L Account as an output, or in the balance sheet as a liability. The point is that *wherever we choose to put the different balances*, as long as we maintain their original polarity as DRs or CRs, *the figure reported as profit or loss will adjust to ensure that the balance sheet will always balance*, and no striking anomalies will be visible in the final accounts.

This is a point raised before in connection with the valuation of closing stock, and one to which we must return. It means that a firm's reported profit is always open to adjustment by judgement or choice of the accountant who prepares the P&L Account and balance sheet. Box 24.6 provides an illustration, showing how the reported profit of the firm in our example can be increased by the simple expedient of copying a DR from the TB into the balance sheet as an asset, instead of the P&L Account as an expense. The example shows how there may be good reason for such an adjustment, but what can be done for good reasons, can also be done for bad.

## BOX 24.6

### Adjusting Reported Profit by Moving Values between the P&L Account and the Balance Sheet

Imagine that the firm in our example discovers that the £50 DR for insurance in the trial balance is in respect of insurance coverage for the following year. This input has not yet been consumed, and should therefore be shown in the balance sheet as an asset, rather than the P&L Account as an expense.

Notice that when the error is corrected (merely by moving the £50 from one column to another), the firm's reported profit will automatically increase from £500 to £550, and the balance sheet will remain in balance.

| | Trial Balance | | P&L Account | | Balance Sheet | |
| --- | --- | --- | --- | --- | --- | --- |
| | DR | CR | DR | CR | DR | CR |
| sales | | 5 000 | | 5 000 | | |
| purchases | 4 000 | | 4 000 | | | |
| stock | 1 600 | | 1 600 | 1 500 | 1 500 | |
| wages | 200 | | 200 | | | |
| rent | 100 | | 100 | | | |
| insurance | 50 | | | ~~50~~ | 50 | |
| electricity | 30 | | 30 | | | |
| interest | 20 | | 20 | | | |
| bank | 800 | | | | 800 | |
| trade debtors | 700 | | | | 700 | |
| trade creditors | | 300 | | | | 300 |
| loan | | 1 000 | | | | 1 000 |
| capital | | 1 200 | | | | 1 200 |
| profit | | | 550 | | | 550 |
| total | 7 500 | 7 500 | 6 500 | 6 500 | 3 050 | 3 050 |

## REVIEW

This chapter has demonstrated the use of the extended trial balance. It also showed how the extended trial balance can provide an insight into the nature of debits and credits. Finally, the chapter used the extended trial balance to draw attention to the fact that reported profit or loss depends not so much on the values in the trial balance, but rather on how those values are assigned by the accountant to the P&L Account or the balance sheet.

# DRILLS AND EXERCISES

## 24.1 A drill to practise extending the trial balance

For each trial balance given below, copy the relevant balances into the appropriate columns, and determine the firm's profit or loss for the period.

### BUSINESS A

NOTE: closing stock is valued at £1 490.

|  | TRIAL BALANCE | | P&L ACCOUNT | | BALANCE SHEET | |
|---|---|---|---|---|---|---|
|  | DR | CR | DR | CR | DR | CR |
| sales |  | 7 500 |  |  |  |  |
| purchases | 5 700 |  |  |  |  |  |
| stock | 1 100 |  |  |  |  |  |
| wages | 1 230 |  |  |  |  |  |
| rent | 120 |  |  |  |  |  |
| insurance | 56 |  |  |  |  |  |
| electricity | 144 |  |  |  |  |  |
| interest | 40 |  |  |  |  |  |
| bank | 900 |  |  |  |  |  |
| trade debtors | 850 |  |  |  |  |  |
| trade creditors |  | 740 |  |  |  |  |
| loan |  | 400 |  |  |  |  |
| capital |  | 1 500 |  |  |  |  |
| profit |  |  |  |  |  |  |
| total | 10 140 | 10 140 |  |  |  |  |

## BUSINESS B

NOTE: closing stock is valued at £1 000.

| | TRIAL BALANCE | | P&L ACCOUNT | | BALANCE SHEET | |
|---|---|---|---|---|---|---|
| | DR | CR | DR | CR | DR | CR |
| sales | | 7 500 | | | | |
| purchases | 6 300 | | | | | |
| stock | 1 300 | | | | | |
| wages | 1 100 | | | | | |
| rent | 450 | | | | | |
| advertising | 100 | | | | | |
| interest | 40 | | | | | |
| bank | | 600 | | | | |
| trade debtors | 1 400 | | | | | |
| trade creditors | | 800 | | | | |
| capital | | 1 790 | | | | |
| total | 10 690 | 10 690 | | | | |

## BUSINESS C

NOTE: closing stock is valued at £950.

The accountant of Business C is uncertain as to whether or not input A has been consumed. Compare the P&L Account and balance sheet prepared under the assumption that input A has been consumed, with the same prepared under the assumption that input A remains in the business as an asset.

| | TRIAL BALANCE | | P&L ACCOUNT | | BALANCE SHEET | |
|---|---|---|---|---|---|---|
| | **DR** | **CR** | **DR** | **CR** | **DR** | **CR** |
| sales | | 3 400 | | | | |
| purchases | 2 300 | | | | | |
| stock | 800 | | | | | |
| wages | 780 | | | | | |
| **input A** | **100** | | | | | |
| interest | 20 | | | | | |
| bank | 500 | | | | | |
| trade debtors | 900 | | | | | |
| trade creditors | | 800 | | | | |
| capital | | 1 200 | | | | |
| total | 5 400 | 5 400 | | | | |

## 24.2  An exercise on the relation between the Income Statement and the balance sheet, and the trial balance

Reconstruct the trial balance on which the Income Statement and balance sheet below are based. (This is a somewhat artificial exercise, but useful for understanding.)

| ABC INCOME STATEMENT FOR THE PERIOD ENDED 30 JUNE 2050 | | |
|---|---:|---:|
| | £ | £ |
| SALES | | 23 500 |
| purchases | 15 000 | |
| opening stock | 3 000 | |
| closing stock | (2 500) | |
| COST of SALES | | (15 500) |
| GROSS PROFIT | | 8 000 |
| rent | 2 200 | |
| electricity | 1 350 | |
| salaries | 3 450 | |
| | | (7 000) |
| OPERATING PROFIT | | 1 000 |
| interest receivable | | 200 |
| interest payable | | (300) |
| NET PROFIT | | £900 |

**ABC BALANCE SHEET
AS AT 30 JUNE 2050**

|  | £ | £ |
|---|---|---|
| ASSETS |  |  |
| stock |  | 2 500 |
| trade receivables |  | 4 300 |
| finance debtor |  | 1 500 |
| bank |  | 200 |
|  |  | 8 500 |
| LIABILITIES |  |  |
| trade payables | 3 600 |  |
| finance payable | 1 400 |  |
|  |  | (5 000) |
| NET ASSETS |  | £3 500 |
| CAPITAL |  | £3 500 |

# PART THREE

# Reporting Results – Profit and Net Assets

Part 3 deals with more advanced accounting matters, and approaches the major problems which require the accountant to intervene and adjust the information recorded in the accounts of a business, including depreciation, accruals, provisions, and the valuation of stock and debtors. It begins with a brief discussion of the principles which govern and constrain the accountant's interventions, and concludes with a brief look at insolvency and its consequences.

# CHAPTER 25

# An Introduction to Accounting Principles

## OBJECTIVES

*The objectives of this chapter are:*

- to outline the major accounting principles of useful information, accruals, prudence, and neutrality
- to consider the problem of accountability and historical cost
- to show how the major accounting principles have evolved in response to changes in the structure of business and the behaviour of investors

## ACCOUNTING RULES AND PRINCIPLES

Previous chapters have shown that the profit or loss reported by a firm depends really upon which figures from the trial balance are included in the P&L Account, and which are left to appear in the balance sheet. The accountant who makes these dispositions is therefore possessed of the power to determine precisely how a firm's results will be presented. In the exercise of that power, the accountant's choices may be governed by rules or guided by principles.

A rule-based approach is attractive insofar as it offers certainty. Follow the rule and the right answer will emerge. Or if the right answer doesn't emerge, the rule will be at fault and not your judgement. The problem with rules is that they cannot cover every case, and they can become absurdly complicated if they try. And no rule can be constructed without loop-holes. Technical compliance with a rule need not entail compliance with its spirit.

Outside the United States, accountants have mostly preferred to be guided by principles. Accounting principles were first derived from accounting practice. The procedure was to start with what accountants seemed to be agreed upon, then to articulate the principle behind it, and then to apply the principle to new and marginal cases. More recently, that approach has been reversed. The attempt has been made to start with a set of principles, self-evident or universally acceptable in the abstract, from which best practice, which ought to be agreed upon, can then be arrived at by deduction.

In the following chapters we shall consider some of the problems to which accounting principles must be applied. In this chapter, as a preliminary, we shall examine the four most basic accounting principles: the principles of useful information, accruals, prudence, and neutrality.

# THE PRINCIPLE OF USEFUL INFORMATION

The principle of useful information is the doctrine that financial statements should provide information that is useful to a range of users. Users of accounting information are assumed to be economic decision-makers, and useful information is information that is relevant to their decisions.

## USERS OF FINANCIAL STATEMENTS

If financial information is to be useful, we must specify its users and the uses to which it will be put. The seven user-groups most commonly identified are:

- investors
- lenders
- suppliers and trade creditors
- employees
- customers
- governments and their agencies, and
- the public.

Each of these groups has a legitimate interest in the financial affairs of a business they are dealing with, or contemplating dealing with.

As the law stands, however, the only groups with any effective power to demand financial information from a business are governments, and those investors with some claim to actual ownership of the business. (Governments, however, may exercise their powers to demand financial information on behalf of other groups.) It follows that despite the interests of other groups, financial statements largely cater to the needs of investors.

In summary, then, the doctrine of useful information is reduced to this: investors make decisions about whether to buy, sell or hold investments. To make those decisions, they need information about the performance and financial position of a business. That, therefore, is the useful information financial statements should provide.

## INFORMATION AND ACCOUNTABILITY

The doctrine of useful information may be true but is certainly incomplete. Financial statements do, and should, provide some useful information for investors – as does the telephone book for its users, or the speaking clock for those who want to know the time. But unlike the telephone book or the speaking clock, a set of financial statements has other purposes beyond and even above the provision of information.

In particular, financial statements are concerned with accountability – not just facts about outcomes, but explanations of what people did and why they did it. Accountability is not in itself about the provision of information, but rather about the imposition of responsibility. The external form of accountability is that A provides information to B, but the moral structure of the relation is that *B imposes a duty upon A* to explain himself – and thus to regulate his conduct in compliance with B's wishes or best interests. The importance of accountability is shown by the continuing use of historical costs in financial statements.

# HISTORICAL COST

Historical cost could well be called transaction cost. The historical cost of an item is the value at which it was exchanged in the transaction which caused it to be recorded in the accounts of a business. Most financial statements are based on historical costs, which means they are based on transactions. In terms of usefulness for investors' decision-making, historical cost compares rather badly with current cost (which is, broadly speaking, the present value of an item). On the face of it, current costs carry information that is useful for investors, while historical costs carry only back-ward-looking, useless information.

However, statements about current costs and statements about historical costs are not in fact truly comparable on that basis. For all their surface similarity, they are talking about different things. A current cost statement like 'This machine is worth £100' will indeed tell you something useful about the resources in a business. But an historical cost statement like 'We paid £80 for this machine' will tell you something else, and something no less useful – about who did what and why – which is the essence of accountability.

Note: it is possible, and sometimes very desirable, to adapt the information collected in transaction-based (historical cost) accounting records, to enable the production of current cost financial statements. But the adjustments raise theoretical issues that are rather beyond the scope of an introductory text.

# THE PRINCIPLE OF ACCRUALS

The principle of accruals is the doctrine that profit or loss should be measured as a difference between value created and value consumed. As we have seen, this definition forms the basis of the accounting model of a business. Notable mainly for what it *excludes* from being an acceptable measure of profit, the principle of accruals means that profit should *not* be measured as the difference between money paid out and money taken in. Neither should profit be measured as the difference between the value of outputs paid for and inputs paid for – even if we allow that payment can be made in money or in promises.

While the principle of accruals may seem to be self-evident, its explicit formulation is relatively new in the history of accounting – a reflection of modern conditions in which business is a continuous process, rather than a series of separate ventures.

# MATCHING – APPLYING THE PRINCIPLE OF ACCRUALS

The principle of accruals is also known as the principle of *matching* – the idea being that the value of outputs created in a period should be matched (in the same P&L Account) against the value of inputs consumed in the creation of those outputs. In practice, this kind of matching is more difficult than it may sound.

One difficulty is the problem of measurement. Recall that the creation of outputs and consumption of inputs are not transactions. They are processes which occur inside the business, unobserved by the accountant. Moreover, they are not instantaneous. It takes time to consume business inputs, and time to create business outputs. At any particular moment, therefore, whenever we choose to prepare a P&L Account for an ongoing business, there will always be some inputs whose value has not yet been wholly consumed, and some outputs awaiting comple-tion or sale. Until such changes in value have been realized in a transaction, accountants can only estimate their effect.

A second difficulty is the problem of properly matching outputs against the particular inputs consumed in their creation. Sometimes, as we shall see, the causal connection between consumption of input and creation of output may be tenuous or obscure. Sometimes also, to compound the difficulty, the connection in time may be very remote – an input may be paid for in one period, consumed in another period (before or after it has actually been paid for), and enter into an output which is sold in yet another period.

We have already seen one application of the principle of accruals in the treatment of opening and closing stock in the P&L Account. There will be more examples in the chapters that follow.

## THE PRINCIPLE OF PRUDENCE

Prudence is 'wisdom shown in the exercise of reason, forethought and self-control'. The accounting principle of prudence is the doctrine that accountants should take special care to avoid the overstatement of profit or net assets. According to this principle, revenue should not be recognized in a firm's accounts until the firm has actually made delivery of the relevant goods or services; and any increase in the value of an asset should not be recognized until it is realized in the course of a transaction. Meanwhile expenses, losses and liabilities should be recognized as soon as they become apparent (that is, without waiting for them to be realized in the course of a transaction). Alternatively, in a more recent statement of the principle, prudence requires that we should seek more and better evidence for the recognition of revenue and the value of assets, than we should for the recognition of losses and the value of liabilities.

## THE NEED FOR PRUDENCE

Why is prudence needed in accounting? Why should we take more care to avoid the overstatement of profit and net assets than we do to avoid their understatement? Two reasons. First, the temptation among those responsible is almost always in the direction of overstatement. A number of forces are at work, including personal psychology. Entrepreneurs and business managers are by nature inclined to accentuate the positive – that is, they are (in a Darwinian sense) selected for ability to talk up the performance of their business. The structure of modern industry and finance is also far from neutral. Directors and managers are in competition to attract capital from investors, and a history (real, imaginary, or projected) of ever-rising profits, must be to their advantage. In addition, at all levels in the hierarchy of management, bonuses and promotion flow more copiously and more frequently to those reporting higher profits. Even shareholders, the principal victims of any scheme or practice for the overstatement of profit, may not be too inclined to prevent or detect the abuse. Higher reported profits translate into higher prices for shares, which mean real gains for shareholders – but such gains will not survive the revelation of the truth.

The second reason why we should take more care to avoid the overstatement of profit and net assets than we do to avoid their understatement, is the fact that overstatement of profit and net assets is objectively more dangerous than understatement. There are two reasons also for this. Recall first that profit, as an increase in net assets, means an increase in the value inside the business, which is claimed by the owner. In past times, and still in law, the investor's profit was taken to be the extra value which owners could safely take out of the business and spend as income, while still preserving all of the value they had originally invested. In this context, any overstatement of profit is dangerous, because it may lead owners or investors inadvertently to consume their own capital – taking more than they should out of the business and spending it, until finally they are left with nothing. While understatement of profit and net assets is at worst conducive to economy and saving, overstatement of profit may lead to waste and consumption of capital.

In the more modern context of a market for shares in the profits of a company, the danger is that any overstatement of a firm's profit or net assets will lay a deadly trap for investors, artificially inflating share prices such that the investor who buys on the basis of exaggerated past results, in the expectation that the future will resemble the mis-reported past, can only suffer a loss when the truth at last emerges. On the scale of society at large, therefore, the modern argument for prudence in accounting is this: prudence promotes a stable capital market, while lack of prudence may lead to a cycle of boom and bust.

## THE PRINCIPLE OF NEUTRALITY

The principle of neutrality is the doctrine that accounting information should be presented as far as possible without bias. Clearly freedom from bias is a desirable attribute of any information. But clearly also, the principle of neutrality is in conflict with the principle of prudence, which demands a bias on the downside of reported profit and net assets. This clash of principles is best understood as the symptom of an underlying conflict of interest.

## PRUDENCE VS NEUTRALITY

Prudence is a doctrine of restraint. It assumes a world in which investors see themselves as traditional owners of an enterprise, who seek to benefit from the profits of the business they invest in, and to preserve the value of their capital.

The principle of neutrality, however, is a response to an emerging pattern of investor behaviour, in which investors are no more than dealers in the market for shares, indifferent to the actual profit or loss of any particular firm, but seeking rather to gain from movements in share prices. These investors profit as much from selling an overpriced share as they do from buying a share that is underpriced. But their lack of concern for the fate of any individual company is reflected in their demand for neutral, unbiased information, on which to base their calculations.

The conflict between prudence and neutrality therefore reflects a clash between the interests of investors who follow a more traditional pattern of behaviour, demanding prudence for the preservation of their capital, and the interests of investors who follow the emerging pattern, demanding neutral information for the fixing of share prices in the market. The case is a convenient illustration of how theoretical issues in accounting are often in fact a sign of deeper social developments.

## REVIEW

After briefly describing the difference between accounting rules and accounting principles, this chapter has outlined the significance of four basic accounting principles: the principles of useful information, accruals, prudence, and neutrality. In connection with useful information, the chapter also considered the relative importance of accountability, and the use of historical costs in financial statements.

## DRILLS AND EXERCISES

There are no drills or exercises on this chapter.

# CHAPTER 26

# The Presentation of the Balance Sheet

## OBJECTIVES

*The objectives of this chapter are:*

- to explain the order in which items are presented in a balance sheet
- to show the importance of matching the maturity of assets and liabilities
- to describe the relation between inputs, assets and expenses

## HEADINGS, SUB-HEADINGS, AND ORDER OF PRESENTATION

A balance sheet is a list of all balances on all accounts after transfers to and from the P&L Account (some balances may be added together and included in the balance sheet in aggregate). The balance sheet is also defined by the manner of its presentation: it is arranged to represent the accounting equation. Main headings in the balance sheet therefore correspond directly to the three elements of the accounting equation – assets, liabilities, and capital. Further sub-headings are inserted to divide current assets from non-current assets, and current liabilities from non-current liabilities. The headings themselves, and the balances listed under each sub-heading, are usually listed in a fairly strict conventional order. This chapter explores the logic of these divisions and the conventional order of presentation.

## CURRENT ASSETS

The division between current and non-current assets is based on how easily, quickly, or certainly the asset could be turned asset into money. *Current assets* consist of money itself, and assets held for use, sale, or conversion to money in the short term (within one year of the balance sheet date).

'Money itself' means whatever can be used to make immediate payment – that is, bank deposits (promises received in respect of value deposited with the bank), as well as currency notes and coins. 'Assets held for use, sale, or conversion to money in the short term' would include inventories, such as any stock of goods which the firm intends to sell, as well as receivables, such as promises from debtors, which are held for conversion into money.

# NON-CURRENT ASSETS AND FIXED ASSETS

*Non-current assets* are those which fail to qualify for inclusion in the class of current assets (that is, they are any assets which are *not* held for use, sale, or conversion to money in the short term). This is a residual class, the idea being that assets must be either current or non-current – there is no third alternative, and if assets do not meet the criteria for inclusion among current assets, then they must be classified as non-current. In principle, non-current assets need share no positive characteristics, but in practice many, if not most, non-current assets fall into the class traditionally called fixed assets, which are positively defined as assets acquired *for use* by the business (not for sale or conversion) *in the long term*.

Fixed assets would include such things as land and buildings, plant, machinery, and vehicles (provided these are held for use in the long term and not for resale – for example a building just constructed by a builder, and waiting to be sold, would be classified as stock, and included in inventory, a current asset). For present purposes the long term is defined as longer than one year. Thus an asset held for use, but in the short term, such as for example a supply of heating oil, would again be classified as stock, a current asset.

# TANGIBLE AND INTANGIBLE ASSETS

Tangible assets are, literally, those which can be touched – that is, they are physical objects. Many non-current assets however, are intangible – they cannot be touched. Essentially these consist of legal rights, private knowledge, and/or the simple power to enjoy or extract some economic benefit, or deny it to others. Examples would include trademarks, patents, licenses, as well as business names, goodwill, and know-how. As long as they are saleable, such rights and powers will have a value which can be recognized in the accounts of a business.

# INVESTMENTS

A firm may also hold investments, such as shares in other firms. Such investments are assets – things of value – and they may either be current or non-current. Investments held for short-term gain are current assets. Investments held for the long-term are non-current assets. Often these are held for strategic reasons – for example, to control or influence another company, or to gain access to its markets or technology.

# FINANCIAL ADAPTABILITY AND A FIRM'S MIX OF ASSETS

Why is the division between current and non-current assets so important? Few firms could operate without a mixture of current and non-current assets, but information about the actual balance between them is held to be useful for investors because it reflects a firm's financial adaptability.

By definition, current assets are easily turned into money, and money can be used for any purpose at a moment's notice. An adequate holding of current assets, therefore, makes a firm fast-moving, and fit for any challenge. By contrast (so the theory goes) an excess of non-current assets may render a firm slow-moving, overcommitted to its present strategy, and less able to cope with the risks and opportunities that fortune may throw in its way.

The message is not unmixed, however. Non-current assets, especially tangible fixed assets, offer ideal security for borrowing. A firm with much in the way of land, buildings and productive machinery will always be able to borrow more and at lower rates than a firm possessed of only current assets, and this in itself will contribute to the firm's financial adaptability.

## CURRENT AND NON-CURRENT LIABILITIES

*Current liabilities* are liabilities that are payable within one year of the balance sheet date. This category would include trade creditors or payables (suppliers normally require payment within one or two months of invoice date, unless otherwise agreed) and any bank overdraft (a bank may allow an overdraft to continue indefinitely, but should the bank change its mind, an overdraft is repayable on demand).

*Non-current liabilities* are liabilities that need not be paid within one year. This would include any liability to repay a loan at an agreed date which is more than one year from the balance sheet. Notice that as time passes, and the date of repayment draws closer, a non-current liability will inevitably change into a current liability. Where a loan is repayable by instalments, the value payable within one year of the balance sheet date will be listed among current liabilities, while the remainder, payable after more than one year from the balance sheet date, will be listed among non-current liabilities.

## MATCHING THE MATURITY OF ASSETS AND LIABILITIES

When we classify assets and liabilities as current or non-current, we are essentially dividing them on the basis of their *maturity*. The maturity of an asset is the length of time before the asset will be consumed or sold. The maturity of a liability is the length of time before it must be paid. As a general rule, it is important for a firm to ensure as far as possible that the maturity of its liabilities is matched by the maturity of its assets. In principle, current liabilities, payable within one year, should be matched by current assets, which can be used or sold to generate money within one year. Meanwhile, non-current liabilities (often called long-term liabilities) should be covered by the value of non-current assets.

This general rule for the matching of maturities is most evidently applicable to a firm's borrowing decisions. While it might make sense to use an overdraft (repayable on demand) to finance the purchase of stock (which can be quickly sold), it would be folly to use an overdraft to purchase a machine with an expected useful life of several years. Conversely, while it might be quite reasonable to take out a long-term loan in order to purchase a machine with many years of useful life, it would be madness to take out a long-term loan in order to buy a stock of goods for immediate resale.

## MAIN HEADINGS: ORDER OF PRESENTATION

Under each main heading in the balance sheet there will be a list of balances belonging to that category. But the main headings form the skeleton of the balance sheet, and are conventionally presented in this order:

- non-current assets
- current assets
- current liabilities
- non-current liabilities.

As shown in Box 26.1, the figures in a balance sheet can be arranged (often by the use of separate columns) to generate a sub-total for *net current assets* (current assets – current liabilities), and a final total for *net assets*, which is balanced by the figure for *capital*.

**BOX 26.1**

### The Order of Main Headings in a Standard Balance Sheet

XYZ Balance Sheet at end of Period 1

|                               |   £    |   £    |
|-------------------------------|--------|--------|
| Non-current (or Fixed) Assets |        |  600   |
| Current Assets                |  150   |        |
| Current Liabilities           |  (50)  |        |
| Net Current Assets            |        |  100   |
| Non-current Liabilities       |        | (200)  |
| Net Assets                    |        | £500   |
|                               |        |        |
| Capital                       |        | £500   |

## ASSETS AND THE ORDER OF ITEMS UNDER EACH MAIN HEADING

Under non-current assets, intangibles are generally grouped together and listed before tangibles, and within each of those sub-categories, items with a longer life are listed before those with a shorter life. Thus, for example, under tangible non-current assets, land and buildings would be listed before machinery, equipment, or vehicles, and so on.

Current assets are generally classified under three sub-headings, which are listed in this order:

- inventories
- receivables
- cash and cash equivalents.

Notice how assets in general are listed in order of increasing liquidity. Liquidity means the degree of closeness, speed or certainty of conversion to cash. Non-current assets, often difficult to sell and in any case held for use in the long term, are listed first, then current assets. Within the class of current assets, cash itself, the most liquid asset, is listed last, after inventories and receivables. (The idea is that inventories or stocks are sold or converted into promises or receivables, and promises are collected and turned into cash.)

## CAPITAL

The rights and responsibilities of owning a business may be shared in different ways between a number of different individuals. Depending on these arrangements, it may be necessary to present a balance sheet in which capital, the owner's claim, is divided into several different parts. Thus for example:

- in a partnership, each separate partner will have a separate capital account to record the value of his or her own personal claim on the business; while
- in a limited company, the balance sheet must show the owners' claim not divided among individuals, but divided in various ways, to show how each part of the total claim came into being.

Later chapters, in Part 4, will deal with the problems of accounting for capital in limited companies. For the moment, however, our interest is confined to the net asset side of the balance sheet, and we shall present our balance sheets with one single undivided figure for capital. Subject to that limitation, Box 26.2 shows an example of a balance sheet with most of the usual headings and sub-headings on the net asset side, in the usual order.

## BOX 26.2

**Standard Format for a Balance Sheet (Net Asset Side)**

XYZ Balance Sheet at end of Period 1

|  | £ | £ | £ |
|---|---|---|---|
| Intangible Fixed Assets | | | |
| Goodwill | | | 100 |
| Patents | | | 150 |
| | | | 250 |
| Tangible Fixed Assets | | | |
| Land & Buildings | | 25 | |
| Plant & Machinery | | 325 | |
| | | | 350 |
| Total Fixed Assets | | | 600 |
| Current Assets | | | |
| Stock | | 60 | |
| Debtors | | 40 | |
| Bank | | 30 | |
| Cash | | 20 | |
| | | 150 | |
| Current Liabilities | | | |
| Trade Creditors | 40 | | |
| Bank Overdraft | 10 | | |
| | | (50) | |
| Net Current Assets | | | 100 |
| | | | 700 |
| Long-term Liabilities | | | |
| Bank Loan | | | (200) |
| NET ASSETS | | | £500 |
| CAPITAL | | | £500 |

## INPUTS, EXPENSES, AND ASSETS

Taking the P&L Account and the balance sheet together, we have now effectively divided inputs into three separate categories. Some inputs are consumed immediately on entry to the firm (as for example heat and light, or use of the telephone). Because they are consumed immediately, these inputs hardly ever qualify as assets. They are shown as expenses in the P&L Account of the period in which they are acquired.

Other inputs, like for example purchases, may be held within the firm for some relatively short time before they are used or sold. For as long as these unconsumed inputs are held in the firm, they are classified as current assets, and will appear in the balance sheet under the general heading of inventories. As soon as they are used or sold, they become inputs consumed, and will be included in the P&L Account as part of the cost of sales.

Finally, there is a third class of inputs, being those which the firm intends to hold for the long term. For as long as they stay within the firm, these will be listed in the balance sheet under the heading of non-current assets. Note, however, that in the end, *all inputs are eventually consumed*, and their value must pass through the P&L Account. Nothing retains its value in a business forever.

This three-way analysis of inputs is summarized in Box 26.3.

## BOX 26.3

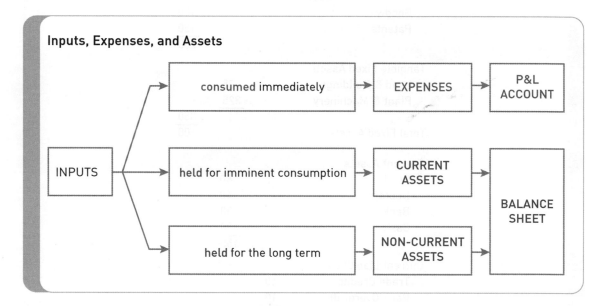

**Inputs, Expenses, and Assets**

## REVIEW

This chapter has introduced the standard headings used on the net asset side of the balance sheet, explaining the difference between current and non-current assets and liabilities, as well as the difference between tangible and non-tangible assets, and the order in which they are presented.

The chapter also considered the importance of the distinction between current and non-current assets and liabilities in the context of the practical need to match the maturity of assets and liabilities, and the investors' need to assess the financial adaptability of the firm. (These issues are discussed at greater length in Part 5).

# DRILLS AND EXERCISES

## 26.1  A drill to practise the presentation of the balance sheet

Put each list of balances below into the form of a standard balance sheet.

| FIRM A | |
|---|---|
| bank | 30 |
| bank overdraft | 10 |
| capital | 250 |
| cash | 20 |
| debtors | 40 |
| land and buildings | 25 |
| long-term loan | 200 |
| plant & machinery | 325 |
| stock | 60 |
| trade creditors | 40 |

| FIRM B | |
|---|---|
| trade creditors | 50 |
| stock | 45 |
| plant & machinery | 150 |
| long-term loan | 300 |
| land and buildings | 340 |
| debtors | 60 |
| capital | 215 |
| bank overdraft | 45 |
| bank | 15 |

## 26.2 Some exercises on the significance of balance sheet categories

1. What, if anything, would be the advantage gained by classifying current liabilities as non-current liabilities? (How would it affect the interpretation of the firm's balance sheet?)

2. What, if anything, would be the advantage gained by classifying current assets as non-current assets?

3. A firm has the option of borrowing to finance the purchase of a fixed asset, or leasing the fixed asset for a regular annual payment. What presentational difference would the choice make to the balance sheet?

4. State, giving your reasons, how you would finance each of the following (use cash savings, overdraft, short-term loan, long-term loan):

   (a) to purchase a stock of goods for immediate resale
   (b) to pay for a holiday
   (c) to buy a house
   (d) to pay for professional training

# CHAPTER 27

# Fixed Assets and Depreciation

## OBJECTIVES

*The objectives of this chapter are:*

- to explain what accountants mean by depreciation
- to show the most basic method of accounting for depreciation

## DEPRECIATION

Depreciation means loss or consumption of value. Any asset may depreciate or lose value, but as an accounting problem, depreciation is particularly associated with the loss in value suffered by those non-current assets traditionally known as fixed assets. Recall that fixed assets are assets acquired *for use* by the business *in the long term*. Examples would include land and buildings, plant and machinery, equipment, vehicles, and so on.

Although a fixed asset may retain its usefulness, and therefore its value, for a considerable time, it remains true that (with the possible exception of freehold land), *every fixed asset has a finite useful economic life*. Which is to say that throughout its life, the value of every fixed asset must be declining towards nil as the asset approaches the end of its useful life. Ultimately then, the value of every fixed asset, except land, will be lost through the passage of time, even if it is not already worn-out or consumed in use.

While such loss in value is generally inevitable, some particular causes of depreciation are easily identifiable. These causes may operate separately or together. They include but are not limited to:

- wear and tear in use;
- decay through the passage of time; and
- obsolescence through technological or market changes.

## ACCOUNTING FOR DEPRECIATION

Depreciation means loss of *value*, not loss of *money*. Money or promises are involved only when an asset is bought or sold. However, if we observe that an asset is losing value while it remains in use, the principle of prudence requires us to recognize the loss in value in the accounts of a business as it happens, even if that is long before the loss in value is realized in a transaction. Meanwhile, the principle of accruals requires us to match the loss in value of a fixed asset in each period, against the revenue generated from its use in each period.

Notice however, that *depreciation* itself is an economic process, which occurs regardless of whether or how we account for it, while *accounting for* depreciation is a matter of choice. We could simply choose to ignore any loss in value until the loss is realized in a transaction. In modern times at least, that would be foolish. Modern industry is characterized by huge investment in fixed assets, and the loss in value suffered by those assets in any period must be correspondingly large. Depreciation therefore cannot be ignored, and in this chapter we shall begin to examine how it can be accounted for.

## FIXED ASSETS AS INPUTS

To begin with, a fixed asset is an input, just like any other. When a firm pays wages, for example, money or promises go OUT of the firm, and labour comes IN. Likewise when a firm buys a fixed asset, money or promises go OUT, and the fixed asset comes IN.

The difference arises at the end of the accounting period (we shall assume a standard accounting period of one year). We may assume that most inputs, like labour, will be entirely consumed within the year of acquisition, with no value remaining at the year-end. A fixed asset is different because at the end of the year it will remain present inside the firm, probably retaining most of its value. Being one year closer to the end of its useful life, however, some of its value will have been lost or consumed. The question is, how do we account for the part of its value that has been consumed?

## ACCOUNTING FOR THE DEPRECIATION OF A NEWLY ACQUIRED FIXED ASSET

Ordinarily, the whole value of any input coming IN to a business during a year will be transferred to the P&L Account at the end of the year, because it can be assumed that the whole value of the input has been consumed in the course of the year. In the case of a newly acquired fixed asset, however, only a part of the value that came IN during the year will have been consumed, so only a part of the value that came IN will be transferred to the P&L Account, with the rest remaining as a balance on the fixed asset account.

Thus at the end of a year:

● That part of a fixed asset's value that has been lost or consumed in the period will be transferred to the P&L Account, where it will be listed as an operating expense and called the *depreciation charge* for the year, or the *depreciation expense* for the year.

Meanwhile:

● the remaining (unconsumed) value of the fixed asset, as represented by the balance remaining on the Fixed Asset Account, will be shown in the balance sheet as an asset at the end of the year.

Box 27.1 shows an example.

## BOX 27.1

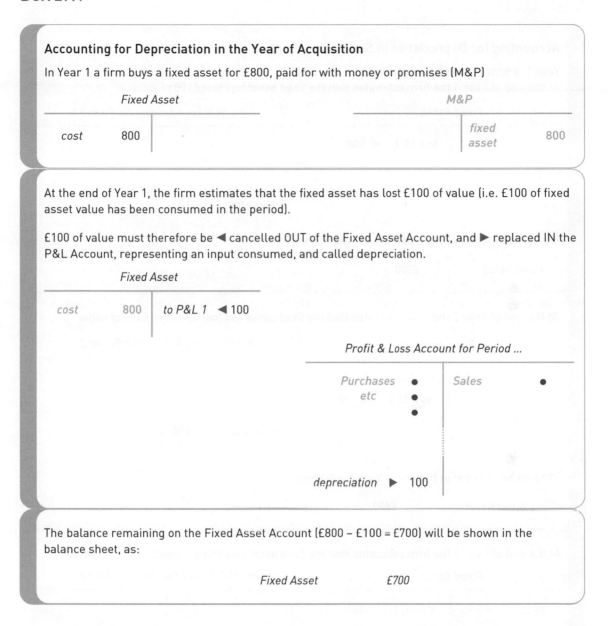

**Accounting for Depreciation in the Year of Acquisition**

In Year 1 a firm buys a fixed asset for £800, paid for with money or promises (M&P)

| | | Fixed Asset | | | | | M&P | |
|---|---|---|---|---|---|---|---|---|
| cost | 800 | | | | | | *fixed asset* | 800 |

At the end of Year 1, the firm estimates that the fixed asset has lost £100 of value (i.e. £100 of fixed asset value has been consumed in the period).

£100 of value must therefore be ◄ cancelled OUT of the Fixed Asset Account, and ► replaced IN the P&L Account, representing an input consumed, and called depreciation.

*Fixed Asset*

| cost | 800 | *to P&L 1* ◄ 100 |
|---|---|---|

*Profit & Loss Account for Period ...*

| Purchases | ● | Sales | ● |
|---|---|---|---|
| etc | ● | | |
| | ● | | |

| depreciation ► | 100 | |
|---|---|---|

The balance remaining on the Fixed Asset Account (£800 − £100 = £700) will be shown in the balance sheet, as:

| *Fixed Asset* | *£700* |
|---|---|

## ACCOUNTING FOR DEPRECIATION IN SUCCESSIVE PERIODS

A fixed asset will continue to lose value throughout its life. At the end of each period, therefore, the value lost in that period (or an estimate of the value lost in the period) should be taken OUT of the Fixed Asset Account, and put IN to the P&L Account as an expense. Thus, as shown in Box 27.2:

- each period's P&L Account will show an expense in respect of the fixed asset value lost in that period; and
- the balance sheet at the end of each period will show only the remaining value of the fixed asset, and this balance sheet value will steadily decline over the life of the fixed asset.

BOX 27.2

### Accounting for Depreciation in Successive Years

Year 1: a firm acquires a fixed asset at a cost of £800.
At the end of Year 1 the firm estimates that the fixed asset has lost £100 of value.

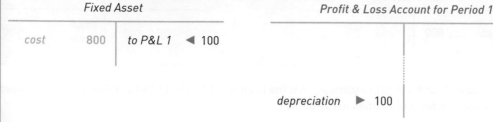

| *Fixed Asset* | | | *Profit & Loss Account for Period 1* |
| --- | --- | --- | --- |
| cost | 800 | to P&L 1 ◄ 100 | |
| | | depreciation ► 100 | |

The **balance sheet** at the end of Year 1 will show:

*Fixed Asset*      £700

At the end of **Year 2** the firm estimates that the fixed asset has lost a further £100 of value.

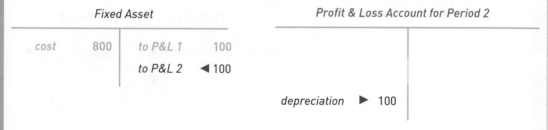

| *Fixed Asset* | | | *Profit & Loss Account for Period 2* |
| --- | --- | --- | --- |
| cost | 800 | to P&L 1      100 | |
| | | to P&L 2 ◄ 100 | |
| | | depreciation ► 100 | |

The **balance sheet** at the end of Year 2 will show

*Fixed Asset*      £600

At the end of **Year 3** the firm estimates that the fixed asset has lost yet another £100 of value.

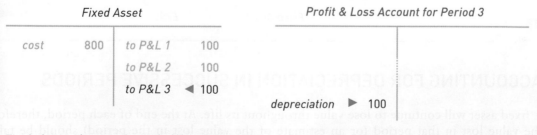

| *Fixed Asset* | | | *Profit & Loss Account for Period 3* |
| --- | --- | --- | --- |
| cost | 800 | to P&L 1      100 | |
| | | to P&L 2      100 | |
| | | to P&L 3 ◄ 100 | |
| | | depreciation ► 100 | |

The **balance sheet** at the end of Year 3 will show

*Fixed Asset*      £500

# THE DOUBLE ENTRY FOR DEPRECIATION

As shown in our examples, the basic double entry required to account for depreciation at the end of each period has been:

| | | |
|---|---|---|
| DR | P&L Account (depreciation expense) | £● |
| CR | Fixed Asset Account | £● |

The next chapter will introduce a slight modification to this procedure, but the principle will remain unchanged.

# REVIEW

This chapter has introduced the idea of depreciation, and has shown the basic procedure involved in accounting for the depreciation of a fixed asset, so that the P&L Account of each period will include depreciation as an expense, and so that the balance sheet at the end of each period will show only the remaining value of any fixed asset.

# DRILLS AND EXERCISES

## 27.1 Drills to practise basic accounting for depreciation

For each separate business below, show

1. a Fixed Asset Account and an account for money or promises (M&P), plus
2. relevant extracts concerning the fixed asset from:

   ● the P&L Account for YEAR 1 and the balance sheet at the end of YEAR 1
   ● the P&L Account for YEAR 2 and the balance sheet at the end of YEAR 2
   ● the P&L Account for YEAR 3 and the balance sheet at the end of YEAR 3

### BUSINESS 1

YEAR 1: the business buys a fixed asset at a cost of £10 000. During the year, the fixed asset loses £2 000 of value.
YEAR 2: the fixed asset loses a further £1 500 of value.
YEAR 3: the fixed asset loses a further £1 000 of value.

### BUSINESS 2

YEAR 1: a fixed asset is purchased at cost £24 000. During the year, the fixed asset loses £4 000 of value.
YEAR 2: the fixed asset depreciates by £3 000.
YEAR 3: the fixed asset depreciates by £2 000.

## BUSINESS 3

YEAR 1: a fixed asset is purchased at cost £4 000. At the end of the year, the fixed asset is valued at £3 200.
YEAR 2: at the end of the year the fixed asset is valued at £2 800.
YEAR 3: at the end of the year the fixed asset is valued at £2 500.

## BUSINESS 4

The business purchases a fixed asset at cost £16 000 in YEAR 1. The fixed asset is estimated to lose £4 000 of value in each year of use.

## BUSINESS 5

The business purchases a fixed asset in YEAR 1 for £20 000. In each year of use, the fixed asset is estimated to lose 10% of its value at the start of that year.

## BUSINESS 6

The business purchases a fixed asset in YEAR 1 for £15 000. The business estimates that the fixed asset will be used for ten years, after which it will be thrown away with no value.

## BUSINESS 7

A fixed asset is acquired in YEAR 1 for £100 000. The business estimates that the fixed asset will be used for eight years, after which it will be sold for £20 000.

## BUSINESS 8

The business purchases a fixed asset at a cost of £50 000 in YEAR 1. At the end of YEAR 1 the fixed asset is valued at £44 000.

At the end of YEAR 2 it is valued at £43 000, and at the end of YEAR 3 it is valued at £33 000.

## 27.2 Some exercises on the nature of depreciation

1. Simon inherits £20 000 from his uncle, and uses it to buy a fixed asset in order to start a new business. At the end of the accounting period, Simon has attracted no customers, and has engaged in no further transactions. Has he made a profit or a loss for the period? Explain your answer.
2. What are the objects of accounting for depreciation?
3. What would happen if we failed to account for depreciation?

# CHAPTER 28

# The Provision for Depreciation Account

## OBJECTIVES

*The objectives of this chapter are:*

- to explain why the single Fixed Asset Account is usually split down the middle into a Fixed Asset Cost Account and a separate Provision for Depreciation Account
- to show how to account for depreciation using a separate Provision for Depreciation Account

## FIXED ASSETS IN THE BALANCE SHEET

If we are accounting for depreciation each year in the manner shown in the previous chapter, then the balance sheet at the end of each year will show the remaining value of the firm's fixed assets.

However, on its own, the remaining value of a fixed asset is a frustratingly incomplete piece of information. Recall that most readers of a firm's financial statements are outside the firm, with no right to see the underlying accounts. Thus, when they see the remaining value of a fixed asset in the balance sheet, they have no way of knowing what exactly it may represent. It could be a small remaining part of a large original value, now almost entirely worn out. Or it could be a large remaining part of a small original value which is nearly new. Box 28.1 shows an example of the problem.

BOX 28.1

### Fixed Assets in the Balance Sheet

A firm's balance sheet at the end of Year 4 shows

*Fixed Asset* £5 000

Without access to the underlying accounts, we cannot tell exactly what this represents.

**BOX 28.1**    Continued

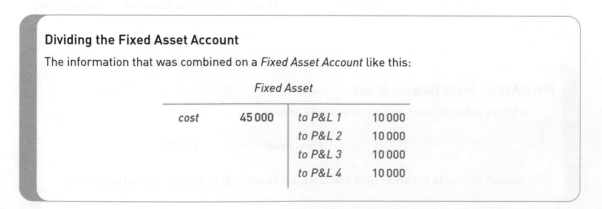

| It could represent for example, Fixed Asset A which is relatively costly, but was bought four years ago and is now almost worn out. | Fixed Asset A | | | |
| --- | --- | --- | --- | --- |
| | cost | 45 000 | to P& L 1 | 10 000 |
| | | | to P& L 2 | 10 000 |
| | | | to P& L 3 | 10 000 |
| | | | to P& L 4 | 10 000 |

| Fixed Asset B | | | | OR it could represent Fixed Asset B which is less costly but nearly new (it was bought in Year 4) |
| --- | --- | --- | --- | --- |
| cost | 6 000 | to P&L 4 | 1 000 | |

## DIVIDING THE FIXED ASSET ACCOUNT

As a remedy for this situation, accountants now divide the single Fixed Asset Account into two separate accounts, called:

- the Fixed Asset Cost Account; and
- the Provision for Depreciation Account.

As its name suggests, the Fixed Asset Cost Account is used only to record the value of the fixed asset coming IN to the firm at its original cost. The Provision for Depreciation Account is then used only to record the values that are consumed and transferred OUT to the P&L Account in successive years.

The advantage of the new arrangement is that both the original fixed asset cost, and the total value that has been consumed so far, can be shown in the balance sheet, with one deducted from the other to show the remaining value, which now is called the *Net Book Value* (or NBV).

Box 28.2 provides an illustration.

**BOX 28.2**

### Dividing the Fixed Asset Account

The information that was combined on a *Fixed Asset Account* like this:

| Fixed Asset | | | | |
| --- | --- | --- | --- | --- |
| cost | 45 000 | to P&L 1 | 10 000 | |
| | | to P&L 2 | 10 000 | |
| | | to P&L 3 | 10 000 | |
| | | to P&L 4 | 10 000 | |

**BOX 28.2**   Continued

is now recorded separately on a *Fixed Asset Cost Account* and a *Provision for Depreciation Account* like this:

| *Fixed Asset Cost* | | | | *Provision for Depreciation* | |
|---|---|---|---|---|---|
| cost | 45 000 | | | *to P&L 1* | 10 000 |
| | | | | *to P&L 2* | 10 000 |
| | | | | *to P&L 3* | 10 000 |
| | | | | *to P&L 4* | 10 000 |

which means that the balance sheet now can show

| | £ |
|---|---|
| *Fixed Asset Cost* | 45 000 |
| *less Provision for Depreciation* | (40 000) |
| *Net Book Value* | £5 000 |

## USING THE PROVISION FOR DEPRECIATION ACCOUNT

At the end of each period, the fixed asset value consumed in that period is now transferred OUT of the Provision for Depreciation Account and IN to the P&L Account as an operating expense. The double entry is:

| DR | P&L Account (depreciation expense) | £● | |
|---|---|---|---|
| CR | Provision for Depreciation Account | | £● |

Notice that the Fixed Asset Cost Account will remain untouched with a constant balance throughout the life of the fixed asset. But the balance on the Provision for Depreciation Account will steadily increase as more and more of the fixed asset's value is consumed. For each period therefore:

● the P&L Account will show the fixed asset value consumed in that period; and

● the closing balance sheet will show both the original fixed asset cost, *and* the total value consumed over the asset's life up to the balance sheet date.

Box 28.3 shows an example covering the first two years of a fixed asset's life.

## BOX 28.3

### Using the Provision for Depreciation Account

YEAR 1

A firm has already recorded the acquisition of a fixed asset for £850, as shown on the Fixed Asset Cost Account below:

*Fixed Asset Cost*

| | | |
|---|---|---|
| *cost* | 850 | |

At the end of Year 1, the firm estimates that the fixed asset has lost £100 of value. This value is taken OUT of the Provision for Depreciation Account, and transferred IN to the P&L Account as an expense:

*P&L Account 1*

*Provision for Depreciation*

| | |
|---|---|
| *to P&L 1* ◀ 100 | |

| | |
|---|---|
| *dep'n* ▶ 100 | |

The balance sheet at the end of Year 1 will show

| | £ |
|---|---|
| *Fixed Asset Cost* | 850 |
| less *Provision for Depreciation* | (100) |
| *Net Book Value* | £750 |

---

YEAR 2

The Fixed Asset Cost Account remains unchanged as shown below:

*Fixed Asset Cost*

| | | |
|---|---|---|
| *cost* | 850 | |

But at the end of Year 2, the firm estimates that the fixed asset has lost a further £150 of value. This further loss in value must be transferred OUT of the Provision for Depreciation Account and IN to the P&L Account as an expense:

*Provision for Depreciation*

| | |
|---|---|
| *to P&L 1*    100 | |
| *to P&L 2* ◀ 150 | |

*P&L Account 2*

| | |
|---|---|
| *dep'n* ▶ 150 | |

The balance sheet at the end of Year 2 will now show

| | £ |
|---|---|
| *Fixed Asset Cost* | 850 |
| less *Provision for Depreciation* | (250) |
| *Net Book Value* | £600 |

## UNDERSTANDING THE PROVISION FOR DEPRECIATION ACCOUNT

Once separated from each other, the Fixed Asset Cost Account and the Provision for Depreciation Account may appear to be free-standing, with each one complete in itself. However, it is important to realize that these two accounts are no more than two halves of an original Fixed Asset Account, which has been unnaturally split down the middle. In particular, it would be a mistake to interpret the Provision for Depreciation Account as recording anything other than 'the part of the fixed asset cost that has been consumed and transferred to the P&L Account'. The provision for depreciation is therefore not a thing in itself, but a deduction from a thing. It can exist only as a deduction from fixed asset cost.

This warning may seem to be self-evident, but there is a natural tendency to assume that the existence of an account for something, indicates that the something itself exists. Moreover, language itself seems to conspire against a proper understanding of depreciation. Expressions like 'providing for depreciation', or 'making provision' for depreciation seem to imply that accounting for depreciation is somehow comparable to saving up, or providing for old age or sickness. We also say, for example, that the provision 'builds up' over the years, as though it has a bulk and being of its own. All of these expressions seem to imply, quite falsely, that the provision is itself perhaps some kind of asset which might replace the original fixed asset, rather than a deduction from its value.

Any such impression would be absolutely wrong. Accounting for depreciation, or creating a provision for depreciation, in no way involves building up another asset or a store of value. Quite the contrary. Accounting for depreciation means recognizing loss of value. The provision for depreciation is a statement of value lost. It is not a replacement of value lost. It is a negative value, and exists only as a deduction from the original cost of a fixed asset.

## ACCUMULATED DEPRECIATION

Because the balance on the Provision for Depreciation Account seems to build up throughout the life of the fixed asset, it is also sometimes called *accumulated depreciation*, or *cumulative depreciation*. These expressions mean nothing more than the balance on the Provision for Depreciation Account.

## THE DEPRECIATION EXPENSE ACCOUNT

As well as a Provision for Depreciation Account, many firms also maintain a separate Depreciation Expense Account. Instead of entering the fixed asset value consumed in a period directly in the P&L Account as we have done, they enter it first in a Depreciation Expense Account, and then transfer the balance on that account to the P&L Account like any other expense. This approach is useful where, for example, the firm has many fixed assets and would prefer to show just one line item for depreciation expense in the P&L Account. It is also useful where the firm operates a computerized system of accounting which does not allow entries to be made directly into the P&L Account.

## REVIEW

This chapter has shown how and why the single Fixed Asset Account is usually split down the middle into a Fixed Asset Cost Account, and a separate Provision for Depreciation Account, and how the net book value of a fixed asset is shown in the balance sheet.

# DRILLS AND EXERCISES

## 28.1 Drills to practise using the Provision for Depreciation Account

For each separate business and fixed asset below show:

1. a Fixed Asset Cost Account and an account for money or promises (M&P)
2. a Provision for Depreciation Account

plus relevant extracts concerning the fixed assets from:

- the P&L Account for YEAR 1 and the balance sheet at the end of YEAR 1
- the P&L Account for YEAR 2 and the balance sheet at the end of YEAR 2
- the P&L Account for YEAR 3 and the balance sheet at the end of YEAR 3

### BUSINESS 1

YEAR 1: the business buys a pressing machine at a cost of £10 000, and a delivery van at cost of £15 000. During the year, the pressing machine loses £2 000 of value, and the delivery van loses £3 000 of value.

YEAR 2: the machine depreciates by a further £1 500, and the van loses £2 000 of value.

YEAR 3: the machine loses a further £1 500 of value, and the van depreciates by £500.

### BUSINESS 2

YEAR 1: fixtures and fittings are purchased at a cost of £4 000, and plant and machinery is purchased at a cost of £8 000. At the end of the year, the fixtures and fittings are valued at £3 200, and the plant and machinery is valued at £6 000.

YEAR 2: at the end of the year, fixtures and fittings are valued at £2 800, and plant and machinery is valued at £5 000.

YEAR 3: at the end of the year, fixtures and fittings and plant and machinery are both valued at £2 000.

### BUSINESS 3

YEAR 1: the business buys a truck at cost £100 000 and a refrigeration unit at a cost of £16 000.

The truck is driven hard and is expected to lose £30 000 of value in each year of use. The refrigeration unit is expected to lose £2 000 of value in each year of use.

### BUSINESS 4

YEAR 1: the business purchases a grinding machine and a polishing machine, each at a cost of £20 000.

In each year of use, the grinding machine is expected to lose 10% of its original value or cost, while the polishing machine is expected to lose 10% of its value at the start of that year.

## BUSINESS 5

YEAR 1: the business acquires a steam generator at a cost of £100 000, and a steam hammer at a cost of £20 000.

The business estimates that the steam generator will be used for 15 years before it is scrapped with a value of £10 000. The steam hammer will be used for ten years, after which it will be sold for £5 000.

## BUSINESS 6

YEAR 1: the business buys a diamond drilling machine for £120 000. The business estimates that it will be possible to use the machine for 200 000 cutting operations before it is sold for £20 000 and replaced.

The machine is used to perform the following number of cutting operations in the first three years of its life:

Year 1      30 000 cutting operations
Year 2      20 000 cutting operations
Year 3      40 000 cutting operations

## BUSINESS 7

YEAR 1: the business buys a truck for £50 000. The business estimates that the truck will be driven for 500 000 miles before it is scrapped with no value. The mileage driven by the truck in the first three years of its life is: Year 1, 100 000 miles; Year 2, 140 000 miles; Year 3, 80 000 miles.

## 28.2  More drills to practise using the Provision for Depreciation Account

### BUSINESS A

At 30 November, Year 10, the balance sheet of a business showed the following in relation to fixed assets:

|  | £ | £ |
| --- | --- | --- |
| **machinery** | | |
| cost | 80 000 | |
| provision for depreciation | (28,800) | |
| **Net Book Value** | | 51 200 |
| **motor vehicles** | | |
| cost | 40 000 | |
| provision for depreciation | (24,000) | |
| **Net Book Value** | | 16 000 |

The business believes that in each year of use, the machinery loses 20% of its value at the start of that year, while the motor vehicles lose 20% of their original value.

Show relevant extracts concerning the fixed assets from the P&L Account for the year to 30 November, Year 11, and from the balance sheet at 30 November, Year 11.

## BUSINESS B

At the end of the year to 31 December, Year 20, the trial balance of a business included the following:

|  | DR £ | CR £ |
|---|---|---|
| fixed asset cost | 90 000 | |
| provision for depreciation | | 18 000 |

The business believes that the fixed asset loses 10% of its original value (cost) in every year of use.

Show relevant extracts concerning the fixed assets from the P&L Account for the year to 31 December, Year 20, and from the balance sheet at 30 December, Year 20. (Notice that the trial balance is drawn up *before* transfers to the P&L Account.)

## 28.3 An exercise on accounts concerning depreciation

Apart from looking at their different names, how could you tell the difference between a Provision for Depreciation Account and a Depreciation Expense Account?

# CHAPTER 29

# Accounting for Fixed Asset Disposals

## OBJECTIVES

*The objectives of this chapter are:*

- to show how to account for the disposal of a fixed asset
- to explain the true meaning of 'profits' and losses' on disposal

## DISPOSAL AND DISPOSAL PROCEEDS

At the end of its useful life within the firm, a fixed asset will be disposed of. If it has no remaining value, it may be thrown away. If it still retains some value, it may be sold for scrap or further use, or given in part exchange for a replacement asset. Any value that a firm does receive on disposal of a fixed asset is called 'disposal proceeds'.

Notice that the actual loss in value suffered by a fixed asset can only be known with certainty at the time of disposal. During the active life of a fixed asset, we can only make an estimate of the value it is losing in each period. Any estimate is bound to contain some degree of error, and when the truth is discovered, the error must be corrected.

## THE FIXED ASSET DISPOSAL ACCOUNT

Accounting for the disposal of a fixed asset involves three related tasks:

- accounting for receipt of the disposal proceeds;
- cancelling the values shown on the Fixed Asset Cost and Provision for Depreciation accounts (these are no longer needed since the firm no longer has the fixed asset); and
- correcting any error in the previous estimate of value consumed.

Each of these tasks is usually accomplished through the use of a Fixed Asset Disposal Account.

# ACCOUNTING FOR DISPOSAL PROCEEDS

When a fixed asset is sold, money or promises come IN to the firm. The movement OUT is recorded on a Fixed Asset Disposal Account. Notice that the sale of a fixed asset is *not* recorded on the Sales Account, which is reserved for goods or services sold in the ordinary course of business.

The double entry to account for disposal proceeds is:

| DR | M&P (money or promises) | £● |
|----|-------------------------|-----|
| CR | Fixed Asset Disposal Account | £● |

Box 29.1 shows an example with the appearance of the relevant accounts at this stage.

## BOX 29.1

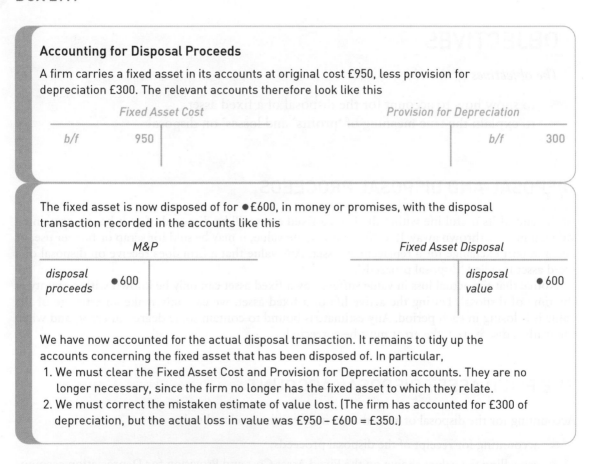

### Accounting for Disposal Proceeds

A firm carries a fixed asset in its accounts at original cost £950, less provision for depreciation £300. The relevant accounts therefore look like this

| Fixed Asset Cost | | Provision for Depreciation | |
|-----|-----|-----|-----|
| b/f  950 | | | b/f  300 |

The fixed asset is now disposed of for ●£600, in money or promises, with the disposal transaction recorded in the accounts like this

| M&P | | Fixed Asset Disposal | |
|-----|-----|-----|-----|
| disposal proceeds  ●600 | | disposal value  ●600 | |

We have now accounted for the actual disposal transaction. It remains to tidy up the accounts concerning the fixed asset that has been disposed of. In particular,
1. We must clear the Fixed Asset Cost and Provision for Depreciation accounts. They are no longer necessary, since the firm no longer has the fixed asset to which they relate.
2. We must correct the mistaken estimate of value lost. (The firm has accounted for £300 of depreciation, but the actual loss in value was £950 – £600 = £350.)

# CANCELLING FIXED ASSET COST

Once a fixed asset has been disposed of, the record of its cost should be taken OUT of the Fixed Asset Cost Account, and replaced IN the Fixed Asset Disposal Account. The double entry is:

| DR | Fixed Asset Disposal Account | £● |
|----|------------------------------|-----|
| CR | Fixed Asset Cost Account | £● |

This will leave the Fixed Asset Cost Account with a nil balance, in effect cancelling the record, to reflect the fact that the fixed asset has gone out of the business. Box 29.2 continues the example.

## BOX 29.2

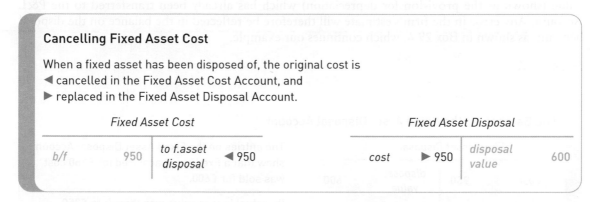

**Cancelling Fixed Asset Cost**

When a fixed asset has been disposed of, the original cost is
◀ cancelled in the Fixed Asset Cost Account, and
▶ replaced in the Fixed Asset Disposal Account.

| Fixed Asset Cost | | | | Fixed Asset Disposal | | | |
|---|---|---|---|---|---|---|---|
| b/f | 950 | to f.asset disposal | ◀ 950 | cost | ▶ 950 | disposal value | 600 |

Notice how, at this stage, the Fixed Asset Disposal Account presents a comparison between the disposal value of the fixed asset and its original cost. It therefore shows the true loss in value of the fixed asset over the course of its life.

## CANCELLING THE PROVISION FOR DEPRECIATION

The provision for depreciation is also no longer necessary once the fixed asset has been disposed of. It too should also be transferred to the Fixed Asset Disposal Account. The double entry will be

| DR | Provision for Depreciation Account | £● |
|---|---|---|
| CR | Fixed Asset Disposal Account | £● |

Box 29.3 continues the example.

## BOX 29.3

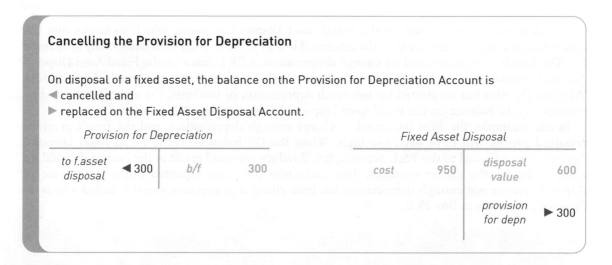

**Cancelling the Provision for Depreciation**

On disposal of a fixed asset, the balance on the Provision for Depreciation Account is
◀ cancelled and
▶ replaced on the Fixed Asset Disposal Account.

| Provision for Depreciation | | | | Fixed Asset Disposal | | | |
|---|---|---|---|---|---|---|---|
| to f.asset disposal | ◀ 300 | b/f | 300 | cost | 950 | disposal value | 600 |
| | | | | | | provision for depn | ▶ 300 |

# CORRECTING THE PREVIOUS ESTIMATE OF VALUE CONSUMED

At this stage the Fixed Asset Disposal Account allows a comparison between the actual loss in value suffered by the fixed asset (shown as cost minus disposal value), and the firm's estimate of its loss in value (shown as the provision for depreciation) which has already been transferred to the P&L Account. Any error in the firm's estimate will therefore be reflected in the balance on the disposal account, as shown in Box 29.4, which continues our example.

## BOX 29.4

### The Balance on the Fixed Asset Disposal Account

*Fixed Asset Disposal*

| cost | 950 | disposal value | 600 |
|------|-----|----------------|-----|
|      |     | provision for depn | 300 |

The entries on the Fixed Asset Disposal Account show that a fixed asset acquired for £950 cost was sold for £600.

Its actual loss in value was therefore **£350**

Meanwhile, however, the firm has already accounted for a loss in value of **£300**

*Fixed Asset Disposal*

| cost | 950 | disposal value | 600 |
|------|-----|----------------|-----|
|      |     | provision for depn | 300 |
|      |     | balance c/f | 50 |
|      | 950 |             | 950 |
| balance b/f | 50 |        |     |

The balance on the Fixed Asset Disposal Account therefore represents the extra £50 loss in value that remains to be accounted for

Box 29.4 shows a DR balance on the Fixed Asset Disposal Account, which indicates that the actual loss in value was greater than the estimated loss in value that the firm has already accounted for. The firm has not accounted for enough depreciation. A CR balance on the Fixed Asset Disposal Account would indicate that the firm had previously accounted for too much depreciation. Whether the firm has accounted for too much depreciation or too little, the error is corrected by transferring the balance on the Fixed Asset Disposal Account to the P&L Account.

In our example, the firm has failed to charge enough depreciation, and the firm's previous reported profits will have been too high. When the DR balance on the Fixed Asset Disposal Account is transferred to the P&L Account, it will reduce reported profit in the year of disposal, to compensate for the earlier mistakes. This correction (reducing reported profit in the year of disposal because not enough depreciation has been charged in previous years) is called a 'loss on disposal', as shown in Box 29.5.

## BOX 29.5

### Correcting the Previous Estimate of Value Consumed

*Fixed Asset Disposal*

| | | | |
|---|---|---|---|
| cost | 950 | disposal value | 600 |
| | | provision for depn | 300 |
| | | balance c/f | 50 |
| | 950 | | 950 |
| balance b/f | 50 | to P&L ◄ | 50 |

In our example the DR balance on the Fixed Asset Disposal Account indicates that the firm has not charged enough depreciation during the life of the fixed asset.

The correction is to transfer the balance to the P&L Account.

When a DR is transferred into the P&L Account, it will reduce reported profit.

This reduction in reported profit in the year of disposal, to compensate for failure to charge enough depreciation in earlier years, is called a loss on disposal

*P&L  Account for Year of Disposal*

| | |
|---|---|
| loss on disposal ► 50 | |

If the firm has charged too much depreciation during the life of the fixed asset, the correction will appear as a CR in the P&L Account, where it is called 'profit on disposal'.

All of the steps required in our example are now shown together in Box 29.6, which also shows how the relevant accounts should look when the procedure is complete.

## BOX 29.6

### Accounting for the Disposal of a Fixed Asset

A fixed asset is sold for £600. The fixed asset was recorded in the accounts at cost £950, less provision for depreciation £300.

The accounting steps to be followed are:

- account for receipt of any disposal proceeds●
- ◄ transfer original cost to Fixed Asset Disposal a/c ►
- ◄ transfer provision for depreciation to Fixed Asset Disposal a/c ►
- ◄ balance the Fixed Asset Disposal a/c ►
- ◄ transfer the balance on the Fixed Asset Disposal a/c to the P&L a/c ►

**BOX 29.6**   Continued

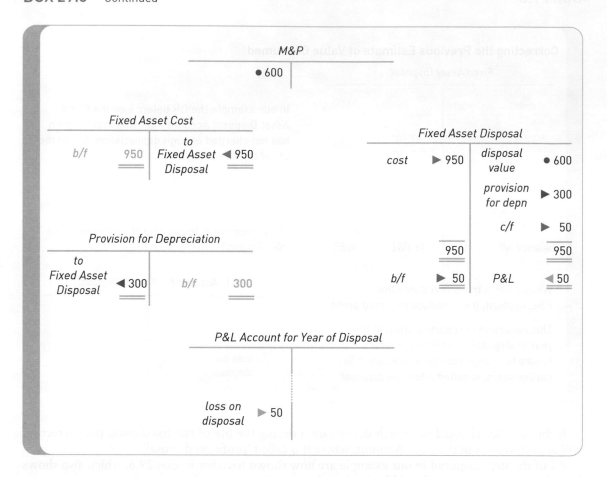

## A SHORT-CUT TO TRANSFERRING BALANCES

Recall that balancing an account means cancelling the individual movements already present on the account, and replacing them with a single net movement. And, transferring a value from one account to another means cancelling the value on the first account, and replacing it on the second account. Thus when we balance the Fixed Asset Disposal Account and then transfer the balance to the P&L Account, we are cancelling the individual movements and replacing them with a net movement, then cancelling the net movement and replacing it on the P&L Account. It is simpler and quicker to cancel the individual movements on the Disposal Account and replace them immediately with a single movement on the P&L Account. Box 29.7 shows two examples.

## BOX 29.7

### The Transfer from Fixed Asset Disposal Account to P&L Account

1. A fixed asset has been disposed of for £200. The fixed asset was recorded in the accounts at cost £725, less provision for depreciation £500.

   There will be a loss on disposal of £25, which can be transferred directly from the Fixed Asset Disposal Account to the P&L Account like this:

| Fixed Asset Disposal | | | | | P&L Account | |
|---|---|---|---|---|---|---|
| cost | 725 | disposal value | 200 | | | |
| | | provision for depn | 500 | | loss on disposal ▶ 25 | |
| | | to P&L ◀ 25 | | | | |
| | 725 | | 725 | | | |

2. A fixed asset recorded in the accounts at cost £500 less provision for depreciation £400, has been sold for £140.

   There will be a profit on disposal of £40, which can be transferred directly from the Fixed Asset Disposal Account to the P&L Account like this:

| Fixed Asset Disposal | | | | | P&L Account | |
|---|---|---|---|---|---|---|
| cost | 500 | disposal value | 140 | | | |
| | | provision for depn | 400 | | profit on disposal ▶ 40 | |
| to P&L ◀ 40 | | | | | | |
| | 540 | | 540 | | | |

## PROFITS AND LOSSES ON DISPOSAL

'Profits' and 'losses' on disposal are badly named. They are not really profits or losses. Real profits indicate success, superior business acumen, or luck. Real losses indicate failure. Profits and losses on disposal, however, have no relation to success or failure. They do not indicate that a fixed asset was well or badly sold. They are merely adjustments, or corrections of previous estimates. If a firm has charged too much depreciation during the life of a fixed asset, it must record a 'profit' on disposal in the final year to correct the previous error. If a firm has charged too little depreciation during the life of a fixed asset, it must record a 'loss' on disposal to correct the error.

# REVIEW

This chapter has shown the procedures involved in accounting for the disposal of a fixed asset, including the use of the Fixed Asset Disposal Account to record the receipt of the disposal proceeds, cancel the fixed asset cost and provision for depreciation, and account for the 'profit' or 'loss' on disposal (that is, the adjustment required to compensate for errors in the previous estimates of depreciation).

# DRILLS AND EXERCISES

## 29.1 Drills to practise using the Fixed Asset Disposal Account

For each example below show:

1. the Fixed Asset Cost Account;
2. the Provision for Depreciation Account;
3. the Fixed Asset Disposal Account and an account for money or promises (M&P);
4. an extract from the P&L Account in the year of disposal.

### BUSINESS 1

A fixed asset in the accounts of a business at cost £18 000 less depreciation £8 000, is disposed of with disposal proceeds £7 000.

### BUSINESS 2

A fixed asset in the accounts of a business at cost £33 000 less provision for depreciation £29 000, is disposed of with disposal proceeds £5 000.

### BUSINESS 3

A fixed asset in the accounts of a business at cost £14 000 less accumulated depreciation £12 000, is scrapped with no value.

### BUSINESS 4

A fixed asset in the accounts of a business at cost £27 000 less provision for depreciation £17 000, is destroyed in an accident. The insurers of the business agree to pay a claim of £9 000.

### BUSINESS 5

A fixed asset in the accounts of a business at cost £70 000 less provision for depreciation £50 000, is stolen. The insurers of the business agree to pay a claim of £25 000.

## 29.2 More drills to practise accounting for fixed asset disposals

For each example below, state the double entry necessary to account for the disposal, and show the Fixed Asset Disposal Account, with an extract from the P&L Account in the year of disposal.

### BUSINESS 1

A fixed asset in the accounts of a business at cost £5 000 less accumulated depreciation £4 000, is disposed of with disposal proceeds of £750.

### BUSINESS 2

A fixed asset in the accounts of a business at cost £15 000 less depreciation £8 000, is disposed of with disposal proceeds of £7 500.

### BUSINESS 3

A fixed asset in the accounts of a business at cost £42 000 less provision for depreciation of £38 000, is disposed of with nil value.

### BUSINESS 4

A fixed asset in the accounts of a business at cost £27 000 less provision for depreciation of £9 000, is destroyed in an accident, at which time it is not insured.

### BUSINESS 5

A fixed asset in the accounts of a business at cost £120 000 less provision for depreciation of £70 000, is damaged in an accident, and sold as scrap for £10 000. The insurers of the business agree to pay a claim of £35 000.

## 29.3 A drill to practise accounting for loss in value throughout the life of a fixed asset

For each example below show:

1. the Fixed Asset Cost Account;
2. the Provision for Depreciation Account;
3. the Fixed Asset Disposal Account and an account for money or promises (M&P);
4. relevant extracts concerning the fixed asset from the P&L Accounts of YEAR 1, YEAR 2 and YEAR 3.

NOTE: assume no depreciation is charged in the year of disposal.

### BUSINESS 1

A fixed asset is purchased in YEAR 1 at a cost of £130 000. The business uses the fixed asset for two years, believing that it loses £30 000 of value in the first year of use and £20 000 in the second year.

In Year 3 the fixed asset is sold for £70 000.

### BUSINESS 2

A fixed asset is purchased in YEAR 1 at a cost of £10 000. The business uses the fixed asset for two years, believing that it loses £2 000 of value in each year of use.

In Year 3 the fixed asset is sold for £7 000.

### BUSINESS 3

A fixed asset is purchased in YEAR 1 at a cost of £20 000. The business believes that the fixed asset will lose 10% of its original value (cost) in each year of use.

In Year 3 the fixed asset is sold for £17 000.

### BUSINESS 4

A fixed asset is purchased in YEAR 1 at a cost of £16 000. The business believes that in each year of use, the fixed asset will lose 25% of the value it had at the start of the year.

In Year 3 the fixed asset is sold for £8 500.

## 29.4 A drill to show how the profit or loss on disposal works to correct previous errors in the estimation of value lost by a fixed asset

### BUSINESS 1

A fixed asset is acquired at a cost of £120 000 in YEAR 1.

In YEAR 3 the fixed asset is disposed of for £57 500.

Treating each assumption separately, show how the actual loss in value of the fixed asset would have been accounted for in the P&L Accounts of YEAR 1, YEAR 2 and YEAR 3

1. if the business believed that the fixed asset would lose 25% of its original value in each year of use.
2. if the business believed that in each year of use, the fixed asset would lose 25% of the value it had at the start of the year.

### BUSINESS 2

A fixed asset is acquired at a cost of £20 000 in YEAR 1.

In YEAR 3 the fixed asset is disposed of for £16 500.

Treating each assumption separately, show how the actual loss in value of the fixed asset would have been accounted for in the P&L Accounts of YEAR 1, YEAR 2 and YEAR 3

1. if the business believed that the fixed asset would lose 10% of its original value in each year of use.
2. if the business believed that the fixed asset would lose £3 000 of value in YEAR 1 and £2 000 of value in YEAR 2.

# CHAPTER 30

# Fixed Asset Disposals – Quick Method

## OBJECTIVE

*The objective of this chapter is:*

- to show a quick method of accounting for the disposal of a fixed asset

## IS A DISPOSAL ACCOUNT REALLY NEEDED?

Recall from Chapter 29 that accounting for the disposal of a fixed asset involves three related tasks:

- accounting for the receipt of disposal proceeds;
- cancelling the Fixed Asset Cost and Provision for Depreciation;
- correcting any error in the previous estimate of value consumed.

We have presented these tasks as three continuous steps in an unbroken sequence. In practice, however, the tasks are often separately performed. Usually a firm will account for the receipt of any disposal proceeds immediately when the disposal transaction occurs. But the firm will wait until the end of the period before undertaking the next two tasks, which are essentially just tidying up the accounts (cancelling the fixed asset cost and provision for depreciation, and correcting the previous estimate of loss in value).

It is only the breaking of the sequence in this way that demands the use of a Fixed Asset Disposal Account. To account for the receipt of disposal proceeds, requires a DR in an account for money or promises. That DR requires a corresponding CR. Where else to put the CR except in a Fixed Asset Disposal Account?

However, if all of the steps can in fact be taken in an unbroken sequence, the Fixed Asset Disposal Account ceases to be necessary. Recall that the balance on the Fixed Asset Disposal Account is ultimately transferred to the P&L Account. The Disposal Account therefore begins and ends the sequence of steps with a nil balance. So here is a paradox: making *all* of the relevant entries on the Fixed Asset Disposal Account is equivalent to making *no* entries at all on the account.

## THE QUICK METHOD

The quick method of accounting for a fixed asset disposal involves performing all three essential steps, without using a Fixed Asset Disposal Account:

● To account for the receipt of disposal proceeds, we need only DR the relevant account for money or promises.

● To cancel fixed asset cost, we CR the Fixed Asset Cost Account, and to cancel the provision for depreciation, we DR the Provision for Depreciation Account.

● To correct any error in our previous estimate of value lost by the fixed asset, we DR the P&L Account (in the case of a loss on disposal) or CR the P&L Account (in the case of a profit on disposal).

These three steps will balance and will fully account for the disposal of a fixed asset. Box 30.1 shows an example.

## BOX 30.1

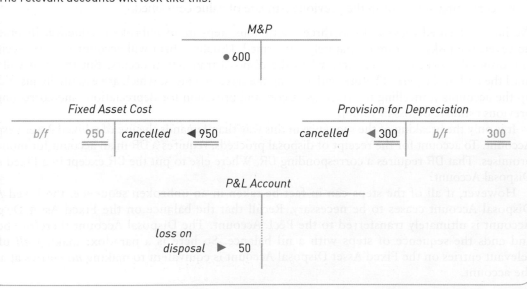

### Accounting for the Disposal of a Fixed Asset – Quick Method

A fixed asset recorded in the accounts at cost £950, less provision for depreciation £300, is sold for £600.

Accounting entries are necessary to:

 ● record the receipt of disposal proceeds
 ◀ cancel fixed asset cost
 ◀ cancel provision for depreciation
 ▶ show the profit or loss (in this case, loss) on disposal in the P&L Account.

The relevant accounts will look like this:

*M&P*

● 600

| | *Fixed Asset Cost* | | |
|---|---|---|---|
| *b/f* | 950 | *cancelled* ◀ 950 | |

| | *Provision for Depreciation* | | |
|---|---|---|---|
| *cancelled* ◀ 300 | | *b/f* | 300 |

*P&L Account*

*loss on disposal* ▶ 50

# JOURNAL ENTRIES FOR THE QUICK METHOD

The journal entries for the quick method are only slightly complicated by the requirement to show all of the DR entries before any of the corresponding CR entries. To begin with, we know that DR entries are definitely required to show the disposal proceeds coming in, and to cancel the provision for depreciation, so those can be written first. A CR entry is definitely required to cancel the fixed asset cost, so that can be done last. Between those DRs and that CR, we can insert the entry for profit or loss on disposal. If there is a loss on disposal, the relevant DR will attach itself to the preceding DRs, so that all DRs are shown together, and if there is a profit on disposal the relevant CR will attach itself to the following CR, so that all CRs are shown together. Box 30.2 shows an example.

## BOX 30.2

### Journal Entries for the Disposal of a Fixed Asset – Quick Method

A fixed asset recorded in the accounts at cost £700, less provision for depreciation £500, is sold for £220.

Journal entries to record the disposal will involve DRs to record the disposal proceeds coming IN and to cancel the Provision for Depreciation, a DR or a CR in the P&L Account to record the loss or profit on disposal, and a CR to cancel the fixed asset cost:

| DR | M&P (money or promises) | £220 | |
|----|-------------------------|------|------|
| DR | Provision for Depreciation Account | £500 | |
| ? | P&L Account (loss or profit on disposal) | ? | ? |
| CR | Fixed Asset Cost Account | | £700 |

On this occasion a CR of £20 in the P&L Account is needed to make the journal entry balance. There is evidently a profit on disposal (an asset with a net book value of £200, was sold for £220).

The completed journal entry will be

| DR | M&P (money or promises) | £220 | |
|----|-------------------------|------|------|
| DR | Provision for Depreciation Account | £500 | |
| CR | P&L Account (profit on disposal) | | £20 |
| CR | Fixed Asset Cost Account | | £700 |

# JOURNAL ENTRIES TO TIDY UP

It sometimes happens that the disposal transaction has already been recorded, and the accountant is invited to tidy up the accounts at the end of the period. In this case the DR entry to an account for money or promises has already been made, with a corresponding CR to the Fixed

Asset Disposal Account. Tidying up will involve cancelling this CR (so that the Fixed Asset Disposal Account will end with a nil balance), as well as cancelling the fixed asset cost and provision for depreciation, and accounting for the profit or loss on disposal. Box 30.3 shows an example of the relevant journal entries.

## BOX 30.3

### Journal Entries to Complete the Accounting for a Disposal of a Fixed Asset

A firm has already recorded the receipt of £600 proceeds on disposal of a fixed asset. However the fixed asset remains recorded in the accounts at cost £950, less provision for depreciation £300.

Journal entries to complete the job of accounting for the disposal will involve DRs to cancel the entry on the Fixed Asset Disposal Account and to cancel the provision for depreciation, a DR or a CR in the P&L Account to record the loss or profit on disposal, and a CR to cancel the fixed asset cost:

| DR | Fixed Asset Disposal Account | £600 | |
|----|------------------------------|------|------|
| DR | Provision for Depreciation Account | £300 | |
| ? | P&L Account (loss or profit on disposal) | ? | ? |
| CR | Fixed Asset Cost Account | | £950 |

A DR of £50 in the P&L Account is needed to make the journal entry balance. Here there is a loss on disposal (an asset with a net book value of £650, was sold for £600).

The completed journal entry will be

| DR | Fixed Asset Disposal Account | £600 | |
|----|------------------------------|------|------|
| DR | Provision for Depreciation Account | £300 | |
| DR | P&L Account (loss on disposal) | £50 | |
| CR | Fixed Asset Cost Account | | £950 |

# REVIEW

This chapter has presented a quick method of accounting for the disposal of a fixed asset, without using a Fixed Asset Disposal Account. It has also shown a quick method of tidying up the accounts when the receipt of disposal proceeds has already been recorded, but no other accounting entries have been made.

# DRILLS AND EXERCISES

## 30.1 Drills to practise the quick method of accounting for the disposal of a fixed asset

For each example below, show the double entry for the quick method to account for the disposal of the fixed asset, or to complete the accounting for the disposal.

1. A fixed asset with original cost £10 000 and provision for depreciation £7 000 is sold with disposal proceeds £3 500.
2. A fixed asset with original cost £4 500 and provision for depreciation £3 000 is sold with disposal proceeds £1 200.
3. A fixed asset with original cost £9 700 and provision for depreciation £4 200 is sold with disposal proceeds £5 500.
4. A fixed asset with original cost £3 400 is sold for £1 000. Provision for depreciation on the fixed asset was £2 550.
5. A fixed asset with original cost £81 900 is sold for £22 600. The loss on disposal is £1 700.
6. A fixed asset is sold with £1 250 profit on disposal. Provision for depreciation on the fixed asset was £3 200, and disposal proceeds were £11 000.
7. A fixed asset is sold for £10 400, giving rise to a profit on disposal of £3 700. Total depreciation charged on the fixed asset during its life was £27 800.
8. A fixed asset is sold with profit on disposal £5 000. Original cost and cumulative depreciation were £89 000 and £43 000 respectively.
9. A fixed asset has been sold for £5 000. The firm has properly accounted for the disposal transaction but has not yet cancelled the fixed asset cost £40 000 and the provision for depreciation £36 000.
10. A fixed asset has been sold for £7 500. The firm has properly accounted for the disposal transaction but has not yet cancelled the fixed asset cost £30 000 and the provision for depreciation £20 000.

# CHAPTER 31

# Estimating Annual Depreciation

## OBJECTIVES

*The objectives of this chapter are:*

● to describe the four most commonly used methods of estimating annual depreciation
● to comment on the appropriate uses of each method

## FOUR COMMON METHODS

Changes in value can only be known with certainty when they are realized in the course of a transaction. To account for depreciation during the life of a fixed asset, therefore, as it happens, we must rely on estimates of the value lost in each period. Any reasonable method of estimation may be used, although at least four methods are so obvious, and so frequently used, that they have names of their own. These are:

● the valuation method;
● the 'straight line' method;
● the 'reducing balance' method; and
● the usage or depletion method.

While the names may be new, the methods are no more than common sense, and readers who have attempted the examples in the Drills and Exercises will have invented and used the methods for themselves.

Notice that in all of our examples in this chapter, we shall as usual assume a standard accounting period of one year. This corresponds to the usual accounting period of most firms in practice, although longer or shorter periods are of course possible.

## THE VALUATION METHOD

This method involves valuing the relevant fixed asset at the end of each year. The loss in value to be accounted for in any year will then be the difference between the value at the end of the year, and the value at the end of the previous year, or (if the asset was acquired during the year) the value at acquisition. Box 31.1 on the following page shows a simple example.

## BOX 31.1

### The Valuation Method of Estimating Annual Depreciation

**YEAR 1**

A fixed asset is acquired in Year 1 at a cost of £900. At the end of Year1 the fixed asset is valued at £700.

The depreciation charge in the P&L Account for Year 1 will therefore be £200 (being £900 minus £700).

Since this is the first year of the asset's life, the provision for depreciation in the balance sheet will also be £200.

**YEAR 2**

At the end of Year 2 the fixed asset is valued at £650.

The depreciation charge in the P&L Account for Year 2 will therefore be £50 (being £700 minus £650).

Provision for depreciation in the balance sheet will now be £250, representing the total loss in value so far.

## COMMENT ON THE VALUATION METHOD

At first sight, the valuation method seems the simplest and perhaps even the best method of estimating annual depreciation. However, it is open to objections in practice and in theory.

In practice the valuation method may be costly and unreliable. Valuation requires time and attention at the least, and possibly professional expertise as well, which is costly. In any case, valuation is always difficult and subjective unless there is an active market in the relevant kind of asset, where current values may be observed.

Theoretical objections to the valuation method are focussed on two points. These concern first, the appropriate meaning of 'value' in this context, and secondly, the ultimate purpose of accounting for depreciation, and the relative importance of the P&L Account against the balance sheet.

As regards the appropriate meaning of value, there are at least three possibilities. The value of a fixed asset could mean

- its value in the open market, if it were to be sold;
- its value to the business; or
- its replacement cost – that is, what the firm would have to pay in order to replace the fixed asset.

Box 31.2 presents an example to show how these may differ quite considerably.

## BOX 31.2

### Three Possible Meanings of Value

A firm buys a highly specialized fixed asset, constructed to its own specifications, at a cost of £100 000.

The firm expects the fixed asset to remain in use for several years, although it is so specialized that no other firm would have any use for it except as scrap.

*Market Value*
At the end of Year 1, the market value of the fixed asset would be very low, corresponding to its scrap value. Based on market value, the depreciation charge for the year would be very high.

*Value to the Firm*
Since the asset is expected to remain in use for several years, its value to the firm at the end of Year 1 must be not much less than the £100 000 that was just paid for it. Using this basis of valuation, the depreciation charge for the year would be comparatively low.

*Replacement Cost*
At the end of Year 1, the replacement cost of the fixed asset could be almost anything, depending on changes in technology, markets, and relative prices. The depreciation charge for the year would vary accordingly.

Which of these different concepts of value we choose as the most appropriate, depends upon our purpose in accounting for depreciation, and perhaps in whose interests we are doing the accounting. If our focus is on the balance sheet as a basis for investment decisions, then perhaps we would choose market value or replacement cost as the basis of valuation. If on the other hand our attention is focussed on the P&L Account and the value of inputs consumed in the period, then we might choose value to the firm as the basis of valuation, and hence as the basis of the depreciation charge. Here is not the place to dig deeper into such questions, though we shall return to some of them in a later chapter on depreciation in context.

## THE STRAIGHT LINE METHOD

The straight line method of estimating annual depreciation is based on the original cost of the fixed asset, and essentially depends on the assumption that the amount of value lost by a fixed asset is the same in each year of its life. An estimate of the value lost in each year is usually expressed as a percentage of original cost. Box 31.3 shows a simple example.

## BOX 31.3

### The Straight Line Method of Estimating Annual Depreciation

A fixed asset is acquired in Year 1 at a cost of £4 000. The firm charges depreciation at 25% per year on the straight line method.

The depreciation charge in each year of the fixed asset's life will be £1,000 (i.e. 25% × £4 000).

The provision for depreciation in the balance sheet at the end of Year 1 will be £1 000.
At the end of Year 2, the provision for depreciation will be £2 000, and so on.

If by chance the fixed asset should remain in the firm for longer than four years, then after Year 4 no further depreciation will be charged.

Having chosen to use the straight line method, how does a firm decide on the appropriate percentage rate to charge? The honest answer is probably just by experience or educated guess. If an asset looks as though it will last for about four years, the firm will charge straight line depreciation at 25% per year. If it looks as though the asset will last for about 50 years, straight line depreciation will be charged at 2% per year, and so on. An example of the calculations that may be involved is shown in Box 31.4.

## BOX 31.4

### Determining the Annual Rate of Straight Line Depreciation

A fixed asset is acquired in Year 1 at a cost of £10 000. The firm expects to use the fixed asset for six years, after which it will be sold for an estimated £1 000.

The annual charge for depreciation on the straight line basis can be calculated like this:

|                                | £        |
| ------------------------------ | -------- |
| original cost                  | 10 000   |
| *less* estimated residual value | (1000)   |
| 'depreciable amount'           | £9 000   |
|                                |          |
| estimated useful life          | 6 years  |
|                                |          |
| annual depreciation charge     | £9 000/6 = £1 500 per year |

Since £1 500 is 15% of £10 000, the firm's depreciation policy will be described as charging straight line depreciation at 15% per year, or as charging depreciation at 15% per year on cost.

## COMMENT ON THE STRAIGHT LINE METHOD

The straight line method is certainly the simplest and cheapest method of estimating annual depreciation. For that reason, it is almost certainly the method most frequently used in practice. However, there are some assets for which the straight line method would not be entirely appropriate.

The problem is that the straight line method seems to assume that loss in value is occasioned simply by the passage of time, with time itself flowing evenly throughout the life of a fixed asset. But loss in value is also accelerated or slowed by intensity of use. If a fixed asset is used very little in a given year, it may lose very little value. If used a lot, it may lose a lot of value. In addition to intensity of use, the rate at which a fixed asset loses value may also be affected by changes in technology and the economy at large.

It follows, perhaps, that the straight line method is most applicable when a fixed asset will be used evenly throughout its life, and when it exists in a stable economic and technological environment. Outside of those conditions, other methods may be more appropriate.

## THE REDUCING BALANCE METHOD

The reducing balance method of estimating annual depreciation is again based on the original cost of the fixed asset. Here, the assumption is that the value lost in each year is always the same percentage of the value that remained at the start of the year. An example, as shown in Box 31.5, is probably more useful than further abstract description.

### BOX 31.5

**The Reducing Balance Method of Estimating Annual Depreciation**

A firm buys a fixed asset for £16 000. The firm estimates that in any year the fixed asset will lose 25% of the value it had at the beginning of the year.

This policy will be described as charging depreciation at 25% per year on the reducing balance. Relevant calculations will be:

|  | £ |
|---|---|
| original cost | 16 000 |
| Year 1 depreciation 25% × 16 000 | (4 000) |
| remaining value | 12 000 |
| Year 2 depreciation 25% × 12 000 | (3 000) |
| remaining value | 9 000 |
| Year 3 depreciation 25% × 9 000 | (2 250) |
| etc. | etc. |

## COMMENT ON THE REDUCING BALANCE METHOD

The reducing balance method is characterized by an annual charge for depreciation which gets smaller as the asset gets older, which is probably a fair reflection of the way in which most fixed assets do actually lose value. In the early years of its life, a fixed asset will tend to lose value quickly, but towards the end of its life, the rate of loss in value will slow down – that is, the value lost in each year will be progressively less as there is less value left to lose.

The reducing balance method may therefore seem to be a more faithful representation of what happens in real life. However, this truth may be irrelevant or even perhaps misleading, as shown by the example in Box 31.6.

## BOX 31.6

### Reducing Balance and Cost per Unit

A firm acquires a fixed asset in Year 1 for £16 000, and charges depreciation at 25% per year on the reducing balance, as shown in Box 31.5. Assume for simplicity that other costs or expenses are negligible.

Production is 1 000 units per year for the first three years of the asset's life.
The cost per unit for each year is there fore as given in the table below

|  | Year 1 | Year 2 | Year 3 |
|---|---|---|---|
| depreciation charge | £4 000 | £3 000 | £2 250 |
| annual production | 1 000 units | 1 000 units | 1 000 units |
| cost per unit | £4.00 | £3.00 | £2.25 |

In terms of cost per unit, this result is highly misleading. It falsely implies that the firm is becoming progressively more efficient, with lower unit costs in successive years. It also raises the possibility that older machines will appear to be more efficient than newer machines.

Advocates of the reducing balance method argue that its results are not so misleading as our example would seem to indicate. In fact, the reducing balance method may well give a more stable cost per unit than the straight line method. This is because the total cost of using a fixed asset is actually composed of two elements – depreciation, and repairs and maintenance. As a fixed asset gets older, we expect the cost of repairs and maintenance to increase. Meanwhile, with the reducing balance method of estimation, the reported cost of depreciation will decrease from year to year. The combined total cost of using the asset (increasing repair cost, and decreasing depreciation expense), as reported in the P&L Account, will therefore remain roughly constant, and the absurdities suggested above will not arise in practice.

## THE USAGE OR DEPLETION METHOD

With the usage method, the estimate of value lost in any year depends on how intensively the fixed asset is used in that year. The example in Box 31.7 is probably clearer than further abstract description.

BOX 31.7

### The Usage Method of Estimating Annual Depreciation

A firm acquires a delivery van as a fixed asset, at a cost of £12 000. The van is expected to run for 240 000 miles before it is scrapped with no remaining value.

Depreciation per mile is therefore £12 000/240 000 = 5p per mile.

In Year 1, the van runs 16 000 miles.
Applying the usage method of estimation, the firm's depreciation charge for Year 1 will be
$$16 000 \times 5p = £800$$

In Year 2, the van runs for 24 000 miles.
Applying the usage method of estimation, the firm's depreciation charge for Year 2 will be
$$24 000 \times 5p = £1 200$$

## DEPLETION

In extractive industries like drilling for oil, mining, and quarrying, 'depletion' means the rate at which reserves are extracted. Oil wells, mines and quarries are of course fixed assets, and they lose value as their reserves are extracted. The depletion method of charging depreciation recognizes this, and charges depreciation accordingly. It is therefore similar in principle to the usage method. If it costs £10 million to dig a new mine which contains one million tonnes of valuable ore, then the depreciation charge for the mine as a fixed asset should be £10 per tonne of ore extracted in the period. And so on.

## COMMENT ON THE USAGE OR DEPLETION METHOD

Although usage is not the only factor which contributes to the loss in value of a fixed asset, the usage method of estimating annual depreciation does carry a certain logical appeal. It means that periods when production is high, will also carry a high depreciation charge. When production is low, the depreciation charge also will be low. This seems to be fair.

The principal drawback of the usage method is the cost of applying it. While it is simple enough in a textbook to say for example that 'in Year 1 the van runs for 16 000 miles' (or whatever), in real life it would be inordinately costly to record, collect and process such detailed information for a vast number of fixed assets. It is no wonder that other methods of estimation are preferred in practice, except when the firm is required to make a record of the usage of a fixed asset in any case, for legal, safety, or other economic reasons. Having said that, however, we must recognize that developments in information technology may soon make it possible to monitor fixed asset usage automatically and to process the information at very low cost. Where and when that happens, we may well expect the usage method to replace some of the other, cruder methods that were developed in the days when data collection and information processing were labour intensive, prone to error and expensive.

# DEPRECIATION AND ACCOUNTING FOR DEPRECIATION

In the context of making an estimate of annual depreciation, it is worth remarking that the word depreciation is commonly used to mean either actual loss in value, or the process of accounting for loss in value. Thus, for example, if we read that 'depreciation is 20% per year', it is not quite certain whether this means that a fixed asset does actually lose 20% of its value in each year, or merely that the firm has decided to account for that much loss in value in each year.

The distinction is not trivial, and the ambiguity should be avoided. Depreciation in its primary sense (loss in value) is an economic process which takes place regardless of whether or how we account for it. Depreciation in its secondary sense (accounting for loss in value) is a matter of choice and policy. Moreover, depreciation in its primary sense (what actually happens) has an unavoidable effect on the real profits of a firm. Depreciation in its secondary sense (how we account for it) affects only the reported profits of a firm, and can be altered or adjusted at will.

# AMORTIZATION

Amortization means accounting for loss in value. The word amortization is particularly favoured in connection with the loss in value of intangible fixed assets like goodwill, or purely time-based assets like a lease on a property for a fixed number of years. To amortize an asset or an item of expenditure means to account for its loss in value over a number of years.

# FIXED ASSETS OWNED FOR ONLY PART OF A PERIOD

It seldom happens that a firm will buy a fixed asset on the very first day of an accounting period, or that a firm will dispose of a fixed asset on the very last day of an accounting period. When the firm has adopted a time-based method of estimating depreciation, like straight line or reducing balance, this can present a problem. In general, these methods tell us what the depreciation charge should be *for a year*. The question then is: should the annual depreciation charge be reduced proportionately, if, in the year of acquisition or disposal, the firm has held the asset for less than a year?

In practice it would seem that free choice is allowed, and the simplest way is:

- to charge a full year's depreciation in the year of acquisition; and
- no depreciation in the year of disposal.

Whatever choice is made, it should be realized that it will make no difference to the overall reported profit or loss of the firm in the year of disposal. (The profit or loss on disposal will always adjust to ensure that the total loss in value accounted for is equal to the actual loss in value experienced by the fixed asset.) For the same reason, although it may make a small difference to the reported profit or loss of the firm in the year of acquisition, whatever choice we make will not affect the aggregate reported profit or loss of the firm over the life of the fixed asset.

Where it is necessary to specify the chosen method, accountants often rely on a slight difference of expression. If depreciation is charged *at* x% per year on fixed assets held at the balance sheet date, it means that no depreciation will be charged on disposals made during the year and a full year's depreciation will be charged on all other fixed assets, including new acquisitions. If depreciation is charged *at the rate of* x% per year, it means that where a fixed asset has been held for part of a year (because it was acquired or disposed of during the year), then part of a year's depreciation should be charged in the P&L Account. Examiners set questions on this sort of thing to see if candidates are capable of reading instructions with due care (a valuable skill, and not only for prospective accountants). Otherwise, in theory and in practice, its significance is vanishingly small.

## CHOICE OF METHOD

Exactly how the annual charge for depreciation should be estimated, is not yet rigidly prescribed in theory or in practice. The rule is only that depreciation should be accounted for 'in a consistent manner which reflects as fairly as possible the pattern in which the asset's economic benefits are consumed by the firm'.

The appropriate method will, therefore, vary from one kind of asset to another and from one firm to another. Note, however, that the depreciation charge for the year is another figure which must be brought in from outside the accounts, and which is self-balancing, like the figure for the value of closing stock. To avoid the manipulation and deliberate mis-statement of profits or losses, it is important that it should be estimated fairly and by a method consistently applied from one year to the next.

## REVIEW

This chapter has described the four most frequently used methods of estimating the annual depreciation of a fixed asset. It has also made some general comments on the relative merits of each method.

## DRILLS AND EXERCISES

### 31.1  To practise the different methods of estimating annual depreciation

#### BUSINESS 1

At the beginning of a year, a fixed asset is in the balance sheet of a business at cost £12 000, less depreciation £3 000.

At the end of the year, the fixed asset remains in the business.

Show a P&L Account extract for the year, and an extract from the closing balance sheet, as they would be under each of the following assumptions:

1. depreciation is charged at 25% per year on cost;
2. depreciation is charged at 25% per year on the reducing balance;
3. the fixed asset is valued at £7 500 at the end of the year.

#### BUSINESS 2

At the beginning of a year, a fixed asset is in the balance sheet of a business at cost £16 000, less depreciation £5 000.

At the end of the year, the fixed asset remains in the business.

Show a P&L Account extract for the year, and an extract from the closing balance sheet, as they would be under each of the following assumptions:

1. depreciation is charged at 10% per year on the straight line method;
2. depreciation is charged at 10% per year on the reducing balance.

## BUSINESS 3

A fixed asset with original cost £100 000 has been held by a business for three years.

Calculate the total depreciation charged to date (to the end of YEAR 3) and the net book value of the asset, under each of the following assumptions:

1. the policy of the firm has been to charge depreciation at 20% per year on the reducing balance;
2. the policy of the firm has been to charge depreciation at 20% per year on cost.

For each assumption, also calculate the profit or loss on disposal that would be reported if the fixed asset were sold for £45 000 at the start of YEAR 4.

## 31.2 An exercise on the choice of different methods of estimating annual depreciation

Identify the depreciation policy that might probably be applied to each of the following fixed assets:

1. a 20-year lease on land and buildings
2. antique fixtures and fittings in the boardroom of a large company
3. a freehold building kept in good repair
4. a computerized accounting system
5. freehold land
6. a passenger aircraft
7. a motor vehicle
8. a durable machine expected to have a long useful life
9. a new factory built by a military uniform manufacturer at the start of a war, to cater for increased demand (when such equipment would normally have a useful life of 10 years)

## 31.3 An exercise on the effects of depreciation policy

1. You are the financial director of a company which has just started with high investment in fixed assets. Investors in the firm are prepared to tolerate low profits in the early years, as the new firm establishes itself, but they do expect profits to rise steadily over time.

   State the depreciation policy you would advise your fellow directors to adopt, and explain why.

2. State the effect on reported profits of the following changes in accounting assumptions:

   (a) longer asset lives
   (b) higher residual values (that is, higher expected disposal proceeds)
   (c) faster technological change in the industry
   (d) shorter asset lives

# CHAPTER 32

# Revenue and Capital

## OBJECTIVES

*The objectives of this chapter are:*

- to describe the distinction between a revenue transaction and a capital transaction
- to explain the associated differences between expenditure and expense, and receipt and income
- to show the importance of these distinctions for the avoidance of fraudulent mis-statements

## REVENUE TRANSACTIONS AND CAPITAL TRANSACTIONS

A revenue transaction is a transaction which has, or should have, a direct and immediate effect on the Income Statement or P&L Account. A capital transaction is one which does not, or should not, immediately affect the income statement or P&L Account.

## EXPENDITURE AND EXPENSES

Accounting terminology is fluid and often inconsistent, but a useful distinction is generally observed between *expenditure* and *expenses*:

- expenditure means spending – that is, actually paying out money or promises;
- expenses means the value of inputs consumed in a period.

While expenses evidently reduce profit, expenditure does not in itself affect profit or loss. Money or promises are exchanged for something else of equal value – an input. Actual profit is affected only when the relevant input is consumed, and reported profit is affected only when the DR recording the input is transferred to the P&L Account.

# REVENUE EXPENDITURE AND CAPITAL EXPENDITURE

Revenue expenditure is expenditure (spending money or promises) on inputs which are consumed immediately, or at least in the same period as the spending. Each item of revenue expenditure therefore involves an expense, and a reduction in profit for the period. Examples would include spending on electricity, heat and light, transport and suchlike inputs which are apparently consumed on entry into the firm.

Capital expenditure is expenditure on an input which is *not* consumed immediately. Capital expenditure includes most obviously any spending involved in the acquisition of a fixed asset. The significant point is that capital expenditure entails no corresponding expense in the P&L Account of the period. Profit is not reduced immediately or in the same period as the spending, but gradually as the value of the input is consumed.

In terms of the double entry, all expenditure is recorded with a CR to show money or promises going OUT, and a DR to show the relevant input coming IN. The distinction between revenue expenditure and capital expenditure is relevant only to the treatment of the DR at the end of the period. In the case of revenue expenditure (relating to an input consumed in the period) the DR is (or ought to be) transferred in full to the P&L Account as an expense. In the case of capital expenditure (relating to an input that is not consumed) the DR is (or ought to be) left on its own account, to be listed in the balance sheet as a fixed asset. In this context, there is even a verb 'to capitalize' expenditure, which means to show the object of the expenditure as an asset in the balance sheet (and not, therefore, as an expense in the P&L Account).

For accountants, the problem of what to do with the DR is often a question of judgement. It might be fair to say therefore, that calling a transaction 'revenue expenditure' merely indicates a decision to treat the expenditure as relating to an expense, while calling it 'capital expenditure' would indicate a decision to treat the expenditure as relating to the creation or acquisition of a fixed asset.

# FRAUD AND THE MISCLASSIFICATION OF EXPENDITURE

While the difference between a fixed asset (capital expenditure) and an expense (revenue expenditure) may seem to be gross and self-evident, it does not in fact require much imagination to find cases where there could be room for doubt, error, or deception. For example, there is a fine line between repairs and maintenance (revenue expenditure) and renewal or improvement of a fixed asset (capital expenditure). There is also often good reason for classifying certain items as capital expenditure, which at first sight may appear to be revenue expenditure. Thus the total cost of a fixed asset, all of it legitimately classified as capital expenditure, would include not only the purchase cost of the asset itself, but also all the costs of legal advice and contract negotiation, plus delivery, installation, testing and so on. In the case of development property, even the interest on a loan to purchase or develop the property is allowable as capital expenditure (part of the cost of the fixed asset). In a firm which constructs its own fixed assets, even such items as wages (paid to the persons making the fixed asset) can be properly classified as capital expenditure.

When revenue expenditure is misclassified as capital expenditure, what should be an expense in the P&L Account is shown as a fixed asset in the balance sheet, and profit is overstated. The deliberate misclassification of expenditure can therefore seem to make expenses vanish, and is a well-known fraudulent method of boosting reported profits. Box 32.1 shows the effect through a simplified extract from an extended trial balance.

## BOX 32.1

### The Classification of Inputs and Reported Profit

In the extended trial balance below, input 1 is classified as revenue expenditure and included in the P&L Account.

On the basis of the figures shown, the firm would report a **profit of £1 500**, with no fixed assets.

| | Trial Balance | | P&L Account | | Balance Sheet | |
|---|---|---|---|---|---|---|
| | DR | CR | DR | CR | DR | CR |
| sales | | 2 000 | | 2 000 | | |
| | | | | | | |
| **input 1** | 500 | | 500 | | | |
| etc | | | | | | |

Input 1 has now been reclassified as capital expenditure and included in the balance sheet as a fixed asset.

On the basis of these figures, the firm will report a **profit of £2 000**, with a fixed asset of £500.

| | Trial Balance | | P&L Account | | Balance Sheet | |
|---|---|---|---|---|---|---|
| | DR | CR | DR | CR | DR | CR |
| sales | | 2 000 | | 2 000 | | |
| | | | | | | |
| **input 1** | 500 | | | | 500 | |
| etc | | | | | | |

Misclassification of expenditure to boost reported profit is a favourite method among fraudsters, in part because of the availability of grey areas to exploit, but also because it is difficult at first to detect from outside. Fraudulent overstatement of profit is often detectable because despite its apparent profits, the firm is often short of cash. However, misclassification of expenditure contains its own excuse for a shortage of cash and the story is quite plausible: the firm is short of cash because it is investing in fixed assets, in order to expand and take advantage of its profitability.

As a matter of principle, accountants are encouraged to treat all expenditure as revenue expenditure, unless there is clear evidence that the expenditure has given rise to a fixed asset or some other future benefit. (The principle is prudence.) Every input is, as it were, presumed guilty of being an expense until proven innocent.

# REVENUE INVESTMENT

Strictly speaking, 'revenue investment' is a contradiction in terms. There is revenue expenditure and there is capital investment, but there is no such thing as revenue investment. However, the expression is sometimes used to indicate expenditure which must be treated as an expense under normal accounting rules (applying the principle of prudence), but which, in the opinion of the speaker, should be regarded as capital expenditure because it will result in some future benefit to the firm. An example might be the expenditure on an extensive advertising campaign. Prudence would dictate that this should be treated as an expense of the year in which it occurs, but it may yet be called revenue investment because, if successful, it could establish the firm or the product and generate sales for years into the future.

# RECEIPTS AND INCOME

The distinction between expenditure and expenses is matched by a similar distinction between *receipts* and *income*. Any money coming in to the firm, for whatever reason, is a receipt. Income, however, refers to the value that comes in, in exchange for the value of outputs created by a firm. The value of such outputs (being equal to the income they have drawn in to the firm) is matched against expenses (inputs consumed) in the P&L Account or Income Statement. Income, therefore, contributes to profit, while receipts could come from anywhere.

# CAPITAL RECEIPTS AND REVENUE RECEIPTS

A *capital* receipt means a payment coming in to the firm from the owner (or possibly from a lender). Such receipts have no connection with the generation of profit or the P&L Account. By contrast a *revenue* receipt is a receipt of money in exchange for some output created. A revenue receipt represents income, in the same way that revenue expenditure represents an expense.

# FRAUD AND THE MISCLASSIFICATION OF RECEIPTS

For those who wish to perpetrate a fraud by the overstatement of profits, misclassifying capital receipts as revenue receipts is an extremely attractive option, albeit difficult to achieve. Essentially, it involves falsely claiming that money coming in from investors is in fact coming in to the firm in respect of sales, and therefore contributing to profit. If capital receipts can be successfully disguised as revenue, the more money that investors pay in to the firm, the higher will be its reported profits. Furthermore, the higher the firm's reported profits, the more investors will be willing to pay in. (Notice that this fraud has the special attraction of actually accumulating cash within the firm. Most other accounting frauds are self-limiting. They provoke suspicion and collapse when the firm runs out of money.) Fortunately the distinction between revenue receipts and capital receipts is in general very clear-cut and it takes considerable skill and ingenuity to set up a situation in which a fraud of this nature can be executed and concealed, even temporarily.

# REVIEW

This chapter has introduced the distinction between revenue expenditure and capital expenditure, and the corresponding distinction between revenue receipts and capital receipts. It has also outlined the significance of the distinction in each case and the way in which profits can be mis-stated by accidental or deliberate failure to make the appropriate distinction.

# DRILLS AND EXERCISES

## 32.1  A drill to practise the different year-end treatments of revenue expenditure and capital expenditure

### REQUIRED

(a) Show how each of the following transactions would be initially recorded in the accounts of the business concerned;

(b) show any necessary transfers (to the P&L Account or otherwise) at the year-end; and

(c) show how any remaining balances would be shown in the balance sheet at the year-end.

1. At the start of a year, a business purchases a machine for use in the business, paying a total price of £7 650 to the supplier. The price paid is made up as follows:

|  | £ |
|---|---|
| machine | 4 500 |
| installation | 1 000 |
| one year's insurance | 150 |
| one year's servicing | 200 |
| delivery charge | 300 |
| training for machine operators | 1 500 |
|  | £7 650 |

The business expects to use the machine for 15 years before it is scrapped with no value.

2. The payments made by a building firm during a period include wages £540 000 and building materials £400 000.

   Included in these amounts are wages of £20 000 in respect of work done on a new storage shed which the firm has built for itself, and materials costing £30 000 which were also used in the construction of the new shed.

3. A pharmaceutical business pays total salaries of £500 000 in a period.

   Analysis at the end of the period shows that this includes salaries of production managers £300 000, and salaries of research scientists £200 000.

Of the salaries paid to research scientists, £120 000 relates to general research with no specific project yet envisaged, while £80 000 relates to final testing of a new drug to be marketed in the following year.

## 32.2 An exercise on the distinction between capital expenditure and revenue expenditure

### REQUIRED

State whether the following should be treated as capital expenditure or revenue expenditure. Give reasons for your decision and/or state any further information you may need in order to make a decision.

In the case of capital expenditure, also outline the depreciation policy you would propose for the relevant fixed asset.

1. legal fees in connection with the purchase of land for construction of a new factory
2. major repairs to the roof of a building
3. purchase of a pencil sharpener and stapler for use in an office
4. purchase of hand-tools by a self-employed craftsman
5. purchase of hand-tools by an engineering factory
6. purchase of overalls for factory workers
7. purchase of costumes by a nightclub artiste
8. staff training costs
9. patent registration fees
10. advertising to promote a special offer
11. advertising to promote 'name awareness'
12. legal fees in connection with defence of patent rights
13. costs of setting up a new accounting system
14. costs of recruiting skilled staff
15. major costs associated with arranging a very large long-term loan
16. cost of farm-workers' labour in digging drainage ditches
17. a football transfer fee of £8 million
18. market research prior to the launch of a new product

## 32.3

The government of an oil-producing country has plans for a tax on the profits of the foreign oil company that is licensed to drill and operate in the country.

The company argues that it should be able to deduct all exploration costs as an expense in the year of expenditure. The government argues that exploration costs should be treated capital expenditure and amortized at 8% per year.

Comment, and explain some of the consequences of the point at issue.

## 32.4

Research a company called WorldCom, and write a brief account of the fraud that led to its collapse in 2002.

# CHAPTER 33

# Depreciation in Context

## OBJECTIVES

*The objectives of this chapter are:*

- to show how the modern accounting treatment of depreciation has evolved in response to changes in the wider business environment
- to emphasize that depreciation relates to loss of value, not loss of money, and to outline the relation between accounting for depreciation and the problem of capital maintenance

## HISTORY

Accounting for depreciation is only significant to the extent that commercial investment in fixed assets is significant. The problem of accounting for depreciation was therefore quite safely ignored until quite recent times, because commercial investment in fixed assets was relatively small. Serious thinking about depreciation began with the industrial revolution of the 19th century and its development has been influenced as much by successive social changes as by its own internal logic.

## DEPRECIATION AND THE PROBLEM OF CAPITAL MAINTENANCE

The industrial revolution of the 19th century required unprecedented amounts of capital to invest in fixed assets of an entirely new kind – costly and long-lived, but ultimately subject to obsolescence through technological advance, as well as physical decay. Entrepreneurs and company projectors raised the necessary finance for investment in these new fixed assets partly by borrowing, and partly by selling shares in the expected profits of the companies they founded. To further their own careers and to enhance the value of the shares they held personally, it was vital for them to promise high profits, to report high profits, and to pay impressive annual dividends to shareholders. Meanwhile, shareholders bought their shares in the expectation that they were buying a source of income that could, and should, continue indefinitely into the future.

At the time it seemed clear to both entrepreneurs and investors that once the new machinery had been bought, or once a railway had been built and equipped with signals, engines, and rolling stock, then with just a little regular repair and maintenance, it would last indefinitely. Any cash receipts in excess of maintenance and running costs could be counted as profit and distributed as dividend to shareholders.

However, even with the finest programme of repairs and maintenance, no fixed asset will last forever. Moreover, physical decay is probably not the major problem. Even if a machine or industrial building could last forever, the increasing pace of technological change would sooner or later require it to be replaced with another one to do a different job, or to do the same job more efficiently. Without allowing for this loss in value when they calculated profit, many early shareholders found out too late that the dividends they thought they could spend as income, actually contained some element that was in fact a depletion or repayment of their capital. Ultimately they could be left with nothing, as their fixed assets became worn out or obsolete, and there was nothing left in the company to replace them. This is the problem of capital maintenance – preserving sufficient value in the business for it to continue to generate profits indefinitely into the future.

The solution was to require companies to account for depreciation. 'Profit' should be reduced to reflect the loss in value suffered by fixed assets. With the reduction in reported profits, would come a reduction in company dividends. Thus value would be retained in the company, to make up for the consumption of fixed asset value. The company would therefore be able to renew itself and preserve its value indefinitely. It would be safe for shareholders to assume that their dividends would continue without end. (An alternative solution might have been to warn shareholders that the assets in their company were wearing out, and advise them that in order to preserve their wealth they should not treat all of their annual dividends as disposable income, but rather save and reinvest some part of it.)

## DEPRECIATION AND PRICE CONTROL

The next strong influence on our thinking about depreciation was the development of price controls in certain industries, and the use of 'cost-plus' contracts to prevent profiteering by government suppliers. On the whole, entrepreneurs tend to disfavour accounting for depreciation – it reduces reported profits, and is therefore a handicap as they compete to raise capital from investors. However, price controls and cost-plus contracts will encourage a firm to search for, and even to exaggerate, every possible item of cost to justify demands for higher selling prices. Depreciation is obviously one such item, and the proper method or rate of depreciation to be used in determining the real cost of a unit of output became a matter of serious study, entering into the negotiation of contracts and even into the law, in the case of regulated industries.

## THE NEEDS OF THE CAPITAL MARKET

A third development which concentrated attention on the problem of accounting for depreciation was the increasing acceptance, throughout the last century, of the idea that the object of buying a share in the profits of a company was not to gain an income from regular dividends, but rather to benefit from the movement of share prices. To run this game fairly, it became ever more important for stock market investors to receive fair and adequate information on which to base their estimates of the 'true' value of a share in the profits of a company. Any area of accounting that involved judgement (including depreciation) therefore became subject to closer examination and tighter constraints, designed to ensure that accounting information was as far as possible objective and comparable over time and between different companies.

## DEPRECIATION AND INFLATION

The final development which occasioned serious thinking about accounting for depreciation was the steady increase in the rate of inflation which occurred in most of the developed economies in the second half of the 20th century, and especially in the 1970s. Under the unadjusted rules of historical cost accounting, an input is recorded at its acquisition value and remains in the accounts of a firm at that value until it is consumed. Where there is inflation, therefore, the value of a long-lived fixed asset held in the firm may well be far in excess of the value at which it is recorded in the accounts. As we shall see, it is possible to adjust the accounts and revalue fixed assets, but where there is inflation, and historical costs are unadjusted, balance sheets will tend to understate the real value of fixed assets.

The problem here is not loss in value, but what appears to be an increase in value, and in the face of inflation it is fair to ask why we should bother to account for depreciation, or indeed whether there is any loss in value to be accounted for at all. Rigorous pursuit of these questions would lead us far into accounting theory, but the questions do arise in practice and cannot safely be ignored in further studies.

## MODERN THEORY OF DEPRECIATION

The modern theory of accounting for depreciation is largely a response to the problems raised by inflation. It has been contrived to allow the upward revaluation of fixed assets, which we shall consider in a later chapter, while avoiding any suggestion that a firm can legitimately avoid accounting for depreciation, even when the relevant asset appears to have increased in value. The logical basis of the theory is the proposition that *all fixed assets with a finite useful economic life must experience depreciation*, which must be accounted for through the P&L Account.

The proposition that *all fixed assets with a finite useful economic life must experience depreciation* is true by definition: every fixed asset with a finite useful life will eventually have no value at all (that is what it means to have a finite useful life). It follows that every such asset must experience depreciation, since, throughout its life, its value is progressively approaching nil. Freehold land being the only asset which conceivably has a more than finite useful economic life, this means that depreciation is suffered by every fixed asset except land, and this must be true, even in times of inflation. Box 33.1 shows a simple example of how the argument works.

## BOX 33.1

### Depreciation and Inflation

At the START of YEAR 1, a business acquires a fixed asset for £100. The asset has a well-known useful life of four years, after which it will have no remaining value, and will be replaced with another exactly equivalent fixed asset.

Assume now that by the END of YEAR 1, the price of a new, exactly equivalent fixed asset has doubled to £200.

This change in the price of new assets will (plausibly) cause an increase in the value of the one-year-old asset held by the firm, and so perhaps the firm has made a profit, and need not account for any depreciation.

## BOX 33.1   Continued

BUT the asset now held by the firm is worth less than it would have been if it were new.

THEREFORE by holding and using the asset for one year, the firm has actually experienced a loss in value, as shown in the figures below

| | start of YEAR 1 £ | end of YEAR 1 £ |
|---|---|---|
| price of new fixed asset with four-year life | 100 | 200 |
| price of one-year-old used fixed asset with three-year remaining life | | (150) |
| VALUE LOST in YEAR 1 | | £50 |

While the argument above may seem to be rather abstract and contrived, there is also a practical basis for the argument that firms should account for depreciation on all fixed assets, even if they appear to be increasing in value. It is grounded in the concept of capital maintenance. If in the end the purpose of accounting for depreciation is the maintenance of capital (the capacity to generate profits into the future), then at times of rising asset prices we should in fact restrict profits even more (with a higher depreciation charge) to ensure that sufficient resources are kept in the firm to allow for the replacement of fixed assets at higher prices in the future. Capital maintenance will be discussed at greater length in Part 4.

## DEPRECIATION AND MONEY

Finally, once again: depreciation means loss of value, not loss of money. Accounting for depreciation means making entries in accounts. It does not involve handling, moving, keeping or storing up money. There is no connection between depreciation and money, and no truth in the suggestion that accounting for depreciation somehow involves building up a store of cash to replace fixed assets when they are retired.

As we have seen in the discussion of capital maintenance, there is a relation between accounting for depreciation and the ability to replace fixed assets, but the relation is entirely indirect. Depreciation is an expense in the P&L Account and so accounting for depreciation will reduce reported profit. Prudent owners who wish to maintain their wealth, will try to ensure that the value they take out of a business each year and spend, is less than the real profit or increase in value that the business has generated. So accounting for depreciation, by reducing reported profit, should also reduce the value taken out of the business by its owners. In principle therefore (and in the absence of losses), accounting for depreciation should ensure that the business will at least maintain its net asset value, or, which is equivalent, it should preserve owners from the risk of taking out and consuming their own capital. Notice however, that this logic and this procedure cannot guarantee that the firm will have the *cash* required to replace its fixed assets when necessary, because the value thus kept in the business need not be in the form of money. It may be in the form of increased stock, or increased promises from debtors. If it ever did exist in the form of extra money, it may have been applied to reducing the firm's liabilities. Accounting for depreciation will preserve net assets in the firm. It will not in itself provide a store of cash.

# REVIEW

This chapter has looked at the context in which ideas about accounting for depreciation have developed, with reference to the problems of capital maintenance, price regulation, the information needs of the capital market and inflation. It briefly considered the present theory of accounting for depreciation and returned once more to the difference between accounting for depreciation and saving up a store of cash.

# DRILLS AND EXERCISES

There are no drills and exercises on this chapter.

# CHAPTER 34

# Profits, Losses, and Movements of Money

## OBJECTIVES

*The objectives of this chapter are:*

- to establish the difference between profits and losses and cash flows
- to describe the main causes of the difference, and how they work
- to show how to reconcile operating profit and cash flow from operations

## PROFIT AND CASH

The object of a business is to make a profit. But a business needs cash in order to operate and *profit* does not necessarily mean *more money* – indeed a firm which makes a profit in a period may very well end the period with less money than it started with. The importance of this distinction between profit and cash can hardly be overemphasized, for a firm which is perfectly profitable may fail entirely if it runs out of cash.

The distinction between making a profit and getting more money can be seen as a matter of definition: profit is made by a difference between the value of outputs created and the value of inputs consumed in order to create those outputs (it is not the difference between money coming in and money going out). Or, alternatively, the substance of profit is an increase in net assets (it is not an increase in money, which is only one of the elements involved). However, in this chapter we shall consider the four basic causes of the disjuncture between cash and profit. They are:

- Transactions on credit.
- Timing differences – that is, differences between the time at which inputs are paid for and the time at which they are consumed. (These differences arise in connection with stock and also in connection with fixed assets and depreciation.)
- Financial transactions – that is, borrowing, lending and repayment of loans.
- Transactions between the firm and its owner(s).

These causes, and the way in which they operate to separate the making of profit or loss from the getting or spending of money are summarized in Box 34.1.

## BOX 34.1

**Profit and Cash – Causes of the Difference**

| BASIC CAUSE | these events AFFECT PROFIT but NOT CASH | these events AFFECT CASH but NOT PROFIT |
|---|---|---|
| Transactions on Credit | sales on credit | cash received from debtors |
| | purchases on credit | cash paid to creditors |
| Timing Differences | consumption of stock | purchase of stock |
| | depreciation | purchase of fixed assets |
| | profit/loss on disposal | sale of fixed assets |
| Financial Transactions | | borrowing, lending, repayment of loans |
| Transactions with Owners | | new investment or cash withdrawn |

## TRANSACTIONS ON CREDIT

A transaction on credit is an exchange of goods or services for a promise to pay *later*. At some stage the promises involved in a transaction on credit must be exchanged for money, but in the interim there will be a difference between the sales and purchases which contribute to profit or loss and the flows of money which contribute to an increase or decrease of cash. Thus, a firm which buys for cash and sells on credit – paying out money for its purchases and collecting only promises for its sales – will certainly suffer a loss of cash, even if it is trading at a profit. (Its profits will take the form of more and more promises from debtors.) Meanwhile a firm which buys on credit and sells for cash will initially accumulate cash, even if it is trading at a loss, because it will be paying only promises out to its suppliers, while collecting money from its customers.

In the long term, with trading on credit, the difference between profit and cash flow is essentially governed by the rate of debtor collection and creditor payment.

## SALES ON CREDIT AND DEBTOR COLLECTION

In general, if sales go faster than debtor collection, the value of sales reported in the P&L Account will be greater than the value of money collected from debtors and some of the firm's profit will take the form of an increase in debtors, rather than an increase in money. On the other hand, a decrease in debtors would indicate that the firm is collecting cash faster than it is making sales and the value of cash collected from customers will be greater than the value of the sales reported in the P&L Account.

All other things being equal, the effects of debtor collection on the relation between profit and cash are as summarized in Box 34.2.

### BOX 34.2

**Profit and Cash – Effects of Debtor Collection**

|  | £ |  |
|---|---|---|
| PROFIT | X | PROFIT |
| *minus increase in Debtors* | (X) | minus sales not matched by money from customers |
| *plus decrease in Debtors* | X | plus money from customers in excess of sales for period |
| = INCREASE in CASH | X | = INCREASE in CASH |

## PURCHASES ON CREDIT AND CREDITOR PAYMENT

If a firm is making purchases at a faster rate than it is paying its suppliers, then there will be more purchases in the P&L Account than the firm has actually paid for. The firm will conserve its money for the moment, but will see an increase in creditors. On the other hand, a reduction in creditors would indicate that the firm has paid out money to suppliers in excess of the value of purchases made in the period. Thus, to reconcile profit and changes in cash, the adjustment in respect of creditors (all other things being equal) will be as shown in Box 34.3.

### BOX 34.3

**Profit and Cash – Effects of Creditor Payment**

|  | £ |  |
|---|---|---|
| PROFIT | X | PROFIT |
| *plus increase in Creditors* | X | add back purchases not matched by money paid to |
| *minus decrease in Creditors* | (X) | suppliers deduct money paid to suppliers in excess of purchases for period |
| = INCREASE in CASH | X | = INCREASE in CASH |

## TIMING DIFFERENCES – STOCK

When a firm increases its stock, it is paying out money for purchases which are not yet consumed. These purchases will not affect the profit of the current period. When a firm decreases its stock, it is consuming inputs in the current period (and thereby reducing its profit) but not reducing its money, for the inputs were already paid for in a previous period. The effect of these timing differences, concerning stock, on the relation between profit and cash can be summarized as shown in Box 34.4.

## BOX 34.4

**Profit and Cash – Effect of Changes in Stock**

|  | £ |  |
|---|---|---|
| PROFIT | X | PROFIT |
| *minus increase in Stock* | X | minus money spent on purchases not yet consumed |
| *plus decrease in Stock* | (X) | add back value consumed, that was already paid for |
| = INCREASE in CASH | X | = INCREASE in CASH |

# TIMING DIFFERENCES – DEPRECIATION AND PROFITS OR LOSSES ON DISPOSAL

Accounting for depreciation means accounting for loss or consumption of value, not loss of money. There is no corresponding loss of money in the period. (The relevant cash flow occurred when the fixed asset was first acquired.) Thus, if we want to move from reported profit to actual cash flow in a period, we must add back any depreciation charged in the P&L Account.

Also recall that profits and losses on disposal are in fact adjustments to depreciation, so to get back from profit to cash flow, any loss on disposal charged in the P&L Account must also be added back and any profit on disposal included in the P&L Account must be taken out again.

To get from profit to cash, therefore, we must strip out or reverse the non-cash adjustments made in the P&L Account in respect of depreciation, as shown in Box 34.5.

## BOX 34.5

**Profit and Cash – Effects of Depreciation and Related Adjustments**

|  | £ |
|---|---|
| PROFIT | X |
| *plus* depreciation for the period | X |
| *minus* Profit on Disposal | (X) |
| *plus* Loss on Disposal | X |
| = INCREASE in CASH | X |

# RECONCILING PROFIT AND CASH FROM OPERATIONS

In accounting, a reconciliation is a statement or explanation of differences, showing how one figure relates to another. With the adjustments in respect of debtors, creditors, stock and depreciation, we are now in a position to produce a complete reconciliation between operating profit and cash from operations, as shown in Box 34.6.

## BOX 34.6

**Reconciling Operating Profit and Cash from Operations**

The pro forma reconciliation statement below includes all the factors that will cause a difference between operating profit and cash flow from operations.

|  | £ |
|---|---|
| OPERATING PROFIT | X |
| *(minus increase) / plus decrease* in Debtors | (X) |
| *plus increase / (minus decrease)* in Creditors | X |
| *(minus increase) / plus decrease* in Stock | (X) |
| *plus* depreciation for the period | X |
| *(minus profit) / plus loss* on disposal | (X) |
| = CASH FROM OPERATIONS | X |

# PROFIT AND CASH FROM OPERATIONS – THE LOGIC OF THE RECONCILIATION

The possibility of an increase or a decrease in each of the separate elements, and the consequent reversal of its sign from plus to minus, or from minus to plus, make the reconciliation of operating profit and cash flow a rather daunting prospect, but there is no need to learn it blindly just by rote. One way to work out the sign attaching to each element, and understand the logic of the statement, is to recall that profit is an increase in net assets.

Thus, an increase in any non-cash asset (like debtors or stock) must mean that less of the firm's profit will take the form of an increase in cash. Meanwhile a decrease in any non-cash asset must mean that more of any profit must be in the form of money.

On the other hand, an increase in creditors must mean that the firm has kept hold of more money, by postponing payment to its suppliers. Conversely, a decrease in creditors will mean that the firm must have less money, having used it to pay off past suppliers.

# NON-OPERATIONAL CASH FLOWS

Operations are (only) those activities directly related to the making of a profit or a loss. A firm's total increase or decrease in cash over a period, however, will reflect not only its cash from operations, but also any cash flows in connection with non-operational activities, such as the purchase and sale of fixed assets, the payment of tax, financial transactions (borrowing, lending and repayment of loans) and transactions with the owner.

These non-operational cash flows need very little analysis. They contribute to a difference between cash and profit because, while they have no effect on the profit or loss reported by a firm, they have self-evident and often substantial effects on its holdings of cash. A profitable firm, for example, may experience a decrease in cash if it is buying new fixed assets, or using its cash to repay loans. Conversely, a loss-making firm may experience an increase in cash if it disposes of fixed assets, or raises a loan, or draws in fresh investment from its owners.

## REVIEW

This chapter has considered the four general factors giving rise to a difference between a firm's profit or loss for a period and its increase or decrease in cash. These are:

- transactions on credit;
- timing differences between purchase and consumption of inputs (stock as well as fixed assets);
- financial transactions, and
- transactions with the owner.

The chapter showed how to prepare a statement reconciling a firm's operating profit to its cash flow from operations and briefly considered the effect of non-operational cash flows, which affect a firm's holding of cash without affecting its profit or loss for a period.

## DRILLS AND EXERCISES

### 34.1

For each separate business below, produce a reconciliation between operating profit and the increase or decrease in cash held by the business during the period.

You may assume that there have been no transactions with the owner, and that the business has made no fixed asset purchases or disposals (any change in fixed asset value will be solely attributable to the depreciation charge for the year).

Remember that profit is reflected in an increase in net assets.

## BUSINESS 1

| OPENING BALANCE SHEET | | | CLOSING BALANCE SHEET | | |
|---|---|---|---|---|---|
| | £ | £ | | £ | £ |
| ASSETS | | | ASSETS | | |
| Fixed Assets | | 400 | Fixed Assets | | 375 |
| Stock | | 250 | Stock | | 200 |
| Trade debtors | | 125 | Trade debtors | | 100 |
| Bank | | 100 | Bank | | 90 |
| | | 875 | | | 765 |
| LIABILITIES | | | LIABILITIES | | |
| Trade Creditors | 160 | | Trade Creditors | 20 | |
| Overdraft | | | Overdraft | | |
| | | (160) | | | (20) |
| NET ASSETS | | £715 | NET ASSETS | | £745 |
| CAPITAL | | £715 | CAPITAL | | £745 |

## BUSINESS 2

| OPENING BALANCE SHEET | | | CLOSING BALANCE SHEET | | |
|---|---|---|---|---|---|
| | £ | £ | | £ | £ |
| ASSETS | | | ASSETS | | |
| Fixed Assets | | 350 | Fixed Assets | | 325 |
| Stock | | 220 | Stock | | 200 |
| Trade debtors | | 140 | Trade debtors | | 210 |
| Bank | | 130 | Bank | | 120 |
| | | 840 | | | 855 |
| LIABILITIES | | | LIABILITIES | | |
| Trade Creditors | 45 | | Trade Creditors | 55 | |
| Overdraft | | | Overdraft | | |
| | | (45) | | | (55) |
| NET ASSETS | | £795 | NET ASSETS | | £800 |
| CAPITAL | | £795 | CAPITAL | | £800 |

## BUSINESS 3

| OPENING BALANCE SHEET | £ | £ | CLOSING BALANCE SHEET | £ | £ |
|---|---|---|---|---|---|
| ASSETS | | | ASSETS | | |
| Fixed Assets | | 325 | Fixed Assets | | 300 |
| Stock | | 200 | Stock | | 280 |
| Trade debtors | | 210 | Trade debtors | | 190 |
| Bank | | 120 | Bank | | 150 |
| | | 855 | | | 920 |
| LIABILITIES | | | LIABILITIES | | |
| Trade Creditors | 55 | | Trade Creditors | 105 | |
| Overdraft | | | Overdraft | | |
| | | (55) | | | (105) |
| NET ASSETS | | £800 | NET ASSETS | | £815 |
| CAPITAL | | £800 | CAPITAL | | £815 |

## BUSINESS 4

| OPENING BALANCE SHEET | £ | £ | CLOSING BALANCE SHEET | £ | £ |
|---|---|---|---|---|---|
| ASSETS | | | ASSETS | | |
| Fixed Assets | | 300 | Fixed Assets | | 275 |
| Stock | | 280 | Stock | | 100 |
| Trade debtors | | 190 | Trade debtors | | 50 |
| Bank | | 150 | Bank | | 450 |
| | | 920 | | | 875 |
| LIABILITIES | | | LIABILITIES | | |
| Trade Creditors | 105 | | Trade Creditors | 155 | |
| Overdraft | | | Overdraft | | |
| | | (105) | | | (155) |
| NET ASSETS | | £815 | NET ASSETS | | £720 |
| CAPITAL | | £815 | CAPITAL | | £720 |

## BUSINESS 5

| OPENING BALANCE SHEET | | | CLOSING BALANCE SHEET | | |
|---|---|---|---|---|---|
| | £ | £ | | £ | £ |
| ASSETS | | | ASSETS | | |
| Fixed Assets | | 275 | Fixed Assets | | 250 |
| Stock | | 100 | Stock | | 300 |
| Trade debtors | | 250 | Trade debtors | | 240 |
| Bank | | 450 | Bank | | 50 |
| | | 875 | | | 840 |
| LIABILITIES | | | LIABILITIES | | |
| Trade Creditors | 155 | | Trade Creditors | 100 | |
| Overdraft | | | Overdraft | | |
| | | (155) | | | (100) |
| NET ASSETS | | £720 | NET ASSETS | | £740 |
| CAPITAL | | £720 | CAPITAL | | £740 |

## BUSINESS 6

| OPENING BALANCE SHEET | | | CLOSING BALANCE SHEET | | |
|---|---|---|---|---|---|
| | £ | £ | | £ | £ |
| ASSETS | | | ASSETS | | |
| Fixed Assets | | 250 | Fixed Assets | | 225 |
| Stock | | 300 | Stock | | 350 |
| Trade debtors | | 240 | Trade debtors | | 300 |
| Bank | | 50 | Bank | | |
| | | 840 | | | 875 |
| LIABILITIES | | | LIABILITIES | | |
| Trade Creditors | 100 | | Trade Creditors | 100 | |
| Overdraft | | | Overdraft | 25 | |
| | | (100) | | | (125) |
| NET ASSETS | | £740 | NET ASSETS | | £750 |
| CAPITAL | | £740 | CAPITAL | | £750 |

## 34.2 A drill to practise the relation between operating profit and cashflow (with fixed asset purchases and disposals)

For each separate business below, produce a reconciliation between operating profit and the increase or decrease in cash held by the business during the period. You may assume there have been no tranactions with the owner.

### BUSINESS 7

| BUSINESS 7 OPENING BALANCE SHEET | | | BUSINESS 7 CLOSING BALANCE SHEET | | |
|---|---|---|---|---|---|
| | £ | £ | | £ | £ |
| ASSETS | | | ASSETS | | |
| Fixed Assets | | 225 | Fixed Assets | | 360 |
| Stock | | 350 | Stock | | 300 |
| Trade debtors | | 300 | Trade debtors | | 260 |
| Bank | | | Bank | | |
| | | 875 | | | 920 |
| LIABILITIES | | | LIABILITIES | | |
| Trade Creditors | 100 | | Trade Creditors | 110 | |
| Overdraft | 25 | | Overdraft | 45 | |
| | | (125) | | | (155) |
| NET ASSETS | | £750 | NET ASSETS | | £765 |
| CAPITAL | | £750 | CAPITAL | | £765 |

| | |
|---|---|
| During the period, the business acquired a new fixed asset for | £300 |
| and disposed of a fixed asset for | £150 |
| Net book value of the disposal was | £125 |
| Depreciation charged in the year was | £40 |

## BUSINESS 8

| BUSINESS 8<br>OPENING BALANCE SHEET | | | BUSINESS 8<br>CLOSING BALANCE SHEET | | |
|---|---|---|---|---|---|
| | £ | £ | | £ | £ |
| ASSETS | | | ASSETS | | |
| Fixed Assets | | 360 | Fixed Assets | | 270 |
| Stock | | 300 | Stock | | 300 |
| Trade debtors | | 260 | Trade debtors | | 260 |
| Bank | | | Bank | | 130 |
| | | 920 | | | 960 |
| LIABILITIES | | | LIABILITIES | | |
| Trade Creditors | 110 | | Trade Creditors | 145 | |
| Overdraft | 45 | | Overdraft | | |
| | | (155) | | | (145) |
| NET ASSETS | | £765 | NET ASSETS | | £815 |
| CAPITAL | | £765 | CAPITAL | | £815 |

| | |
|---|---|
| During the period, the business | |
| acquired a new fixed asset for | £100 |
| disposed of a fixed asset for | £140 |
| Net book value of the disposal was | £160 |
| Depreciation charged in the year was | £30 |

# CHAPTER 35

# Accruals and Prepayments

## OBJECTIVES

*The objectives of this chapter are:*

- to explain the difference between the value recorded on an expense account, and the value consumed in a period
- to explain the meaning of the terms accrual and prepayment
- to show how to account for accruals and prepayments at the end of a period

## THE PRINCIPLE OF ACCRUALS

The principle of accruals, or matching, is the doctrine that a firm's P&L Account or Income Statement should show the value of outputs actually delivered in a period, matched against the value of inputs consumed in order to create those outputs. In practice, however, the ledger accounts of a business are used to record transactions – movements of money or promises. Thus, inputs and outputs are not recorded when they are consumed or created, but only when they are required to explain a movement of money or promises.

It follows that an input or an output can be recorded in an account only if/when it has been paid for in money or in promises. The actual delivery of outputs and consumption of inputs are non-financial, physical events which are not recorded in the accounts. Box 35.1 on the following page is an illustration of the problem insofar as it concerns inputs.

BOX 35.1

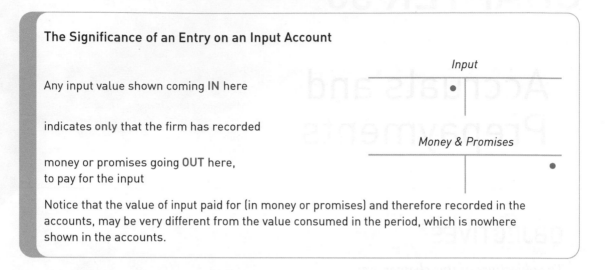

**The Significance of an Entry on an Input Account**

Any input value shown coming **IN** here

indicates only that the firm has recorded

money or promises going **OUT** here,
to pay for the input

Notice that the value of input paid for (in money or promises) and therefore recorded in the accounts, may be very different from the value consumed in the period, which is nowhere shown in the accounts.

## PREPARING THE P&L ACCOUNT

So far as concerns expenses, preparing a firm's P&L Account for a period involves transferring the value of any inputs consumed OUT of the original input account and IN to the P&L Account. We now recognize however, that the account for an input does not show the value consumed, but only the value paid for in the period.

The simplest way around the problem is to simply ignore the value recorded on the input account. Being the value *paid for*, it is not the value we need to know. Instead we find the value *consumed* in the period from some other source, and transfer that value OUT of the input account and IN to the P&L Account.

Box 35.2 shows an example of the procedure. This solves the problem with respect to the P&L Account, but as we shall see, it may leave behind a problem in the form of a balance on the input account.

BOX 35.2

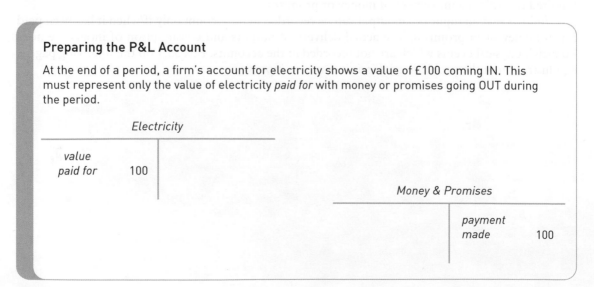

**Preparing the P&L Account**

At the end of a period, a firm's account for electricity shows a value of £100 coming IN. This must represent only the value of electricity *paid for* with money or promises going OUT during the period.

BOX 35.2   Continued

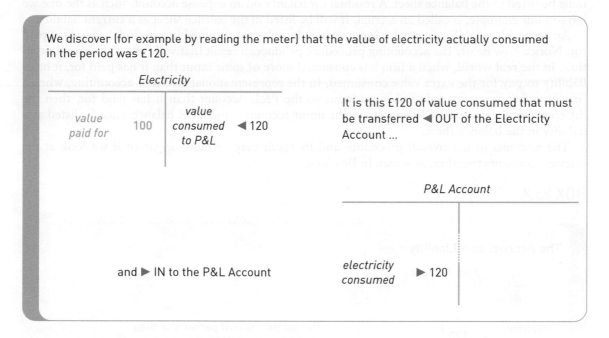

We discover (for example by reading the meter) that the value of electricity actually consumed in the period was £120.

*Electricity*

| value paid for | 100 | value consumed to P&L | ◀ 120 |

It is this £120 of value consumed that must be transferred ◀ OUT of the Electricity Account ...

*P&L Account*

and ▶ IN to the P&L Account

| | | electricity consumed | ▶ 120 | |

## ACCRUALS

In our example in Box 35.2 the value of the input (electricity) consumed is greater than the value paid for. In such a situation, when the P&L Account is prepared the value transferred OUT of the input account is greater than the value shown as coming IN, and after the transfer the input account will be left with a residual CR balance, as shown in Box 35.3.

BOX 35.3

### A Residual CR Balance on an Input Account

The firm in our example has paid for £100 of electricity, and has therefore recorded an input of ●£100 coming IN to the Electricity Account.

But the firm has consumed £120 of electricity and has therefore transferred ◀ £120 OUT of the Electricity Account to the P&L Account.

After the transfer, the Electricity Account will therefore be left with a **residual CR balance**, as shown below.

*Electricity*

| value paid for | ● 100 | value consumed to P&L | ◀ 120 |
|---|---|---|---|
| bal c/f | 20 | | |
| | 120 | | 120 |
| | | bal b/f | 20 |

Any balance on an account, after transfers to and from the P&L Account at the end of a period, must be listed in the balance sheet. A residual *CR* balance on an expense account, such as the one we have in our example, is called an accrual. It will be listed in the balance sheet as a current liability.

An accrual is a liability to pay for inputs which have been consumed in a period, but not yet paid for. Notice how neatly the accounting procedure produces a result that will reflect the actual situation. In the real world, when a firm has consumed more of some input than it has paid for, it has a liability to pay for the extra value consumed. In the representational world of accounting, when a firm transfers a greater value of some input to the P&L Account than it has paid for, then the difference will generate a CR balance on the input account – and a CR balance must be listed as a liability in the balance sheet.

The neatness of the overall procedure and its result may be more apparent if we look at the relevant accounts together, as shown in Box 35.4.

**BOX 35.4**

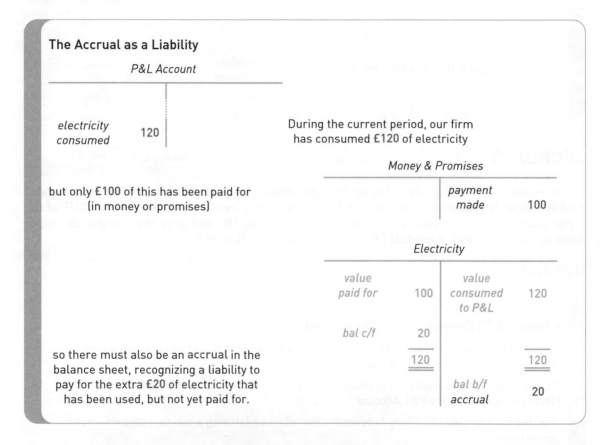

**The Accrual as a Liability**

P&L Account

electricity consumed    120

During the current period, our firm has consumed £120 of electricity

but only £100 of this has been paid for (in money or promises)

*Money & Promises*

payment made    100

*Electricity*

| value paid for | 100 | value consumed to P&L | 120 |
| bal c/f | 20 | | |
| | 120 | | 120 |
| | | bal b/f accrual | 20 |

so there must also be an accrual in the balance sheet, recognizing a liability to pay for the extra £20 of electricity that has been used, but not yet paid for.

# PREPAYMENTS

A prepayment arises when a firm has paid (in money or promises) for a greater value of some input than it has yet received. As a consequence, the value shown coming IN to the input account will be greater than the value transferred OUT to the P&L Account at the end of the period. Box 35.5 shows an example.

## BOX 35.5

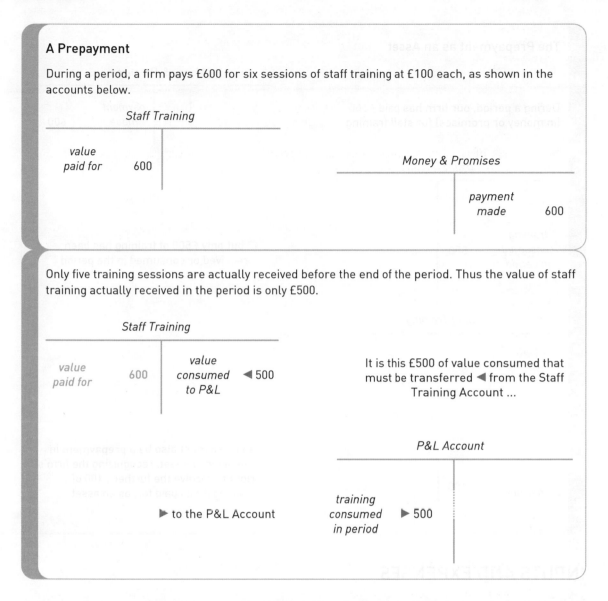

### A Prepayment

During a period, a firm pays £600 for six sessions of staff training at £100 each, as shown in the accounts below.

*Staff Training*

value
paid for     600

*Money & Promises*

payment
made     600

Only five training sessions are actually received before the end of the period. Thus the value of staff training actually received in the period is only £500.

*Staff Training*

value
paid for     600

value
consumed    ◀ 500
to P&L

It is this £500 of value consumed that must be transferred ◀ from the Staff Training Account ...

*P&L Account*

▶ to the P&L Account

training
consumed    ▶ 500
in period

In this instance, the input account will be left with a residual DR balance after the year-end transfer to the P&L Account. Any such residual DR balance is called a prepayment. It will be listed in the balance sheet as a current asset. A prepayment is an asset, not only because it is a DR balance, but because it represents a firm's right to enjoy a value it has paid for, but not yet received.

Notice once again how neatly the accounting procedure produces a result that is a fair reflection of legal or commercial reality, as shown in Box 35.6.

## BOX 35.6

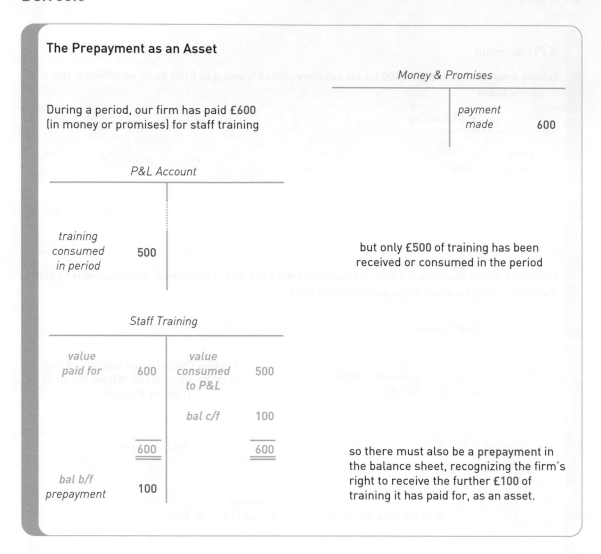

### The Prepayment as an Asset

*Money & Promises*

During a period, our firm has paid £600 (in money or promises) for staff training

| | | payment made | 600 |

*P&L Account*

| training consumed in period | 500 | |

but only £500 of training has been received or consumed in the period

*Staff Training*

| value paid for | 600 | value consumed to P&L | 500 |
| | | bal c/f | 100 |
| | 600 | | 600 |
| bal b/f prepayment | 100 | | |

so there must also be a **prepayment** in the balance sheet, recognizing the firm's right to receive the further £100 of training it has paid for, as an asset.

## INPUTS AND EXPENSES

The problem of accruals and prepayments draws particular attention to the two ways in which accountants use the word expense. Strictly, an expense, as shown in the P&L Account or Income Statement, is the value of any input consumed in a period. Since all inputs are eventually consumed, we can say that all inputs are on their way to becoming expenses. But at the time of the transaction when an input is acquired, we cannot know for certain whether its value will be consumed within the period or not. It is only at the end of the period that we can distinguish between unconsumed inputs (which are assets), and inputs consumed (which are expenses).

However, there are many inputs, like labour, rent, electricity and so on, which we can plausibly imagine to be consumed almost immediately on entry to the firm. Because they are generally consumed so quickly, these and similar inputs are traditionally called *expenses* without regard to whether or not they have yet been consumed; and the accounts on which they are recorded are called expense accounts. The issue of prepayments depends on large part on the difference between these two meanings: *loosely*, things may be called expenses because they are likely to be consumed immediately, but *strictly* they become expenses only when they are actually consumed.

# REVIEW

This chapter has shown (in respect of inputs) the contrast between the value recorded on an account, which is the value paid for; and the value that must be transferred to the P&L Account, which is the value consumed in the period. The chapter showed how this difference between value paid for and value consumed may leave a residual balance on an input account, after the appropriate period-end transfer to the P&L Account.

If the residual balance is a CR it must be listed in the balance sheet as a current liability called an accrual. An accrual represents the firm's liability to pay for things consumed but not yet paid for, in money or in promises. If the residual balance is a DR it must be listed in the balance sheet as a current asset, called a prepayment. A prepayment represents the firm's right to enjoy inputs it has already paid for but has not yet received or consumed.

# DRILLS AND EXERCISES

## 35.1

REQUIRED: For each set of data below show:
(a) relevant extracts from an account for money and/or promise;
(b) the relevant expense account; and
(c) relevant extracts from the P&L Account for the period and from the balance sheet at the end of the period.

1. During a period, a firm records £2 400 as payment, in money or promises, for labour.
   Labour actually used during the period was valued at £2 450.
2. During a period, a business receives and records invoices for legal services to the value of £1 500.
   Legal services actually used during the period were valued at £1 700.
3. A firm uses a credit control agency to check the records of customers who ask to be supplied on credit and has paid £400 for the right to make 40 searches in the agency's database at £10 per search.
   At the end of the period, the firm has made only 30 searches.
4. During a period, a firm receives and records invoices from its accountants, to the value of £3 450.
   Accounting services actually used during the period were valued £3 200.
5. The Electricity Account of a business at the end of a period (before transfers to the P&L Account) shows a balance of £500 DR.
   During the period, the business actually used electricity to the value of £520.
6. The Waste Disposal Account of a business at the end of a period (before transfers to the P&L Account) shows a balance of £230.
   During the period, the firm actually used waste disposal services to the value of £200.
7. During a period in which it recorded no transactions and made no payments in money or promises in respect of advertising, a firm actually used its advertising agency to do work to the value of £4 000.
8. In the final month of its accounting period, a firm pays £300 for a year's subscription to a trade magazine, their first copy of the magazine to be received in the following month (that is, in the following accounting period).

## 35.2

Describe and explain the different accounting treatments of
closing stock
fixed assets
prepayments

In what way are these items similar? Why is the accounting procedure for each of them
different, at the end of a period?

# CHAPTER 36

# Deferred Income and Accrued Income

## OBJECTIVES

*The objectives of this chapter are:*

- to explain the difference between the value recorded on a Sales Account and the value of sales delivered by the firm in a period
- to explain the meaning of the terms deferred income and accrued income
- to show how to account for deferred income and accrued income at the end of a period

## SALES AND THE PRINCIPLE OF ACCRUALS

During a period, the value recorded going OUT of a firm's Sales Account must be the value of sales paid for – that is, the value of sales for which the firm has received payment (in money or promises) coming IN from customers. At the end of the period, however, according to the principle of accruals, the value transferred from the Sales Account to the P&L Account should be the value of sales actually delivered to customers in the period. The value of sales paid for and the value of sales delivered may of course be entirely different and in such cases the Sales Account will be left with entries that will generate a residual balance, as happens in Box 36.1.

## BOX 36.1

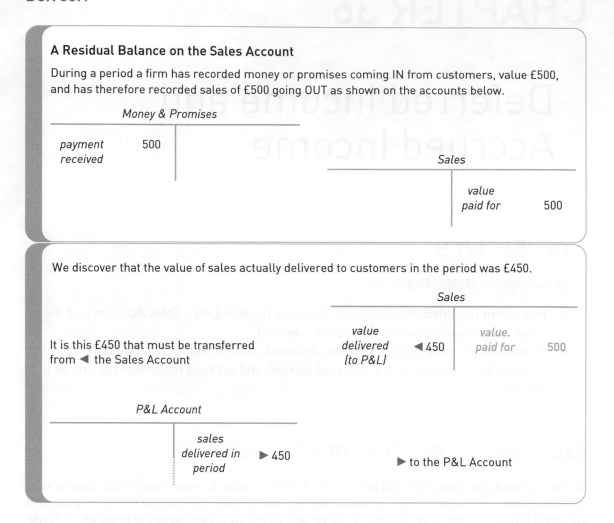

### A Residual Balance on the Sales Account

During a period a firm has recorded money or promises coming IN from customers, value £500, and has therefore recorded sales of £500 going OUT as shown on the accounts below.

*Money & Promises*

payment received    500

*Sales*

value paid for    500

We discover that the value of sales actually delivered to customers in the period was £450.

*Sales*

It is this £450 that must be transferred from ◄ the Sales Account

value delivered (to P&L)   ◄ 450     value. paid for    500

*P&L Account*

sales delivered in period   ► 450      ► to the P&L Account

## DEFERRED INCOME

If the residual balance on the Sales Account is a CR, it is called deferred income. Deferred income is listed in the balance sheet as a current liability. It represents the firm's liability to deliver goods or services in the future, for which it has already received and recorded payment from customers.

Box 36.2 returns to our example, to show how deferred income arises, how it appears as a CR balance on the Sales Account, and why it should be recognized as a liability in the balance sheet.

## BOX 36.2

### Deferred Income as a Liability

*Money & Promises*

| | |
|---|---|
| *payment received*   500 | |

Our firm has received payment of £500 from customers

*P&L Account*

| | |
|---|---|
| | *sales delivered in period*   450 |

but in this period, the firm has only delivered sales value £450

*Sales*

| | |
|---|---|
| *value delivered (to P&L)*   450 | *value paid for*   500 |
| *bal c/f*   50 | |
| 500 | 500 |

so the firm must show **deferred income** as a liability in the balance sheet, recognizing its liability to deliver the extra £50 value of sales that has been paid for.

| |
|---|
| *bal b/f deferred income*   50 |

## ACCRUED INCOME

Accrued income arises when the value of sales delivered by a firm is greater than the value it has been paid for. In this situation the value transferred from the Sales Account to the P&L Account at the end of the period will be greater than the value recorded as going OUT of the Sales Account during the period. In consequence the Sales Account will be left with entries that will generate a residual DR balance. Box 36.3 presents an example.

## BOX 36.3

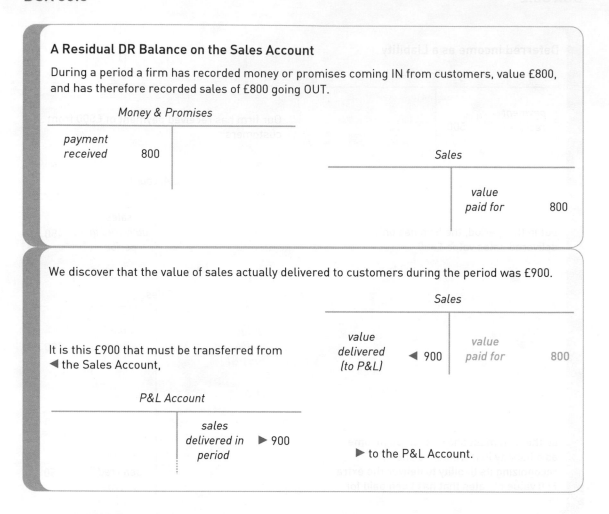

### A Residual DR Balance on the Sales Account

During a period a firm has recorded money or promises coming IN from customers, value £800, and has therefore recorded sales of £800 going OUT.

*Money & Promises*

| | | | |
|---|---|---|---|
| *payment received* | 800 | | |

*Sales*

| | |
|---|---|
| | *value paid for*  800 |

We discover that the value of sales actually delivered to customers during the period was £900.

*Sales*

| | | | |
|---|---|---|---|
| *value delivered (to P&L)* ◄ 900 | *value paid for*  800 |

It is this £900 that must be transferred from ◄ the Sales Account,

*P&L Account*

| | |
|---|---|
| | *sales delivered in period* ► 900 |

► to the P&L Account.

A residual DR balance on a Sales Account, after the transfer to the P&L Account, is called accrued income. Accrued income is listed as a current asset in the balance sheet. It represents the firm's right to collect payment for goods or services delivered to customers in excess of the value they have already paid for.

Box 36.4 demonstrates how accrued income arises, how it appears as a DR balance on the Sales Account and why it should be recognized as an asset in the balance sheet.

## BOX 36.4

### Accrued Income as an Asset

During a period, a firm has delivered sales to the value of £900.

*P&L Account*

| | | |
|---|---|---|
| | sales delivered in period | 900 |

*Money & Promises*

| | |
|---|---|
| payment received   800 | |

but the firm has received only £800 payment in money and promises from its customers

*Sales*

| | | | |
|---|---|---|---|
| value delivered (to P&L) | 900 | value paid for | 800 |
| | | bal c/f | 100 |
| | 900 | | 900 |
| bal b/f accrued income | 100 | | |

so the firm must show accrued income as an asset in its balance sheet, representing its right to collect payment for the extra £100 of sales that it has delivered in the period.

## REVIEW

This chapter has introduced deferred income and accrued income. Deferred income is a residual CR balance remaining on the Sales Account after transfers to the P&L Account. In the balance sheet, deferred income is listed as a current liability representing the firm's obligation to deliver goods or services for which it has already been paid. Accrued income is a residual DR balance remaining on the Sales Account after transfers to the P&L Account. In the balance sheet accrued income is listed as a current asset representing the firm's right to collect payment for goods or services delivered in the current period, but not yet paid for or properly recorded in the accounts.

# DRILLS AND EXERCISES

## 36.1

REQUIRED: For each set of data below show:
(a) relevant extracts from an account for money and/or promise;
(b) the Sales Account; and
(c) relevant extracts from the P&L Account for the period and from the balance sheet at the end of the period.

1. During a period, a firm receives payment, in money or promises, for sales to the value of £5 000.
   Sales actually delivered during the period are valued at £5 200.
2. During a period, a firm receives payment, in money or promises, for sales to the value of £9 250.
   Sales actually delivered during the period are valued at £9 000.
3. During a period, a firm issues sales invoices to the value of £8 360.
   Sales actually delivered during the period are valued at £8 200.
4. During a period, a firm issues sales invoices to the value of £100 000.
   Sales actually delivered during the period are valued at £103 000.
5. The Sales Account at the end of a period (before transfers to the P&L Account) shows a balance of £15 400 CR.
   During the period, the business actually delivered goods and services to the value of £15 000.
6. At the end of a period (before transfers to the P&L Account) the Sales Account of a business shows a balance of £24 700.
   During the period, the business actually delivered goods and services to the value of £25 000.
7. A firm of engineers in Xanadu has a single client from whom it has received a payment of £30 000 under a contract to advise on the construction of a pleasure dome.
   By the end of the firm's accounting period, construction work had not yet commenced and the firm had given no advice to the client.
8. A firm of accountants has a single client for whom it has completed work during a period with a sales value of £4 500.
   By the end of the period, the firm has issued no sales invoice in connection with this work.

## 36.2

You are the financial director of a major travel and holiday firm in the northern hemisphere. In what month would you choose to have the end of your accounting year? (Give reasons for your answer.)

# CHAPTER 37

# Accruals etc. in the Extended Trial Balance

## OBJECTIVES

*The objectives of this chapter are:*

- to show how the extended trial balance can be used to account for accruals, etc.
- to explain how the same trial balance can be the basis of very different final accounts
- to explain the difference between recording a value in the accounts of a business and recognizing a value in the P&L Account or the balance sheet

## ACCRUALS ETC.

*Accruals etc.* means accruals, prepayments, deferred income and accrued income taken together as a group of related phenomena and all arising from the same cause. This is the difference between the financial events or transactions recorded in the ledger accounts of a business and the physical processes of consumption and creation that we should like to see reflected in the P&L Account.

## USING THE EXTENDED TRIAL BALANCE TO ACCOUNT FOR ACCRUALS ETC.

The extended trial balance was introduced in Chapter 24 as a framework for assigning balances from the ledger accounts, as listed in the trial balance, to their proper place in either the P&L Account or the balance sheet. We shall see now, however, that it is not necessary to assign *whole* balances to one category or another. Through the perspective of the extended trial balance, it is possible to see accruals etc. as adjustments concerning the proper *division* of a ledger account balance between the P&L Account and the balance sheet. The topic is best developed by way of examples.

## PREPAYMENTS IN THE EXTENDED TRIAL BALANCE

Prepayments arise in connection with expenses. In the case of a prepayment, the original DR balance on an expense account in the trial balance is divided into two DR balances – one of which (representing the value consumed in the period) is assigned to the P&L Account as an expense, while the other (representing value paid for but not yet received) is assigned to the balance sheet as an asset. Box 37.1 shows an example.

## BOX 37.1

### Prepayments in the Extended Trial Balance

In a firm's trial balance at the end of a period, an expense account is listed with a DR balance of £1 000, as shown here.

| | Trial Balance | | P&L Account | | Balance Sheet | |
|---|---|---|---|---|---|---|
| | DR | CR | DR | CR | DR | CR |
| | | | | | | |
| expense | 1 000 | | | | | |
| | | | | | | |

On enquiry, it appears that only £750 of the value paid for and recorded on the account has been received and consumed in the period. The remaining £250 of the value paid for has not yet been received.

The £1 000 DR in the TB must therefore be divided into a £750 DR in the P&L Account, to represent the value consumed in the period, and a £250 DR in the balance sheet, to represent the remaining value as an asset (a prepayment), as shown below.

| | Trial Balance | | P&L Account | | Balance Sheet | |
|---|---|---|---|---|---|---|
| | DR | CR | DR | CR | DR | CR |
| | | | | | | |
| expense | 1 000 | | 750 | | 250 | |
| | | | | | | |
| | | | | | | |

## DEFERRED INCOME IN THE EXTENDED TRIAL BALANCE

Deferred income arises in connection with sales. In the case of deferred income, the original CR balance on the Sales Account in the trial balance is divided into two CR balances – one of which (representing the value of sales delivered) is assigned to the P&L Account, while the other (representing the value of sales paid for by customers but not yet delivered) is assigned to the balance sheet as a liability. Box 37.2 on the following page shows an example.

## BOX 37.2

### Deferred Income in the Extended Trial Balance

The Sales Account in a firm's trial balance at the end of a period carries a CR balance of £2 500, as shown here.

| | Trial Balance | | P&L Account | | Balance Sheet | |
|---|---|---|---|---|---|---|
| | DR | CR | DR | CR | DR | CR |
| | | | | | | |
| sales | | 2 500 | | | | |
| | | | | | | |

On enquiry, it appears that only £2 000 of the sales paid for and recorded on the account have been delivered to customers in the period. The firm has not yet delivered the remaining £500 of sales paid for.

The £2 500 CR in the TB must therefore be divided into a £2 000 CR in the P&L Account, to represent the value of sales delivered in the period, and a £500 CR in the balance sheet, to represent deferred income – that is, the firm's liability to deliver the remaining value of sales it has been paid for – as shown below.

| | Trial Balance | | P&L Account | | Balance Sheet | |
|---|---|---|---|---|---|---|
| | DR | CR | DR | CR | DR | CR |
| | | | | | | |
| sales | | 2 500 | | 2 000 | | 500 |
| | | | | | | |

## ACCRUALS IN THE EXTENDED TRIAL BALANCE

Accruals arise in connection with expenses. In the case of an accrual, the DR balance on an expense account in the TB is 'divided' into a *larger* DR which goes into the P&L Account (to represent the total value consumed in the period), and a smaller counterbalancing CR which goes into the balance sheet (to represent a liability to pay for extra value consumed). Box 37.3 on the following page shows an example.

## BOX 37.3

### Accruals in the Extended Trial Balance

An expense account in a firm's trial balance at the end of a period carries a DR balance of £3 500, as shown here.

|         | Trial Balance | | P&L Account | | Balance Sheet | |
|---------|------|------|------|------|------|------|
|         | DR   | CR   | DR   | CR   | DR   | CR   |
| expense | 3 500 |     |      |      |      |      |
|         |      |      |      |      |      |      |
|         |      |      |      |      |      |      |

The £3 500 DR in the TB indicates the value of this particular input that has been paid for during the period.

Investigation reveals that a further £500 of this particular expense has been consumed, but not yet paid for, in money or in promises, and therefore not yet properly recorded in the accounts. The extra £500 of value consumed, and the liability to pay for it, must now be included in the firm's P&L Account and balance sheet.

The £3 500 DR in the TB must therefore be 'divided' into a £4 000 DR in the P&L Account (to represent the whole value consumed in the period) and a £500 CR in the balances represent the accrual – that is, the firm's liability to pay for the extra value consumed.

|         | Trial Balance | | P&L Account | | Balance Sheet | |
|---------|------|------|------|------|------|------|
|         | DR   | CR   | DR   | CR   | DR   | CR   |
| expense | 3 500 |     | 4 000 |     |      | 500  |
|         |      |      |      |      |      |      |
|         |      |      |      |      |      |      |

Notice that the procedure involved in accounting for accruals makes it possible to include completely new expenses in the P&L Account, even where nothing at all has been recorded in the ledger accounts. If a £3 500 DR in the trial balance can be divided into a P&L DR of £4 000 and a balance sheet CR of £500, then a zero in the trial balance can be divided into a P&L DR and a balance sheet CR of any value, as long as they are equal.

## ACCRUED INCOME IN THE EXTENDED TRIAL BALANCE

Accrued income arises in connection with sales. With accrued income, the CR balance on the Sales Account in the TB is split into a larger CR which goes into the P&L Account, and a smaller counter-balancing DR which goes into the balance sheet, as shown in Box 37.4.

## BOX 37.4

### Accrued Income in the Extended Trial Balance

The Sales Account in a firm's trial balance at the end of a period carries a CR balance of £6 000, as shown below.

| | Trial Balance | | P&L Account | | Balance Sheet | |
|---|---|---|---|---|---|---|
| | DR | CR | DR | CR | DR | CR |
| | | | | | | |
| sales | | 6 000 | | | | |
| | | | | | | |

The £6 000 CR in the TB indicates the value of sales paid for by customers (in money or promises) during the period.

It appears that the firm has also delivered another £2 000 of sales in the period, which has not yet been recorded in the accounts. The extra value of sales delivered, and the firm's right to collect payment from the customer, must now be included in the firm's P&L Account and balance sheet.

The £6 000 CR in the TB must therefore be 'divided' into an £8 000 CR in the P&L Account (to represent the whole value of sales delivered in the period) and a £2 000 DR in the balance sheet (to represent accrued income – that is, the firm's right to collect payment for the extra sales it has delivered but not yet recorded).

| | Trial Balance | | P&L Account | | Balance Sheet | |
|---|---|---|---|---|---|---|
| | DR | CR | DR | CR | DR | CR |
| | | | | | | |
| sales | | 6 000 | | 8 000 | 2 000 | |
| | | | | | | |
| | | | | | | |

As with accruals, the procedure involved in adjusting the accounts for accrued income can also be used to bring values into the P&L Account and balance sheet, which have never been recorded in the ledger accounts. Box 37.5 presents an example.

## BOX 37.5

### Unrecorded Income and Expenses in the Extended Trial Balance

During a period, a firm has recorded no sales and no expenses, as shown in the extract from its trial balance shown below:

|  | Trial Balance | | P&L Account | | Balance Sheet | |
|---|---|---|---|---|---|---|
|  | DR | CR | DR | CR | DR | CR |
|  |  |  |  |  |  |  |
| sales |  |  |  |  |  |  |
| expense |  |  |  |  |  |  |
|  |  |  |  |  |  |  |

On enquiry it seems that the firm has in fact delivered sales value £4 000 during the period, and has consumed inputs value £3 000, but none of these events have yet been recorded in the accounts.

In the extract from the extended trial balance below, we see that despite recording no transactions, the firm will be able to report sales of £4 000 and expenses of £3 000 in the P&L Account, with accrued income of £4 000 and an accrual of £3 000 in the balance sheet.

|  | Trial Balance | | P&L Account | | Balance Sheet | |
|---|---|---|---|---|---|---|
|  | DR | CR | DR | CR | DR | CR |
|  |  |  |  |  |  |  |
| sales |  |  |  | 4 000 | 4 000 |  |
| expense |  |  | 3 000 |  |  | 3 000 |
|  |  |  |  |  |  |  |
|  |  |  |  |  |  |  |

## THE TRIAL BALANCE AND THE P&L ACCOUNT

The examples above are striking evidence that *any* P&L Account can be derived from the information recorded in *any* trial balance. They reinforce the point made in Chapter 25 that, in the end, the profit or loss reported by a firm will depend entirely on what the accountant decides to put into the P&L Account, and what he or she decides to put into the balance sheet. Professional accountants (individually and collectively) are therefore in a position of great power. They cannot avoid the associated responsibility.

## RECOGNIZING, REALIZING, AND RECORDING

In accounting a value is *recognized* when it is included in the P&L Account or the balance sheet. To recognize a value in the P&L Account means to include it there as a sale or expense of the period.

To recognize a value in the balance sheet means to include it there as an asset or a liability, or as part of the owner's claim. The value of an item is *realized* (in the form of money) when it is sold or exchanged for money. A transaction is *recorded* in the accounts of a business when there is a movement of money into or out of the business and when the business sends or receives an invoice.

Notice the distinction between recording transactions in the ledger accounts of a firm, and recognizing effects in the final accounts (P&L and balance sheet). Recording transactions is a matter of book-keeping routine. If the appropriate trigger event occurs, a transaction must be recorded in the accounts. If the trigger event does not occur, nothing will be recorded in the accounts. Recognition, however, is a matter of judgement and expertise. In what is almost a separate exercise at the end of every period, the accountant must decide what to recognize in the P&L Account as income or expense, and what to recognize in the balance sheet as an asset, a liability, or part of the owner's claim.

## REVIEW

This chapter has used the extended trial balance to show how accruals etc. can be seen as a method of dividing the balance on a sales or expense account between the P&L Account for the period and the balance sheet at the end of the period. The chapter also introduced the significance of the distinction between recording transactions in the accounts of a business and recognizing values in the P&L Account and the balance sheet. Using the extended trial balance, the chapter showed once again how, while the transactions recorded by a firm may be a matter of fact, the profit or loss reported by a firm will depend on decisions made by the accountant as to what values are recognized, and how they are recognized, in the final accounts – whether in the P&L Account as income or expenses, or in the balance sheet as assets or liabilities.

# DRILLS AND EXERCISES

## 37.1

REQUIRED: for each separate extract from an extended trial balance below, with notes, show the values that should be included in the P&L Account and the values that should be included in the balance sheet. Where values are to be included in the balance sheet, state what they should be called.

### FIRM A

|         | TRIAL BALANCE | | P&L ACCOUNT | | BALANCE SHEET | |
|---------|------|------|------|------|------|------|
|         | DR   | CR   | DR   | CR   | DR   | CR   |
| sales   |      | 4 000 |     |      |      |      |
| expense | 1 500 |     |      |      |      |      |

## OPTION 1

Note: the value of sales actually delivered in the period was £4 500, and it is estimated that only £1 300 of the expense paid for has actually been consumed.

## OPTION 2

Note: the value of sales actually delivered in the period was £3 700, and it is estimated that £2 200 of the expense paid for has actually been consumed.

## FIRM B

|  | TRIAL BALANCE | | P&L ACCOUNT | | BALANCE SHEET | |
|  | DR | CR | DR | CR | DR | CR |
|---|---|---|---|---|---|---|
| sales |  | 6 000 |  |  |  |  |
| expense | 2 000 |  |  |  |  |  |

## OPTION 1

Note: the value of sales actually delivered in the period was only £6 000, while in fact a total of £2 300 of the expense has actually been consumed.

## OPTION 2

Note: the value of sales actually delivered in the period was £6 750, while only £1 800 of the expense has actually been consumed.

## 37.2 A drill to practise understanding the terms accrual, prepayment, deferred income and accrued income

1. A firm's P&L Account shows an expense of £650 in respect of electricity. The balance sheet shows an accrual of £50.
   State what this means, then say what was the original balance on the Electricity Account after all transactions had been recorded and before transfers to the P&L Account.
2. A firm's P&L Account shows an expense of £500 in respect of rent. The balance sheet shows a prepayment of £70.
   State what this means, then say what was the original balance on the Rent Account after all transactions had been recorded and before transfers to the P&L Account.
3. A firm's P&L Account shows sales value £650 for the year. The balance sheet shows deferred income of £50.
   State what this means, then say what was the original balance on the Sales Account after all transactions had been recorded and before transfers to the P&L Account.
4. A firm's P&L Account shows sales value £1 000 for the year. The balance sheet shows accrued income of £200.
   State what this means, then say what was the original balance on the Sales Account after all transactions had been recorded and before transfers to the P&L Account.

# CHAPTER 38

# Accruals etc. as Time-Shifts

## OBJECTIVES

*The objectives of this chapter are:*

- to show how the adjustments for prepayments and deferred income can be seen as devices for pushing expenses and sales recorded in one period into the P&L Account of the next period
- to show how the adjustments for accruals and accrued income can be seen as devices for pulling expenses and sales that will be recorded in the next period, into the P&L Account of the current period

## TIME-SHIFTS

The need to adjust accounts for accruals, prepayments, deferred income and accrued income is occasioned by a timing difference – that is, a difference between the period in which inputs and outputs are recorded in the accounts and the period in which they should be recognized in the P&L Account or Income Statement. With that in mind, it is possible to see the procedures involved in accounting for accruals etc. as time-shifting manoeuvres – ways of pushing income and expenses recorded in one period into the P&L Account of the next period, or of pulling income and expenses that will be recorded in the next period, into the P&L Account of the current period.

## PREPAYMENTS AS TIME-SHIFTS

An expense account is used to record the value of certain inputs paid for (in money or promises) during a period. If, at the end of the period, some of the value paid for has not yet been consumed, it should not be included in the current P&L Account, but left behind as a balance on the expense account, to appear in the balance sheet as a prepayment.

We are now concerned with the next period, when the expense account will start with an opening prepayment. This DR will be added to the values recorded on the account in the following period. It will therefore be included in the total available for transfer to the next P&L Account. In effect, with the adjustment for a prepayment, we shall have moved an expense recorded in the current period, into the P&L Account of the next period. Box 38.1 presents an illustration.

## BOX 38.1

### The Adjustment for a Prepayment as a Time-Shift

During a period, a firm has paid for £300 of some input, as shown on the Expense Account below.

*Expense Account*

| | |
|---|---|
| *value paid for and recorded in this period* | 300 |

At the end of the period, it is found that £100 of the value paid for has not yet been received or consumed. It must be left behind on the account, to be added to the values that will be paid for and recorded in the following period.

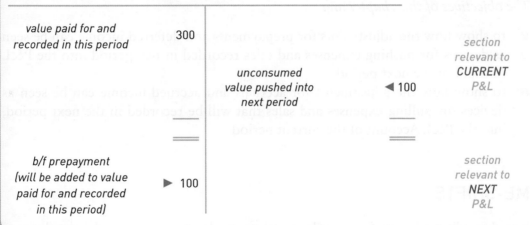

*Expense Account*

| | | | |
|---|---|---|---|
| *value paid for and recorded in this period* | 300 | | |
| | | *unconsumed value pushed into next period* ◀ 100 | *section relevant to* **CURRENT** *P&L* |
| | ═══ | ═══ | |
| *b/f prepayment (will be added to value paid for and recorded in this period)* ▶ 100 | | | *section relevant to* **NEXT** *P&L* |

The £200 value remaining in the section relevant to the current P&L Account (that is, the £200 value consumed in the current period) can now be transferred to the P&L Account.

*Expense Account*

| | | | |
|---|---|---|---|
| *value paid for and recorded in this period* | 300 | *transferred to P&L – net value consumed in this period* ◀ 200 | *section relevant to* **CURRENT** *P&L* |
| | | *unconsumed value pushed into next period* 100 | |
| | 300 | 300 | |
| *b/f prepayment (will be added to value paid for and recorded in this period)* | 100 | | *section relevant to* **NEXT** *P&L* |

# ACCRUALS AS TIME-SHIFTS

While the adjustment for a prepayment involves pushing an expense recorded in the current period into the P&L Account of the next period, from a time-shift point of view the adjustment for an accrual involves pulling an expense that will be recorded in the next period, into the P&L Account of the current period.

Imagine an input has been consumed in the current period, but not yet recorded because the trigger event for recording a transaction (payment of money or receipt of an invoice) has not yet occurred. We wish to recognize the extra value consumed in the P&L Account of the current period. But we must also acknowledge that the trigger event for recording the transaction is bound to occur in the next period and therefore, in accordance with standard procedures, the value involved will be recorded in the expense account of the next period. From there, unless we are careful, it may find its way into the P&L Account of the next period as well.

The procedure involved in accounting for an accrual will automatically correct the potential error. When we account for an accrual, we leave a CR balance on the expense account, which will still be there at the start of the following period. In the following period that CR will serve to cancel the DR that will be entered on the account when the trigger event to record the transaction finally occurs. In effect, when we account for an accrual, we are dragging an expense that will be recorded in the next period, into the P&L Account of the current period, as shown in Box 38.2.

## BOX 38.2

### The Adjustment for an Accrual as a Time-Shift

During a period, a firm has recorded payment, in money or promises, for £500 of some input, as shown on the Expense Account below.

*Expense Account*

| | | |
|---|---|---|
| *value paid for and recorded in this period* | 500 | |

**BOX 38.2**   Continued

At the end of the period, it is found that a further £150 of the input has been consumed in the period, although not yet recorded. The extra value consumed must be included in the Expense Account for the current period, with a CR in the next period, to ensure that the value is cancelled when it is eventually recorded there.

*Expense Account*

| | | | | |
|---|---|---|---|---|
| *value paid for and recorded in this period* | 500 | | | *section relevant to* |
| | | | | **CURRENT** |
| *add extra value consumed (this value will be recorded in the next period)* | ▶ 150 | | | *P&L* |
| | | *b/f accrual (this will cancel the value already consumed, when it is finally recorded opposite)* | ◀ 150 | *section relevant to* **NEXT** *P&L* |

The total £650 value now included in the section relevant to the current P&L Account can now be transferred to the P&L Account.

*Expense Account*

| | | | | |
|---|---|---|---|---|
| *value paid for and recorded in this period* | 500 | *value consumed in this period – transferred to P&L* | ◀ 650 | *section relevant to* **CURRENT** *P&L* |
| *add extra value consumed (this value will be recorded in the next period)* | 150 | | | |
| | 650 | | 650 | |
| | | *b/f accrual (this will cancel the value already consumed, when it is finally recorded opposite)* | 150 | *section relevant to* **NEXT** *P&L* |

## DEFERRED INCOME AS A TIME-SHIFT

The adjustment for deferred income is comparable to the adjustment for a prepayment. In the case of deferred income, part of the value of sales recorded in the current period is not delivered by the end of the period, and will have to be delivered in the following period. The undelivered value is left as a CR balance on the Sales Account, where it will be added to the value of sales recorded in the following period. The adjustment for deferred income therefore pushes a sale recorded in one period into the P&L Account of the following period. Box 38.3 shows an illustration.

## BOX 38.3

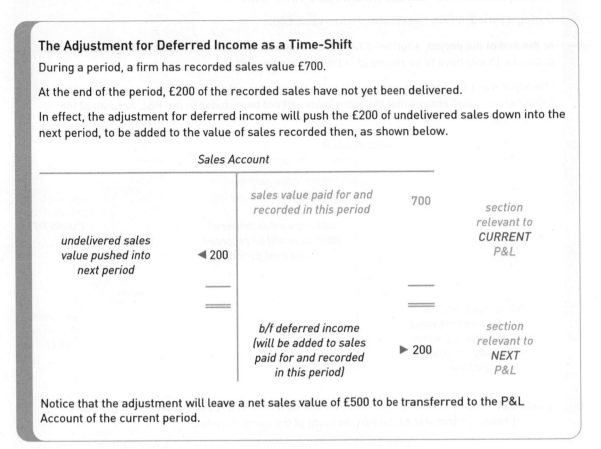

**The Adjustment for Deferred Income as a Time-Shift**

During a period, a firm has recorded sales value £700.

At the end of the period, £200 of the recorded sales have not yet been delivered.

In effect, the adjustment for deferred income will push the £200 of undelivered sales down into the next period, to be added to the value of sales recorded then, as shown below.

*Sales Account*

|  |  |  |
|---|---|---|
| *undelivered sales value pushed into next period* ◀ 200 | *sales value paid for and recorded in this period* 700 | *section relevant to* CURRENT P&L |
| | *b/f deferred income (will be added to sales paid for and recorded in this period)* ▶ 200 | *section relevant to* NEXT P&L |

Notice that the adjustment will leave a net sales value of £500 to be transferred to the P&L Account of the current period.

## ACCRUED INCOME AS A TIME-SHIFT

Accrued income arises when a sale is delivered in the current period, but the firm is unable to record the relevant sales transaction before the end of the period. The firm will therefore have to record the sale in the next period.

The accrued income adjustment is comparable to the adjustment for an accrual. First we make a CR entry in the current section of the Sales Account, to include the value of the extra sales delivered but not recorded in the current period. Then we make a DR entry in the section of the Sales Account that is relevant to the *next* P&L Account, so that when the transaction is eventually recorded there with a CR, it will be of no effect. The overall effect will be to drag the value of a sale that will be recorded in the next period, back into the P&L Account of the current period. Box 38.4 shows an example.

## BOX 38.4

### The Adjustment for Accrued Income as a Time-Shift

During a period, a firm has recorded sales value £800.

At the end of the period, a further £125 of sales have been delivered, but not yet recorded in the accounts. (It will have to be recorded in the following period.)

The adjustment for accrued income will bring these extra sales into the current section of the Sales Account, and ensure that the extra value will not be included in the P&L Account of the next period.

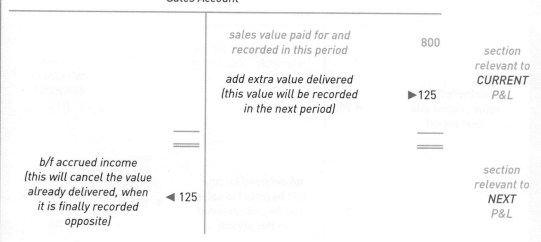

*Sales Account*

|  | sales value paid for and recorded in this period | 800 | section relevant to **CURRENT** P&L |
|  | add extra value delivered (this value will be recorded in the next period) | ▶125 |  |
| b/f accrued income (this will cancel the value already delivered, when it is finally recorded opposite)  ◀ 125 |  |  | section relevant to **NEXT** P&L |

Notice that following the adjustment, there will be a total of £925 in the section of the Sales Account ready for transfer to the P&L Account of the current period.

## RECONCILING VALUE PAID FOR AND VALUE IN THE P&L ACCOUNT

With the idea of accruals etc. as a device for moving recorded values backwards or forwards between one reporting period and the next, we must recognize that an expense account for any period may have opening as well as closing accruals or prepayments. Likewise, a sales account may have opening accrued income or deferred income as well as closing accrued income or deferred income.

Whether as opening balances or as closing balances, accruals etc. will always contribute to a difference between the value of transactions occurring in a period (that is the value paid for during the period, in money or in promises) and the value reported in the P&L Account. Box 38.5 shows how these differences work, in two pro forma reconciliations.

## BOX 38.5

### Reconciling Sales Transactions and Sales Reported in the P&L Account

|  | £ |
|---|---|
| SALES TRANSACTIONS occurring in the period <br> *(value paid for in money or promises in current period)* | X |
| plus opening deferred income <br> *(value paid for in previous period, but delivered in this period)* | X |
| minus closing deferred income <br> *(value paid for in this period, but not yet delivered)* | (X) |
| minus opening accrued income <br> *(value paid for in this period, but delivered in previous period)* | (X) |
| plus closing accrued income <br> *(value delivered but not yet paid for)* | X |
| SALES REPORTED in P&L ACCOUNT = value *delivered* in current period | X |

### Reconciling Expense Transactions and Expenses Reported in the P&L Account

|  | £ |
|---|---|
| EXPENSE TRANSACTIONS occurring in the period <br> *(value paid for in money or promises in current period)* | X |
| plus opening prepayment <br> *(value paid for in previous period, but consumed in this period)* | X |
| minus closing prepayment <br> *(value paid for in this period, but not yet consumed)* | (X) |
| minus opening accrual <br> *(value paid for in this period, but consumed in previous period)* | (X) |
| plus closing accrual <br> *(value consumed but not yet paid for)* | X |
| EXPENSE REPORTED in P&L ACCOUNT = value *consumed* in current period | X |

# REVIEW

This chapter has shown how accounting for accruals etc. can be seen and used as a technique for shifting the effect of a transaction backwards or forwards in time – from the period in which it is recorded, to the period in which it is recognized in the P&L Account. From this point of view the adjustment for a prepayment or deferred income involves pushing a value recorded in the current period forward into the P&L Account of the following period. The adjustment for an accrual or accrued income involves dragging a value that will be recorded in the next period, back into the P&L Account of the current period.

# DRILLS AND EXERCISES

## 38.1

REQUIRED: For each set of data below show:

(a) a relevant extract from an account for money or promises;
(b) the relevant expense or sales account with transactions recorded in the current year;
(c) any adjustments necessary to ensure that the P&L Accounts of the current year and the next year will reflect the actual value of inputs consumed or outputs created in the period (rather than the values paid for in the period);
(d) the necessary transfer to the P&L Account for the current year, with extracts from the P&L Account for the year and the balance sheet at the end of the year.

1. Before transfers to the P&L Account, the balance on a firm's account for repair work, an expense, is £10 500DR.
   Of this value recorded in the current year, £1 500 relates to work not yet done, which will be done in the following year.
2. Before transfers to the P&L Account, the balance on a firm's account for building maintenance, an expense, is £1 600DR.
   Further maintenance work to the value of £400 has been done in the period, but no invoice for this work has been received, and the work will have to be recorded in the ledger account next year.
3. During a period, a firm has issued invoices, and therefore recorded sales, to the value of £33 000.
   This includes certain sales, value £3 000, which the business has not yet been able to deliver and which will be delivered in the next period.
4. In its accounts for a period, a business has recorded transactions in respect of sales to the value of £37 000.
   In addition to these recorded sales, the firm has also delivered sales to the value of £2 000, which will be recorded in the accounts of the following period, when the relevant invoices are issued to customers.
5. For many firms in the Democratic Republic of Accrulia, a recent postal strike has delayed the receipt of invoices from the suppliers of goods and services.
   A business in Accrulia has received invoices from suppliers in respect of expenses totalling £45 000, but the business suspects that further invoices for work done in the

period, totalling £5 000, have been delayed in the post, and will have to be recorded in the ledger accounts of the following period.

## 38.2

Each separate business below operates on a cash only basis and does not keep double entry accounts. In each case, explain the significance of the information given, and produce a reconciliation between the value of sales or expenses paid for in the period, and the value to be reported in the P&L Account.

1. Cash paid for rent during the period, £8 000. Opening prepayment £300. Closing accrual £700.
2. Cash paid for electricity during the period, £5 000. Opening accrual £250. Closing prepayment £750.
3. Cash paid for insurance during period, £450. Opening prepayment £40. Closing prepayment £50.
4. Cash paid for subscription to trade association during period, £60. Opening accrual £15. Closing accrual £20.
5. Cash received for sales during the period, £8 000. Opening accrued income £750. Closing deferred income £250.
6. Cash received for sales during the period, £5 000. Opening deferred income £700. Closing accrued income £300.
7. Cash received for sales during the period, £7 900. Opening accrued income £400. Closing accrued income £100.
8. Cash received for sales during the period, £4 800. Opening deferred income £200. Closing deferred income £700.

# CHAPTER 39

# Accounting Software and Post-Trial Balance Adjustments

## OBJECTIVES

*The objectives of this chapter are:*

- to explain the manner in which accounting software requires us to make the adjustments for accruals etc. at the end of a period
- to show how and why those adjustments must be reversed at the start of the next period

## ACCRUALS ETC. IN ACCOUNTING SOFTWARE

Accounting software is generally based on the assumption of a trial balance or chart of accounts in which there are:

- 'income and expense' accounts (like sales, purchases and expenses); and
- 'balance sheet' accounts (like the accounts for bank, debtors, creditors, fixed assets, and so on).

The idea is that whole balances from each of the 'income and expense' accounts will be included in the income statement or P&L Account, and whole balances from the 'balance sheet' accounts will be included in the balance sheet.

There is therefore no question of taking a single balance in the TB and dividing it as we have done in previous chapters – transferring some of it to the P&L Account and leaving some of it as a residual balance to appear in the balance sheet. Instead, the software designers propose a three-stage process to prepare a set of final accounts at the end of each period, beginning with the production of a First Trial Balance, followed by post-trial balance adjustments, and concluding with a Final Trial Balance from which whole balances can be transferred to either the income statement or the balance sheet.

The 'First Trial Balance' is a list of all balances on all accounts, extracted after all the transactions of a period have been recorded. This is the standard trial balance with which we are already familiar.

Post-trial balance adjustments essentially involve transferring relevant values from income and expense accounts to separate balance sheet accounts for deferred income, accrued income, accruals and prepayments.

The 'Final Trial Balance' is then a list of all balances on all accounts, after the post-trial balance adjustments have been made. It is, in effect, a list of balances which can be sorted and summarized automatically into the form of an income statement and a balance sheet.

This approach makes life simpler, perhaps, at the end of a period. However, it does create work at the beginning of the next period, for, as we have seen, adjustments for accruals etc. affect more than just the closing balance sheet. They also affect the following period's P&L Account. The subject is best explored by way of examples.

## THE ADJUSTMENT FOR DEFERRED INCOME

Deferred income arises when a firm has been paid for, and therefore recorded, sales which it has not yet delivered. The post-trial balance adjustment for deferred income involves transferring the undelivered value from the Sales Account, to a Deferred Income Account, such that the whole of the final balance on the Sales Account can be transferred to the P&L Account (representing the value of sales delivered in the period), while the balance on the Deferred Income Account can be listed in the balance sheet (representing the firm's liability to deliver the extra value it has already been paid for). Box 39.1 presents an example of the adjusting entries to be made and the appearance of the relevant accounts.

## BOX 39.1

### The Adjustment for Deferred Income

At the end of a period, having recorded all of its transactions, a firm has produced a First Trial Balance including the Sales Account shown below.

*Sales Account*

| | |
|---|---|
| | transactions recorded  500 |

On enquiry we find that the whole balance on the Sales Account can not be transferred to the P&L Account because £100 of the sales recorded there have not yet been delivered. The adjustment required to account for this deferred income, and the appearance of the relevant accounts, will be as shown below.

| DR | Sales Account | ◄ £100 | |
|----|---------------|--------|--------|
| CR | Deferred Income | | ► £100 |

*Sales Account*

| | | | |
|---|---|---|---|
| to deferred income ◄ 100 | transactions recorded  500 | | |

*Deferred Income*

| | |
|---|---|
| | sales not yet delivered ► 100 |

BOX 39.1    Continued

When the accounts are balanced again for the Final Trial Balance, they will now carry the balances shown below, which can be included directly in the Income Statement or the balance sheet.

*Sales Account*

| to deferred income | 100 | transactions recorded | 500 |
|---|---|---|---|
| c/f | 400 | | |
| | 500 | | 500 |
| | | b/f sales value delivered | 400 |

*Deferred Income*

| | | sales not yet delivered | 100 |
|---|---|---|---|

*the balance on this account can now be listed in the balance sheet*

*the balance on this account can now be transferred in full to the P&L Account*

## REVERSING THE ADJUSTMENT FOR DEFERRED INCOME

Deferred income at the end of a period is properly included in the balance sheet as a liability to deliver goods that customers have already paid for. However, at the start of the next period, that same value must be returned to the Sales Account because that is when the sales will be delivered.

It follows that the post-trial balance adjustment made in respect of deferred income at the end of any period, must be reversed at the beginning of the next period. Box 39.2 presents an example.

BOX 39.2

### Reversing the Adjustment for Deferred Income

At the beginning of a period, a firm's Deferred Income Account carries an opening balance as shown below.

*Deferred Income*

| | | b/f balance | 100 |
|---|---|---|---|

This balance relates to sales recorded in the previous period, which the firm must deliver in the current period. This value should therefore be transferred to the Sales Account of the current period.

**BOX 39.2**   Continued

In effect, the adjustment made at the end of the previous period in respect of deferred income, must now be reversed.

The necessary accounting entries, and the appearance of the relevant accounts, are as shown below.

| DR | Deferred Income | ◄ £100 | |
| CR | Sales Account | | ► £100 |

*Deferred Income*

| | | | |
|---|---|---|---|
| *to Sales A/c*  ◄ 100 | *b/f balance*  100 | | |

*Sales Account*

| | |
|---|---|
| | *b/f deferred income*  ► 100 |

The sales that were excluded from the P&L Account of the previous period, will now be added to the sales recorded in the current period, as shown below.

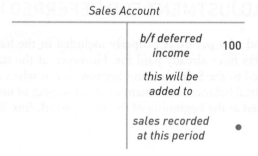

*Sales Account*

| |
|---|
| *b/f deferred income*  100 |
| *this will be added to* |
| *sales recorded at this period*  ● |

# THE ADJUSTMENT FOR ACCRUED INCOME

Accrued income arises when a firm has delivered a greater value of goods and services than it has yet recorded in the accounts. The post-trial balance adjustment for accrued income involves adding the extra value delivered, to the value already recorded in the Sales Account and showing the firm's right to receive payment for the extra sales as an asset ('Accrued Income') in an account created for the purpose. Box 39.3 presents an example.

## BOX 39.3

**The Adjustment for Accrued Income**

At the end of a period, having recorded all of its transactions, a firm has produced a First Trial Balance including the Sales Account shown below.

*Sales Account*

|  | transactions recorded | 700 |

A further £150 of sales have been delivered, but not yet recorded in the accounts. The adjustment required to account for this accrued income, and the appearance of the relevant accounts, will be as shown below.

| DR | Accrued Income | ◄ £150 |  |
| CR | Sales |  | ► £150 |

*Accrued Income*

| right to extra payment | ◄ 150 |

*Sales Account*

|  | transactions recorded | 700 |
|  | extra value delivered | ► 150 |

When the accounts are balanced again for the Final Trial Balance, they will now carry the balances shown below, which can be included directly in the Income Statement or the balance sheet.

*Accrued Income*

| right to extra payment | 150 |

*the balance on this account can now be listed in the balance sheet*

*Sales Account*

| c/f | 850 | transactions recorded | 700 |
|  |  | extra value delivered | 150 |
|  | 850 |  | 850 |
|  |  | b/f total sales delivered | 850 |

*the balance on this account can now be transferred to the P&L Account*

# REVERSING THE ADJUSTMENT FOR ACCRUED INCOME

As well as representing the right to be paid for goods already delivered, which is an asset at the end of a period, accrued income also represents a value that must be excluded from the sales recorded in the next period, because it has already been included in the P&L Account of the current period.

Thus, at the start of the next period, any balance on the Accrued Income Account must transferred to the Sales Account. When the sales already delivered are eventually recorded, this DR will be there to cancel their effect, and ensure that they do not go into the next P&L Account as well. Box 39.4 presents an example.

## BOX 39.4

At the beginning of a period, a firm's Accrued Income Account carries an opening balance as shown below.

| Accrued Income | |
|---|---|
| *right to extra payment* 150 | |

This balance relates to sales delivered in the previous period (and included in the P&L Account of the previous period), which will be recorded in the current period.

To prevent these sales being double counted, the DR on the Accrued Income Account must now be transferred to the Sales Account, where it will cancel the entries that will eventually be made to record the relevant sales.

In effect, the adjustment made at the end of the previous period in respect of accrued income, must now be reversed.

The necessary accounting entries, and the appearance of the relevant accounts, are as shown below.

| DR | Sales Account | ►£150 | |
|---|---|---|---|
| CR | Accrued Income | | ◄£150 |

| *Sales Account* | | | *Accrued Income* | | |
|---|---|---|---|---|---|
| *b/f accrued income* ►150 | | | *right to extra payment* 150 | *to Sales A/c* ◄150 | |

## BOX 39.4   Continued

When the extra sales that were included in the P&L Account of the previous period are eventually. recorded in the Sales Account, the effect of the entries in the Sales Account will now be cancelled by the opening DR balance, as shown below.

*Sales Account*

| | | | |
|---|---|---|---|
| *b/f accrued income* | 150 | | |
| this DR will cancel entries made opposite when the sales already delivered are finally recorded | | *recorded now but included in previous P&L* | ● |

# THE ADJUSTMENT FOR AN ACCRUAL

An accrual arises when a firm has consumed a greater value of an input than it has recorded in the accounts. Box 39.5 shows an example of the post-trial balance adjustment for an accrual.

## BOX 39.5

### The Adjustment for an Accrual

A firm has produced a First Trial Balance showing an Expense Account with a balance of £800 DR.

But in addition to the value recorded on the account, the firm has also consumed another £125 of the relevant input.

The adjustment required to account for this accrual is shown below.

| DR | Expense Account | ▶ £125 | |
|---|---|---|---|
| CR | Accrual | | ◀ £125 |

Following the adjustment, the relevant accounts will look like this:

| *Expense Account* | | *Accrual* | |
|---|---|---|---|
| *transactions recorded*   800 | | | *liability to pay for extra value consumed*   ◀ 125 |
| *extra value consumed*   ▶ 125 | | | |

**BOX 39.5** Continued

In the Final Trial Balance, the Expense Account will now carry a balance of £925, representing the total value consumed in the period, which can be transferred to the P&L Account, and the Accrual Account will show a balance which can be listed in the balance sheet, as shown below.

| *Expense Account* | | | | *Accrual* | | |
|---|---|---|---|---|---|---|
| *transactions recorded* | 800 | | | | *liability to pay for extra value consumed* | 125 |
| *extra value consumed* | 125 | *c/f* | 925 | *the balance on this account can now be listed in the balance sheet* | | |
| | 925 | | 925 | | | |
| *b/f total value consumed* | 925 | | | | | |

*the balance on this account can now be transferred to the P&L Account*

## ACCRUALS – REVERSAL IN THE FOLLOWING PERIOD

As well as representing a liability to pay for inputs already consumed, although not yet recorded, an accrual also represents a value that must be excluded from the expenses recorded in the next period, because it has already been included in the P&L Account of the current period.

Thus, at the start of the next period, any balance on an Accrual Account must be transferred to the relevant Expense Account. When the inputs already consumed are eventually recorded, this CR will be there to cancel their effect, and ensure that they do not go into the next P&L Account as well. Box 39.6 presents an example.

## BOX 39.6

### Reversing the Adjustment for an Accrual

A firm begins a period with a balance of £125 CR on an Accrual Account, arising in respect of inputs consumed in the previous period, but not yet recorded.

This CR must be transferred to the relevant Expense Account for the current period, so that when the input is eventually recorded there, the effect of the entry will be cancelled. In effect the closing adjustment of the previous period must now be reversed.

BOX 39.6    Continued

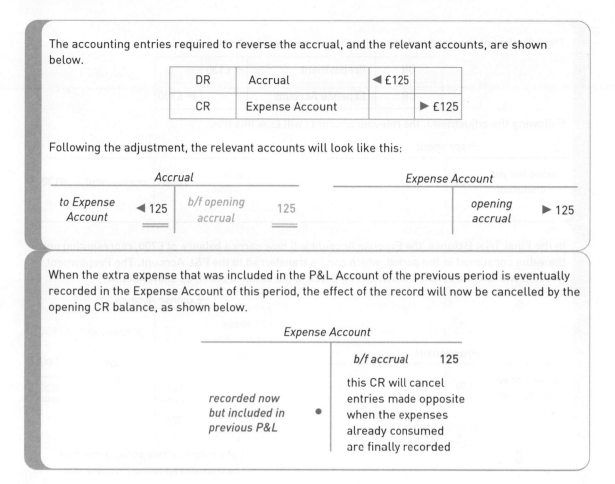

The accounting entries required to reverse the accrual, and the relevant accounts, are shown below.

| DR | Accrual | ◄ £125 | |
|----|---------|--------|--|
| CR | Expense Account | | ► £125 |

Following the adjustment, the relevant accounts will look like this:

**Accrual**

| to Expense Account | ◄ 125 | b/f opening accrual | 125 |
|---|---|---|---|

**Expense Account**

| | | opening accrual | ► 125 |
|---|---|---|---|

When the extra expense that was included in the P&L Account of the previous period is eventually recorded in the Expense Account of this period, the effect of the record will now be cancelled by the opening CR balance, as shown below.

**Expense Account**

| | b/f accrual | 125 |
|---|---|---|
| recorded now but included in previous P&L • | this CR will cancel entries made opposite when the expenses already consumed are finally recorded | |

# THE ADJUSTMENT FOR A PREPAYMENT

A prepayment arises when a firm has paid for and recorded more of an expense than it has in fact consumed in a period. After the First Trial Balance, an adjustment is necessary to take the unconsumed value out of the Expense Account, and replace it in a Prepayment Account, to be listed in the balance sheet as an asset. Box 39.7 presents an example.

BOX 39.7

**The Adjustment for a Prepayment**

A firm has produced a First Trial Balance showing an Expense Account with a balance of £830 DR.

But the balance on the account includes £130 of expense which has not yet been received or consumed.

**BOX 39.7**   Continued

The adjustment required to account for this prepayment is shown below.

| DR | Prepayment | ◄ £130 | |
|----|------------|--------|---|
| CR | Expense Account | | ► £130 |

Following the adjustment, the relevant accounts will look like this:

| Prepayment | | Expense Account | | |
|---|---|---|---|---|
| value not yet consumed ►130 | | value recorded 830 | prepayment ◄130 | |

In the Final Trial Balance, the Expense Account will now carry a balance of £700, representing only the value consumed in the period, which can be transferred to the P&L Account. The Prepayment Account will show a balance which can be listed in the balance sheet, as shown below.

Expense Account

| | | value recorded | 830 | prepayment | 130 |
|---|---|---|---|---|---|
| | | | | c/f | 700 |
| | | | 830 | | 830 |

Prepayment

| value not yet consumed | 130 | |
|---|---|---|

the balance on this account can now be listed in the balance sheet

| b/f = value consumed | 700 | |
|---|---|---|

the balance on this account can now be transferred to the P&L Account

## REVERSING THE ADJUSTMENT FOR A PREPAYMENT

At the start of the following period, any previous adjustment for a prepayment must be reversed, to allow for the fact that the input will be received and consumed in the period now beginning. Box 39.8 presents an example.

**BOX 39.8**

### Reversing the Adjustment for a Prepayment

A firm begins a period with a balance of £130 DR on a Prepayment Account, arising in respect of inputs recorded but not yet consumed.

These inputs will be consumed in the current period, and so this DR must be returned to the Expense Account from which it was transferred at the end of the previous period.

**BOX 39.8**   Continued

The accounting entries required to reverse the year-end adjustment and return the prepayment to the Expense Account are shown below.

| DR | Expense Account | ▶ £130 | |
|----|-----------------|--------|--------|
| CR | Prepayment | | ◀ £130 |

Following the adjustment, the relevant accounts will look like this:

| | Prepayment | | | | | Expense Account | |
|---|---|---|---|---|---|---|---|
| opening balance | 130 | to Expense A/c | ◀ 130 | | b/f prepayment | ▶ 130 | |

The expenses that were excluded from the P&L Account of the previous period, will now be added to the expenses recorded in the current period, as shown below.

Expense Account

| b/f prepayment | 130 |
|---|---|
| this will be added to | |
| expenses recorded in this period | ● |

# REVIEW

This chapter has summarized the accounting procedures necessary to adapt to the needs of accounting software, in which an account must be designated in advance as wholly feeding into the P&L Account, or wholly feeding into the balance sheet. The chapter described the usual approach, in which a First Trial Balance is produced after the firm's transactions have been recorded. This First Trial Balance is adjusted to allow for accruals, etc. by the intervention of the accountant, after which a second trial balance is produced, from which whole balances can be incorporated into the P&L Account or the balance sheet.

One consequence of this approach, with separate 'balance sheet' accounts for deferred income, accrued income, accruals and prepayments, is that the accountant's year-end adjustments must be reversed at the start of the following period.

# DRILLS AND EXERCISES

## 39.1

State and explain the accounting entries necessary to account for the following year-end adjustments in a computerized accounting system. Also state and explain the accounting entries necessary to reverse the adjustments in the following period.

1. deferred income
2. accrued income
3. a prepayment
4. an accrual

# CHAPTER 40

# Matching: Accruals etc. in Context

## COMPONENTS OF THE ACCOUNTING MODEL

The problem of accruals, etc. can be seen as a problem in the evolution of the accounting model of a business. The model is shown again in Box 40.1.

BOX 40.1

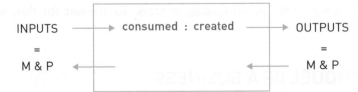

**The Double Entry Model of a Business**

INPUTS  ⟶  consumed : created  ⟶  OUTPUTS

=  ⟵  ⟵  =

M & P  M & P

- a transaction is a movement of money or promises (M&P) across the boundary IN to or OUT of a business

- every transaction is recorded as an exchange of equal value

- inside the business, inputs are consumed while outputs are created

This model is in fact an amalgam, easily separable into two quite different components – the double entry model of a transaction and the profit model of a business.

## THE DOUBLE ENTRY MODEL OF A TRANSACTION

A transaction is a movement of money or promises IN or OUT across the boundary of a business. In the double entry model, a transaction is recorded as an exchange of equal value, but the inputs and outputs involved are no more than reasons or explanations for movements of money or promises. What happens inside the business can be ignored or left blank, as it is in Box 40.2.

## BOX 40.2

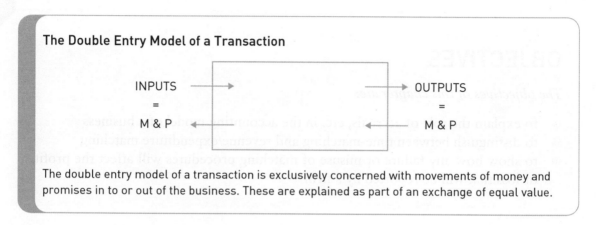

**The Double Entry Model of a Transaction**

INPUTS $\longrightarrow$     $\longrightarrow$ OUTPUTS

=     =

M & P $\longleftarrow$     $\longleftarrow$ M & P

The double entry model of a transaction is exclusively concerned with movements of money and promises in to or out of the business. These are explained as part of an exchange of equal value.

This focus on transactions, and this model of a transaction, reflect an original concern with financial accountability.

Accountability is not, as some would have it, a backward looking obsession with past events which cannot be undone. It is a means of control. Financial accounting, including the double entry model of a transaction, was first developed to control those who handle other people's money, by imposing upon them the obligation to explain what they have done with it, and why.

For many organizations, especially those like governments and their agencies which do not sell their goods or services for profit, the double entry model of a transaction is enough for all accounting purposes, without much further elaboration. Business, however, is also concerned with profit, and the efficiency of the profit-making process. To account for this, we need the profit model of a business.

## THE PROFIT MODEL OF A BUSINESS

The profit model is a separate and more recent development than the transaction model. It is essentially concerned with how profit is made. The model assumes a process of consumption and creation which takes place inside the business. It is presented not as a diagram but as a summary description of the profit-making process and its result, as shown in Box 40.3.

## BOX 40.3

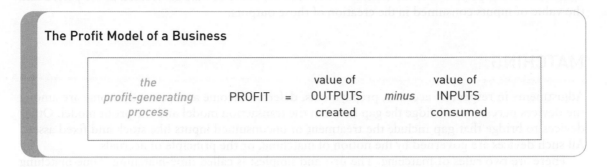

**The Profit Model of a Business**

|  | | | |
|---|---|---|---|
| *the* *profit-generating* *process* | PROFIT = | value of OUTPUTS created | *minus* | value of INPUTS consumed |

This model, comparing outputs against inputs, can be associated with the regime of managerial capitalism that emerged in the 19th and 20th centuries, with its emphasis on the efficiency of production.

## THE OVERALL ACCOUNTING MODEL

In the overall accounting model of a business, the profit model is embedded within the transaction model, like the nucleus in a living cell, as shown in Box 40.4.

## BOX 40.4

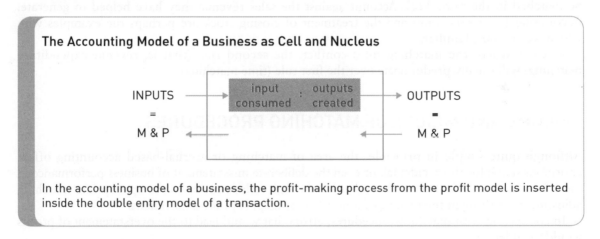

**The Accounting Model of a Business as Cell and Nucleus**

In the accounting model of a business, the profit-making process from the profit model is inserted inside the double entry model of a transaction.

The essential link between these two components is that the inputs and outputs which are consumed or created inside a business (in the profit model) cannot get into or out of the business except by way of a transaction with the outside world (in the transaction model).

The disjoint between the two components is in the dimension of time. The financial event by which an input is acquired may take place at a different time (and in a different period) from the physical process in which the value of the input is consumed. Likewise the financial event by which the value of an output is realized may occur at a different time (and in a different period) from the physical process by which the value of the output is created.

In addition to these timing differences (one between purchase and consumption of input, the other between creation and sale of output), there is also a further potential timing difference – between the consumption of inputs (one part of the profit-making process) and the creation of related outputs (the other part of the profit-making process). This difference is significant, for the profit of a period is not the difference between the values created in the period and the values consumed in the period. It is the difference between the value of outputs created in the period and the value of inputs consumed in the creation of those outputs.

## MATCHING

Adjustments in respect of accruals, prepayments, deferred income and accrued income are among the devices necessary to bridge the gap between the transaction model and the profit model. Other devices to bridge that gap include the treatment of unconsumed inputs like stock and fixed assets. All such devices are governed by the notion of matching, or the principle of accruals.

There are two rules of matching. The first and simplest is called time-matching. Time-matching is the rule that items of income or expense should appear in the P&L Account of the period in which they were earned or incurred (and not the P&L Account of the period in which they were paid for).

Time-matching applies in particular to the treatment of sales revenue. Sales should be recognized in the P&L Account of the period in which the sales were delivered, regardless of when the sales were ordered, when they were paid for, or when the outputs were created. Time-matching also applies to such things as rent and interest, which may be paid in advance or in arrears, but should always be recognized in the P&L Account of the period to which the payment relates, rather than the period in which the payment is made.

The second rule of matching is called revenue/expenditure matching. Revenue/expenditure matching demands that the consumption of an input should be recognized in the same P&L Account as the creation of the output with which it is associated. In other words expenses should be matched in the same P&L Account against the sales revenue they have helped to generate. Accounting for depreciation and the treatment of closing stock are perhaps the examples with which we are most familiar.

In cases where the matching rules conflict, the second rule (that is, revenue/expenditure matching) will usually predominate over the first rule (time matching).

## FAILURE AND MISUSE OF MATCHING PROCEDURES

Although quite simple in principle, the area of matching or accrual-based accounting offers enormous scope for the accidental, or even the deliberate misstatement of business performance in the P&L Account. Mis-statement may arise through failure to make the appropriate matching adjustment, or through the making of unjustified or inappropriate adjustments.

In connection with matching procedures, errors that would lead to the overstatement of profits would include:

- failure to account for deferred income when customers have paid in advance for goods or services;
- improper inclusion of accrued income, when future sales are merely expected and have not yet been delivered;
- failure to account for an accrual when the firm has used inputs which it has not yet paid for;
- improper adjustment for a prepayment when an input has in fact been completely consumed in the period.

Evidently, opposite errors would lead to understated profits.

Other procedures associated with the idea of matching may also fail and generate mis-statements, including:

- misclassification of revenue expenditure as capital expenditure;
- underestimation of periodic depreciation charges; and
- overstatement of the value of closing stock.

All of these, again, would lead to overstated profits, while opposite errors would lead to understated profits.

## REVIEW

This chapter has discussed accruals, etc. in the context of the interplay between the two components of the accounting model of a business – the transaction model and the profit model – noting that the transaction model is part of a regime of personal accountability, while the profit model is mostly concerned with business efficiency. The chapter examined the rules of matching or accrual-based accounting and described both time-matching and revenue/expenditure matching. Finally, the chapter showed how the failure or misuse of matching devices like accruals, etc. may result in the mis-statement of a firm's profit or loss for the period.

# DRILLS AND EXERCISES

## 40.1

State and explain the effect of each of the following actions or situations on the *reported profit* of the current period and on the firm's *net assets* at the end of the period:

1. making an inappropriate (excessive) adjustment for deferred income
2. making an inappropriate (excessive) adjustment for accrued income
3. making an inappropriate (excessive) adjustment for a prepayment
4. making an inappropriate (excessive) adjustment for an accrual
5. failing to make an appropriate adjustment for deferred income
6. failing to make a necessary adjustment for accrued income
7. failing to make a necessary adjustment for a prepayment
8. failing to make a necessary adjustment for an accrual
9. overestimating the useful life of a fixed asset
10. underestimating the residual value of a fixed asset

## 40.2

Is the principle of accruals fully consistent with the principle of prudence? Identify two cases in which you think they may conflict and explain how you would resolve the difficulty.

# CHAPTER 41

# Provisions and Potential Liabilities

## OBJECTIVES

*The objectives of this chapter are:*

- to explain what is meant by the term provision in accounting
- to show how to create a provision
- to explain how provisions can be used to account for potential or contingent liabilities

## CREATING A PROVISION

A provision is a dummy claim or liability, created by reducing profit. (Profit is claimed by the owner, so reducing profit is a way of reducing capital, the owner's claim.) Making a provision, therefore, takes away part of the owner's claim and replaces it with a dummy claim. Box 41.1 shows the accounting procedures involved in creating a provision and the balance sheet of a firm before and after the making of a provision.

### BOX 41.1

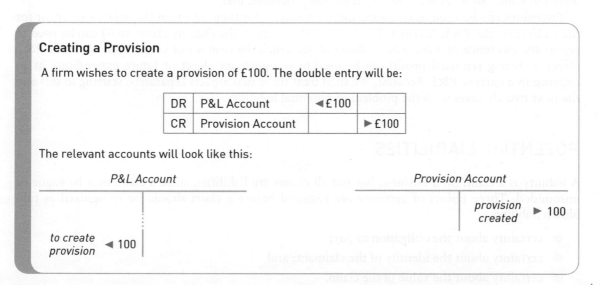

**Creating a Provision**

A firm wishes to create a provision of £100. The double entry will be:

| DR | P&L Account | ◀£100 | |
|----|-------------|-------|-------|
| CR | Provision Account | | ▶£100 |

The relevant accounts will look like this:

| P&L Account | | Provision Account | |
|-------------|---|-------------------|---|
| | | | provision created ▶ 100 |
| to create provision ◀ 100 | | | |

**BOX 41.1**   Continued

Now, assuming that the firm starts with a balance sheet like the one on the left below, the effect of making the provision can be seen in the balance sheet on the right below.

| | *BALANCE SHEET*<br>*before provision* | | | *BALANCE SHEET*<br>*after provision* | |
|---|---|---|---|---|---|
| | £ | | | £ | |
| assets | 700 | | assets | 700 | |
| liabilities | (200) | | liabilities | (200) | |
| | | | provision | (100) | |
| | 500 | | | 400 | |
| | | | capital b/f | 500 | |
| | | | loss occasioned by<br>creation of provision | (100) | |
| capital | 500 | | capital c/f | 400 | |

## CREATING A PROVISION WITH ACCOUNTING SOFTWARE

Accounting software does not normally permit entries to be made directly in the P&L Account. The procedure, therefore, to create a provision is to put the DR in an expense account, which will be transferred to the P&L Account at the end of the period.

## WHAT ARE PROVISIONS FOR?

Notice that creating a provision does not affect the assets or the proper liabilities of a business in any way whatsoever. All that happens is that part of the owner's claim is taken away and given a different name. So what is the point? What are provisions for?

Provisions can be used in two quite different ways – for their effect on the balance sheet, or for their effect on the P&L Account. The balance sheet effect (the dummy claim itself) can be used to report the existence of a *potential* liability about which the firm is not yet certain, while the P&L effect (reducing reported profit) can be used to recognize an object of future expenditure as an expense in a current P&L Account. We shall treat these two aspects separately, starting in this and the next two chapters with the problem of potential liabilities.

## POTENTIAL LIABILITIES

A liability is a claim on a business, but not all claims are liabilities, since a claim may be vague or unfounded. Three points of certainty are required before a claim should be recognized as full-blown liability:

- certainty about the obligation to pay;
- certainty about the identity of the claimant; and
- certainty about the value of the claim.

These are strict conditions, and many liabilities start off in life as mere claims, lacking one or more of the three essential certainties. Such claims are proto-liabilities – they have the potential to develop into proper liabilities as the various uncertainties are clarified. Because of their size or significance, however, these proto-liabilities may well merit disclosure in the accounts of a business at an early stage, despite the uncertainty attaching to them.

Thus, for example, a business may be aware that some customers claim to have suffered damage from its products. Some customers may have begun legal proceedings to gain compensation, and others may follow. Is the firm liable at all for the alleged damage? To whom exactly is it liable? How much must it pay them? For the moment, none of the three certainties is present, so the business has no proper liability. On the other hand, it may be possible to estimate the likelihood and size of the potential liability, and if so, in accordance with the principle of prudence, it may be desirable to show it in the firm's accounts. The ability to create provisions allows us to do just that.

## CONTINGENT LIABILITIES

A contingent liability is a potential liability, existing now, which may or may not develop into a full liability, depending on the occurrence or non-occurrence of a future precipitating event. Thus, if X has promised to pay Y £10 if Andorra win the next World Cup (the precipitating event), X has a contingent liability to pay Y £10.

If a firm has a contingent liability, but the precipitating event is highly unlikely to occur, the contingent liability may be ignored in the firm's accounts. If on the other hand the event is judged likely to occur, then prudence would indicate that the firm should make a provision. At points in between *highly unlikely* and *probable*, the accountant must make a judgement as to whether or not the firm should create a provision. A possible compromise for contingencies at the lower end of probability, is not to make a provision in the accounts, but to disclose the existence of the contingency in a note to the accounts.

## THE MEANING OF MAKING A PROVISION

It is vital to recognize that in accounting the word *provision*, and expressions like *making a provision* or *providing for* are used in a strictly technical sense, which does not fully correspond with their everyday non-technical meaning.

In the everyday non-accounting sense, provisions are supplies. Making provisions in this sense, and providing for, say, old age or a dependent relative means setting aside cash or other assets for some specific purpose.

In the technical accounting sense, as we have said, a provision is a dummy claim or liability. In accounting, making a provision means making entries in the accounts, so as to show a dummy claim or liability in the balance sheet. It does not mean setting aside cash or any other asset to pay the liability. In short: making a provision in the everyday sense means doing something with assets, while making a provision in the accounting sense means doing something with claims in double entry. In itself, therefore, creating a provision does nothing to ensure that a potential liability can be paid, or will be paid if and when it becomes a definite liability.

Merely juggling with DRs and CRs to set up a provision may seem an inadequate response in the face of a potential claim. However, the purpose of a provision is essentially to warn of the existence of a potential liability. In a balance sheet, there are assets, representing the value of things in the business, and there are liabilities, the definite claims of other people. In theory, what remains can be claimed by the owner. Creating a provision says in effect to the owner 'Wait – you cannot be certain of all the value that remains after the definite claims of other people. There are also these potential claims that may have to be met before you may claim whatever is left'. Once warned, the firm or those responsible for its financial affairs may take steps to ensure that the liability can be paid, but any such steps are not part of making a provision.

## PROVISIONS ASSOCIATED WITH SPECIFIC ASSETS

It is a mistake to expect a 1:1 correspondence between words and things in any natural language. One of the functions of a science, therefore, is to establish an unambiguous technical language, and one of the difficulties in accounting is the near impossibility of this work, given the close relation between accounting and everyday life. In accounting the same concept is often covered by several different words, or the same word is often attached to some quite different concepts. This is most confusing when it is most likely to occur – that is, when the different concepts do indeed have some superficial resemblance to each other.

Provision is such a word. Its primary meaning in accounting is that of a dummy claim, as we have seen above.

However, accountants also use the word provision to describe a deduction from the recorded value of some specific asset, made in recognition of a loss in value. We have met with this use of the word before, in the 'provision for depreciation', which is a deduction from the recorded value of a fixed asset. We shall meet with it again in other cases, such as the 'provision for doubtful debts'. These provisions are not free-standing dummy claims. They have no meaning in isolation. Each such 'provision' is best considered as a separate case and best explained in connection with the specific asset to which it is related.

## REVIEW

This chapter has introduced provisions, which are dummy claims or liabilities, and shown how provisions are created by reducing profit for a period (and thereby reducing the owner's claim). The chapter outlined how provisions can be used to warn of potential and contingent liabilities. It drew attention to the difference between the everyday meaning of provisions and the technical meaning of the word in accounting. The chapter also outlined the difference between free-standing true provisions and those deductions from the value of specific assets, which are also called provisions.

# DRILLS AND EXERCISES

## 41.1

FIRM A has been notified that it will almost certainly have to pay a fine of £1 000 in the near future, while FIRM B has been notified that it will almost certainly be awarded a prize of £1 000 in the near future.

How should each firm account for the news? Explain your answer with reference to the accounting principle of prudence.

## 41.2

A firm is sued for damages of £100. According to the best advice, there is a 50% chance that the firm will lose the case and have to pay £100, and a 50% chance that the case will be dismissed and the firm will have nothing to pay. Should the firm make a provision? If so, for how much?

# CHAPTER 42

# Maintaining, Changing, or Releasing a Provision

## OBJECTIVES

*The objectives of this chapter are:*

- to show how an existing provision can be maintained at the same level, adjusted, or released in a later period
- to explain how and why the reported figures relevant to a provision will be different in the P&L Account and the balance sheet

## MAINTAINING A CONSTANT LEVEL OF PROVISION

Once a provision has been created, the balance on the provision account will stay there and appear in successive balance sheets forever – or at least until something is done to change it. Having once established a provision, therefore, a firm need do nothing to maintain the provision at the same level in successive periods, as shown in Box 42.1.

BOX 42.1

---

**Maintaining an Existing Provision**

In Period 1 a customer alleges that she has suffered damage from the activities of a firm, and claims £500 compensation. The firm contests the claim but decides in any case to set up a provision for the potential liability of £500. The double entry will be:

| DR | P&L Account | ◄ £500 | |
| CR | Provision for Compensation | | ► £500 |

---

**BOX 42.1**  Continued

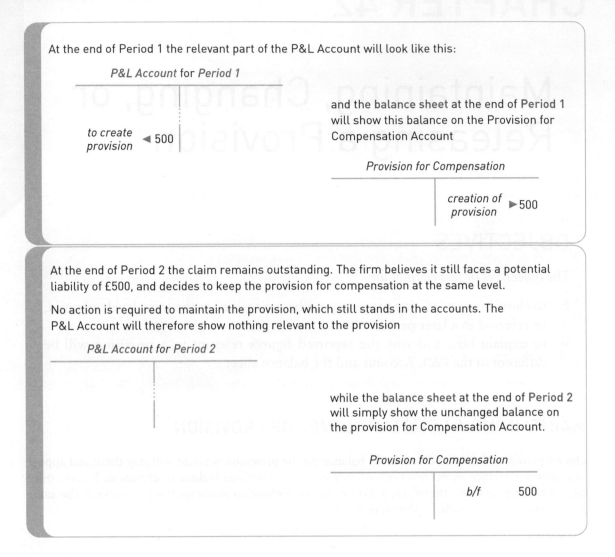

At the end of Period 1 the relevant part of the P&L Account will look like this:

P&L Account for *Period 1*

to create provision  ◄ 500

and the balance sheet at the end of Period 1 will show this balance on the Provision for Compensation Account

Provision for Compensation

creation of provision  ► 500

At the end of Period 2 the claim remains outstanding. The firm believes it still faces a potential liability of £500, and decides to keep the provision for compensation at the same level.

No action is required to maintain the provision, which still stands in the accounts. The P&L Account will therefore show nothing relevant to the provision

P&L Account for Period 2

while the balance sheet at the end of Period 2 will simply show the unchanged balance on the provision for Compensation Account.

Provision for Compensation

b/f          500

## INCREASING A PROVISION

To change a provision at any time after it has been created – that is, to change the balance on a Provision Account – we need only to make accounting entries for the *difference* between the old provision and the new. Since a provision is a CR balance, to increase an existing provision will require an extra CR in the Provision Account. The corresponding DR will be in the P&L Account, to reduce the owner's claim (thereby making way for the increase in the dummy claim). Box 42.2 shows an example.

**BOX 42.2**

### Increasing a Provision

It is the end of Period 3. A firm has previously made a provision of £500 in respect of a claim for compensation made by a customer in Period 1, as shown on the Provision for Compensation Account below.

*Provision for Compensation*

|  |  |
|---|---|
|  | b/f    500 |

Lawyers now advise that if the case comes to court, the firm may well have to pay compensation of £600.

At the end of Period 3 therefore, the firm decides that the existing provision of £500 should be increased by £100 to £600. The double entry for the increase in provision will be:

| DR | P&L Account | ◄ £100 |  |
|---|---|---|---|
| CR | Provision for Compensation |  | ► £100 |

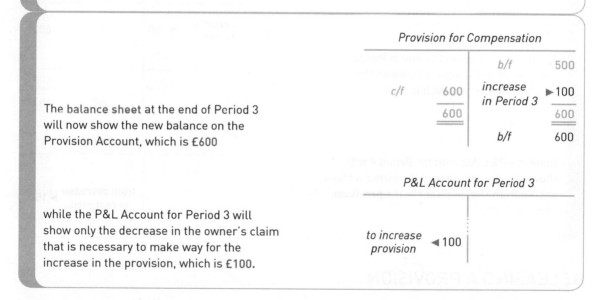

*Provision for Compensation*

The balance sheet at the end of Period 3 will now show the new balance on the Provision Account, which is £600

| | | | |
|---|---|---|---|
| | | b/f | 500 |
| c/f | 600 | increase in Period 3 | ►100 |
| | 600 | | 600 |
| | | b/f | 600 |

while the P&L Account for Period 3 will show only the decrease in the owner's claim that is necessary to make way for the increase in the provision, which is £100.

*P&L Account for Period 3*

| | | |
|---|---|---|
| to increase provision | ◄ 100 | |

## DECREASING A PROVISION

Decreasing a provision requires a DR entry in the Provision Account. This will decrease the dummy claim. The corresponding CR will be in the P&L Account, ultimately increasing the owner's claim to take up the slack created by the decrease in the dummy claim. Box 42.3 shows an example.

## BOX 42.3

### Decreasing a Provision

It is the end of Period 4. A firm has an existing provision of £600 in respect of a claim for compensation made by a customer, as shown below.

*Provision for Compensation*

|  |  |  |  |
|--|--|--|--|
|  | b/f | 600 |  |

The firm is now advised that the maximum compensation payable in cases of this kind is only £450.

At the end of Period 4 therefore, the firm decides that the existing provision of £600 should be decreased by £150 to a new level of £450. The double entry for the decrease in provision will be:

| DR | Provision for Compensation | ◀ £150 |  |
|----|---------------------------|--------|--------|
| CR | P&L Account |  | ▶ £150 |

*Provision for Compensation*

| period 4 decrease | ◀ 150 | b/f | 600 |
|-------------------|-------|-----|-----|
| c/f | 450 |  |  |
|  | 600 |  | 600 |
|  |  | b/f | 450 |

The balance sheet at the end of Period 4 will now show the new balance on the Provision Account, which is £450

*P&L Account for Period 4*

|  |  |  |
|--|--|--|
|  | from decrease in provision | ▶ 150 |

while the P&L Account for Period 4 will show only the increase in the owner's claim arising from the decrease in the provision, which is £150.

## RELEASING A PROVISION

A provision may in the end prove unnecessary. As events unfold, it may become clear that there is no longer any chance of the potential liability developing into a definite liability. In such circumstances the provision must be released, or cancelled. The accounting entries are the opposite of those required to set up the provision in the first place. To release a provision requires a DR in the Provision Account to cancel the dummy claim, and a CR in the P&L Account to restore the full value of the owner's claim by increasing reported profit. Box 42.4 shows an example.

## BOX 42.4

### Decreasing a Provision

It is the end of Period 5. A firm has an existing provision of £450 in respect of a claim for compensation made by a customer, as shown below.

*Provision for Compensation*

|   |   |   |   |
|---|---|---|---|
|   |   | b/f | 450 |

The firm is now advised that the customer has dropped her claim for compensation. The existing provision must therefore be released. The double entry will be:

| DR | Provision for Compensation | ◄ £450 |   |
|----|----------------------------|--------|---|
| CR | P&L Account |   | ► £450 |

The Provision for Compensation Account will now carry a nil balance. The balance sheet at the end of Period 5 will therefore show nothing in respect of the provision

*Provision for Compensation*

| release of provision | ◄ 450 | b/f | 450 |
|----------------------|-------|-----|-----|

*P&L Account for Period 5*

while the P&L Account for Period 5 will show the £450 increase in the owner's claim arising from the release of the dummy claim.

|   |   | from release of provision | ► 450 |
|---|---|---------------------------|-------|

When a provision is created, the reported value of the owner's claim is decreased. When a provision is released, the decrease is reversed. The overall effect is neutral in the end.

This is not to say that the making of provisions should be lightly undertaken, because their effect may be so easily reversed. Making provisions and unmaking them if they are wrong are not actions that are neutral in their effect on the reported profit of individual periods. Creating a new provision (or increasing an existing one) will reduce the reported profit of the period in which it occurs. Releasing a provision (or just decreasing it) will increase the reported profit of the period in which it occurs. No matter how easily they may be reversed, these short-term signals may be vitally important. In business and for investors, the reported profit or loss of the latest period may be the basis of significant decisions, and is often the only information we have by which to judge the performance of a firm and those responsible for its management.

## PROVISIONS AS REPORTED IN THE BALANCE SHEET AND THE P&L ACCOUNT

In the accounting for provisions, different figures appear in the balance sheet and in the P&L Account. In the balance sheet the figure we see is the balance on the Provision Account – that is, we see the whole amount of the dummy claim. Meanwhile in the P&L Account the figure we see is only the amount of any change in the provision; and we see this through an entry in the P&L Account which actually shows how the change in the provision affects the owner's claim. An increase in a provision comes at the expense of the owner's claim – there must be a DR in the P&L Account. A decrease in a provision leaves extra value to be claimed by the owner – there must be a CR in the P&L Account. To summarize the rules concerning the accounting for provisions in the P&L Account:

- If there is no change in a provision during a period, there will be no entry in the P&L Account.

- If a provision is increased, the amount of the change must be recorded as a DR in the P&L Account, reflecting the decrease in the owner's claim that is needed to make way for the increase in the dummy claim. In an Income Statement, where there are no DRs and CRs, the cause of this reduction in the owner's claim will be listed as an expense.

- If a provision is decreased in a period, the amount of the change must be recorded as a CR in the P&L Account, reflecting the increase in the owner's claim, taking up the slack left by the decrease in the dummy claim. In an Income Statement, this increase in the owner's claim will be listed as a negative expense.

In the balance sheet, provisions will be listed among current liabilities if the potential liability they warn about is likely to be payable within 12 months of the balance sheet date. If the potential liability is not likely to be payable within 12 months, the provision will be listed among the firm's long-term liabilities.

## REVIEW

This chapter has shown the accounting entries necessary to increase or decrease a provision, and has contrasted the information relevant to provisions that are shown in the P&L Account for any period and the information that is shown in the balance sheet at the end of any period.

# DRILLS AND EXERCISES

## 42.1

REQUIRED: for each set of data below, show a P&L Account extract for each of the relevant years and an account for the relevant provision with the balance at the end of each year.

### BUSINESS 1

YEAR 1: A business dismisses an employee for (alleged) gross misconduct. The employee sues the business for wrongful dismissal. The business is advised by its lawyers that it may be found liable for damages in the sum of £200 000 if the case comes to court.
YEAR 2: The case remains undecided.
YEAR 3: The case remains undecided, but lawyers advise the firm that the maximum liability it would face is probably not more than £150 000.

### BUSINESS 2

YEAR 1: An engineering firm builds a bridge which falls down. The firm is sued for damages and expects to lose £200 000.
YEAR 2: Lawyers advise the firm that it will probably be found liable for damages of £250 000.
YEAR 3: The case remains undecided.

### BUSINESS 3

YEAR 1: A customer visiting the premises of a business falls down, breaks her leg, and sues the business for £15 000. The business denies liability, and at the end of the year the case is not yet decided, but the business is advised by its lawyer that it is likely to be found liable for damages in the sum of £12 000.
YEAR 2: The case remains undecided.
YEAR 3: It emerges that the customer ignored repeated safety warnings and forced the lock on a door in order to enter the area where she fell down. The case is therefore dropped.

### BUSINESS 4

YEAR 1: A business decides to close a branch of its operations. Closure will actually take place in Year 2. It is estimated that the costs of closure (mainly redundancy payments) will be £400 000.
YEAR 2: Revival of demand in the area means that the firm abandons its plans to close the branch.

## 42.2

A customer sues a food manufacturer, having consumed a contaminated product. The manufacturer is likely to lose the case, but the contamination is traced to an ingredient bought in from another supplier. The food manufacturer sues the supplier, and is likely to win the case.

Should the food manufacturer make a provision for the damages claimed by the customer? Give reasons for your answer.

# CHAPTER 43

# Transactions That Have Been Provided For

## OBJECTIVES

*The objectives of this chapter are:*

- to show the two possible ways of accounting for a transaction that has already been provided for
- to demonstrate that the two methods will show the same result in the P&L Account and the balance sheet

## THE BASIC APPROACH

A provision is made in anticipation of a real liability or a real payment that may arise in the future. So what do we do when the real event occurs? How do we account for a real transaction that has already been provided for?

There are two possible treatments in the ledger accounts. One approach is to record the real transaction as though no provision had been made, and then simply cancel or release the provision (once the real transaction has occurred, there is no more need for the provision). Box 43.1 presents an example.

## BOX 43.1

### Accounting for a Transaction Already Provided For

In Period 1, a firm made a provision of £300 in respect of a potential liability to pay a registration tax. It is now Period 2, and the real tax liability has been fixed at £250.

1. The double entry to record the real liability will be:

| DR | P&L Account – tax expense | ●£250 | |
|----|---------------------------|-------|------|
| CR | Tax Liability (= promise to pay tax) | | ●£250 |

2. The double entry to release the provision will be:

| DR | Provision for Tax | ◄ £300 | |
|----|-------------------|--------|--------|
| CR | P&L Account – release of provision | | ► £300 |

After these entries the relevant accounts will look like this:

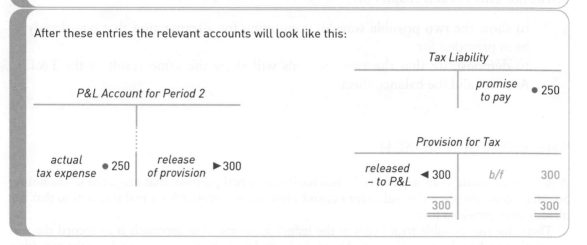

Notice first that the value involved in the real transaction may well be different from the value provided for, as it is in our example. This will often happen, since uncertainty about the relevant value is one of the reasons why a provision (instead of a real liability) may have been recorded in the first place.

Notice also that this treatment generates two accounting entries in the P&L Account when the actual event occurs: a DR to record the actual transaction, and a CR to release the provision. The net effect of these two entries in the current P&L Account, in conjunction with the original entry in an earlier P&L Account when the provision was created, will ensure that the total reduction of profit/the owner's claim is, finally, exactly equal to the value involved in the real transaction. Box 43.2 provides a demonstration.

## BOX 43.2

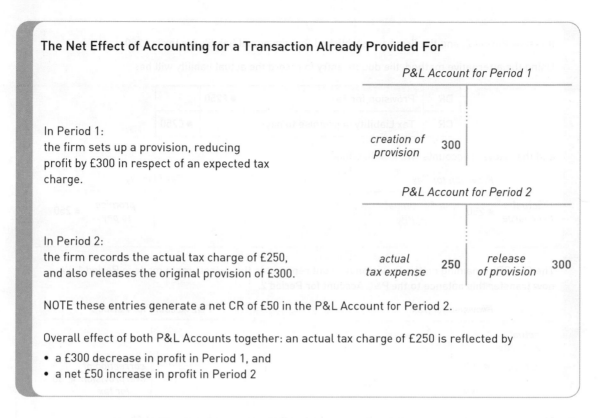

**The Net Effect of Accounting for a Transaction Already Provided For**

*P&L Account for Period 1*

In Period 1:
the firm sets up a provision, reducing profit by £300 in respect of an expected tax charge.

creation of provision | 300

*P&L Account for Period 2*

In Period 2:
the firm records the actual tax charge of £250, and also releases the original provision of £300.

actual tax expense | 250 | release of provision | 300

NOTE these entries generate a net CR of £50 in the P&L Account for Period 2.

Overall effect of both P&L Accounts together: an actual tax charge of £250 is reflected by

- a £300 decrease in profit in Period 1, and
- a net £50 increase in profit in Period 2

# AN ALTERNATIVE APPROACH

An alternative approach, achieving exactly the same effect, is to DR the Provision Account instead of the P&L Account when the actual transaction occurs; and then to transfer the balance on the Provision Account to the P&L Account. Box 43.3 reworks our example using this approach.

## BOX 43.3

**Accounting for a Transaction Already Provided For – an Alternative**

In Period 1, a firm made a provision of £300 in respect of an expected tax charge

*Provision for Tax*

potential liability | 300

*P&L Account for Period 1*

creation of provision | 300

## BOX 43.3  Continued

It is now Period 2, and the firm has established that the actual liability for tax is £250.

Using the alternative method, the double entry to record the actual liability will be:

| DR | Provision for Tax | ● £250 | |
|----|----|----|----|
| CR | Tax Liability (= promise to pay) | | ● £250 |

and the relevant accounts will look like this:

| Provision for Tax | | | | Tax Liability | |
|----|----|----|----|----|----|
| actual tax charge | ● 250 | b/f potential liability | 300 | promise to pay | ● 250 |

The £50 CR remaining on the Provision Account represents the overestimate made in Period 1. We now transfer this balance to the P&L Account for Period 2.

| Provision for Tax | | | | P&L Account for Period 2 | |
|----|----|----|----|----|----|
| actual tax charge | 250 | b/f potential liability | 300 | | |
| to P&L | ◄ 50 | | | | correction of overprovision ► 50 for tax |
| | 300 | | 300 | | |

The overall result here, as with the basic method, is that the actual tax charge of £250 is represented as an expense of £300 in the P&L Account of Period 1, and (to correct the mistaken estimate) an increase in profit of £50 in Period 2

# REVIEW

This chapter has introduced two methods of accounting for an actual transaction which has previously been provided for. Either the actual transaction is recorded as though it had not been provided for, and the provision is cancelled by release to the P&L Account. Or the actual transaction is recorded in the Provision Account, and *the balance* on the Provision Account is transferred to the P&L Account. Both methods achieve the same effect.

# DRILLS AND EXERCISES

## 43.1

REQUIRED: For each set of data below, show the necessary entries on a provision account, with an extract from the P&L Account for each relevant year, plus an account for money and promises.

### BUSINESS 1

YEAR 1: A firm is investigated, and conclusive evidence is found that the firm has been breaking regulations for which there is a mandatory fine £50 000. The case will come to court in Year 2.

YEAR 2: The case comes to court and the firm is duly fined £50 000.

### BUSINESS 2

YEAR 1: A firm discovers a major crack in the wall of a building which will have to be repaired in Year 2. It is estimated that the repair will cost £15 000.

YEAR 2: The crack is repaired at an actual cost of £14 000.

### BUSINESS 3

YEAR 1: All firms operating in Dystopia are informed that they will be required to make a one-off contribution to a fund for the development of the capital city. Firm A believes that it will be required to make a contribution of £900.

YEAR 2: Firm A pays its actual contribution, which is actually fixed at £950.

### BUSINESS 4 (SLIGHTLY TRICKIER)

YEAR 1: The chairman of a baby-food manufacturing firm promises to give one million pounds to a global fund for fighting child poverty.

YEAR 2: The firm pays £500 000 to the fund.

YEAR 3: The firm pays another £500 000 to the fund.

## 43.2

REQUIRED: Describe at least two ways in which the following events or situations could or should be accounted for in Year 1 and Year 2, and state which way you would choose if you were responsible for preparing the firm's final accounts.

YEAR 1: A firm decides to upgrade its manufacturing capacity, and places an order for a new fixed asset costing £30 000.

YEAR 2: The fixed asset is delivered at a cost of £30 000 as expected, and paid for.

Are there any further facts, not stated above, that might be relevant to your decision?

# CHAPTER 44

# Provisions: Matching Future Expenditure Against Current Revenue

## OBJECTIVES

*The objectives of this chapter are:*

- to explain why it may be necessary, on occasion, to recognize future expenditure as an expense in a current P&L Account
- to show how the creation of a provision can be used to achieve this effect

## PROVISIONS AND EXPENSES

To create a provision requires a DR entry and a CR entry. The CR, creating a dummy claim in the balance sheet, can be used to represent a potential liability, as we have seen in preceding chapters. This chapter will consider the use of the DR, which appears in the P&L Account. This can be used to show an object of future expenditure as an expense in a current P&L Account.

What does this mean and why is it useful? First, recall the difference between expenditure and expense. Expenditure means spending, or paying out money or promises. Expense means the consumption of value. Remember also the concept of matching, and especially the rule that expenses should be matched in the same P&L Account against the revenue or sales they have helped to generate.

In general, expenditure will precede expense – an input must be paid for, at least with a promise (it must be the object of expenditure) before its value can be consumed (before it becomes an expense). However, there are cases in which activities that generate revenue now, involve a consumption of value that can only be paid for later. The classic example is clean-up costs. The costs, for example, of cleaning up the site of a coal mine or a nuclear power station can only be paid when mining or power generation has ceased. These clean-up costs, payable in the future, are expenses which should in all fairness be matched against the revenues earned from operations in the present. Box 44.1 presents an example of how provisions can be used to achieve this effect, with an object of future expenditure being shown as an expense in a current P&L Account.

## BOX 44.1

### Provisions – Recognizing Future Expenditure as a Current Expense

A firm has held the right to run open-air concerts in a city centre park for the whole of Year 1.

It is now the end of Year 1, and the firm has received £500 net revenue from concerts in the year.

On the basis of actual transactions in Year 1, the firm could report a profit of £500 in Year 1, as shown below

*P&L Account for Year 1*

| | |
|---|---|
| *net revenue from concerts* | 500 |

However, that would be misleading, since the firm has also agreed to clean and restore the park to its normal condition in Year 2. It is estimated that the clean-up cost payable in Year 2 will be £100.

It would seem fairer to match the cost of cleaning up, payable in Year 2, against the revenue earned in Year 1. This can be done by the use of a provision, as shown below.

Double entry to create the provision would be

| DR | P&L Account – estimated clean-up costs | ● £100 | |
|---|---|---|---|
| CR | Provision for Clean-Up Costs | | ● £100 |

As a result the estimated clean-up costs will appear in the P&L Account for Year 1, and the firm will report a much fairer net profit of only £400, with a provision for the expected liability in the balance sheet.

At the end of Year 1, relevant accounts will look like this:

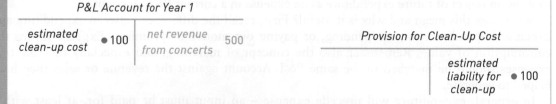

*P&L Account for Year 1*

| | | | | |
|---|---|---|---|---|
| *estimated clean-up cost* | ● 100 | *net revenue from concerts* | 500 | |

*Provision for Clean-Up Cost*

| | |
|---|---|
| | *estimated liability for clean-up* ● 100 |

Note that in our example the P&L Account for Year 2 will include the actual cost of cleaning up the park (as a DR), and the release of the provision (as a CR). Any difference between the two will reflect an error in the earlier estimate, and will automatically correct that error with a compensating adjustment of the P&L Account for Year 2.

## PROVISIONS, ACCRUALS, AND DEPRECIATION

As used in cases like the one above, to recognize future expenditure in a current P&L Account, provisions are not unlike accruals, and take their place in the range of devices used by accountants to ensure that the revenues reported in a P&L Account are fairly matched against the costs of earning those revenues.

It is interesting also to compare this use of provisions to recognize future expenditure in a current P&L Account, against the use of the provision for depreciation. Both are matching devices, although they work in opposite directions:

● the provision for depreciation is used to recognize past expenditure (the purchase of a fixed asset) as an expense in future P&L accounts (matching the expenditure bit by bit against the revenues earned as the value of the fixed asset is consumed);

● the freestanding provision as we have used it here, is used to recognize future expenditure as an expense in a current P&L Account (matching the future expenditure against the revenues generated here and now by activities that will make the expenditure necessary).

# REVIEW

This chapter has shown how the DR entry to the P&L Account, made in connection with the creation of a provision, may be used to show an object of future expenditure as an expense in the current P&L Account.

# DRILLS AND EXERCISES

## 44.1

REQUIRED: For each set of data below, show the necessary entries on a provision account, with an extract from the P&L Account for each relevant year, plus an account for money and promises.

### BUSINESS 1

YEAR 1: A firm runs a small lottery, selling 100 tickets for £1 each, and offering a prize of £90.
   At the end of Year 1, all 100 tickets have been sold, but the winner has not yet been selected.
YEAR 2: The winner of the lottery is selected and given the prize of £90.

### BUSINESS 2

YEAR 1: A farmer rents a field to a motor-cycling club for the whole of Year 1, for a rent of £1 000. The farmer expects that he will have to pay costs of £300 to restore the land to agricultural use in Year 2.
YEAR 2: The actual cost to restore the land is £310.

### BUSINESS 3

YEAR 1: A business takes a three-year lease on a property, with an undertaking to fully redecorate the property before leaving at the end of the third year. It is estimated that the cost of redecoration will be £1 500.

YEAR 2: The business continues to occupy the property.

YEAR 3: The business occupies the property until the end of the year, and redecorates at a cost of £1 400 before leaving.

## BUSINESS 4

YEAR 1: A mining business develops a new site which it believes will have a three-year useful life. Environmental legislation demands that the business must clean up the site after its operations., and it is estimated that after three years of operations, the cost of cleaning up (to be paid in Year 4) will be £600 000.

YEAR 2: As a result of stricter environmental legislation, it is now estimated that the cost of cleaning up will be £800 000.

YEAR 3: The business continues to operate the site until the end of the year. However, technological improvements indicate that the cost of cleaning up will probably be only £700 000.

YEAR 4: The site is cleaned up at an actual cost of £670 000.

# CHAPTER 45

# Rolling Provisions

## OBJECTIVES

*The objectives of this chapter are:*

- to explain the concept of a rolling provision
- to explain the accounting entries needed to set up and adjust a rolling provision
- to show how actual expenditure covered by a rolling provision is normally accounted for

## ROLLING PROVISIONS

Many provisions relate to the expectation of a specific future event. They last only as long as the likelihood of the event and are cancelled when the actual event occurs, or when it ceases to be likely. However, some provisions seem to be almost perpetual, relating to a state of affairs rather than any individual expected event. These are what we shall call rolling provisions.

Rolling provisions would include, for example, provisions relating to a firm's liability to repair or replace defective goods. Each year's sales will generate a new potential liability to repair or replace some of the goods sold, and as the firm continues to sell goods, so it will continue to renew its potential liability to repair or replace the defective ones.

## ACCOUNTING FOR ROLLING PROVISIONS

Rolling provisions are not technically different from other provisions, but understanding the accounting for rolling provisions does seem to cause particular problems. Box 45.1 on the following page shows an example of the standard accounting approach.

## BOX 45.1

### A Rolling Provision

A firm offers a full refund to all customers who return goods for any reason within 12 months of the year of the original sale. The firm estimates that 10% of its sales in any year will be returned for refund in the following year.

Sales in Year 1 are £5 000. The firm therefore creates a provision for refunds of ● £500, as shown below.

| P&L Account for Year 1 | | | Provision for Refunds | |
|---|---|---|---|---|
| | Sales | 5 000 | | |
| creation of provision for refunds | ● 500 | | balance at end of YR 1 | ● 500 |

Sales in Year 2 are £4 000, requiring a provision of £400. A provision of £500 already exists. The provision must therefore be reduced by ●£100 as shown below.

| P&L Account for Year 2 | | | Provision for Refunds | | | |
|---|---|---|---|---|---|---|
| | Sales | 4 000 | decrease | ● 100 | balance at end of YR 1 | 500 |
| gain from decrease in provision for refunds | ● 100 | | c/f | 400 | | |
| | | | | 500 | | 500 |
| | | | | | balance at end of YR 2 | 400 |

Sales in Year 3 are £6 000, requiring a provision of £600. A provision of £400 already exists. The provision must therefore be increased by ● £200 as shown below.

| | | | Provision for Refunds | | | |
|---|---|---|---|---|---|---|
| | | | decrease | 100 | balance at end of YR 1 | 500 |
| P&L Account for Year 3 | | | c/f | 400 | | |
| | | | | 500 | | 500 |
| | Sales | 6 000 | | | balance at end of YR 2 | 400 |
| to increase provision for refunds | ● 200 | | c/f | 600 | increase | ● 200 |
| | | | | 600 | | 600 |
| | | | | | balance at end of YR 3 | 600 |

## COMMENT ON ACCOUNTING FOR ROLLING PROVISIONS

The procedure to set up a rolling provision in Year 1 is very straightforward. It is the procedure in later years that seems to raise objections. If the value of the provision required at the end of the year is related to the value of sales during the year, for many students it seems somehow wrong for the P&L Account to show the whole of the year's sales, while it only shows the change in the related provision.

One way out of this puzzle is to recognize that the one entry made in the P&L Account to reflect the change in the provision, represents in fact the net effect of two things that are happening at the end of each period. First the old provision, relating to last year's sales, is released, then a new provision relating to the current year's sales is created. Box 45.2 shows these two effects separately for Year 2 of our example.

### BOX 45.2

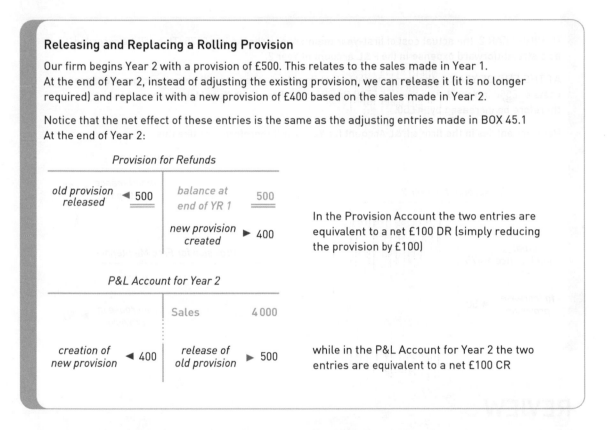

**Releasing and Replacing a Rolling Provision**

Our firm begins Year 2 with a provision of £500. This relates to the sales made in Year 1.
At the end of Year 2, instead of adjusting the existing provision, we can release it (it is no longer required) and replace it with a new provision of £400 based on the sales made in Year 2.

Notice that the net effect of these entries is the same as the adjusting entries made in BOX 45.1
At the end of Year 2:

*Provision for Refunds*

| old provision released ◀ 500 | balance at end of YR 1 500 |
| | new provision created ▶ 400 |

In the Provision Account the two entries are equivalent to a net £100 DR (simply reducing the provision by £100)

*P&L Account for Year 2*

| | Sales 4000 |
| creation of new provision ◀ 400 | release of old provision ▶ 500 |

while in the P&L Account for Year 2 the two entries are equivalent to a net £100 CR

## ACTUAL EXPENDITURE COVERED BY A ROLLING PROVISION

Rolling provisions are made in expectation of real expenditure – thus the firm in our example, which guarantees to give refunds, will eventually face real expenditure in the form of repayments to customers, and so on. These real transactions are normally accounted for as though no provision had been made – they are treated as normal expenses of the period in which they arise. Box 45.3 on the following page presents an example.

## BOX 45.3

### Rolling Provisions and Actual Transactions

A firm sells bicycles, and offers to do a free first-year maintenance check on all bicycles sold.

AT THE END OF YEAR 1, the firm estimates that customers who have bought during the year, will claim maintenance work costing £500 during Year 2. A Provision for Free Maintenance is made accordingly, and the provision account will look like this:

*Provision for Free Maintenance*

| | *potential liability* | 500 |
|---|---|---|

DURING YEAR 2, the actual cost of first-year maintenance checks is ●£475. This will be recorded as a straightforward expense in the P&L account of Year 2.

AT THE END OF YEAR 2, the firm estimates that its sales in the year will give rise to maintenance costs of £550 in Year 3. The existing £500 Provision for Free First-Year Maintenance should therefore be increased by ◀£50.

Relevant entries in the firm's P&L Account for Year 2 will therefore look like this:

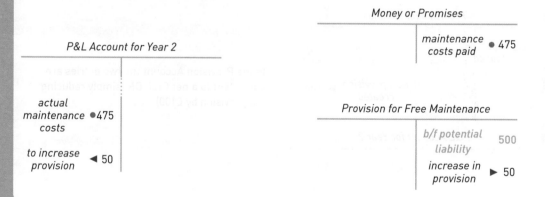

*P&L Account for Year 2*

| *actual maintenance costs* ●475 | |
|---|---|
| *to increase provision* ◀ 50 | |

*Money or Promises*

| | *maintenance costs paid* ● 475 |
|---|---|

*Provision for Free Maintenance*

| | *b/f potential liability* | 500 |
|---|---|---|
| | *increase in provision* ▶ 50 | |

## REVIEW

This chapter has introduced the idea of rolling provisions, showing how they are adjusted from year to year and explaining how the transactions they provide for should be accounted for when they actually occur.

# DRILLS AND EXERCISES

## 45.1

REQUIRED: For each set of data below, show an extract from the P&L Account for each relevant year, plus an account for the relevant provision.

### BUSINESS 1

The business guarantees to repair, free of charge, any of its sales that prove defective within one year of sale.

YEAR 1: Sales for the year are £600 000. The business estimates that repair costs on these goods will be 5% of their sales value.

YEAR 2: Actual repair costs are £31 000. Sales for the year are £800 000, and the business continues to estimate that repair costs will be 5% of the value of goods sold.

YEAR 3: Actual repair costs are £38 000. Sales for the year are £900 000. The business has made improvements to the quality of its goods and now believes that repair costs will be only 4% of the value of goods sold.

### BUSINESS 2

A school offers courses which last one year. Students pay for the whole course in advance, but are guaranteed a full refund of their fees if they do not pass the public examination at the end of their course. Unfortunately, the accounting year-end of the school falls between the end of the course and the announcement of the examination results.

YEAR 1: Sales for the year are £250 000. The school estimates that 10% of the students awaiting results at the end of the year will fail the examination and require a refund.

YEAR 2: Actual refunds to the previous year's students are £23 000. Sales for the year are £300 000. Higher standards are now expected in the examination, and the school estimates that 15% of the students will fail the examination and require a refund.

YEAR 3: Actual refunds to the previous year's students are £45 000. Sales for the year are £280 000. Once again, the school estimates that 15% of the students will fail the examination and require a refund.

# CHAPTER 46

# The Misuse of Provisions

## OBJECTIVES

*The objectives of this chapter are:*

- to give examples of the potential misuse of accounting provisions
- to point out the need for integrity as well as principles in accounting

## PROVISIONS, PRINCIPLES, AND MISUSE

Provisions may be used for two legitimate purposes: to warn of the existence of potential liabilities and to recognize future expenditure in a current P&L Account (reducing reported profit now, to allow for expenses that may have to be paid in the future). The first of these uses is associated with the principle of prudence. The second is also associated with the principle of accruals or matching. Both of these uses are beneficial, but the ability to create and release provisions is also open to misuse.

## PROFIT SMOOTHING

Investors are interested in profits and the growth of profits, but erratic and unpredictable growth is undesirable. Investors would rather see a smoothly rising trend of profits. Thus, a company director faced with an unexpectedly large actual profit in any period, and wishing to please investors, might well be tempted to create or increase unnecessary provisions, to ensure that the reported profit for the period is not so far above the expected trend. This is known as profit smoothing. The added advantage of creating a provision in these circumstances is of course that any unnecessary provision will be available for release in a future period, when actual profits may fall below the expected trend.

## INCREASING LOSSES

A second, related misuse of provisions may occur when a firm cannot avoid reporting weak results for a period, and ideally when this happens for external reasons for which the firm itself bears no responsibility. In such circumstances the temptation is to throw in all kinds of extra provisions to make reported profits even worse. This move can be seen as a protection against the need to report further disappointing results in the future. The idea is to present investors with one big announcement of bad news, to be followed by steady improvements in reported profits (which may be helped by the release of unnecessary provisions), rather than a trickle of bad news over a number of successive periods.

## THE BIG BATH

A third and very similar misuse of provisions is almost irresistibly attractive to a newly appointed incoming management team. The technique is to find as many potential liabilities and likely expenditures as possible (all attributable to the failings of the outgoing management team). The incoming team will be forced to report some very bad results in their first year as they clear up the mess left by their predecessors, but this can be presented as proof of their courage in facing up to unpleasant facts. Thereafter, though, as provisions are found to be unnecessary and quietly released, the firm should be able to report a rising trend of profits – confirming the superior business ability of the incoming management team.

## HIDING EXPENSES

Provisions may also be misused to hide expenses. Recall that once a provision has been created, expenses may be debited to the provision, and not to the P&L Account. Such expenses are effectively hidden from the public gaze. While investors, analysts and others may examine the P&L Account with some degree of rigour, few of them will give comparable attention to movements on a provision account, even if the details are made available.

## NEUTRALITY

According to the principle of neutrality, accounting judgements should be made without bias, on the facts of the case, and without regard to a predetermined outcome. The making of excessive or unnecessary provisions should therefore be countered by the principle of neutrality. This is good: explicit rules and principles do help the cause of honest accounting. But accountants, and those who train them, should not neglect the role of personal integrity.

## REVIEW

This chapter has considered some of the ways in which provisions may be misused to present a misleading picture of the affairs of a business.

# DRILLS AND EXERCISES

### 46.1

State how the following actions would affect the reported profit of a firm in the current period and in the next period(s):

(a)  failure to make a provision when required;
(b)  making a provision when not required.

### 46.2

'A provision is a warning sign'. But what is its purpose? What does it warn us to do or abstain from doing?

### 46.3

While provisions are commonplace, there is no device in accounting for the recognition of potential assets or revenue that will be earned in the future.

   If such a device did exist, how would it work? Give a numerical example. Explain why no such device is openly used in accounting.

# CHAPTER 47

# Accounting for Discounts

## OBJECTIVES

*The objectives of this chapter are:*

- to explain the working of settlement discounts
- to show how to account for transactions involving discounts allowed and discounts received

## PRICE DISCOUNTS

A price discount is a reduction in the selling price of goods or services. This would include bulk or quantity discounts, trade discounts, and discounts for special groups such as students or senior citizens, as well as time-limited special offers, and so on. In accounting, price discounts are normally considered only insofar as they affect the calculation of a selling price. Once a selling price has been determined, the transaction is recorded at that price, with no separate record of the discount. Price discounts are not, in general, an accounting problem.

## SETTLEMENT DISCOUNTS

A settlement discount is a deduction from the value owed by a debtor, which is allowable only if the debtor pays within a certain limited period. Box 47.1 presents an example.

BOX 47.1

---

**Settlement Discounts**

A firm sells goods on credit, offering a 2% discount for payment within 30 days.

Assume a sale on credit for, say, £100.

If the debtor pays within 30 days, the firm will allow a discount of 2% × £100 = £2, accepting £98 cash as full payment of the original £100 promise.

If the debtor does not pay within 30 days, the whole £100 of the original promise must be paid.

---

Settlement discounts are also known as discounts for prompt payment, or even as cash discounts. Their obvious purpose is to encourage debtors to pay their debts promptly, thus providing a firm with cash which it can use, instead of promises. A settlement discount may be *allowed* by the firm which is expecting a payment, or *received* by the firm which is making a payment. Notice that, at the time of the initial transaction, it cannot be known whether or not the offer of a settlement discount will be taken. Sales or purchases on credit, therefore, must always be recorded at full value, even though a settlement discount may be offered.

## DISCOUNTS ALLOWED

A discount allowed is given by a firm to a debtor, as a reward for prompt payment. Part of the debtor's promise is given back, not in exchange for money, but in exchange for paying promptly. The discount allowed is best imagined as a gift going out to the debtor, with the value given away being recognized as an expense or loss in the P&L Account. Thus, when a firm is owed a certain amount, but allows a discount and receives a lesser payment from the debtor, it must record:

- a DR in the Cash Account to record the actual value of the cash coming in, after discount;
- a DR in the P&L Account to recognize the expense or loss incurred in allowing the discount; and
- a CR in the debtor's account (the account for promises from/to the debtor), to show the whole value of the debtor's promise being given back (part of it given back in exchange for money and part of it given back as a gift or reward for prompt payment).

Box 47.2 shows an example.

### BOX 47.2

**Accounting for Discount Allowed**

A firm has sold goods for £200 on credit, as shown in the accounts below.

| Debtor | | | | Sales | | |
|---|---|---|---|---|---|---|
| *promise received* | 200 | | | | *output* | 200 |

The firm offers a 2.5% discount for payment within 30 days, and the debtor pays within 30 days, taking advantage of the discount.

2.5% × £200 = £5, so the discount allowed is £5, and the firm receives £195.

The double entry to account for the transaction and the discount allowed will be:

| | | | |
|---|---|---|---|
| DR | Cash | ●£195 | |
| DR | P&L Account – expense of discount allowed | ● £5 | |
| CR | Debtor (promise given back out) | | ●£200 |

**BOX 47.2** Continued

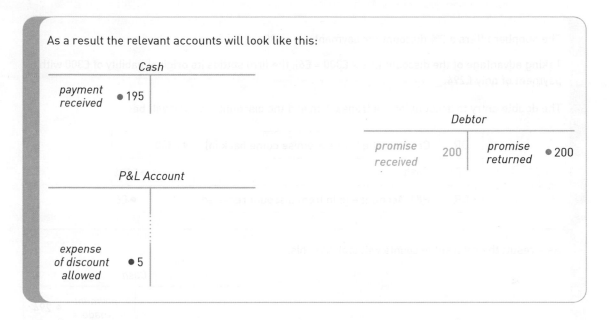

As a result the relevant accounts will look like this:

- Cash: payment received ● 195
- Debtor: promise received 200 | promise returned ● 200
- P&L Account: expense of discount allowed ● 5

## DISCOUNTS RECEIVED

A discount received is a reduction received by a firm in exchange for prompt payment. The firm pays less than it owes, but pays promptly, and therefore receives back the full value of the promise originally given. Discount received is best imagined as a gift received from the creditor, in the form of a promise returned, that has not been fully paid for. The value thus gained by the firm must be recognized with a CR in the P&L Account, as a form of income. Thus, when a firm makes a payment to a creditor net of a discount received, the firm must record:

- a DR in the creditor's account (the account for promises from/to the creditor), to show the whole of the firm's original promise coming back;
- a CR in Cash Account to show the actual value of cash paid out; and
- a CR in the P&L Account to record the firm's gain from the discount received.

Box 47.3 shows an example.

**BOX 47.3**

**Accounting for Discount Received**

A firm owes a supplier (a creditor) £300 for goods purchased on credit, as shown in the accounts below

- Purchases: goods paid for 300
- Creditor: promise given out 300

## BOX 47.3   Continued

The supplier offers a 2% discount for payment within 30 days.

Taking advantage of the discount (2% × £300 = £6), the firm settles its original liability of £300 with a payment of only £294.

The double entry to account for the transaction and the discount received will be:

| DR | Creditor (the firm's promise come back in) | ●£300 | |
|----|--------------------------------------------|--------|--------|
| CR | Cash | | ●£294 |
| CR | P&L Account – gain from discount received | | ●£6 |

As a result the relevant accounts will look like this:

*Cash*

| | |
|---|---|
| | payment made ● 294 |

*Creditor*

| promise returned ●300 | promise given out · 300 |
|---|---|

*P&L Account*

| | |
|---|---|
| | gain from discount received ● 6 |

# FACTORING

Factoring is an arrangement under which a factor (often a large financial institution) will advance money to a firm in exchange for the right to collect money from the firm's debtors. Factoring *without recourse* means in effect selling debts entirely. The factor takes on the risk of bad debts, and should any debtor fail to pay, the factor has no recourse against the firm to whom the debt was originally owed. Factoring *with recourse* means that the factor merely takes on the task of collecting the debt and bears no risk of loss if the debt turns bad.

Factors provide a valuable service to those who need it. They provide immediate access to cash, for which a firm might otherwise have to wait. They are also equipped to collect payments efficiently and by doing so they save work for the firm whose debts they collect.

If debts are transferred to a third party for cash, they must be transferred at a discount, because in general a promise of £1 must be worth less than £1 of real money. Once stated this may be obvious, but why? First, because whoever buys the promise will no doubt incur expenses to collect the money; secondly because there is always a risk, however small, that the debtor may default; and thirdly because money is by definition immediately acceptable in exchange, while promises from debtors are not.

Assuming then that a debtor's promise is transferred or sold at a discount, the transaction will be recorded with a DR in the Cash Account, to record the money coming in, a DR in the P&L Account to recognize the loss involved in selling the promise for less than its face value, and a CR in the debtor's account to show the promise going out. Box 47.4 shows an example.

## BOX 47.4

### Selling Debtors

A firm holds a promise of £500 from a debtor, but the firm needs cash and there is no chance of immediate payment. The firm therefore sells the debt, at a discount of £50, for £450.

The double entry to show the money coming in, to recognize the loss, and to cancel the debtor's original promise will be:

| DR | Cash | ● £450 | |
|----|------|--------|--------|
| CR | P&L Account – loss from discount debt | ● £50 | |
| CR | Debtor (the debtor's promise being given away) | | ● £500 |

As a result the relevant accounts will look like this:

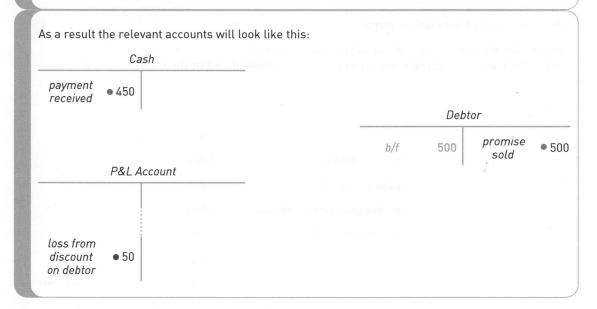

## SEPARATE ACCOUNTS FOR DISCOUNT ALLOWED AND DISCOUNT RECEIVED

Settlement discounts and discounts in connection with the factoring of debts may arise throughout an accounting period. It is not practical, therefore, to record the gains or losses arising directly in the P&L Account, as we have done for simplicity. Usually in practice a firm will have a separate Discount Allowed Account in which to record (as a DR) the loss or expense involved each time the firm allows a discount. The balance on this account can then be transferred to the P&L Account as an expense at the end of the period.

Likewise in practice a firm will usually have a Discount Received Account in which to record (with a CR) the income or gain arising each time the firm receives a discount. The balance on this account will then be transferred to the P&L as a kind of income at the end of the period.

In an Income Statement, discount allowed will be shown as an expense. Discount received is normally shown as a negative expense.

# REVIEW

This chapter has described the difference between price discounts and settlement discounts and has explained the rules of accounting for discounts allowed and for discounts received. It has also shown how to account for the sale or factoring of debtors' promises at a discount.

# DRILLS AND EXERCISES

## 47.1

From each set of data below prepare:

(a)  a debtors account and/or a creditors account, and
(b)  a P&L Account extract concerning discounts allowed and/or discounts received.

### BUSINESS 1

|  | £ |
|---|---|
| opening debtors | 11 000 |
| sales on credit | 48 000 |
| cash received from debtors | 50 960 |
| discount allowed | 1 040 |

|  | £ |
|---|---|
| opening creditors | 7 000 |
| purchases on credit | 26 000 |
| cash paid to creditors | 26 325 |
| discount received | 675 |

## BUSINESS 2

| | £ |
|---|---|
| opening debtors | 13 000 |
| sales on credit | 57 000 |
| cash received from debtors | 56 550 |
| discount allowed | 1 450 |

| | £ |
|---|---|
| opening creditors | 8 000 |
| purchases on credit | 32 000 |
| cash paid to creditors | 28 275 |
| discount received | 725 |

## BUSINESS 3

A firm sells only on credit, and offers a discount of 2% to customers who pay within four weeks of invoice. Debtors at the start of the year are £20 000, and sales for the year are £250 000. Customers originally owing £100 000 pay within the relevant period, taking the discount allowed. £140 000 is received from other customers.

## BUSINESS 4

A firm buys exclusively on credit. One major supplier offers a discount of 2.5% for payment within 30 days of invoice. The firm always takes advantage of this discount. Creditors at the start of the year are £25 000. Purchases during the year are £300 000. The firm pays a total of £275 000 to creditors during the year, including a payment in respect of an original £200 000 owed to the supplier who offers the discount.

# 47.2

In accounting, price discounts are normally considered only as insofar as they affect the calculation of a selling price. Once a selling price has been determined, the transaction is recorded at that price, with no separate record of the discount.

## BUSINESS 5

At the height of the 'dot.com boom' (leading up to the year 2000) when the commercial exploitation of the Internet seemed to offer immeasurable wealth to the firms that got there first, new companies building a business on the Internet were rated by investors and analysts on the basis of sales growth. Profits were not expected. The essential thing was to gain customers and sales, from which it was expected that profits would flow in the future.

One such firm offered a *price* discount of £50 on all sales of £50 or more, and was immediately swamped with orders for goods with a value of exactly £50, or very little more.

Describe at least two ways in which these transactions *could* be reported in a firm's P&L Account, and state the way in which the company (in the circumstances) would be most likely to account for them. Comment.

# CHAPTER 48

# Bad Debt Write off and Recovery

## OBJECTIVES

*The objectives of this chapter are:*

- to show how a bad debt can be written off and explain the accounting treatment of a dishonoured cheque
- to explain the accounting treatment of a bad debt which is eventually recovered
- to outline some of the most usual and basic credit control procedures

## WRITING OFF A BAD DEBT

When a business sells on credit or makes a loan, there is always a chance that the debtor's promise to pay or repay may come to nothing in the end. Sometimes debtors cannot pay the value they have promised. Sometimes they abscond or will not pay, and it is not worthwhile for a firm that holds their promises to find them or force them to pay. In such cases the firm has a bad debt – a promise that is worthless.

Bad debts or worthless promises should be written off – that is to say, the value shown as coming IN to the Debtor's Account (the account for the debtor's promises), now being worthless, should be cancelled with a CR, and there should be a corresponding DR in the P&L Account to recognize the loss incurred. Box 48.1 shows an example.

BOX 48.1

### Writing Off a Bad Debt

A firm has previously made a sale on credit to Customer A, who is now a debtor to the firm for £500, as shown in the account below.

| Customer A | | |
|---|---|---|
| b/f existing debt | 500 | |

## BOX 48.1    Continued

It now appears that Customer A cannot or will not pay, and the firm has decided to write off the whole of the existing debt.

The double entry to write off the debt will be

| DR | P&L Account – bad debt written off | ► £500 | |
| CR | Customer A's Account | | ◄ £500 |

As a result the relevant accounts will look like this:

|  | *P&L Account* |  |  | *Customer A* |  |
| --- | --- | --- | --- | --- | --- |
| | | | *b/f*<br>*existing debt* | 500 | *bad debt*<br>*– to P&L*   ◄ 500 |
| *bad debt*<br>*written off*   ► 500 | | | | | |

# ACCOUNTING FOR THE RECOVERY OF A BAD DEBT

If a customer has proved to be a bad debtor, a firm will offer no further credit, and will probably notify credit control agencies and other firms of the risks involved in dealing with the bad debtor. It is only fair, then, that if a bad debt is eventually recovered after being written off, the debtor's account should be adjusted to remove the stain on his or her character.

Thus, if a firm receives payment in respect of a debt previously written off, there are two things to be done in the accounts. First will be the correction of the previous write-off, with a DR in the debtor's account to restore the original promise, and a CR in the P&L Account to reverse the loss that was recognized when the debt was written off. Secondly, the money received must be accounted for in the normal way, with a DR in the bank or cash account (money coming in) and a CR in the debtor's account (promise returned to debtor). Box 48.2 shows an example.

## BOX 48.2

### Recovery of a Bad Debt

In a previous period, a firm has written off a bad debt of £500 owed by Customer A, whose account therefore looks like this:

| | *Customer A* | | |
| --- | --- | --- | --- |
| *b/f*<br>*existing debt* | 500 | *bad debt*<br>*– to P&L* | 500 |

**BOX 48.2**   Continued

Now, in the current period, the firm has received a cheque for £500 in full payment of the debt previously written off as bad.

First the firm will reinstate the bad debt, by reversing the entries that were previously made to write it off. The double entry will be

| DR | Customer A – bad debt reinstated | ●£500 | |
|----|----------------------------------|-------|------|
| CR | P&L Account – recovery of bad debt | | ●£500 |

Next, the firm will account for the payment received in the usual way, showing the cash coming IN and the customer's promise being given back OUT. The double entry will be

| DR | Cash | ● £500 | |
|----|------|--------|------|
| CR | Customer A | | ●£500 |

As a result, the relevant accounts will look like this:

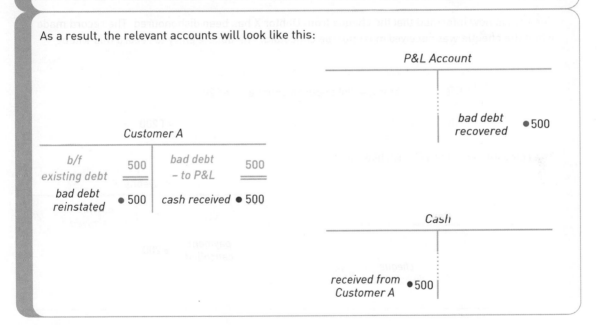

# DISHONOURED CHEQUES

A dishonoured cheque is an instruction that the bank refuses to obey. When a firm first receives a cheque, it must presume that the cheque will be honoured and the firm will receive its payment from the bank in the normal way. All cheques received, therefore, are accounted for in the normal way as a promise coming IN from the bank. If the cheque is to be dishonoured, it will only happen when it reaches the issuer's bank.

When a cheque is dishonoured, it does not mean that the underlying debt is a bad debt and will never be paid. The bank's refusal to pay may reflect just a temporary problem for the debtor, or a misunderstanding between the debtor and his or her bank. It follows that news of a dishonoured cheque does not mean that the underlying debt should be written off. It simply means that the debtor still owes the money which the firm mistakenly thought it had received in the form of the cheque. The accounting entries that were made when the cheque was received, must be reversed. Box 48.3 shows an example.

BOX 48.3

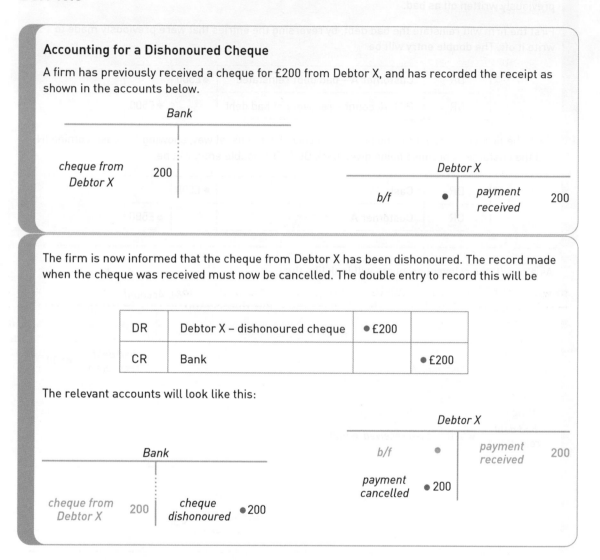

### Accounting for a Dishonoured Cheque

A firm has previously received a cheque for £200 from Debtor X, and has recorded the receipt as shown in the accounts below.

The firm is now informed that the cheque from Debtor X has been dishonoured. The record made when the cheque was received must now be cancelled. The double entry to record this will be

| DR | Debtor X – dishonoured cheque | • £200 | |
| CR | Bank | | • £200 |

The relevant accounts will look like this:

# CREDIT CONTROL

Credit control means all of the procedures and practices involved in collecting payment from customers and minimizing the occurrence of bad debts. The simplest and most effective means of credit control is a refusal to sell except for cash. In certain circumstances (when for example the trade is illegal, or where the law itself is erratic and unenforced) it may even be impossible to trade on credit. However, under normal circumstances, the benefits of trading on credit, for both buyer and seller, are such that few firms can afford to insist on immediate payment in cash.

Credit control is in itself a specialized occupation, but some of the standard credit control procedures of which accountants should be aware would include measures such as these:

- investigate the credit worthiness of prospective customers (there are agencies that will do this for a fee);
- set a credit limit for each customer – that is, set a maximum value that each customer is allowed to owe, after which further sales will be refused until some payment is made;
- produce a regular 'aged debtor' listing – analyzing debts by how long they have been outstanding. Usual categories are debts 0–30 days old; 31–60 days old; 61–90 days old, and more than 90 days;
- stay in regular contact with debtors, and issue increasingly stern reminders to those who are falling behind with payments;
- state the firm's terms of credit, such as 'payment within 30 days' and offer discounts for prompt payment.

There are also legal devices available to protect against bad debts, some of which will be considered in Chapter 56.

## RELUCTANCE TO WRITE OFF BAD DEBTS

One basic measure of credit control which certainly concerns accountants, should be a reluctance to write off bad debts. It is true that writing off a bad debt does not in itself create a loss – it will merely recognize a loss that has already happened. But the accountant should be quite sure that a debt really cannot be collected, before the debt is written off. Once a debt is written off as bad, it will no longer appear among the firm's outstanding debts, and the firm will no longer pursue the debtor for payment. Writing off a debt as bad may therefore become a self-fulfilling prophecy – few debtors will pay if no one bothers to ask them. Thus, writing off a bad debt is usually delayed until it can no longer be avoided, and there may well be a number of debts in a firm at any time that are not yet written off, but which are unlikely ever to be paid. The treatment of these and other doubtful debts will be considered in the next two chapters.

## REVIEW

This chapter has shown how to write off a bad debt, and how to account for the recovery of a debt which has previously been written off. It has also shown the accounting procedure necessary to deal with a dishonoured cheque, and outlined some of the procedures involved in credit control.

# DRILLS AND EXERCISES

## 48.1

REQUIRED: For each set of data below, prepare a Debtors Account and a P&L Account extract concerning (where necessary): discounts allowed, bad debts written off, and/or bad debts recovered.

|   |   | £ |
|---|---|---|
| A | opening debtors | 12 000 |
|   | sales on credit | 72 500 |
|   | cash received from debtors | 70 000 |
|   | bad debts written off | 3 500 |

|   |   | £ |
|---|---|---|
| B | opening debtors | 19 500 |
|   | sales on credit | 210 500 |
|   | cash received from debtors | 207 000 |
|   | bad debts written off | 4 000 |

|   |   | £ |
|---|---|---|
| C | opening debtors | 5 600 |
|   | sales on credit | 68 400 |
|   | cash received from existing debtors | 67 000 |
|   | cash received from debtors previously written off | 750 |

| | | £ |
|---|---|---|
| D | opening debtors | 57 500 |
| | sales on credit | 500 000 |
| | cash received from existing debtors | 510 000 |
| | cash received from debtors previously written off | 2 500 |

| | | £ |
|---|---|---|
| E | opening debtors | 57 500 |
| | sales on credit | 678 000 |
| | discount allowed | 10 500 |
| | cash received from existing debtors | 675 000 |
| | cash received from debtors previously written off | 4 500 |
| | bad debts written off | 5 500 |

| | | £ |
|---|---|---|
| F | opening debtors | 27 400 |
| | sales on credit | 172 600 |
| | discount allowed | 3 200 |
| | cash received from existing debtors | 169 300 |
| | cash received from debtors previously written off | 4 500 |
| | bad debts written off | 2 700 |

# CHAPTER 49

# Provision for Doubtful Debts

## OBJECTIVES

*The objectives of this chapter are:*

- to explain why a firm may need to create a provision for doubtful debts
- to show how a provision for doubtful debts is created and explain how it must be adjusted at the end of every period
- to show how debtor transactions are recorded when there is a provision for doubtful debts

## DOUBTFUL DEBTS

A firm is often able to predict the proportion of its debts that will turn bad in the near future, even though it may not able identify the specific debtors that will be involved. In such a situation there are no debts that can be written off, but the firm's promises from debtors as a whole will be worth less than the total value recorded in the accounts.

When such a situation exists, the firm should create a general provision for doubtful debts, to ensure that the value of debtors as a whole is not overstated (an example of the principle of prudence). A provision for doubtful debts is a CR balance on an account, which will be shown in the balance sheet as a deduction from the DR balance on the Debtors Account. The object is to show promises from debtors at their true value, allowing for the fact that some may never be collected. (We have come across provisions of this kind before, in the form of the provision for depreciation, which is shown in the balance sheet as a deduction from the recorded value of a fixed asset.)

## CREATING A PROVISION FOR DOUBTFUL DEBTS

To create a provision for bad or doubtful debts requires a CR in a Provision for Doubtful Debts Account, with the corresponding DR in the P&L Account to recognize the probable loss to the firm. The Debtors Account itself is not affected. Box 49.1 shows an example.

## BOX 49.1

### Creating a General Provision for Doubtful Debts

At the end of Period 1, a firm has total debtors of £500, as shown by the balance on the Debtors Account below:

```
                         Debtors
        balance
                          500
      (total debtors)
```

The firm believes that 10% of these debts (value £50) will turn bad in the course of the next period, and therefore wishes to create a general provision for doubtful debts.

The double entry to create the provision will be

| DR | P&L Account – reducing profit in respect of doubtful debts | • £50 | |
| CR | Provision for Doubtful Debts | | •£50 |

The P&L Account and the Provision for Doubtful Debts Account will look like this:

```
          P&L Account for Period 1

                                                            Provision for Doubtful Debts

                                                                 period 1 –
     to create
                                                                 provision      • 50
   provision for     • 50
                                                                  created
   doubtful debts
```

In the ledger accounts we now have the recorded value of debtors shown as a £500 DR balance, and the provision shown as a £50 CR balance.

In the balance sheet at the end of Period 1, the provision will appear as a deduction from the recorded value of debtors, as shown in the balance sheet extract below

|  | £ |
|---|---|
| debtors | 500 |
| *less* provision for doubtful debts | (50) |
|  | 450 |

## PROVISIONS AND DEBTOR TRANSACTIONS

The existence of a provision for doubtful debts will make no difference to the recording of any actual transaction concerning debtors. *All* actual transactions concerning debtors, including the write off and recovery of bad debts, should be recorded with the standard accounting entries in the Debtors Account, regardless of whether or not there is an existing provision for doubtful debts.

Entries in the Provision Account, meanwhile, should reflect only the creation, release, or adjustment of the provision. Such entries are made only at the end of a period, after all transactions have been recorded, when the firm is preparing a P&L Account and balance sheet. It follows that the first trial balance at the end of a period, before period-end adjustments, will always show the closing balance on the Debtors Account, and the opening balance on the Provision for Doubtful Debts Account. Box 49.2 presents an example.

## BOX 49.2

### Existing Provisions and Actual Debtor Transactions

At the beginning of Period 2, a firm has opening debtors and an opening provision for doubtful debts as shown below

| | Debtors | | | | Provision for Doubtful Debts | |
|---|---|---|---|---|---|---|
| b/f | 500 | | | | b/f | 50 |

**During Period 2**, the following transactions occur

1. firm makes sales on credit (receiving new promises from debtors) of ●£700

2. firm receives payment of £740 from debtors, (and therefore returns promises of ●£740)

3. debtors of ●£60 are written off.

**At the end of Period 2**, the Debtors Account and the Provision for Doubtful Debts Account will look like this

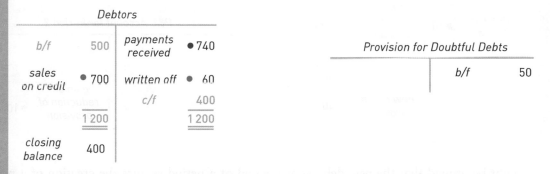

| | Debtors | | | | | Provision for Doubtful Debts | |
|---|---|---|---|---|---|---|---|
| b/f | 500 | payments received | ●740 | | | | |
| sales on credit | ●700 | written off | ●60 | | | b/f | 50 |
| | | c/f | 400 | | | | |
| | 1 200 | | 1 200 | | | | |
| closing balance | 400 | | | | | | |

Notice that Provision Account remains unchanged. A trial balance at this stage would therefore show the opening balance on the Provision Account, and the closing balance on the Debtors Account.

## ADJUSTING A PROVISION FOR DOUBTFUL DEBTS

At the end of each successive period, a firm will have a different set of debtors. Old debtors will have paid their debts and new debtors will have taken their place. The potential loss of value through bad debts will also necessarily be different. The provision for doubtful debts should therefore be adjusted, as shown in Box 49.3.

## BOX 49.3

### Adjusting an Existing Provision for Doubtful Debts

At the end of Period 2, the accounts of a firm have been balanced and show closing debtors of £400, and an existing provision for doubtful debts of £50 (this being the opening balance on the Provision Account, representing the provision created at the end of Period 1).

| Debtors | | | Provision for Doubtful Debts | | |
|---|---|---|---|---|---|
| new closing debtors | 400 | | | old existing provision | 50 |

The firm now considers that 10% of its closing debtors are doubtful and likely to turn bad. The provision for doubtful debts should therefore be reduced from the existing £50 to a new level of £40.

The double entry to reduce the provision will be

| DR | Provision for Doubtful Debts – reduction | ●£10 | |
|---|---|---|---|
| CR | P&L Account – gain on reduction of provision for doubtful debts | | ●£10 |

The Provision for Doubtful Debts Account, with its new balance, and the P&L Account for Period 2 will then look like this:

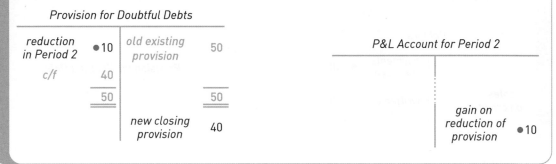

| Provision for Doubtful Debts | | | | | |
|---|---|---|---|---|---|
| reduction in Period 2 | ●10 | old existing provision | 50 | | |
| c/f | 40 | | | | |
| | 50 | | 50 | | |
| | | new closing provision | 40 | | |

| P&L Account for Period 2 | | |
|---|---|---|
| | gain on reduction of provision | ●10 |

It might be argued that the new debtors at the end of a period require the creation of a new provision, rather than the adjustment of an old provision. This is in fact what happens, except that, at the same time as the new provision is created, the old provision must be released (because it referred to old debtors that have now been replaced). The net effect, as shown in Box 49.4, is the same as simply making an adjustment to the old provision.

## BOX 49.4

### Releasing and Replacing a Provision for Doubtful Debts

A firm begins Period 2 with an existing Provision for Doubtful Debts of £50 as shown below

*Provision for Doubtful Debts*

|  |  | b/f | 50 |
|---|---|---|---|

At the end of Period 2, after various transactions, the firm has a different set of debtors, but believes that £40 of its new debtors are doubtful, and wishes to make a provision for doubtful debts accordingly.

The old provision should be ◄ released ► to the P&L Account
and a ●new provision● should be created, as shown in the accounts below.

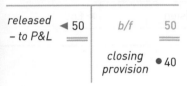

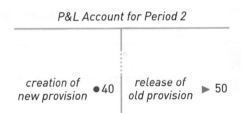

Notice how the release of the old provision of £50 and the creation of the new provision of £40 will have the same net effect in the P&L Account and in the Provision Account, as merely reducing the existing provision by £10.

## RELEASING A PROVISION FOR DOUBTFUL DEBTS

If a firm has an existing provision for doubtful debts and wishes to have no provision, it must take steps to release the provision. Otherwise the provision will continue to appear in all future balance sheets. The accounting entries necessary to release a provision for doubtful debts are a DR in the provision account (to cancel the existing CR), and a CR in the P&L Account (for the owner to claim the value no longer thought to be at risk). Box 49.5 shows an example of the procedure, which is of course the opposite of the procedure required to set up a provision.

## BOX 49.5

### Releasing a Provision for Doubtful Debts

At the start of a period, a firm has a £40 provision for doubtful debts, as shown on the account below.

*Provision for Doubtful Debts*

|  |  |
|---|---|
|  | b/f    40 |

At the end of the period, the firm no longer requires any provision for doubtful debts. The existing provision must therefore be released.

The double entry to release the provision will be

| DR | Provision for Doubtful Debts | ◄ £40 | |
|----|------------------------------|--------|--------|
| CR | P&L Account – gain on release of provision | | ► £40 |

And the relevant accounts will look like this:

*Provision for Doubtful Debts*

| released – to P&L | ◄ 40 | b/f | 40 |
|---|---|---|---|

*P&L Account for Period 2*

gain on release of provision ► 40

## REVIEW

This chapter has shown how to create, maintain, release, and increase or decrease a general provision for doubtful debts. It has also shown how the existence of a provision for doubtful debts should not affect the recording of any transactions concerning debtors.

# DRILLS AND EXERCISES

## 49.1

REQUIRED: For each set of data below, prepare a Debtors Account and a Provision for Doubtful Debts Account, with relevant extract from the P&L Account for each year, and extracts from the balance sheet at the end of each year concerning debtors and the provision for doubtful debts.

|   | | YEAR 1 £ | YEAR2 £ |
|---|---|---|---|
| A | sales on credit | 60 000 | 72 500 |
| | discount allowed | 1 200 | 950 |
| | bad debts written off | 4 500 | 3 500 |
| | cash received from existing debtors | 52 000 | 63 000 |
| | cash received from debtors previously written off | | 1 500 |
| | general provision for bad debts required | 8.0% | 7.5% |

|   | | YEAR 1 £ | YEAR2 £ |
|---|---|---|---|
| B | sales on credit | 45 600 | 53 000 |
| | discount allowed | | 870 |
| | bad debts written off | 2 350 | 3 000 |
| | cash received from existing debtors | 39 000 | 45 000 |
| | cash received from debtors previously written off | | 1 350 |
| | general provision for bad debts required | 5.0% | 6.0% |

|   |   | £ |
|---|---|---:|
| C | opening debtors | 45 000 |
|   | opening provision for doubtful debts | 2 250 |
|   | sales on credit | 382 500 |
|   | discount allowed | 5 750 |
|   | cash received from debtors | 385 000 |
|   | bad debts written off | 4 000 |
|   | general provision for bad debts required | 6.0% |

|   |   | £ |
|---|---|---:|
| D | opening debtors | 62 000 |
|   | opening provision for doubtful debts | 3 100 |
|   | sales on credit | 527 000 |
|   | discount allowed | 9 500 |
|   | cash received from existing debtors | 385 000 |
|   | cash received from debtors previously written off | 2 500 |
|   | bad debts written off | 7 000 |
|   | general provision for bad debts required | 8.0% |

## 49.2

List the factors or evidence you would consider in deciding whether to create or change a firm's general provision for doubtful debts.

# CHAPTER 50

# Specific Provisions and Year-End Accounting for Debtors

## OBJECTIVES

*The objectives of this chapter are:*

- to explain the use of specific provisions for doubtful debts
- to summarize the year-end procedures involved in accounting for bad and doubtful debts
- to consider the practice of setting off debtor and creditor balances involving the same individual or firm

## SPECIFIC PROVISION FOR DOUBTFUL DEBTS

A general provision for doubtful debts is made on the basis of statistics and probability. It involves no judgement on the reliability of any individual debtor, merely a recognition that that some debtors will not pay what they owe. However, a firm may also know of individual debtors who are unlikely to pay some or all of the amount they owe. In such cases it is appropriate to make a *specific* provision for doubtful debts. A specific provision for a doubtful debt is a deduction from the value owed by a specific debtor, recognizing the likelihood that some or all of the debt may not be paid.

Specific provision for one or more identifiable doubtful debts does not preclude a general provision for other doubtful debts that cannot yet be specified. However, we should take care to ensure that any debt which is the subject of a specific provision (or indeed any debt which is written off) is excluded from the value of debtors requiring a general provision. Box 50.1 offers an example of the relevant working. Notice that specific provisions for doubtful debts and general provisions for doubtful debts are recorded in separate accounts.

## BOX 50.1

### Specific Provision for Doubtful Debts

At the end of a period a firm has debtors of £560. This includes ◄£15 owed by Debtor X which should be written off, and ●£45 owed by Debtor Y, in respect of which the firm has decided to make a specific provision. The firm also wishes to have a 10% general provision for doubtful debts. There is an existing general provision for doubtful debts of £70.

The calculation of the general provision now required will be

|  | £ |
|---|---|
| debtors before write off | 560 |
| *less* Debtor X (written off) | (15) |
| *less* Debtor Y (specifically provided for) | (45) |
| debtors requiring general provision | £500 |
|  |  |
| general provision required:  10% × £500 | £50 |

The existing general provision for doubtful debts is £70, and the required provision is £50. The existing general provision must therefore be reduced by ●£20.

The relevant accounts and a balance sheet extract concerning debtors will look like this:

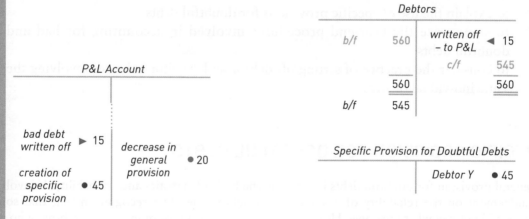

*Debtors*

| | | | | |
|---|---|---|---|---|
| b/f | 560 | written off – to P&L ◄ | 15 |
| | | c/f | 545 |
| | 560 | | 560 |
| b/f | 545 | | |

*P&L Account*

| | | | | |
|---|---|---|---|---|
| bad debt written off ► | 15 | decrease in general provision ● | 20 |
| creation of specific provision ● | 45 | | |

*Specific Provision for Doubtful Debts*

| | | |
|---|---|---|
| | Debtor Y ● | 45 |

*General Provision for Doubtful Debts*

| | | | | |
|---|---|---|---|---|
| decrease ● | 20 | b/f | 70 |
| c/f | 50 | | |
| | 70 | | 70 |
| | | b/f | 50 |

*Balance Sheet Extract*

| | £ |
|---|---|
| debtors | 545 |
| less: specific provision | (45) |
| general provision | (50) |
| | 450 |

# ADJUSTING A SPECIFIC PROVISION FOR DOUBTFUL DEBTS

Like a general provision, a specific provision for doubtful debts will continue to appear with the same value in successive balance sheets until it is changed or released.

Specific provisions should therefore be reviewed at the end of each year. If there has been no change in circumstances, then the existing provision should be allowed to stand without adjustment – no accounting entries are necessary. If the debt provided against has been paid or written off, or the dispute about it has been resolved, then the provision must be released.

# A SEPARATE BAD AND DOUBTFUL DEBTS EXPENSE ACCOUNT

Decisions about the write-off of bad debts, and about the nature and level of provision for doubtful debts usually take place at the end of a period, when a firm is preparing its P&L Account and balance sheet. Where such decisions affect profit, we have shown the relevant accounting entries being made directly in the P&L Account.

In practice, however, this procedure may be untidy, and in any case many firms now employ accounting software which does not permit them to make entries directly in the P&L Account. It is possible instead to have a separate Bad and Doubtful Debt Expense Account – an intermediate account for recording all 'P&L Account' DRs and CRs in connection with bad debt provisions, write-offs and recoveries. The balance on this account can then be transferred to the P&L Account as a single item. Box 50.2 presents an example.

## BOX 50.2

### The Bad and Doubtful Debts Expense Account

At the end of a period, a firm wishes to record the following events and situations in its accounts:

- a debt of £50, previously written off as bad, has been recovered

- a debt of £45 cannot now be collected and should be written off

- a debt of £25, owed by Debtor X, against which the firm had previously made specific provision, has now been paid

- a debt of £30, owed by Debtor Y, against which the firm had previously made a specific provision of 100%, now seems to be entirely lost. The debt should be written off and the specific provision should be released■.

- a specific provision should be made in respect of Debtor Z, who owes £95

- an existing general provision for doubtful debts should be decreased by £10

**BOX 50.2** Continued

The relevant accounting entries in the Bad and Doubtful Debts Account would look like this:

### Bad and Doubtful Debt Expense Account

| bad debt written off | 45 | bad debt recovered | 50 |
|---|---|---|---|
| | | Debtor X – release of specific provision | 25 |
| Debtor Y – written off | 30 | Debtor Y – release of specific provision | 30 |
| Debtor Z – creation of specific provision | 95 | decrease in general provision | 10 |

This account may now be balanced, and the balance transferred to the P&L Account.

## SUMMARY OF YEAR-END ACCOUNTING FOR BAD AND DOUBTFUL DEBTS

The year-end procedures involved in accounting for debtors can now be summarized in six successive steps:

1. balance the Debtors Account(s);
2. review the list of debtors for bad debts and write them off;
3. review the list for identifiable doubtful debts;
4. release any specific provisions that are no longer necessary, and create new specific provisions if needed;
5. on the basis of the debts remaining without specific provision, calculate the new level of general provision for doubtful debts that may be required;
6. adjust the existing level of general provision for doubtful debts to the new level of provision required.

## SETTING OFF DEBTOR AND CREDITOR BALANCES

A firm may supply goods and services to another firm from which it also buys goods and services. In such cases, the firm may have one account for promises IN from the other firm as a customer or debtor, and another account for promises OUT to the other firm as a supplier or creditor. Under normal circumstances the balance on one of these accounts may be offset against the balance on the other account, and the difference settled with a single payment. Box 50.3 provides an example.

## BOX 50.3

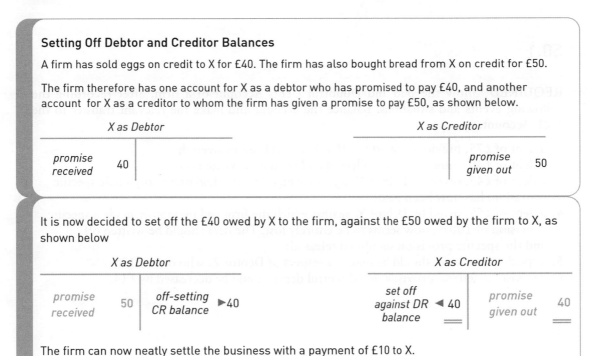

**Setting Off Debtor and Creditor Balances**

A firm has sold eggs on credit to X for £40. The firm has also bought bread from X on credit for £50.

The firm therefore has one account for X as a debtor who has promised to pay £40, and another account for X as a creditor to whom the firm has given a promise to pay £50, as shown below.

| X as Debtor | | X as Creditor | |
|---|---|---|---|
| promise received   40 | | | promise given out   50 |

It is now decided to set off the £40 owed by X to the firm, against the £50 owed by the firm to X, as shown below

| X as Debtor | | X as Creditor | |
|---|---|---|---|
| promise received   50 | off-setting CR balance   ►40 | set off against DR ◄ 40 balance | promise given out   40 |

The firm can now neatly settle the business with a payment of £10 to X.

Setting off debtor and creditor balances in this way is not unusual, but it should be done with care. In particular, it must be agreed that there is a right of set-off, and neither of the debts must be disputed. Your claim, and your right to full payment from me in respect of one transaction, are legally quite separate from my claim, and my right to full payment from you, in respect of another transaction.

# REVIEW

This chapter has described how to make specific provisions for doubtful debts, and has shown how specific provisions for identifiable debts affect the calculation of the general provision for doubtful debts. The chapter also demonstrated the use of a separate Bad and Doubtful Debt Expense Account, summarized the year-end procedures involved in accounting for debtors, and showed how debtor and creditor balances may be off-set.

# DRILLS AND EXERCISES

## 50.1

REQUIRED: Show the Bad and Doubtful Debts Account of a firm, after recording the following events and situations. Balance the account and make the relevant transfer to the P&L Account.

1. a debt of £75, previously written off as bad, has been recovered;
2. a debt of £30 cannot now be collected and should be written off;
3. a debt of £47, owed by Debtor X, against which the firm had previously made specific provision, has now been paid;
4. a debt of £55, owed by Debtor Y, against which the firm had previously made a specific provision of 100%, now seems to be entirely lost. The debt should be written off and the specific provision should be released;
5. a specific provision should be made in respect of Debtor Z, who owes £125;
6. an existing general provision for doubtful debts should be decreased by £14.

## 50.2

REQUIRED: Below is a Bad and Doubtful Debts expense account with DR and CR entries. State where you would find the CR corresponding to each DR in the account, and where you would find the DR corresponding to each CR. Balance the account and make the relevant transfer to the P&L Account.

*Bad and Doubtful Debt Expense Account*

| | | | | |
|---|---|---|---|---|
| bad debt written off | 60 | bad debt recovered | | 65 |
| | | Debtor A – release of specific provision | | 25 |
| Debtor A – written off | 45 | Debtor Z – release of specific provision | | 30 |
| Debtor B – creation of specific provision | 125 | | | |
| increase in general provision | 20 | | | |

## 50.3

List the factors or evidence you would consider in deciding whether to create or change a firm's provision for doubtful debts.

# CHAPTER 51

# Accounting for VAT

## OBJECTIVES

*The objectives of this chapter are:*

- to explain the basic principles of Value Added Tax, and show how to account for VAT on inputs and outputs
- to outline the procedures involved in quarterly accounting for VAT

## VALUE ADDED TAX

Value Added Tax (VAT) is a tax on the final consumers of goods and services. The tax is collected by registered suppliers of goods and services, who add a certain percentage for VAT to the sales price of their outputs, and collect the total, including VAT, from the customer. The supplier, having collected VAT, is then responsible for paying the value on to the tax authorities.

## APPLICABLE RATES OF VAT

For ease of computation, we shall assume a rate of 10% for VAT in our examples. Actual rates of VAT may vary. At the time of writing, the standard rate of VAT in the United Kingdom is 17.5%, which makes for unpleasant arithmetic. In Ireland it is 21% and in France it is 19.6%. As with all taxes there are special rates, exemptions, limits, and peculiar definitions of who and what are subject to the tax. Our purpose here is not to describe the tax in detail, but only to show the basic procedures involved in accounting for VAT.

## OUTPUT VAT

Output VAT means the VAT collected on a firm's outputs or sales. A firm which makes a sale subject to VAT must account for three movements of value:

- the total value of money or promises coming IN from the customer (including the element of VAT that has been added to the selling price);
- the value of the sale itself going OUT; and
- the liability to pass on the value of the tax collected to the tax authorities. This liability is recorded on an Output VAT Account.

An example of the accounting for output VAT is shown in Box 51.1.

## BOX 51.1

### Accounting for Output VAT

A firm sells goods for £150. The firm is registered for VAT, and the applicable rate of VAT is 10%. The total amount charged to the customer will be £165, calculated as below:

|  | £ |
|---|---|
| sales value | 150 |
| *add* VAT at 10% | 15 |
| total | 165 |

The double entry to account for the transaction will be

| DR | Money or Promise from Customer | ● £165 |  |
|---|---|---|---|
| CR | Sales |  | ● £150 |
| CR | Output VAT (liability) |  | ● £15 |

and the relevant accounts will look like this

*Sales*

| | value of sale ● 150 |

*Money or Promises*

| total receivable from customer, including VAT ● 165 | |

*Output VAT*

| | liability to pay Tax Authority ● 15 |

## INPUT VAT

Input VAT is the VAT that is paid on inputs. Evidently, for every supplier of goods or services collecting output VAT, there must also be a purchaser who is paying input VAT.

Although all purchasers of goods and services must pay VAT to the supplier, the burden of VAT is intended to fall only on the final consumers of goods and service. Final consumers are in general non-trading individuals. A registered *provider* of goods and services (that is, a commercial firm) is therefore allowed to claim back the VAT it has paid on its inputs.

A firm which buys goods or services subject to VAT therefore must account for:

● the total value of money or promises going OUT to the supplier, including the element payable in respect of VAT;

● the actual value (before VAT) of the goods or services coming IN; and

● the right to recover the VAT, also coming IN.

The right to recover input VAT is shown on an Input VAT Account. An example of the necessary accounting is shown in Box 51.2.

## BOX 51.2

### Accounting for Input VAT

A firm buys goods or services for £100. The firm is registered for VAT, and the applicable rate of VAT is 10%. The total amount payable to the supplier will be £110, calculated as below:

|  | £ |
|---|---|
| input cost | 100 |
| *add* VAT at 10% | 10 |
| total | 110 |

The double entry to account for the transaction will be

| DR | Goods or Services | ●£100 | |
|---|---|---|---|
| DR | Input VAT (right to reclaim) | ●£10 | |
| CR | Money or Promise to Supplier | | ●£110 |

and the relevant accounts will look like this

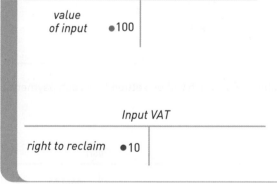

## QUARTERLY ACCOUNTING FOR VAT

Every three months, a firm that is registered for VAT must settle its account with Her Majesty's Revenue and Customs (HMRC) – the tax authority. At this stage, the firm's right to reclaim the VAT paid on its inputs may be offset against its liability to hand over the VAT collected on its outputs. If the firm has collected more VAT from its customers than it has paid to its suppliers, then it must pay over the difference to HMRC. If the firm has paid more VAT than it has collected, then the firm may claim a refund of the difference from HMRC. Box 51.3 shows an example of this quarterly accounting procedure where the firm has collected more VAT than it has paid.

## BOX 51.3

### Quarterly Accounting for VAT

At the end of a quarter, a firm has the right to reclaim £10 in respect of VAT paid on its inputs, and has a liability to pass on to the government £15 in respect of VAT which it has collected on its outputs, as shown on the accounts below.

| Input VAT | | | | Output VAT | |
|---|---|---|---|---|---|
| *right to reclaim* | 10 | | | *liability to pay* | 15 |

Every quarter the right to reclaim input VAT and the liability to pass on output VAT are transferred to a single VAT Settlement Account, as shown below.

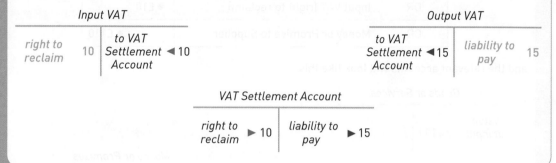

The VAT Settlement Account now shows a *net* liability of £5, which will be settled by a cash payment to HM Revenue & Customs, as shown below:

It is of course possible for a firm to have paid more VAT on its inputs than it has collected on its outputs. In such a case, the firm will receive a cash payment from HM Revenue & Customs to settle the difference, as shown in Box 51.4.

## BOX 51.4

### Reclaiming Surplus Input VAT

During a quarter a firm has paid £80 of VAT on its inputs, which it has the right to reclaim, and has collected £60 of VAT on its outputs, which it has a liability to pass on to the government.

At the end of the quarter, the firm has transferred the right and the liability to a single VAT Settlement Account, as shown below.

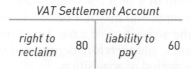

| VAT Settlement Account | | | |
|---|---|---|---|
| right to reclaim | 80 | liability to pay | 60 |

This indicates that the firm has a *net* right to reclaim £20, which will be settled by receipt of a cash payment from HM Revenue & Customs.

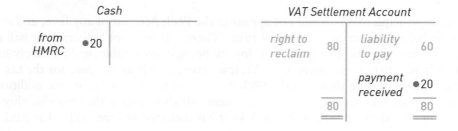

| Cash | | | VAT Settlement Account | | |
|---|---|---|---|---|---|
| from HMRC | •20 | | right to reclaim | 80 | liability to pay | 60 |
| | | | | | payment received | •20 |
| | | | | 80 | | 80 |

## VAT AND SETTLEMENT DISCOUNTS

When a firm sells on credit, the VAT on each sale must be calculated at the time the invoice is issued. If the firm offers a discount for prompt payment, it cannot tell at that stage whether or not the discount will be taken. How, then should we calculate the VAT on the sale? The rule is that when a firm offers a discount for prompt payment, VAT is calculated on the value payable *after* the discount. It cannot be re-calculated if the discount is not taken. Thus, if a firm sells goods on credit for £100, offering a 2% discount for payment within 30 days, VAT should be based on the after discount value of £98, and that calculation will stand, whether or not the discount is in fact taken.

## REGISTRATION LIMITS

Although the financial burden of VAT is intended to fall on consumers rather than providers, VAT does impose administrative burdens on the registered firms who must collect and account for the tax. In general, therefore, a firm need not register for VAT unless/until its taxable outputs exceed a certain limit. Registration limits are bound to change, but as a general indication, a firm would have had to register for VAT in 2007 if its taxable outputs had exceeded £61 000 in the previous year.

## EXEMPT, ZERO RATED, AND IRRECOVERABLE VAT

There are various ways in which VAT is adapted to meet the demands of fairness and political economy. For example, certain goods and services are exempt from VAT, which is to say that a firm supplying such goods and services is not required to collect VAT on its outputs, but may not reclaim the VAT paid on its inputs.

Also, different rates may be applied to the provision of different goods and services. Most significantly, some goods and services may be zero-rated. A firm which supplies zero-rated goods or services must collect VAT at 0% on its outputs (that is, it need not in fact collect any VAT from its customers), but it is entitled to reclaim any VAT paid on its inputs.

Finally, the VAT on certain inputs may be deemed irrecoverable. With respect to irrecoverable VAT, a firm is effectively in the position of a final consumer – any irrecoverable VAT paid on an input becomes part of the cost of the input and may not be reclaimed. One consequence of this is that any irrecoverable VAT paid on the acquisition of a fixed asset must be included in the cost of the fixed asset for depreciation purposes, and therefore depreciated over the life of the fixed asset – it is not treated as an expense of the period of acquisition.

## VAT IN THE P&L ACCOUNT AND THE BALANCE SHEET

Notice that in principle, VAT should not appear in the P&L Account of any firm, and should only appear in the balance sheet of a registered firm. Where a firm is not registered, it will collect no VAT on its outputs, and the VAT paid on its inputs, being irrecoverable, will be simply included in their cost. Where a firm is registered for VAT, it is acting simply as an agent for the tax authority. Sales and purchases will be shown in the P&L Account at their price before the addition of VAT, and the only sign of VAT will be in the balance sheet, which will show the firm's liability to pay, or right to reclaim, the difference between the VAT it has collected and the VAT it has paid.

## REVIEW

This chapter has briefly outlined the workings of VAT, describing output and input VAT and showing how they are accounted for.

# DRILLS AND EXERCISES

## 51.1

REQUIRED: Record the following transactions and events in the accounts of the business, which is registered for VAT at a standard rate of 20%, and produce a simple P&L Account and balance sheet at the end of the period.

1. business begins when owner puts £10 000 into a business bank account
2. business buys goods on credit for £40 000, plus VAT
3. business sells goods on credit for £60 000 plus VAT
4. first quarterly accounting
5. business buys goods on credit for £35 000, plus VAT

6. business sells goods on credit for £25 000, plus VAT
7. second quarterly accounting
8. business buys goods on credit for £45 000, plus VAT
9. business sells goods for £65 000, plus VAT
10. business receives payment of £140 000 by cheque from customers
11. business pays £100 000 by cheque to suppliers
12. end of period. Closing stock is valued at £15 000

## 51.2

Explain the effect of VAT on the profit of a business, and on its cash flow.

Find more questions and answers at www.cengage.co.uk/hodge

# CHAPTER 52

# Cost of Sales in a Manufacturing Firm

## OBJECTIVES

*The objectives of this chapter are:*

- to explain the use of a Manufacturing Account to determine cost of sales in a manufacturing firm
- to describe or define the major categories involved, including direct costs and indirect costs or overheads, prime cost and inventory including work-in-progress
- to present a standard format for the Manufacturing Account

## COST OF SALES: COST TO BUY OR COST TO MAKE?

In the standard Trading Account as we have presented it so far, the figure for Cost of Sales is based on purchases in the period, adjusted if necessary for opening and closing stock. The assumption has been that the firm does not make the goods it sells, but merely buys and sells them, virtually unchanged. In this context, 'cost of sales' means only 'what it cost to *buy* the goods that were sold in the period'.

In a manufacturing firm, however, cost of sales should mean 'what it cost to *make* the goods that were sold in the period'. The figure for cost of sales should therefore be based on the factory cost of goods produced in the period, adjusted if necessary for opening and closing stock. Box 52.1 points out the contrast between a trader's cost of sales, based on purchases (cost to buy), and a manufacturer's cost of sales, based on factory cost (cost to make).

## BOX 52.1

**Cost of Sales for a Trader and a Manufacturer**

| SIMPLE TRADING FIRM | |
| --- | --- |
| | £ |
| Purchases | X |
| *plus* opening stock | X |
| *minus* closing stock | (X) |
| Cost of Sales<br>   = *cost to buy* | X |

In a purely trading firm
Cost of Sales means what it
cost to buy the goods that were
sold in the period

| MANUFACTURING FIRM | |
| --- | --- |
| | £ |
| Factory Cost of<br>   finished goods produced | X |
| *plus* opening stock<br>   of finished goods | X |
| *minus* closing stock<br>   of finished goods | (X) |
| Cost of Sales<br>   = *cost to make* | X |

In a manufacturing firm
Cost of Sales means what it
cost to make the goods that were
sold in the period

## THE ELEMENTS OF FACTORY COST

The factory cost of finished goods produced in a period is a total that will comprise a large number of separate elements, including not only raw materials and production wages, but also factory rent, light and heat, the depreciation of machinery and all the other costs of running a factory. All such inputs are naturally recorded on their own separate accounts when they are acquired, and at the end of a period they must be gathered together to find a single total figure for the cost of finished goods produced. This is done through the use of a Manufacturing Account.

## THE MANUFACTURING ACCOUNT

A Manufacturing Account is a single account in which all factory costs of production are gathered together, prior to transfer to the P&L Account as a single total figure. Each separate element of factory cost is recorded first in its own account. Then at the end of each period, each element of factory cost is transferred OUT of its own account and IN to the Manufacturing Account. The balance on the Manufacturing Account can then be transferred to the P&L Account as one single figure representing Factory Cost of Finished Goods Produced.

Notice that there will also be many other inputs recorded in the firm's accounts, in connection with selling and distribution, administration and other general expenses. These inputs are not at all related to the cost of *making* things, and therefore should not be included in the Manufacturing Account. They should be transferred directly to the P&L Account in the normal manner of expenses, after gross profit has been determined. The Manufacturing Account is exclusively for *factory* costs.

Box 52.2 demonstrates the basic procedure involved in the preparation of a Manufacturing Account.

## BOX 52.2

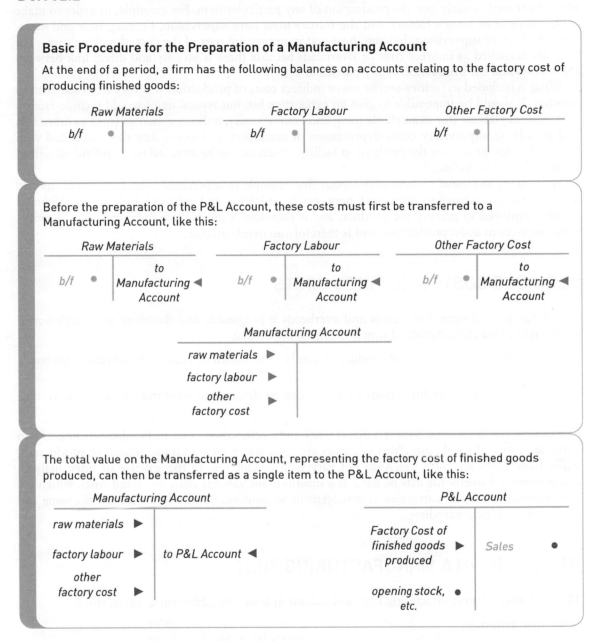

### Basic Procedure for the Preparation of a Manufacturing Account

At the end of a period, a firm has the following balances on accounts relating to the factory cost of producing finished goods:

| Raw Materials | Factory Labour | Other Factory Cost |
|---|---|---|
| b/f • | b/f • | b/f • |

Before the preparation of the P&L Account, these costs must first be transferred to a Manufacturing Account, like this:

| Raw Materials | Factory Labour | Other Factory Cost |
|---|---|---|
| b/f • | to Manufacturing ◄ Account | b/f • | to Manufacturing ◄ Account | b/f • | to Manufacturing ◄ Account |

**Manufacturing Account**

raw materials ▶
factory labour ▶
other factory cost ▶

The total value on the Manufacturing Account, representing the factory cost of finished goods produced, can then be transferred as a single item to the P&L Account, like this:

| Manufacturing Account | P&L Account |
|---|---|
| raw materials ▶ | |
| factory labour ▶    to P&L Account ◄ | Factory Cost of finished goods ▶ produced | Sales • |
| other factory cost ▶ | opening stock, • etc. |

## DIRECT COSTS AND INDIRECT COSTS

By convention factory costs, or costs of production, are divided into direct costs and indirect costs (also known as overheads).

Direct costs are those which are easily traced directly into the production of a particular item. Direct costs would therefore include the cost of raw materials and/or components and the cost of the labour directly employed in making things. All of these costs can be observed going into the product and measured as each item is made. Other direct costs may not be open to physical observation, but their attachment to individual items of production is easily open to reason. Thus, direct costs would also include, for example, any payments under a license, where the firm has agreed to pay per unit produced for the right to use a patented design.

Indirect costs or overheads are costs associated with production, which nevertheless cannot easily be traced directly into the production of any particular item. For example, in order to make cars, a firm must have a factory, and the factory must have supervision, lighting, heat and insurance. So factory supervision, lighting, heat and insurance are part of the cost of making cars – but they are classified as indirect costs or overheads because there is no easy and direct link between these costs and the production of any particular car.

What is included in factory overheads or indirect costs of production will vary from one firm to another. It would be impossible to give an exhaustive list, but typical items would include factory rent, indirect labour (for example cleaning and maintenance), indirect materials (such as lubricants and abrasives), supervisory costs, depreciation of machinery and so on. Any cost associated with the production process or the production facility, which cannot be attached to an individual unit of output, should be included.

Since many overhead costs involve labour (for example in supervision, cleaning, or repairs and maintenance), it is usual to distinguish between direct labour, and indirect labour. Direct labour is visibly employed in making the product, and is therefore a direct cost. Indirect labour provides other services to assist production, and is therefore an overhead cost.

## VARIABLE COSTS AND FIXED COSTS

The difference between direct costs and overheads is pragmatic, and therefore necessarily somewhat vague. One characteristic distinction appears to be that

- the direct costs of a unit of production can be determined by reason or inspection, *without the use of averaging*; while
- the overhead or indirect costs of a unit can be determined only indirectly, on an average basis.

In this way the distinction between direct costs and overheads is close to the distinction between variable costs and fixed costs. (Variable costs are costs which vary with the volume of production, while fixed costs are costs which do not vary with production. In the absence of finer analysis, direct costs and overheads may be used as a substitute for variable costs and fixed costs, which are well-defined and useful categories in management accounting. But the terms are not the same and the results may be misleading.

## INVENTORY IN A MANUFACTURING FIRM

The inventory of a manufacturing firm will include at least three different kinds of stock:

- raw materials;
- work-in-progress; and
- finished goods.

Raw materials in themselves need no explanation, but it should be noted that the cost of raw materials would include not just the purchase cost, but also any associated costs of getting the raw materials into the factory and ready to use. Thus, for example, any customs duties payable on imported raw materials should be included in the cost of the materials, as well as any costs of 'carriage in' (that is, any costs of bringing materials into the firm).

Finished goods also form a category needing little explanation. But note once again that the full cost of finished goods produced in a period should include indirect costs (overheads) as well as direct costs such as raw materials and direct labour.

Work-in-progress (WIP) means incomplete goods, still in the process of production. The cost of WIP would depend on its degree of completion, but would include a proportion of each of the elements included in the cost of finished goods. Where the production process is relatively quick, a firm may have little or no work-in-progress at the balance sheet date, but where the production process takes weeks, months, or even longer, WIP may constitute the major part of a firm's inventory.

## PRIME COST

Prime cost is the total *direct* cost of production, including raw materials consumed and direct labour, plus any other direct costs. Note that the cost of raw materials *consumed* in a period is based on raw material purchases, but the figure for purchases must be adjusted for opening and closing stock. Box 52.3 presents an example of the standard prime cost calculation.

## BOX 52.3

### Elements of Prime Cost

**Prime Cost** means the total direct cost of production. Some of the more usual elements of prime cost are included in the pro-forma statement below:

|  | £ |
|---|---|
| purchases of raw materials | X |
| customs duties paid | X |
| carriage in | X |
|  | X |
| *plus* opening stock of raw materials | X |
| *minus* closing stock of raw materials | (X) |
| cost of raw materials consumed | X |
| direct labour | X |
| other direct cost | X |
| PRIME COST | X |

## OVERHEADS, WIP, AND COST OF PRODUCTION

The total cost of finished goods produced in a period will consist of prime cost, plus indirect costs of production (overheads). But this total must be adjusted for stocks of work-in-progress. The cost of goods *completed* in the current period must include the cost of opening WIP (started in the previous period, but completed in the current period), just as it must exclude the cost of closing WIP (started in the current period, but not yet completed).

## PRESENTATION OF THE MANUFACTURING ACCOUNT

Although the Manufacturing Account is clearly a part of the double entry system, with DRs and CRs as we have shown above in Box 52.2, it is more usually presented in a vertical or columnar format (comparable to the presentation of the Income Statement). In this format, the Manufacturing Account is essentially a list of costs, leading down to a total factory cost of finished goods produced.

Box 52.4 shows a model of the standard 'list of costs' format of the Manufacturing Account, beginning with the determination of prime cost as shown above, including some typical indirect costs or overheads, and concluding with the adjustment for work-in-progress.

## BOX 52.4

### A Manufacturing Account:Standard Format

XYZ Manufacturing Account for the Year Ended (date)

|  | £ |
|---|---|
| **purchases of raw materials** | X |
| customs duties paid | X |
| carriage in | X |
| *plus* opening stock of raw materials | X |
| *minus* closing stock of raw materials | (X) |
| **cost of raw materials consumed** | X |
| direct labour | X |
| other direct cost | X |
| **PRIME COST** | **X** |
| Production Overheads | |
| indirect labour | X |
| indirect materials | X |
| factory rent | X |
| factory insurance | X |
| power | X |
| light and heat | X |
| etc. | X |
|  | X |
| *plus opening stock* of WIP | X |
| *minus closing stock* of WIP | (X) |
| **FACTORY COST of FINISHED GOODS PRODUCED** | **X** |

## REVIEW

This chapter has described how the Manufacturing Account is used to gather together the various costs of production in a manufacturing firm, so that the firm's Cost of Sales will reflect the cost of making the goods that were sold in the period. The chapter also outlined the distinction between direct costs and indirect costs, or overheads and explained what is typically included in prime cost. It described the three kinds of stock that will appear in the inventory of a manufacturing firm (raw materials, work-in-progress and finished goods) and concluded with a Manufacturing Account in standard format, presented as a list of costs.

# DRILLS AND EXERCISES

## 52.1

REQUIRED: From the information listed below, compile a Manufacturing Account in standard form and an Income Statement.

|  | £ |
|---|---|
| opening stock |  |
| raw materials | 20 000 |
| WIP | 11 000 |
| finished goods | 13 000 |
| purchases of raw materials | 140 000 |
| direct labour | 58 000 |
| sales | 430 000 |
| factory heat and light | 9 000 |
| factory supervision | 8 000 |
| machinery (net book value) | 80 000 |
| office equipment (net book value) | 12 000 |
| general office expenses | 15 000 |
| indirect materials | 2 000 |
| indirect labour | 5 000 |
| selling expenses | 13 000 |
| administrative expenses | 4 000 |
| insurance | 6 000 |
|  |  |
| NOTES |  |
| closing stocks are valued at: |  |
| raw materials | 22 000 |
| WIP | 10 000 |
| finished goods | 16 000 |
| Insurance is to be divided two thirds for the factory and one third for the office. |  |
| Depreciation on machinery and office equipment for the period should be charged at 25% of the NBV |  |

## 52.1

WIP is easy to recognize in a manufacturing business. Is there anything resembling WIP in a service providing business, such as a firm of lawyers or accountants?

# CHAPTER 53

# Stock Valuation: Cost and Net Realizable Value

## OBJECTIVES

*The objectives of this chapter are:*

- to explain the rule that stock should be valued at the lower of cost and net realizable value
- to show how the rule works to ensure that any expected losses on stock are recognized in the P&L Account of the current period, while any expected profit is not recognized until the stock is sold

## THE PROFIT-MAKING PROCESS, CLOSING STOCK AND PRUDENCE

The profit-making process is one in which inputs come in to a firm at cost, and as they pass through the firm, they are consumed or converted into outputs. In the normal course of events, outputs leave the firm with a higher value than the inputs that went into their creation. In general, therefore, the process that takes place inside a firm is one in which value is added, although there may be accidental or unexpected outcomes in which value is actually lost.

Closing stock consists of inputs whose passage through the firm has not yet been completed. That is to say, closing stock is part-way through the value-changing process that takes place inside the firm. How should such stock be valued? According to the principle of prudence, if stock has gained any value inside the firm, the gain should not be recognized in the P&L Account until it is realized in a transaction. On the other hand, if stock has lost value inside the firm, the loss should be recognized in the P&L Account immediately. The operational rule that puts this doctrine into effect is this:

- *stock should be valued at the lower of cost and net realizable value.*

## COST

The cost of closing stock means all the costs of bringing the stock to its current condition and location. This would include the cost of any work done to change, combine, or move the stock and, as we have seen in the Manufacturing Account, any associated overheads.

# NET REALIZABLE VALUE

The net realizable value (NRV) of stock is the value at which it is expected to be sold, minus all expected *future* costs to complete, make good, repair, bring to market and sell the stock. Box 53.1 shows an example of the NRV calculation.

## BOX 53.1

### The Net Realizable Value Calculation

A firm has goods in stock with a cost of £50.

After further work expected to cost £30, the firm will be able to sell the goods at an expected sales value of £70.

The Net Realizable Value of the stock is calculated like this:

|  | £ |
| --- | --- |
| expected sales value | 70 |
| *minus* further costs | (30) |
| NET REALIZABLE VALUE | 40 |

In DR and CR form, the Net Realizable Value calculation could be presented as the following entries in an expected *future* P&L Account. Notice that these entries would generate a net CR of £40 in the future P&L Account, and would exactly balance any opening stock brought in at NRV.

*Future P&L Account*

| | | | |
| --- | --- | --- | --- |
| expected further costs | 30 | expected sales value | 70 |

# COST AND NET REALIZABLE VALUE: WHAT THE COMPARISON MEANS

At any moment in time, NRV is in effect the value that a firm will be able to get out of its stock, while cost is the value it has already put in to its stock.

If NRV is greater than cost, then the firm will make a profit when the stock is finally sold (it will get more value out of the stock than it has already put in). This profit should not be recognized in the P&L Account until the stock is actually sold at some future date.

However, if NRV is lower than cost, then the firm will make a loss when the stock is finally sold (what it gets out of the stock will be less than the value it has already put in). Prudence demands that this loss be recognized in the P&L Account immediately, even before the loss is realized in a transaction.

## VALUING STOCK AT COST

The rule that stock should be valued at the lower of cost and net realizable value means that stock can never be valued at anything more than cost. This gives effect to the first part of the doctrine of prudence: profit should not be recognized in the P&L Account until it is realized in a transaction. Box 53.2 shows how the rule works to this effect.

## BOX 53.2

### Prudence and Cost as a Maximum Value of Closing Stock

For simplicity, assume a firm whose only cost of any kind is purchases. The firm's only transaction in Period 1 is to buy goods for £50.

At the end of the period, the firm has made no sales. The entire batch of purchases therefore remains in stock, and the firm's P&L Account for the period will look something like this

*P&L Account for Period 1*

| | | | |
|---|---|---|---|
| purchases at cost | 50 | closing stock | ?? |

If stock must be valued at the lower of cost and NRV, then cost is the maximum value of stock.

If stock cannot be valued at anything more than cost, then our firm's stock cannot be valued at anything more than its cost of £50.

As a result, the firm can never report a profit on these goods until they are sold. This puts into effect the first part of the doctrine of prudence.

## VALUING STOCK AT NET REALIZABLE VALUE

If NRV is less than cost, a loss will be realized when the stock is sold. The rule that stock should be valued at the lower of cost and NRV means that any such loss will be recognized in the P&L Account of the current period, even before the stock is sold. This gives effect to the second part of the doctrine of prudence: that losses should be recognized as soon as they become apparent. Box 53.3 shows the working of the rule.

## BOX 53.3

### Valuing Stock at Net Realizable Value

COST: A firm has made purchases value £50 in Period 1, but has made no sales. At the end of Period 1 therefore all purchases remain in stock with a cost of £50.

NET REALIZABLE VALUE: After the completion of further work expected to cost £30, the goods are expected to sell for £70. NRV of the stock is therefore £70 – £30 = £40

**BOX 53.3**   Continued

Since NRV of ●£40 is lower than cost of £50, it is clear that
1. the firm is expecting to realize a loss of £10 when the stock is sold; and
2. the stock must be valued at NRV in the P&L Account, as shown below.

*P&L Account for Period 1*

| *purchases at cost* | 50 | *closing stock at NRV* | ●40 |
|---|---|---|---|

Notice the effect of valuing stock at NRV (when NRV is lower than cost):

the loss of £10 will be recognized in the P&L Account of Period 1, even though the stock is not yet sold and the loss is not yet realized.

## COST AND NRV: THE EFFECT ON THE NEXT PERIOD

Choosing between cost and NRV for the valuation of closing stock can also be seen as a way of choosing *when* to recognize the profit or the loss that will arise when the stock is finally sold:

- if stock is valued at cost, any profit or loss arising on its sale will be recognized in the next period, when the stock is sold;
- if stock is valued at NRV, any profit or loss arising on its sale will be recognized in the current P&L Account.

Box 53.4 presents an illustration.

## BOX 53.4

**Cost and NRV, and Choosing When to Recognize Profit or Loss**

COST: The firm in our example has made purchases value £50 in Period 1, but has made no sales. At the end of Period 1 therefore all purchases remain in stock with a cost of £50.

NET REALIZABLE VALUE: After the completion of further work expected to cost £30, the goods are expected to sell for £70. NRV of the stock is therefore £70 – £30 = £40

**BOX 53.4**   Continued

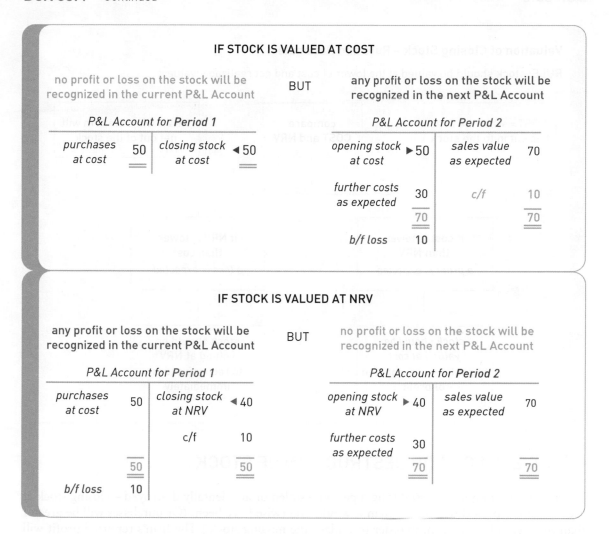

## A SUMMARY OF THE RULE

Box 53.5 presents a summary of the rule for the valuation of closing stock and its rationale.

BOX 53.5

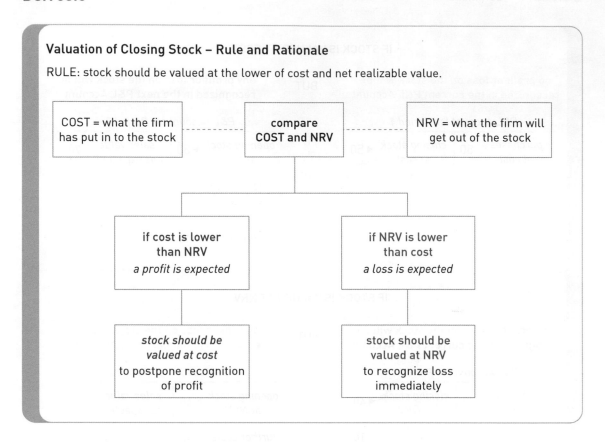

**Valuation of Closing Stock – Rule and Rationale**

RULE: stock should be valued at the lower of cost and net realizable value.

| COST = what the firm has put in to the stock | compare **COST and NRV** | NRV = what the firm will get out of the stock |

| if cost is lower than NRV *a profit is expected* | if NRV is lower than cost *a loss is expected* |

| *stock should be valued at cost* to postpone recognition of profit | stock should be valued at NRV to recognize loss immediately |

## COMPLETE LOSS OR DESTRUCTION OF STOCK

When stock is completely lost during a period – stolen or accidentally destroyed – closing stock at the end of the period will be less than it would otherwise have been. (Or purchases will be greater than they would have been, in order to replace the missing stock.) The firm's reported profit will therefore *automatically* reflect the loss.

It follows that an accountant interested only in overall profit or loss needn't do anything to record the loss or destruction of stock.

However, if we are interested in precisely how a firm's profit or loss is made, we should take the value of stock lost OUT of purchases or cost of sales, and put it IN to expenses in the P&L Account. This will not affect the firm's overall reported profit, but it will allow the P&L Account to show that some of the firm's inputs were not consumed, not by conversion into sales, but by theft or accident before they could be sold.

## STOCK VALUATION FOR OTHER PURPOSES

The rule that stock should be valued at the lower of cost and net realizable value applies only to the valuation of closing stock for the purposes of financial accounting (the production of a P&L Account and a balance sheet). For other purposes, it may be quite appropriate to value stock on an entirely different basis. Thus, for an insurance claim, it may be proper to value stock at replacement cost. Or for job-costing purposes, where a job will require the consumption of materials held in stock, it would be better to value the stock at opportunity cost. Financial accounting is not the only reason for valuing stock, and lower of cost and NRV is not the only rule.

## THE OWNERSHIP OF STOCK

A final note: only the stock that is actually owned by a firm should be included in the firm's accounts as an asset. This is unsurprising and mostly will not cause a problem. Under normal circumstances, the ownership of stock will pass to the buyer on delivery. However, goods may be provided to a shop or retail outlet on what is known as *sale or return*. Such goods will continue to belong to the supplier, until the recipient has sold them on to a retail customer. Goods on sale or return should therefore be included in the stock of the supplier to whom they still belong and excluded from the stock of the retail outlet where they happen to be held.

## REVIEW

This chapter has introduced the rule in financial accounting that closing stock should be valued at the lower of cost and net realizable value. It explained what should be included in the cost of stock, and how NRV is calculated. The chapter also explained how the rule fulfilled the two requirements of the principle of prudence: that profits should not be recognized in the P&L Account until they are realized, while impending losses should be recognized immediately. Finally, the chapter considered how losses of stock should be accounted for, how stock should be valued for different purposes, and how to account for stock that is held on sale or return.

# DRILLS AND EXERCISES

## 53.1

REQUIRED: For each of the following sets of data:

1. determine the net realizable value of the closing stock;
2. compare the cost of the stock against its net realizable value and state the profit or loss expected when the stock is ultimately disposed of;
3. state whether the closing stock should be valued at cost or at net realizable value and explain your decision with reference to the accounting principle of prudence.

| STOCK | A £ | B £ | C £ | D £ | E £ |
|---|---|---|---|---|---|
| cost | 1 000 | 20 000 | 40 000 | 4 800 | 12 000 |
| expected sales value | 1 500 | 30 000 | 50 000 | 7 000 | 16 000 |
| expected future costs | 300 | 12 000 | 10 000 | 3 000 | 3 000 |

## 53.2

A firm in its first period (with no opening stock) has recorded purchases £550 and sales £750. Closing stock is valued at £50. There are no other costs or expenses, but it is known that halfway through the year, stock valued at £20 was stolen.

Produce a P&L Account for the firm's first period.

Find more questions and answers at www.cengage.co.uk/hodge

# CHAPTER 54

# Stock Flow Assumptions:
# LIFO, FIFO, and AVCO

## OBJECTIVES

*The objectives of this chapter are:*

- to describe the LIFO, FIFO, and AVCO methods of assigning a cost to closing stock
- to compare the results of the different methods, and their effect on the reported profit of a firm in periods when input prices are changing

## THE PROBLEM

A firm will often buy identical items of stock at different prices during a period. If any such items remain in stock at the end of the period, they should be valued at the lower of cost and net realizable value. The problem, though, is this: how do we determine the cost of the items that remain in stock, when identical items were purchased at different prices?

Management accountants face the same problem from a different point of view. We (as financial accountants) are interested in which of the items purchased remain in stock at the end of the period. Management accountants, however, are interested in which of the items are selected to go out in each particular sale. From this, they will be able to determine the cost of each particular sale and therefore, able to set an appropriate selling price, or determine the profit made on the sale.

The management accountants have named three alternative assumptions that can be made to identify which items are going out of the firm in any particular sale. These are:

- LIFO ('last in, first out');
- FIFO ('first in, first out'); and
- AVCO (average cost).

LIFO is the assumption that in any sale, the items sold (that is, the items going out of the firm) are the very last ones that came in. FIFO is the assumption that in any sale, the items sold are the first ones that came in to the firm. AVCO meanwhile is more of a rule than an assumption. The AVCO rule is that in any sale, the cost assigned to the items sold should be calculated as the weighted average cost of all the items in stock at the time of the sale.

Since the management accountants deal with each particular sale as it is made, and financial accountants deal with closing stock only at the end of the period, we (financial accountants) must make do with what they (management accountants) have left behind, because closing stock for us is a residual. Thus, under LIFO (last in, first out), closing stock must consist of the first items that came into the firm. Under FIFO (first in, first out), closing stock must consist of the last items that came into the firm. Box 54.1 presents a very simple illustration. In practice, however, there are complications.

## BOX 54.1

### Stock Valuation: LIFO, FIFO, and AVCO

First, a firm buys one item of stock for £4. Later, the firm buys another identical item for £6.

At the end of the period, only one item remains in stock.

LIFO means we assume that the second item (the last one in) has been sold. Closing stock must therefore consist of the first item, with a cost of £4.

FIFO means we assume that the first item has been sold. Closing stock must therefore consist of the second item, with a cost of £6.

AVCO means that the item in closing stock should be valued at the average cost of (4 + 6)/2 = £5.

## LIFO

LIFO (last in, first out) is an assumption made in order to determine the cost of sales *each time a sale is made*, thus leaving the cost of closing stock as a residual. The assumption is that the goods sold in any transaction are taken from the latest available batch of goods to come in. It is probably easier to demonstrate how the assumption is applied, than to describe it in any further detail. First, each batch of purchases must be separately recorded. Box 54.2 shows an example.

## BOX 54.2

### LIFO – the Analysis of Purchases

A firm which trades in goods begins a period with a stock of 60 units, each of which originally cost £12. The firm then purchases another 26 units at £14 each. To apply the LIFO technique, the firm's opening stock and subsequent purchases must be recorded like this:

| | | units in stock | opening stock | purchase 1 | purchase 2 | purchase 3 |
|---|---|---|---|---|---|---|
| Notice how the units acquired in each separate purchase transaction will be copied into a separate analysis column. | cost per unit | | £12 | £14 | | |
| | opening stock | 60 | 60 | | | |
| | purchase 1 | 26 | | 26 | | |

The LIFO assumption is that any goods sold will be taken from the last batch of goods to come in, or, if that batch is exhausted, from the previous available batch, as shown in Box 54.3.

## BOX 54.3

### LIFO – the Identification of Goods Sold and Cost of Sales

The firm in our previous example now makes a sale of 48 units. Applying the LIFO assumption, these are taken to be all 26 units of the last batch of purchases to come in, with a further 22 units taken from the goods that were in opening stock.

As a result, the analysis of stock movements will look like this:

| | units in stock | opening stock | purchase 1 | purchase 2 | purchase 3 |
|---|---|---|---|---|---|
| cost per unit | | £12 | £14 | | |
| opening stock | 60 | 60 | | | |
| purchase 1 | 26 | | 26 | | |
| sale 1 | (48) | (22) | (26) | | |
| | 38 | 38 | – | | |

Each further purchase of goods should be copied into a separate analysis column, and the goods that go out in each successive sale should be identified according to the same LIFO rules, so that the cost of each sales transaction can be calculated as it happens. Box 54.4 continues the example with some further transactions.

## BOX 54.4

### LIFO – the Analysis of Stock Movements

The firm in our previous example continues to make purchases and sales transactions in this order:
buying 53 units @ £18 in Purchase 2, selling 23 units in Sale 2, selling another 42 units in Sale 3, buying 44 units @£20 in Purchase 3, and finally selling 24 units in Sale 4.

These movements should be analyzed so that the origin (according to the LIFO assumption) of the units sold in each sale transaction can be identified as shown below:

| | units in stock | opening stock | Purchase 1 | Purchase 2 | Purchase 3 |
|---|---|---|---|---|---|
| cost per unit | | £12 | £14 | £18 | £20 |
| opening stock | 60 | 60 | | | |
| Purchase 1 | 26 | | 26 | | |
| Sale 1 | (48) | (22) | (26) | | |
| | 38 | 38 | – | | |
| Purchase 2 | 53 | | | 53 | |
| Sale 2 | (23) | | | (23) | |
| | 68 | 38 | – | 30 | |
| Sale 3 | (42) | (12) | | (30) | |
| | 26 | 26 | – | – | |
| Purchase 3 | 44 | | | | 44 |
| Sale 4 | (24) | | | | (24) |
| | 46 | 26 | – | – | 20 |

# LIFO AND CLOSING STOCK

The LIFO assumption and the related analysis of stock movements shown above were developed to determine the cost of each sale as it occurs. However, as financial accountants we are more interested in the cost of closing stock at the end of the period. To that end we can ignore the cost of sales calculations, using the analysis only to identify the assumed origin, and therefore the cost, of the units that remain in closing stock. Box 54.5 completes the example and shows how the LIFO cost of closing stock is finally computed.

## BOX 54.5

### LIFO and the Cost of Closing Stock

The firm in our example has made purchases and sales which have been analyzed according to the LIFO assumption as shown below:

|  | units in stock | opening stock | Purchase 1 | Purchase 2 | Purchase 3 |
|---|---|---|---|---|---|
| cost per unit |  | £12 | £14 | £18 | £20 |
| opening stock | 60 | 60 |  |  |  |
| Purchase 1 | 26 |  | 26 |  |  |
| Sale 1 | (48) | (22) | (26) |  |  |
|  | 38 | 38 | – |  |  |
| Purchase 2 | 53 |  |  | 53 |  |
| Sale 2 | (23) |  |  | (23) |  |
|  | 68 | 38 | – | 30 |  |
| Sale 3 | (42) | (12) |  | (30) |  |
|  | 26 | 26 | – | – |  |
| Purchase 3 | 44 |  |  |  | 44 |
| Sale 4 | (24) |  |  |  | (24) |
| Closing Stock | 46 | 26 | – | – | 20 |

From this analysis we can move directly to calculate the cost of closing stock as shown below:

**LIFO COST of CLOSING STOCK:**

|  | units |  |  | cost £ |
|---|---|---|---|---|
| from Purchase 3 | 20 | @ | £20 | 400 |
| from opening stock | 26 | @ | £12 | 312 |
| Total Cost |  |  |  | **£712** |

# FIFO

FIFO (first in, first out) is also an assumption made with the purpose of identifying the items (and therefore the cost of the items) going out each time a sale is made. However, if items are assumed to go out of the firm on a FIFO basis, the items remaining in stock at the end of a period will *always* be the latest items to come in to the firm. This makes it extremely simple to determine a FIFO cost for closing stock. Box 54.6 on the following page presents an example.

## BOX 54.6

### FIFO Analysis and the Cost of Closing Stock

A firm which trades in only one variety of goods begins a period with 60 units in stock, which originally cost £12 per unit.

The firm then makes a series of purchases and sales throughout the period, as shown here.

|  | units |  |
|---|---|---|
| opening stock | 60 | at £12 per unit |
| purchase 1 | 26 | at £14 per unit |
| sale 1 | (48) | |
| purchase 2 | 53 | at £18 per unit |
| sale 2 | (23) | |
| sale 3 | (42) | |
| purchase 3 | 44 | at £20 per unit |
| sale 4 | (24) | |
| closing stock | 46 | |

If we assume that stock is selected for sale on a FIFO basis, then the 46 items remaining in stock at the end of the period will consist of the last 46 to come in to the firm, and the cost of closing stock is easily calculated as shown below:

### FIFO COST of CLOSING STOCK:

|  | units |  |  | cost £ |
|---|---|---|---|---|
| from Purchase 3 | 44 | @ | £20 | 880 |
| from Purchase 2 | 2 | @ | £18 | 36 |
| Total Cost |  |  |  | **£916** |

# AVCO

AVCO (average cost) is again a method devised to determine a figure for cost of sales each time a sale is made. It follows that the 'average' referred to in AVCO is not the average cost of all the purchases made in a period (this cannot be known at the time each sale is made). Rather, the 'average' in AVCO is the average cost of goods in stock at the time each sale is made. Unfortunately, this means that unlike LIFO and FIFO, the AVCO method does not allow us to skip straight to the cost of closing stock without calculating the cost of each sale.

There are two essential procedures in the AVCO method. First, each time there is a purchase, we must recalculate the average cost of items in stock, as shown in Box 54.7.

## BOX 54.7

### The AVCO Method and Purchases

A firm begins a period with 60 units in stock, held at an average cost of £12.00 each. The firm then purchases a further 26 units at £14.00 each, as shown below.

|  | units | cost per unit | £ |
|---|---|---|---|
| opening stock | 60 | £12.00 | 720.00 |
| Purchase 1 | 26 | £14.00 | 364.00 |

After each purchase, the AVCO method requires us to recalculate the average cost of the units held in stock, based on the new total number of units in stock, and the new total cost, like this:

|  | units | cost per unit | £ |
|---|---|---|---|
| opening stock | 60 | £12.00 | 720.00 |
| Purchase 1 | 26 | £14.00 | 364.00 |
| average | 86 | $\dfrac{£1\,084.00}{86}$ = £12.60 | 1 084.00 |

Secondly, each time there is a sale, the units sold must be taken out of stock at the prevailing average cost, until there is a further purchase, which will cause the average cost to be recalculated. Box 54.8 continues the example.

## BOX 54.8

### The AVCO Method and Sales

The firm in our example now **sells** 48 units which are taken out of stock at the prevailing average cost, and purchases a further 53 units at a cost of £18.00 each, which causes the average cost to be recalculated as shown below.

|  | units | cost per unit | £ |  |
|---|---|---|---|---|
| opening stock | 60 | £12.00 | 720.00 |  |
| Purchase 1 | 26 | £14.00 | 364.00 |  |
| average | 86 | $\dfrac{£1\,084.00}{86}$ = £12.60 | 1 084.00 |  |
| Sale 1 | (48) | £12.60 | (604.80) | ◄ Cost of Sale 1 |
| Purchase 2 | 53 | £18.00 | 954.00 |  |
| average | 91 | $\dfrac{£1\,433.20}{91}$ = £15.75 | 1 433.20 |  |

## AVCO AND CLOSING STOCK

Box 54.9 completes the example and concludes with the cost of closing stock as it would be reported under the AVCO rules.

## BOX 54.9

### AVCO and Closing Stock

The firm in our previous example continues to make sales and purchase transactions in this order: selling 23 units in Sale 2, selling another 42 units in Sale 3, buying 44 units at a cost of £20 each in Purchase 3, and finally selling 24 units in Sale 4.

The AVCO analysis of stock movements for the period, and the resulting cost of closing stock will therefore look like this:

| | units | cost per unit | £ | |
|---|---|---|---|---|
| opening stock | 60 | £12.00 | 720.00 | |
| Purchase 1 | 26 | £14.00 | 364.00 | |
| average | 86 | $\frac{£1\,084.00}{86}$ = £12.60 | 1 084.00 | |
| Sale 1 | (48) | £12.60 | (604.80) | ◀ Cost of Sale 1 |
| Purchase 2 | 53 | £18.00 | 954.00 | |
| average | 91 | $\frac{£1\,433.20}{91}$ = £15.75 | 1 433.20 | |
| Sale 2 | (23) | **£15.75** | (362.25) | ◀ Cost of Sale 2 |
| Sale 3 | (42) | **£15.75** | (661.50) | ◀ Cost of Sale 3 |
| Purchase 3 | 44 | £20.00 | 880.00 | |
| average | 70 | $\frac{£1\,289.45}{70}$ = **£18.42** | 1 289.45 | |
| Sale 4 | (24) | **£18.42** | (442.08) | ◀ Cost of Sale 4 |
| Closing Stock | 46 | **£18.42** | **£847.37** | |

As shown in the table, under AVCO rules, the cost of closing stock will be £18.42 per unit, and with 46 units in stock, the total cost of closing stock will be £847.32.

Readers may verify for themselves that the AVCO cost of units in closing stock is not the same as the average cost of units purchased in the period.

## ACCOUNTING ASSUMPTIONS AND THE ACTUAL FLOW OF STOCKS

In practice, we may imagine that most firms would attempt to arrange an orderly flow of inputs through the business, and therefore try to sell their stock on a FIFO basis. However, there is no requirement or expectation that the accountant's assumptions should be consistent with the actual flow of stocks through a firm. Nor is there any requirement for a firm to make its actual flow of stocks consistent with whichever of the LIFO, FIFO, or AVCO assumptions the accountant may have made.

# COMPARING STOCK FLOW ASSUMPTIONS

The choice between LIFO, FIFO and AVCO is significant only when input prices are changing rapidly, and changing consistently in the same direction throughout the accounting period. Our example in earlier sections was constructed with quite sharply rising input prices, and as a result the LIFO, FIFO and AVCO costs of closing stock were quite significantly different. This in turn would affect the reported cost of sales and hence the firm's reported profit. Box 54.10 presents a summary and comparison of the different results in our example.

## BOX 54.10

### LIFO, FIFO and AVCO Results Compared

Our firm has faced consistently rising inputs prices throughout the period. As a result, LIFO, FIFO and AVCO methods give quite different costs for closing stock, therefore different figures for cost of sales, as shown below.

|  | LIFO £ | FIFO £ | AVCO £ |
|---|---|---|---|
| purchases | 2 198 | 2 198 | 2 198 |
| opening stock | 720 | 720 | 720 |
| closing stock | (712) | (916) | (847) |
| Cost of Sales | £2 206 | £2 002 | £2 071 |

# CHOOSING BETWEEN LIFO AND FIFO

Closing stock is taken out of the P&L Account of one period and put into the P&L Account of the next period. Overall, therefore, the method of stock valuation will make no difference to the aggregate reported profits of a number of periods. However, it will make a consistent difference in respect of the timeliness of different figures in the financial statements.

The LIFO method (last in, first out) means that cost of sales in the P&L Account will reflect the latest and most up-to-date costs, while closing stock in the balance sheet will reflect the cost of older inputs. Meanwhile, the FIFO method (first in, first out) means that cost of sales in the P&L Account will reflect the cost of older inputs, while closing stock in the balance sheet will reflect the latest and most up-to-date costs. In times of consistently rising input prices, therefore, the lagging effect of FIFO in the P&L Account will consistently plump up a firm's reported profits with an out-of-date figure for cost of sales. Box 54.11 shows a summary of the P&L Account and balance sheet effects of the LIFO/FIFO choice.

## BOX 54.11

### LIFO and FIFO: P&L Account and Balance Sheet Effects

LIFO and FIFO have different and contrasting effects on the timeliness of the figures in the P&L Account and the balance sheet, as summarized below.

|  | LIFO | FIFO |
|---|---|---|
| P&L ACCOUNT<br>Cost of Sales | latest costs | older costs |
| BALANCE SHEET<br>Closing Stock | older costs | latest costs |

## LIFO

LIFO is not looked upon with favour by financial accountants. In part this may reflect a preference for the timeliness and relevance of figures in the balance sheet over figures in the P&L Account. (This in turn may be a response to the interests of conservative lenders, who are generally more interested in the strength of a firm's balance sheet, than in its P&L Account.) In part, it may reflect a simple fear that under LIFO, the cost of closing stock in the balance sheet may get further and further out of date until it is entirely meaningless.

Whatever may be the reason, readers should be aware that the LIFO assumption is not generally regarded as acceptable in European financial accounting. This does not destroy its relevance for internal purposes within the firm, and especially its use for the setting of sales prices. Firms that operate in a context of rapidly changing input prices often seem to justify and base their selling prices on a LIFO cost of sales. We are all aware that when crude oil prices rise today, the price of petrol will rise tomorrow, even though the petrol in the pumps is made from crude oil that was lifted several weeks ago.

## REVIEW

This chapter has introduced LIFO, FIFO and AVCO as three different management accounting assumptions about which of a firm's purchases are sold in any particular sales transaction. The chapter showed how these assumptions impact on the cost of closing stock as a residual, and how the cost of closing stock should be determined under each assumption. The chapter also briefly considered the effects of the choice between LIFO and FIFO in times of changing input prices, and contrasted the timeliness, or otherwise, of figures in the P&L Account and the balance sheet under LIFO, and under FIFO.

# DRILLS AND EXERCISES

## 54.1

From each set of data below, compute the cost of closing stock on a LIFO, FIFO, and AVCO basis.

| A | STOCK MOVEMENTS | UNITS IN/(OUT) | UNIT COST |
|---|---|---|---|
| | opening stock | 500 | £10 |
| | purchase 1 | 1 000 | £12 |
| | purchase 2 | 750 | £14 |
| | sale | (1 500) | |
| | purchase 3 | 1 800 | £15 |
| | sale | (1 600) | |
| | sale | (200) | |
| | closing stock (units) | 750 | |

| B | STOCK MOVEMENTS | UNITS IN/(OUT) | UNIT COST |
|---|---|---|---|
| | opening stock | 850 | £10 |
| | sale | (200) | |
| | purchase 1 | 350 | £22 |
| | sale | (80) | |
| | purchase 2 | 250 | £16 |
| | sale | (270) | |
| | purchase | 50 | £12 |
| | closing stock (units) | 950 | |

# CHAPTER 55

# Absorption Costing and Marginal Costing

## OBJECTIVES

*The objectives of this chapter are:*

- to explain the difference between absorption costing and marginal costing and show its true significance
- to show how absorption costing may encourage overproduction
- to outline the use of standard costing for overheads

## ABSORPTION COSTING AND MARGINAL COSTING

There are two possible treatments of production overheads in a firm's P&L Account and balance sheet:

- absorption costing means including an appropriate share of production overheads in the cost of closing stock;
- marginal costing means including only direct costs in the cost of closing stock.

Box 55.1 presents an example.

## BOX 55.1

### Absorption Costing and Marginal Costing

A firm manufactures goods with a direct cost of £2 per unit. Production overheads are £400 for the period, and 100 units are produced. The total cost of production for the period is as shown below.

|  | £ |
|---|---|
| direct cost of production  (100 units at £2 per unit) | 200 |
| production overheads | 400 |
| total cost of production | £600 |

#### ABSORPTION COSTING

With a total cost of production (including overheads) of £600, and 100 units produced, the absorption cost of any units remaining in stock at the end of the period would be

$$£600/100 = £6 \text{ per unit}$$

#### MARGINAL COSTING

The marginal cost of any units remaining in stock at the end of the period would include only the direct cost of production, and would therefore be

$$£2 \text{ per unit}$$

## WHAT DIFFERENCE DOES IT MAKE?

These standard definitions are true enough, but they tend to obscure the real difference between absorption costing and marginal costing, which is seen in the P&L Account. Under absorption costing, production overheads are included in the P&L Account as part of cost of sales, while under marginal costing, production overheads are included in the P&L Account as expenses of the period. This may have important consequences, as shown in Box 55.2.

## BOX 55.2

### Absorption Costing and Marginal Costing – the Real Difference

Assume that the firm in our example has only the costs and expenses included in the schedule below.

|  | £ |
|---|---|
| direct cost of production  (100 units at £2 per unit) | 200 |
| production overheads | 400 |
| total cost of production | £600 |

**BOX 55.2**   Continued

Assume now that only half of the units produced are actually sold in the period, for a total of say £800, with the remaining half of the units produced going into closing stock. For simplicity we shall also assume there is no opening stock.

Under absorption costing, the total cost of production is introduced into cost of sales, so half of the total cost (including half of the overhead costs) can be taken out as closing stock.

Under marginal costing, only the direct cost of production is introduced into cost of sales, so only half of the direct cost can be taken out as closing stock. Meanwhile production overheads must be included in the P&L Account as an expense.

The P&L Account under each method will therefore look like this:

| ABSORPTION COSTING | £ | £ | MARGINAL COSTING | £ | £ |
|---|---|---|---|---|---|
| SALES | | 800 | SALES | | 800 |
| total cost of production | 600 | | direct cost of production | 200 | |
| closing stock | (300) | | closing stock | (100) | |
| COST of SALES | | (300) | COST of SALES | | (100) |
| Gross Profit | | 500 | Gross Profit | | 700 |
| expenses | | – | production overheads | | (400) |
| NET PROFIT | | £500 | NET PROFIT | | £300 |

The example in Box 55.2 shows that a firm may report a very different profit or loss for a period, depending on whether it adopts absorption costing or marginal costing. It also reminds us of the perverse and perhaps unexpected result of including any items in the cost of stock. Closing stock is taken OUT of the P&L Account. It follows that whatever is *included* (or absorbed) in the cost of stock, is *excluded* from the P&L Account, with consequent effects on the reported profit or loss of the period.

## ABSORPTION COSTING AND OVERPRODUCTION

Most firms have some degree of spare capacity (they have the power to produce goods faster than they can be sold), but a slump in demand may leave them with more than they would wish for. In such cases, absorption costing may encourage a firm to overproduce, rather than cut production in line with falling demand. Overproduction is undesirable and even dangerous because, in effect, it means turning useful money into useless stock. With absorption costing, however, overproduction is encouraged, or at least rewarded, because it has the effect of boosting reported profit. Box 55.3 presents an example.

## BOX 55.3

### Absorption Costing and Over production

A firm produces goods with a direct cost of £2 per unit. The goods are sold at a price of £3 per unit, and the firm must pay production overheads of £1 000 per year.

There are no other costs or expenses, but let us say for the purpose of our example that the firm is not allowed to sell more than 1 000 units per year.

Before we proceed, it must be clear that

**if this firm cannot sell more than 1 000 units in a year, it can never make a profit.**

Let us imagine however that the firm has spare capacity, and decides to produce 2 000 units in year 1, with 1 000 units being sold, and 1 000 units going into stock. The total cost of production will look like this:

|  | £ |
|---|---|
| direct cost of production (2 000 units at £2 per unit) | 4 000 |
| production overheads for year | 1 000 |
| total cost of production (2 000 units) | £5 000 |

Now, under absorption costing, this firm will be able to report a profit for Year 1, with a P&L Account that will look like this:

| P&L a/c for YEAR 1 (absorption costing) | | |
|---|---|---|
|  | £ | £ |
| SALES   (1 000 units at £3) |  | 3 000 |
| total cost of production (2 000 units) | 5 000 |  |
| less: absorption cost of closing stock (1 000 units) | (2 500) |  |
| COST of SALES |  | (2 500) |
| Gross Profit |  | 500 |
| expenses |  | - |
| NET PROFIT |  | £500 |

What is happening here? It seems as though the firm in Box 55.3 has conjured a profit from thin air. The point is, however, that under absorption costing a firm which produces more than it can sell, will be able to absorb some of its overheads in closing stock – and closing stock is taken OUT of the P&L Account. With absorption costing, more unsold goods means more overheads taken OUT of the P&L Account and that means higher reported profits. Overproduction, therefore, is rewarded – at least in the short term, for the costs taken out in this year's closing stock are only moved into next year's P&L Account. However, as long as stock levels are never reduced, recognition of such costs can in fact be indefinitely postponed. It is only when the additional stock is converted into sales, that its cost will reappear in the P&L Account. Absorption costing, therefore, not only rewards overproduction with higher reported profits, it also punishes de-stocking with lower reported profits.

## STANDARD OVERHEAD COSTS

Although absorption costing is potentially misleading and dangerous, it is still generally agreed that the cost of stock in a manufacturing firm should include a proportion of overhead costs, *based on normal production*. The idea is to keep the benefits of absorption costing, while avoiding the dangers by absorbing a 'standard' overhead cost per unit, rather than an actual average overhead cost per unit.

In practice, when a firm has many overhead costs, many production departments, and many different products, the determination of a standard overhead cost per unit is not at all a simple matter. But the basic idea is very simple, as shown in Box 55.4.

### BOX 55.4

**Determining a Standard Overhead Cost per Unit**

A firm's production overheads for the current year are expected to be £7 000, and the firm expects to produce 1 000 units to meet demand for the product.

Standard overhead cost per unit will therefore be

$$\frac{£7\,000}{1\,000} \ = \ £7 \text{ per unit}$$

## ABSORPTION OF STANDARD OVERHEAD COST PER UNIT

Once a standard overhead cost per unit has been determined, it must be absorbed into the cost of goods produced. The procedure is first to record actual overhead costs, in the normal way, as they are incurred. Then, at the end of the period, the *standard* overhead cost of the units produced in the period is transferred from the overhead account to the Manufacturing Account, where it will enter into the cost of finished goods produced in the period (and therefore form part of cost of sales). Box 55.5 presents an example.

## BOX 55.5

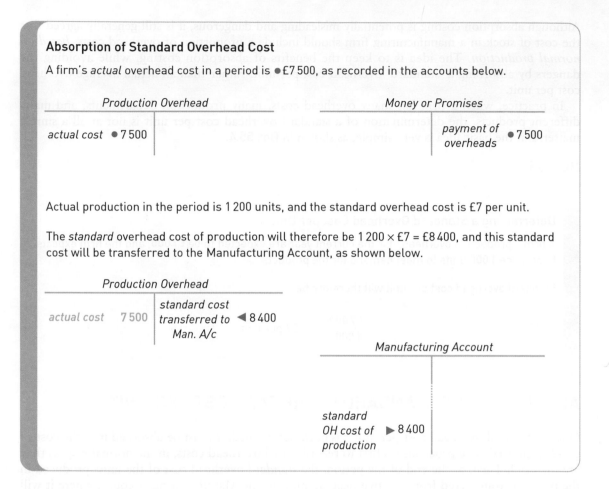

**Absorption of Standard Overhead Cost**

A firm's *actual* overhead cost in a period is ●£7 500, as recorded in the accounts below.

| Production Overhead | | Money or Promises | |
|---|---|---|---|
| actual cost ●7 500 | | | payment of ●7 500 overheads |

Actual production in the period is 1 200 units, and the standard overhead cost is £7 per unit.

The *standard* overhead cost of production will therefore be 1 200 × £7 = £8 400, and this standard cost will be transferred to the Manufacturing Account, as shown below.

| Production Overhead | |
|---|---|
| *actual cost* 7 500 | standard cost transferred to ◀8 400 Man. A/c |

| Manufacturing Account | |
|---|---|
| standard OH cost of ▶8 400 production | |

## OVER-ABSORPTION OF OVERHEAD

Overhead is over-absorbed when (as in Box 55.5) the standard overhead transferred to the Manufacturing Account is greater than the actual overhead cost incurred. This will have two effects: the Manufacturing Account will overstate the cost of goods produced and the Production Overhead Account will be left with a CR balance. The solution is quite simple: while the overstated balance on the Manufacturing Account is transferred to the P&L Account as part of Cost of Sales (a DR), the balance on the Production Overhead Account, representing the amount of over-absorbed overhead, will be transferred to the expenses section of the P&L Account (as a CR). The 'error' will therefore correct itself in the P&L Account overall, but with this crucial difference: Cost of Sales and closing stock, will include only the standard overhead cost of production. Box 55.6 continues the example.

## BOX 55.6

### Over-Absorption of Overheads

A firm's actual production overhead cost for a period is £7 500, but the standard overhead cost absorbed through the Manufacturing Account is £8 400. There is a £900 over-absorption of overhead, which is remedied as shown on the accounts below.

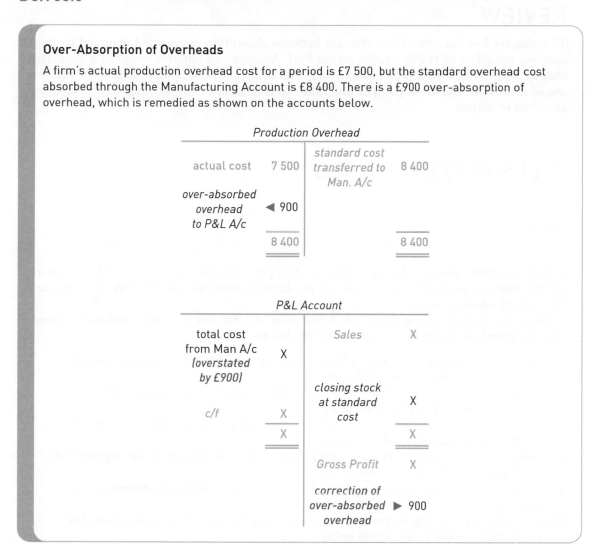

*Production Overhead*

| | | | |
|---|---|---|---|
| actual cost | 7 500 | *standard cost transferred to Man. A/c* | 8 400 |
| *over-absorbed overhead to P&L A/c* | ◄ 900 | | |
| | 8 400 | | 8 400 |

*P&L Account*

| | | | |
|---|---|---|---|
| total cost from Man A/c *(overstated by £900)* | X | *Sales* | X |
| | | *closing stock at standard cost* | X |
| *c/f* | X | | X |
| | X | | X |
| | | *Gross Profit* | X |
| | | *correction of over-absorbed overhead* | ► 900 |

## UNDER-ABSORPTION OF OVERHEAD

Overhead is under-absorbed when the standard overhead cost transferred to the Manufacturing Account is less than the actual overhead cost incurred. When overhead is under-absorbed, the Manufacturing Account will understate the cost of goods produced, and the Production Overhead Account will be left with a DR balance representing the amount of the understatement. Once again the situation is remedied by transfer of the under-absorbed overhead from the Overhead Account to the expenses section of the P&L Account. As a result, the P&L Account as a whole will contain all of the overhead cost of the period, but Cost of Sales and closing stock will reflect only the standard production overheads.

## REVIEW

This chapter has described the difference between absorption costing and marginal costing, showing the effect of the difference on the P&L Account and reported profit of a firm. The chapter showed how absorption costing may encourage over-production. It also showed the use of a standard overhead cost per unit, and the treatment of any eventual under- or over-absorbed overhead.

## DRILLS AND EXERCISES

### 55.1

A firm produces goods with a sales price of £12 per unit and a direct cost of £8 per unit. 3 200 units are sold in a year and actual production overheads are £10 000 for the year. There is no opening stock.

Standard production for the year is 3 200 units and, for this year, the standard overhead and the actual overhead are the same (£10 000 for the year).

(a) using *marginal costing*, prepare a P&L Account for the firm on the assumption that production for the year is 3 500 units;

(b) using *marginal costing*, prepare a P&L Account for the firm on the assumption that production for the year is 7 000 units;

(c) using *absorption costing*, prepare a P&L Account for the firm on the assumption that production for the year is 3 500 units;

(d) using *absorption costing*, prepare a P&L Account for the firm on the assumption that production for the year is 7 000 units;

(e) using *standard costing*, prepare a P&L Account for the firm on the assumption that production for the year is 3 500 units;

(f) using *standard costing*, prepare a P&L Account for the firm on the assumption that production for the year is 7 000 units;

(g) using *standard costing*, prepare a P&L Account for the firm on the assumption that production for the year is 3 500 units, but that the standard overhead cost was £12 000 for the year (this will lead to an over-absorption of overhead);

(h) using *standard costing*, prepare a P&L Account for the firm on the assumption that production for the year is 7 000 units, but again, the standard overhead cost was £12 000 for the year.

### 55.2

The authorities in Gotham are concerned to increase the efficiency of their health service. Each hospital in the city has been required to calculate its total cost per operation performed in the year to date. Money will be saved as more patients are directed to hospitals with the lowest cost per operation.

Comment on the Gotham policy.

# CHAPTER 56

# Insolvency and its Consequences

## OBJECTIVES

*The objectives of this chapter are:*

- to explain how insolvency may arise
- to outline the effects of a firm's insolvency on its creditors
- to describe the different consequences of insolvency for sole traders, partnerships and limited companies
- to explain the going-concern assumption

## INSOLVENCY AND NET LIABILITIES

A firm is insolvent if it cannot pay its liabilities as they fall due. Insolvency is strictly a matter of access to cash, not value. A firm may have assets enough to cover its liabilities eventually, but the firm will be insolvent if it cannot turn its assets into cash when cash is needed.

Temporary difficulties in making payments are potentially dangerous, but not always fatal to the firm. Far more dangerous is the case when payment appears to be impossible, now or at any time in the future, because the firm has *net liabilities* rather than net assets – that is, when the firm's liabilities are greater than the value of its assets.

A firm may find itself insolvent with net liabilities because the value of its assets has fallen, or because of the sudden appearance of involuntary liabilities. Box 56.1 shows the case when insolvency is caused by a fall in the value of the firm's assets.

## BOX 56.1

### Insolvency and Net Liabilities

|  | OPENING BALANCE SHEET | |
|---|---|---|
|  |  | £ |
| A firm begins a period with the opening balance sheet shown opposite. | ASSETS | |
|  | Stock | 900 |
|  | LIABILITIES | |
|  | Loan | (400) |
|  | NET ASSETS | £500 |
|  |  | |
|  | CAPITAL | £500 |

Now assume there is a collapse in the value of the goods held in stock by the firm, which are ultimately sold for only £100 cash (realizing a loss of £800).

|  | CLOSING BALANCE SHEET | |
|---|---|---|
|  |  | £ |
|  | ASSETS | |
|  | Cash | 100 |
| The firm's closing balance sheet will therefore look like this: | LIABILITIES | |
|  | Loan | (400) |
|  | NET LIABILITIES | £(300) |
|  |  | |
|  | CAPITAL b/f | 500 |
|  | loss | (800) |
|  | CAPITAL c/f | £(300) |

## NET LIABILITIES AND NEGATIVE CAPITAL

If a firm does arrive at a situation of net liabilities (where the claims of other people are greater than the value of the assets in the firm) then, in principle, the owner should put further assets into the firm, so that the claims of other people can be met. The argument works by a kind of symmetry: since the owner is the person entitled to claim whatever is left in the firm after meeting the claims of other people, the owner is also the person obliged to pay into the firm, if there are insufficient assets to pay the claims of other people. Where there are net liabilities instead of net assets, therefore, the usual relation between firm and owner is reversed – instead of the owner having a claim on the firm, the firm has a claim on the owner and capital will appear as a negative value in the balance sheet.

In the Capital Account, this negative capital will be represented by a DR balance, which can be interpreted as a promise taken IN from the owner. Box 56.2 shows an example.

BOX 56.2

---

### A DR Balance on the Capital Account

A firm's Capital Account will normally carry a CR balance, with the owner's claim on the business represented by promises going OUT from the business to the owner, as shown here

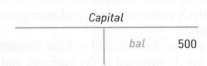

|  | Capital |  |  |
|---|---|---|---|
|  |  | bal | 500 |

However, if the business incurs large losses, and ends with net liabilities, the Capital Account will end with a DR balance, indicating that the business has a claim on the owner.

In this case, we assume a loss of •£800, turning net assets of £500 into net liabilities of £300, and more than wiping out the opening CR balance of £500 on the Capital Account, leaving it with a DR balance of •£300.

| Capital |  |  |  |
|---|---|---|---|
| loss | •800 | bal. b/f | 500 |
|  |  | bal c/f | 300 |
|  | 800 |  | 800 |
| bal b/f | •300 |  |  |

The DR balance on the Capital Account represents the firm's claim on the owner for the extra value needed to pay the claims of other people. It is shown in the form of a promise taken IN from the owner.

---

## INSOLVENCY AND THE RISKS OF BUSINESS OWNERSHIP

For business owners, the consequences of a firm's insolvency will vary depending on the legal structure of the firm. There are three main possibilities:

- sole trading;
- partnership; and
- limited company.

## SOLE TRADING

A sole trader is an individual who has the single undivided ownership and control of his or her own business. The difficulty in accounting for sole traders is the difference between the accounting view of a sole trader's business and the legal view.

In the accounting view, a business (regardless of whatever may be its actual legal structure) is *always* regarded as an entity with an existence of its own, which is separate from the existence or identity of its owners. As accountants, therefore, we maintain a clear distinction between *business* transactions and *personal* transactions, as also between *business* assets and liabilities and *personal* assets and liabilities. We adopt this *separate entity concept* because without it we cannot usefully determine the profit or loss made by the business, nor even the value invested in it (and without knowing the profit or the value invested, we cannot tell if the investment in the business is worthwhile).

However, while a sole trader or an accountant may look at a transaction, an asset, or a liability, and say 'this is business' or 'this is personal', the law recognizes no such distinction. In law there is a single pool of assets owned by the sole trader, and there is a single set of creditors with claims against the value of those assets. Whether the owner chooses to call them business or personal, is of no consequence to the law. This means that the sole trader's 'personal' assets can take no shelter from the claims of 'business' creditors. If there are not enough assets in a sole trader's business to meet the claims of business creditors, then the creditors of the business may pursue their claims against the trader's personal assets, and even against his or her future earnings in another business or a different trade.

As a result, sole traders are said to have *unlimited liability* – that is, they may lose far more than they have knowingly invested in the business, and there is no limit to the value they may be liable to pay into their business, should the business end with net liabilities. Box 56.3 shows an extreme but frightening example of the possible consequences of unlimited liability, in which an owner who invests (and knowingly risks the loss of) a mere £500, ends with a liability of £500 000.

## BOX 56.3

### A Sole Trader's Unlimited Liability

A business begins when a sole trader invests £500 to buy a stock of fireworks for resale.

At this stage, the business balance sheet will look like this:

**BALANCE SHEET 1**

| | £ |
|---|---|
| ASSETS | 500 |
| LIABILITIES | ( – ) |
| NET ASSETS | £500 |
| | |
| CAPITAL | £500 |

The fireworks are lost in an explosion, which also causes £500,000 of damage to neighbouring property.

In the manner of accountants, we show the neighbours' claim for damages as a claim against the business, and the firm's balance sheet will look like this:

**BALANCE SHEET 2**

| | £ |
|---|---|
| ASSETS | – |
| LIABILITIES | (500 000) |
| NET LIABILITIES | £(500 000) |
| | |
| CAPITAL | £(500 000) |

#### NOTE
Although Balance Sheet 2 shows creditors claiming against the business, and the business claiming against the owner, in practice the creditors will of course pursue their claims directly against the owner and his personal assets.

## PARTNERSHIP

English law defines partnership in the abstract, as the relation which subsists between persons carrying on a business in common with a view of profit. More concretely, for accountants, a partnership is a business which is owned by two or more individuals (partners) who share in its profits and losses.

Like sole traders, partners face unlimited personal liability to pay the creditors of their business if the business becomes insolvent. For partners, this liability is 'joint and several', which means that creditors of the firm may pursue their claims against the partners jointly, or they may seek payment in full from any individual partner. A partner therefore is not just liable to pay *a share* of any value claimed by creditors of the partnership – each partner is personally liable to pay the full value of any claim against the partnership. A partner who is caught in this way may of course try to recover a contribution from his or her fellow partners, but a partner cannot delay or avoid making full payment to a creditor of the partnership on the grounds that his or her fellow partners cannot or will not contribute.

## PARTNERSHIP WITH LIMITED LIABILITY

The rigours of joint and several liability fall particularly hard on professional partnerships, where the fraud or negligence of one partner may lead to substantial claims against the firm as a whole, which are ultimately paid out of the personal fortunes of other, entirely innocent, partners.

For a long time, this situation was accepted as a bracing and necessary incentive towards the greatest of care in the selection of fellow professional partners. Recently, however, with the existence of larger partnerships, and larger claims against them, the law has created an alternative in the form of the limited liability partnership (LLP). In an LLP, claims arising from the misconduct of an individual partner can be pursued against the partnership as a whole, but cannot be pursued against the personal assets of any other partner. Thus a 'guilty' partner in an LLP must still face the perils of unlimited liability, while his or her 'innocent' partners are liable to lose no more than the value they have already invested or agreed to invest in the business.

## THE LIMITED COMPANY

As its name implies, the limited company (or company with limited liability) is a form of business organization specifically designed to limit the potential liability of its owners, or rather its members. (Strictly speaking the investors who share the profits of a limited company should not be called its owners. They are more properly called *members* or *shareholders*.) In law, the creditors of a limited company have claims against the company only and not against its individual members. If there are insufficient assets in the company to pay its creditors in full, then the creditors must share whatever assets there are, accepting part payment or even no payment from the company, with no further recourse against its members. The liability of the members or shareholders of a limited company is therefore limited to this extent: in the event of business failure and insolvency, they are not liable to lose any more than the value they have already invested or agreed to invest in the company.

## CREDITORS' CLAIMS IN THE EVENT OF INSOLVENCY

When a business is insolvent with net liabilities *and* the owner(s) cannot be made to pay in any further value, the creditors of the firm must share what assets there are, in proportion to the value of their claims. Box 56.4 presents an example of the procedure.

## BOX 56.4

**Creditors' Claims in the Event of Insolvency**

A firm is insolvent with net liabilities, as shown in the statement below:

|  |  |  | £ | £ |
|---|---|---|---|---|
| ASSETS |  |  |  | 100 |
| LIABILITIES |  |  |  |  |
| Creditors: | X | 60 |  |  |
|  | Y | 30 |  |  |
|  | Z | 30 |  |  |
|  |  |  | (120) |  |
| NET LIABILITIES |  |  |  | £(20) |

If the owner cannot be made to pay another £20 into the firm, to pay off all creditors in full, then the creditors will have to share the existing assets in proportion to their claims, as shown below:

$$\text{to X} \quad \frac{60}{120} \times £100 = £50$$

$$\text{to Y} \quad \frac{30}{120} \times £100 = £25$$

$$\text{to Z} \quad \frac{30}{120} \times £100 = £25$$

## LENDING AND SECURITY

Finance creditors (lenders) may reduce their risk of loss in the event of the borrower's insolvency by ensuring that they have security for their loans. A secured loan is secured by a charge over an asset. If the debtor fails to pay interest when due, or fails to make appropriate repayments, the lender has the right to seize the asset subject to the charge, sell it, and take what he or she is owed out of the proceeds. Any excess realized on disposal of the asset must be returned for sharing among the other, unsecured creditors. A secured lender who is *not* repaid in full from the proceeds of the asset subject to the charge, may pursue the rest of his claim on equal terms with other unsecured creditors. Box 56.5 presents an example.

## BOX 56.5

### Insolvency with a Secured Loan

A firm is insolvent with net liabilities, as shown in the statement below:

|  |  | £ | £ |
|---|---|---|---|
| ASSETS |  |  | 100 |
| LIABILITIES |  |  |  |
| Creditors: | X | 60 |  |
|  | Y | 30 |  |
|  | Z | 30 |  |
|  |  |  | (120) |
| NET LIABILITIES |  |  | £(20) |

---

**CASE 1**

Assume that X is a lender, whose loan of £60 is secured on an asset which is sold for £60 or more.

X will be repaid £60 in full, leaving £40 in the firm, which will be shared between Y and Z in proportion to their claims, which happen to be equal, as shown below:

| to X | £60 | (payment in full) |
|---|---|---|
| to Y | £20 | (equal share of remaining £40) |
| to Z | £20 | (equal share of remaining £40) |

---

**CASE 2**

Assume that X is a lender, whose loan of £60 is secured on an asset which is sold for only £45.

X will take the £45 from the disposal of the asset, but will still have a claim for the additional £15 of the original loan. At this stage, the firm's remaining assets and liabilities will be as follows

|  |  | £ | £ |
|---|---|---|---|
| ASSETS |  |  | 55 |
| LIABILITIES |  |  |  |
| Creditors: | X | 15 |  |
|  | Y | 30 |  |
|  | Z | 30 |  |
|  |  |  | (75) |
| NET LIABILITIES |  |  | £(20) |

The remaining £55 in the firm will be shared among X, Y and Z in proportion to their outstanding claims, with a final distribution among the creditors as shown below:

$$\text{to X} \quad \frac{15}{75} \times £55 \ = \ £11 + £45 \text{ from secured asset} = £56$$

$$\text{to Y} \quad \frac{30}{75} \times £55 \ = \ £22$$

$$\text{to Z} \quad \frac{30}{75} \times £55 \ = \ £22$$

## ASSETS AND SECURITY

A firm without assets, which cannot offer security for a loan, may be unable to borrow, or may be required to pay a higher rate of interest, to compensate the lender for the higher risk. Access to loan capital may therefore depend on the nature and value of the firm's assets, rather than its profit-earning potential.

However, not all assets are equally acceptable as security for a loan. The ideal security is an asset that the business will not need or want to sell, and one that will maintain its value – at least for the duration of the loan. Land and buildings are the obvious examples, although other fixed assets like plant and machinery may also be acceptable.

Assets such as stock or debtors, which are constantly turned into money and renewed, are not acceptable as security for a loan to a sole trader or a partnership. For such firms, the particular asset subject to a charge must always be individually identified. A limited company, however, may offer to secure its borrowings with a *floating charge* over all of its assets, including stock and debtors. This means that stock and debtors may flow freely through the firm, but in the event of the firm's insolvency, the charge will crystallize and fall upon whatever stock or debtors happen to be held in the company at the relevant time.

## RESERVATION OF TITLE

Under normal circumstances, ownership of goods passes to the buyer on delivery. This means that in the case of the buyer's insolvency, unpaid suppliers (trade creditors) may claim *payment* for the goods they have supplied, but they may not simply take them back. Instead, the goods must be sold, and the proceeds divided among all of the creditors in the normal way, in proportion to their claims.

Suppliers may avoid this situation if they make sales with reservation of title. Title, here, means ownership, and goods sold on credit with reservation of title do not belong to the buyer until they are fully paid for. An unpaid supplier may, therefore, simply take them back. (There are however limitations, if the goods involved have been incorporated into something else. An unpaid supplier of bricks to a builder may not destroy a house in order to recover the bricks, even if they were provided under reservation of title.)

For accounting purposes, goods sold subject to reservation of title are treated as genuine sales – that is to say, they are included in the stock of the purchaser, even if they are not yet paid for.

## THE GOING CONCERN ASSUMPTION

A going concern is a business which has the capacity to continue operations into the foreseeable future. When a business ceases to be a going concern, by reason of insolvency or any other cause, the value of its assets may be severely impaired. The firm may be unable to sell its remaining stock through normal channels at normal prices. Unable to make further use of its fixed assets, it may be obliged to sell them at knock-down prices.

By ceasing to be a going concern, a business may also incur involuntary liabilities. It may be unable to fulfil its contracts and so face lawsuits from its customers and suppliers. Most notably, it may be obliged to make redundancy payments to its employees. Whether or not a business is a going concern, therefore, may make a substantial difference to the values reported in the firm's accounts.

The going concern assumption is the assumption that unless otherwise stated in a set of accounts:

(a) the firm actually is a going concern; and

(b) the accounts have been drawn up on the basis that the firm is a going concern.

It is therefore not a fair criticism of a set of accounts to say that if the firm closed down tomorrow, its assets would be worth far less than the value shown in the balance sheet, or that it would face additional liabilities. All of that may well be true. It is irrelevant, however, as long as the firm is a going concern and has no prospect or intention of closing down tomorrow.

Notice that the going concern assumption also imposes a duty on the accountant preparing a set of accounts, to check and ensure that business actually is a going concern. Allowing others to make a false assumption (that the business is a going concern) is as deceptive or negligent as making a false statement to the same effect.

## REVIEW

This chapter concludes our study of the accounting for profit and loss and the net asset side of the balance sheet.

The chapter explained the meaning of insolvency, showing how a business may become insolvent with net liabilities, and outlining the different consequences of this for sole traders, partnerships, and limited companies. The chapter also showed some of the ways in which creditors may protect themselves against the consequences of a firm's insolvency. Finally, the chapter described the going concern assumption and the duty it imposes upon accountants.

# DRILLS AND EXERCISES

## 56.1

A firm is insolvent with net liabilities, as shown in the statement below:

|  |  | £ | £ |
|---|---|---|---|
| ASSETS |  |  | 1 200 |
| LIABILITIES |  |  |  |
| Creditors: | A | 900 |  |
|  | B | 700 |  |
|  | C | 400 |  |
|  |  |  | (2 000) |
| NET LIABILITIES |  |  | £(800) |

Determine how much will be received by each creditor under each of the following assumptions:

1. if all creditors are unsecured and rank equally for payment;
2. if the liability to A is secured on an asset which is disposed of for £900 or more, and all other creditors are unsecured and rank equally for payment;
3. if the liability to A is secured on an asset which is disposed of for £500, and all other creditors are unsecured and rank equally for payment;
4. if the liability to A is secured on an asset which is disposed of for £400, and the liability to B is secured on an asset which is sold for £600, while the liability to C is unsecured.

## 56.2

It is sometimes argued that the shareholders of a limited company should have the exclusive right to control the affairs of the company, because they (the shareholders) are the ultimate bearers of risk, if the company's affairs miscarry.

Comment.

## 56.3

Research 'micro-credit' and 'Grameen bank' and comment on the utility of these institutions.

# PART FOUR

# The Limited Company

Part 4 describes the distinctive features of the limited company, and shows how these are reflected in the company's accounts and financial statements. It explains the rules that limit the payment of dividends, and the factors that influence the market value of a share. Part 4 concludes with an introduction to two additional financial statements: the Statement of Changes in Equity and the Cash Flow Statement.

# CHAPTER 57

# Incorporation and the Limited Company

## OBJECTIVES

*The objectives of this chapter are:*

- to describe what is meant by incorporation and limited liability
- to explain how a limited company is formed
- to distinguish between a private limited company, a public limited company and a listed company

## INCORPORATION

Incorporation means forming a corporation. A corporation is an organization or body composed of different members, but possessing its own legal identity, with its own permanent existence being separate from the coming and going of its members. A university is perhaps the prime example. In law, a university founded, say, a hundred years ago or more, is still the same institution today, even though its members have been constantly in flux and even though its founder members are by now all dead – among its other attributes, a corporation has the power to go on forever.

Historically, the right to form a corporation – that is, the right to combine with others, forming one legal body instead of a mass of relatively powerless individuals – was once an enormous privilege. It was granted only by special permission of the state and in England an Act of Parliament or a Royal Charter were required. Now, however, the right of incorporation is open to all. Since about 1850, it has been possible to create a limited company with a very minimum of formality and the limited company is a species of corporation.

## THE LIMITED COMPANY

The limited company is a creation of the law, and since its first invention, the law relating to limited companies has been refined in a series of Companies Acts of increasing length and complexity. The latest, Companies Act 2006, now weighs in at well over 700 pages. Essentially, however, company law permits one or more individuals to form a company with themselves as members (others may be admitted later without limit). The members then put resources (usually money) into the company, to enable it to operate, and in exchange the company gives them shares in its future profits. The members of a limited company and its shareholders, therefore, are the same people, called by a different name.

Shares are normally given to members in proportion to the value they put into the company and (in general) each ordinary share carries a vote in meetings of the company. Meetings must take place at least once a year and members may vote to elect themselves or others (who need not be members) as directors, to manage the company. Members (in their capacity as members) may not otherwise interfere in the company's affairs, although the company's directors must prepare annual accounts of its activities for presentation to the members. For the information and protection of the company's creditors, the same annual accounts must be filed for public inspection at Companies House, the official registry of company information. The content of these accounts is specified by law and in general they must also be audited, or examined, by a qualified accountant, who must express an opinion as to whether they present a true and fair view of the company's profit or loss and its state of affairs.

Although members or shareholders enjoy the profits of a company, strictly speaking it is wrong to say that they are the company's owners. Unlike the owners of, say, a dog or a bonfire, the members of a company are not responsible for any damage it may cause. Unlike the owners of a house or a car, the members of a company have little direct control over its affairs, unless they also happen to be directors of the company. The point is that as a corporation, a body composed of people, a company has no need of owners. It has members and what the members actually own are shares – that is, certificates which give them various rights in the company (the right to vote in meetings, the right to claim a share of profits and so on).

Members who wish to leave a company may not normally return their shares and get their money back. They may, however, sell their shares to other investors, who will take their place as members of the company.

## LIMITED LIABILITY

Once established, a company may buy and sell assets, enter contracts and incur liabilities in its own name, without disturbing its members. It is understood, therefore, that the assets of a company belong to the company itself and not to its several members. With regard to liabilities, however, it is explicitly stated that a *limited* company may be incorporated *with limited liability* for its members. This means that the creditors of a limited company may pursue their claims only against the company itself and not against its individual members. As we saw in Chapter 56, if there are not sufficient assets in a limited company to meet the claims of its creditors, then the creditors must simply be content to share whatever assets there may be, according to the rank and proportion of their different claims.

From the members' point of view, limited liability means that if a company cannot pay its creditors, the worst that can happen to them as members is that the company will fail, and their shares in the company will be worthless. But, as members, they can lose no more than the value they have already paid, or agreed to pay, for their shares. Even the company itself lacks any power to make its members pay in any more than they agree to, when their shares are issued. When they buy a share in a limited company, therefore, shareholders know exactly the limit of what they can lose. That is the meaning of limited liability.

## FORMING A LIMITED COMPANY

The steps required to form a limited company are deliberately simple, with ready-made standard forms available for all of the necessary documentation. First, prospective members ('subscribers') must sign a Memorandum of Association stating their intention to form a company, and a set of Articles of Association (rules for the governance and conduct of the company).

The memorandum must state the name and the objects of the company (that is, its purpose) and the fact that the liability of its members is to be limited. It must also state the maximum number of shares the company may issue and the minimum value in exchange for which they may be issued.

These limits are set by the members themselves and may be changed by vote of the members in the future. They are expressed in what is known as the authorized capital clause of the memorandum, where the minimum value at which a share may be issued is also called its nominal value.

The subscribers must also agree to put some value into the company, in exchange for which the company will issue shares or share certificates conferring all the rights of membership. Finally, the subscribers must appoint a company secretary and at least one person to be a company director. The relevant documentation must then be sent to the Registrar of Companies, with the requisite fee. Assuming that the documents are in order, they must be filed by the registrar and made available for public inspection at Companies House. The registrar must then issue a certificate of incorporation and the company is born.

## PRIVATE, PUBLIC, AND QUOTED COMPANIES

A private limited company (XYZ *Ltd*) is one whose shares may not be sold to the public at large. Thus, the company may only sell its shares to those with whom it has an existing connection. It is assumed that such individuals, because of their connections with the company, will be in a position to make their own enquiries into the company's affairs, both before and after they invest. Small and medium sized private limited companies, therefore, are not required to publish their accounts in the same exhaustive detail as a public limited company, and the accounts of some small private limited companies need not be subject to an independent audit.

A public limited company (XYZ *plc*) is a company which may issue its shares to be traded among the public at large. Except for their shareholding, therefore, the members of a plc may have no other connection with the company and thus, no personal ability to access any information concerning its affairs. A plc is, therefore, required to publish detailed and extensive annual accounts, which must be audited. A company may not become a public limited company unless it has already issued shares with a nominal value of at least £50 000 in total. It would seem that this requirement was designed to ensure the existence of enough shares and shareholders in a plc for there to be a reasonable market in which the shares can be traded.

A quoted or listed company is one whose shares are listed for trading on a recognized stock exchange. As a condition of access to the exchange, the company must have at least one sponsor willing and able at any time to quote a price at which it will buy or sell the company's shares, so that investors wishing to trade will always find a counterparty. The law now requires quoted companies to publish their accounts and other information on a website. However, when a company is listed, the stock exchange itself is likely to impose requirements for disclosure of information that are far more stringent than the minimum required by the law. Stock exchange authorities are charged with the responsibility of ensuring a smooth and continuous market in shares, and one which is fair to all participants. A fundamental requirement is the prompt and accurate disclosure of any information that is likely to affect the price of a share, and the information must be simultaneously available to all.

## ADVANTAGES OF INCORPORATION

Incorporation, especially with limited liability, affords enormous advantages to business enterprise. These include:

- easier access to capital, especially for those very large quoted companies with millions of shares in issue, who need to attract vast quantities of investment from around the world;
- flexibility for investors, who may withdraw their investment by selling their shares, without disrupting the affairs of the company;

- limited liability, which is of benefit not only to the passive investor in the very large company, but also to the owner of even the very small firm, who may wish to escape the *unlimited* liability of the sole trader or the partnership;
- ease of transfer and succession – it is easier to transfer the ownership of shares in a company, than it would be to transfer the ownership of all the separate assets in a business.

## ACCOUNTING AND THE PUBLIC INTEREST

It is only with the invention of the limited company that accounting becomes a matter of genuinely public interest. For, in addition to all of its potential benefits, incorporation with limited liability also brings tremendous risks of recklessness and fraudulent abuse. For example:

- it creates an asymmetrical pattern of business risk, allowing investors to take unlimited profits from a company, should they arise, while limiting their liability to pay for any losses it may cause to other people;
- it offers unparalleled opportunity for fraud by those in control of a company or its assets, against the distant uncoordinated members who entrusted them with that control.

At the same time, the size and power of the modern corporation make it essential that those who control and direct its activities should be held accountable, not just for their use of shareholders' capital, but also for their stewardship of such a large proportion of the planet's limited resources.

Since its inception therefore, there has been an ever-developing framework of laws, regulations, principles, standards, codes of practice and other requirements intended to prevent, detect, or expose successive abuses of the limited company as a vehicle of fraud, oppression, or social irresponsibility, and it is this framework which has mostly shaped the development of modern accounting.

The following chapters, therefore, will concern themselves in somewhat greater detail with the nature of the limited company and with some of its peculiar requirements in accounting.

## REVIEW

This chapter has considered the nature of a corporation and some of the essential characteristics of the limited company as a species of corporation. The chapter briefly outlined how a limited company may be formed and the importance of incorporation with limited liability for members. Finally, the chapter pointed out how the development of the limited company has changed accounting from a matter of private concern into a matter of public interest.

## DRILLS AND EXERCISES

There are no drills or exercises on this chapter, but for the understanding of subsequent chapters, readers should ensure that they have a clear understanding of the nature of a corporation and of limited liability.

# CHAPTER 58

# The Issue of Shares in a New Company

## OBJECTIVES

*The objectives of this chapter are:*

- to describe the issue of shares in a limited company
- to explain the significance of a company's authorized share capital and the nominal value of a share
- to show how to account for the issue of shares at par, at a premium and part-paid

## AUTHORIZED CAPITAL

The authorized capital of a limited company is a statement of the maximum number of shares the company may issue and the minimum value in exchange for which they may be issued. The law requires the company itself to set these limits and they may be changed by agreement of the members at a later date. Box 58.1 presents an example, with particular numbers, of how a company's authorized capital may be stated.

BOX 58.1

> **Authorized Capital**
>
> ABC Limited is formed with authorized capital £500, divided into 100 shares of £5 each.
>
> This means that:
>
>> 100 is the maximum number of shares the company may issue; and
>>
>> £5 is the minimum value in exchange for which a share may be issued.
>
> Notice that the authorized capital clause may consist of any workable combination of numbers. The authorized capital of DEF Ltd might be £100, divided into 400 shares of 25p each, and so on.

The minimum value at which a share may be issued is also known as its nominal value, or (sometimes) its par value.

## WHY SHOULD SHARES HAVE A NOMINAL VALUE?

One reason why a company must give its shares a nominal value – that is, why it must set a minimum on the value in exchange for which it may issue a share – is to ensure that all the members of a company will have made a real investment and therefore have something to lose in the event of the company's failure. In the United States, where each separate state has a company law of its own, and some regimes are quite permissive, a company may issue shares of no par value. There is no theoretical objection to this, except perhaps that it would seem to be unfair on all of those who had actually paid for their shares, by making it possible for those in control of a company to give out further shares among their friends for nothing.

## WHY LIMIT THE NUMBER OF SHARES THAT CAN BE ISSUED?

A company must issue at least one ordinary share (without which it would have no members) but the company may decide for itself how many more shares it will issue, subject to the authorized maximum. The purpose of making the company state the maximum number of shares it may issue, is connected with the fact that each share carries a vote, and the value of a vote on any matter must depend on the total number of votes that may be cast. One vote out of a maximum possible two votes is 50% of the votes and carries substantial power. One vote, or even 100 votes, out of a maximum possible 100 000 votes, will carry very little power.

## ISSUING SHARES: THE BASIC TRANSACTION

The basic transaction involved in any issue of shares is this: coming IN to the company is something of value (usually in the form of money), while going OUT is a promise which will form the basis of the shareholder's claim on the company. Precisely how the transaction should be recorded, however, will depend on the value received. It matters whether the shares are issued at par or at a premium and whether they are issued fully paid or part-paid.

## THE ISSUE OF SHARES AT PAR

Shares issued at par, are issued at their nominal value – that is, they are issued in exchange for the minimum value specified in the company's Memorandum of Association.

When shares are issued at par, value comes IN to the company, and the whole of the promise given OUT to the new shareholders is called 'Issued Share Capital'. Box 58.2 shows the double entry for an issue of ordinary shares at par, with the relevant accounts and the resulting balance sheet.

BOX 58.2

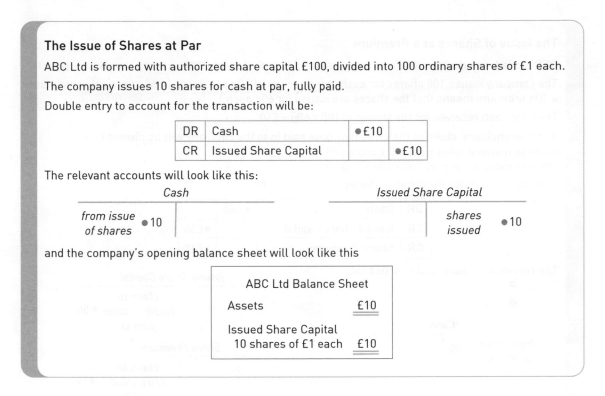

**The Issue of Shares at Par**

ABC Ltd is formed with authorized share capital £100, divided into 100 ordinary shares of £1 each.

The company issues 10 shares for cash at par, fully paid.

Double entry to account for the transaction will be:

| DR | Cash | ●£10 | |
|----|------|------|------|
| CR | Issued Share Capital | | ●£10 |

The relevant accounts will look like this:

| Cash | | Issued Share Capital | |
|------|------|------|------|
| from issue of shares ●10 | | | shares issued ●10 |

and the company's opening balance sheet will look like this

ABC Ltd Balance Sheet

| Assets | £10 |
|--------|-----|
| Issued Share Capital 10 shares of £1 each | £10 |

Notice that 'Issued Share Capital' is recorded as a single item in the accounts. There is no attempt in a company's accounts to record a separate claim for each individual shareholder, although a company should maintain a separate register of shareholders. Also, notice how it is customary in the balance sheet to state the nominal value of the shares that have been issued.

## THE ISSUE OF SHARES AT A PREMIUM

Shares issued at a premium are issued in exchange for more than the minimum (nominal) value specified in the company's Memorandum of Association. Why should shareholders pay in any more for their shares than they have to? A fair question, to which one answer is, why shouldn't they? As long as shares are issued in proportion to the value paid into the company, so that an investor who pays in twice as much gets twice as many shares and so on; as long as shareholders have a claim to all of the value they put in to a company; and as long as the company gets the resources it needs, it really doesn't matter how much shareholders actually pay for each individual share.

## ACCOUNTING FOR THE ISSUE OF SHARES AT A PREMIUM

When shares are issued at a premium:

- the shareholders' claim to the basic nominal value they have paid for their shares is recorded in the Issued Share Capital Account; and
- a further claim to the extra value they have paid is recorded in an account created for the purpose, which is called the Share Premium Account.

Box 58.3 presents an example.

## BOX 58.3

### The Issue of Shares at a Premium

DEF Ltd is formed with authorized share capital £100, divided into 200 ordinary shares of 50p each.

The company issues 100 shares for cash at a premium of 10p per share. (A 50p nominal value plus a 10p premium means that the shares are issued for 60p each.)

The total cash received for the shares is 100 x 60p = £60.

The shareholders' claim to the value they have paid in to the company will be divided into:
claim to nominal value paid 100 x 50p = £50
claim to extra value paid 100 x 10p = £10

The double entry for the issue of shares therefore will be:

| DR | Cash | ●£60 | |
|----|------|------|------|
| CR | Issued Share Capital | | ●£50 |
| CR | Share Premium | | ●£10 |

The relevant accounts will look like this:

*Issued Share Capital*

claim to
nominal value ● 50
paid in

*Cash*

from issue ● 60
of shares

*Share Premium*

claim to
extra value ●10
paid in

and the balance sheet after the issue of shares will look like this:

DEF Ltd Balance Sheet
Assets                                   £60

Issued Share Capital
  100 shares of 50p each   50
Share Premium                    10
                                            £60

## THE ISSUE OF SHARES PART-PAID

Although a company may not issue shares at a discount (in exchange for anything less than their nominal value), it is possible for a company to issue shares on receipt of only part of the full issue price. Such shares are said to be issued 'part paid'. Box 58.4 presents an example.

## BOX 58.4

**Issue of Shares Part Paid**

GHI Ltd is formed with authorized share capital £100, divided into 400 ordinary shares of 25p each.

The company issues 100 shares for cash at par, part paid 20p.

The cash received by the company will be 100 × 20p = £20, and the company's balance sheet will look like this:

| GHI Ltd Balance Sheet | |
|---|---|
| Assets | £20 |
| Issued Share Capital | |
| 100 shares of 25p each, part paid 20p | £20 |

Holders of part paid shares are obliged, when asked, to pay the remainder of the issue price into the company, thus making their shares fully paid. Box 58.5 continues the example.

## BOX 58.5

**Making Shares Fully Paid**

GHI Ltd, formed with authorized share capital £100, divided into 400 ordinary shares of 25p each, has previously issued 100 shares for cash at part part-paid 20p, as shown in balance sheet 1 below.

Shareholders are now required to make their shares fully paid.

100 shares were issued part paid, and the unpaid part of the shares' issue price is 25p – 20p = 5p. The cash received by the company therefore will be 100 × 5p = £5.

The company's balance sheets before and after the shares are made fully paid will look like this:

| GHI Ltd Balance Sheet (1) | |
|---|---|
| Assets | £20 |
| Issued Share Capital | |
| 100 shares of 25p each, **part paid 20p** | £20 |

| GHI Ltd Balance Sheet (2) | |
|---|---|
| Assets | £25 |
| Issued Share Capital | |
| 100 shares of 25p each, **fully paid** | £25 |

The power to issue shares part paid is perhaps most useful when the company wishes to finance a long-term project which need not be paid for all at once. Issuing shares part-paid means that shareholders need not pay in more than is needed at the beginning, yet the company has the assurance that it can require them to pay in the remaining value when it is needed. Box 58.6 shows a simple example.

## BOX 58.6

### Use of the Power to Issue Shares Part Paid

J, K, and L have formed a company, JKL Ltd, to build and equip a new hotel. They estimate that building costs, payable in YEAR 1, will be £300, and equipment costs, payable in YEAR 2, will be £200. The hotel will open in YEAR 3, after which any further investment should be financed out of profits.

A suitable plan for the new company would be to give itself authorized share capital of £500, divided into 100 shares of £5 each.

The company could begin in YEAR 1 with the issue of all 100 authorized shares, for cash, part paid £3. This would raise the necessary £300 for building costs.

At the beginning of YEAR 2, the company could require shareholders to make their shares fully paid, thus raising the extra £200 necessary for equipping the hotel.

## THE ISSUE OF PART PAID SHARES AT A PREMIUM

Part-paid shares may be issued at a premium. In such a case, shareholders are deemed to be paying the share premium before they pay the nominal value of their shares. Box 58.7 presents an example.

## BOX 58.7

### The Issue of Part Paid Shares at a Premium

MNO Ltd is formed with authorized share capital £300, divided into 300 shares of £1 each.

The company issues 100 shares for cash at £1.20 each, part-paid 70p.

There is a share premium of 20p per share. The 70p paid for each share will go:
• first to pay the whole of the 20p premium on each share;
• then to pay part of the nominal value.

The company's balance sheet will therefore look like this

| MNO Ltd Balance Sheet | |
| --- | --- |
| Assets | £70 |
| | |
| Issued Share Capital | |
|    100 shares of £1 each, part-paid 50p | £50 |
| Share Premium | £20 |
| | £70 |

# REVIEW

This chapter has explained the significance of authorized share capital, and has shown the basic procedures involved in accounting for the issue of shares at par, at a premium, and part-paid.

# DRILLS AND EXERCISES

## 58.1

For each of the companies below:

(a) state the double entry necessary to account for the issue of shares;
(b) show the entries in the relevant accounts;
(c) show a summary balance sheet for the company after the share issue.

1. ABC Ltd is formed with authorized share capital £100, divided into 400 ordinary shares of 25p each nominal value.
   100 shares are issued for cash at par, fully paid.
2. DEF Ltd is formed with authorized share capital £10 000, divided into 20 ordinary shares of nominal value £500 each.
   The company issues five shares for cash at par, fully paid.
3. GHI Ltd is formed with authorized share capital £2 000, divided into 4 000 ordinary shares of nominal value 50p each.

   (a) The company issues 100 shares for cash at par, part-paid 30p per share;
   (b) The issued shares are made fully paid.

4. JKL Ltd is formed with authorized share capital £1 000, divided into 5 000 ordinary shares of nominal value 20p each.

   (a) The company issues 1 000 shares for cash at par, part-paid 15p per share;
   (b) The issued shares are made fully paid.

5. MNO Ltd is formed with authorized share capital £100, divided into 200 ordinary shares of nominal value 50p each.
   The company issues 100 shares for cash at 60p each (i.e. at a premium of 10p per share) fully paid.
6. PQR Ltd is formed with authorized share capital £500, divided into 500 ordinary shares of nominal value £1 each.
   The company issues 300 shares for cash at £1.50 each (i.e. at a premium of 50p per share) fully paid.
7. STU Ltd is formed with authorized share capital £1 000, divided into 1 000 ordinary shares of nominal value £1 each.

   (a) The company issues 100 shares for cash at £1.20 each, part-paid 90p;
   (b) The issued shares are made fully paid.

8. VWX Ltd is formed with authorized share capital £5 000, divided into 500 ordinary shares of nominal value £10 each.

   (a) The company issues 400 shares for cash at £12 each, part-paid £11;
   (b) The issued shares are made fully paid.

9. Robert has invented and patented a new engineering process.

   Various investors are interested, and Robert has formed RHA Ltd to exploit the idea, with an authorized share capital of £50 000, divided into 200 000 shares of 25p each.

   The company initially issues a total of 160 000 shares at a premium of 75p per share, fully paid. 90 000 shares are allotted to Robert, in exchange for the exclusive right to use his patent, and 70 000 shares are allotted to Audrey for cash.

10. X, Y, and Z have formed XYZ Ltd with an authorized share capital of £500 000, divided into 100 000 shares of £5 each.

    The company issues 20 000 shares at par, fully paid, as follows:

    8 000 shares are issued to X in exchange for delivery vehicles;
    7 000 shares are issued to Y in exchange for machinery;
    5 000 are allotted to Z for cash.

# CHAPTER 59

# Accounting for Profits and Losses

## OBJECTIVES

*The objectives of this chapter are:*

- to show how profits and losses are accounted for in a limited company
- to describe the consequences of a limited company continuing to trade while insolvent

## THE RETAINED EARNINGS ACCOUNT

In a sole trader, when the business makes a profit (increasing its net assets), the extra value is claimed by the owner, and we record the increase in the owner's claim by transferring the balance on the P&L Account to the Capital Account. In a limited company, the procedure is essentially the same, except that the extra value is claimed by shareholders, and the increase in the shareholders' claim is recorded by transferring the balance on the P&L Account to a Retained Earnings Account, which forms a separate part of the shareholders' total claim on the company.

The Retained Earnings Account in the balance sheet, therefore, shows the shareholders' claim to the extra value in the company that is there as a result of having made a profit. Box 59.1 on the following page presents an example.

BOX 59.1

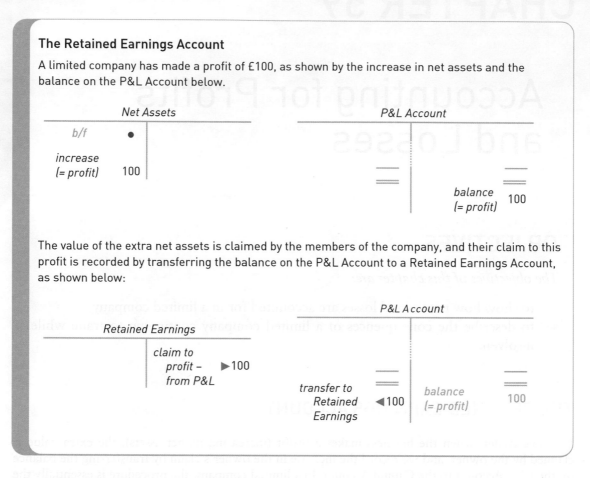

### The Retained Earnings Account

A limited company has made a profit of £100, as shown by the increase in net assets and the balance on the P&L Account below.

The value of the extra net assets is claimed by the members of the company, and their claim to this profit is recorded by transferring the balance on the P&L Account to a Retained Earnings Account, as shown below:

In future periods, further profits will increase the balance on the Retained Earnings Account to match the company's increase in net assets, while losses will decrease the balance on the Retained Earnings Account, to match the company's decrease in net assets. The effect of profits and losses on successive balance sheets is shown in Box 59.2 on the following page.

## BOX 59.2

### Profits and Losses in Successive Balance Sheets

ABC Limited has formed with authorized share capital £1 000, divided into 1 000 shares of £1 each.

200 shares are issued at £1.25 each for cash. The company's opening balance sheet will therefore look like this:

ABC Ltd Opening Balance Sheet

| | |
|---|---|
| Net Assets | £250 |
| Issued Share Capital | |
| 200 shares of £1 each | 200 |
| Share Premium | 50 |
| | £250 |

If the company makes a profit of £100 in Year 1 and a loss of £40 in Year 2, successive balance sheets will look like this:

| ABC Ltd Balance Sheet at END OF YEAR 1 after *£100 profit in year* | | ABC Ltd Balance Sheet at END OF YEAR 2 after *£40 loss in year* | |
|---|---|---|---|
| **Net Assets** (250 + 100) | **£350** | **Net Assets** (350 – 40) | **£310** |
| Issued Share Capital | | Issued Share Capital | |
| 200 shares of £1 each | 200 | 200 shares of £1 each | 200 |
| Share Premium | 50 | Share Premium | 50 |
| **Retained Earnings** | 100 | Retained Earnings (100 – 40) | 60 |
| | £350 | | £310 |

## RETAINED LOSS

It is quite possible for a company's losses to exceed any pre-existing retained earnings. In such a case, the Retained Earnings Account will carry a DR balance, and will be shown in the balance sheet as a Retained Loss, to be deducted from the other elements of the shareholders' claim. Box 59.3 shows an example of a company with successive profits and losses, including at times a retained loss.

## BOX 59.3

### Retained Loss

DEF Ltd, having issued a number of shares at a premium, starts with this summarized balance sheet:

DEF Ltd Opening Balance Sheet

| | |
|---|---|
| Net Assets | £500 |
| Issued Share Capital | 300 |
| Share Premium | 200 |
| | £500 |

## BOX 59.3    Continued

In successive periods, the company then makes a profit of £100, a loss of £150, a profit of £20, and a profit of £40.

Summary balance sheets at the end of each period will look like this:

| DEF Ltd Balance Sheets | opening | after £100 profit | after £150 loss | after £20 profit | after £40 profit |
|---|---|---|---|---|---|
| Net Assets | £500 | £600 | £450 | £470 | £510 |
| Issued Share Capital | 300 | 300 | 300 | 300 | 300 |
| Share Premium | 200 | 200 | 200 | 200 | 200 |
| Retained Earnings (Loss) | | 100 | (50) | (30) | 10 |
| | £500 | £600 | £450 | £470 | £510 |

## NET LIABILITIES AND TRADING WHILE INSOLVENT

A company with repeated or catastrophic losses may ultimately find itself with net liabilities – that is, with liabilities exceeding the value of assets remaining in the company. On the capital side of the balance sheet, this would be reflected by a Retained Loss exceeding the sum of all other parts of the shareholders' claim.

A company with net liabilities is insolvent – it has insufficient assets to cover the value of its liabilities. In a sole trader or a partnership, the creditors who would suffer from this shortfall are allowed to pursue their claims against the personal assets of the owner(s) of the business. In a limited company, however, creditors have no claim against the shareholders. They can claim only against the assets of the company.

It follows that net liabilities and insolvency in a limited company are far more serious for creditors than they would be in a sole trader or a partnership. The law therefore attempts to protect them. A company which is insolvent with net liabilities must cease to trade. If the company continues to trade while insolvent, thus exposing its creditors to even greater losses, its directors may face criminal charges, and they may become personally liable to pay the creditors of the company.

## ELEMENTS OF THE LIMITED COMPANY BALANCE SHEET

Like the owners of an unincorporated business, the members of a limited company claim whatever value remains in the business after the claims of other people. The net asset side of the balance sheet for a limited company is therefore essentially the same as it would be for a sole trader. However, there are differences, as we have seen, on the capital side of the balance sheet.

The essential difference is that in the balance sheet of a sole trader, the total of the owner's claim can be presented as a single lump – the balance on the one and only Capital Account. In the balance sheet of a limited company, however, the total shareholders' claim must be divided into several constituent parts, depending on how each part came into existence. Thus we have seen already that:

- Issued Share Capital shows the shareholders' claim arising in respect of the minimum value they originally had to pay into the company for their shares;

- Share Premium shows the shareholders' claim arising in respect of any extra value they have paid into the company for their shares; and

- Retained Earnings shows the shareholders' claim to any extra value accumulated in the company, arising as a result of profitable operations.

Box 59.4 presents an illustration.

## BOX 59.4

### Some Elements of the Shareholders' Claim on a Limited Company

|  | £ |  |
|---|---|---|
| Assets | 850 | —— value of things in the company |
| Liabilities | (500) | —— value claimed by other people |
| Net Assets | £350 | —— value left for members to claim |
|  |  |  |
| Issued Share Capital | 200 | ┐ claims arising in respect of value paid in to the company |
| Share Premium | 50 | ┘ |
| Retained Earnings | 100 | —— claim arising in respect of extra net assets (profits) |
| Total Shareholders' Claim | £350 |  |

## REVIEW

This chapter has shown the use of the Retained Earnings Account in a limited company to show the result of those changes in the shareholders' claim that arise in respect of successive profits (increases in net assets) and losses (decreases in net assets). The chapter also briefly considered the possibility of a Retained Loss and, at the extreme, the potential consequences of a company continuing to trade while insolvent. Finally, the chapter summarized the way in which the total shareholders' claim on a limited company is divided into separate parts, depending on how each different part of the claim came into existence.

# DRILLS AND EXERCISES

## 59.1

ABC Ltd has issued 100 shares of £1 each for £1.50. The Company therefore shows net assets £150, issued share £100, and share premium £50.

Show the company's balance sheet at the end of each successive year, if it reports profits and losses as follows:

Year 1 £25 profit
Year 2 £20 loss
Year 3 £60 profit

Year 4 £80 loss
Year 5 £10 profit
Year 6 £100 loss
Year 7 £50 loss

## 59.2

For each of the following companies, state the total value of the shareholders' claim on the company and explain the origin of its different components.

| DEF LTD | |
|---|---|
| Net Assets | £200 |
| Issued Share Capital | |
| 800 shares of 25p | £200 |

| GHI LTD | |
|---|---|
| Net Assets | £120 |
| Issued Share Capital | |
| 100 shares of £1 | 100 |
| Share Premium | 20 |
| | £120 |

| JKL LTD | |
|---|---|
| Net Assets | £190 |
| Issued Share Capital | |
| 500 shares of 20p | 100 |
| Share Premium | 50 |
| Retained Earnings | 40 |
| | £190 |

| MNO LTD | |
|---|---|
| Net Assets | £550 |
| Issued Share Capital | |
| 1 000 shares of 50p | 500 |
| Share Premium | 250 |
| Retained Loss | (200) |
| | £550 |

| PQR LTD | |
|---|---|
| Net Assets | £2 000 |
| Issued Share Capital | |
| 1 000 shares of £5 | 5 000 |
| Share Premium | 3 000 |
| Retained Loss | (6 000) |
| | £2 000 |

| STU LTD | |
|---|---|
| Net Assets | £(1 000) |
| Issued Share Capital | |
| 1 000 shares of £5 | 5 000 |
| Share Premium | 3 000 |
| Retained Loss | (9 000) |
| | £(1 000) |

# CHAPTER 60

# Accounting for the Payment of Dividends

## OBJECTIVES

*The objectives of this chapter are:*

- to show how to account for the payment of a dividend
- to explain the significance of the entries, and the balance, on the Retained Earnings Account
- to show the different ways in which the amount of a dividend can be described

## DIVIDENDS

A dividend is a payment of value out of a limited company, to be divided among its members or shareholders. Dividends are normally paid in the form of money, although it is possible for a company to pay out dividends in some other form. (The East India Company once paid a dividend by distributing surplus stocks of tea among its shareholders.)

Accounting for dividends in a limited company is essentially the same as accounting for drawings in a sole trader. When a sole trader makes drawings, assets go out of the business, and the owner's claim must be reduced. In a limited company when a dividend is paid, assets go out of the company, and the shareholders' claim must be reduced. The particular part of the shareholders' claim that must be reduced when a dividend is paid, is Retained Earnings. Box 60.1 presents an illustration.

## BOX 60.1

**Accounting for Dividends**

|  | £ |  |
|---|---|---|
| **Assets** | 850 | —— any value taken out of here by shareholders |
| Liabilities | (500) | |
| Net Assets | £350 | |
| | | |
| Issued Share Capital | | |
| 200 shares of £1 each | 200 | |
| Share Premium | 50 | |
| **Retained Earnings** | 100 | —— must be matched by a reduction in their claim here |
| | £350 | |

# THE PAYMENT OF A DIVIDEND

Accounting for the payment of a dividend requires a CR in the Cash Account, to record the cash going out, and a DR in the Retained Earnings Account to reduce the shareholders' claim on the company (that is, to take back part of the promise going out to the shareholders). Box 60.2 presents an example.

## BOX 60.2

**Accounting for the Payment of a Dividend**

ABC Ltd has been operating for some time and has assets £850, liabilities £500, issued share capital £200, share premium £50, and retained profit £100.

The company now decides to pay a dividend of £20. Double entry to account for the dividend will be

| DR | Retained Earnings | ●£20 | |
|---|---|---|---|
| CR | Cash (Assets) | | ●£20 |

The relevant accounts will look like this:

| | *Retained Earnings* | | | | *Assets* | | | |
|---|---|---|---|---|---|---|---|---|
| *reduction of claim* | ●20 | b/f | 100 | | b/f | 850 | *payment of dividend* | ●20 |

**BOX 60.2**  Continued

And the company's balance sheet before and after payment of the dividend will look like this

| ABC Ltd Balance Sheets | before dividend | after £20 dividend |
|---|---|---|
| | £ | £ |
| Assets | 850 | 830 |
| Liabilities | (500) | (500) |
| Net Assets | £350 | £330 |
| | | |
| Issued Share Capital | 200 | 200 |
| Share Premium | 50 | 50 |
| Retained Earnings (Loss) | 100 | 80 |
| | £350 | £330 |

## THE CONTENT OF THE RETAINED EARNINGS ACCOUNT

The Retained Earnings Account now represents a cumulative record of changes in the shareholders' claim to the extra net assets in the company, above the values put there by the shareholders themselves. These changes arise in respect of profits, losses and dividends – recall that profits are increases in net assets as a result of successful operations, losses are decreases in net assets as a result of unsuccessful operations and dividends are decreases in net assets as a result of payments out to shareholders.

Box 60.3 now shows an abstract summary of the contents of the Retained Earnings Account.

## BOX 60.3

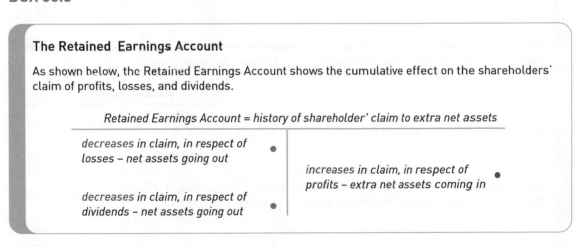

**The Retained Earnings Account**

As shown below, the Retained Earnings Account shows the cumulative effect on the shareholders' claim of profits, losses, and dividends.

*Retained Earnings Account = history of shareholder' claim to extra net assets*

- *decreases in claim, in respect of losses – net assets going out*
- *decreases in claim, in respect of dividends – net assets going out*
- *increases in claim, in respect of profits – extra net assets coming in*

## THE BALANCE ON THE RETAINED EARNINGS ACCOUNT

By law, the only claim that may be reduced when shareholders take value out of a company is the Retained Earnings Account. It follows that the balance on the Retained Earnings Account represents the maximum dividend that a company is allowed to pay. Thus:

- if there is a CR balance on the Retained Earnings Account, then the company may pay a dividend up to the value of the claim it represents;
- if there is no balance on the Retained Earnings Account, then there is no claim that may be reduced and the company may not pay a dividend;
- if there is a DR balance on the Retained Earnings Account, representing a negative claim, then the company may not pay a dividend, and must not pay a dividend until it has made sufficient profit to turn the DR balance into a CR balance.

It also follows that a company may pay a dividend in a period in which it makes a loss, as long as the loss is not enough to wipe out an existing CR balance on the Retained Earnings Account. On the other hand, there may be periods in which a company may not pay a dividend even though it has made a profit, if there was an existing DR balance on the Retained Earnings Account, and the profit was not enough to wipe it out. Box 60.4 presents a sequence of examples.

## BOX 60.4

### The Balance on the Retained Earnings Account

DEF Ltd issues 200 shares of £1 each at a premium of 50p per share. The company pays no dividends, but generates profits and losses as shown in the series of balance sheets below:

| DEF Ltd Balance Sheets | end of YR 1 after £50 loss | end of YR 2 after £20 profit | end of YR 3 after £140 profit | end of YR 4 after £10 loss |
|---|---|---|---|---|
| Net Assets | £250 | £270 | £410 | £400 |
| Issued Share Capital | 200 | 200 | 200 | 200 |
| Share Premium | 100 | 100 | 100 | 100 |
| Retained Earnings (Loss) | (50) | (30) | 110 | 100 |
| | £250 | £270 | £410 | £400 |

The maximum dividend payable at the end of each period can be seen by inspection of the balance sheet, or by examination of the Retained Earnings Account, as shown below.

*Retained Earnings*

at the end of YR 1, the company may not pay a dividend until it has made enough profit to wipe out this DR balance

| balance at end of YR 1 | 50 | YR 2 – profit | 20 |
| | | c/f | 30 |
| | 50 | | 50 |

even though the company made a profit in YR 2, with a DR balance remaining here, it still may not pay a dividend

| balance at end of YR 2 | 30 | YR 3 – profit | 140 |
| c/f | 110 | | |
| | 140 | | 140 |

even though the company made a profit of £140 in YR3 the maximum dividend it may pay for the year is only £110

| YR 4 – loss | 10 | balance at end of YR 3 | 110 |
| c/f | 100 | | |
| | 110 | | 110 |

even though the company made a loss in YR 4, with a CR balance here it still may pay a dividend of up to £100

| | | balance at end of YR 4 | 100 |

# DESCRIBING THE AMOUNT OF A DIVIDEND

The dividends in our examples have been described in terms of the total amount payable by the company. However, the individual shareholder is probably less concerned about the total payment out of the company and rather more concerned about the value he or she is going to receive. For the individual shareholder, therefore, dividends are also described in terms of pence per share. (This being the total amount of the dividend, divided by the number of shares in issue and qualifying for the dividend.) The individual shareholder may then determine the value that he or she will receive by multiplying the dividend in pence per share by the number of shares in his or her portfolio. Box 60.5 presents an example.

## BOX 60.5

### Dividends in Pence per Share

GHI Ltd proposes to pay a dividend of £700. The company has 10 000 shares in issue and qualifying for dividend.

This dividend could be described in terms of pence per share as follows:

$$\frac{£700}{10\ 000} = 7 \text{ pence per share}$$

X is a shareholder who holds 600 shares. The dividend receivable by X therefore will be

600 shares × 7 pence per share = £42

Dividends may also be described as a *percentage of the nominal* value of the relevant shares. Thus, a dividend of 5p per share on shares with a nominal value of 50p, could be described as a 10% dividend. In the past, dividends were quite commonly described as a percentage of nominal value, but in recent years, the pence per share description has become predominant and the per cent of nominal value method has become almost defunct.

# REVIEW

This chapter has introduced the topic of dividends, showing how dividends are accounted for, how the balance on the Retained Earnings Account shows the maximum dividend a company may pay and how dividends are commonly described.

# DRILLS AND EXERCISES

## 60.1

Show a summarized balance sheet at the end of each year for each of the following companies.

1. ABC Ltd is incorporated with authorized share capital £1 000 divided into 1 000 shares of £1 each. All of the shares are issued fully paid, at par.

   YEAR 1: net profit £230, dividend £170
   YEAR 2: net profit £180, dividend 10p per share
   YEAR 3: net loss £50, dividend 3p per share
   YEAR 4: net profit £90, dividend 8%

2. DEF Ltd is incorporated with authorized share capital £500 divided into 1 000 shares of 50p each. All of the shares are issued for 75p each, fully paid.

   YEAR 1: net profit £105, dividend £100
   YEAR 2: net profit £80, dividend 4.5p per share
   YEAR 3: net loss £5, dividend 3p per share
   YEAR 4: net profit £60, dividend 5%

3. GHI Ltd is incorporated with authorized share capital £2 000 divided into 2 000 shares of £1 each. 1 500 of the shares are issued at a premium of 10p each, fully paid.

   YEAR 1: net loss £50
   YEAR 2: net profit £350, dividend £150
   YEAR 3: net profit £200, dividend 9p per share
   YEAR 4: net loss £45, dividend nil

4. JKL Ltd is incorporated with authorized share capital £500 divided into 5 000 shares of 10p each. 3 000 of the shares are issued at par, part paid 7p per share.

   YEAR 1: net profit £95, dividend £45
   YEAR 2: net loss £20, dividend 10%
   YEAR 3: during this year, the company required the shares to be paid up in full, and reported net profit £140, dividend 2p per share
   YEAR 4: net profit £50, dividend 10%

# CHAPTER 61

# Capital Maintenance and Dividend Policy

## OBJECTIVES

*The objectives of this chapter are:*

- to describe the concept of capital maintenance
- to show how the law imposes the doctrine of capital maintenance by restricting the dividends payable by a limited company
- to explain the difference between the maintenance of financial capital and the maintenance of physical capital

## CAPITAL MAINTENANCE AND THE LAW

The legal doctrine of capital maintenance is the idea that:

- any value paid into a company by its shareholders should be locked in and may not normally be taken out again.

The law relates only to limited companies and its main purpose is the protection of creditors. We shall see first how the law is applied in practice and then consider its purpose and effects.

## HOW THE LAW IS APPLIED

When a company's original shareholders first acquire their shares, they put things of value into the company. The law is that they, or their successors if they sell their shares to other investors, may not normally take this value out again. Although apparently quite simple, in practice this law would seem quite difficult to apply. It would be pointless, for example, to say that any particular thing put in to a company by its shareholders may not be taken out again, because a company is always using, selling and replacing its assets.

The law therefore adopts an indirect approach, applying the principles of double entry. It places no restriction on what a company may do with its assets, choosing instead to restrict what shareholders may do with their claims.

It works like this: when shareholders put value into a company, the company gives them a claim to that value, which is recorded in the Share Capital Account and, if necessary, in the Share Premium Account. When shareholders take any value out of a company, they must reduce their claim. The law simply states that the claims recorded on the Share Capital Account and Share Premium Account may not be reduced. The value they represent – that is, the value put into the company by its shareholders – is therefore locked into the company.

To make quite certain of the matter, the law also states, as we have seen, that the only claim that can be reduced when shareholders take any value out of a company is the claim recorded in the Retained Earnings Account. This is the claim to the *extra* net assets accumulated in the company as a result of profit-making operations.

Box 61.1 provides an illustration of how the law is applied.

## BOX 61.1

### Imposing the Law on Capital Maintenance

The value that shareholders may take out of a company is governed by restrictions on their claims, as shown in the balance sheet below:

|  | £ |  |
|---|---|---|
| Assets | 850 | —— any value taken out of here by shareholders must be matched by a reduction in their total claim below |
| Liabilities | (500) | |
| Net Assets | £350 | |
| | | |
| Issued Share Capital | 200 | but these claims are locked in, and may not be reduced |
| Share Premium | 50 | |
| Retained Earnings | 100 | —— and  this is the only claim that can be reduced  when shareholders take value out of the company |
| | £350 | |

It follows from the restriction on their claims, that shareholders are in fact prevented from taking more than £100 of assets out of this company.

## THE PURPOSE OF THE LAW

The main purpose of the law on capital maintenance is the protection of creditors. As we know, the creditors of a limited company may not pursue their claims against its members. Any value that members can contrive to remove from a company is therefore removed entirely from the grasp of creditors. It follows that there has to be a limit on what shareholders may take out of a company, for if shareholders had the right to take as much as they liked, they could strip the company entirely, leaving nothing for the creditors to claim.

A secondary purpose of the law is the protection of shareholders themselves. Most shareholders are passive investors, with no direct knowledge of the companies in which they invest. They invest nevertheless, in the hope of receiving dividends which they can take and spend, without reducing the value of the capital they have invested. For this system to work, shareholders must be confident that what they receive as a dividend from a company genuinely is a payment out of extra net assets, and not in fact a repayment of their capital, merely masquerading as a profit.

## THE EFFECT OF THE LAW

The effect of the law on capital maintenance is not to give creditors any absolute protection against unforeseen company losses, but to ensure at least that shareholders allow them a protective - cushion. Thus shareholders must always leave assets in a company of sufficient value to exceed its liabilities by at least the amount of the company's issued share capital, plus any balance on the Share Premium Account. If, by reason of losses, the margin of assets over liabilities should fall below this amount, shareholders are not required to put further assets into the company, but they are prevented from taking any more value out. Box 61.2 presents an illustration.

### BOX 61.2

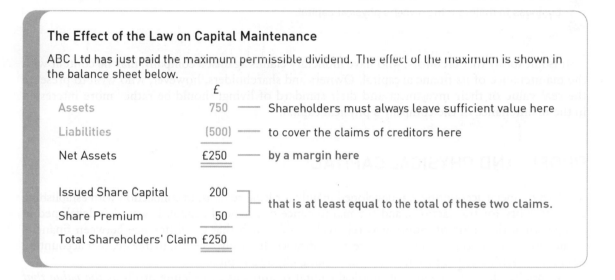

**The Effect of the Law on Capital Maintenance**

ABC Ltd has just paid the maximum permissible dividend. The effect of the maximum is shown in the balance sheet below.

|  | £ |  |
|---|---|---|
| Assets | 750 | —— Shareholders must always leave sufficient value here |
| Liabilities | (500) | —— to cover the claims of creditors here |
| Net Assets | £250 | —— by a margin here |
|  |  |  |
| Issued Share Capital | 200 | ⌉ that is at least equal to the total of these two claims. |
| Share Premium | 50 | ⌋ |
| Total Shareholders' Claim | £250 |  |

## FINANCIAL CAPITAL AND PHYSICAL CAPITAL

The legal doctrine of capital maintenance, as we have described it, refers to what is called financial capital. There is also physical capital, which is capital of a different kind. Financial capital is a claim to the monetary value invested in a business, as shown in the capital section of the balance sheet. Maintaining the financial capital of a company means ensuring that the value, as expressed in £'s, that shareholders first put in to a company when their shares are issued, is not later taken out again. This is largely for the protection of creditors, who have financial claims (expressed in £'s and payable in money) against the company.

Physical capital means productive capacity. It is measured, not in £'s, but, for example, in the rate at which a firm can produce units of output. Maintaining the physical capital of a company would mean maintaining its productive capacity. The maintenance of physical capital is not mandated by law, but it is a prudent objective, and in times of changing prices it is clear that the maintenance of financial capital will not guarantee the maintenance of physical capital. Box 61.3 provides a very simple example.

## BOX 61.3

**Financial Capital and Physical Capital**

A small business begins on Monday when the owner invests £500 to buy a stock of goods for resale.

On Tuesday the goods are sold for £600, yielding a profit of £100.

To preserve the owner's financial capital, it is enough to keep £500 in the business to buy new stock.

**BUT** if on Tuesday an equivalent stock of goods would cost £560, then £560 must be kept in the business to maintain the owner's physical capital.

It is fair to say that creditors, who have monetary claims against a company, may be content with the maintenance of its financial capital. Owners and shareholders, however, who wish to preserve the real value of their investment and their standard of living, should be rather more interested in the maintenance of the company's physical capital.

# PROFIT AND PHYSICAL CAPITAL

Modern financial accounting was developed mainly for legal reasons, in connection with establishing accountability for transactions, and the maintenance of financial capital. It was also developed in an age when the value of money was relatively stable, such that the difference between financial capital and physical capital was not of great significance. It is only recently, therefore, that accounting has begun to address the problems of maintaining physical capital.

Essentially, the maintenance of physical capital requires us to redefine profit as *the value that can be taken out of a business at the end of a period and spent, without reducing the productive capacity of the business.* Box 61.4 illustrates the definition with the data from our simple example.

## BOX 61.4

**Profit and Physical Capital**

A small business begins on Monday when the owner invests £500 to buy a stock of goods for resale.

On Tuesday the goods are sold for £600, yielding a financial profit of £100.

**HOWEVER**, if on Tuesday an equivalent stock of goods would cost £560, then £560 must be kept in the business to maintain the owner's physical capital.

The real profit of the business (the value that can be taken out of the business without reducing its productive capacity) would therefore be only £40.

At times of rapid change in the value of money, fully articulated schemes have been advanced for producing or adapting financial statements to reflect this 'real' or physical definition of profit, but then when the value of money has been stabilized, the problem has been shelved for lack of urgency. In practice, it would seem that accounting for changes in physical capital, although in theory very attractive, has always met with stiff resistance from among the ranks of accountants themselves. This may be because accounting for value would necessarily entail some neglect of accounting for transactions, which is the basis of accountability.

## DIVIDEND POLICY

Capital maintenance is not simply a problem in connection with the definition of profit, but also one of the factors determining a company's dividend policy. The directors of a company have the power to pay interim dividends at times throughout the year, and to propose a final dividend for approval by the members in their annual meeting. Within the limits imposed by the law, a number of factors may govern their decision as to how much dividend should be paid. These would include most obviously:

- preservation of the company's productive capacity (physical capital);
- opportunities for growth and further investment in the company; and
- the availability of cash.

In theory, a company need not, and even should not, pay a dividend at all, if it can profitably keep the extra resources for itself and invest in an expansion of the business. The theory is that the company's shareholders will thereby benefit from an increase in the value of their shares, rather than the receipt of a dividend. Any shareholders who actually need an income in money from their shares will be able, if they want, to realize some of the extra value by selling off a small proportion of their holding. (This is the theory known as 'dividend irrelevance'.)

In practice, however, most companies do pay a dividend and one limiting factor is the availability of cash. A company may be allowed to pay a dividend, and it may even want to pay a dividend, but it cannot pay a dividend unless it has the cash to pay it with.

A major intangible factor governing the size of a company's dividend is the way in which dividend policy is often used to send a signal to investors, about how the directors view the company's prospects. Thus, for example, in the face of weak results for a period, the directors may well maintain the dividend, to indicate their belief that the problem is only temporary. Or a massive dividend cut may be used to show that brutal surgery is underway. And so on.

## REVIEW

This chapter has considered the topic of capital maintenance, drawing a distinction between financial capital and physical capital. The chapter showed how the legal requirement for the maintenance of financial capital is imposed by restrictions on the use of shareholders' claims. It then outlined how the legal requirement works for the protection of both creditors and shareholders. Finally, the chapter described how the concept of physical capital may demand a redefinition of profit, and briefly considered some of the factors that might govern the dividend policy of a company.

# DRILLS AND EXERCISES

## 61.1

Go to www.wikipedia.com and research 'Ponzi scheme'.

## 61.2

According to the dividend irrelevance theory, investors should be indifferent as to whether or not a company pays a dividend. How would the system work if *no* companies ever paid a dividend?

# CHAPTER 62

# The Market Value
# of a Share

## OBJECTIVES

*The objectives of this chapter are:*

- to describe the primary and secondary markets for shares
- to identify the elements which contribute to the market value of a share
- to explain the nature of goodwill and show how its value can be measured

## THE PRIMARY AND SECONDARY MARKETS FOR SHARES

The primary market for shares is the market between companies and investors – where companies raise the capital they need by selling shares in their future profits to investors. The secondary market is the market in which investors buy and sell those shares among themselves.

Small companies may impose restrictions on the transfer of their shares, but in general, once a share has been issued by a company to an original investor in the primary market, it becomes freely transferable in the secondary market – the original shareholder may sell his or her shares to another investor, that other investor may sell them to another, and so on. Thus, in most cases when we buy the shares of a company, we buy them from an existing shareholder, and our payment goes not into the company itself, but into the hands of the existing shareholder, from whom we buy the shares in the secondary market.

Evidently, the price at which shares are transferred in this secondary market between investors will be determined by the investors themselves. It will not depend upon the nominal value of the shares (the minimum value at which the company could have issued them). Nor will it depend upon the actual price at which the shares were issued in the primary market – what the original investor may have paid for a share some time ago is of no relevance to what another investor would be willing to pay for it now.

## THE MARKET VALUE OF A SHARE

The market value of a share depends upon what the prospective buyer hopes to get, and what the prospective seller may be giving up. In this context, a share is essentially a package, composed of three basic elements:

- a claim on the net assets of a company;
- the right to claim a share of all future profits of the company; and
- the right to vote in meetings of the company.

## THE NET ASSET VALUE OF A SHARE

The shareholders' claim on the net assets of a company is shown in the company's balance sheet and we can in fact determine the net asset value of a share by dividing the value of the company's net assets by the number of shares in issue. Box 62.1 presents an example.

BOX 62.1

**The Net Asset Value of a Share**

ABC Ltd has the following balance sheet:

|  | £ |  |
|---|---|---|
| Assets | 8 500 | —— value of things in the company |
| Liabilities | (5 000) | —— value claimed by other people |
| Net Assets | £3 500 | —— value left for members to claim |
| Issued Share Capital | | |
| 1 000 shares of £2 each | 2 000 | |
| Share Premium | 500 | |
| Retained Earnings | 1 000 | |
| | £3 500 | —— total shareholders' claim |

The Net Asset Value of a share will be $\dfrac{£3\,500}{1\,000}$ = £3.50

Notice, however, that the net asset value of a share, based on balance sheet values, is open to all the criticisms of historical cost accounting. Strictly speaking, it is a misuse of the information given, for historical cost accounting is not in fact about current values. With respect to assets for example, historical cost accounting presents us with a balance sheet which says 'we paid £x for this'. It does not pretend to say that 'this is worth £x.'

## GOODWILL AND THE RIGHT TO CLAIM ALL FUTURE PROFITS

The claim to net assets is probably not the most significant element in the market value of a share. What matters most of all is the element called goodwill, which is the right to claim a share of all the future profits of the company. At moments of euphoria in the stock market, the future profits of a company may seem set for boundless growth, and share prices will soar as goodwill becomes enormously valuable. At moments of despair, future losses may seem more likely than profits and share prices will tumble. At most times, however, a company whose shares are traded in the stock market will try to ensure that the price of its shares will adjust quite smoothly, by relatively small amounts, by keeping the market fully informed of its latest results and its future prospects.

## THE VALUE OF A VOTE

Buying a share also means buying the right to vote in meetings of the company. Mostly, this right is of little value. A large company, with shares quoted on a recognized stock exchange, may have millions of shares in issue, and the individual shareholder with just a few hundred shares has very little effective power. However, in the event of a takeover bid or struggle for control of the company, the right to vote may have considerable value. (A takeover bid is when one company attempts to take over and control another company by acquiring a majority of its voting shares.)

## MARKET CAPITALIZATION AND THE MEASURE OF GOODWILL

The market capitalization of a company is the total market value of all its issued shares. In practical terms, the market capitalization of a company is found by multiplying the market price of a share in the company by the number of shares in issue.

If we assimilate the right to vote with the right to claim all future profits, then we can measure the value of goodwill. Traditionally this has been defined by accountants as the difference between the value of a business as a whole and the value of its separable net assets. Thus, the value of goodwill in a quoted company will be given by the difference between its market capitalization and the value of net assets in its balance sheet. (Subject always to the qualification that values in an historical cost balance sheet do not necessarily correspond with actual current values. A true valuation of goodwill should be based on market capitalization and the actual fair value of net assets in the company.)

## GOODWILL AND NET ASSET VALUES

Although a company will only hold assets in order to make a profit from using or selling them, a company's power to generate profits into the future is only partly related to the value of assets or net assets presently in its balance sheet.

Some companies, for example, make their profits mainly from the exploitation of ideas, or from their name and reputation. Such things are indeed assets, insofar as they are valuable, but they are seldom acquired in the course of a transaction and so will not generally appear in the balance sheet of a company. (Assets appear in the balance sheet only if they have entered the firm in the course of a transaction.) In such companies, which trade on their knowledge or their name, high profits can be generated from a low net asset base, and goodwill will contribute a larger proportion of the company's share price and its market capitalization. (This is what we would expect, although there may be some anomalies.) Box 62.2 presents some real-world examples from four different quoted companies.

## BOX 62.2

**Market Capitalization and Goodwill: Four Sample Companies**

| company activity | office rental | public transport | department store | professional training |
|---|---|---|---|---|
| | £M | £M | £M | £M |
| Market Capitalization | 1 295.2 | 1 436.0 | 11 771.8 | 321.3 |
| Net Asset Value | (654.7) | (542.5) | (1 646.8) | (10.6) |
| Goodwill | 640.5 | 893.5 | 10 125.0 | 310.7 |
| Goodwill as % of share value | 49.5% | 62.2% | 86.0% | 96.7% |

# REVIEW

This chapter has looked at why the market value of a share should differ from its issue price, identifying the three major factors that determine the market price of a share, and introducing the concept of goodwill and its valuation in the market for shares.

# DRILLS AND EXERCISES

## 62.1

Review the comparisons of market capitalization and net asset values in Box 62.2 and consider possible causes for the large differences in the importance of goodwill in the share prices of the different companies.

# CHAPTER 63

# Rights Issues

## OBJECTIVES

*The objectives of this chapter are:*

- to explain the nature of a rights issue
- to show how to account for a rights issue
- to consider the effects of a rights issue on the market value of a share in the company

## THE ISSUE OF FURTHER SHARES BY AN ESTABLISHED COMPANY

An established company, which has already issued shares, may at some stage wish to issue further shares – perhaps to expand the business, or to pay off debt. For a number of reasons, however, this will cause a problem for the interests of existing shareholders and for the market price of the company's shares. For example:

- the funds raised from the new issue will change the profit-making power of the company (and the change will not necessarily be for the better);
- the new shares will carry votes, and therefore dilute the voting power of existing shareholders.

But above all:

- the new shareholders must be allowed to share in all of the future profits of the company – not just the extra profits attributable to the new investment they bring in. This will give them part of a valuable right which currently belongs exclusively to the existing shareholders.

English law responds to these problems by giving existing shareholders the right to buy any new shares issued by a company, in proportion to the shares they already hold. Thus, if all shareholders take up their rights, none will be able to complain, because the distribution of power and profits among shareholders will remain unchanged. These *pre-emption rights* are not enjoyed by investors everywhere (for example, they do not generally apply in the United States), but here they mean that the issue of new shares by an established company is generally known as a rights issue.

## RIGHTS ISSUES

A rights issue is an issue of new shares for value by an established company, in which existing shareholders have the right to buy the new shares in proportion to the shares they already hold.

A rights issue is typically described as shown in Box 63.1.

## BOX 63.1

**Describing a Rights Issue**

Example:

ABC plc announces a 3 for 5 rights issue at £1.20

This means that
- existing shareholders have the right to buy three new shares for every five shares they already hold
- the new shares are to be issued at £1.20 each

A shareholder currently holding five shares, would therefore end with eight shares – if he or she took up the right to buy the three new shares at a price of £1.20 each.

## ACCOUNTING FOR A RIGHTS ISSUE

Accounting for a rights issue involves a preliminary working to determine how much cash the company will raise (we assume the rights issue will be for cash) and the share premium involved.

This will be followed by the double entry to account for the transaction. Box 63.2 presents an example.

## BOX 63.2

**Accounting for a Rights Issue**

DEF plc is an established company, whose summarized balance sheet is shown below:

| | |
|---|---|
| Net Assets | £3 200 |
| | |
| Issued Share Capital | |
| 1 200 shares of £1 each | 1 200 |
| Share Premium | 900 |
| Retained Earnings | 1 100 |
| | £3 200 |

The company now decides to make a 2 for 3 rights issue at £2.10.

Standard preliminary working for a rights issue:

| | | | |
|---|---|---|---|
| number of new shares | $2 \times \dfrac{1\,200}{3}$ | = | 800 |

| | | | £ |
|---|---|---|---|
| • cash raised | 800 × £2.10 | = | 1 680 |
| • nominal value of new shares | 800 × £1.00 | = | (800) |
| • Share Premium | | | £880 |

## BOX 63.2    Continued

The double entry to account for the rights issue will be

| DR | Cash (included in Net Assets) | • £1 680 | |
|---|---|---|---|
| CR | Issued Share Capital | | • £800 |
| CR | Share Premium | | • £880 |

And the balance sheet after the rights issue will look like this:

Net Assets (3 200 + 1 680)   £4 880

Issued Share Capital
2 000 shares of £1 each      2 000
Share Premium (900 + 880)  1 780
Retained Earnings              1 100

£4 880

# THE VALUE OF A RIGHT

To ensure the success of a rights issue, a company will normally issue any new shares at less than the prevailing market price. But recall that the rights to buy new shares at this special price belong exclusively to existing shareholders. These rights have a value, which can be determined if we first compute the 'theoretical ex-rights price' of a share, as shown in Box 63.3.

## BOX 63.3

### The Theoretical Ex-Rights Price of a Share and the Value of a Right

The market value of a share in DEF plc is £3.60 per share.

The company now announces a 2 for 3 rights issue at £2.10.

Imagine the holding of an investor who starts with 3 shares, and takes up the right to buy an extra 2 at £2.10. After the rights issue, the holding will look like this

| | number of shares | | price per share | | value £ |
|---|---|---|---|---|---|
| initial holding | 3 | × | £3.60 | = | 10.80 |
| rights issue | 2 | × | £2.10 | = | 4.20 |
| after rights issue | 5 | × | ? | = | £15.00 |

It follows from the table above, that with 5 shares now costing a total of £15.00, the price of a share after the rights issue should be £3.00. This is the theoretical ex-rights price of a share.

## BOX 63.3    Continued

Upshot: for every three shares already held, an existing investor in DEF plc has rights to buy 2 shares with a market value of £3.00 each, at an exclusive price of £2.10.

These rights are worth 90p × 2 = £1.80 for every three shares the investor already holds.

It follows that the value of the right attaching to every one existing share is £1.80/3 = 60p.

Given that these rights have a value, existing investors who do not wish to exercise their rights may sell them. Readers who wish to follow it through will therefore see that the rights issue mechanism has two effects:

● It allows a company to issue its new shares at less than the prevailing market price, ensuring the success of the issue.

while also:

● It allows existing investors who do not want to buy the new shares at the special price, to compensate themselves for the fall in the value of their shares by selling their rights to other investors.

## REVIEW

This chapter has described what is meant by a rights issue, explaining why existing shareholders are given these pre-emption rights, showing how to account for a rights issue, and outlining the effect of a rights issue on an existing investor and on the market price of a share.

# DRILLS AND EXERCISES

## 63.1

For each of the companies below:
(a) show the standard working for the rights issue;
(b) state the double entry to account for the rights issue;
(c) show the balance sheet of the company after the rights issue.

1.   ABC Ltd begins with this balance sheet:

| | |
|---|---:|
| Net Assets | £550 |
| Issued Share Capital 700 Shares of 50p | 350 |
| Retained Earnings (Loss) | 200 |
| | £550 |

The company makes a 3 for 7 rights issue at 80p.

2.   DEF Ltd begins with this balance sheet:

| | |
|---|---:|
| Net Assets | £300 |
| Issued Share Capital 1000 Shares of 10p | 100 |
| Share Premium | 50 |
| Retained Earnings (Loss) | 150 |
| | £300 |

The company makes a 2 for 5 rights issue at 16p.

3.   GHI Ltd begins with this balance sheet:

| | |
|---|---:|
| Net Assets | £2 000 |
| Issued Share Capital 4000 Shares of 25p | 1 000 |
| Share Premium | 250 |
| Retained Earnings (Loss) | 750 |
| | £2 000 |

The company makes a 3 for 8 rights issue at 60p.

4.  JKL Ltd begins with this balance sheet:

| | |
|---|---:|
| Net Assets | <u>£10 000</u> |
| Issued Share Capital 2100 Shares of £1 | 2 100 |
| Share Premium | 3 780 |
| Retained Earnings (Loss) | 4 120 |
| | <u>£10 000</u> |

The company makes a 1 for 3 rights issue at £1.90p.

## 63.2

For each of the situations below, show the standard working for the theoretical ex-rights price of a share.

1.  Market value of a share in ABB Ltd before rights issue: 62p.
    Rights issue: 2 for 5 at 50p.
2.  Market value of a share in BCC Ltd before rights issue: £1.10.
    Rights issue: 3 for 7 at 60p.
3.  Market value of a share in CDD Ltd before rights issue: 81p.
    Rights issue: 3 for 8 at 59p.
4.  Market value of a share in DFF Ltd before rights issue: 55p.
    Rights issue: 1 for 3 at 35p.

# CHAPTER 64

# Debentures, Preference Shares, and Earnings

## OBJECTIVES

*The objectives of this chapter are:*

- to describe the features of a debenture and show how to account for the issue of a debenture
- to describe the characteristics and claims attaching to preference shares
- to explain the difference between profit and earnings in a company which has issued preference shares

## DEBENTURES

A debenture is essentially a certificate, which formally acknowledges a duty to repay a loan. A debenture may also be called a bond. Not all borrowing is accompanied by the issue of a debenture, but a company will often issue a debenture when it borrows any large amount, and especially when the conditions of the loan are complex and strictly defined. In the context of corporate finance, therefore, issuing a debenture means a kind of borrowing.

A company which has borrowed and issued a debenture will include the cash raised among its assets, and show the liability to repay the relevant value in its balance sheet, normally with a note of the annual rate of interest payable and the date at which the loan must be repaid. Box 64.1 on the following page presents an example.

## BOX 64.1

### The Issue of a Debenture

ABC Ltd has the following balance sheet

ABC Ltd Balance Sheet

| | |
|---|---|
| Assets | £ 600 |
| | |
| Issued Share Capital | |
| 500 shares of £1 each | 500 |
| Share Premium | 100 |
| | £ 600 |

The company now issues a 7% debenture for £300. That is to say, the company borrows £300, promising under the terms of a debenture to pay interest at 7% per year. The debenture also specifies that the loan will be repaid at some time in the period 2050–2060.

The debenture will be shown as a liability in the company's balance sheet like this:

ABC Ltd Balance Sheet

| | £ |
|---|---|
| Assets (600 + 300) | 900 |
| Liabilities | |
| 7% Debenture 2050 – 2060 | (300) |
| | £ 600 |
| | |
| Issued Share Capital | |
| 500 shares of £1 each | 500 |
| Share Premium | 100 |
| | £ 600 |

## MARKETABLE DEBENTURES

The transaction costs of issuing a debenture (legal fees, investigations, etc.) are such that debentures normally cover long-term loans for substantial amounts. Although a company may issue a debenture in connection with private borrowings from an individual or a bank, debentures are often associated with large-scale borrowing from investors drawn from the general public. In such cases, there may be many individual lenders, each of whom receives a separate certificate in respect of each £100 lent to the company under the debenture. Each separate debenture certificate will then give its holder the right to be paid interest on £100 each year at the relevant rate and to be repaid £100 at the specified date of redemption.

Crucially, these debenture certificates are designed to be readily negotiable, like ordinary shares. They may even be traded on a recognized stock exchange. This arrangement allows the company to borrow large amounts, from many people, for the long-term. Meanwhile, it allows each individual lender to contribute a sum that is relatively small and (in effect) it allows them to get repayment at any time, by selling their debenture certificates to other investors in the market.

# THE MARKET VALUE OF A DEBENTURE

The debenture holder who approaches the market to sell a debenture is selling a set of promises, including the promise of:

● a regular income from the company (in the form of interest payments) for a number of years; followed by

● the (re)payment of a capital sum.

What the debenture holder originally paid in order to acquire those promises (the original loan made to the company) is irrelevant to the value at which the promises can be sold and resold in the market at a later date. If, for example, unfolding events cast doubt on a company's ability to make the promised payments, the market value of its promises will fall.

Prevailing interest rates will also affect the market value of a debenture. In general, if interest rates rise, the market value of a debenture will fall, and if interest rates fall, the market value of a debenture will rise. Box 64.2 on the following page presents an illustration.

## BOX 64.2

### Interest Rates and the Market Value of a Debenture

The prevailing interest rate for loans to companies like DEF Ltd is 5%.

DEF Ltd issues a 5% debenture.

Individual G lends £100 to the company, and receives a certificate promising to pay her £5 per year (being interest calculated at 5% per year on £100).

Interest rates now rise throughout the economy, such that the prevailing interest rate for loans to companies like DEF Ltd increases to 10%.

Notice that this makes no difference to the £5 per year that DEF has promised to pay to the debenture holder G.

G's real problem, however, is this: with interest rates now at 10%, an investor who wants an income of £5 per year from lending to a company like DEF Ltd, can now get it by lending only £50.

It follows that G's debenture certificate, promising an income of £5 per year, is now worth only £50. Its market value has fallen as interest rates have risen.

# THE TERMS OF A DEBENTURE

The terms of a debenture would normally include at least a schedule for the payment of interest and repayment of capital, with details of any security for the loan.

Otherwise, the terms of a debenture are almost infinitely variable. Some debentures are irredeemable – with the company offering no date of repayment, and effectively promising to pay interest for as long as it continues to exist. Other debentures may allow one or more representatives of the debenture-holders to sit on the company's board of directors, or they may include undertakings by the company not to impair its solvency by, for example, raising further loans.

Some debentures may also include special features designed to increase their appeal to investors. Thus, for example, some debentures are not repayable, but convertible into ordinary shares at a future given date. This somewhat blurs the line between equity (the claim to value invested by shareholders) and liabilities (the claims of other people). Nevertheless, even convertible debentures are not shares. For as long as they are unconverted, they must be classified as liabilities.

## PREFERENCE SHARES

Although a company must issue at least one ordinary share, it may also issue shares of a different class (or different classes), with different rights in the company. Preference shares are among the most common of these different shares.

Like convertible debentures, preference shares are a hybrid form of company finance. In the case of preference shares, while they are rightly called shares, and qualify under the law as shares, in practice they rather resemble a loan. The rights attaching to preference shares will vary in detail from one company to another, but in general:

- preference shares have the right to be paid a fixed amount of dividend per year before the company may pay any ordinary dividend;
- as long as the preference dividend is paid up to date, preference shares do not carry the right to vote;
- if the company is wound up, preference shareholders must be repaid the nominal value of their shares in full before anything may be repaid to ordinary shareholders.

Less commonly, but nevertheless often enough:

- preference shares may be convertible into ordinary shares at some given date in the future; or alternatively
- preference shares may be redeemable – that is, they may be issued on the basis that the company will have the power (or the obligation) at some future date to buy them back and cancel them.

## THE PREFERENCE DIVIDEND AND PREFERENCE IN A WINDING UP

The fixed amount of the preference dividend is usually expressed as a percentage of the nominal value of the shares, so for example a 7.5% preference share of nominal value £1 would qualify for a dividend of 7.5p per year, and so on. Notice however, that preference shareholders have no absolute right to receive this or any other amount of dividend. (They are not like debenture holders, who have a right to the payment of interest come what may.) In respect of dividends, the only right given to preference shareholders is the right to be preferred over ordinary shareholders – that is, the right to be paid their dividend before any ordinary dividend is paid. Thus, if a company cannot pay a dividend because it has no retained profits, or if it chooses not to pay an ordinary dividend, it has no obligation to pay any preference dividend in that period.

As a measure of protection for preference shareholders, however, the preference dividend is usually cumulative – that is to say, arrears of unpaid preference dividend can build up, and must be paid in full before any further ordinary dividend can be paid. As stated above, preference shareholders will usually have the right to vote in meetings of the company for as long as their dividend remains in arrears.

Box 64.3 offers an example of how preference shares appear in the balance sheet of a company and a demonstration of their significance for the distribution of a company's net assets in the event of a winding up.

## BOX 64.3

### Preference Shares

GHI Ltd has just produced the following balance sheet:

|  | £ |
|---|---|
| Assets | 850 |
| Liabilities | (350) |
|  | £ 500 |
|  |  |
| Issued Share Capital |  |
| Ordinary Shares of 50p each | 600 |
| 6% Preference Shares | 200 |
| Share Premium | 100 |
| Retained Loss | (400) |
|  | £ 500 |

1. The Preference Dividend:
   Under normal circumstances, before any ordinary dividend could be paid, the holders of the 6% preference shares would be entitled to a total dividend of £12 (being 6% of the £200 nominal value of their shares) before any ordinary dividend could be paid.

   However, since the company has a retained loss, no dividend of any kind may be paid.

2. Preference in a Winding Up:
   If the company decided now to be wound up, because, say, further losses were inevitable, then after payment of the company's creditors, the preference shareholders would have to be repaid the whole of the nominal value of their shares (£200), before any payment could be made to ordinary shareholders.

   In this instance, after paying off first the creditors, and then the preference shareholders, ordinary shareholders would be left with only £300 to share among themselves.

Notice that, although preference shares may be issued at a premium, no attempt is made to keep a separate account of the premium paid on ordinary shares and the premium paid on preference shares. There is only one Share Premium Account in a company's balance sheet.

## EARNINGS

The issue of preference shares in a company means that ordinary shareholders are no longer entitled to claim the whole of the company's profits after tax. We therefore need a new word or name to indicate 'that part of a company's annual profit, after payment of the preference dividend, that remains to be claimed by ordinary shareholders.' *Earnings* is the word that has been pressed into service.

A company's earnings for a period, therefore, means the company's net profit after tax, minus any preference dividend payable for the period. The record of a company's earnings, as we shall see, is a major determinant of its share price, and may be of greater significance than its profit.

# REVIEW

This chapter has described the essential features of debentures, preference shares, and earnings.

# DRILLS AND EXERCISES

## 64.1

ABC plc has the following balance sheet:

|  | £ |
|---|---|
| Assets | 570 000 |
| Liabilities | (95 000) |
| Net Assets | £475 000 |
| Issued Share Capital 300 000 ordinary shares of 50p | 150 000 |
| Share Premium | 75 000 |
| Retained Earnings | 250 000 |
| Net Assets | £475 000 |

The company issues a 5% debenture for £100 000, repayable in 2040.
Show the company's balance sheet after the issue of the debenture.

## 64.2

DEF plc has issued a 6% irredeemable debenture for £250 000.
   X lends the company £1 000 and becomes the holder of £1 000 debenture stock.
   What will be the approximate market value of X's holding:

   (a) if interest rates rise so that companies like DEF plc are having to pay 9% per year
       on their borrowings?
   (b) if interest rates fall, so that companies like DEF plc are able to borrow at 3%
       interest per year?

## 64.3

GHI plc has the following balance sheet:

|  | £ |
|---|---|
| Assets | 685 000 |
| Liabilities | (140 000) |
| Net Assets | £545 000 |
|  |  |
| Issued Share Capital 800 000 ordinary shares of 25p | 200 000 |
| Share Premium | 45 000 |
| Retained Earnings | 300 000 |
| Net Assets | £545 000 |

The company issues 100 000 8% preference shares of £1 each nominal value for cash at £1.05 per share.

(a)   show the company's balance sheet after the issue of the preference shares;
(b)   state what the company's earnings will be, if the profit for the year after the issue of the preference shares is £18 000.

## 64.4

Three companies have balance sheets as follows:

| A | £ | B | £ |
|---|---|---|---|
| Assets | 680 000 | Assets | 310 000 |
| Liabilities | (230 000) | Liabilities | (120 000) |
| Net Assets | £450 000 | Net Assets | £190 000 |
|  |  |  |  |
| Issued Share Capital |  | Issued Share Capital |  |
| ordinary shares of 10p | 250 000 | ordinary shares of 25p | 200 000 |
| 7% preference shares | 100 000 | 8% preference shares | 100 000 |
| Share Premium | 40 000 | Share Premium | 50 000 |
| Retained Earnings | 60 000 | Retained Loss | (160 000) |
|  | £450 000 |  | £190 000 |

| **C** | **£** |
|---|---|
| Assets | 135 000 |
| Liabilities | (45 000) |
| Net Assets | £90 000 |
| Issued Share Capital | |
| ordinary shares of 25p | 150 000 |
| 6% preference shares | 100 000 |
| Share Premium | 30 000 |
| Retained Loss | (190 000) |
| | £90 000 |

The directors now decide to wind up each company. Assuming that the balance sheets show fair values for assets and liabilities, state for each company how much will be received by preference shareholders and how much by ordinary shareholders.

# CHAPTER 65

# Equity: Share Capital and Reserves

## OBJECTIVES

*The objectives of this chapter are:*

- to explain the meaning of equity and its division into issued share capital and reserves
- to describe the five reserves most commonly found in the balance sheet of a limited company
- to show how to account for the revaluation of an asset and a simple redemption of share capital out of profits

## EQUITY

Equity, also known as shareholders' funds, means the total shareholders' claim on a company. Since the shareholders in a company, like the owners of a business, claim whatever value is left after the claims of other people have been met, the value of equity must be equal to the value of net assets in the company.

As the *total* shareholders' claim, equity is the sum of a number of separate claims, each arising for a different reason. In a limited company it is important to distinguish between these separate claims. Equity therefore is divided into:

- issued share capital; and
- a number of reserves;

with each reserve reflecting the different origin of the claim it represents.

## ISSUED SHARE CAPITAL

Issued share capital is the shareholders' claim arising in the respect of the minimum or nominal value they (the original shareholders) had to pay into the company, in exchange for the issue of their shares. For reasons of capital maintenance and the protection of creditors, as explained in Chapter 61, shareholders may not take this value out again. The value is locked in the company, and to ensure that shareholders do not take it out again, their claim to Issued Share Capital is a claim that may not be reduced.

# RESERVES

The five reserves most commonly found in the balance sheet of a limited company are:

- Share Premium Account
- Revaluation Reserve
- Capital Redemption Reserve
- General Reserve
- Retained Earnings (also known as Retained Profit)

Notice that, in accounting:

- *a reserve* means *part of the total shareholders' claim on a company.*

This contrasts with the use of the word reserve in everyday language, where a reserve is a supply of something kept back for future use (which in accounting would be an asset).

In the technical language of accounting, however, readers should always be aware that a reserve is not an asset but a claim. In particular, a reserve is not, as one might otherwise reasonably imagine, a supply of cash or anything else kept back for future use. Thus, for example, the statement that a company has reserves of, say, £60, tells us nothing about the value of cash held in the company. To be precise, it means only that the total shareholders' claim on the company is £60 greater than the nominal value of its issued share capital. Box 65.1 shows a pair of examples to demonstrate the point.

## BOX 65.1

### The Meaning of Reserves

In accounting, reserves are part of the shareholders' claim on the company.
Reserves are NOT a secret supply of cash.

| COMPANY A | £ |
|---|---|
| Cash | – |
| Other Assets | 360 |
| | 360 |
| Liabilities | (200) |
| Net Assets | £160 |
| | |
| Issued Share Capital | 100 |
| Share Premium | 50 |
| Retained Profit | 10 |
| | £160 |

This company has reserves of £60
It has no cash

| COMPANY B | £ |
|---|---|
| Cash | 200 |
| Other Assets | 450 |
| | 650 |
| Liabilities | (500) |
| Net Assets | £150 |
| | |
| Issued Share Capital | £150 |

This company has no reserves
It has cash of £200

## THE SHARE PREMIUM ACCOUNT

When shares are issued in exchange for more than their nominal value, the shareholders' claim to the extra value paid into the company must be recorded in a Share Premium Account. Because this procedure is mandated by law, the Share Premium Account is called a statutory reserve.

As we saw with issued share capital, any value put into a company by its shareholders may not be taken out again. The Share Premium Account, therefore, represents a claim to value that is locked in the company and to keep that value locked in the company, the balance on the Share Premium Account may not normally be reduced.

One exception to the rule arises in connection with the expenses of a share issue. If a company has issued shares at a premium, the expenses of the share issue (legal and professional fees, commissions and so on) may be written off against the Share Premium Account, instead of appearing as expenses in the P&L Account or Income Statement. Box 65.2 presents an illustration.

## BOX 65.2

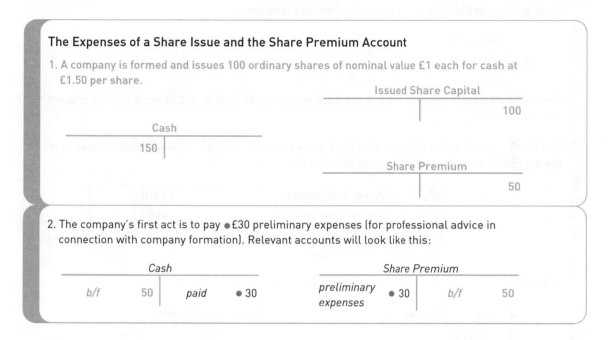

**The Expenses of a Share Issue and the Share Premium Account**

1. A company is formed and issues 100 ordinary shares of nominal value £1 each for cash at £1.50 per share.

Issued Share Capital

|  | 100 |

Cash

| 150 | |

Share Premium

|  | 50 |

2. The company's first act is to pay ●£30 preliminary expenses (for professional advice in connection with company formation). Relevant accounts will look like this:

Cash

| b/f | 50 | paid | ● 30 |

Share Premium

| preliminary expenses | ● 30 | b/f | 50 |

Beyond this exception, a reduction in the Share Premium Account is not normally permitted – unless the amount of the reduction is immediately replaced with the creation or increase of another locked in and equally irreducible claim (as we shall see later in connection with bonus issues).

## THE REVALUATION RESERVE

In general, fixed assets ('non-current assets') are likely to depreciate or lose value with the passage of time. It may happen, however, that a fixed asset will increase in value over time, and a company may decide to recognize such an increase in value in its accounts, by revaluing the asset.

Revaluation means replacing the existing net book value of an asset with a new and usually higher valuation. In the balance sheet this higher valuation will mean more value to be claimed by shareholders, and it is standard accounting practice to record the claim to this extra value in a Revaluation Reserve. A Revaluation Reserve, therefore, represents the shareholders' claim to any additional value recognized in the accounts of a company when an asset is revalued.

Accounting for a revaluation involves three steps:

● opening a new account to record the fixed asset at valuation;

● cancelling the existing net book value (cancelling the original fixed asset cost and any related provision for depreciation); and finally

● using the Revaluation Reserve to record the shareholders' claim to the relevant increase in value.

Box 65.3 presents an example.

## BOX 65.3

### Accounting for a Revaluation

A company holds a fixed asset on its accounts at a Net Book Value of £100 (cost £150 less provision for depreciation £50). Relevant accounts therefore look like this

| | *Fixed Asset Cost* | | | *Provision for Depreciation* | |
|---|---|---|---|---|---|
| b/f | 150 | | | b/f | 50 |

The company now decides to revalue the fixed asset at £170 (that is, at £70 more than its present net book value).

The shareholders' claim to this extra £70 of value will be recorded in a Revaluation Reserve, and the acccounting for the resolution will look like this

| DR | Fixed Asset Revaluation | ●£170 | |
|---|---|---|---|
| DR | Provision for Depreciation | ●£50 | |
| CR | Fixed Asset Cost | | ●£150 |
| CR | Revaluation Reserve | | ●£70 |

After the revaluation, the relevant accounts will look like this:

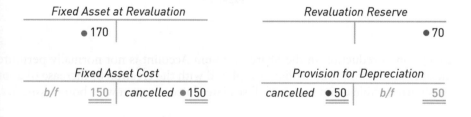

| | *Fixed Asset at Revaluation* | | | *Revaluation Reserve* | |
|---|---|---|---|---|---|
| | ● 170 | | | | ● 70 |

| | *Fixed Asset Cost* | | | *Provision for Depreciation* | |
|---|---|---|---|---|---|
| b/f | 150 | cancelled ●150 | cancelled | ● 50 | b/f | 50 |

Once a fixed asset has been revalued, the company should open a new Provision for Depreciation Account and continue to account for depreciation in the normal way, basing its calculations on the new valuation of the fixed asset and the latest estimate of its remaining useful life.

Like Retained Profit (or 'Retained Earnings'), the Revaluation Reserve represents a claim to extra value accumulated in the company. In the case of a revaluation, however, the extra value accumulated in the company remains a matter of opinion as long as it remains unrealized (that is, as long as the fixed asset remains unsold). Shareholders may not, therefore, remove this extra value. It follows that the Revaluation Reserve, like the Share Premium Account, is a claim to value that is locked in the company, and to prevent its removal, the shareholders' claim to the extra value may not be reduced.

When a revalued fixed asset is finally disposed of, there will be a normal profit or loss on disposal, calculated on the net book value of the asset. At the same time, however, we must also recognize that the extra value claimed in the Revaluation Reserve has now been realized, and may be taken out of the company. Any balance on a Revaluation Reserve relating to a fixed asset sold in a period should therefore be released or transferred to the P&L Account.

# THE CAPITAL REDEMPTION RESERVE

As a general rule, a company is not allowed to redeem or buy back its own shares from shareholders. This follows from the principle of capital maintenance, that any value put in to a company by its shareholders may not be taken out again. Two exceptions to this rule are:

- when the shares are redeemed out of the proceeds of a new share issue; and
- when the shares are redeemed 'out of profits'.

When existing shares are redeemed out of the proceeds of a new share issue, the cash raised from issuing the new shares is used to buy back and cancel the old shares. This is a fairly simple operation in which, essentially,

- one set of shareholders replaces another set of shareholders;
- overall, no value leaves the company; and
- the total value locked in the company is not diminished.

When shares are redeemed 'out of profits', however, value does leave the company. But, for the protection of creditors, the value locked in the company must remain the same. How is this done?

A redemption 'out of profits' means that the shares to be redeemed are paid for out of the extra net assets accumulated in the company as a result of successful operations. Clearly it is not possible to identify which particular assets are in a company because the shareholders put them there, and which are there because the company has made a profit. It is however possible, by looking at issued share capital and reserves, to identify the value that is in a company because the shareholders put it there, and the value that is there because the company has made a profit. Box 65.4 presents an illustration.

## BOX 65.4

### Values in a Company, and Where They Came From

|  | £ |  |
|---|---|---|
| Assets | 8 900 | value of things in the company |
| Liabilities | (5 000) | value claimed by other people |
| Net Assets | £3 900 | value left for shareholders to claim |
|  |  |  |
| Issued Share Capital | 2 000 | these claims represent value put in to the company by shareholders |
| Share Premium | 500 | |
| Other Reserves | 400 | |
| Retained Earnings | 1 000 | this claim represents the value of extra net assets now in the company because it has made profits |
|  | £3 900 | |

So, when shares are redeemed 'out of profits', assets go out of the company, and because the payment is out of profits (read 'out of extra net assets accumulated because the company has made profits'), the claim that must be reduced is the claim to Retained Earnings.

At the same time, the Issued Share Capital that has been redeemed must also be cancelled. But, for the protection of creditors, share capital can only be cancelled in these circumstances if it is replaced with another claim that cannot be reduced. This replacement for cancelled share capital is called the Capital Redemption Reserve. With one non-reducible claim (part of Issued Share Capital) being replaced by another non-reducible claim (the Capital Redemption Reserve), it follows that the value locked in the company will remain the same.

Any redemption of shares 'out of profits' must therefore be accounted for in two stages:

- first, we account for the payment of money, reducing cash and the claim to Retained Earnings;
- then we account for the cancellation of the shares, replacing the claim to share capital with a claim recorded in the Capital Redemption Reserve.

As a result, assets go out of the company, but the value locked in the company remains the same. Box 65.5 presents an example.

## BOX 65.5

### Redemption of Shares Out of Profits

ABC Ltd has the following balance sheet:

| | |
|---|---|
| Net Assets | £4 000 |
| | |
| Issued Share Capital | 2 000 |
| Share Premium | 600 |
| Other Reserves | 400 |
| Retained Profit | 1 000 |
| | £4000 |

The company now decides to redeem shares with a nominal value of £250, at par, out of profits.

The double entry to account for the payment out of profits, and the relevant accounts, will look like this

| DR | Retained Profit | ●£250 | |
|---|---|---|---|
| CR | Cash (Net Assets) | | ●£250 |

| Retained Profit | | | | Net Assets | | | |
|---|---|---|---|---|---|---|---|
| redemption | ●250 | b/f | 1 000 | b/f | 4 000 | payment | ●250 |

**BOX 65.5**   Continued

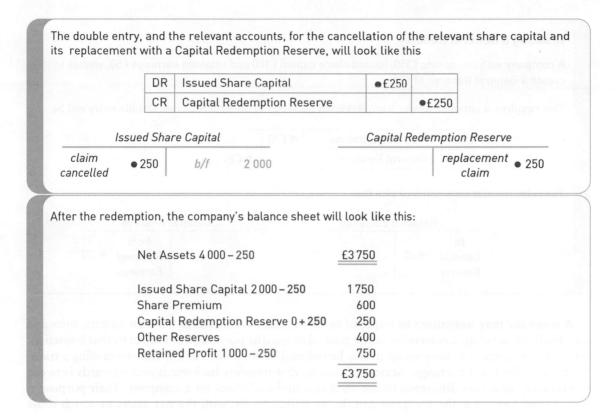

The double entry, and the relevant accounts, for the cancellation of the relevant share capital and its replacement with a Capital Redemption Reserve, will look like this

| | | | |
|---|---|---|---|
| DR | Issued Share Capital | ●£250 | |
| CR | Capital Redemption Reserve | | ●£250 |

| Issued Share Capital | | | | | Capital Redemption Reserve | |
|---|---|---|---|---|---|---|
| claim cancelled | ●250 | b/f | 2 000 | | replacement claim | ●250 |

After the redemption, the company's balance sheet will look like this:

| | |
|---|---|
| Net Assets 4 000 – 250 | £3 750 |
| | |
| Issued Share Capital 2 000 – 250 | 1 750 |
| Share Premium | 600 |
| Capital Redemption Reserve 0 + 250 | 250 |
| Other Reserves | 400 |
| Retained Profit 1 000 – 250 | 750 |
| | £3 750 |

## RETAINED EARNINGS

The Retained Earnings Account (also known as Retained Profit) is a reserve representing the shareholders' claim to profit – that is, their claim to the extra net assets that have accumulated in the company as a result of past successful operations. As we saw in Chapter 60, Retained Earnings represents the only part of the shareholders' claim that may be reduced to reflect the reduction in a company's assets that will occur when the company pays a dividend. It follows that in most circumstances the balance on the Retained Earnings Account will represent the maximum dividend legally payable by a company.

## GENERAL AND OTHER RESERVES

A General Reserve is essentially a part of Retained Earnings (that is, part of the shareholders' claim to extra net assets in the company), which has been transferred to a separate account to indicate that the company wishes to keep an equivalent value of net assets in the company (a value which it *could* otherwise pay out as a dividend). If it is resolved to keep net assets in the company for some specific purpose, a reserve with that name may be created at will, by transfer from Retained Earnings. Box 65.6 presents an example of the creation of a General Reserve.

## BOX 65.6

### Creating a General Reserve

A company with net assets £150, issued share capital £100 and retained earnings £50, wishes to create a General Reserve of £20.

This requires a simple transfer from Retained Earnings to General Reserve. Double entry will be

| DR | Retained Earnings | ◄ £20 |        |
|----|-------------------|-------|--------|
| CR | General Reserve   |       | ►£20   |

The relevant accounts will look like this

| Retained Earnings | | | General Reserve | | |
|---|---|---|---|---|---|
| *to General Reserve* | ◄ 20 | b/f   50 | | *from Retained Earnings* | ► 20 |

A company may sometimes be required by its Articles of Association (its own internal rules and constitution) to set up a reserve for some general or specific purpose, but subject to that limitation, once such a reserve has been set up it may be reduced or eliminated at any time by making a transfer back to Retained Earnings. Notice, of course, that transfers backwards and forwards between reserves can make no difference to the total shareholders' claim on a company. Their purpose is only to indicate what the company can do, or wishes to do, with the net assets to which those reserves represent a claim.

## REVIEW

This chapter has shown how equity, the total shareholders' claim on a company, is divided into Issued Share Capital and a number of different reserves. The chapter considered the five most commonly occurring reserves in a limited company, showing the different circumstances under which each claim could arise, and explaining why certain claims may not be reduced, because they are claims to value that shareholders are not permitted to remove from the company.

# DRILLS AND EXERCISES

## 65.1

Carefully describe the different claims on the assets of the company whose balance sheet is shown below, stating as far as possible the origin of each claim, how or when it may be reduced, and why some claims may not normally be reduced at all.

|  | £ |
|---|---|
| Assets | £1 680 000 |
| Liabilities | (650 000) |
| Net Assets | £1 030 000 |
| Issued Share Capital ordinary shares of 25p | 250 000 |
| 6% preference shares | 100 000 |
| Share Premium | 120 000 |
| Revaluation Reserve | 60 000 |
| Capital Redemption Reserve | 50 000 |
| General Reserve | 75 000 |
| Retained Earnings | 375 000 |
|  | £1 030 000 |

## 65.2 Revaluation reserves

For each of the companies below, state the double entry required to account for the given situation, and show the entries on the relevant accounts.

1.  ABC plc has a fixed asset in its accounts at cost £400 000, less provision for depreciation £250 000. The company now wishes to revalue the fixed asset at £500 000.
2.  Five years after the revaluation above, during which time the company has been providing £10 000 per year depreciation on the revalued fixed asset, ABC plc disposes of the fixed asset for £420 000.
3.  DEF plc has a fixed asset in its accounts at cost £750 000, less provision for depreciation £350 000. The company now wishes to revalue the fixed asset at £600 000.
4.  Ten years after the revaluation above, during which time the company has been providing £12 000 per year depreciation on the revalued fixed asset, DEF plc disposes of the fixed asset for £400 000.

## 65.3 Capital redemption and general reserves

For each of the companies below, state the double entry required to account for the given situation, and show the entries on the relevant accounts.

1.  ABB plc has the balance sheet shown below:

| | |
|---|---|
| Net Assets | £4 700 |
| Issued Share Capital | 2 500 |
| Share Premium | 700 |
| Other Reserves | 300 |
| Retained Profit | 1 200 |
| | £4 700 |

The company now wishes to redeem £500 of share capital at par, out of profits.

2.  BCC plc has the balance sheet shown below:

| | |
|---|---|
| Net Assets | £5 500 |
| Issued Share Capital | 3 000 |
| Share Premium | 500 |
| Revaluation Reserve | 750 |
| Retained Profit | 1 250 |
| | £5 500 |

The company now wishes to establish a General Reserve of £250.

3.  CDD plc has the balance sheet shown below:

| | |
|---|---|
| Net Assets | £3 900 |
| Issued Share Capital | 1000 |
| Share Premium | 1 200 |
| Revaluation Reserve | 300 |
| Retained Profit | 1 400 |
| | £3 900 |

The company now wishes to reduce its General Reserve to £200.

# CHAPTER 66
# Reserves and Bonus Issues

## OBJECTIVES

*The objectives of this chapter are:*

- to explain the classification and use of reserves
- to describe a bonus issue
- to show how to account for a bonus issue

## CLASSIFICATION OF RESERVES

The reserves in a company's balance sheet may be classified in a number of ways, depending on how and why they are created. The principal distinctions are between:

- statutory reserves and other reserves;
- revenue reserves and capital reserves;
- distributable reserves and non-distributable reserves.

## STATUTORY RESERVES

Statutory reserves are reserves created in compliance with statute law (that is, the law established in an Act of Parliament). This applies to two reserves, with which we are already familiar:

- the Share Premium Account; and
- the Capital Redemption Reserve.

Section 610 of the Companies Act 2006 requires the creation of a Share Premium Account when shares are issued at a premium, while section 733 requires the creation of a Capital Redemption Reserve when shares are redeemed out of profits. An outline of how these reserves are created, and why they are needed, was offered in Chapter 64.

## REVENUE RESERVES AND CAPITAL RESERVES

A revenue reserve is a part of the shareholders' claim on a limited company which arises in respect of profits (increases in the value of net assets) which have been recognized in the P&L Account or Income Statement. The basic revenue reserve, therefore, is Retained Earnings, although revenue reserves would also include any General Reserve created by transfer out of Retained Earnings.

A capital reserve is a part of the shareholders' claim on a limited company which has arisen either:

- in respect of values that shareholders themselves have put into the company; or
- in respect of any unrealized increase in value that has been recognized in the company's accounts.

Capital reserves would include the Share Premium Account, the Capital Redemption Reserve and the Revaluation Reserve.

## DISTRIBUTABLE RESERVES AND NON-DISTRIBUTABLE RESERVES

A distributable reserve is a claim to value in a company which shareholders are permitted to remove and distribute among themselves. In accounting terms, therefore, a distributable reserve is a claim which it is permissible to reduce when shareholders take assets out of the company. Retained Earnings is in effect the only distributable reserve to be found in a limited company.

A non-distributable reserve is a claim to value in a company that shareholders are *not* permitted to remove and distribute among themselves. Non-distributable reserves, therefore, are claims which cannot be reduced when shareholders take assets out of a company. All capital reserves are by definition non-distributable, but by decision of the company, non-distributable reserves could also include a General Reserve, or any other reserve created to keep net assets in the company for some particular purpose. Non-distributable reserves would therefore include the Share Premium Account, the Revaluation Reserve, the Capital Redemption Reserve and the General Reserve.

Box 66.1 presents a table to illustrate the classification of reserves.

## BOX 66.1

**The Classification of Reserves**

|  | DISTRIBUTABLE | NON-DISTRIBUTABLE |
|---|---|---|
| CAPITAL |  | Share Premium<br>Revaluation Reserve<br>Capital Redemption Reserve |
| REVENUE | Retained Earnings | General Reserve |

## RESERVE ACCOUNTING

Reserve accounting is the practice of transferring income or expenses (gains or losses) directly to reserves at the end of a period, instead of transferring them first to the P&L Account. In conventional year-end accounting, income and expenses are first transferred to the P&L Account, then wrapped up together in the balance on the P&L Account, and finally transferred to a reserve in the balance sheet (Retained Earnings). Cutting out the transfer to the P&L Account and transferring all or some of the relevant items directly to a reserve in the balance sheet would clearly be feasible and would achieve the same effect (that is, it would result in the same closing balance sheet, but the P&L Account would be different).

Reserve accounting is, therefore, a means by which a company may recognize the effect of an event or a transaction in its balance sheet, while avoiding the need to show its effect in the P&L

Account. Sometimes, this may be desirable or necessary, but it should be fully disclosed, and in recent years accountants have invented an entirely new financial statement for this purpose (it is called the Statement of Changes in Equity, which is described in the following chapter). In general, however, reserve accounting has a sorry history of use as a means of obscuring the facts and avoiding accountability.

## HIDDEN OR SECRET RESERVES

Hidden or secret reserves are parts of the shareholders' claim on a company, disguised in the balance sheet as liabilities or provisions. The procedure for creating or releasing a hidden reserve is exactly the procedure for creating or releasing a provision, as shown in Chapter 42. Banks were once quite regularly accused of using hidden reserves to smooth the ups and downs of their reported profits. Whatever the facts, the charge was plausible – wild swings in profit are not conducive to the trust that banks then felt they had to earn.

## BONUS ISSUES

A bonus issue is a conversion of reserves into issued share capital. The total shareholders' claim on a company will therefore remain the same after a bonus issue as it was before, but with a different composition – more of it will be shown in Issued Share Capital and less of it will be shown in reserves.

   To all outward appearances, however, a bonus issue is an issue of new shares, free of charge to existing shareholders, in proportion to the number of shares they already hold. Box 66.2 shows how a bonus issue is normally described.

BOX 66.2

---

**Describing a Bonus Issue**

Example:

ABC plc announces a 3 for 5 bonus issue.

This means that:

● the company will issue three new (additional) shares to every shareholder, for every five share they already hold;

● the shares will be issued free of payment.

---

## ACCOUNTING FOR A BONUS ISSUE

Accounting for a bonus issue involves a preliminary working to determine the number and the total nominal value of the new shares to be issued. This will be followed by the double entry necessary to reduce the relevant reserve(s), and increase Issued Share Capital. Note that a bonus issue involves no new assets entering the company. Box 66.3 presents an example.

## BOX 66.3

### Accounting for a Bonus Issue

ABC Ltd is an established company, whose summarized balance sheet is shown below:

| | |
|---|---:|
| Net Assets | <u>£3 700</u> |
| | |
| Issued Share Capital | 2 100 |
| 4 200 shares of 50p each | |
| Share Premium | 500 |
| Retained Profit | 1 100 |
| | <u>£3 700</u> |

The company now decides to make a 2 for 7 bonus issue.

---

Standard preliminary working for a bonus issue:

number of new shares $\qquad 2 \times \dfrac{4\,200}{7} = 1\,200$

- nominal value of new shares $1\,200 \times 50p = £600$

---

£600 of reserves must be converted into issued share capital. If we convert the £500 Share Premium first, and £100 from Retained Profit, the double entry to account for the bonus issue, and the relevant accounts, will look like this:

| DR | Share Premium | ● £500 | |
|----|---------------|--------|--------|
| DR | Retained Profit | ● £100 | |
| CR | Issued Share Capital (ISC) | | ● £600 |

*Share Premium*

| to ISC | ● <u>500</u> | b/f | <u>500</u> |
|--------|--------------|-----|------------|

*Retained Profit*

| to ISC | ● 100 | b/f | 1 100 |
|--------|-------|-----|-------|

*Issued Share Capital*

| | b/f | 2 100 |
|---|-----|-------|
| | bonus | ● 600 |

**BOX 66.3**  Continued

And the balance sheet after the bonus issue will look like this:

| | |
|---|---|
| Net Assets (unchanged) | £3 700 |
| | |
| Issued Share Capital (2 100 + 600) | 2 700 |
| 5 400 shares of 50p each | |
| Share Premium (500 – 500) | – |
| Retained Profit (1 100 – 100) | 1 000 |
| | £3 700 |

## BONUS ISSUES AND RIGHTS ISSUES

Readers may have noticed the resemblance between the ways in which bonus issues and rights issues are described. This should not be allowed to cause confusion:

- a rights issue is an issue of new shares *for value* – 'three for five *at £1.20*' (or whatever). In a rights issue, new value enters the company, net assets are increased, and the total shareholders' claim on the company is increased.

- a bonus issue is an issue of new shares *for nothing*, where an increase in issued share capital is paid for by a reduction in some other part(s) of the shareholders' claim. In a bonus issue, no new value enters the company, the company's net assets are unchanged, and the total shareholders' claim on the company will remain the same.

## WHICH RESERVES SHOULD BE CONVERTED FIRST?

In a bonus issue, a company may convert any of its reserves into Issued Share Capital. There are no restrictions. However, a company will normally choose to convert capital reserves before revenue reserves. Capital reserves are in any case just like Issued Share Capital, insofar as they represent claims to value in the company that shareholders are not permitted to remove.

Retained Earnings, on the other hand, is a claim to value in the company that shareholders are permitted to remove. Any conversion of Retained Earnings into Issued Share Capital, therefore, would automatically reduce the value that shareholders would be allowed to take out of the company. It follows that normally in a bonus issue, Retained Earnings will be the *last* reserve to be converted into issued share capital.

## BONUS ISSUES AND THE MARKET VALUE OF A SHARE

In a bonus issue, no new resources come in to the firm. Net assets remain the same, but there is a larger number of shares. Each share, therefore, will be smaller. Members will find themselves with a greater number of shares, but the total value of their shareholding, like the total value of the company, will remain the same. It follows that the market value of a share after a bonus issue will be lower than the market value of a share before the bonus issue. Box 66.4 provides an illustration.

## BOX 66.4

### Bonus Issues and the Market Value of a Share

The market value of a share in DEF Ltd is £1.20 per share.

The company now announces a 1 for 3 bonus issue.

Imagine the holding of an investor who starts with 3 shares, and receives 1 extra share in the bonus issue. After the bonus issue, the holding will look like this:

|  | number of shares |  | price per share |  | value £ |
|---|---|---|---|---|---|
| initial holding | 3 | × | £1.20 | = | 3.60 |
| bonus issue | 1 |  | free | = |  |
| after bonus issue | 4 | × | ? | = | £3.60 |

value of 1 share after bonus issue will be $\dfrac{£3.60}{4}$ = **90 pence**

## THE PURPOSE OF A BONUS ISSUE

It is fair to ask why a company should bother to make a bonus issue. It brings no new resources into the company, and while it gives members more shares, it also makes each share worth less, such that overall there is no benefit for shareholders. There are, however, a number of possible motives for a bonus issue, including:

- to tidy up the balance sheet;
- to reduce the price of each share; and
- to signal a permanent increase in the dividend payout.

Evidently, converting reserves into issued share capital will simplify the balance sheet, and if the reserves in question are in any case capital or non-distributable reserves, it will make no difference to the situation of the company or its shareholders.

The benefit of using a bonus issue to reduce the price of each share is less obvious. It seems, however, that investors who trade in shares do not like share prices to become too 'heavy'. Thus, for example, rather than having a relatively small number of shares in a company, each with a - market price of, say, £5 000, they would prefer to have 1 000 times as many shares, each with a market price of only £5, and so on. For a successful, growing company, periodic bonus issues are a way of keeping the individual share price within the range that seems to be preferred by market traders.

With respect to dividends and bonus issues, companies do not, in general, like to reduce their dividend in terms of pence per share. Giving shareholders more shares in a bonus issue may therefore be used as a means of telling them that the company expects to make a bigger total dividend payout in future years.

No doubt also, in the past, there were investors simple-minded enough to believe that a bonus issue gave them something for nothing. Nor was that an utter misconception. In the past, though very rarely now, investors bought shares not to sell them at a profit in the short-term, but to hold them as a source of income in the long term. The idea then was to keep the same number of shares and spend the dividend income. Under such circumstances, the market in shares could become very illiquid, and shareholders, committed to holding the number of shares they originally bought, would not benefit from any increase in the market value of their shares. A bonus issue, however, would definitely benefit these permanent shareholders, by giving them a gift of extra shares which they might feel free to sell, without the feeling that they were in any way reducing their original investment.

# REVIEW

This chapter has considered the different ways in which reserves are classified, and how reserves may be misused through reserve accounting and the creation of hidden reserves. The chapter also explained what is meant by a bonus issue, showing the effects of a bonus issue for the company and for the shareholder, and suggesting some possible motives for the making of a bonus issue.

# DRILLS AND EXERCISES

## 66.1

For each of the companies below:

(a) show the standard working for the bonus issue;
(b) state the double entry to account for the bonus issue;
(c) show the balance sheet of the company after the bonus issue.

1.  ABC Ltd begins with this balance sheet:

| | |
|---|---:|
| Net Assets | £480 |
| Issued Share Capital | |
| 560 shares of 50p | 280 |
| Retained Earnings | 200 |
| | £480 |

The company makes a 2 for 7 bonus issue.

2.  DEF Ltd begins with this balance sheet:

| | |
|---|---:|
| Net Assets | £350 |
| Issued Share Capital | |
| 1500 shares of 10p | 150 |
| Share Premium | 50 |
| Retained Earnings | 150 |
| | £350 |

The company makes a 1 for 5 bonus issue.

3.  GHI Ltd begins with this balance sheet:

| | |
|---|---:|
| Net Assets | £1 725 |
| Issued Share Capital | |
| 4000 of 25p | 1 000 |
| Captial Redemption Reserve | 100 |
| Retained Earnings | 625 |
| | £1 725 |

The company makes a 3 for 8 bonus issue.

4.  JKL Ltd begins with this balance sheet:

| | |
|---|---:|
| Net Assets | £6 420 |
| Issued Share Capital | |
| 1 800 shares of £1 | 500 |
| Revaluation Reserve | 500 |
| Retained Earnings | 4 120 |
| | £6 420 |

The company makes a 1 for 3 bonus issue.

## 66.2

For each of the situations below, show the standard working for market value of a share after the bonus issue.

1.   Market value of a share in ABB Ltd before bonus issue: 63p
     Bonus issue: 2 for 5
2.   Market value of a share in BCC Ltd before bonus issue: £1.10
     Bonus issue: 3 for 7
3.   Market value of a share in CDD Ltd before bonus issue: 88p
     Bonus issue: 3 for 8
4.   Market value of a share in DFF Ltd before bonus issue: £1.60
     Bonus issue: 1 for 3

# CHAPTER 67

# Additional Financial Statements

## OBJECTIVES

*The objectives of this chapter are:*

- to describe the purpose and content of the Statement of Changes in Equity
- to describe the purpose and content of the Cash Flow Statement

## FOUR FINANCIAL STATEMENTS

A listed company is required to report to its shareholders in four annual financial statements, with relevant notes attached. Two of these are the traditional financial statements that have long been the centre of accounting attention, namely:

- an Income Statement or P&L Account; and
- a balance sheet.

The other two are additional statements invented more recently, and produced in order to fill certain gaps in the information provided by the two traditional statements. They are:

- a Statement of Changes in Equity; and
- a Cash Flow Statement.

## THE STATEMENT OF CHANGES IN EQUITY

Equity is the total shareholders' claim on a company, which is composed of issued share capital and reserves. The Statement of Changes in Equity is, therefore, a statement of changes in issued share capital and reserves. These changes may come about for a number of reasons:

- through the making of a profit or loss in the commercial operations of the business;
- through unrealized changes in value which the company has decided to recognize in its accounts (as with the revaluation of fixed assets);
- through the payment of dividends to shareholders; and
- through the issue or redemption of shares.

# THE PURPOSE OF THE STATEMENT OF CHANGES IN EQUITY

Before the requirement to present a Statement of Changes in Equity was imposed, any record of movements on reserves was deeply buried in the notes to the balance sheet, and often ignored. The statement is now required, mainly in order to give due prominence to a small number of changes in value which, although they ought to be recognized in the accounts of a company, ought not to be recognized as profits or losses in the P&L Account or Income Statement.

Such changes in value may be unrealized, and/or they may arise from events outside the usual operations of the business. The revaluation of a fixed asset (as shown in Chapter 65) is perhaps the simplest example. If a fixed asset still held in the company has increased in value, it may be quite reasonable to recognize the increase in value in the accounts, but it would be quite unreasonable to record the shareholders' claim to the increased value as a profit in the P&L Account. The claim to the increased value should be recorded in a reserve.

There are other cases where a change in the value of an asset or a liability should be recognized in the accounts, but where it would not be proper to report the effect on the shareholders' claim as a profit or a loss in the P&L Account. For example, if a company has assets or liabilities denominated in a foreign currency, and exchange rates vary between balance sheet dates, then there will be an apparent gain or loss in value, arising solely from the currency translation. Thus, the same $100, worth £70 at the end of one year, may be worth only £60 at the end of the next year, and so on. Depending on the circumstances, there may be good reason to recognize such gains or losses in a reserve, rather than in the P&L Account of the period. Another example might be changes in the valuation of pension scheme liabilities. Such liabilities are often only payable in the distant future and can only be estimated on the basis of actuarial assumptions. A change in the estimate of such liabilities would evidently represent a gain or a loss to shareholders, but the gain or loss would not be strictly comparable with the gains or losses normally reported in the P&L Account. It might be better, therefore, to report such gains or losses in a reserve rather than in the P&L Account.

# THE PRESENTATION OF THE STATEMENT OF CHANGES IN EQUITY

An example of a Statement of Changes in Equity, in standard form with sample numbers, is given in Box 67.1.

## BOX 67.1

**Sample Presentation of the Statement of Changes in Equity**

XYZ plc – Statement of Changes in Equity for the Year Ended 31 December 2050

| | Share Capital £ | Share Premium £ | Other Reserves £ | Currency Translation £ | Retained Earnings £ | Total £ |
|---|---|---|---|---|---|---|
| Balance at 1 January 2050 | 363 | 180 | 570 | 145 | 761 | 2 019 |
| Loss on currency translation | | | | (89) | | (89) |
| Gain on revaluation | | | 26 | | | 26 |
| Profit for period | | | | | 549 | 549 |
| Total Recognized Gains and Losses for the Period | | | 26 | (89) | 549 | 486 |
| Dividends | | | | | (172) | (172) |
| Issue of Share Capital | 120 | 680 | | | | 800 |
| Balance at 31 December 2050 | 483 | 860 | 596 | 56 | 1 138 | 3 133 |

# THE STATEMENT OF RECOGNIZED INCOME AND EXPENSE

In the Statement of Recognized Income and Expense, the words income and expense are used (in a rather perverse international accounting sense) to mean gains and losses in value. The statement itself is essentially a truncated version of the Statement of Changes in Equity, the difference being that:

- the Statement of Changes in Equity includes all changes in the shareholders' claim on a business, including changes arising from transactions between the company and its shareholders (payment of dividends, issue and redemption of shares, etc.); while
- the Statement of Recognized Income and Expense includes only those changes in the value of net assets in a company that have arisen independently of transactions with the shareholders.

A company may, therefore, present a Statement of Recognized Income and Expense instead of a Statement of Changes in Equity, as long as the information relating to transactions between the company and its shareholders is presented elsewhere in the financial statements.

# THE CASH FLOW STATEMENT

A cash flow statement is a detailed analysis of the cash flows into and out of a company in the period between two balance sheets. In the standard format, cash flows are analyzed under three main headings:

- *cash flows from operating activities* – these are the company's regular activities in the creation and sale of goods and services;
- *cash flows from investing activities* – investing activities include the purchase and sale of fixed assets, as well as lending, the purchase and sale of shares in other companies, and the receipt of associated interest and dividends;
- *cash flows from financing activities* – these include the issue and redemption of shares, borrowing and the repayment of loans, as well as the payment of dividends.

# CASH FLOW FROM OPERATING ACTIVITIES

Cash flow from operating activities is generally derived by adjustment of operating profit to allow for those causes of difference between cash and profit that were analyzed in Chapter 34. Recall that the extra net assets accumulated in a business when it makes a profit need not take the form of money. Extra net assets may take the form of an increase in stocks or promises from debtors, or they may be the result of a decrease in creditors. Also, profit includes such non-cash items as depreciation and profits or losses on the disposal of fixed assets. All of these must be adjusted for, as shown in Chapter 34, if we wish to move from operating profit to cash from operations.

# FORMAT OF THE CASH FLOW STATEMENT

After the derivation of the net cash flow from operating activities, the remaining elements of the Cash Flow Statement are largely self-explanatory. An example of a Cash Flow Statement, in standard form with sample numbers, is given in Box 67.2 on the following page.

## BOX 67.2

**Standard Format for a Cash Flow Statement, with sample figures**

ABC plc Cash Flow Statement for the year ended 31 December 2050

|  | £ |
|---|---:|
| **Cash Flows from Operations** | |
| Operating Profit | 495 |
| add back depreciation | 100 |
| *less* profit on disposal | (20) |
| add decrease in stock | 60 |
| *less* increase in debtors | (35) |
| add increase in creditors | 11 |
|  | 611 |
| interest paid | (15) |
| tax paid | (25) |
| **Net Cash Flow from Operating Activities** | **571** |
| **Cash Flows from Investing Activities** | |
| purchase of fixed assets | (563) |
| proceeds on disposal of fixed assets | 470 |
| interest received | 13 |
| dividends received | 4 |
|  | **(76)** |
| **Cash Flows from Financing Activities** | |
| proceeds from issue of shares | 53 |
| repayment of loans | (250) |
| new borrowings | 100 |
| dividends paid | (10) |
| **Net Cash used in Financing Activities** | **(107)** |
| **Net Increase in Cash** | **388** |
| Overdraft at 1 January 2050 | (30) |
| **Cash at 31 December 2050** | **£ 358** |

Notice how at the end of the statement, the net movement in cash for the year is added to the opening cash balance, to reach the closing balance, which should agree with the value shown in the balance sheet.

## PURPOSE OF THE CASH FLOW STATEMENT

The purpose of the Cash Flow Statement is to provide useful information about a company's liquidity, solvency and financial adaptability. Liquidity is ease or speed of access to cash and the Cash Flow Statement is designed to show whether, and how, the company has been able to generate cash in the period under review. Liquidity is needed both for solvency (the vital ability to pay the company's liabilities when they fall due) and for financial adaptability (the power conferred by money to adapt to changing circumstances).

## INFORMATION GAINS FROM THE CASH FLOW STATEMENT

Although its purpose is to draw attention to movements of cash, the Cash Flow Statement could be seen as a line by line explanation of differences between a company's opening and closing balance sheets. This brings much useful information into prominence, which might otherwise be neglected. Thus, for example, a wholesale repayment and replacement of a company's borrowings, with little net change, might easily escape notice if our information is confined to the opening and closing balance sheets, without the actual movements that are shown in the Cash Flow Statement. Similarly, changes in fixed assets are now far more readily apparent in the Cash Flow Statement, than they previously were in the notes to the balance sheet.

## REVIEW

This chapter has introduced two additional statements: the Statement of Changes in Equity and the Cash Flow Statement. Quoted companies are required to produce these statements in addition to the traditional Income Statement and balance sheet. The chapter outlined the purpose of these statements and showed examples of their standard format.

## DRILLS AND EXERCISES

### 67.1

Consider the sample Statement of Changes in Equity presented in Box 67.1, and explain as far as you can the significance of each figure in the statement.

### 67.2

Figures based on the published Cash Flow Statements of two comparable companies are presented side by side below.

Compare the two statements, comment on the differences, and state, on the basis of the available evidence, with reasons, which company appears to you to be in a better financial position.

| CASH FLOW STATEMENTS | A | B |
|---|---|---|
| Cash Flows from Operations | 2 116 | 3 412 |
| interest paid | (159) | (364) |
| tax (paid) received | 3 | (429) |
| **Net Cash Flow from Operating Activities** | **1 960** | **2 619** |
| Cash Flows from Investing Activities | | |
| purchase of fixed assets | (2 018) | (2 700) |
| proceeds on disposal of fixed assets | 151 | 664 |
| interest received | 112 | 96 |
| | (1 755) | (1 940) |
| Cash Flows from Financing Activities | | |
| proceeds from issue of shares | 22 | 123 |
| repayment of loans | (2 049) | (109) |
| new borrowings | 2 056 | |
| dividends paid | (131) | (510) |
| Net Cash used in Financing Activities | (102) | (496) |
| **Net Increase in Cash** | **103** | **183** |
| Cash at 1 January 2050 | 700 | 1 146 |
| Cash at 31 December 2050 | £ 803 | £1 329 |

Find more questions and answers at www.cengage.co.uk/hodge.

# PART FIVE

# Understanding Company Financial Statements

Part 5 shows some of the more powerful ways in which the published accounts of a company can be analyzed to reveal the working of the underlying business. It introduces the concept of profitability, before discussing the gearing ratio and the working capital cycle. Part 5 concludes with a review of the ratios commonly used by investors to support their investment decisions.

# CHAPTER 68

# Profitability

## OBJECTIVES

*The objectives of this chapter are:*

- to distinguish between profit and profitability
- to show how profitability can be measured as a rate of return on equity or as a rate of return on capital employed
- to consider how investors balance the promise of profitability against the risk of failure, in the light of some real world examples

## PROFIT AND PROFITABILITY

When comparing investment opportunities, what matters to the investor is not so much the amount of profit previously achieved or offered in the future, but the profitability of the undertaking.

Profitability is the power to generate profit, taking into account:

- how much capital is required to generate each £1 of profit; and
- how fast the profit can be generated.

The three variables are profit, capital and speed. A business or a project is more profitable:

- if it can generate more profit without requiring more capital or more time;
- if it can generate the same profit in the same time, while requiring the investment of less capital (because the surplus capital can be invested elsewhere at a profit); or
- if it can generate the same profit with the same capital, but faster (because the sooner the profit arises, the sooner the capital involved can be used again to generate more profit).

## MEASURING PROFITABILITY

Profitability is measured as a rate of return on capital, which is defined like this:

*profitability = £'s income or profit per year per £100 of capital invested*

Since companies are required to produce annual accounts, our standard unit of time for measuring profitability is one year. Choosing £100 as the standard unit of capital means that the return on capital can be very neatly summarized in terms of a percentage rate per year. Box 68.1 presents an illustration.

## BOX 68.1

---

### Determining the Rate of Return on Capital

Three investment possibilities, A, B, and C offer profits per year and require capital as shown below.

|  | A | B | C |
|---|---|---|---|
|  | £ | £ | £ |
| Profit per year | 50 000 | 60 000 | 70 000 |
| Capital invested | 200 000 | 360 000 | 400 000 |

Clearly C offers the most profit per year, but it also requires more capital. A calculation of the rate of return on each project will reveal which one promises to be the most profitable.

|  | A | B | C |
|---|---|---|---|
|  | £ | £ | £ |
| Profit per year | 50 000 | 60 000 | 70 000 |
| Capital invested | 200 000 | 360 000 | 400 000 |
| working | $\dfrac{50\,000}{200\,000}$ | $\dfrac{60\,000}{360\,000}$ | $\dfrac{70\,000}{400\,000}$ |
|  | = | = | = |
| **Rate of Return** | 25.0% per year | 16.7% per year | 17.5% per year |

A is now revealed to be the most profitable investment, despite its lower profit per year, because it requires so much less capital investment.

NOTE even an investor with £400 000 to invest would maximize his or her income by investing £200 000 in A, and the remaining £200 000 in half of C. This would generate a total income of £85 000 per year.

---

## PROFITABILITY, RISK, AND SHARE PRICES

The investment that promises to be the most profitable, is not necessarily the best. There is always the risk that an investment may fail to generate profits as expected, or even that it will result in losses. Investors are aware of this and in general, they will not invest in a riskier business unless it offers the prospect (if all goes well) of providing a higher rate of return. On the other hand, if a business is thought to be relatively safe, investors will be happy to accept the prospect of a lower rate of return on the capital they invest.

Modern investors now invest largely in the hope of achieving a gain from an increase in the price of their shares. It is the job of a company's directors, therefore, to increase the market value of the company's shares. This can be done by improving the company's profitability. An increase in profitability, generating more profits more quickly, or with less capital, should translate into a higher share price. But changes intended to increase a company's profitability should be balanced against the potential cost of making the business more risky. If it comes to the notice of the capital market, any increase in risk will reduce demand for the company's shares and, therefore, cause the company's share price to fall as investors begin to fear losses.

A proper assessment of risk would depend upon detailed knowledge of the company's environment and activities and it would be hard to embody such information in a set of purely financial statements. Financial statements should, however, include enough for us to assess a company's profitability.

## THE PROFITABILITY OF A COMPANY

There are two possible measures of the profitability of a company. These are:

● return on capital employed (ROCE); and
● return on equity (ROE). Since the value of equity is equal to the value of net assets, this measure may also be called return on net assets (RONA).

## RETURN ON EQUITY

Return on equity measures the profitability or profit generating power of the value invested in a company *by its shareholders*. (Recall that some of the value invested in a company may also come from lenders.)

The value invested by shareholders is represented by equity, the total shareholders' claim on the company. The annual return that shareholders get, is the company's net profit after tax. Return on equity is calculated therefore according to the formula:

$$\text{return on equity} = \frac{\text{net profit after tax}}{\text{equity}} \times 100\%$$

Box 68.2 shows the calculation of return on equity, with figures taken from the published accounts of three sample listed companies.

BOX 68.2

**Return on Equity for Three Sample Companies**

|  | pharmaceutical company | manufacturing company | supermarket company |
|---|---|---|---|
| Net Profit after Tax | 5 498 | 889 | 1 576 |
| Equity | 9 386 | 4 527 | 9 444 |
| working | $\dfrac{5\,498}{9\,386}$ | $\dfrac{889}{4\,527}$ | $\dfrac{1\,576}{9\,444}$ |
|  | = | = | = |
| **Return on Equity** | 58.6% per year | 19.6% per year | 16.7% per year |

Two points may need clarification. First, in this context, the value invested in the company by shareholders means the value actually paid into the company by shareholders, plus the extra value in the company, arising as a result of past profits, which shareholders have decided to keep in the

516 Part V Understanding Company Financial Statements

company. It does not mean the value that shareholders may have actually paid for their shares, because most shareholders will have bought their shares in the secondary capital market – not from the company itself, but from previous investors.

Secondly, we take it that the return that shareholders get is the whole of the company's net profit for the year. It does not matter whether all or any of this gain is actually paid out to shareholders in the form of a dividend. All of it belongs to shareholders. If they do not benefit from it by receiving a dividend, they benefit instead from its reinvestment in the company, to generate further profits into the future.

# RETURN ON CAPITAL EMPLOYED

Return on capital employed measures the profitability or profit generating power of the total value invested in a company. Recall that lenders are investors as well as shareholders, and the total value invested in a company consists of equity plus borrowings or financial liabilities.

The return to *all* investors in a business is *operating profit* – that is, profit before the deduction of interest. Return on capital employed is calculated therefore according to the formula:

$$\text{return on capital employed} = \frac{\text{operating profit}}{\text{equity} + \text{loan capital}} \times 100\%$$

Box 68.3 shows the calculation of return on capital employed, with figures taken from the same three sample companies.

## BOX 68.3

### Return on Capital Employed for Three Sample Companies

|  | pharmaceutical company | manufacturing company | supermarket company |
|---|---|---|---|
| Operating Profit | 7 808 | 1 574 | 2 280 |
| Equity | 9 386 | 4 527 | 9 444 |
| Financial Liabilities | 5 490 | 4 739 | 5 921 |
| Capital Employed | 14 876 | 9 266 | 15 365 |
| working | $\frac{7\,808}{14\,876}$ | $\frac{1\,574}{9\,266}$ | $\frac{2\,280}{15\,365}$ |
|  | = | = | = |
| Return on Capital Employed | 52.5% per year | 17.0% per year | 14.8% per year |

# INTERPRETING MEASURES OF PROFITABILITY

The rates of return we have calculated for each of our sample companies are summarized in Box 68.4.

## BOX 68.4

### Return on Capital Employed for Three Sample Companies

|  | pharmaceutical company | manufacturing company | supermarket company |
|---|---|---|---|
| **Return on Equity** | 58.6% per year | 19.6% per year | 16.7% per year |
| **Return on Capital Employed** | 52.5% per year | 17.0% per year | 14.8% per year |

What do these figures mean? Profitability should always be assessed against the background of risk. At the time of writing it is possible for investors to receive a rate of return of about 5.5% per year on bank or building society deposits, with very little risk of loss. Each of our companies, therefore, seems to be producing a rate of return sufficient to reward the undertaking of at least some measure of additional risk.

The pharmaceutical company appears to enjoy a very high rate of return on its investment (over 52% per year ROCE). This partly reflects the very high risks of developing new drugs – because of the high risk, a pharmaceutical company will not undertake the development of a new drug, unless it promises *if successful* to be extremely profitable. In any event this result should be compared against competing firms (it is a little better than most pharmaceutical companies, but not very far out of line) and against the company's own track record.

Supermarkets claim to face extremely intense competition, driving down their rates of profit. With the supermarket in our (very arbitrary) sample producing the lowest ROCE, which is not very far adrift from other companies in the sector, there is perhaps some evidence to support their claim.

It is difficult to say very much about the manufacturing company, without reference to its own past history, the nature of its markets, the risks it may face, and the performance of comparable companies in the same sector.

# PROBLEMS WITH ACCOUNTING RATIOS

There are a number of problems associated with the use of accounting ratios, especially in connection with investment decision-making. Accounting ratios are based on financial statements, which must relate to the past because they are mainly produced for reasons of accountability. Investors, however, are more concerned with future prospects, and although we do not live in a chaos – the future will resemble the past more often than not – the past is not always the best or the only guide to the future.

At a technical level, we must also acknowledge that accounting ratios depend on prior accounting judgements that may or may not be open to question. Thus for example, the very high rate of return shown by our pharmaceutical company might not be so high, if the company were allowed to treat some of its research costs as capital expenditure – an investment in fixed assets – rather than expenses. Similarly, a company which chooses to revalue its fixed assets (building up a revaluation reserve) will show more equity in its balance sheet than a company which does not revalue its assets. It will therefore show a lower rate of return on equity, not for any objective underlying reason, but solely because it has chosen a different accounting policy. So, if we are to understand accounting ratios, we must also understand accounting policies and their effect upon financial statements.

## REVIEW

This chapter has introduced and defined the idea of profitability and, has shown the possibility of measuring a company's profitability in terms of its rate of return on equity, and its rate of return on capital employed. The chapter showed how investors balance the rate of return promised by a business, against the risk of loss it may entail. Finally, the chapter briefly considered some of the problems associated with the interpretation of profitability and other accounting ratios.

# DRILLS AND EXERCISES

## 68.1

Consider each of the investment projects below, and determine which is the most profitable.

|  | A | B | C |
|---|---|---|---|
| investment required | £ 200 000 | £ 800 000 | £1 000 000 |
| projected profit | £ 50 000 | £ 120 000 | £1 |
| expected time to generate profit | 1 year | 6 months | 1 minute |

Assuming that each project could be repeated indefinitely, and that all carry the same degree of risk, which would you prefer to invest in?

## 68.2

The figures below are taken from the published accounts of five listed companies. For each company:

(a)  calculate the rate of return on equity achieved in the year under consideration;

(b)  calculate the return on capital employed.

In your opinion, do your results support the theory that investors will only support higher risk investments if they produce higher rates of return?

| COMPANY ACTIVITY | MICRO-CHIP MAKER | CEMENT PRODUCER | PRECISION ENGINEER | MILK WHOLESALER | SATELLITE BROADCASTER |
|---|---|---|---|---|---|
| operating profit | 49 898 | 2 678 | 692 | 27 495 | 877 |
| profit after tax | 48 588 | 1 589 | 994 | 18 450 | 551 |
| borrowings | | | | | |
| current | – | 1 664 | 400 | 2 291 | 163 |
| non-current | – | 9 421 | 990 | 5 024 | 1 825 |
| total borrowings | – | 11 085 | 1 390 | 7 315 | 1 988 |
| equity | 663 204 | 11 794 | 2 725 | 119 258 | 121 |
| capital employed | 663 204 | 22 879 | 4 115 | 126 573 | 2 109 |

# CHAPTER 69

# Borrowing and the Effects of Gearing

## OBJECTIVES

*The objectives of this chapter are:*

- to explain the significance of gearing
- to show how to calculate a company's gearing ratio
- to describe some of the benefits of borrowing and some of the associated dangers

## EQUITY AND DEBT

Investment in a company comes either from shareholders or from lenders. The value invested by each of these two classes is shown in the balance sheet by their claim on the company. Equity, the total shareholders' claim on the company, represents the value invested by shareholders. 'Borrowings', 'loans' or 'debt' represent the values claimed by lenders, in respect of the values invested by them.

## GEARING

In a financial context, gearing describes the extra power over assets that can be acquired through borrowing. The name is derived by obvious analogy with the mechanical effect of gearing. In American English, gearing is called by the simpler name of leverage – a concept very much easier to capture in a diagram. Box 69.1 on the following page presents a simplified example.

## BOX 69.1

### Gearing or Leverage – the Power of Borrowing

As shown in the balance sheet below, the effect of borrowing ('gearing') in this firm is that: £100 of equity (investment by share holders) **controls** £500 of assets.

|                | £       |
|----------------|---------|
| Assets         | 500     |
| Borrowing      | (400)   |
| Net Assets     | £100    |
|                |         |
| Equity         | £100    |

This power is very simply illustrated if we use the alternative analogy of leverage

EQUITY
£100

ASSETS
£500

## THE GEARING RATIO

A firm's gearing ratio describes its financial structure in terms of the proportion invested by lenders. Gearing can be measured in two ways:

- as the ratio of debt to equity; or
- as the ratio of debt to total investment in the firm (debt + equity).

Using the debt to equity gearing ratio:

$$\text{gearing} = \frac{\text{debt}}{\text{equity}} \times 100\%$$

and we can say: 'this firm's borrowings are $x$ per cent of the value invested by owners'. Using the debt to total investment (debt + equity) gearing ratio:

$$\text{gearing} = \frac{\text{debt}}{\text{equity} + \text{debt}} \times 100\%$$

and we can say 'y per cent of the total investment in this firm comes from lenders'.

Since each measure of gearing is equally acceptable, and both are equally understandable, the choice would seem to be a matter of personal preference or ease of calculation. For the avoidance of misunderstanding, however, one should always state which formula for gearing has been used. Box 69.2 presents an example of the basic calculations.

## BOX 69.2

### The Gearing Ratio

A gearing ratio for the firm below may be calculated in two ways.

|  |  | £ |
|---|---|---|
| Assets |  | 500 |
| Borrowing |  | (400) |
| Net Assets |  | £100 |
| | | |
| Equity |  | £100 |

| Gearing debt/equity | working | $\dfrac{400}{100}$ |
|---|---|---|
| | ratio | $=$ 4 |

| Gearing debt/(equity + debt) | working | $\dfrac{400}{100 + 400}$ |
|---|---|---|
| | ratio | $=$ 80.0% |

## THE BENEFITS OF BORROWING

Gearing is about borrowing, which has both benefits and dangers for a firm. The benefits of borrowing must be assessed against the alternative of owners or shareholders themselves providing further value for investment in the firm. Sometimes owners or shareholders do not have the extra value to invest and the firm is forced to borrow. Sometimes, however, it is advantageous for a firm to borrow, even if it does not have to. Lenders, facing less risk than equity investors (especially if the firm can offer security for loans), will not demand so high a rate of return on their investment. The rate of return on equity, therefore, will increase if extra value for investment is borrowed. Box 69.3 presents an illustration.

## BOX 69.3

### Borrowing and the Rate of Return on Equity

X is an entrepreneur with a business idea. The business will require an investment of £2 000 to acquire assets, and is expected to generate operating profits of £300 per year. X has two options for the financing of the firm:

Option A – entirely self-financing: X herself would provide £2 000 of equity

Option B – with borrowing: X would invest only £1 000 of her own equity, and the firm would borrow the remaining £1 000, paying interest at 10 per cent per year.

Comparative opening balance sheets and expected P&L Accounts for the first year are shown below:

|  | Option A<br>all equity | Option B<br>with borrowing |
|---|---|---|
|  | £ | £ |
| assets | 2 000 | 2 000 |
| liabilities |  | (1 000) |
|  | £2 000 | £1 000 |
| Equity | £2 000 | £1 000 |
|  | £ | £ |
| operating profit | 300 | 300 |
| interest |  | (100) |
| Net Profit | £ 300 | £ 200 |

Evidently (if all goes well) X would enjoy more profit under Option A. But so she should – she would have invested twice as much of her own capital. The significant point is that by borrowing X will not only save £1 000 of her own capital for investment elsewhere, but also increases the rate of return on the £1 000 she has invested here, as shown below

|  | all equity | with borrowing |
|---|---|---|
| Rate of Return<br>on equity | $\dfrac{300}{2\ 000}$ | $\dfrac{200}{1\ 000}$ |
|  | = | = |
|  | 15% | 20% |

The benefit of borrowing gets better if the profits of the business grow. As operating profits increase, the annual amount of interest payable will stay the same, and a higher proportion of operating profits will be left for equity investors. Box 69.4 presents an example of the effect.

## BOX 69.4

### Borrowing and Growing Profits

ABC Ltd is financed in part by £1 500 of loan capital, on which interest must be paid at 10% per year.

In Year 1, the firm generates an operating profit of £200. In Year 2, operating profit is doubled, to £400.

Comparative income statements for each year will look like this:

|  | Year 1 £ |  | Year 2 £ |
|---|---|---|---|
| operating profit | 200 | × 2 | 400 |
| interest | (150) | the same | (150) |
| Net Profit | £ 50 |  | £ 250 |

The effect of borrowing here is that:

- while operating profit has doubled from Year 1 toYear 2;
- the net profit for equity investors has increased by a factor of five – from £50 to £250.

## THE DANGERS OF BORROWING

While some borrowing may be beneficial, borrowing always carries extra risk for equity investors. It represents a commitment to pay interest and ultimately repay loans, regardless of the firm's eventual profits or cash flow. In the worst case, failure to meet such commitments may destroy the firm, and a downturn in operating profits (or an increase in interest rates, if the firm has borrowed at variable rates) may prove fatal. Box 69.5 continues our example to show one of the potential dangers.

## BOX 69.5

### Borrowing and Falling Profits

ABC Ltd is financed in part by £1 500 of loan capital, on which interest must be paid at 10% per year.

In Year 3, operating profit falls to only £100.

A summary income statement for the year will look like this:

|  | Year 3 £ |
|---|---|
| operating profit | 100 |
| interest | (50) |
| Net Profit (Loss) | (50) |

Here, with falling profits, the effect of borrowing and interest payments is:

- to convert an operating profit;
- into a net loss for equity investors.

High borrowing also reduces a firm's capacity to make further borrowings – that is, the more a firm has borrowed already, the longer it will take to find another lender, and the higher the rate of interest that will be demanded on the next loan. This affects a firm's adaptability. Borrowing represents a source of finance which can be used to escape from trouble in the event of a sudden crisis, or to take advantage of a sudden opportunity. Thus any inability to borrow easily and quickly, as shown by a gearing ratio that is already high, will restrict the speed and effectiveness of a firm's response to changing business circumstances.

# REVIEW

This chapter has introduced the concept of financial gearing or leverage, showing the two ways in which a gearing ratio may be calculated, and considering some of the advantages and problems associated with borrowing for a commercial firm.

# DRILLS AND EXERCISES

Chapter 70 will be followed by exercises on the gearing of a selection of actual listed companies.

# CHAPTER 70

# The Gearing Ratio

## OBJECTIVES

*The objectives of this chapter are:*

- to consider the main factors that will influence a firm's gearing ratio, with reference to the gearing ratio of three real world examples
- to explain what is meant by 'borrowing capacity'
- to describe the measure of interest cover
- to outline the nature of 'off-balance sheet' financing

## UNDERSTANDING THE GEARING RATIO

In theory, a high gearing ratio (reflecting high borrowing), represents a danger sign. But much depends on the nature of the business. Box 70.1 presents some sample gearing ratios, based on the published accounts of three large listed companies.

BOX 70.1

**Sample Gearing Ratios**

| Liabilities (in respect of borrowing) | a water company | a manufacturing company | an employment agency |
|---|---|---|---|
| current | 632 | 1 047 | 6 981 |
| non-current | 2 639 | 7 006 | |
| **Total Debt** | 3 271 | 8 053 | 6 981 |
| **Equity** | 1 137 | 19 607 | 68 896 |
| Gearing debt/equity — working | $\frac{3271}{1137}$ | $\frac{8053}{19607}$ | $\frac{6981}{68896}$ |
| ratio | = 287.6% | = 41.1% | = 10.1% |
| Gearing debt/(equity + debt) — working | $\frac{3271}{3271+1137}$ | $\frac{8053}{8053+19607}$ | $\frac{6981}{6981+68896}$ |
| ratio | = 74.2% | = 29.1% | = 9.2% |

Here we have:

- a water company with a very high gearing ratio – borrowings almost three times greater than the equity investment in the company (debt/equity 287.6%).

By contrast:

- in the manufacturing company not much more than a quarter of the investment (actually 29.1%) has come from lenders; while
- in the employment agency less than 10% of the investment in comes from lenders.

These figures must be interpreted in the light of each firm's borrowing capacity, and its ability to pay interest.

## BORROWING CAPACITY

The point at which high gearing may become dangerous for a firm will depend on its borrowing capacity. At one end of the spectrum would be firms with a high proportion of long-lived immovable fixed assets and a stable revenue stream. Such a firm (as for example our water company, with a network of pipes, reservoirs, and treatment plants as well as a virtually guaranteed demand for its product or service) may borrow heavily with relative safety. The high proportion of immoveable fixed assets would provide for security for lenders, while the steady, predictable income stream would reassure both borrowers and lenders that annual interest payments could be made.

At the other end of the spectrum would be firms with a low proportion of immoveable fixed assets and an unpredictable income stream. Such might be an employment agency or a high fashion retailer. These firms would be ill-advised to borrow heavily, although the natural caution of lenders would probably make it difficult for them to do so even if they tried.

As a very rough guide to borrowing capacity, we may consider the relative weight of non-current (fixed) assets and current assets in a company's balance sheet. Box 70.2 compares the gearing of three of our sample companies against this crude measure of their borrowing capacity.

BOX 70.2

**Gearing and Borrowing Capacity**

|  | water company | manufacturing company | employment agency |
|---|---|---|---|
| **Gearing** | | | |
| debt/equity | 287.6% | 41.1% | 10.1% |
| debt/(equity + debt) | 74.2% | 29.1% | 9.2% |
| Non-Current Assets | 5 682 | 16 351 | 33 778 |
| Current Assets | 567 | 29 887 | 125 331 |
| **Proportion of assets that are non-current** | 90.9% | 35.4% | 21.2% |

Here we see that the very high gearing of the water company is in fact supported by a very high borrowing capacity (more than 90% of its assets are fixed assets), while the low gearing of the employment agency reflects its much lower borrowing capacity (scarcely more than 20% of its assets are fixed assets).

# INTEREST COVER

High gearing is not necessarily a problem, if a firm is well able to meet its interest payments as they fall due. A firm's ability to pay interest is shown by its interest cover, which is the ratio of operating profit to interest payable. The interest cover ratio tells how many times the firm could have paid its interest expense for the last period out of its operating profit. Thus, an interest cover of (say) 6 would indicate that the firm could have paid up to six times as much interest without incurring a net loss, or alternatively that the firm's operating profit could decline to one sixth of its present level and the firm would still be able to pay its annual interest without falling into loss. Box 70.3 shows the calculation of interest cover and continues our example to show the relation between gearing ratio and interest cover.

## BOX 70.3

### Gearing and Interest Cover

The three examples below, based on actual company results, show the interaction between gearing and interest cover, and the way in which both are (or should be) related to the nature of the underlying business.

|  | water company | manufacturing company | employment agency |
|---|---|---|---|
| **Gearing** | | | |
| debt/equity | 287.6% | 41.1% | 10.1% |
| debt/(equity + debt) | 74.2% | 29.1% | 9.2% |
| | | | |
| Operating Profit | 430 | 6 707 | 66 519 |
| Interest | 240 | 389 | 776 |
| | | | |
| interest cover working | $\dfrac{430}{240}$ | $\dfrac{6\,707}{389}$ | $\dfrac{66519}{776}$ |
| **Interest cover ratio** | 1.8 | 17.2 | 85.7 |

High gearing (heavy borrowing) means high interest payments, and therefore must mean lower interest cover.

The employment agency (able to pay its interest more than 86 times over out of operating profit) and the manufacturing company (able to pay its interest more than 17 times over) are clearly not at risk from over-borrowing.

The highly geared water company is not quite able to pay its interest twice over. With a predictable income stream, it is not currently at risk of being unable to meet its interest payments, but it may be exposed to future increases in interest rates.

# SIGNIFICANCE OF THE TREND

As with all ratios, the gearing and interest cover ratio should be interpreted not just in relation to the structure of the firm, but also in relation to preceding figures. Are the ratios changing? If so, in what direction? Is any change an improvement or a deterioration? Is it a result of deliberate policy, or just a matter of drift? Is it part of a general trend, or more of a sudden shock? These and other questions must be asked to put the ratio into context.

## PREFERENCE SHARE CAPITAL AND GEARING

Preference share capital has some of the marks of equity, and some of the marks of debt. Thus, for example, preference shareholders receive a dividend out of profits, like equity shareholders, but their dividend is a fixed amount, like the interest paid to lenders. In their claims on the company, preference shareholders rank below lenders and creditors on the one hand, but above ordinary shareholders on the other hand, and so on.

So, when we calculate a gearing ratio, is preference share capital to be counted as part of debt or part of equity? The consensus seems to be that preference share capital should *not* be counted as part of equity. Equity is *usually* reserved to mean, exclusively, ordinary share capital. The term debt, therefore, is stretched to cover every claim, including preference share capital, that ranks above the claims of ordinary shareholders. It follows that preference share capital will usually count as debt, for the purpose of the gearing ratio.

## OFF-BALANCE SHEET FINANCING

Off-balance sheet financing is the name given to a number of techniques designed to achieve the same effect as borrowing, without the appearance of a liability in the balance sheet and therefore without an increase in the gearing ratio. Much ingenuity is given to the devising of such schemes. Box 70.4 presents a very crude example.

BOX 70.4

### Off-balance Sheet Financing

ABC Ltd wishes to acquire a fixed asset with a four year useful life at a cost of £4 000.

The firm may borrow £4 000 to buy the asset, paying 10% interest per year and repaying the loan after four years. With the liability to repay the loan in the balance sheet, this would increase the company's gearing ratio.

Alternatively the firm is offered an opportunity to enter a binding agreement to lease the machine for four years at a cost of £1 400 per year.

This is off-balance sheet financing. It achieves the same effect as borrowing, but instead of showing a liability to repay £4 000 in the balance sheet, the firm has a liability to make four annual payments, each of which is paid in the year it arises, and therefore never appears in the balance sheet.

## REVIEW

This chapter has considered the importance of gearing, and the two possible measurements of the gearing ratio, with the benefits and dangers of borrowing. The chapter also discussed the interpretation of the gearing ratio in relation to the borrowing capacity of a company and its interest cover. Finally, we also briefly examined the intermediate status of preference share capital, between debt and equity, and the problem of off-balance sheet financing.

# DRILLS AND EXERCISES

## 70.1

Below are extracts from the published accounts of two listed companies. One is a producer of luxury goods, the other owns and operates an electricity distribution network.

Calculate gearing ratios for each company and state, with reasons, your opinion as to which is which.

|  | A | B |
|---|---|---|
| Equity | 4 136 | 11 868 |
| borrowings |  |  |
| current | 1 025 | 3 376 |
| non-current | 14 686 | 4 443 |

## 70.2

The figures given in question 70.1 are now supplemented with figures from the published accounts of the prior year.

For each company separately, calculate and compare gearing ratios for the current year and the prior year. Comment on any differences you may find, from one year to the next.

|  | A | | B | |
|---|---|---|---|---|
|  | CURRENT YEAR | PRIOR YEAR | CURRENT YEAR | PRIOR YEAR |
| Equity | 4 136 | 3 493 | 11 868 | 10 065 |
| borrowings |  |  |  |  |
| current | 1 025 | 2 839 | 3 376 | 2 984 |
| non-current | 14 686 | 10 287 | 4 443 | 5 092 |

Find more questions and answers at www.cengage.co.uk/hodge.

# CHAPTER 71

# Working Capital and Liquidity

## OBJECTIVES

*The objectives of this chapter are:*

- to explain the distinction between fixed capital and working capital
- show how working capital is measured
- to describe the working capital ratio and the quick ratio, and their use in assessing the liquidity of a company

## FIXED CAPITAL AND WORKING CAPITAL

Capital, the value invested in a firm, can be analyzed as equity or debt on the basis of where it came from, or who claims the relevant value. It can also be analyzed as fixed capital or working capital, on the basis of how it is used and embodied in assets.

Fixed capital is used to provide a firm with facilities or productive capacity, in the form of fixed or non-current assets (such as land, buildings, machinery, patents, licenses and so on). Working capital is used in order to work or operate those facilities. It is invested in the purchase of stocks and the payment of wages and expenses.

## THE WORKING CAPITAL CYCLE

In the absence of radical changes in markets or technology, fixed assets in general have a long and predictable life. Fixed capital, therefore, is stable and its renewal is easily planned and controlled.

Working capital has a shorter and less predictable life. The value involved, however, is caught within a recurring cycle, where the investment in working capital is continuously made, realized and renewed. Thus:

- money is invested in purchases, labour and overheads to create inventory (goods or services for sale);
- inventory is sold and turned into receivables (promises from debtors);
- receivables are collected and turned into money; and
- money is once again invested in inventory.

For this reason, working capital was in the past called circulating capital.

Because of its short life-cycle and the need for continuous renewal, working capital is notoriously difficult to manage, and problems with working capital are probably the most frequent cause of company collapse.

## MEASUREMENT OF WORKING CAPITAL

Working capital is the value invested in getting or making things for sale. This value is captured:

- in the form of inventories (where things remain unsold); and
- in the form of trade receivables or promises from debtors (where things have been sold, but no payment has yet been received).

However, the firm itself need not invest the whole of the value captured in working capital. Where there is trading on credit, there will always be some part of the firm's inventory that has not yet been paid for. So at least part of the investment in working capital may be provided free of charge – by suppliers waiting to be paid (trade payables).

A simple measure of the value invested by the firm in working capital, therefore, would be: inventories, plus trade receivables, minus trade payables.

But also, to operate with any freedom, a firm will need access to cash. Otherwise the system would be so tight that the firm could never pay a creditor without first receiving payment from a debtor. The value held by the firm in the form of cash, therefore, is also normally included in the measure of working capital. Further complications arise with accruals and prepayments, and so in the end, unless otherwise defined for some specific purpose, working capital is generally assumed to be the value of all current assets, minus current liabilities – a figure also known as net current assets. Box 71.1 shows sample figures for fixed and working capital, taken from the published accounts of three listed companies.

## BOX 71.1

### Fixed and Working Capital for Three Sample Companies

|  | house-building company | industrial supply company | supermarket company |
|---|---|---|---|
| Non-current Assets fixed capital | 23 739 | 2 723 | 18 644 |
| Current Assets | 92 337 | 5 348 | 3 919 |
| Current Liabilities | (19 265) | (2 995) | (7 518) |
| Working Capital net current assets (liabilities) | 73 072 | 2 353 | (3 599) |

Notice how firms in different sectors require a different distribution of investment between fixed capital and working capital.

Also notice that a firm may have negative working capital, or net current liabilities.

# THE CURRENT RATIO

The current ratio, also called the working capital ratio, is an attempt to measure the liquidity of a firm. Liquidity means ease, speed, or certainty of access to cash. A firm which is not liquid, without such access to cash, is in danger of insolvency, because it may not be able to pay its liabilities as they fall due.

The working capital ratio is the ratio of current assets to current liabilities, with the formula:

$$\text{current ratio} = \frac{\text{current assets}}{\text{current liabilities}}$$

Recall that current assets are cash itself and assets held for use or conversion to cash within one year, while current liabilities are liabilities payable within one year. Thus the current ratio compares:

● the cash a firm can get within one year; against
● the liabilities it must pay within one year.

It would seem, therefore, that a firm with a current ratio of more than 1 (indicating current assets greater than current liabilities) should have access to enough cash within the year to pay its immediate liabilities, while a firm with a current ratio of less than 1 (indicating current assets less than current liabilities) would be in danger of being unable to pay its liabilities as they fall due. However, things are not quite so simple. Box 71.2 presents actual data from the published accounts of our three sample listed companies.

## BOX 71.2

**Some Sample Current Ratios**

|  | house-building company | industrial supply company | supermarket company |
|---|---|---|---|
| Current Assets | 92 337 | 5 348 | 3 919 |
| Current Liabilities | 19 265 | 2 995 | 7 518 |
| working | $\frac{92\,337}{19\,265}$ | $\frac{5\,348}{2\,995}$ | $\frac{3\,919}{7\,518}$ |
|  | = | = | = |
| Working Capital or Current Ratio | 4.8 | 1.8 | 0.5 |

A simple reading of the ratios here would indicate that the house-builder has access to nearly five times as much cash within the coming year as will be required to pay its current liabilities.

The industrial supply company also looks quite comfortable, with current assets nearly twice the value of current liabilities.

Meanwhile the supermarket appears to be in trouble, with current assets scarcely more than half the value of its current liabilities.

And yet: builders are notoriously short of cash, and supermarkets are well known to be awash with money.

Clearly there is something wrong with our analysis.

# THE QUICK RATIO OR ACID TEST

One weakness of the current ratio is the fact that inventories or stocks are included in the ratio as part of current assets. In theory of course stocks should be sold and turned into cash within the year, but one reason why firms run out of money may be precisely because they are building up stocks they cannot sell. But a surplus of stocks, instead of sending a danger signal through the current ratio, would actually tend to make the current ratio bigger and therefore apparently better.

The quick ratio or acid test is an attempt to correct this weakness of the current ratio, by excluding the value of stocks from the calculation. Thus the quick ratio is the ratio of current assets *excluding stock* to current liabilities.

$$\text{quick ratio} = \frac{\text{current assets excluding stock}}{\text{current liabilities}}$$

Box 71.3 shows quick ratios for our three sample companies.

## BOX 71.3

### Sample Quick Ratios

|  | house-building company | industrial supply company | supermarket company |
|---|---|---|---|
| Current Assets | 92 337 | 5 348 | 3 919 |
| inventories | (75 808) | (1 954) | (1 464) |
| Current Assets excluding inventories | 16 529 | 3 394 | 2 455 |
| Current Liabilities | 19 265 | 2 995 | 7 518 |
| working | $\frac{16\,529}{19\,265}$ | $\frac{3\,394}{2\,995}$ | $\frac{2\,455}{7\,518}$ |
|  | = | = | = |
| Quick Ratio or Acid Test | 0.9 | 1.1 | 0.3 |

Here, the house-builder looks a lot less healthy, with the value of current assets excluding stock (that is, in fact, the total of cash and debtors) actually less than the value of current liabilities.

The industrial supply company still looks fairly safe, with current assets excluding stock still bigger than current liabilities.

The supermarket, however, looks even sicker. But since these figures come from a very well known and successful supermarket, and are in line with many years of previously reported figures, it is clearly wrong to suggest that a low current ratio or quick ratio are necessarily any indication of an imminent liquidity crisis.

## UNDERSTANDING WORKING CAPITAL RATIOS AND LIQUIDITY

Our examples have shown that the interpretation of working capital ratios is by no means simple. If they are to be used at all, they must be used with care, and with reference to the nature of the firm, the sector in which it operates and the overall trend of previously reported results. While there is no value of either the current ratio or the quick ratio that is necessarily good or bad in itself, it is possible perhaps to use the ratios to compare one company against another in the same sector, or to compare a company's state of affairs in the present against its state of affairs in the past.

Notice also how these ratios may be affected by purely accounting decisions at an earlier stage in the preparation of the financial statements – how to value stock, for example, or what kind of provision should be made for doubtful debts.

## REVIEW

This chapter has introduced the topic of working capital and the possible use of working capital ratios (the current ratio and the quick ratio) to assess the liquidity of a firm. The chapter observed how these ratios may differ quite markedly for firms in different sectors and commented on some of the difficulties of interpretation. The following chapter will explore the topic further.

## DRILLS AND EXERCISES

Chapter 72 will be followed by exercises on the working capital of a selection of actual listed companies.

# CHAPTER 72

# The Working Capital Cycle

## OBJECTIVES

*The objectives of this chapter are:*

- to explain the need for working capital
- to show the importance of time and the length of the working capital cycle
- to show how the length of the working capital cycle can be measured in terms of transit time for inventory, time taken to collect payment from debtors and time taken to pay creditors
- to examine the different working capital needs of three contrasting real world companies

## THE NEED FOR WORKING CAPITAL

The need for working capital is occasioned by a timing difference – the gap between the time at which a firm must pay out money for its inputs and the time at which it takes in money for its outputs. If the firm can narrow that gap or make it shorter, it will need less working capital and become more profitable. If the firm allows the gap to widen, then it will need more working capital and become less profitable. Journey time or speed of throughput is the crucial factor. Box 72.1 presents an illustration, loosely based on actual historical developments.

## BOX 72.1

### Working Capital and Speed of Throughput

In the early 19th century, before railways, a group of merchants discovers it is possible to buy a waggon-load of goods in Manchester for £10, with transport to London included, and sell the load in London for £12. Demand in London is one load per day.

The business proceeds like this:

|  | total value invested |
|---|---|
| DAY 1 the merchants buy one load and send it on its way | £10 |
| DAY 2 they buy and dispatch a further load of goods | £20 |
| DAY 3 etc. | £30 |

**BOX 72.1**    Continued

By DAY 10, the total value invested in the business will be £100 (that is 10 waggon-loads, each with £10 worth of goods, spread out along the road to London).

On DAY 11, the first load will reach London and be sold for £12. After the sale, £2 can be taken out of the business as profit, and £10 can be reinvested to dispatch a further load from Manchester, and so on in subsequent days.

AFTER DAY 10 therefore, the business will be stable, with
- a permanent working capital investment of £100
- yielding a profit of £2 *per day*.

Now imagine the whole process speeded up by the opening of a railway taking goods from Manchester to London in just two days – that is, five times faster than the previous journey.

Our merchants' business will now require an investment of only £20, but will still yield a profit of £2 per day. Because throughput is five times faster, the investment in working capital will be five times more profitable.

## WORKING CAPITAL AND THE BENEFITS OF SPEED

The story in Box 72.1 shows that narrowing the gap in time between payment of supplier and collection of money from customer will free up working capital, which can be used to generate yet more profits somewhere else. The gap can be narrowed by:

- speeding up the flow of inventory through production, distribution and sales;
- speeding up the collection of cash from customers; and (it must be said) by;
- slowing down the payment of suppliers.

## WORKING CAPITAL AND THE DANGERS OF A SLOWDOWN

Reflection on the story also shows how any slowing down of the process – that is, any widening of the gap in time – will cause the firm to soak up cash in working capital. In terms of our story, one extra day taken for the production or selling of goods, or a day's delay in collection of debtors, is like an extra day on the journey. It means a day on which the firm makes payments out, without receiving any payment in. Any such gap must be bridged by the provision of extra working capital and that must come from the firm's investors.

If the rate of throughput continues to slow down, and the gap in time gets wider, the danger is that a point will come at which no further cash will be available. This is the classic working capital crisis. At this point the firm is in danger of collapse, not least because with trading on credit, cash is needed not to buy new things, but to pay suppliers for things already bought that cannot be sent back. (A firm might survive a temporary stop on purchases, but creditors are unlikely to accept a stop on payments due to them, and the law gives them the power to strike back.)

## WORKING CAPITAL AND PROFIT

Notice that problems with working capital may arise, irrespective of the firm's capacity to make a profit. If the timing of payments and receipts escapes control, a firm may be in trouble, regardless of its profits. This is especially significant when the firm is growing. Inputs take time to pass through the business. Thus, a firm which grows and continues to grow will find itself continuously paying out for a volume of inputs that is greater than the volume of outputs for which it is collecting payment – with consequent strains on its supplies of cash. That is why business managers and lenders insist upon cash flow projections as well as forecast P&L Accounts as part of their planning procedures.

## COMPONENTS OF WORKING CAPITAL

In practice the analysis of working capital is complicated by the introduction of trading on credit. Trading on credit means that the point of purchase is not the point of payment, at which the investment in working capital is actually made. Likewise trading on credit means that the point of sale is not the point at which money is received and the cycle is complete. Thus:

- Purchase is separated from payment by the time the firm takes to pay its creditors. During this time the firm will show *trade payables* (promises to suppliers) in its balance sheet.
- Sale of output is separated from purchase of input by the time the firm takes to produce, distribute, and sell its goods or services. During this time the firm will show *inventories* in its balance sheet.
- Finally, collection of money is separated from sale by the time it takes for the firm to collect its debts. During this time the firm will show *trade receivables* (promises from customers) in its balance sheet.

Box 72.2 illustrates the processes behind the need for working capital and how they are reflected in the balance sheet.

## BOX 72.2

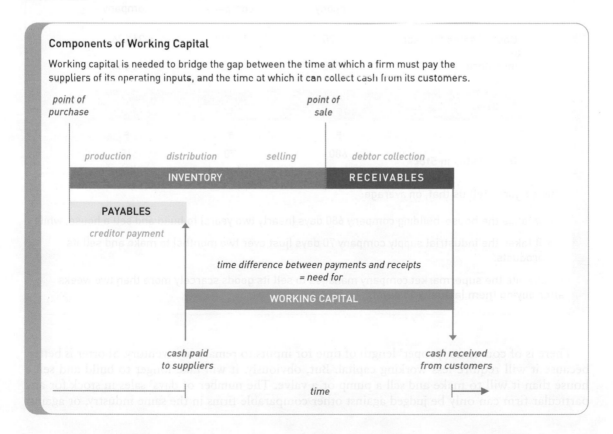

**Components of Working Capital**

Working capital is needed to bridge the gap between the time at which a firm must pay the suppliers of its operating inputs, and the time at which it can collect cash from its customers.

# TRANSIT TIME FOR INVENTORY

It is possible, from analysis of a firm's financial statements, to determine the length of time that inputs spend in inventory (that is, the time taken for production, distribution and selling). The logic follows a two-step process:

- first, determine the *average daily cost of sales* (divide the year's cost of sales by 365, the number of days in a year);
- then, see how many days' sales there are in inventory (divide the cost of inventory, by the average daily cost of sales).

The resulting figure should tell us the transit time for inventory – how long it takes, in days, on average, for inputs to pass through the firm, from day of purchase to day of sale.

In practice, the calculation can be reordered and simplified into a formula:

$$\text{days' sales in stock} = \frac{\text{inventory} \times 365}{\text{cost of sales}}$$

Box 72.3 presents the calculation of number of days' sales in stock for each of the three sample companies used in Chapter 71.

## BOX 72.3

**Transit Time for Inventory, or Days' Sales in Stock: Three Sample Companies**

|  | house-building company | industrial supply company | supermarket company |
|---|---|---|---|
| Cost of sales for year | 40 720 | 10 222 | 36 426 |
| inventories | 75 808 | 1 954 | 1 464 |
| working | $\dfrac{75\,808 \times 365}{40\,720}$ | $\dfrac{1\,954 \times 365}{10\,222}$ | $\dfrac{1\,464 \times 365}{36\,426}$ |
|  | = | = | = |
| **Days' Sales in Stock** | 680 days | 70 days | 15 days |

These figures tell us that, on average:

- it takes the house-building company 680 days (nearly two years) to build and sell a house; while

- it takes the industrial supply company 70 days (just over two months) to make and sell its products.

Meanwhile the supermarket company manages to sell its goods scarcely more than two weeks after buying them (actually 15 days).

There is of course no 'proper' length of time for inputs to remain in inventory. Shorter is better, because it will require less working capital. But, obviously, it will take longer to build and sell a house than it will to make and sell a pump or a valve. The number of days' sales in stock for any particular firm can only be judged against other comparable firms in the same industry, or against the past record of the same firm (is the process slowing down or speeding up? is it taking more time to make and sell goods or services, or less time?).

# THE DEBTOR COLLECTION PERIOD

It is also possible to determine the length of time taken for a firm to collect payment from its debtors. The logic again follows a two-step process:

- first, determine the average value of *sales per day* (divide the year's sales revenue by 365, the number of days in a year);
- then, see how many days' sales there are in debtors or trade receivables (divide the value of trade receivables, by the average value of sales in a day).

The resulting figure should tell us how long it takes, in days, on average, for the firm to collect payment from its debtors.

In practice, the calculation can be simplified into this formula:

$$\text{days' sales in debtors} = \frac{\text{trade receivables} \times 365}{\text{sales}}$$

Box 72.4 presents the calculation of number of days' sales in debtors for each of our three sample companies.

## BOX 72.4

**Debtor Collection Period, or Days' Sales in Debtors: Three Sample Companies**

|  | house-building company | industrial supply company | supermarket company |
|---|---|---|---|
| Sales revenue for year | 59 729 | 14 158 | 39 454 |
| trade receivables | 2 245 | 2 650 | 892 |
| working | $\frac{2\,245 \times 365}{59\,729}$ | $\frac{2\,650 \times 365}{14\,158}$ | $\frac{892 \times 365}{39\,454}$ |
|  | = | = | = |
| Days' Sales in Debtors | 14 days | 68 days | 8 days |

These figures tell us that, on average:

- it takes the house-building company 14 days to collect payment for the sale of a house; while
- it takes the industrial supply company 68 days to collect payment from its customers.

Mean while on average the supermarket company collects cash from customers within eight days of sale.

Most firms selling on credit will aim to collect payment by the end of the month that follows the sale. That would give an average debtor collection period of one month and a half – round about 45 days. Less than 30 days would be very good, while more than 90 days would be considered poor.

However, different industries have different practices. A supermarket generally makes its sales for cash, so even an eight-day average cash collection period would require some explanation. Also the sale of a house in England is not normally completed before receipt of money from the buyer, so a debtor collection period of 14 days for the house-building company might also merit further questioning.

With the debtor collection period, as with other financial ratios, the figure itself is of little value, except in comparison with the firm's past history, and with other similar firms.

## THE CREDITOR PAYMENT PERIOD

The length of time taken by a firm to pay its creditors can also be determined through a very similar process:

- first, determine the average value of *purchases per day* (divide the year's purchases by 365, the number of days in a year);
- then, see how many days' purchases there are in creditors or trade payables (divide the value of trade payables, by the value of a purchases in a day).

The resulting figure should tell us how long it takes, in days, on average, for the firm to pay its creditors.

Once again, in practice, the calculation can be simplified into a formula:

$$\text{days' purchases in creditors} = \frac{\text{trade payables} \times 365}{\text{purchases}}$$

The only difficulty here is the problem of finding the value of purchases. Normally, the P&L Account (Income Statement) of a company will show only the figure for cost of sales. There will, however, be comparative balance sheets – this year's showing closing stock and last year's showing what will now be opening stock. Cost of sales from the P&L Account can therefore be adjusted back to find the value of purchases in the year.

Box 72.5 presents the calculation of number of days' purchases in creditors for each of our three sample companies.

## BOX 72.5

**Creditor Payment Period, or Days' Purchases in Creditors: Three Sample Companies**

|  | house-building company | industrial supply company | supermarket company |
|---|---|---|---|
| Trade Payables | 4 426 | 2 294 | 5 083 |
| Cost of Sales for year | 40 720 | 10 222 | 36 426 |
| closing stock | 75 808 | 1 954 | 1 464 |
| opening stock | (78 137) | (1 706) | (1 309) |
| Purchases for year | 38 391 | 10 470 | 36 581 |
| working | $\dfrac{4\,426 \times 365}{38\,391}$ | $\dfrac{2294 \times 365}{10\,470}$ | $\dfrac{5\,083 \times 365}{36\,581}$ |
|  | = | = | = |
| **Days' Purchases in Creditors** | 42 days | 80 days | 51 days |

These figures tell us that, on average:

- the house-building company pays its suppliers 42 days after purchase; and

- the industrial supply company pays its creditors after 80 days.

Mean while the supermarket company takes 51 days' credit.

It is, of course, beneficial for a firm to delay making payment to its creditors. It is also damaging for the creditor, and an ethical company will try to pay its suppliers without undue delay. In this context, a lengthening creditor payment period is almost certainly a danger sign. It may indicate that the firm has difficulty finding the cash to make payments. It may also make suppliers reluctant to do further business with the firm.

## THE WORKING CAPITAL CYCLE AND WORKING CAPITAL RATIOS

It is possible now to determine the length of the working capital cycle by adding the inventory transit time to the debtor collection period, and deducting the creditor payment period. This finally explains why supermarkets and similar businesses can survive with net current liabilities (very low working capital ratios). Because they buy on credit, and sell their stock for cash extremely quickly, they are able to collect the cash for selling goods even before they pay their suppliers. They therefore need no working capital at all. By contrast, the very high working capital ratio of the house-building company reflects the extreme length of its working capital cycle. Box 72.6 presents the figures.

## BOX 72.6

### The Working Capital Cycle and Working Capital Ratios

| | house-building company | industrial supply company | supermarket company |
|---|---|---|---|
| Current Assets | 92 337 | 5 348 | 3 919 |
| Current Liabilities | (19 265) | (2 995) | (7 518) |
| *less* Working Capital Net Current Assets (Liabilities) | 73 071 | 2 353 | (3 599) |
| Working Capital or Current Ratio | 4.79 | 1.79 | 0.52 |
| Days' Sales in Stock or Inventory Transit Time | 680 | 70 | 15 |
| Days' Sales in Debtors or Debtor Collection Period | 14 | 68 | 8 |
| Days' Purchases in Creditors or Creditor Payment Period | (42) | (80) | (51) |
| **Number of Days in Cycle** | 652 | 58 | (28) |

## STOCK, DEBTOR, AND CREDITOR TURNOVER RATIOS

Instead of calculating how long it takes to process inventory through the firm, how long it takes to collect debtors and how long it takes the firm to pay its creditors, it is possible to calculate how many times each one of these elements is turned over in a year. We begin by assuming that the balance sheet shows one batch of stock, one batch of debtors and one batch of creditors. Then:

- *Stock turnover* means how many times a batch of stock like this was sold and replaced in the year. If stock turnover is 12 times per year, it means 12 such batches in the year were sold and then replaced, with each batch, therefore, taking just one month in transit through the business. Stock turnover is calculated by dividing cost of sales for the year by the value of the batch of stock in the closing balance sheet.
- *Debtor turnover* means how many times a batch of debtors were collected and renewed within the year. If debtors are turned over 52 times in a year, it means that it takes one week to collect each batch of debtors. Debtor turnover is calculated by dividing sales for the year by the value of the batch of debtors shown in the balance sheet.
- *Creditor turnover* means how many times creditors are paid off and renewed within the year. If creditors are turned over six times in a year, it means the firm is taking two months for the payment of its creditors. Creditor turnover is calculated by dividing purchases by the value of the batch of creditors in the balance sheet.

Formulae for the relevant ratios are given in Box 72.7.

## BOX 72.7

### Stock, Debtor, and Creditor Turnover Ratios

These ratios can be calculated according to the formulae below:

$$\text{stock turnover} = \frac{\text{cost of sales}}{\text{inventory}} \text{ times per year}$$

$$\text{debtor turnover} = \frac{\text{sales}}{\text{debtors}} \text{ times per year}$$

$$\text{creditor turnover} = \frac{\text{purchases}}{\text{creditors}} \text{ times per year}$$

## REVIEW

This chapter has examined the working capital cycle, showing how the need for working capital arises, and how it is sensitive to growth and speed of throughput. With examples from different industries, the chapter showed how to calculate the inventory transit time for a firm, the debtor collection period, and the creditor payment period. The chapter also briefly considered the alternative measures of stock turnover, debtor turnover, and creditor turnover.

## DRILLS AND EXERCISES

### 72.1

Below are extracts from the published accounts of two listed companies. A is a producer of dairy foods, while B produces consumer durables or 'white goods' – washing machines, fridges, etc.

Calculate the following ratios for each company:
current ratio
quick ratio
days' sales in stock
days' sales in debtors
days' purchases in creditors
Comment on your findings.

|  | A | B |
|---|---|---|
| Sales | 1 355.2 | 103 848 |
| Cost of Sales | 1 033.5 | 79 664 |
| inventories at year end | 192.6 | 12 041 |
| trade receivables | 142.8 | 20 905 |
| total current assets | 350.1 | 44 091 |
| trade payables | 173.3 | 15 320 |
| total current liabilities | 222.3 | 36 304 |
| opening inventories | 172.7 | 18 606 |

## 72.2

The figures given in question 72.1 are now supplemented with figures from the published accounts of the prior year.

For each company separately, calculate and compare working capital ratios for the current year and the prior year. Comment on any differences you may find, from one year to the next.

|  | A | | B | |
|---|---|---|---|---|
|  | CURRENT YEAR | PRIOR YEAR | CURRENT YEAR | PRIOR YEAR |
| Sales | 1 355.2 | 1 260.6 | 103 848 | 100 701 |
| Cost of Sales | 1 033.5 | 928.0 | 79 664 | 77 270 |
| inventories at year end | 192.6 | 172.7 | 12 041 | 18 606 |
| trade receivables | 142.8 | 124.0 | 20 905 | 24 269 |
| total current assets | 350.1 | 323.9 | 44 091 | 52 827 |
| trade payables | 173.3 | 147.9 | 15 320 | 18 798 |
| total current liabilities | 222.3 | 187.8 | 36 304 | 37 387 |
| opening inventories | 172.7 | 188.5 | 18 606 | 19 170 |

## 72.3

A supermarket, currently selling only food, is considering whether to expand into the sale of household goods. Comment on the possible effects of the change on the firm's working capital requirement.

# CHAPTER 73

# Profit and Sales Ratios

## OBJECTIVES

*The objectives of this chapter are:*

- to show how to calculate the gross profit ratio and the net profit ratio
- to consider, through two contrasting real world pairs of companies, the significance of these two ratios
- to examine, with reference to one pair of companies, the strategic choice between profit margin and speed of throughput
- to introduce the possibility of using activity and other ratios to review the performance of a company

## THE GROSS PROFIT RATIO

The gross profit ratio, (also known as the gross profit margin, or margin on sales) is the ratio of gross profit to sales, normally expressed as a percentage, as given by the formula:

$$\text{gross profit ratio} = \frac{\text{gross profit}}{\text{sales}} \times 100\%$$

This ratio shows the extent of the difference between sales and cost of sales – that is, the difference between what a firm gets from selling its goods or services and what it must pay to make or buy them. Box 73.1 shows the calculation with figures from the published accounts of four sample listed companies.

## BOX 73.1

**Sample Gross Profit Ratios**

| | Food Producers | | Motor Manufacturers | |
|---|---|---|---|---|
| | branded | commodity | luxury | mass market |
| Sales | 7 427 | 1 438 | 71 227 | 51 832 |
| Cost of Sales | (3 666) | (1 056) | (37 346) | (43 888) |
| Gross Profit | 3 761 | 382 | 33 881 | 7 944 |
| Gross Profit Ratio working | $\dfrac{3761}{7427}$ | $\dfrac{382}{1438}$ | $\dfrac{33881}{71227}$ | $\dfrac{7944}{51832}$ |
| | = | = | = | = |
| ratio | 50.6% | 26.6% | 47.6% | 15.3% |

The gross profit ratio is often taken as an indicator of a firm's competitive power – a measure of how much the firm can escape the rigours of price-based competition. The figures in our sample would appear to support this interpretation. The maker of brand-name foods is able to compete on the basis of name and reputation rather than price and secures a gross profit margin of more than 50%. The maker of unbranded foods is forced to compete more on the basis of price and achieves a gross profit margin of only just over 26%.

The story with the motor manufacturers is much the same. In the period to which these figures relate, with chronic overcapacity in the European mass car market, there was fierce competition on price, such that the mass-market producer in our sample could achieve a gross profit ratio of only just over 15% (not very far out of line with other mass-market producers). Meanwhile, the smaller-scale luxury producer, competing on perceptions of quality rather than price, was able to achieve a gross profit ratio more than three times greater, at 47.6%.

The gross profit margin is also sensitive to changes in market conditions. When supply prices increase, or there is a fall in demand, firms will usually feel it first in a squeeze on their gross profit margins.

## THE NET PROFIT RATIO

The net profit ratio is the ratio of net profit to sales, normally expressed as a percentage, as given by the formula

$$\text{net profit ratio} = \frac{\text{net profit}}{\text{sales}} \times 100\%$$

The 'net profit' used may be net profit before tax or after tax. In our examples in this section we shall use profit before tax. (However, if tax is regarded as a cost like any other, which the firm should be able to plan for and manage, then there is an argument for using profit after tax.)

The net profit ratio shows what proportion of each sale goes as profit for the business. Box 73.2 shows the calculation for our four sample companies.

## BOX 73.2

### Sample Net Profit Ratios

| | Food Producers | | Motor Manufacturers | |
| --- | --- | --- | --- | --- |
| | branded | commodity | luxury | mass market |
| Sales | 7 427 | 1 438 | 71 227 | 51 832 |
| Cost of Sales | (3 666) | (1 056) | (37 346) | (43 888) |
| Gross Profit | 3 761 | 382 | 33 881 | 7 944 |
| operating expenses | (2 852) | (312) | (12 712) | (5 993) |
| Operating Profit | 909 | 70 | 21 169 | 1 951 |
| net financial costs | (171) | (25) | (68) | (310) |
| Profit before Tax | 738 | 45 | 21 101 | 1 641 |
| Net Profit Ratio  working | $\frac{738}{7\,427}$ | $\frac{45}{1\,438}$ | $\frac{21\,101}{71\,227}$ | $\frac{1\,641}{51\,832}$ |
| ratio | = 9.9% | = 3.1% | = 29.6% | = 3.2% |

Here we see the producers of branded and luxury goods also enjoying higher *net* profits per unit sold. But note that this is not necessarily so and the differences are smaller. Maintaining the quality of a brand often means high expenses on advertising, quality assurance, packaging, public relations, after-sales service and so on.

## THE NET PROFIT RATIO AND INVENTORY TRANSIT TIME

A weakness of the net profit ratio is the way it neglects the dimension of time. It tells us the proportion of profit in each £1 of sales, but not how fast the sales are made. This is important. If you and I make sales at £100 per unit and both have costs of £90 per unit, we will both enjoy £10 net profit on each sale and both of us will have a 10% net profit ratio. But if I sell two units in a year and you sell only one, my business will be twice as profitable as yours. In this context, it is interesting to compare the net profit ratio and the inventory transit time of the branded food producer and the commodity food producer in our sample, as shown in Box 73.3.

BOX 73.3

**Net Profit Ratio and Inventory Transit Time**

The net profit ratio and the inventory transit time of our two food producers are shown below

|  | Food Producers | |
|---|---|---|
|  | branded | commodity |
| Net Profit Ratio | 9.9% | 3.1% |
| inventory transit time | 72 days | 24 days |

Although each £1 of sales yields more than three times as much net profit for the branded food producer, the unbranded producer is making sales three times faster (taking only 24 days to sell inventory as against 72 for the branded producer).

This means that although the profitability of each sale may be lower for the unbranded producer, the profitability of the business as a whole will not necessarily be less.

Although, ideally, a firm would aim for both high margin and high throughput, in general a firm must make a basic strategic decision whether to go for one or the other: supermarkets typically go for lower margins and high throughput, while luxury goods producers go for higher margins and low throughput.

## ACTIVITY RATIOS

Activity ratios are essentially measure of how busy a company has been with its assets, or with the value invested by its shareholders. Activity can be measured in two ways:

- as the ratio of sales to total assets in the firm;
- as the ratio of sales to equity (the shareholders' investment).

Using the sales to total assets activity ratio:

$$\text{activity ratio} = \frac{\text{sales}}{\text{total assets}}$$

we can say 'this firm has generated £$x$ of sales for every £1 of assets it can use'. Using the sales to equity activity ratio:

$$\text{activity ratio} = \frac{\text{sales}}{\text{equity}}$$

we can say 'this firm has generated £$y$ of sales for every £1 invested by its shareholders. Box 73.4 presents activity ratios for our four sample companies.

BOX 73.4

**Sample Activity Ratios**

| | Food Producers | | Motor Manufacturers | |
|---|---|---|---|---|
| | branded | commodity | luxury | mass market |
| Sales | 7 427 | 1 438 | 71 227 | 51 832 |
| Total Assets | 6 945 | 566 | 101 363 | 30 224 |
| Equity | 3 696 | 152 | 53 761 | 10 036 |

| | | branded | commodity | luxury | mass market |
|---|---|---|---|---|---|
| Activity Ratio (sales to total assets) | working | $\dfrac{7427}{6945}$ | $\dfrac{1438}{566}$ | $\dfrac{71227}{101363}$ | $\dfrac{51832}{30224}$ |
| | | = | = | = | = |
| | ratio | 1.1 | 2.5 | 0.7 | 1.7 |
| Activity Ratio (sales to equity) | working | $\dfrac{7427}{3696}$ | $\dfrac{1438}{152}$ | $\dfrac{71227}{53761}$ | $\dfrac{51832}{10036}$ |
| | | = | = | = | = |
| | ratio | 2.0 | 9.5 | 1.3 | 5.2 |

Notice first that the lower margin producers simply must work harder to make up for their lower margin.

Also notice the profound effects of gearing in the lower margin producers. It may be a coincidence that our two lower margin producers are both very highly geared, but equity seems to be working so much harder in the lower margin producers because it has the help of quite a lot of debt.

## RATIO ANALYSIS AND OTHER RATIOS

Company financial statements are rich in information, but very hard of access. Numbers on a page are quite inscrutable and few of us can read them like a novel. They demand the very closest concentration, with constant comparison between one figure and another and an unrelenting effort to imagine what is happening in the underlying business. Ratios are helpful in this undertaking and many more of them could be suggested: the ratio of operating costs to sales, for example, or of fixed to total assets, or the capital employed and profit earned per employee and so on. All or any of these ratios could be useful, depending on the nature of our query. Readers may think of others for themselves. But financial statements tell you nothing if you do not ask them. It is essential to approach them with a set of questions, rather than a thoughtless set of ratios.

# REVIEW

This chapter has considered some of the commonly used accounting ratios involving profit and sales, including especially the gross profit ratio, the net profit ratio and two possible versions of the activity ratio. The chapter also briefly discussed the use of accounting ratios in general and the importance of approaching all financial statements in a spirit of intelligent inquiry.

# DRILLS AND EXERCISES

## 73.1

Below are extracts from the published accounts of three listed companies. Two are pharmaceutical companies and the other is a supermarket.
Calculate the following ratios for each company:
gross profit ratio
net profit ratio (use the profit before tax)
activity ratio (sales/equity)
activity ratio (sales/capital employed)
Identify the odd one out and state whether, in your opinion, the sample consists of two supermarkets and one pharmaceutical company, or two pharmaceutical companies and one supermarket.
Explain your opinion and comment on your findings.

| | A | B | C |
|---|---|---|---|
| Sales | 26 475 | 39 454 | 23 225 |
| Cost of Sales | (5 559) | (36 426) | (5 010) |
| Gross Profit | 20 916 | 3 028 | 18 215 |
| Profit before Tax | 8 543 | 2 235 | 7 799 |
| Equity | 15 416 | 9 444 | 9 648 |
| Current Debt | 136 | 1 646 | 718 |
| Long-term Debt | 1 087 | 3 742 | 4 772 |
| Total Debt | 1 223 | 5 388 | 5 490 |
| Capital Employed | 16 639 | 14 832 | 15 138 |

## 73.2

The figures given in question 73.1 are now supplemented for companies A and B with figures from the published accounts of the prior year.

For each company separately, calculate and compare the same ratios as above for the current year and the prior year. Comment on any differences you may find, from one year to the next.

|  | A | | B | |
|  | CURRENT YEAR | PRIOR YEAR | CURRENT YEAR | PRIOR YEAR |
| --- | --- | --- | --- | --- |
| Sales | 26 475 | 23 950 | 39 454 | 33 866 |
| Cost of Sales | (5 559) | (5 356) | (36 426) | (31 231) |
| Gross Profit | 20 916 | 18 594 | 3 028 | 2 635 |
| Profit before Tax | 8 543 | 6 667 | 2 235 | 1 894 |
| Equity | 15 416 | 13 691 | 9 444 | 8 654 |
| Current Debt | 136 | 90 | 1 646 | 482 |
| Long-term Debt | 1 087 | 1 111 | 3 742 | 4 563 |
| Total Debt | 1 223 | 1 201 | 5 388 | 5 045 |
| Capital Employed | 16 639 | 14 892 | 14 832 | 13 699 |

## 73.2

The figures given in question 73.1 are now supplemented for companies A and B with figures from the published accounts of the prior year.

For each company, separately, calculate and compare the same ratios as above for the current year and the prior year. Comment on any differences you may find, from one year to the next.

|  | A | | B | |
|---|---|---|---|---|
|  | CURRENT YEAR | PRIOR YEAR | CURRENT YEAR | PRIOR YEAR |
| Sales | 26,175 | 23,950 | 24,154 | 23,866 |
| Cost of Sales | (5,359) | (5,358) | (14,424) | (21,231) |
| Gross Profit | 20,816 | 18,592 | 9,028 | 2,635 |
| Profit before Tax | 8,823 | 6,627 | 2,735 | 1,874 |
| Equity | 15,716 | 13,627 | 9,466 | 8,466 |
| Current Debt | 124 | 90 | 1,646 | 287 |
| Long-term Debt | 1,087 | 1,111 | 3,972 | 1,543 |
| Total Debt | 1,223 | 1,201 | 5,308 | 5,345 |
| Capital Employed | 16,939 | 14,847 | 14,832 | 13,694 |

# CHAPTER 74

# Investment Ratios

## OBJECTIVES

*The objectives of this chapter are:*

- to describe the basic investment ratios: earnings per share, price/earnings, dividend yield and dividend cover
- to compare the investment ratios of three contrasting real-world companies
- to explain the interpretation of these ratios in terms of comparative risk, and investor preferences for growth or income

## THE CAPITAL MARKET AND INVESTMENT DECISIONS

Competition between companies extends beyond competing for customers in the market for goods and services. Companies also compete to attract funds from investors in the market for shares and capital. Investors and their advisers, therefore, need to compare investment opportunities, choosing which shares to buy or sell and when to buy or sell them.

For this they need information, and to simplify matters, many investors rely, at least initially, on a small number of investment ratios.

## EARNINGS PER SHARE

When an investor buys an ordinary share, what he or she gets is a claim on the future earnings of the company. The market value of a share therefore reflects expected future earnings and much effort is expended on the making of estimates, forecasts and predictions.

Estimates of future earnings will generally start from the latest actual figures available in the company's financial statements. The critical figure is earnings per share.

Earnings per share (often shortened to eps) is the total of the company's earnings for the year, divided by the number of ordinary shares in issue. (Recall that earnings are profits after tax and after payment of any preference dividend – that is, the profit left for ordinary shareholders in any year.) The standard formula for the calculation is:

$$\text{earnings per share} = \frac{\text{profit after tax and preference dividend}}{\text{number of ordinary shares in issue}}$$

Normally, for a listed company, this figure is given on the face of the Income Statement, and for good reasons. It may in fact involve quite complex calculations if new shares have been issued in the period. We shall ignore such complications. Box 74.1 presents two very simple examples.

BOX 74.1

**The Earnings per Share Calculation**

|  | A plc |  | B plc |
|---|---|---|---|
|  | £ |  | £ |
| Assets | 3 500 | Assets | 3 500 |
| Liabilities | (1 000) | Liabilities | (1 000) |
| Net Assets | £2 500 | Net Assets | £2 500 |
| | | | |
| Issued Share Capital | | Issued Share Capital | |
| 1 000 shares of £1 each | 1 000 | 4 000 shares of 25p each | 1 000 |
| Reserves | 1 500 | Reserves | 1 500 |
| | £2 500 | | £2 500 |
| | | | |
| earnings for year | £480 | | £480 |

Earnings per Share

$$\frac{£480}{1\,000}$$
=
48p per share

$$\frac{£480}{4\,000}$$
=
12p per share

Notice first that earnings per share cannot be used as a comparison between companies. It is strictly a comparison between shares. The two companies in our example are identical except that one has issued 1 000 shares, while the other has issued 4 000 shares. It follows from this purely arbitrary fact that earnings per share in A plc will be four times greater than earnings per share in B plc, and one share in A plc should be equal in price to four shares in B plc. But that is no reflection on the merits of the different companies.

## THE TREND IN EARNINGS PER SHARE

Share prices are extremely sensitive to changes in earnings per share, and it is the principal objective of most chief executives to report a steady rise in their company's earnings per share from one year to the next.

Given the importance of the earnings per share figure, companies sometimes also like to provide alternatives to the full or total earnings per share – for example, by excluding the effect of events that are not expected to recur, or by excluding the effect of activities that have since been discontinued.

# DILUTED EARNINGS PER SHARE

A company may have made commitments to issue more shares in the future. For example, it may have issued preference shares or debentures with the option to convert them into ordinary shares, or it may have offered incentives to its senior executives by giving them options to buy the company's shares in the future at less than market price, providing some set of performance targets have been met. The eventual issue of these shares will make more issued shares in total, and therefore reduce or dilute the earnings of the shares already issued. In such situations, a company is also required to publish a figure for 'fully diluted' earnings per share, taking into account the expected effect of issuing the new shares.

# THE P/E RATIO

The P/E (or price to earnings) ratio of a share is the ratio of the current share price to the latest reported earnings per share, according to the formula:

$$\text{P/E ratio} = \frac{\text{current price per share}}{\text{last reported earnings per share}}$$

P/E ratios will change from day to day, as share prices change in the market. By comparing the price an investor must pay for a share against the benefit he or she would have got for the previous period, the P/E ratio shows how expensive a share is. However, while we may say that a share with a high P/E ratio is expensive, we cannot say without further investigation why it is expensive – it may be expensive because it is a good, high quality investment, or it may be expensive because it is a poor investment which is overpriced.

# EARNINGS YIELD

The earnings yield on a share is a ratio which measures how profitable it would be to invest in a share at its current price, and benefit from a repeat of its last reported earnings per share. It is therefore calculated according to the formula:

$$\text{earnings yield} = \frac{\text{last reported earnings per share}}{\text{current price per share}} \times 100\%$$

It will be seen that the earnings yield (earnings/price) is the reciprocal of the P/E ratio (price/earnings).

# INTERPRETING P/E AND EARNINGS YIELD

Because the P/E ratio and the earnings yield are so closely related, it is helpful to consider them together, with the P/E ratio as a quick indicator of the expensiveness of a share, and the earnings yield as a measure of the rate of return available to an investor if the company's annual earnings were to remain the same into the future.

The earnings yield on a share should be compared against the rate of return available to an investor in government bonds. These are considered to be 'risk-free' investments. No investment is in fact risk-free, but it must be recognized that the risk of any government defaulting on its loans is far less than the risk of any company becoming insolvent. The point is that investors should only accept higher risks if they are offered higher returns. Thus the riskiest companies should offer the highest rates of return, and all shares should offer a higher rate of return than the yield on government bonds.

Figures based on actual ratios for ordinary shares in three sample companies, with the rate of return available on government bonds at the same date, are shown in Box 74.2.

## BOX 74.2

### P/E and Earnings Yield

|  | electricity generating company | advertising agency | search engine company |
|---|---|---|---|
| P/e ratio | 16.0 | 20.9 | 45.8 |
| **Earnings Yield** | **6.25%** | **4.78%** | **2.18%** |
| 'Risk free' rate of return available to investors in British government bonds | | 5.50% (approximate) | |

Those who are paying nearly 46 times annual earnings for a share in the search engine company are evidently gambling on the expectation that those earnings will rise very sharply in the future. Otherwise the investment, currently generating less than half the risk-free rate of return, would make no sense.

Similarly, those who are paying more than 20 times annual earnings for a share in the profits of the advertising agency (such that their rate of return will be less than 4.8% per year, when they could be getting 5.5% per year from a risk-free investment in government bonds) must also be gambling on the expectation that the company's earnings will rise in the future.

On the basis of most recent actual earnings, as opposed to expectations, the only company in our sample whose shares seem near to being fairly priced, is the electricity generator. This is understandable. Given the nature of this company's business, any growth is likely to be slow, so it would make sense to value its shares on the basis of current earnings. The business is also relatively safe, with little risk. Investors have therefore put a value on the company's shares which, at 16 times earnings, will give them a rate of return that is just above the risk-free rate available for lending to the government (an earnings yield of 6.25% per year, against a yield on government bonds of 5.50% per year).

## DIVIDEND YIELD

While the whole of a company's earnings is claimed by ordinary shareholders, usually only part of it is paid to them as dividend. The remainder is kept in the company where it will be invested to generate further profits, and enhance the future share price. Such is the importance given to increasing the company's share price that the dividend may in fact be only the smallest part of a shareholder's total return on investment.

The dividend yield on a share is the rate of return on investment that would be provided by the dividend alone. It is measured by the formula

$$\text{dividend yield} = \frac{\text{dividend paid for previous year}}{\text{current share price}} \times 100\%$$

Box 74.3 presents examples of the dividend yield for ordinary shares in each of our three sample companies.

## BOX 74.3

### Dividend Yield for Three Sample Companies

|  | electricity generating company | advertising agency | search engine company |
|---|---|---|---|
| Dividend per Share | 25.0p | 11.2p | nil |
| Price per Share | 762.5p | 756.5p | $443.03 |
| dividend yield working | $\frac{25.0}{762.5}$ | $\frac{11.2}{756.5}$ | not applicable |
| **Dividend Yield** | 3.3% | 1.5% | 0.0% |

## INVESTOR PREFERENCES: GROWTH OR INCOME

Investors can be broadly divided into those who are looking for capital growth (shares that are likely to increase in value) and those who are looking for income (shares that will pay a regular and reliable dividend). Companies also differ in what they offer to investors.

At one extreme in our small sample is the search engine company, which at present pays no dividend at all. This is a company for investors who are looking for capital growth. All profits are reinvested to expand the company and enhance the future share price.

At the other extreme is the electricity generating company, which provides a dividend yield of 3.3% per year. Here, in an established, low-risk industry, there are limited opportunities for growth and the company would attract investors who are looking for a safe and reliable income. Notice, however, that even for this company the dividend yield is less than the risk-free rate of return on government bonds. Why? Essentially because the return on government bonds comes largely in the form of a fixed amount of interest, exposing the investor to the erosion of real value through inflation. It may be expected by contrast that the dividends of our electricity generating company will keep their real value and rise at least in line with inflation.

## DIVIDEND COVER

Dividend cover is a ratio showing the number of times a company could have paid its last annual dividend out of its earnings for the year. A high dividend cover would indicate that even future falls in earnings would not impair the company's ability to pay a dividend out of current profits. Investors may therefore rely on the firm making the same or even bigger dividend payments into the foreseeable future.

A high dividend cover ratio also means that the company is growing larger by retaining a higher proportion of the extra net assets it accumulated in the year.

Dividend cover may be calculated on a total basis, as:

$$\text{dividend cover} = \frac{\text{total earnings}}{\text{total ordinary dividend for year}} \text{ times}$$

or, alternatively, the same answer can be reached if dividend cover is calculated on a per share basis, as:

$$\text{dividend cover} = \frac{\text{earnings per share}}{\text{dividend per share}} \text{ times}$$

Box 74.4 presents the calculation for our three sample companies.

## BOX 74.4

### Three Sample Dividend Cover Ratios

|  | electricity generating company | advertising agency | search engine company |
|---|---|---|---|
| Earnings per Share | 47.7p | 36.2p | $9.67 |
| Dividend per Share | 25.0p | 11.2p | nil |
| dividend cover working | $\frac{47.7}{25.0}$ | $\frac{36.2}{11.2}$ | not applicable |
| **Dividend Cover** | 1.9 times | 3.2 times | not applicable |

Notice in our examples how dividend cover must also be considered in the light of the firm's activities and financial structure. With what is presumably a very predictable revenue stream, our electricity generating company can afford a lower dividend cover ratio, because it has less cause to fear a fall in earnings. By contrast, the advertising agency, with what is potentially a much more volatile revenue stream, may need to maintain a higher dividend cover in its good years, to avoid any dividend cuts in bad years.

Our examples also show that dividend cover is not just a matter of reassuring investors about the viability of future dividends. With a high fixed asset base as well as a predictable revenue stream, our electricity generating company will almost certainly have the highest borrowing capacity. If the company needs to expand, it can borrow easily and cheaply. It can therefore afford to distribute a high proportion of the extra net assets it accumulates as profit in a year. By contrast, however, the advertising agency, with a low fixed asset base and a less predictable revenue stream, will find it much harder to borrow in order to grow. Such a company's easiest way to grow is to retain a high proportion of the extra net assets it gains in a year as profits. As a result it will generally show a higher dividend cover ratio.

## UNCOVERED DIVIDENDS

A company may of course pay a dividend that is not covered by its current earnings, and it may pay a dividend even if it has made a loss in the current period, as long as it has profits retained from previous periods. A company will sometimes pay an uncovered dividend to reassure investors that current problems are merely temporary, but it should be noted that an uncovered dividend will always ensure that the total value invested in the company will be less at the end of the year than it was at the beginning.

## REVIEW

This chapter has examined the principal ratios used by investors in deciding which shares to buy or sell, and when to buy or sell them. The chapter also considered the importance of risk and the prospects of growth and showed how some investors aim for capital growth (increases in share prices), while others are looking for a reliable source of income (dividends).

## DRILLS AND EXERCISES

### 74.1

Below are extracts from the five-year historical record published with the accounts of six listed companies, with their P/E ratio at the time of writing.
Study the table and:

(a) compute the dividend cover for each company for each year;
(b) identify any periods in which the 'adjusted' earnings per share has turned out to be lower than the basic earnings per share. Comment on your findings;
(c) identify any periods in which there was a fall in earnings per share, and compare the movement in that period of the dividend per share (increase, decrease or stay the same). Comment on your findings;
(d) identify any period in which there was a cut in dividend;
(e) compare each company's present P/E ratio against its trend of past earnings per share and dividends per share. Is there any relation?

| | CURRENT P/E RATIO | YEAR 1 | YEAR 2 | YEAR 3 | YEAR 4 | YEAR 5 |
|---|---|---|---|---|---|---|
| **Water Company** | 22 | | all figures in pence | | | |
| earnings per share | | | | | | |
| basic | | 43.40 | 80.30 | 39.00 | 52.90 | 106.10 |
| adjusted | | 87.20 | 92.10 | 52.60 | 70.40 | 82.40 |
| dividends per share | | 45.90 | 47.04 | 48.51 | 51.13 | 61.45 |
| **Office Rental Co** | 5.9 | | | | | |
| earnings per share | | | | | | |
| basic | | 2.10 | (10.10) | 15.10 | 39.30 | 91.70 |
| adjusted | | 12.70 | 13.30 | 12.80 | 11.60 | 10.20 |
| dividends per share | | 10.00 | 10.25 | 10.50 | 10.75 | 11.00 |
| **Department Store** | 19.1 | | | | | |
| earnings per share | | | | | | |
| basic | | 21.80 | 24.20 | 17.60 | 31.30 | 39.10 |
| adjusted | | | | | | |
| dividends per share | | 23.30 | 24.70 | 19.20 | 31.40 | 40.40 |
| **Public Transport Co** | 17.7 | | | | | |
| earnings per share | | | | | | |
| basic | | 38.00 | 28.70 | 42.60 | 43.70 | 51.80 |
| adjusted | | | | | | |
| dividends per share | | 17.20 | 18.00 | 18.90 | 19.84 | 20.83 |
| **Pharmaceutical Co** | 14.6 | | | | | |
| earnings per share | | | | | | |
| basic | | 65.15 | 73.62 | 80.98 | 82.60 | 95.50 |
| adjusted | | | | | | |
| dividends per share | | 40.00 | 41.00 | 42.00 | 44.00 | 48.00 |
| **Satellite Broadcaster** | 18.7 | | | | | |
| earnings per share | | | | | | |
| basic | | −55.50 | 14.90 | 22.40 | 30.20 | 30.20 |
| adjusted | | | | | | |
| dividends per share | | | | 2.75 | 7.25 | 10.50 |

# PART SIX

# Next Steps and Further Reading

Part 6 points the way to further study. For specialists in accounting, it offers a brief review of the bodies involved in setting the accounting standards that they must study next. For non-specialists, it offers a small selection of books for further reading on the business, social, political and economic issues that accounting touches on.

75. Next Steps: Accounting Standards
76. Further Reading

# CHAPTER 75

# Next Steps: Accounting Standards

## OBJECTIVES

*The objectives of this chapter are:*

- for future specialists in accounting, to describe the evolution of the major elements of the standard-setting regime, as a foundation for further detailed study of the standards themselves
- for non-specialists, to point to some of the major issues involved in setting accounting standards, and outline the interests of the different parties to the debate

## ACCOUNTING STANDARDS

Previous chapters have shown the extent to which accounting depends on the exercise of judgement by accountants. Any further study in accounting must approach the detailed study of accounting standards, which exist to help accountants use their judgement wisely and consistently.

In this chapter, as a foundation for further study as well as a matter of general interest, we shall briefly describe the standard-setting regime – in terms of where accounting standards come from, on whose authority they stand, and what basic issues are involved in standard-setting.

## THE EU AND INTERNATIONAL FINANCIAL REPORTING STANDARDS

One of the objects of the European Union is to promote the free movement of capital and entrepreneurship. Pursuant to this aim, Member States have agreed that all companies whose shares are listed on a recognized stock exchange within the EU should no longer present financial statements prepared in accordance with their different national accounting standards. Instead, they must present financial statements drawn up in accordance with International Financial Reporting Standards (IFRSs). The idea is that accounting differences should not prevent a company from anywhere in Europe from having its shares listed on any of the EU's capital markets (or cause such a company to incur any extra cost), and that investors should have access to comparable financial information from all EU listed companies, no matter where in the EU their shares may happen to be listed.

# THE INTERNATIONAL ACCOUNTING STANDARDS BOARD

IFRSs are issued by the International Accounting Standards Board (IASB), which has no institutional connection with the European Union. Members of the IASB are appointed by the trustees of a body called the International Accounting Standards Committee Foundation (IASCF). The trustees of the foundation also raise the funds required to pay for the work of the IASB. (Standard-setting is no mean business: the foundation has a budget of £16 million for 2008. This comes from the voluntary contributions of less than 200 organizations – mostly large companies, as well as the very small number of large international accounting firms.)

The trustees of the IASCF are a self-perpetuating body – they themselves will elect a new trustee to join them when a vacancy arises. But the first trustees of the IASCF were nominated in 2000 by a committee under the then chairman of the US Securities and Exchange Commission (SEC). The nominating committee itself was established by the International Accounting Standards Committee (IASC).

# THE INTERNATIONAL ACCOUNTING STANDARDS COMMITTEE

The IASC was set up in 1973. Its members were representatives of professional accounting bodies from around the world, but predominantly from the Anglo-Saxon and European countries that were home to many multi-national corporations. The principal object of the IASC was to issue International Accounting Standards (IASs).

International Accounting Standards were needed at the time by the large professional accounting firms in the developed world, who were required to audit the accounts of multi-national corporations with subsidiaries in parts of the world with far less effective accounting regulation. Subsidiary accounts which complied with local accounting standards (if any such standards existed) might not meet the standards required for inclusion in the consolidated accounts of the parent company. By creating and demanding compliance with International Accounting Standards, the large auditing firms were able to gain at least some assurance that the accounts of far-flung subsidiaries were prepared according to minimally acceptable standards.

# THE CHANGING NEED FOR INTERNATIONAL STANDARDS

By the year 2000, the focus of the problem had shifted to such an extent that the IASC felt the need to arrange for its own replacement by a different body with a different mission. Larger corporations were beginning to raise capital on stock exchanges around the world, as well as their own domestic markets. They were thus becoming subject to different, and sometimes conflicting accounting standards. The problem was no longer one of imposing basic accounting standards on subsidiaries in places where previously there had been none. Now, the problem was that the developed accounting standards of one regime were inconsistent with the developed accounting standards of another regime. Thus a London-based corporation wanting to have its shares also listed in New York, would have to prepare a completely different set of accounts to comply with US accounting standards, and vice-versa.

# THE INTERNATIONAL ORGANIZATION OF SECURITIES COMMISSIONS

The International Organization of Securities Commissions (IOSCO) is an organization whose ordinary membership is open to the bodies that regulate capital markets around the world. For the

United Kingdom, this is the Financial Services Authority (FSA). For the United States, it is the Securities and Exchange Commission (SEC). In their capacity as domestic regulators, it is the job of these bodies to ensure an orderly capital market within their own jurisdiction. In their capacity as members of IOSCO, they are attempting to establish an orderly and uniform international capital market. Although IOSCO has no constitutional link with the IASB, the transformation of the IASC into the IASB, and with it the replacement of IASs with IFRSs, was provoked in part by a request from IOSCO for the IASC to develop a single set of accounting standards that would be acceptable to the regulators of capital markets around the world.

## THE SECURITIES AND EXCHANGE COMMISSION

While the rest of the world seems to be following Europe in adopting international standards, regulators in the United States, still home to the largest capital markets in the world, are for the moment holding to their own accounting standards. These are issued by the Financial Accounting Standards Board (FASB), which has been designated by the Securities and Exchange Commission (SEC) to develop generally accepted accounting and reporting standards. The SEC is a government agency appointed to regulate the capital markets in the United States, while the FASB, its designated standard-setter, is entirely independent, being appointed and supported by the Financial Accounting Foundation, whose trustees are nominated by professional organizations with an interest in accounting standards.

The SEC and FASB are relevant in Europe, not only because of the number of European companies whose shares are listed in New York, but also because the international standards applicable here are still subject to development and open to the influence of the SEC. Broadly speaking, the SEC is in favour of international accounting standards, but before they agree to adopt international standards, they would rather use their influence to ensure that they bear a closer resemblance to the American standards set by their own FASB.

## THE BASIC STANDARD-SETTING ISSUES

Accounting and financial reporting standards deal with specific questions – for example, how to account for pension costs, or how to disclose contingent liabilities – but current debate recognizes two very basic issues involved in the actual setting of the standards. These concern:

- the proper objectives of financial reporting; and
- the choice between rules and principles.

## THE OBJECTIVES OF FINANCIAL REPORTING

In view of their close connections with the bodies that regulate the capital markets, it is not surprising that the IASB and the FASB seem to agree that the principal objective of financial reporting is, or ought to be, to provide the capital markets (that is, the general class of investors) with information relevant to potential investment decisions. The question still under sharp discussion is, to what extent should financial reporting also be concerned with the accountability of management for their stewardship of the resources entrusted to them by shareholders?

In this context, there is an interesting contrast between accounting standards and the law, which seems to recognize only the objective of accountability. This leaves auditors in the UK in the paradoxical position of reporting that the financial statements they have examined are in compliance with IFRSs (objective: to provide information that is useful to the general class of investors), while emphasizing that their audit report is addressed only to the company's members as a body (objective: reassurance about the accountability of the company's management).

## THE CHOICE BETWEEN RULES AND PRINCIPLES

In general, it might be said that the SEC and FASB have favoured a rule-based approach to accounting standards, while European authorities have favoured an approach based on principles. For an example of what this difference might actually mean in practice, consider two different possible approaches to the question of whether to make provision for a doubtful debt. A system based on principles might declare that a provision should be made if it seems likely that the debt will not be paid. The decision in any particular instance will then depend on the judgement of the accountant, as to whether the debt is likely to be paid. On the other hand, a system based on rules might declare that a provision should be made if and only if a debt is more than 120 days overdue. Rules are more certain, and they are sometimes favoured because they take away the burden of responsibility for making a decision. Yet at the same time, they devalue the expertise of the judge or decision-maker and they open the door to compliance with the letter, but not the spirit, of the law.

## INTERNATIONAL STANDARDS: TEXT AND COMMENTARY

New international standards are published as they are issued, and old standards may be withdrawn or amended, but the IASB publishes a collected text of all standards and official interpretations in force as at 1 January of each calendar year. Details are available on their website: www.iasb.org.

The most detailed and useful critical commentary on the standards is written by a team at the accountancy firm Ernst & Young LLP. It is also updated and published annually, the latest at time of writing being:

- Bonham, M., Curtis, M., Davies, M. *et al* (2006), *International GAAP 2007*, LexisNexis, London.

The account given above, of how the IASC transformed itself into the IASCF, is largely based on this source.

An interesting comment on:

- *Stewardship/Accountability as an Objective of Financial Reporting*
  was issued by the Accounting Standards Board (the UK's own national accounting standard-setter) in June 2007 and is available on the ASB's website at www.apb.org.uk/asb.

## LEGITIMACY AND COMPLIANCE

Accounting standards are concerned with the disclosure of information in financial statements. Such standards would hardly be needed if the disclosures they demand were already perceived to be in the interests of the people to whom the standards are addressed. However, accounting standards are not voted on by a representative assembly and standard-setters cannot simply say, as Parliament does, 'This is the law because we say so'. One way in which standard-setters have attempted to overcome this problem and gain compliance through consent, is through force of logic, presenting individual standards as derived by inescapable logic from undeniable statements of principle. Such an approach is understandable, but nevertheless embarrassing when a standard, once presented as incontrovertibly correct, has to be amended or withdrawn.

## JAPAN

With its own peculiar arrangements for the finance of industry, Japan has come late to the world of accounting standards and, while seeking convergence, Japan still stands aside from both FASB and IASB. As a result, Japanese thinking about accounting standards seems fresher, more tentative, less dogmatic, more aware of the underlying conflicts of interest and more willing to express them. The website of the Accounting Standards Board of Japan carries their statement of principles, as well as some interesting lectures and research papers which have been translated into English. The address is: www.asb.or.jp.

## REVIEW

As a foundation for further study, this chapter has introduced the major bodies involved in the setting of accounting and financial reporting standards. The chapter also briefly discussed some of the basic issues involved in the standard-setting process.

# CHAPTER 76

# Further Reading

## OBJECTIVES

*The objectives of this chapter are:*

- to encourage readers to use and extend their knowledge of accounting with further reading from a variety of disciplines
- to recommend some of the books that I have found most interesting and useful as guides to understanding business and modern society, and the complex relation between them

## FURTHER READING

For readers who wish to pursue their studies and pass examinations in accounting, there is no shortage of courses, qualifications and texts. Relevant books are readily identified and often specified by instructors or examining authorities. However, accounting is not an end in itself. It touches on, or is touched by, almost every field of human activity, and here the connections and relevant books are not so easily identified.

In this final chapter, therefore, I have provided a short list of books that may help to put accounting in a more rounded, responsible and human context. The extent to which I have drawn on the ideas of Galbraith and Chandler to make sense of the history and purpose of accounting will be obvious.

## THE NATURE OF MODERN BUSINESS

On the basic economic factors governing the nature of modern business, a good place to start is:

- Galbraith, J. K. (1991) *The New Industrial State,* Penguin Books Ltd, Harmondsworth, London.

Galbraith's second chapter, on the imperatives of technology, is especially good. For an historical view that defines modern business and describes how it came to pass, the fundamental work is:

- Chandler, A. (1977) *The Visible Hand – The Managerial Revolution in American Business,* Harvard University Press, Cambridge, Massachusetts.

## THE CORPORATION

On the separation of ownership and control the classic work is:

- Berle, A. and Means, G. (1991) *The Modern Corporation and Private Property*, Transaction Publishers, New Brunswick, New Jersey.

First published in 1932, this book is still fresh and relevant. For a view of the modern giant corporation from one of its main architects, try the memoirs of Alfred P. Sloan, Jr. – more exciting than the title makes them sound:

- Sloan, A. (1986) *My Years with General Motors*, Penguin Books Ltd, Harmondsworth.

## SOCIAL AND INSTITUTIONAL CONTROL

Accounting is as much about the general topic of control as it is about recording transactions. Two useful books on the nature of control are:

- Hopwood, A. (1976) *Accounting and Human Behaviour*, Prentice-Hall, Inc., Englewood Cliffs, New Jersey.
- Deming, W. Edwards (2000) *Out of the Crisis*, The MIT Press, Cambridge, Massachusetts.

Hopwood's Chapter 2 on control in organizations is unpretentious, clear and memorable. Deming was the master of statistical quality control (it was he who taught the Japanese). He is savage on the subject of statistical innocents who attempt to manage by numbers.

## THE PRESENTATION OF INFORMATION

Anyone, accountant or otherwise, who is capable of admiring truth, beauty, and clarity of thought should look at:

- Tufte, E. (1983) *The Visual Display of Quantitative Information*, Graphics Press, Cheshire, Connecticut.

## ABOUT ACCOUNTING

Three very different books about accounting are:

- Hopwood, A. and Miller, P. (eds) (1994) *Accounting as Social and Institutional Practice*, Cambridge University Press, Cambridge.
- Johnson, H. and Kaplan, R. (1991) *Relevance Lost – The Rise and Fall of Management Accounting*, Harvard Business School Press, Boston, Massachusetts.
- Whittington, G. (1983) *Inflation Accounting – An Introduction to the Debate*, Cambridge University Press, Cambridge.

Hopwood and Miller is a collection of historical and sociological essays about the social function of accounting. Johnson and Kaplan is mainly about the evolution of accounting for overheads – far more interesting than you ever imagined. Whittington's later chapters on inflation accounting become quite severely technical, but the earlier chapters are very approachable.

# ABOUT BUSINESS AND MANAGEMENT

In an area blighted by poor quality and tricks to trap the gullible, three clear and readable books are:

- Drucker, P. (1968) *The Practice of Management*, Heinemann Ltd, London.
- Porter, M. (1980) *Competitive Strategy*, Free Press, New York.
- Goldratt, M. and Cox, J. (1993) *The Goal*, Gower, Aldershot.

Drucker's Chapter 9 on the Principles of Production is very good. Porter's book is in fact a fascinating description of the ways in which a firm may contrive to escape the rigours of competition. In *The Goal*, Goldratt and Cox have succeeded in writing a very practical and interesting book about production management, in the form of an exciting novel – worth reading just for the story.

# COMPANY LAW

Two books dealing respectively with the basic concepts of corporate law, and the detail of the law as it stands, are:

- Davies, P, (2002) *Introduction to Company Law*, Oxford University Press, Oxford.
- Gower, L. (author) and Davies, P. (editor) (2003) *Gower and Davies' Principles of Modern Company Law*, Sweet and Maxwell, London.

# GENERAL LAW

Accountants, who deal with transactions and claims, are essentially dealing with matters of law. For a closer acquaintance with the law, these two books have plenty of human interest:

- Atiyah, P. S. (1995) *An Introduction to the Law of Contract*, Oxford University Press, Oxford.
- Goode, R. (1995) *Commercial Law*, Penguin Books, Harmondsworth.

# JURISPRUDENCE

Accountants are rule-makers as well as rule-followers. Those of a more philosophical persuasion might be interested in:

- Schauer, F. (1991) *Playing by the Rules*, Oxford University Press, Oxford.
- Twining, W. and Miers, D. (1999) *How To Do Things with Rules*, Butterworths, London.

# HISTORY

To appreciate the peculiar nature of modern business, some readers may like to compare it against what came before. Two treatments of pre-modern economic activity are:

- Braudel, F. (1985) *The Wheels of Commerce*, Fontana Press, London.
- Cipolla, C. (1981) *Before the Industrial Revolution*, Methuen & Co Ltd, London.

Cipolla's is the shorter book. Braudel is also fascinating, but much longer.

# RELIGION

Christians were once as opposed to lending at interest and other capitalistic practices as some Muslims still are. Two books worth reading on religious responses to capitalism are:

- Tawney, R. H. (1964) *Religion and the Rise of Capitalism*, Penguin Books Ltd, Harmondsworth.
- Rodinson, M. (1977) *Islam and Capitalism*, Penguin Books Ltd, Harmondsworth.

# CONTROVERSY

Capitalism and the corporate form of business organization have attracted passionate criticism, and equally passionate defence. For serious criticism, try

- Marx, K. and Engels, F., *The Communist Manifesto* (first published in 1848, countless editions available).
- Bakan, J. (2005) *The Corporation: the Pathological Pursuit of Profit and Power*, Constable and Robinson, London.

Bakan has also produced an entertaining DVD with the same title. For more sanguine views of capitalism and the corporation respectively, consider

- De Soto, H. (2000) *The Mystery of Capital*, Bantam Press, London.
- Micklethwait, J. and Wooldridge, A. (2003) *The Company: A Short History of a Revolutionary Idea*, Phoenix, London.

# COMPANY FINANCIAL STATEMENTS

The financial statements of listed companies are available online. A search engine or Wikipedia.com will take you to the corporate website. Once there, look for a heading like 'investors' or 'investor relations' and then look for headings like 'financial', or 'publications', or especially 'annual reports'. Company information is also available through the market on which the company's shares are listed, for example:

- www.londonstockexchange.com
- www.nyse.com
- www.nasdaq.com

The most practical help available for reading and understanding company financial statements, which is regularly updated with a new edition, is:

- Holmes, G., Sugden, A. and Gee, P. (2004) *Interpreting Company Reports and Accounts*, FT Prentice Hall, Harlow.

# APPENDIX

# Control Accounts

This appendix describes the use of control accounts. These are a frequent source of confusion, largely because of the traditional terminology that is still employed in many cases. The appendix translates into more rational terms, and explains the procedures involved.

## THE SET OF ACCOUNTING LEDGERS

In the days when accounting entries were made in bound books or ledgers, a firm would often have too many accounts to be contained within a single ledger. The usual practice then was to divide the accounts into four separate ledgers. Modern accounting software continues to mimic these divisions, which were (and still are) called:

- the Cash Book, containing the firm's accounts for Bank and for Cash;
- the General Ledger, containing all other double entry accounts;
- the Debtors Ledger, containing a separate account for promises from and to each individual debtor;
- the Creditors Ledger, containing a separate account for promises to and from each individual creditor.

## TOTAL DEBTORS AND TOTAL CREDITORS

Still in the days before computer processing, when a firm made sales on credit to a large number of customers, or made purchases on credit from a large number of suppliers, it became difficult to discover at any time the total value of the firm's debtors or creditors. To find the total value of debtors would involve first balancing all the accounts in the Debtors Ledger, then finding the sum of all the balances. However, by the time the last debtor's account had been balanced, in all probability there would have been a transaction to change the balance on the first debtor's account, and so on. Likewise with creditors, it was difficult to determine at any time the total value owed by the firm to its suppliers.

The solution generally adopted was to have, in the General Ledger:

- a single account for promises from and to all debtors, as though they were the same person, which we might call the Total Debtors Account; and
- a single account for promises to and from all creditors, as though they were the same person, which we might call the Total Creditors Account.

These accounts would be part of the balancing double entry system and by balancing these accounts, the firm would be able to determine the total value receivable from its debtors, or payable to its creditors.

577

At the same time, but now completely outside the double entry system, the firm would maintain separate accounts for each individual debtor in the Debtors Ledger and for each individual creditor in the Creditors Ledger. From these accounts, the firm would be able to know how much was receivable from debtor A or debtor B, and how much was payable to creditor Y or creditor Z.

## HOW THE SYSTEM WORKED

The system, therefore, worked like this. Any transaction involving a debtor would be recorded with:

- balancing double entry in the Total Debtors Account and whatever other account(s) would be concerned in the General Ledger (usually Sales, Cash, or Discount Allowed);

and, quite separately, outside the balancing double entry system:

- a non-balancing single entry in the individual debtor's account in the Debtors Ledger.

Likewise with creditors. Any transaction involving a creditor would be recorded with:

- balancing double entry in the Total Creditors Account and whatever other account(s) would be concerned in the General Ledger (usually Purchases, Cash, or Discount Received);

and, quite separately, outside the balancing double entry system:

- a non-balancing single entry in the individual creditor's account in the Creditors Ledger.

Thus, for example, if the firm made a sale on credit to A, it would record the transaction with the usual double entry in the Total Debtors Account and the Sales Account, and then quite separately and outside the double entry system, it would record a DR in A's account in the Debtors Ledger. When the firm received any payment from A, it would record the transaction with the usual double entry in the Bank or Cash Account and the Total Debtors Account, and then, quite separately and outside the double entry system, it would record a CR in A's account in the Debtors Ledger.

## CONTROL ACCOUNTS

Under modern conditions, with accounting software, all of these entries are made simultaneously. There is no question of an entry being made in the Debtors Ledger which is not paralleled by an entry in the Total Debtors Account and vice versa. In the past, however, when accounting was done by hand and brain, with ink on paper, there were opportunities for errors and discrepancies. These, however, would be revealed by a difference between the balance on the Total Debtors Account, and the total of the individual balances in the Debtors Ledger (or in the case of creditors, by a difference between the balance on the Total Creditors Account, and the total of the individual balances in the Creditors Ledger).

Thus, the total accounts were used as a control on the accuracy of the individual accounts, and accordingly:

- the Total Debtors Account could be called the Debtors Ledger Control Account; and
- the Total Creditors Account could be called the Creditors Ledger Control Account.

(Notice, incidentally, how these alternative names reflect a concern with the control function of accounting, rather than its information content.)

# THE SALES LEDGER AND THE PURCHASE LEDGER

The ability to identify and correct any discrepancies between the Total Debtors Account and the total of Debtors Ledger balances (or between the Total Creditors Account and the total of Creditors Ledger balances) was once highly valued, and is still regarded as a sign of great virtuosity in double entry and book-keeping procedures. It still features in some examination courses, where the issue is often further complicated by the adoption of an extremely perverse traditional terminology:

- because of the connection between debtors and sales (debtors are customers), the Debtors Ledger is sometimes called the Sales Ledger; and
- because of the connection between creditors and purchases (creditors are suppliers); the Creditors Ledger is sometimes called the Purchase Ledger.

It follows that:

- the Total Debtors Account (one account for all debtors, as though they were the same person, which should, and does, carry a DR balance) is also, and most confusingly, called the Sales Ledger Control Account;

while:

- the Total Creditors Account (one account for all creditors, as though they were the same person, which should, and does, carry a CR balance) is also called the Purchase Ledger Control Account.

For those who must find their way through this confusion, the table below may offer some help.

| TRADITIONAL NAME | RATIONAL NAME | CONTENT | COMMENT |
|---|---|---|---|
| Sales Ledger | Debtors Ledger | separate accounts for each individual debtor | NOT normally part of the balancing double entry system |
| Purchase Ledger | Creditors Ledger | separate accounts for each individual creditor | NOT normally part of the balancing double entry system |
| Sales Ledger Control Account | Total Debtors Account | one account in the General Ledger for all debtors as though they were the same person | normally part of the balancing double entry system – should carry a DR balance |
| Purchase Ledger Control Account | Total Creditors Account | one account in the General Ledger for all creditors as though they were the same person | normally part of the balancing double entry system – should carry a CR balance |

# ANSWER SECTION

Fully worked answers to all drills, and comments on the exercises, are provided on the website www.cengage.co.uk/hodge. This section contains a sample of short answers for immediate reference, if needed.

Learning to use the accounting model is to some extent like learning to drive. The procedures are not difficult, but it takes much practice to perform them smoothly and with confidence. Many drills, therefore, have been provided in the text and many of these are quite repetitive (like hill starts, changing gear and so on). In this section we provide enough answers for each kind of drill for students to check that their approach is on the right lines, after which they should be able to proceed with confidence. Students who meet with particular difficulties, or who wish to check their work in detail, may refer to the website. But remember always that accounting is *not* about answers – it is about procedures, the model and the method. Real life has no answer at the back of the book. We must practise doing what we think is right.

## PART ONE *Chapters 1–3*

**2.1**  T = transaction; N = not a transaction; D = debatable – see website

| | |
|---|---|
| 1. T | 6. T |
| 2. T | 7. N |
| 3. N | 8. D |
| 4. T | 9. D |
| 5. N | 10. N |

**2.2**  1. an oil refinery:
input(s): crude oil, energy, labour, machinery
output(s): refined products
process: refining and separation

2. a chocolate factory:
input(s): sugar, cocoa beans, labour, machinery, energy
output(s): chocolate bars, etc.
process: manufacturing

*see website for answers 3–20.*

**2.3**  1. a water company
input(s): pipes, labour
output(s): water
process: collection, purification and distribution

*see website for answers 2–12.*

**2.4**  See text: accountants record transactions; consumption and creation are not transactions.

**2.5**  These questions are worth *thinking* about. Some comments are offered on the website.

**3.1**  V = value; M = money; E = could be either

| | |
|---|---|
| 1. V | 5. E |
| 2. V | 6. V |
| 3. V | 7. M (but see website) |
| 4. V | 8. V |

**3.2**  Value and exchange value

*see website for comments.*

# PART TWO *Chapters 4–24*

**4.1**

**2.**

| IN | cash | £700 | |
|---|---|---|---|
| OUT | sales | | £700 |

**3.**

| IN | cement mixer | £5 000 | |
|---|---|---|---|
| OUT | cash | | £5 000 |

**4.**

| IN | labour | £150 | |
|---|---|---|---|
| OUT | cash | | £150 |

**5.**

| IN | window cleaning | £15 | |
|---|---|---|---|
| OUT | cash | | £15 |

**6.**

| IN | cash | £250 | |
|---|---|---|---|
| OUT | permission to use building | | £250 |

**7.**

| IN | cash | £70 | |
|---|---|---|---|
| OUT | sales | | £70 |

**8.**

| IN | labour | £1 500 | |
|---|---|---|---|
| OUT | cash | | £1 500 |

**9.**

| IN | benefit of advertising | £500 | |
|---|---|---|---|
| OUT | cash | | £500 |

**10.**

| IN | cash | £450 | |
|---|---|---|---|
| OUT | advice/service/sales | | £450 |

*see website for remaining 4.1 answers*

**4.2**

1. firm sells goods for £80 cash
2. firm buys goods for £100 cash
3. firm pays wages £60 cash
4. firm pays rent £450 cash
5. firm pays £95 cash refund on goods previously sold
6. firm receives £18 cash refund on goods returned to supplier
7. firm pays £55 interest in cash
8. firm pays telephone bill £105 in cash
9. legal firm receives £150 cash payment from client
10. firm pays taxi fare £12 cash
11. firm pays £180 cash for insurance
12. school or training centre receives £290 cash for lessons
13. firm buys machinery for £150 cash
14. firm pays £48 cash for membership of trade association
15. firm pays £55 cash for vehicle license.

**5.1**  1.  (a)

| | | | |
|---|---|---|---|
| IN | *purchases* | *£35* | |
| OUT | *promise to A* | | *£35* |

(b)

| | | | |
|---|---|---|---|
| IN | promise from A | £60 | |
| OUT | cash | | £60 |

2.  (a)

| | | | |
|---|---|---|---|
| IN | promise from B | £70 | |
| OUT | sales | | £70 |

(b)

| | | | |
|---|---|---|---|
| IN | cash | £70 | |
| OUT | promise to B | | £70 |

3.  (a)

| | | | |
|---|---|---|---|
| IN | promise from C | £150 | |
| OUT | sales | | £150 |

(b)

| | | | |
|---|---|---|---|
| IN | cash | £150 | |
| OUT | promise to C | | £150 |

*see website for answers 4–15.*

**5.2**  1.  (a)

| | | | |
|---|---|---|---|
| IN | purchases | £15 | |
| OUT | promise to supplier | | £15 |

(b)

| | | | |
|---|---|---|---|
| IN | promise from supplier | £15 | |
| OUT | purchases | | £15 |

2.  (a)

| | | | |
|---|---|---|---|
| IN | promise from customer | £10 | |
| OUT | sales | | £10 |

(b)

| | | | |
|---|---|---|---|
| IN | sales | £10 | |
| OUT | promise to customer | | £10 |

3.  (a)

| | | | |
|---|---|---|---|
| IN | purchases | £65 | |
| OUT | promise to supplier | | £65 |

(b)

| | | | |
|---|---|---|---|
| IN | promise from supplier | £45 | |
| OUT | purchases | | £45 |

*see website for answers 4–10.*

**5.3**  1.  (a) firm sells goods on credit to A for £80
    (b) firm receives £80 cash from A
2.  (a) firm buys goods on credit from S for £60
    (b) firm pays £60 cash to S
3.  (a) firm buys goods on credit from X for £145
    (b) firm returns goods value £45 to X
    (c) firm pays X £100 cash

*see website for answers 4–6.*

**5.4**  There are no definitive answers to these exercises. Some comments may be found on the website.

**6.1**   1.

| IN | labour | £50 | |
|---|---|---|---|
| OUT | (promise to) bank | | £50 |

2.

| IN | (promise to) bank | £300 | |
|---|---|---|---|
| OUT | sales | | £300 |

3.

| IN | purchases | £450 | |
|---|---|---|---|
| OUT | bank | | £450 |

4.

| IN | bank | £75 | |
|---|---|---|---|
| OUT | cash | | £75 |

5.

| IN | cash | £100 | |
|---|---|---|---|
| OUT | bank | | £100 |

*see website for remaining answers.*

**6.2**   1. firm sells goods for £30, receiving payment by cheque
2. firm buys goods for £40, paying by cheque
3. firm pays wages £50 by cheque
4. firm puts £56 cash into the bank
5. firm pays £37 to A by cheque

*see website for remaining answers.*

**6.3**   There are no definitive answers to the exercises. Some comments may be found on the website.

**7.1**   1.   (a)

| IN | bank | £1 000 | |
|---|---|---|---|
| OUT | promise to XYZ | | £1 000 |

(b)

| IN | permission to use money (interest) | £40 | |
|---|---|---|---|
| OUT | bank | | £40 |

(c)

| IN | promise from XYZ | £600 | |
|---|---|---|---|
| OUT | bank | | £600 |

2.   (a)

| IN | promise from ABC | £800 | |
|---|---|---|---|
| OUT | bank | | £800 |

(b)

| IN | bank | £20 | |
|---|---|---|---|
| OUT | permission to use money (interest) | | £20 |

(c)

| IN | bank | £500 | |
|---|---|---|---|
| OUT | promise to ABC | | £500 |

3.

| IN | permission to use money (interest) | £250 | |
|---|---|---|---|
| IN | promise back from lender | £200 | |
| OUT | bank | | £450 |

4.

| | | | |
|---|---|---|---|
| IN | bank | £275 | |
| OUT | permission to use money | | £25 |
| OUT | promise back to borrower | | £250 |

5.

| | | | |
|---|---|---|---|
| IN | bank | £1 000 | |
| IN | cash | £200 | |
| OUT | promise to lender | | £1 200 |

6.

| | | | |
|---|---|---|---|
| IN | promise back from lender | £300 | |
| IN | permission to use money | £100 | |
| OUT | bank | | £350 |
| OUT | cash | | £50 |

**7.2** 1.

| | | | |
|---|---|---|---|
| IN | computer equipment | £500 | |
| IN | software | £200 | |
| OUT | bank | | £300 |
| OUT | promise to supplier | | £400 |

2.

| | | | |
|---|---|---|---|
| IN | truck | £20 000 | |
| IN | trailer | £5 000 | |
| IN | refrigerator unit | £7 000 | |
| IN | fuel | £200 | |
| OUT | bank | | £32 200 |

**7.3**
1. firm borrows £3 000 from XYZ, receiving cheque.
2. firm repays £1 000 by cheque to XYZ.
3. firm pays £1 000 by cheque to lender, being £200 interest and £800 repayment of loan.
4. firm buys equipment for £900, paying £100 cash, £300 by cheque, with the remaining £500 on credit.
5. customer returns goods value £100, and firm gives refund of £30 cash and £70 on account.
6. firm returns goods value £450 to supplier, receiving £50 refund by cheque, and £400 refund on account.

**8.1** 1.

| | | | |
|---|---|---|---|
| IN | 'protection' | £1 400 | |
| OUT | cash | | £1 400 |

2.

| | | | |
|---|---|---|---|
| IN | bank | £500 | |
| OUT | prize (or prize-winning effort) | | £500 |

3.

| | | | |
|---|---|---|---|
| IN | political contribution (influence?) | £1 000 | |
| OUT | cash | | £1 000 |

4.

| | | | |
|---|---|---|---|
| IN | winning ticket | £20m | |
| OUT | bank | | £20m |

5.

| | | | |
|---|---|---|---|
| IN | parking fine | £60 | |
| OUT | cash | | £60 |

6.

| | | | |
|---|---|---|---|
| IN | bank | £5 000 | |
| OUT | prize (or environmental awareness) | | £5 000 |

7.

| | | | |
|---|---|---|---|
| IN | compensation | £50 | |
| OUT | cash | | £50 |

8.

| | | | |
|---|---|---|---|
| IN | bank | £1 000 | |
| OUT | insurance claim | | £1 000 |

9.

| | | | |
|---|---|---|---|
| IN | purchases | £1 000 | |
| OUT | cash | | £1 000 |

10.

| | | | |
|---|---|---|---|
| IN | cash | £2 000 | |
| OUT | sales | | £2 000 |

11. (a)

| | | | |
|---|---|---|---|
| IN | penalty | £2 000 | |
| OUT | promise to pay penalty | | £2 000 |

(b)

| | | | |
|---|---|---|---|
| IN | promise to pay penalty | £2 000 | |
| OUT | bank | | £2 000 |

12. (a)

| | | | |
|---|---|---|---|
| IN | tax assessment | £700 | |
| OUT | promise to pay tax (=tax liability) | | £700 |

(b)

| | | | |
|---|---|---|---|
| IN | promise to pay tax | £700 | |
| OUT | bank | | £700 |

13.

| | | | |
|---|---|---|---|
| IN | theft | £1 800 | |
| OUT | cash | | £1 800 |

14.

| | | | |
|---|---|---|---|
| IN | cash | £250 | |
| OUT | donation | | £250 |

15.

| | | | |
|---|---|---|---|
| IN | negligence | £750 | |
| OUT | promise to pay victim | | £750 |

**8.2**   1. £100 cash is stolen from firm
   2. firm receives notice of liability to pay £450 tax
   3. business pays £120 tax by cheque
   4. business pays £60 blackmail
   5. business pays £16 parking fine
   6. business receives £300 government grant by cheque
   7. business pays £250 to charity by cheque
   8. business receives £600 cheque as prize

**8.3**   *See comments on website.*

**9.1**   1.   (a) no transaction
            (b) no transaction
            (c) transaction: IN money, OUT sales
            (d) transaction: IN purchases, OUT promise to supplier
            (e) transaction: IN promise from supplier, OUT bank

         2.   (a) transaction: IN purchases, OUT bank
            (b) no transaction

         3.   (a) no transaction
            (b) transaction: IN promise from customer, OUT sales
            (c) no transaction
            (d) transaction: IN bank, OUT promise to customer

         4.   (a) transaction: IN bank, OUT sales
            (b) no transaction

         5.   (a) no transaction
            (b) no transaction
            (c) transaction: IN promise from customer, OUT sales

         6.   (a) no transaction
            (b) no transaction
            (c) no transaction
            (d) no transaction
            (e) transaction: IN electricity, OUT promise to Electricity Company

**9.2**   *See website for comments.*

**10.1**  1.

| | | | |
|---|---|---|---|
| IN | cash | £300 | |
| OUT | capital (promise to owner) | | £300 |

         2.

| | | | |
|---|---|---|---|
| IN | machine | £450 | |
| OUT | capital | | £450 |

         3.

| | | | |
|---|---|---|---|
| IN | bank | £500 | |
| OUT | capital | | £500 |

         4.

| | | | |
|---|---|---|---|
| IN | capital (promise back from owner) | £50 | |
| OUT | cash | | £50 |

         5.

| | | | |
|---|---|---|---|
| IN | capital | £40 | |
| OUT | purchases | | £40 |

**10.2**  1. owner puts £100 cash into business
         2. owner takes £20 cash out of business
         3. owner puts machine value £500 into business
         4. owner takes goods value £500 out of business stock

### 11.1 BUSINESS A

#### Cash

| (1) | 1 000 | (4) | 750 |
| (5) | 900 | (8) | 220 |
| (6) | 100 | (9) | 500 |

#### Capital

| (10) | 30 | (1) | 1000 |

#### Purchases

| (2) | 800 | | |
| (7) | 200 | | |

#### Promises from/to Supplier X

| (4) | 750 | (2) | 800 |
| (8) | 220 | (7) | 200 |

#### Promises from/to Customer Y

| (3) | 900 | (5) | 900 |

#### Sales

| | | (3) | 900 |
| | | (6) | 100 |

#### Bank

| (9) | 500 | (10) | 30 |

### BUSINESS B

#### Bank

| (1) | 750 | (7) | 80 |
| (2) | 250 | (9) | 110 |
| (8) | 250 | (10) | 20 |

#### Capital

| | | (1) | 750 |

#### XYZ

| (9) | 100 | (2) | 250 |

#### Purchases

| (3) | 500 | (6) | 80 |

#### Promises from/to S

| (6) | 80 | (3) | 500 |

#### Sales

| (5) | 100 | (4) | 400 |

#### Promises from/to C

| (4) | 400 | (5) | 100 |
| | | (8) | 250 |

#### Wages (labour)

| (7) | 80 | | |
| (10) | 20 | | |

#### Interest (permission to use money)

| (9) | 10 | | |

BUSINESS C

| Bank | | | | Capital | | | |
|---|---|---|---|---|---|---|---|
| (1) | 2 000 | (4) | 200 | (10) | 50 | (1) | 2 000 |
| (5) | 1 200 | (7) | 250 | | | | |
| | | (8) | 50 | | | | |
| | | (9) | 1 000 | | | | |

| Purchases | | | | Promises from/to P | | | |
|---|---|---|---|---|---|---|---|
| (2) | 1 500 | (10) | 50 | (9) | 1 000 | (2) | 1 500 |

| Promises from/to Q | | | | Sales | | | |
|---|---|---|---|---|---|---|---|
| (3) | 1 300 | (5) | 1 200 | (6) | 100 | (3) | 1 300 |
| | | (6) | 100 | | | | |

| Rent (permission to use building) | | Insurance | |
|---|---|---|---|
| (4) | 200 | (7) | 250 |

| Parking Fine | |
|---|---|
| (8) | 50 |

**12.1**      A

1.

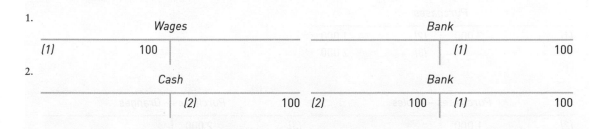

| Wages | | Bank | |
|---|---|---|---|
| (1) | 100 | (1) | 100 |

2.

| Cash | | Bank | |
|---|---|---|---|
| (2) | 100 | (2) | 100 | (1) | 100 |

*see website for B and C.*

**D**

**1.**

| Purchases | | | | Promises from/to X | | | |
|---|---|---|---|---|---|---|---|
| (1) | 1 000 | | | | | (1) | 1 000 |

**2.**

| Purchases | | | | Promises from/to X | | | |
|---|---|---|---|---|---|---|---|
| (1) | 1 000 | (2) | 100 | (2) | 100 | (1) | 1 000 |

**E**

**1.**

| Promises from/to Y | | | | Sales | | | |
|---|---|---|---|---|---|---|---|
| (1) | 1 500 | | | | | (1) | 1 500 |

**2.**

| Promises from/to Y | | | | Promises from/to Z | | | |
|---|---|---|---|---|---|---|---|
| (1) | 1 500 | (2) | 1 500 | (2) | 1 500 | | |

**F**

**1.**

| Purchases | | | | Promises from/to Supplier | | | |
|---|---|---|---|---|---|---|---|
| (1) | 3 000 | | | | | (1) | 3 000 |

**2.**

| Purchases | | | |
|---|---|---|---|
| (1) | 3 000 | (2) | 1 000 |
| | | (3) | 2 000 |

| Purchases – Apples | | | | Purchases – Oranges | | | |
|---|---|---|---|---|---|---|---|
| (2) | 1 000 | | | (3) | 2 000 | | |

G

1.

| Pencils | | | | Bank | | | |
|---|---|---|---|---|---|---|---|
| *(1)* | 10 | | | | | *(1)* | 10 |

2.

| Paper | | | | Bank | | | |
|---|---|---|---|---|---|---|---|
| *(2)* | 40 | | | | | *(1)* | 10 |
| | | | | | | *(2)* | 40 |

3.

| Pencils | | | | Stationery | | | |
|---|---|---|---|---|---|---|---|
| *(1)* | 10 | *(3)* | 10 | *(3)* | 10 | | |
| | | | | *(3)* | 40 | | |

| Paper | | | |
|---|---|---|---|
| *(2)* | 40 | *(3)* | 40 |

*see website for H–O.*

**13.1**     E

1.

| A | | B | |
|---|---|---|---|
| 200 | 100 | 200 | 700 |
| 300 | | 400 | |

2.

| A | | B | |
|---|---|---|---|
| | c/f 400 | c/f 100 | |
| 500 | 500 | 700 | 700 |
| b/f 400 | | | b/f 100 |

| C | | D | |
|---|---|---|---|
| 750 | 50 | 30 | 25 |
| 250 | 150 | 10 | 80 |
| | 300 | 60 | |
| | 100 | | |
| | c/f 400 | c/f 5 | |
| 1 000 | 1 000 | 105 | 105 |
| b/f 400 | | | b/f 5 |

### E

| | | | |
|---|---|---|---|
| | | | 1 000 |
| | | | 4 500 |
| | | | 1 500 |
| c/f | 7 000 | | 7 000 |
| | 7 000 | | 7 000 |
| | | b/f | 7 000 |

### F

| | | | |
|---|---|---|---|
| | | | 600 |
| | | | 400 |
| | | | 250 |
| | | | 750 |
| | | | 500 |
| | | c/f | 2 500 |
| | | | 2 500 |
| b/f | | | 2 500 |

### G

| | | | |
|---|---|---|---|
| | 10 | | 460 |
| | 40 | | 15 |
| | 70 | | 25 |
| | 30 | | |
| | 50 | | |
| c/f | 300 | | |
| | 500 | | 500 |
| | | b/f | 300 |

### H

| | | | |
|---|---|---|---|
| | 350 | | 625 |
| | 450 | | 325 |
| | 200 | | |
| | 300 | | |
| | 175 | | |
| | 225 | | |
| | | c/f | 750 |
| | 1 700 | | 1 700 |
| | | b/f | 750 |

### I

| | | | |
|---|---|---|---|
| | 113 | | 789 |
| | 378 | | 436 |
| | 16 | | 154 |
| | 205 | | |
| | 1 330 | c/f | 663 |
| | 2 042 | | 2042 |
| b/f | 663 | | |

### J

| | | | |
|---|---|---|---|
| | 555 | | 2 361 |
| | 476 | | 1 567 |
| | 450 | | 552 |
| | 3 287 | | 4 513 |
| | 881 | | |
| | 1 858 | | |
| | 97 | | |
| c/f | 1 389 | | |
| | 8 993 | | 8 993 |
| | | b/f | 1 389 |

### K

| | | | |
|---|---|---|---|
| | 1 881 | | 4 361 |
| | 308 | | 4 570 |
| | 330 | | |
| | 2 699 | | |
| | 3 713 | | |
| | 8 931 | | 8 931 |

### L

| | | | |
|---|---|---|---|
| | 5 234 | | 1 442 |
| | 2 839 | | 926 |
| | 542 | | 2 654 |
| | | | 65 |
| | | | 1 457 |
| | | | 146 |
| | | c/f | 1 925 |
| | 8 615 | | 8 615 |
| b/f | | | 1 925 |

**13.2** *See website for comments.*

**14.1**    1. should carry CR balance
      2. should carry DR balance
      3. should carry DR balance
      4. should carry CR balance
      5. could be either
      6. should carry DR or nil balance
      7. should carry CR balance
      8. should carry DR balance
      9. should carry DR balance
    10. should carry DR balance
    11. should carry CR balance
    12. should carry DR balance
    13. should carry CR balance
    14. should carry CR balance
    15. should carry DR balance
    16. should carry CR balance
    17. should carry DR balance
    18. should carry DR balance
    19. should carry DR balance
    20. should carry DR balance
    21. should carry nil balance
    22. should carry nil balance
    23. should carry CR balance
    24. should carry DR balance
    25. should carry DR balance

**14.2**    1. DR should be in cash or debtor's account, to record sale
      2. CR should be in cash or debtor's account, to record refund
      3. CR should be in cash or supplier's account, to record purchase
      4. DR should be in cash or supplier's account, to record refund
      5. CR should be in sales account, to record sale on credit
      6. DR should be in cash account, to record payment from debtor
      7. DR should be in a supplier's account, to record payment to a supplier
      8. CR should be in debtor's account, to record payment received
      9. CR should be in cash account, to record payment to creditor
    10. DR should be in purchases account, to record purchase on credit
    11. CR should be in sales account, to record sale for cash
    12. DR should be in wages account, to record payment of wages
    13. DR should be in bank account, to record value put in by owner
    14. CR should be in bank account, to record value taken out by owner
    15. CR should be in account for Electricity Company, to record use of electricity
    16. DR should be in account for Electricity Company, to record correction of error
    17. CR should be in bank or landlord's account, to record payment or promise to pay
    18. DR should be in bank or landlord's account, to record repayment or promise to repay
    19. CR should be in sales account, to record sale on credit
    20. DR should be in cash or bank, to record payment from customer
    21. CR should be in bank account to record payment, or in purchases account to record return of goods
    22. DR should be in input account, to record supply coming in
    23. DR should be in bank account, to record receipt of borrowed money
    24. CR should be in bank account, to record repayment to lender
    25. CR should be in bank or cash, to record payment of wages
    26. DR should be in bank or cash, to record recovery of overpaid wages
    27. DR should be in cash or supplier's account, to record refund or promise of refund
    28. CR should be in supplier's account, to correct a mistake in recording too big a figure for purchase returns
    29. DR should be in customer's account, to correct a mistake in recording too big a figure for sales returns
    30. CR should be in bank or customer's account, to record repayment or promise to repay
    31. CR should be in bank or advertising supplier's account, to pay for advertising
    32. DR should be in bank or advertising supplier's account, to claim refund or correct mistake

**14.3**   1. customer has overpaid, or paid a deposit in advance of sale
      2. firm has overpaid supplier
      3. overdraft
      4. must be mistake
      5. owner must pay in to firm

**15.1**   A

| TRIAL BALANCE | DR | CR |
|---|---|---|
| sales | | 350 |
| purchases | 260 | |
| capital | | 400 |
| wages | 150 | |
| furniture | 380 | |
| bank | | 80 |
| customer | 100 | |
| interest | 10 | |
| supplier | | 70 |
| TOTAL | 900 | 900 |

this TB does balance, showing that transactions were recorded with equal DR and CR, and the accounts have been properly balanced, and the list of balances is complete.

B

| TRIAL BALANCE | DR | CR |
|---|---|---|
| bank | 40 | |
| capital | | 210 |
| debtor | 110 | |
| machinery | 200 | |
| electricity | 25 | |
| purchases | 130 | |
| sales | | 250 |
| creditor | | 75 |
| wages | 50 | |
| TOTAL | 555 | 535 |

this TB does not balance, indicating either that transactions were not recorded with equal DR and CR, or that the accounts were not properly balanced, or that the list is incomplete.

**15.2**   A

### Bank

| | | | |
|---|---|---|---|
| (1) | 500 | (4) | 400 |
| (5) | 500 | (7) | 100 |
| (9) | 350 | (10) | 40 |
| | | c/f | 810 |
| | 1 350 | | 1 350 |
| b/f | 810 | | |

### Capital

| | | | |
|---|---|---|---|
| | | (1) | 500 |

### Purchases

| | | | |
|---|---|---|---|
| (2) | 400 | | |
| (8) | 300 | | |
| | | c/f | 700 |
| | 700 | | 700 |
| b/f | 700 | | |

### Promises from/to X

| | | | |
|---|---|---|---|
| (4) | 400 | (2) | 400 |
| | | (8) | 300 |
| c/f | 300 | | |
| | 700 | | 700 |
| | | b/f | 300 |

### Sales

| | | | |
|---|---|---|---|
| (6) | 200 | (3) | 700 |
| | | (9) | 350 |
| c/f | 850 | | |
| | 1 050 | | 1 050 |
| | | b/f | 850 |

### Promises from/to Y

| | | | |
|---|---|---|---|
| (3) | 700 | (5) | 500 |
| | | (6) | 200 |
| | 700 | | 700 |

### Wages (labour)

| | |
|---|---|
| (7) | 100 |

### Electricity

| | |
|---|---|
| (10) | 40 |

| TRIAL BALANCE | DR | CR |
|---|---|---|
| bank | 810 | |
| capital | | 500 |
| purchases | 700 | |
| promises from/to X | | 300 |
| sales | | 850 |
| wages | 100 | |
| electricity | 40 | |
| total | 1 650 | 1 650 |

B

**Bank**

| | | | |
|---|---|---|---|
| (1) | 750 | (3) | 600 |
| (2) | 500 | (6) | 150 |
| (10) | 900 | (7) | 50 |
| | | (8) | 300 |
| | | c/f | 1 050 |
| | 2 150 | | 2 150 |
| b/f | 1 050 | | |

**Capital**

| | | | |
|---|---|---|---|
| (7) | 50 | (1) | 750 |
| c/f | 700 | | |
| | 750 | | 750 |
| | | b/f | 700 |

**ABC Finance**

| | | | |
|---|---|---|---|
| | | (2) | 500 |

**Machinery**

| | |
|---|---|
| (3) | 600 |

**Raw Materials**

| | |
|---|---|
| (4) | 300 |

**Promises from/to S**

| | | | |
|---|---|---|---|
| (8) | 300 | (4) | 300 |

**Promises from/to C**

| | | | |
|---|---|---|---|
| (5) | 850 | (10) | 900 |
| (9) | 150 | | |
| | | c/f | 100 |
| | 1 000 | | 1 000 |
| b/f | 100 | | |

**Sales**

| | | | |
|---|---|---|---|
| | | (5) | 850 |
| | | (9) | 150 |
| c/f | 1 000 | | |
| | 1 000 | | 1 000 |
| | | b/f | 1 000 |

**Wages**

| | |
|---|---|
| (6) | 150 |

| TRIAL BALANCE | DR | CR |
|---|---|---|
| bank | 1 050 | |
| capital | | 700 |
| ABC Finance | | 500 |
| machinery | 600 | |
| raw materials | 300 | |
| promises from/to S | | |
| promises from/to C | 100 | |
| sales | | 1 000 |
| wages | 150 | |
| TOTAL | 2 200 | 2 200 |

**15.3** *See website.*

**16.1** BUSINESS 1

| Bank | | |
|---|---|---|
| balance at end of period | 250 | |

| Capital | | |
|---|---|---|
| | | balance at end of period | 50 |

| Purchases | | |
|---|---|---|
| balance at end of period | 600 | to P&L | 600 |

| Sales | | |
|---|---|---|
| to P&L | 800 | balance at end of period | 800 |

| P&L Account for Period 1 | | |
|---|---|---|
| purchases | 600 | sales | 800 |
| | | closing stock | 100 |
| c/f | 300 | | |
| | 900 | | 900 |
| | | b/f profit | 300 |

| Stock | | |
|---|---|---|
| from P&L | 100 | |

*Business 2, 3 and 4: see website.*

**16.2    BUSINESS 1**

| Bank | | | |
|---|---|---|---|
| *(1)* | 1 500 | | |

| Capital | | | |
|---|---|---|---|
| | | to P&L | 1 500 |

| Purchases | | | |
|---|---|---|---|
| *(2)* | 1 800 | *to P&L* | 1 800 |

| Promises from/to Supplier | | | |
|---|---|---|---|
| | | *(2)* | 1 800 |

| Promises from/to Customer | | | |
|---|---|---|---|
| *(2)* | 2 100 | | |

| Sales | | | |
|---|---|---|---|
| *to P&L* | 2 100 | *(3)* | 2 100 |

| P&L Account | | | |
|---|---|---|---|
| purchase | 1 800 | *sales* | 2 100 |
| c/f | 1 100 | closing stock | 800 |
| | 2 900 | | 2 900 |
| | | b/f profit | 1 100 |

| Stock | | | |
|---|---|---|---|
| from P&L | 800 | | |

**BUSINESS 2**

| Bank | | | |
|---|---|---|---|
| *(1)* | 5 000 | | |

| Capital | | | |
|---|---|---|---|
| | | *(1)* | 5 000 |

| Purchases | | | |
|---|---|---|---|
| *(2)* | 4 700 | *to P&L* | 4 700 |

| Promises from/to Supplier | | | |
|---|---|---|---|
| | | *(2)* | 4 700 |

| Promises from/to Customer | | | |
|---|---|---|---|
| *(3)* | 3 000 | | |

| Sales | | | |
|---|---|---|---|
| *to P&L* | 3 000 | *(3)* | 3 000 |

| P&L Account | | | |
|---|---|---|---|
| purchase | 4 700 | *sales* | 3 000 |
| | | closing stock | 700 |
| | | c/f | 1 000 |
| | 4 700 | | 4 700 |
| b/f loss | 1 000 | | |

| Stock | | | |
|---|---|---|---|
| from P&L | 700 | | |

*Business 3 and 4: see website.*

**17.1 BUSINESS 1**

| Bank | | |
|---|---|---|
| *(1)* | 750 | |

| Capital | | |
|---|---|---|
| | | *(1)* | 750 |
| | | profit | 500 |

| Purchases | | |
|---|---|---|
| *(2)* | 900 | to P&L | 900 |

| Promises from/to Supplier | | |
|---|---|---|
| | | *(2)* | 900 |

| Promises from/to Customer | | |
|---|---|---|
| *(3)* | 1 000 | |

| Sales | | |
|---|---|---|
| to P&L | 1 000 | *(3)* | 1 000 |

**P&L Account**

| | | | |
|---|---|---|---|
| purchases | 900 | sales | 1 000 |
| c/f | 500 | closing stock | 400 |
| | 1 400 | | 1 400 |
| to capital | 500 | b/f profit | 500 |

**Stock**

| | |
|---|---|
| from P&L | 400 |

**BUSINESS 2**

| Bank | | |
|---|---|---|
| *(1)* | 2 500 | |

| Capital | | |
|---|---|---|
| loss | 500 | *(1)* | 2 500 |

| Purchases | | |
|---|---|---|
| *(2)* | 2 350 | to P&L | 2 350 |

| Promises from/to Supplier | | |
|---|---|---|
| | | *(2)* | 2 350 |

| Promises from/to Customer | | |
|---|---|---|
| *(3)* | 1 500 | |

| Sales | | |
|---|---|---|
| to P&L | 1 500 | *(3)* | 1 500 |

**P&L Account**

| | | | |
|---|---|---|---|
| purchases | 2 350 | sales | 1 500 |
| | | closing stock | 350 |
| | | c/f | 500 |
| | 2 350 | | 2 350 |
| b/f loss | 500 | to capital | 500 |

**Stock**

| | |
|---|---|
| from P&L | 350 |

*Business 3 and 4: see website.*

**17.2** Rows B and C appear to ignore the fact that capital is the dependent variable in the balance sheet equation. You cannot use the value of capital to find the value of assets or liabilities in the equation, because you cannot know the value of capital unless you already know the value of assets and liabilities.

**17.3**
1. profit £50
2. profit £50
3. profit £350
4. loss £150
5. With an increase in net assets of £50 after the owner has taken out £30, the firm must have made a profit of £80.
6. With an increase in net assets of only £50 after the owner has put in £200, the firm must have made a loss of £150.
7. With an increase in net assets of £350 after the owner has taken out a net value £500, the firm must have made a profit £850.

**18.1** BUSINESS 1

**Sales**

| | | | |
|---|---|---|---|
| | | balance at end of period | 700 |
| to P&L | 700 | | |

**Purchases**

| | | | |
|---|---|---|---|
| balance at end of period | 500 | to P&L | 500 |

**Bank**

| | | |
|---|---|---|
| balance at end of period | 250 | |

**Debtors**

| | |
|---|---|
| balance at end of period | 100 |

**Creditors**

| | | | |
|---|---|---|---|
| | | balance at end of period | 50 |

**Capital**

| | | | |
|---|---|---|---|
| | | balance at end of period | 100 |
| c/f | 380 | profit | 280 |
| | 380 | | 380 |
| | | b/f | 380 |

**P&L Account for Period**

| | | | |
|---|---|---|---|
| purchases | 500 | sales | 700 |
| c/f | 280 | closing stock | 80 |
| | 780 | | 780 |
| to capital | 280 | b/f profit | 280 |

**Stock**

| | | |
|---|---|---|
| from P&L | 80 | |

| BUSINESS 1 BALANCE SHEET AT END OF PERIOD 1 | |
| --- | --- |
| **Assets** | |
| Stock | 80 |
| Debtors | 100 |
| Bank | 250 |
| | 430 |
| **Liabilities** | |
| Creditors | (50) |
| Net Assets | £380 |
| Capital | £ 380 |

*Business 2: see website.*

**18.2    BUSINESS 1**

| Bank | | | | Capital | | | |
| --- | --- | --- | --- | --- | --- | --- | --- |
| (1) | 900 | | | | | (1) | 900 |
| | | | | c/f | 1 350 | profit | 450 |
| | | | | | 1 350 | | 1 350 |
| | | | | | | b/f | 1 350 |

| Purchases | | | | Promises from/to Supplier | | | |
| --- | --- | --- | --- | --- | --- | --- | --- |
| (2) | 850 | to P&L | 850 | | | (2) | 850 |

| Promises from/to Customer | | | | Sales | | | |
| --- | --- | --- | --- | --- | --- | --- | --- |
| (3) | 950 | | | to P&L | 950 | (3) | 950 |

| P&L Account | | | | Stock | | |
| --- | --- | --- | --- | --- | --- | --- |
| purchases | 850 | sales | 950 | from P&L | 350 | |
| c/f | 450 | closing stock | 350 | | | |
| | 1 300 | | 1 300 | | | |
| to capital | 450 | b/f profit | 450 | | | |

### BUSINESS 1 BALANCE SHEET AT END OF PERIOD 1

| Assets | | |
|---|---|---|
| Stock | | 350 |
| Debtors | | 950 |
| Bank | | 900 |
| | | 2 200 |
| Liabilities | | |
| Creditors | | (850) |
| Net Assets | | £1 350 |
| Capital | | £1 350 |

*Business 2: see website.*

**19.1   BUSINESS 1**

*P&L Account*

| purchases | 700 | sales | 900 |
|---|---|---|---|
| opening stock | 120 | closing stock | 160 |
| c/f | 240 | | |
| | 1 060 | | 1 060 |
| to capital | 240 | b/f profit | 240 |

### BUSINESS 1 BALANCE SHEET AT END OF PERIOD 1

| Assets | |
|---|---|
| Stock | 160 |
| Debtors | 250 |
| Bank | 900 |
| | 1 310 |
| Liabilities | |
| Creditors | (760) |
| loan | (130) |
| Net Assets | £420 |
| Capital | £420 |

*Business 2: see website.*

**19.2**   BUSINESS 1

Period 1

#### P&L Account for Period 1

| purchases | 900 | sales | 1 100 |
|---|---|---|---|
| c/f | 500 | closing stock | 300 |
| | 1 400 | | 1 400 |
| to capital | 500 | b/f profit | 500 |

#### BUSINESS 1 BALANCE SHEET AT END OF PERIOD 1

| Assets | |
|---|---|
| Stock | 300 |
| Debtors | 1 100 |
| Bank | 1 000 |
| | 2 400 |
| Liabilities | |
| Creditors | (900) |
| Net Assets | £1 500 |
| Captial | £1 500 |

Period 2

#### P&L Account for Period 2

| purchases | 1 200 | sales | 2 500 |
|---|---|---|---|
| opening stock | 300 | closing stock | 800 |
| c/f | 1 800 | | |
| | 3 300 | | 3 300 |
| to capital | 1 800 | b/f profit | 1 800 |

#### BUSINESS 1 BALANCE SHEET AT END OF PERIOD 2

| Assets | |
|---|---|
| Stock | 800 |
| Debtors | 2 600 |
| Bank | 1 150 |
| | 4 550 |
| Liabilities | |
| Creditors | (1 250) |
| Net Assets | £3 300 |
| Capital | £3 300 |

*Business 2: see website.*

**20.1**   Case 1
1. if closing stock is valued at £75, profit would be £175
2. if closing stock is valued at £50, profit would be £150
3. if closing stock is valued at £25, profit would be £125
Case 2
1. if closing stock is valued at £100, profit would be £150
2. if closing stock is valued at £80, profit would be £130
3. if closing stock is valued at £130, profit would be £180
Case 3
1. if stock levels increase by £50 during the period, profit would be £250
2. if stock levels decrease by £30 during the period, profit would be £170
3. if there is no increase or decrease in stocks over the course of the period, profit would be £200
Case 4
1. if there is no closing stock at the end of Period 1, profit for both periods would be nil
2. if closing stock at the end of Period 1 is valued at £50: period 1, profit £50, period 2, loss £50
3. if closing stock at the end of Period 1 is valued at £100: period 1, profit £100, period 2, loss £100

**20.2**   *See the website for some comments on these exercises.*

**21.1**   FIRM   A

*Firm A Profit & Loss Account for Period . . .*

| | | | |
|---|---|---|---|
| Purchases | 500 | Sales | 700 |
| opening stock | 50 | closing stock | 75 |
| (from Stock A/c) | | (to Stock A/c) | |
| bal c/f | 225 | | |
| | 775 | | 775 |
| | | bal b/f = Gross Profit | 225 |
| wages | 80 | | |
| electricity | 40 | | |
| rent | 60 | | |
| bal c/f | 45 | | |
| | 225 | | 225 |
| | | bal b/f = Operating | |
| | | Profit | 45 |
| interest | 15 | | |
| bal c/f | 30 | | |
| | 45 | | 45 |
| to Capital | 30 | bal b/f = Net Profit | 30 |

**FIRM A: BALANCE SHEET AT END OF PERIOD . . .**

| | |
|---|---|
| Assets | |
| Stock | 75 |
| Debtors | 95 |
| Bank | 26 |
| | 196 |
| Liabilities | |
| Creditors | (86) |
| Net Assets | £110 |
| Capital | £110 |

*see website for Firm B and Firm C.*

## 21.2 BUSINESS A

### Business A Profit & Loss Account for Period . . .

| | | | | |
|---|---|---|---|---|
| Purchases | 5 000 | Sales | 8 000 |
| opening stock (from Stock A/c) | 2 500 | closing stock (to Stock A/c) | 3 000 |
| bal c/f | 3 500 | | |
| | 11 000 | | 11 000 |
| | | bal b/f = Gross Profit | 3 500 |
| rent | 800 | | |
| bal c/f | 2 700 | | |
| | 3 500 | | 3 500 |
| to capital | 2 700 | bal b/f = Operating Profit | 2 700 |

### BUSINESS A: BALANCE SHEET AT END OF PERIOD . . .

| | |
|---|---|
| **Assets** | |
| Stock | 3 000 |
| Debtors | 250 |
| Bank | 3 650 |
| | 6 900 |
| **Liabilities** | |
| Bank | (1 000) |
| Net Assets | £5 900 |
| Capital | £5 900 |

*see website for Business B, Business C, Business D.*

**22.1** Ans A

| | £ | £ |
|---|---|---|
| Sales | | 30 000 |
| purchases | 20 900 | |
| opening stock | 2 250 | |
| closing stock | (2 150) | |
| Cost of Sales | | (21 000) |
| Gross Profit | | 9 000 |
| wages | 1 400 | |
| electricity | 600 | |
| insurance | 300 | |
| advertising | 200 | |
| | | (2 500) |
| Operating Profit | | 6 500 |
| interest payable | | (150) |
| Net Profit | | £6 350 |

Ans B

| | £ | £ |
|---|---|---|
| Sales | | 14 800 |
| purchases | 11 000 | |
| opening stock | 1 200 | |
| closing stock | (1 700) | |
| Cost of Sales | | (10 500) |
| Gross Profit | | 4 300 |
| wages | 2 400 | |
| rent | 1 000 | |
| transport | 800 | |
| | | (4 200) |
| Operating Profit | | 100 |
| interest payable | | (125) |
| Net Profit | | (25) |

Ans C

| C: PROFIT & LOSS ACCOUNT | | | |
|---|---|---|---|
| Purchases | 36 600 | Sales | 50 000 |
| opening stock | 4 000 | closing stock | 5 000 |
| c/f | 15 000 | | |
| | 55 000 | | 55 000 |
| wages | 10 000 | b/f gross profit | 15 000 |
| rent | 2 000 | | |
| insurance | 1 000 | | |
| advertising | 500 | | |
| c/f | 1 500 | | |
| | 15 000 | | 15 000 |
| interest payable | 2 000 | b/f operating profit | 1 500 |
| | | c/f | 500 |
| tot | 2 000 | | 2 000 |
| b/f net loss | 500 | to capital | 500 |

Ans D

| | £ | £ |
|---|---|---|
| Sales | | 46 600 |
| purchases | 32 000 | |
| opening stock | 3 600 | |
| closing stock | (4 000) | |
| Cost of Sales | | (31 600) |
| Gross Profit | | 15 000 |
| wages | 11 350 | |
| rent | 2 650 | |
| insurance | 1 900 | |
| | | (15 900) |
| Operating Loss | | (900) |
| interest payable | | (100) |
| interest receivable | | 1 200 |
| Net Profit | | £200 |

Ans E

### E: PROFIT & LOSS ACCOUNT

| | | | |
|---|---|---|---|
| Purchases | 65 500 | Sales | 87 000 |
| opening stock | 5 700 | closing stock | 4 200 |
| c/f | 20 400 | | |
| tot | 91 600 | | 91 600 |
| wages | 12 150 | b/f gross profit | 20 400 |
| electricity | 1 850 | | |
| transport | 4 400 | | |
| c/f | 2 000 | | |
| | 20 400 | | 20 400 |
| interest payable | 3 000 | b/f operating profit | 2 000 |
| | | interest receivable | 700 |
| | | c/f | 300 |
| | 3 000 | | 3 000 |
| b/f net loss | 300 | to capital | 300 |

**24.1**      BUSINESS A

| | TRIAL BALANCE DR | CR | P&L ACCOUNT DR | CR | BALANCE SHEET DR | CR |
|---|---|---|---|---|---|---|
| sales | | 7 500 | | 7 500 | | |
| purchases | 5 700 | | 5 700 | | | |
| stock | 1 100 | | 1 100 | 1 490 | 1 490 | |
| wages | 1 230 | | 1 230 | | | |
| rent | 120 | | 120 | | | |
| insurance | 56 | | 56 | | | |
| electricity | 144 | | 144 | | | |
| interest | 40 | | 40 | | | |
| bank | 900 | | | | 900 | |
| trade debtors | 850 | | | | 850 | |
| trade creditors | | 740 | | | | 740 |
| loan | | 400 | | | | 400 |
| capital | | 1 500 | | | | 1 500 |
| profit | | | 600 | | | 600 |
| total | 10 140 | 10 140 | 8 990 | 8 990 | 3 240 | 3 240 |

*see website for Business B and Business C.*

24.2

| ABC TRIAL BALANCE AT 30 JUNE 2050 | | |
|---|---|---|
| | £ | £ |
| sales | | 23 500 |
| purchases | 15 000 | |
| opening stock | 3 000 | |
| rent | 2 200 | |
| electricity | 1 350 | |
| salaries | 3 450 | |
| interest receivable | | 200 |
| interest payable | 300 | |
| trade receivables | 4 300 | |
| finance debtor | 1 500 | |
| bank | 200 | |
| trade payables | | 3 600 |
| finance payable | | 1 400 |
| capital | | 2 600 |
| | 31 300 | 31 300 |

# PART THREE *Chapters 25–56*

26.1     FIRM  A

| 26.1 FIRM A BALANCE SHEET | | |
|---|---|---|
| Tangible Fixed Assets | | |
|    Land & Buildings | | 25 |
|    Plant & Machinery | | 325 |
| | | 350 |
| | | |
| Current Assets | | |
|    Stock | 60 | |
|    Debtors | 40 | |
|    Bank | 30 | |
|    Cash | 20 | |
| | 150 | |
| | | |
| Current Liabilities | | |
|    Trade Creditors | 40 | |
|    Bank Overdraft | 10 | |
| | (50) | |
| Net Current Assets | | 100 |
| | | 450 |
| | | |
| Long Term Liabilities | | |
|    Bank Loan | | (200) |
| NET ASSETS | | 250 |
| | | |
| CAPITAL | | 250 |

FIRM B

| 26.1 FIRM B BALANCE SHEET | | |
|---|---:|---:|
| Tangible Fixed Assets | | |
| Land & Buildings | | 340 |
| Plant & Machinery | | 150 |
| | | 490 |
| Current Assets | | |
| Stock | 45 | |
| Debtors | 60 | |
| Bank | 15 | |
| | 120 | |
| Current Liabilities | | |
| Trade Creditors | 50 | |
| Bank Overdraft | 45 | |
| | (95) | |
| Net Current Assets | | 25 |
| | | 515 |
| Long Term Liabilities | | |
| Bank Loan | | (300) |
| NET ASSETS | | 215 |
| CAPITAL | | 215 |

26.2    *Some comments on these exercises are offered on the website.*

**27.1**    BUSINESS 1

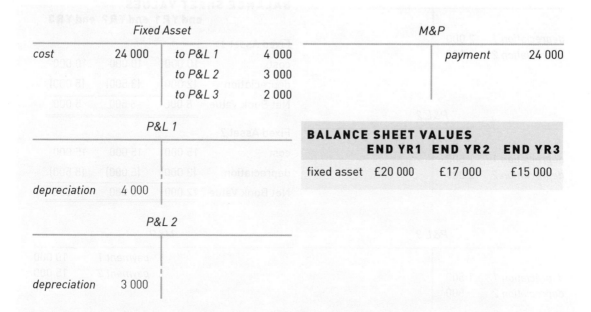

*Fixed Asset*

| cost | 10 000 | to P&L 1 | 2 000 |
| | | to P&L 2 | 1 500 |
| | | to P&L 3 | 1 000 |

*M&P*

| | | payment | 10 000 |

*P&L 1*

| depreciation | 2 000 | |

**BALANCE SHEET VALUES**

| | END YR1 | END YR2 | END YR3 |
|---|---|---|---|
| fixed asset | £8 000 | £6 500 | £5 500 |

*P&L 2*

| depreciation | 1 500 | |

*P&L 3*

| depreciation | 1 000 | |

BUSINESS 2

*Fixed Asset*

| cost | 24 000 | to P&L 1 | 4 000 |
| | | to P&L 2 | 3 000 |
| | | to P&L 3 | 2 000 |

*M&P*

| | | payment | 24 000 |

*P&L 1*

| depreciation | 4 000 | |

**BALANCE SHEET VALUES**

| | END YR1 | END YR2 | END YR3 |
|---|---|---|---|
| fixed asset | £20 000 | £17 000 | £15 000 |

*P&L 2*

| depreciation | 3 000 | |

*P&L 3*

| depreciation | 2 000 | |
|---|---|---|

*see website for Businesses 3–8.*

**27.2** *Comment on these exercises can be found on the website.*

**28.1** BUSINESS 1

*Fixed Asset 1 – Pressing Machine*

| cost | 10 000 | |
|---|---|---|

*Provision for Depreciation 1 – Pressing Machine*

| | | to P&L 1 | 2 000 |
|---|---|---|---|
| | | to P&L 2 | 1 500 |
| | | to P&L 3 | 1 500 |

*Fixed Asset 2 – Delivery Van*

| cost | 15 000 | |
|---|---|---|

*Provision for Depreciation 2 – Delivery Van*

| | | to P&L 1 | 3 000 |
|---|---|---|---|
| | | to P&L 2 | 2 000 |
| | | to P&L 3 | 500 |

*P&L 1*

| depreciation 1 | 2 000 | |
|---|---|---|
| depreciation 2 | 3 000 | |

*P&L 2*

| depreciation 1 | 1 500 | |
|---|---|---|
| depreciation 2 | 2 000 | |

*P&L 3*

| depreciation 1 | 1 500 | |
|---|---|---|
| depreciation 2 | 500 | |

**BALANCE SHEET VALUES**

| | end YR1 | end YR2 | end YR3 |
|---|---|---|---|
| **Fixed Asset 1** | | | |
| cost | 10 000 | 10 000 | 10 000 |
| depreciation | (2 000) | (3 500) | (5 000) |
| Net Book Value | 8 000 | 6 500 | 5 000 |
| **Fixed Asset 2** | | | |
| cost | 15 000 | 15 000 | 15 000 |
| depreciation | (3 000) | (5 000) | (5 500) |
| Net Book Value | 12 000 | 10 000 | 9 500 |

*M&P*

| | | payment 1 | 10 000 |
|---|---|---|---|
| | | payment 2 | 15 000 |

BUSINESS 2

### Fixed Asset 1 – Fixtures and Fittings

| cost | 4 000 | | |
|------|-------|--|--|

### Provision for Depreciation 1 – Fixtures and Fittings

| | | to P&L 1 | 800 |
|--|--|----------|-----|
| | | to P&L 2 | 400 |
| | | to P&L 3 | 800 |

### Fixed Asset 2 – Plant and Machinery

| cost | 8 000 | | |
|------|-------|--|--|

### Provision for Depreciation 2 – Plant and Machinery

| | | to P&L 1 | 2 000 |
|--|--|----------|-------|
| | | to P&L 2 | 1 000 |
| | | to P&L 3 | 3 000 |

### P&L 1

| depreciation 1 | 800 | | |
|----------------|-------|--|--|
| depreciation 2 | 2 000 | | |

### P&L 2

| depreciation 1 | 400 | | |
|----------------|-------|--|--|
| depreciation 2 | 1 000 | | |

### P&L 3

| depreciation 1 | 800 | | |
|----------------|-------|--|--|
| depreciation 2 | 3 000 | | |

### BALANCE SHEET VALUES

| | end YR1 | end YR2 | end YR3 |
|--|---------|---------|---------|
| **Fixed Asset 1** | | | |
| cost | 4 000 | 4 000 | 4 000 |
| depreciation | (800) | (1 200) | (2 000) |
| Net Book Value | 3 200 | 2 800 | 2 000 |
| **Fixed Asset 2** | | | |
| cost | 8 000 | 8 000 | 8 000 |
| depreciation | (2 000) | (3 000) | (6 000) |
| Net Book Value | 6 000 | 5 000 | 2 000 |

### M&P

| | | payment 1 | 4 000 |
|--|--|-----------|-------|
| | | payment 2 | 8 000 |

*see website for Businesses 3–7.*

**28.2**     BUSINESS A

|             | P&L 11  |
| ----------- | ------- |
| *depreciation 1* | 10 240 |
| *depreciation 2* | 8 000 |

| BALANCE SHEET VALUES | END YR11 |
| -------------------- | -------- |
| Machinery            |          |
| cost                 | 80 000   |
| depreciation         | (39 040) |
| Net Book Value       | 40 960   |
| Motor Vehicles       |          |
| cost                 | 40 000   |
| depreciation         | (32 000) |
| Net Book Value       | 8 000    |

BUSINESS B

|                | P&L 20  |
| -------------- | ------- |
| *depreciation* | 9 000   |

| BALANCE SHEET VALUES | END YR20 |
| -------------------- | -------- |
| Fixed Asset          |          |
| cost                 | 90 000   |
| depreciation         | (27 000) |
| Net Book Value       | 63 000   |

**28.3**     The Provision for Depreciation Account will always carry a CR balance. The Depreciation Expense Account will carry a DR balance.

**29.1    BUSINESS 1**

|  | Fixed Asset Cost | | |
|---|---|---|---|
| b/f | 18 000 | F.A. Disposal | 18 000 |

|  | Provision for Depreciation | | |
|---|---|---|---|
| to F.A. Disposal | 8 000 | b/f | 8 000 |

|  | Fixed Asset Disposal | | |
|---|---|---|---|
| cost | 18 000 | disposal value | 7 000 |
|  |  | depreciation | 8 000 |
|  |  | to P&L | 3 000 |
|  | 18 000 |  | 18 000 |

|  | Money and Promises | | |
|---|---|---|---|
| payment received | 7 000 |  |  |

|  | P&L | | |
|---|---|---|---|
| loss on disposal | 3 000 |  |  |

*see website for Businesses 2–5.*

**29.2    BUSINESS 1**

| DR | Money or Promises | £750 | |
|---|---|---|---|
| CR | Fixed Asset Disposal Account | | £750 |
| DR | Fixed Asset Disposal Account | £5 000 | |
| CR | Fixed Asset Cost Account | | £5 000 |
| DR | Provision for Depreciation Account | £4 000 | |
| CR | Fixed Asset Disposal Account | | £4 000 |
| DR | P&L (loss on disposal) | £250 | |
| CR | Fixed Asset Disposal Account | | £250 |

### Fixed Asset Disposal

| | | | |
|---|---|---|---|
| cost | 5 000 | disposal value | 750 |
| | | depreciation | 4 000 |
| | | to P&L | 250 |
| | 5 000 | | 5 000 |

### P&L

| | | | |
|---|---|---|---|
| | | loss on disposal | 250 |

*see website for Businesses 2–5.*

**29.3 BUSINESS 1**

### Fixed Asset Cost

| | | | |
|---|---|---|---|
| cost | 130 000 | to F.A. Disp | 130 000 |

### Provision for Depreciation 1

| | | | |
|---|---|---|---|
| | | to P&L 1 | 30 000 |
| to F.A. Disp | 50 000 | to P&L 2 | 20 000 |

### Fixed Asset Disposal

| | | | |
|---|---|---|---|
| cost | 130 000 | disposal value | 70 000 |
| | | depreciation | 50 000 |
| | | to P&L | 10 000 |
| | 130 000 | | 130 000 |

### Money & Promises

| | | | |
|---|---|---|---|
| | | original payment | 130 000 |
| disposal proceeds | 70 000 | | |

### P&L 1

| | |
|---|---|
| depreciation | 30 000 |

### P&L 2

| | |
|---|---|
| depreciation | 20 000 |

### P&L 3

| | |
|---|---|
| loss on disposal | 10 000 |

*see website for Businesses 2–4.*

**29.4    BUSINESS 1**

**ASSUMPTION 1**

| Fixed Asset Cost | | | |
|---|---|---|---|
| cost | 120 000 | to F.A. Disp | 120 000 |

| Provision for Depreciation | | | |
|---|---|---|---|
| | | to P&L 1 | 30 000 |
| to F.A. Disp | 60 000 | to P&L 2 | 30 000 |

| Fixed Asset Disposal | | | |
|---|---|---|---|
| cost | 120 000 | disposal value | 57 500 |
| | | depreciation | 60 000 |
| | | to P&L | 2 500 |
| | 120 000 | | 120 000 |

| Money & Promises | | | |
|---|---|---|---|
| | | original payment | 120 000 |
| disposal proceeds | 57 500 | | |

| P&L 1 | |
|---|---|
| depreciation | 30 000 |

| P&L 2 | |
|---|---|
| depreciation | 30 000 |

| P&L 3 | |
|---|---|
| loss on disposal | 2 500 |

ASSUMPTION 2

| Fixed Asset Cost | | | |
|---|---|---|---|
| cost | 120 000 | to F.A. Disp | 120 000 |

| Provision for Depreciation | | | |
|---|---|---|---|
| | | to P&L 1 | 30 000 |
| to F.A. Disp | 60 000 | to P&L 2 | 22 500 |

| Fixed Asset Disposal | | | |
|---|---|---|---|
| cost | 120 000 | disposal value | 57 500 |
| | | depreciation | 52 500 |
| | | to P&L | 10 000 |
| | 120 000 | | 120 000 |

| Money & Promises | | | |
|---|---|---|---|
| | | original payment | 120 000 |
| disposal proceeds | 57 500 | | |

| P&L 1 | |
|---|---|
| depreciation | 30 000 |

| P&L 2 | |
|---|---|
| depreciation | 22 500 |

| P&L 3 | |
|---|---|
| loss on disposal | 10 000 |

*see website for Business 2.*

**30.1**

1.

| DR | Money or Promises | £3 500 | |
|----|----|----|----|
| DR | Provision for Depreciation Account | £7 000 | |
| CR | P&L Account (profit on disposal) | | £500 |
| CR | Fixed Asset Cost Account | | £10 000 |

2.

| DR | Money or Promises | £1 200 | |
|----|----|----|----|
| DR | Provision for Depreciation Account | £3 000 | |
| DR | P&L Account (loss on disposal) | £300 | |
| CR | Fixed Asset Cost Account | | £4 500 |

3.

| DR | Money or Promises | £5 500 | |
|----|----|----|----|
| DR | Provision for Depreciation Account | £4 200 | |
| CR | Fixed Asset Cost Account | | £9 700 |

4.

| DR | Money or Promises | £1 000 | |
|----|----|----|----|
| DR | Provision for Depreciation Account | £2 550 | |
| CR | P&L Account (profit on disposal) | | £150 |
| CR | Fixed Asset Cost Account | | £3 400 |

5.

| DR | Money or Promises | £22 600 | |
|----|----|----|----|
| DR | Provision for Depreciation Account | £57 600 | |
| DR | P&L Account (loss on disposal) | £1 700 | |
| CR | Fixed Asset Cost Account | | £81 900 |

6.

| | | | |
|---|---|---|---|
| DR | Money and Promises | £11 000 | |
| DR | Provision for Depreciation Account | £3 200 | |
| CR | P&L Account (profit on disposal) | | £1 250 |
| CR | Fixed Asset Cost Account | | £12 950 |

7.

| | | | |
|---|---|---|---|
| DR | Money and Promises | £10 400 | |
| DR | Provision for Depreciation Account | £27 800 | |
| CR | P&L Account (profit on disposal) | | £3 700 |
| CR | Fixed Asset Cost Account | | £34 500 |

8.

| | | | |
|---|---|---|---|
| DR | Money and Promises | £51 000 | |
| DR | Provision for Depreciation Account | £43 000 | |
| CR | P&L Account (profit on disposal) | | £5 000 |
| CR | Fixed Asset Cost Account | | £89 000 |

9.

| | | | |
|---|---|---|---|
| DR | Fixed Asset Disposal Account | £5 000 | |
| DR | Provision for Depreciation Account | £36 000 | |
| CR | P&L Account (profit on disposal) | | £1 000 |
| CR | Fixed Asset Cost Account | | £40 000 |

10.

| | | | |
|---|---|---|---|
| DR | Fixed Asset Disposal Account | £7 500 | |
| DR | Provision for Depreciation Account | £20 000 | |
| DR | P&L Account (loss on disposal) | £2 500 | |
| CR | Fixed Asset Cost Account | | £30 000 |

**31.1**     BUSINESS 1

**Assumption 1**

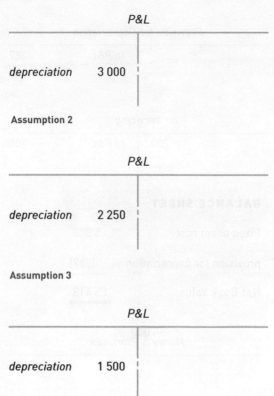

| P&L | |
|---|---|
| depreciation | 3 000 |

| BALANCE SHEET | |
|---|---|
| fixed asset cost | 12 000 |
| provision for depreciation | (6 000) |
| Net Book Value | £6 000 |

**Assumption 2**

| P&L | |
|---|---|
| depreciation | 2 250 |

| BALANCE SHEET | |
|---|---|
| fixed asset cost | 12 000 |
| provision for depreciation | (5 250) |
| Net Book Value | £6 750 |

**Assumption 3**

| P&L | |
|---|---|
| depreciation | 1 500 |

| BALANCE SHEET | |
|---|---|
| fixed asset cost | 12 000 |
| provision for depreciation | (4 500) |
| Net Book Value | £7 500 |

BUSINESS 2

**Assumption 1**

| P&L | |
|---|---|
| depreciation | 1 600 |

| BALANCE SHEET | |
|---|---|
| fixed asset cost | 16 000 |
| provision for depreciation | (6 600) |
| Net Book Value | £9 400 |

**Assumption 2**

| P&L | |
|---|---|
| depreciation | 1 100 |

| BALANCE SHEET | |
|---|---|
| fixed asset cost | 16 000 |
| provision for depreciation | (6 100) |
| Net Book Value | £9 900 |

*see website for Business 3.*

**31.2** *See website for comment on these exercises.*

**32.1** 1.

| Machine Cost | | |
|---|---|---|
| machine | 4 500 | |
| installation | 1 000 | |
| delivery | 300 | |

| Provision for Depreciation | | |
|---|---|---|
| | | to P&L | 387 |

| insurance | | | |
|---|---|---|---|
| | 150 | to P&L | 150 |

| servicing | | | |
|---|---|---|---|
| 200 | to P&L | 200 |

| training | | | |
|---|---|---|---|
| 1 500 | to P&L | 1 500 |

**BALANCE SHEET**

| | |
|---|---|
| Fixed asset cost | 5 800 |
| provision for depreciation | (387) |
| Net Book Value | £5 413 |

| P&L Account | | |
|---|---|---|
| depreciation | 387 | |
| insurance | 150 | |
| servicing | 200 | |
| training | 1 500 | |

| Money & Promises | | |
|---|---|---|
| | | 7 650 |

*see website for answers 2 and 3.*

**32.2** *See website for comments.*

**34.1**     BUSINESS 1

| operating profit | 30 |
|---|---|
| decrease in debtors | 25 |
| decrease in creditors | (140) |
| decrease in stock | 50 |
| depreciation | 25 |
| cash from operations | (10) |
| opening bank | 100 |
| closing bank | 90 |
| decrease in cash | 10 |

BUSINESS 2

| operating profit | 5 |
|---|---|
| increase in debtors | (70) |
| decrease in creditors | 10 |
| decrease in stock | 20 |
| depreciation | 25 |
| cash from operations | (10) |

BUSINESS 3

| operating profit | 15 |
|---|---|
| decrease in debtors | 20 |
| increase in creditors | 50 |
| increase in stock | (80) |
| depreciation | 25 |
| cash from operations | 30 |

BUSINESS 4

| | |
|---|---:|
| operating loss | (95) |
| decrease in debtors | 140 |
| increase in creditors | 50 |
| decrease in stock | 180 |
| depreciation | 25 |
| cash from operations | 300 |

BUSINESS 5

| | |
|---|---:|
| operating profit | 20 |
| increase in debtors | (190) |
| decrease in creditors | (55) |
| increase in stock | (200) |
| depreciation | 25 |
| cash from operations | (400) |

BUSINESS 6

| | |
|---|---:|
| operating profit | 10 |
| increase in debtors | (60) |
| change in creditors | 0 |
| increase in stock | (50) |
| depreciation | 25 |
| cash from operations | (75) |

**34.2**     BUSINESS 7

| | |
|---|---|
| operating profit | 15 |
| decrease in debtors | 40 |
| increase in creditors | 10 |
| decrease in stock | 50 |
| depreciation | 40 |
| profit on disposal | (25) |
| purchase of fixed assets | (300) |
| fixed asset disposal | 150 |
| Cash from operations | (20) |
| opening overdraft | 25 |
| closing overdraft | 45 |
| decrease in cash | 20 |

BUSINESS 8

| | |
|---|---|
| operating profit | 50 |
| change in debtors | 0 |
| increase in creditors | 35 |
| change in stock | 0 |
| depreciation | 30 |
| loss on disposal | 20 |
| purchase of fixed assets | (100) |
| fixed asset disposal | 140 |
| Cash from operations | 175 |
| opening overdraft | 45 |
| closing bank | 130 |
| increase in cash | 175 |

**35.1**     1.

|  Labour | | | |  Money & Promises | | |
|---|---|---|---|---|---|---|
| paid for | 2 400 | to P&L | 2 450 | | payment | 2 400 |
| c/f | 50 | | | | | |
| | 2 450 | | 2 450 | | | |
| | | bal b/f = accrual | 50 | | | |

|  P&L 1 | |
|---|---|
| Labour consumed | 2 450 |

**BALANCE SHEET EXTRACT**

| accrual (current liability) | 50 |
|---|---|

2.

|  Legal services | | | |  Money & Promises | | |
|---|---|---|---|---|---|---|
| paid for | 1 500 | to P&L | 1 700 | | payment | 1 500 |
| c/f | 200 | c/f | | | | |
| | 1 700 | | 1 700 | | | |
| | | bal b/f = accrual | 200 | | | |

|  P&L 1 | |
|---|---|
| Legal services consumed | 1 700 |

**BALANCE SHEET EXTRACT**

| accrual (current liability) | 200 |
|---|---|

*see website for answers 3–8.*

**35.2**     *See website for comments.*

**36.1**    1.

|  | Sales |  |  |
|---|---|---|---|
| to P&L | 5 200 | paid for | 5 000 |
|  |  | c/f | 200 |
|  | 5 200 |  | 5 200 |
| bal b/f |  |  |  |
| accrued income | 200 |  |  |

|  | Money & Promises |  |
|---|---|---|
| payment | 5 000 |  |

|  | P&L 1 |  |
|---|---|---|
|  | Sales delivered | 5 200 |

**BALANCE SHEET EXTRACT**

| accrued income (current asset) | 200 |
|---|---|

2.

|  | Sales |  |  |
|---|---|---|---|
| to P&L | 9 000 | paid for | 9 250 |
| c/f | 250 | c/f |  |
|  | 9 250 |  | 9 250 |
|  |  | bal b/f deferred income | 250 |

|  | Money & Promises |  |
|---|---|---|
| payment | 9 250 |  |

|  | P&L 1 |  |
|---|---|---|
|  | Sales delivered | 9 000 |

**BALANCE SHEET EXTRACT**

| deferred income (current liability) | 250 |
|---|---|

*see website for answers 3–8.*

**36.2**    *See website for comments.*

**37.1**      FIRM A

OPTION 1

| | TRIAL BALANCE | | P&L ACCOUNT | | BALANCE SHEET | |
|---|---|---|---|---|---|---|
| | DR | CR | DR | CR | DR | CR |
| sales | | 4 000 | | 4 500 | 500 | |
| expense | 1 500 | | 1 300 | | 200 | |

£ 500   is accrued income          £ 200   is a prepayment

OPTION 2

| | TRIAL BALANCE | | P&L ACCOUNT | | BALANCE SHEET | |
|---|---|---|---|---|---|---|
| | DR | CR | DR | CR | DR | CR |
| sales | | 4 000 | | 3 700 | | 300 |
| expense | 1 500 | | 2 200 | | | 700 |

£ 300   is deferred income          £ 700   is an accrual

*see website for FIRM B.*

**37.2**      1.   £650 of electricity has been used
                  only £600 has been paid for
                  balance was £600 DR
             2.   £500 worth of rent has been used
                  £570 of rent has been paid
                  balance was £570 DR
             3.   sales value £650 were delivered
                  £700 of sales have been paid for
                  balance was £700 CR
             4.   sales value £1 000 were delivered
                  only £800 of sales have been paid for
                  balance was £800 CR

**38.1**      1.

| *Repair work* | | | |
|---|---|---|---|
| *paid for* | 10 500 | *to P&L* | 9 000 |
| | | *c/f* | 1 500 |
| | 10 500 | | 10 500 |
| *bal b/f* = *prepayment* | 1 500 | | |

| *Money & Promises* | | |
|---|---|---|
| | *payment* | 10 500 |

| *P&L 1* | | |
|---|---|---|
| *Repair work done* | 9 000 | |

**BALANCE SHEET EXTRACT**

prepayment (current asset)     1 500

2.

| B. Maint'ce | | | | | Money & Promises | | |
|---|---|---|---|---|---|---|---|
| paid for | 1 600 | to P&L | 2 000 | | | payment | 1 600 |
| c/f | 400 | | | | | | |
| | 2 000 | | 2 000 | | | | |
| | | bal b/f<br>= accrual | 400 | | | | |

| P&L 1 | | | **BALANCE SHEET EXTRACT** | |
|---|---|---|---|---|
| | | | accrual (current liability) | 400 |
| B. Maint'ce<br>done | 2 000 | | | |

*see website for answers 3–5.*

**38.2**     **1.**

| 1 Rent | £ |
|---|---|
| EXPENSE TRANSACTIONS occurring in the period<br>   *(value paid for in money in current period)* | 8 000 |
| plus opening prepayment<br>   *(value paid for in previous period, but consumed in this period)* | 300 |
| plus closing accrual<br>   *(value consumed but not yet paid for)* | 700 |
| EXPENSE REPORTED in P&L ACCOUNT = value *consumed* in current period | £9 000 |

2.

| 2 Electricity | £ |
|---|---|
| EXPENSE TRANSACTIONS occurring in the period<br>   *(value paid for in current period)* | 5 000 |
| minus closing prepayment<br>   *(value paid for in this period, but not yet consumed)* | (750) |
| minus opening accrual<br>   *(value paid for in this period, but consumed in previous period)* | (250) |
| EXPENSE REPORTED in P&L ACCOUNT = value *consumed* in current period | £4 000 |

*see website for answers 3–8.*

**39.1**    1. Deferred income at the end of the period:

| DR | Sales | X | |
|----|-------|---|---|
| CR | Deferred Income | | X |

to remove undelivered sales from the Sales Account, and show the liability to deliver in the balance sheet.

At the start of the next period:

| DR | Deferred Income | X | |
|----|-----------------|---|---|
| CR | Sales | | X |

to cancel opening liability to deliver, and replace with actual delivery in the Sales Account.

2. Accrued income at the end of the period:

| DR | Accrued Income | X | |
|----|----------------|---|---|
| CR | Sales | | X |

to add sales not yet recorded to value in the Sales Account, and show right to collect payment as an asset in the balance sheet.

At the start of the next period:

| DR | Sales | X | |
|----|-------|---|---|
| CR | Accrued Income | | X |

to cancel opening right to collect payment (it will be replaced by an actual debtor when the sale is properly recorded) and cancel the sale that will be recorded in the Sales Account (because it has already been included in the previous P&L Account).

3. A prepayment at the end of the period:

| DR | Prepayment | X | |
|----|------------|---|---|
| CR | Expense Account | | X |

to remove unconsumed inputs from the Expense Account, and show the right to consume the inputs in the balance sheet.

At the start of the next period:

| DR | Expense Account | X | |
|----|-----------------|---|---|
| CR | Prepayment | | X |

to cancel opening right to consume, and replace with actual expense in the Expense Account.

4. An accrual at the end of the period:

| DR | Expense Account | X | |
|----|-----------------|---|---|
| CR | Accrual | | X |

to add inputs not yet recorded to value in the Expense Account, and show liability to pay in the balance sheet.

At the start of the next period:

| DR | Accrual | X |   |
|----|---------|---|---|
| CR | Expenses Account |   | X |

to cancel opening liability to pay (it will be replaced by an actual creditor when the expense is properly recorded) and cancel the expense that will be recorded in the Expense Account (because it has already been included in the previous P&L Account).

**40.1**
1. making an inappropriate (excessive) adjustment for deferred income-effect: reported profit and net assets will be understated.
2. making an inappropriate (excessive) adjustment for accrued income-effect: reported profit and net assets will be overstated.
3. making an inappropriate (excessive) adjustment for a prepayment-effect: reported profit and net assets will be overstated.
4. making an inappropriate (excessive) adjustment for an accrual-effect: reported profit and net assets will be understated.
5. failing to make an appropriate adjustment for deferred income-effect: reported profit and net assets will be overstated.
6. failing to make a necessary adjustment for accrued income-effect: reported profit and net assets will be understated.
7. failing to make a necessary adjustment for a prepayment-effect: reported profit and net assets will be understated.
8. failing to make a necessary adjustment for an accrual-effect: reported profit and net assets will be overstated.
9. overestimating the useful life of a fixed asset-effect: reported profit and net assets will be overstated.
10. underestimating the residual value of a fixed asset-effect: reported profit and net assets will be understated.

**40.2**   *See website for comments.*
*See website for comments on Exercises 41.1 and 41.2.*

**42.1**   BUSINESS 1

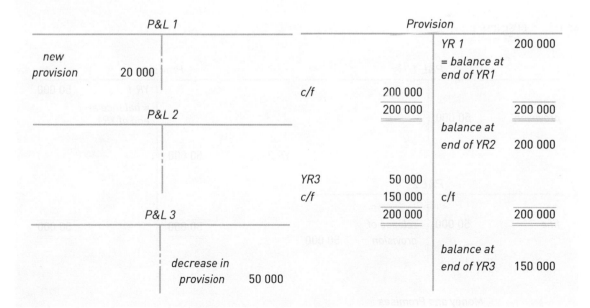

**BUSINESS 2**

| P&L 1 | | | Provision | | |
|---|---|---|---|---|---|
| new provision | 200 000 | | YR 1 = balance at end of YR1 | | 200 000 |

| P&L 2 | | | Provision | | |
|---|---|---|---|---|---|
| | | c/f | 250 000 | YR 2 | 50 000 |
| increase in provision | 50 000 | | 250 000 | | 250 000 |
| | | | | balance at end of YR 2 | 250 000 |

| P&L 3 | | | Provision | | |
|---|---|---|---|---|---|
| | | c/f | 250 000 | | |
| | | | 250 000 | | 250 000 |
| | | | | balance at end of YR3 | 250 000 |

*see website for Business 3 and Business 4.*

**42.2**     *See website for comments.*

**43.1**     BUSINESS 1

| P&L 1 | | | Provision | | |
|---|---|---|---|---|---|
| new provision | 50 000 | | YR 1 = balance at end of YR1 | | 50 000 |
| | | | YR 2 | | 50 000 |

| P&L 2 | | | Provision | | |
|---|---|---|---|---|---|
| fine | 50 000 | release of provision | 50 000 | 50 000 | 50 000 |

| Money and Promises | | |
|---|---|---|
| | fine paid YR 2 | 50 000 |

BUSINESS 2

| P&L 1 | | | | Provision | |
|---|---|---|---|---|---|
| new provision | 15 000 | | | YR 1 = balance at end of YR1 | 15 000 |
| | | | YR 2 | 15 000 | |
| | | | | | |
| | | | 15 000 | | 15 000 |

| P&L 2 | | | |
|---|---|---|---|
| repairs | 14 000 | release of provision | 15 000 |

| Money and Promises | | | |
|---|---|---|---|
| | | paid in YR 2 | 14 000 |

*see website for Business 3 and Business 4.*

**43.2** *See website for comments.*

**44.1** REQUIRED

BUSINESS 1

| P&L 1 | | | | Provision | |
|---|---|---|---|---|---|
| | | Sales | 100 | YR 1 = balance at end of YR 1 | 90 |
| provision for prize | 90 | | | | |
| | | | YR 2 | 90 | |
| | | | 90 | | 90 |

| P&L 2 | | | |
|---|---|---|---|
| prize | 90 | release of provision | 90 |

| Money and Promises | | | |
|---|---|---|---|
| YR 1 sales receipts | 100 | | |
| | | YR 2 prize paid | 90 |

BUSINESS 2

|  | P&L 1 |  |
|---|---|---|
|  | rent received | 1 000 |
| provision for restoration | 300 | |

| Provision | | |
|---|---|---|
|  | YR 1 = balance at end of YR 1 | 300 |
| YR2 | 300 | |
|  | 300 | 300 |

|  | P&L 2 | |
|---|---|---|
| restoration | 310 | release of provision 300 |

|  | Money and Promises | |
|---|---|---|
| YR 1 received | 1 000 | |
|  | YR 2 paid | 310 |

*see website for Business 3 and Business 4.*

**45.1    BUSINESS 1**

|  | P&L 1 | |
|---|---|---|
|  | Sales | 600 000 |
| provision for repairs | 30 000 | |

| Provision | | |
|---|---|---|
|  | YR 1 = balance at end of YR 1 | 30 000 |
|  | YR 2 | 10 000 |
| c/f | 40 000 | |
|  | 40 000 | 40 000 |
|  | balance at end of YR2 | 40 000 |

|  | P&L 2 | |
|---|---|---|
|  | Sales | 800 000 |
| repair cost | 31 000 | |
| increase in provision | 10 000 | |

| YR3 c/f | 4 000 36 000 | |
|---|---|---|
|  | 40 000 | 40 000 |

|  | P&L 3 | |
|---|---|---|
|  | Sales | 900 000 |
| repair cost | 38 000 | |
|  | decrease in provision | 4 000 |

|  | balance at end of YR3 | 36 000 |
|---|---|---|

**BUSINESS 2**

| P&L 1 | | |
|---|---|---|
| | Sales | 250 000 |
| provision for refunds 25 000 | | |

| P&L 2 | | |
|---|---|---|
| | Sales | 300 000 |
| actual refunds 23 000 | | |
| increase in provision 20 000 | | |

| P&L 3 | | |
|---|---|---|
| | Sales | 280 000 |
| actual refunds 45 000 | | |
| | decrease in provision 3 000 | |

| Provision | | |
|---|---|---|
| | YR 1 = balance at end of YR 1 | 25 000 |
| | YR 2 | 20 000 |
| c/f 45 000 | | |
| 45 000 | | 45 000 |
| | balance at end of YR2 | 45 000 |
| YR3 3 000 | | |
| c/f 42 000 | | |
| 45 000 | | 45 000 |
| | balance at end of YR3 | 42 000 |

**46.1**   (a) failure to make a provision when required
    would overstate current profit, understate next period's profit

(b) making a provision when not required
    would understate current profit, overstate future profit (when provision is released)

*see website for comments on exercises 46.2 and 46.3.*

**47.1**   BUSINESS 1

| Debtors | | | |
|---|---|---|---|
| b/f | 11 000 | cash rec'd | 50 960 |
| sales | 48 000 | discount allowed | 1 040 |
| | | c/f | 7 000 |
| | 59 000 | | 59 000 |
| b/f | 7 000 | | |

| Creditors | | | |
|---|---|---|---|
| cash paid | 26 325 | b/f | 7 000 |
| discount received | 675 | purchases | 26 000 |
| c/f | 6 000 | | |
| | 33 000 | | 33 000 |
| | | b/f | 6 000 |

| P&L | | |
|---|---|---|
| discount allowed 1 040 | discount received | 675 |

*BUSINESS 2 – see website.*

**BUSINESS 3**

### Debtors

| | | | |
|---|---|---|---|
| b/f | 20 000 | cash rec'd | 238 000 |
| sales | 250 000 | discount allowed | 2 000 |
| | | c/f | 30 000 |
| | 270 000 | | 270 000 |
| b/f | 30 000 | | |

### P&L

| | | |
|---|---|---|
| discount allowed | 2 000 | |

*BUSINESS 4 – see website.*

**47.2**  *See website for comments.*

**48.1**  A

### Debtors

| | | | |
|---|---|---|---|
| b/f | 12 000 | cash rec'd | 70 000 |
| sales | 72 500 | written off | 3 500 |
| | | c/f | 11 000 |
| | 84 500 | | 84 500 |
| b/f | 11 000 | | |

### P&L

| | |
|---|---|
| written off | 3 500 |

**B**

| Debtors | | | | P&L | | |
|---|---|---|---|---|---|---|
| b/f | 19 500 | cash rec'd | 207 000 | | | |
| sales | 210 500 | written off | 4 000 | written off | 4 000 | |
| | | c/f | 19 000 | | | |
| | 230 000 | | 230 000 | | | |
| b/f | 19 000 | | | | | |

**C**

| Debtors | | | | P&L | | |
|---|---|---|---|---|---|---|
| b/f | 5 600 | cash rec'd | 67 000 | | | |
| sales | 68 400 | from bad debt | 750 | | bad debt | |
| reinstated | 750 | c/f | 7 000 | | reinstated | 750 |
| | 74 750 | | 74 750 | | | |
| b/f | 7 000 | | | | | |

*see website for D, E, and F.*

**49.1**     A

### Provision for Doubtful debts

| | | | | |
|---|---|---|---|---|
| | | YR 1 | | 184 |
| | | adjustment | | |
| | | YR 2 | | 367 |
| c/f | 551 | | | |
| | 551 | | | 551 |
| | | b/f | | 551 |

### Debtors

| | | | | |
|---|---|---|---|---|
| sales | 60 000 | discount allowed | | 1 200 |
| | | bad debts written off | | 4 500 |
| | | cash received | | 52 000 |
| | | c/f | | 2 300 |
| | 60 000 | | | 60 000 |
| b/f | 2 300 | discount allowed | | 950 |
| sales | 72 500 | bad debts written off | | 3 500 |
| bad debt reinstated | 1 500 | cash from existing debtors | | 63 000 |
| | | cash from debtors previously written off | | 1 500 |
| | | c/f | | 7 350 |
| | 76 300 | | | 76 300 |
| b/f | 7 350 | | | |

### P&L 1

| | | |
|---|---|---|
| discount allowed | 1 200 | |
| bad debts written off | 4 500 | |
| creation of provision | 184 | |

### P&L 2

| | | | |
|---|---|---|---|
| discount allowed | 950 | bad debt reinstated | 1 500 |
| bad debts written off | 3 500 | | |
| increase in provision | 367 | | |

| BALANCE SHEET EXTRACTS | | |
|---|---|---|
| | END YR1 | END YR2 |
| Debtors | 2 300 | 7 350 |
| less provision | (184) | (551) |
| Book Value | 2 116 | 6 799 |

B

| Provision for Doubtful Debts | | | | Debtors | | | |
|---|---|---|---|---|---|---|---|
| | | YR 1 | 212 | sales | 45 600 | | |
| | | adjustment YR 2 | 291 | | | bad debts written off | 2 350 |
| c/f | 503 | | | | | cash received | 39 000 |
| | 503 | | 503 | | | c/f | 4 250 |
| | | b/f | 503 | | 45 600 | | 45 600 |
| | | | | b/f | 4 250 | discount allowed | 870 |
| | | | | sales | 53 000 | bad debts written off | 3 000 |
| | | | | bad debt reinstated | 1 350 | cash from existing debtors | 45 000 |
| | | | | | | cash from debtors previously written off | 1 350 |
| | | | | | | c/f | 8 380 |
| | | | | | 58 600 | | 58 600 |
| | | | | b/f | 8 380 | | |

| P&L 1 | | | | P&L 2 | | | |
|---|---|---|---|---|---|---|---|
| bad debts written off | 2 350 | | | discount allowed | 870 | bad debt reinstated | 1 350 |
| creation of provision | 212 | | | bad debts written off | 3 000 | | |
| | | | | increase in provision | 291 | | |

| BALANCE SHEET EXTRACTS | END YR1 | END YR2 |
|---|---|---|
| Debtors | 4 250 | 8 380 |
| less provision | (212) | (503) |
| Book Value | 4 038 | 7 877 |

*see website for C and D.*

**49.2** *See website for comments.*

**50.1**

### Bad and Doubtful Debts

| | | | |
|---|---|---|---|
| (2) bad debt written off | 30 | (1) bad debt reinstated | 75 |
| | | (3) release of specific provision | 47 |
| (4) bad debt written off | 55 | (4) release of specific provision | 55 |
| (5) provision for debtor Z | 125 | (6) decrease of general provision | 14 |
| | | to P&L | 19 |
| | 210 | | 210 |

### P&L

| | | | |
|---|---|---|---|
| bad and doubtful debt expense | 19 | | |

**50.2**     bad debt written off – CR would be in Debtors Account

Debtor A written off – CR would be in Debtor A's account

Debtor B creation of specific provision – CR would be in provision account

increase in general provision – CR would be in provision account

bad debt recovered – DR would be in debtor's account

Debtor A release of specific provision – DR would be in provision account

Debtor Z release of specific provision – DR would be in provision account

A DR of £130 would be transferred from the Bad and Doubtful Debts Account to the P&L Account

**50.3**     *See website for comments.*

**51.1**

### P&L Account for Period 1

| | | | |
|---|---|---|---|
| purchases | 120 000 | sales | 150 000 |
| | | closing stock | 15 000 |
| c/f | 45 000 | | |
| | 165 000 | | 165 000 |
| to capital | 45 000 | b/f profit | 45 000 |

**BALANCE SHEET AT END OF YR 1**

| | |
|---|---|
| stock | 15 000 |
| debtors | 40 000 |
| bank | 48 000 |
| | 103 000 |
| creditors | (44 000) |
| VAT | (4 000) |
| | £55 000 |
| Capital | £55 000 |

**51.2**     *See website for comments.*

**52.1**

**Manufacturing Account for the Year Ended (date)**

| | £ |
|---|---|
| purchases of raw materials | 140 000 |
| *plus* opening stock of raw materials | 20 000 |
| *minus* closing stock of raw materials | (22 000) |
| cost of raw materials consumed | 138 000 |
| direct labour | 58 000 |
| **PRIME COST** | **196 000** |
| Production Overheads | |
| factory heat and light | 9 000 |
| factory supervision | 8 000 |
| machinery depreciation | 20 000 |
| indirect materials | 2 000 |
| indirect labour | 5 000 |
| factory insurance | 4 000 |
| | 244 000 |
| *plus opening stock* of WIP | 11 000 |
| *minus closing stock* of WIP | (10 000) |
| **FACTORY COST of FINISHED GOODS PRODUCED** | **245 000** |

> **Income Statement for the Year Ended (date)**
>
> | | | £ |
> |---|---:|---:|
> | **Sales Revenue** | | **430 000** |
> | Finished goods produced in period | 245 000 | |
> | plus opening stock of finished goods | 13 000 | |
> | less closing stock of finished goods | (16 000) | |
> | **Cost of Sales** | | **(242 000)** |
> | **Gross Profit** | | **188 000** |
> | Expenses | | |
> | office equipment depreciation | 3 000 | |
> | general expenses | 15 000 | |
> | selling expenses | 13 000 | |
> | administrative expenses | 4 000 | |
> | insurance | 2 000 | |
> | | | (37 000) |
> | **Operating Profit** | | **£151 000** |

**52.1**  *See website for comments.*

**53.1**

| | A | B | C | D | E |
|---|---|---|---|---|---|
| net realisable value | 1 200 | 18 000 | 40 000 | 4 000 | 13 000 |
| expected profit (loss) | 200 | (2 000) | 0 | (800) | 1 000 |
| **stock should be valued at** | **cost** | **NRV** | **cost** | **NRV** | **cost** |

**53.2**

*P&L Account for Period 1*

| | | | | |
|---|---:|---|---:|
| Purchases | 550 | Sales | 750 |
| | | stock stolen | 20 |
| c/f | 270 | closing stock | 50 |
| | 820 | | 820 |
| stock stolen | 20 | b/f = gross profit | 270 |
| c/f | 250 | | |
| | 270 | | 270 |
| | | b/f = operating profit | 250 |

**54.1**   A  stock values:

| | |
|---|---|
| LIFO | £8 000 |
| FIFO | £11 250 |
| AVCO | £10 637 |

**54.1**   B  stock values:

LIFO        £12 600

FIFO        £15 300

AVCO       £13 726

**55.1**   (a)

|  | £ | £ |
|---|---|---|
| Sales | | 38 400 |
| direct cost of production | 28 000 | |
| less closing stock | (2 400) | |
| Cost of Sales | | (25 600) |
| Gross Profit | | 12 800 |
| overheads | | (10 000) |
| operating profit | | £2 800 |

(b)

|  | £ | £ |
|---|---|---|
| Sales | | 38 400 |
| direct cost of production | 56 000 | |
| less closing stock | (30 400) | |
| Cost of Sales | | (25 600) |
| Gross Profit | | 12 800 |
| overheads | | (10 000) |
| operating profit | | £2 800 |

(c)

|  | £ | £ |
|---|---|---|
| Sales | | 38 400 |
| total cost of production | 38 000 | |
| less closing stock | (3 257) | |
| Cost of Sales | | (34 743) |
| operating profit | | £3 657 |

(d)

|  | £ | £ |
|---|---|---|
| Sales |  | 38 400 |
| total cost of production | 66 000 |  |
| less closing stock | (35 829) |  |
| Cost of Sales |  | (30 171) |
| operating profit |  | £8 229 |

(e)

|  | £ | £ |
|---|---|---|
| Sales |  | 38 400 |
| standard cost of production | 38 938 |  |
| less closing stock | (3 338) |  |
| Cost of Sales |  | (35 600) |
| Gross Profit |  | £2 800 |

(f)

|  | £ | £ |
|---|---|---|
| Sales |  | 38 400 |
| direct cost of production | 77 875 |  |
| less closing stock | (42 275) |  |
| Cost of Sales |  | (35 600) |
| Gross Profit |  | £2 800 |

(g)

| | £ | £ |
|---|---|---|
| Sales | | 38 400 |
| standard cost of production | 41 125 | |
| less closing stock | (3 525) | |
| Cost of Sales | | (37 600) |
| Gross Profit | | 800 |
| OH overabsorbed | | 3 125 |
| operating profit | | £3 925 |

(h)

| | £ | £ |
|---|---|---|
| Sales | | 38 400 |
| standard cost of production | 82 250 | |
| less closing stock | (44 650) | |
| Cost of Sales | | (37 600) |
| Gross Profit | | 800 |
| OH overabsorbed | | 16 250 |
| operating profit | | £17 050 |

**55.2** *See website for comments.*

**56.1** 1. if all creditors are unsecured and rank equally for payment
A will get £540
B will get £420
C will get £240

2. if the liability to A is secured on an asset which is disposed of for £900 or more, and all other creditors are unsecured and rank equally for payment
A will get £900
B will get £191
C will get £109

3. if the liability to A is secured on an asset which is disposed of for £500, and all other creditors are unsecured and rank equally for payment
A will get £686
B will get £327
C will get £187

4. if the liability to A is secured on an asset which is disposed of for £400, and the liability to B is secured on an asset which is sold for £600, while the liability to C is unsecured.
   A will get £500
   B will get £620
   C will get £80

*see website for comments on 56.2 and 56.3.*

# PART FOUR *Chapters 57–67*

**58.1**   1

| DR | Cash | £25 | |
|----|------|-----|---|
| CR | Issued Share Capital | | £25 |

| | *Cash* | | | | *Issued Share Capital* | |
|---|---|---|---|---|---|---|
| from issue of shares | 25 | | | | claim to nominal value paid in | 25 |

**ABC LTD BALANCE SHEET**

| Assets | £25 |
|--------|-----|
| Issued Share Capital 100 shares of 25p each | £25 |

*see website for answers 2–8.*

9.

| DR | Patent | £90 000 | |
|----|--------|---------|---------|
| DR | Cash | £70 000 | |
| CR | Issued Share Capital | | £40 000 |
| CR | Share Premium | | £120 000 |

| Patent | | | Issued Share Capital | | |
|--------|--------|---|---------------------|---|---|
| from issue of shares | 90 000 | | | claim to nominal value paid in | 40 000 |

| Cash | | | Share Premium | | |
|------|--------|---|--------------|---|---|
| from issue of shares | 70 000 | | | claim to extra value paid in | 120 000 |

### RHA LTD BALANCE SHEET

| Patent | 90 000 |
|--------|--------|
| Cash | 70 000 |
| | £160 000 |
| | |
| Issued Share Capital | |
| shares of 25p each | 40 000 |
| Share Premium | 120 000 |
| | £160 000 |

*see website for answers 10.*

**59.1**

| | | PROFIT 25 | LOSS (20) | PROFIT 60 | LOSS (80) | PROFIT 10 | LOSS (100) | LOSS (50) |
|---|---|---|---|---|---|---|---|---|
| Net Assets | £150 | £175 | £155 | £215 | £135 | £145 | £45 | £(5) |
| Issued Share Capital 400 shares of 25p | 100 | 100 | 100 | 100 | 100 | 100 | 100 | 100 |
| Share Premium | 50 | 50 | 50 | 50 | 50 | 50 | 50 | 50 |
| Retained Earnings (Loss) | | 25 | 5 | 65 | (15) | (5) | (105) | (155) |
| | £150 | £175 | £155 | £215 | £135 | £145 | £45 | £(5) |

**59.2**   DEF Ltd: total shareholders' claim £200, being claim to minimum value shareholders had to pay in for their shares

GHI Ltd: total shareholders' claim £120, being claim to £100 of value shareholders had to pay in for their shares, plus claim to extra £20 also paid in by shareholders

JKL Ltd total shareholders' claim £190, being claim to £100 of value shareholders had to pay in for their shares, plus claim to extra £50 also paid in by shareholders, plus claim to extra net assets (profit) value £40

MNO Ltd total shareholders' claim £550, being claim to £500 of value shareholders had to pay in for their shares, plus claim to extra £250 also paid in by shareholders, minus value of net assets lost by company £200

PQR Ltd total shareholders' claim £2 000, being claim to £5 000 of value shareholders had to pay in for their shares, plus claim to extra £3 000 also paid in by shareholders, minus value of net assets lost by company £6 000

STU Ltd total shareholders' claim is *minus* £1 000. This means that the company is insolvent, and to make it solvent would require a payment in of £1 000 by shareholders. The total negative claim consists of claim to £5 000 of value shareholders had to pay in for their shares, plus claim to extra £3 000 also paid in by shareholders, minus value of net assets lost by company £9 000

**60.1**   1.

| ABC LIMITED BALANCE SHEET AT END OF | YR 1 | YR 2 | YR 3 | YR 4 |
|---|---|---|---|---|
| Net Assets | £1 060 | £1 140 | £1 060 | £1 070 |
| Issued Share Capital 1 000 shares of £1 each | 1 000 | 1 000 | 1 000 | 1 000 |
| Retained Earnings (Loss) | 60 | 140 | 60 | 70 |
| | £1 060 | £1 140 | £1 060 | £1 070 |

2.

**DEF LIMITED**

| BALANCE SHEET AT END OF | YR 1 | YR 2 | YR 3 | YR 4 |
|---|---|---|---|---|
| Net Assets | £ 755 | £1 290 | £1 255 | £1 265 |
| Issued Share Capital 1 000 shares of 50p each | 500 | 1 000 | 1 000 | 1 000 |
| Share Premium | 250 | 250 | 250 | 250 |
| Retained Earnings (Loss) | 5 | 40 | 5 | 15 |
| | £ 755 | £1 290 | £1 255 | £1 265 |

3.

**GHI LIMITED**

| BALANCE SHEET AT END OF | YR 1 | YR 2 | YR 3 | YR 4 |
|---|---|---|---|---|
| Net Assets | £1 600 | £1 800 | £1 865 | £1 820 |
| Issued Share Capital 1 500 shares of £1 each | 1 500 | 1 500 | 1 500 | 1 500 |
| Share Premium | 150 | 150 | 150 | 150 |
| Retained Earnings (Loss) | (50) | 150 | 215 | 170 |
| | £1 600 | £1 800 | £1 865 | £1 820 |

4.

**JKL LIMITED**

| BALANCE SHEET AT END OF | YR 1 | YR 2 | | YR 3 | YR 4 |
|---|---|---|---|---|---|
| Net Assets | £260 | £210 | | £380 | £400 |
| Issued Share Capital | | | | | |
| 3 000 shares of 10p, part paid 7p | 210 | 210 | fully paid | 300 | 300 |
| Retained Earnings (Loss) | 50 | 0 | | 80 | 100 |
| | £260 | £210 | | £380 | £400 |

*see website for comments on exercises 61.1 and 61.2.*

**62.1**    *See website for comments.*

63.1

**ABC**

| | |
|---|---|
| no. of new shares | 300 |
| cash raised | £240 |
| Nominal value of new shares | £(150) |
| Share premium | £90 |

DOUBLE ENTRY

| | | |
|---|---|---|
| DR net assets | £240 | |
| CR issued share capital | | £150 |
| CR Share Premium | | £90 |

BALANCE SHEETS AFTER RIGHTS ISSUE
    ABC

| | |
|---|---|
| Net Assets | £790 |

ISSUED SHARE CAPITAL

| | |
|---|---|
| 1 000 shares of 50p | 500 |
| Share Premium | 90 |
| Retained Earnings (Loss) | 200 |
| | £790 |

## DEF

| | |
|---|---|
| no. of new shares | 400 |
| cash raised | £64 |
| Nominal value of new shares | £(40) |
| Share premium | £24 |

### DOUBLE ENTRY

| | | |
|---|---|---|
| DR net assets | £64 | |
| CR issued share capital | | £40 |
| CR Share Premium | | £24 |

### BALANCE SHEETS AFTER RIGHTS ISSUE
### DEF

| | |
|---|---|
| Net Assets | £364 |

### ISSUED SHARE CAPITAL

| | |
|---|---|
| 1 400 shares of 10p | 140 |
| Share Premium | 74 |
| Retained Earnings (Loss) | 150 |
| | £364 |

**GHI**

| | |
|---|---:|
| no. of new shares | 1500 |
| cash raised | £900 |
| Nominal value of new shares | £(375) |
| Share premium | £525 |

**DOUBLE ENTRY**

| | | |
|---|---|---|
| DR net assets | £900 | |
| CR issued share capital | | £375 |
| CR Share Premium | | £525 |

**GHI BALANCE SHEET**

| | |
|---|---:|
| Net Assets | £2 900 |
| | |
| **ISSUED SHARE CAPITAL** | |
| 5 500 of 25p | 1 375 |
| Share Premium | 775 |
| Retained Earnings (Loss) | 750 |
| | £2 900 |

## JKL

| | |
|---|---|
| no. of new shares | 700 |
| cash raised | £1 330 |
| Nominal value of new shares | £(700) |
| Share premium | £630 |

## DOUBLE ENTRY

| | | |
|---|---|---|
| DR net assets | £1 330 | |
| CR issued share capital | | £700 |
| CR Share Premium | | £630 |

## JKL BALANCE SHEET

| | |
|---|---|
| Net Assets | £11 330 |

## ISSUED SHARE CAPITAL

| | |
|---|---|
| 2 800 shares of £1 | 2 800 |
| Share Premium | 4 410 |
| Retained Earnings (Loss) | 4 120 |
| | £11 330 |

63.2

**1**

| | NUMBER OF SHARES | | PRICE PER SHARE | | VALUE £ |
|---|---|---|---|---|---|
| initial holding | 5 | × | £0.62 | = | 3.10 |
| rights issue | 2 | × | £0.50 | = | 1.00 |
| after rights issue | 7 | × | **£0.59** | = | **£4.10** |

**2**

| | NUMBER OF SHARES | | PRICE PER SHARE | | VALUE £ |
|---|---|---|---|---|---|
| initial holding | 7 | × | £1.10 | = | 7.70 |
| rights issue | 3 | × | £0.60 | = | 1.80 |
| after rights issue | 10 | × | **£0.95** | = | **£9.50** |

**3**

| | NUMBER OF SHARES | | PRICE PER SHARE | | VALUE £ |
|---|---|---|---|---|---|
| initial holding | 8 | × | £0.81 | = | 6.48 |
| rights issue | 3 | × | £0.59 | = | 1.77 |
| after rights issue | 11 | × | **£0.75** | = | **£8.25** |

**4**

| | NUMBER OF SHARES | | PRICE PER SHARE | | VALUE £ |
|---|---|---|---|---|---|
| initial holding | 3 | × | £0.55 | = | 1.65 |
| rights issue | 1 | × | £0.35 | = | 0.35 |
| after rights issue | 4 | × | **£0.50** | = | **£2.00** |

**64.1**

| ABC PLC BALANCE SHEET AFTER DEBENTURE ISSUE | £ |
|---|---|
| Assets | 670 000 |
| Liabilities | (95 000) |
| 5% debenture 2040 | (100 000) |
| Net Assets | £475 000 |
| Issued Share Capital 300 000 ordinary shares of 50p | 150 000 |
| Share Premium | 75 000 |
| Retained Earnings | 250 000 |
| | £475 000 |

**64.2** (a) if interest rates rise so that companies like DEF plc are having to pay 9 per cent per year on their borrowings holding will be worth £667

(b) if interest rates fall, so that companies like DEF plc are able to borrow at 3 per cent interest per year holding will be worth £2 000

**64.3**

| GHI PLC BALANCE SHEET AFTER PREFERENCE SHARE ISSUE | £ |
|---|---|
| Assets | 790 000 |
| Liabilities | (140 000) |
| Net Assets | £650 000 |
| Issued Share Capital 800 000 ordinary shares of 25p | 200 000 |
| 8% Preference shares £1 each | 100 000 |
| Share Premium | 50 000 |
| Retained Earnings | 300 000 |
| | £650 000 |

if profit is £18 000, earnings will be £10 000

**64.4**

| A | |
|---|---|
| preference shareholders will get | £100 000 |
| ordinary shareholders will get | £350 000 |

| B | |
|---|---|
| preference shareholders will get | £100 000 |
| ordinary shareholders will get | £90 000 |

| C | |
|---|---|
| preference shareholders will get | £90 000 |
| ordinary shareholders will get | nil |

**65.1**   Creditors have a claim to £650 000 of value, in respect of promises given to them by the company. Their claims may not be reduced unless/until they are paid.

Preference shareholders have a claim to £100 000 of value, in respect of value they have paid into the company. This claim may not be reduced unless it is replaced by another locked in claim.

Ordinary shareholders have a total claim to £930 000 of value, arising in respect of: minimum value paid in for their shares £250 000; extra value paid in for their shares £120 000; unrealized increase in value of assets in the company £60 000; extra value accumulated by the company (profits), and now locked in by law to replace value originally put in to the company by shareholders but later taken out £50 000; extra value accumulated by the company (profits), and now locked in by choice of the company £75 000; extra value accumulated by the company (profits) which can be reduced by payment of dividend £375 000.

**65.2**   1.

| | |
|---|---|
| DR Fixed Asset Valuation | 500 000 |
| DR Provision for Depreciation | 250 000 |
| CR Fixed Asset Cost | 400 000 |
| CR Revaluation Reserve | 350 000 |

| Fixed Asset Cost | | |
|---|---|---|
| b/f | 400 000 | 400 000 |

| Provision for Depreciation | | |
|---|---|---|
| 250 000 | b/f | 250 000 |

| Fixed Asset at Valuation | | |
|---|---|---|
| 500 000 | | |

| Revaluation Reserve | | |
|---|---|---|
| | | 350 000 |

2.

| | | |
|---|---|---|
| DR Money or Promises | 420 000 | |
| DR Provision for Depreciation | 50 000 | |
| DR P&L (loss on disposal) | 30 000 | |
| CR Fixed Asset at Valuation | | 500 000 |

| | | |
|---|---|---|
| DR Revaluation Reserve | 350 000 | |
| CR P&L Account | | 350 000 |

| Fixed Asset Valuation | | |
|---|---|---|
| b/f | 500 000 | 500 000 |

| Provision for Depreciation | | |
|---|---|---|
| 50 000 | b/f | 50 000 |

| Money or Promises | | |
|---|---|---|
| 420 000 | | |

| Revaluation Reserve | | |
|---|---|---|
| to P&L | 350 000 | b/f | 350 000 |

| P&L Account | | |
|---|---|---|
| loss on disposal | 30 000 | Revaluation Reserve | 350 000 |

*see website for answers 3 and 4.*

**65.3**   1.

| DR Issued Share Capital | 500 | |
|---|---|---|
| CR Net Assets | | 500 |

| DR Retained Profit | 500 | |
|---|---|---|
| CR Capital Redemption Reserve | | 500 |

| Issued Share Capital | | | | Net Assets | | | |
|---|---|---|---|---|---|---|---|
| | 500 | b/f | 2 500 | b/f | 4 700 | | 500 |

| Retained Profit | | | | Capital Redemption Reserve | | | |
|---|---|---|---|---|---|---|---|
| to Capital Redemption | 500 | b/f | 1 200 | | | from Retained Profit | 500 |

2.

| DR Retained Profit | 250 | |
|---|---|---|
| CR General Reserve | | 250 |

| Retained Profit | | | | General Reserve | | | |
|---|---|---|---|---|---|---|---|
| to General Reserve | 250 | b/f | 1 250 | | | from Retained Profit | 250 |

3.

| DR General Reserve | 100 | |
|---|---|---|
| CR Retained Profit | | 100 |

| Retained Profit | | | | General Reserve | | | |
|---|---|---|---|---|---|---|---|
| | | b/f | 1 400 | to Retained Profit | 100 | b/f | 300 |
| | | from General Reserve | 100 | | | | |

**66.1**

| ABC | |
|---|---|
| no. of new shares | 160 |
| nominal value of new shares | £80 |

DOUBLE ENTRY

| DR Retained Earnings | £80 | |
|---|---|---|
| CR Issued Share Capital | | £80 |

ABC AFTER BONUS ISSUE

| Net Assets | £480 |
|---|---|
| Issued Share Capital
720 shares of 50p | 360 |
| Share Premium | – |
| Retained Earnings | 120 |
| | £480 |

**DEF**

| | |
|---|---|
| no. of new shares | 300 |
| nominal value of new shares | £30 |

**DOUBLE ENTRY**

| | | |
|---|---|---|
| DR Share Premium | £30 | |
| CR Issued Share Capital | | £30 |

**DEF AFTER BONUS ISSUE**

| | |
|---|---|
| Net Assets | £350 |
| Issued Share Capital 1 800 shares of 10p | 180 |
| Share Premium | 20 |
| Retained Earnings | 150 |
| | £350 |

## GHI

| | |
|---|---:|
| no. of new shares | <u>1 500</u> |
| nominal value of new shares | <u>£375</u> |

### DOUBLE ENTRY

| | | |
|---|---:|---:|
| DR Capital Redemption Reserve | £100 | |
| DR Retained Earnings | £275 | |
| CR Issued Share Capital | | £375 |

### GHI AFTER BONUS ISSUE

| | |
|---|---:|
| Net Assets | <u>£1 725</u> |
| Issued Share Capital 5 500 of 25p | 1 375 |
| Capital Redemption Reserve Retained Earnings | 350 |
| | <u>£1 725</u> |

**JKL**

| | |
|---|---:|
| no. of new shares | 600 |
| nominal value of new shares | £600 |

**DOUBLE ENTRY**

| | | |
|---|---:|---:|
| DR Revaluation Reserve | £500 | |
| DR Retained Earnings | £100 | |
| CR Issued Share Capital | | £600 |

**JKL AFTER BONUS ISSUE**

| | |
|---|---:|
| Net Assets | £6 420 |
| | |
| Issued Share Capital | |
| 2 400 shares of £1 | 2 400 |
| | |
| Revaluation Reserve | |
| Retained Earnings | 4 020 |
| | £6 420 |

66.2

| **ABB LTD** | **NUMBER OF SHARES** | | **PRICE PER SHARE** | | **VALUE £** |
|---|:---:|:---:|:---:|:---:|---:|
| initial holding | 5 | × | £0.63 | = | 3.15 |
| bonus issue | 2 | | free | = | |
| after bonus issue | 7 | × | **£0.45** | = | £3.15 |

| **BCC LTD** | **NUMBER OF SHARES** | | **PRICE PER SHARE** | | **VALUE £** |
|---|:---:|:---:|:---:|:---:|---:|
| initial holding | 7 | × | £1.10 | = | 7.70 |
| bonus issue | 3 | | free | = | |
| after bonus issue | 10 | × | **£0.77** | = | £7.70 |

| CDD LTD | NUMBER OF SHARES | | PRICE PER SHARE | | VALUE £ |
|---|---|---|---|---|---|
| initial holding | 8 | × | £0.88 | = | 7.04 |
| bonus issue | 3 | | free | = | |
| after bonus issue | 11 | × | **£0.64** | = | **£7.04** |

| DFF LTD | NUMBER OF SHARES | | PRICE PER SHARE | | VALUE £ |
|---|---|---|---|---|---|
| initial holding | 3 | × | £1.60 | = | 4.80 |
| bonus issue | 1 | | free | = | |
| after bonus issue | 4 | × | **£1.20** | = | **£4.80** |

*see website for comments on exercises 67.1 and 67.2.*

# PART FIVE *Chapters 68–74*

**68.1**   Project A: profitability = 25% per year
Project B: profitability = 15% per half-year (*approximately* 30% per year)
Project C: profitability = 0.0001% per minute (*approximately* 52.5% per year)
C is the most profitable, and therefore (if it carries equal risk) the preferable investment.

**68.2**   Ratios:

| COMPANY ACTIVITY | MICRO-CHIP MAKER | CEMENT PRODUCER | PRECISION ENGINEER | MILK WHOLESALER | SATELLITE BROADCASTER |
|---|---|---|---|---|---|
| after tax Return on Equity | 7.3% | 13.5% | 36.5% | 15.5% | 455.4% |
| ROCE | 7.5% | 11.7% | 16.8% | 21.7% | 41.6% |

*see website for comments on risk and profitability.*

**70.1** Ratios:

|  | A | B |
|---|---|---|
| gearing debt/equity | 3.80 | 0.66 |
| gearing debt/(equity+debt) | 79.2% | 39.7% |
|  | electricity distribution | luxury goods producer |

*see website for comments.*

**70.2** Ratios:

|  | ELECTRICITY DISTRIBUTION A | | LUXURY GOODS PRODUCER B | |
|---|---|---|---|---|
|  | CURRENT YEAR | PRIOR YEAR | CURRENT YEAR | PRIOR YEAR |
| gearing debt/equity | 3.80 | 3.76 | 0.66 | 0.80 |
| gearing debt/(equity+debt) | 79.2% | 79.0% | 39.7% | 44.5% |

*see website for comments.*

**72.1** Ratios:

|  | DAIRY FOODS A | CONSUMER DURABLES B |
|---|---|---|
| current ratio | 1.6 | 1.2 |
| quick ratio | 0.7 | 0.9 |
| days' sales in stock | 68 | 55 |
| days' sales in debtors | 38 | 73 |
| days' purchases in creditors | 60 | 76 |
| working capital cycle (days) | 46 | 52 |

*see website for comments.*

**72.2** Ratios:

| | DAIRY FOODS A | | CONSUMER DURABLES B | |
| --- | --- | --- | --- | --- |
| | CURRENT YEAR | PRIOR YEAR | CURRENT YEAR | PRIOR YEAR |
| current ratio | 1.6 | 1.7 | 1.2 | 1.4 |
| quick ratio | 0.7 | 0.8 | 0.9 | 0.9 |
| days' sales in stock | 68 | 68 | 55 | 88 |
| days' sales in debtors | 38 | 36 | 73 | 88 |
| days' purchases in creditors | 60 | 59 | 76 | 89 |
| working capital (days) | 46 | 45 | 52 | 86 |

*see website for comments.*

**72.3** *See website for comments.*

**73.1** Ratios:

| | PHARMA A | SUPERMARKET B | PHARMA C |
| --- | --- | --- | --- |
| Gross Profit Ratio | 79.0% | 7.7% | 78.4% |
| Net Profit Ratio | 32.3% | 5.7% | 33.6% |
| activity sales/equity | 1.72 | 4.18 | 2.41 |
| activity sales/cap employed | 1.59 | 2.66 | 1.53 |

**73.2**    Ratios:

| | PHARMA A | | SUPERMARKET B | |
|---|---|---|---|---|
| | **CURRENT YEAR** | **PRIOR YEAR** | **CURRENT YEAR** | **PRIOR YEAR** |
| Gross Profit Ratio | 79.0% | 77.6% | 7.7% | 7.8% |
| Net Profit Ratio | 32.3% | 27.8% | 5.7% | 5.6% |
| activity sales/equity | 1.72 | 1.75 | 4.18 | 3.91 |
| activity sales/cap employed | 1.59 | 1.61 | 2.66 | 2.47 |

*see website for comments.*

**74.1**    *See website for comments.*

# INDEX